Mathematics for Economics

Mathematics for Economics

An integrated approach

Third edition

Mik Wisniewski
University of Strathclyde

palgrave
macmillan

First published 2013 by
PALGRAVE MACMILLAN

Palgrave Macmillan in the UK is an imprint of Macmillan Publishers Limited, registered in England, company number 785998, of Houndmills, Basingstoke, Hampshire RG21 6XS.

Palgrave Macmillan in the US is a division of St Martin's Press LLC, 175 Fifth Avenue, New York, NY 10010.

Palgrave Macmillan is the global academic imprint of the above companies and has companies and representatives throughout the world.

Palgrave® and Macmillan® are registered trademarks in the United States, the United Kingdom, Europe and other countries.

ISBN 978–0–230–27892–9

This book is printed on paper suitable for recycling and made from fully managed and sustained forest sources. Logging, pulping and manufacturing processes are expected to conform to the environmental regulations of the country of origin.

A catalogue record for this book is available from the British Library.

A catalog record for this book is available from the Library of Congress.

10   9   8   7   6   5   4   3   2   1
22   21   20   19   18   17   16   15   14   13

Printed and bound in China

Brief Contents

1   Introduction   1

SECTION A   THE BUILDING BLOCKS OF ECONOMIC ANALYSIS
A1   Tools of the trade: the basics of algebra   13
A2   Linear relationships in economic analysis   34
A3   Non-linear relationships in economic analysis   55

SECTION B   LINEAR MODELS IN ECONOMIC ANALYSIS
B1   The principles of linear models   83
B2   Market supply and demand models   96
B3   National income models   111
B4   Matrix algebra: the basics   130
B5   Matrix algebra: inversion   149
B6   Economic analysis with matrix algebra   171
B7   Input−output analysis   186

SECTION C   OPTIMIZATION IN ECONOMIC ANALYSIS
C1   Quadratic functions in economic analysis   201
C2   The derivative and the rules of differentiation   215
C3   Derivatives and economic analysis   235
C4   The principles of optimization   253
C5   Optimization in economic analysis   266
C6   Optimization in production theory   283

SECTION D   OPTIMIZATION WITH MULTIPLE VARIABLES
D1   Functions of more than two variables   295
D2   Analysis of multivariable economic models   314
D3   Unconstrained optimization   330
D4   Constrained optimization   345

SECTION E   FURTHER TOPICS IN ECONOMIC ANALYSIS
E1   Integration and economic analysis   363
E2   Financial analysis I: interest and present value   376

E3 Financial analysis II: annuities, sinking funds and growth
models 396
E4 An introduction to dynamics 413
E5 Probability in economic analysis 430

APPENDICES
1 The Greek alphabet in mathematics 454
2 Solutions to Knowledge Check activities 455
3 Solutions to Progress Check activities 457
4 Outline solutions to end-of-module exercises 478

Contents

Preface   xv

1   Introduction   1
   1.1   **The need for mathematics in economics**   3
   1.2   **Economic theory, economic models and mathematics**   6
   1.3   **Summary**   9
        Exercises   9

SECTION A   THE BUILDING BLOCKS OF ECONOMIC ANALYSIS

A1   Tools of the trade: the basics of algebra   13
        Learning Objectives   13
   A1.1   **Algebraic notation**   14
   A1.2   **Arithmetic in algebra**   14
   A1.3   **Brackets in algebra**   17
   A1.4   **Inequalities**   21
   A1.5   **Fractions**   23
   A1.6   **Transposing an expression**   27
   A1.7   **Summary**   30
        Learning Check   30
        Exercises   30
        Appendix A1 Powers and exponents 31

A2   Linear relationships in economic analysis   34
        Learning Objectives   34
   A2.1   **Economic relationships**   35
   A2.2   **Using graphs to show economic relationships**   35
   A2.3   **Functions**   40
   A2.4   **Functional notation**   44
   A2.5   **Linear functions**   44
   A2.6   **Summary**   47
        Learning Check   47
        Worked Example   47
        Exercises   49
        Appendix A2 Graphs in Excel   51

A3 Non-linear relationships in economic analysis   55

Learning Objectives   55
A3.1 Polynomial functions   56
A3.2 Graphs of non-linear functions   57
A3.3 Other non-linear functions   58
A3.4 Logarithms and logarithmic functions   60
A3.5 Exponential functions   62
A3.6 Functions with more than one independent variable   66
A3.7 Inverse functions   69
A3.8 Summary   70
Learning Check   70
Worked Example   70
Exercises   73
Appendix A3 Non-linear graphs in Excel   75

SECTION B   LINEAR MODELS IN ECONOMIC ANALYSIS

B1 The principles of linear models   83

Learning Objectives   83
B1.1 Linear functions   83
B1.2 A simple breakeven model   87
B1.3 Simultaneous equations   89
B1.4 Obtaining linear equations from graphs   91
B1.5 Summary   92
Learning Check   92
Worked Example   92
Exercises   94

B2 Market supply and demand models   96

Learning Objectives   96
B2.1 Market demand and supply   96
B2.2 A partial equilibrium model   98
B2.3 An excise tax in a competitive market   101
B2.4 Elasticity   104
B2.5 Summary   107
Learning Check   107
Worked Example   107
Exercises   109

B3 National income models   111

Learning Objectives   111
B3.1 A national income model   111
B3.2 The national income model in diagram form   118
B3.3 A national income model including a government sector   120
B3.4 A national income model with a government sector and foreign trade   123
B3.5 A national income model with a monetary sector   124
B3.6 Summary   126
Learning Check   127
Worked Example   127
Exercises   129

B4 Matrix algebra: the basics   130

	Learning Objectives	130
B4.1	The vocabulary of matrix algebra	131
B4.2	Special matrices	133
B4.3	Matrix algebra	133
B4.4	Matrix addition	134
B4.5	Matrix subtraction	135
B4.6	Multiplication by a scalar	135
B4.7	Matrix multiplication	135
B4.8	Using matrix algebra to represent economic models	138
B4.9	Summary	140
	Learning Check	140
	Worked Example	140
	Exercises	142
	Appendix B4 Matrix algebra with Excel	143

B5 Matrix algebra: inversion   149

	Learning Objectives	149
B5.1	The matrix inverse	149
B5.2	Using a matrix inverse	150
B5.3	Calculating the matrix inverse	152
B5.4	Determinants	154
B5.5	Calculating the matrix inverse using determinants	158
B5.6	The determinant and non-singularity	159
B5.7	Cramer's rule	161
B5.8	Summary	163
	Learning Check	163
	Worked Example	163
	Exercises	165
	Appendix B5.1 Matrix inverse with Excel	166
	Appendix B5.2 Confirmation of the determinant method	168

B6 Economic analysis with matrix algebra   171

	Learning Objectives	171
B6.1	A partial equilibrium market model	171
B6.2	The effect of an excise tax on market equilibrium	175
B6.3	A basic national income model	177
B6.4	A national income model with government activity	179
B6.5	Summary	181
	Learning Check	181
	Worked Example	182
	Exercises	184

B7 Input–output analysis   186

	Learning Objectives	186
B7.1	Input–output tables	186
B7.2	Input–output coefficients	188
B7.3	Input–output analysis	190
B7.4	Summary	195
	Learning Check	195

Worked Example   195
Exercises   198

SECTION C   OPTIMIZATION IN ECONOMIC ANALYSIS

C1 Quadratic functions in economic analysis   201
Learning Objectives   201
C1.1   Quadratic functions   201
C1.2   Characteristics of quadratic functions   202
C1.3   Breakeven analysis   205
C1.4   Market equilibrium   209
C1.5   Quadratic functions with no real roots   210
C1.6   Summary   211
Learning Check   211
Worked Example   211
Exercises   212
Appendix C1 Derivation of the roots formula   213

C2 The derivative and the rules of differentiation   215
Learning Objectives   215
C2.1   The slope of linear and non-linear functions   215
C2.2   The derivative   219
C2.3   Rules of differentiation   223
C2.4   Non-differentiable functions   228
C2.5   Summary   229
Learning Check   230
Worked Example   230
Exercises   232

C3 Derivatives and economic analysis   235
Learning Objectives   235
C3.1   Curve sketching   235
C3.2   The derivative and the concept of marginality   237
C3.3   Analysing elasticity   238
C3.4   Analysing other types of elasticity   241
C3.5   Analysing revenue   242
C3.6   Analysing production   244
C3.7   Analysing costs   246
C3.8   The consumption function   247
C3.9   National income   248
C3.10 Summary   249
Learning Check   249
Worked Example   249
Exercises   251

C4 The principles of optimization   253
Learning Objectives   253
C4.1   An example of optimization   253
C4.2   Optimization in general   257
C4.3   Local and global maxima and minima   259

C4.4   Points of inflection   260
C4.5   Summary   262
        Learning Check   263
        Worked Example   263
        Exercises   264

C5 Optimization in economic analysis   266
        Learning Objectives   266
C5.1   Profit maximization   266
C5.2   Profit maximization: perfect competition   267
C5.3   Profit maximization: monopoly   270
C5.4   The effect of tax on profit maximization   272
C5.5   The imposition of a lump-sum tax   272
C5.6   The imposition of a profit tax   274
C5.7   The imposition of an excise tax   275
C5.8   Maximizing taxation revenue   276
C5.9   Summary   279
        Learning Check   279
        Worked Example   279
        Exercises   281

C6 Optimization in production theory   283
        Learning Objectives   283
C6.1   The theory of production   283
C6.2   The theory of costs   287
C6.3   Relationship between the cost functions   289
C6.4   Summary   290
        Learning Check   290
        Worked Example   290
        Exercises   292

SECTION D   OPTIMIZATION WITH MULTIPLE VARIABLES

D1 Functions of more than two variables   295
        Learning Objectives   295
D1.1   Partial differentiation   295
D1.2   Second-order partial derivatives   299
D1.3   Generalization to n-variable functions   302
D1.4   Differentials   304
D1.5   The total differential   305
D1.6   The total derivative   307
D1.7   Implicit functions   309
D1.8   Summary   310
        Learning Check   310
        Worked Example   311
        Exercises   311
        Appendix D1 Rules for partial differentiation   312

D2 Analysis of multivariable economic models   314
        Learning Objectives   314
D2.1   Partial market equilibrium   314

D2.2	A national income model	317
D2.3	Elasticity of demand	319
D2.4	Production functions	320
D2.5	Utility functions	323
D2.6	Summary	327
	Learning Check	327
	Worked Example	327
	Exercises	328

D3 Unconstrained optimization

		330
	Learning Objectives	330
D3.1	General principles of unconstrained optimization	330
D3.2	Profit maximization	335
D3.3	Price discrimination	336
D3.4	Profit maximization revisited	338
D3.5	Summary	340
	Learning Check	340
	Worked Example	341
	Exercises	342
	Appendix D3 The Hessian matrix	343

D4 Constrained optimization

		345
	Learning Objectives	345
D4.1	The principles of constrained optimization	345
D4.2	Lagrange multipliers	348
D4.3	Interpretation of the Lagrange multiplier	349
D4.4	Output maximization subject to a cost constraint	352
D4.5	Cost minimization subject to an output constraint	354
D4.6	Maximizing consumer utility subject to a budget constraint	355
D4.7	Summary	357
	Learning Check	357
	Worked Example	357
	Exercises	358
	Appendix D4 The bordered Hessian matrix	359

SECTION E   FURTHER TOPICS IN ECONOMIC ANALYSIS

E1 Integration and economic analysis

		363
	Learning Objectives	363
E1.1	Notation and terminology	363
E1.2	Rules of integration	364
E1.3	Definite integrals	366
E1.4	Definite integrals and areas under curves	367
E1.5	Consumer's surplus	369
E1.6	Producer's surplus	371
E1.7	Capital stock formation	371
E1.8	Summary	372
	Learning Check	373

| | Worked Example | 373 |
| | Exercises | 374 |

E2 Financial analysis I: interest and present value   376

	Learning Objectives	376
E2.1	Financial mathematics	376
E2.2	Time preference	377
E2.3	Arithmetic and geometric series	377
E2.4	Simple and compound interest	379
E2.5	Nominal and effective interest rates	381
E2.6	Depreciation	382
E2.7	Present value	384
E2.8	Basic investment appraisal	385
E2.9	Internal rate of return	386
E2.10	Interest rates and the price of government bonds	388
E2.11	Summary	390
	Learning Check	390
	Worked Example	391
	Exercises	392
	Appendix E2 Financial calculations in Excel	393

E3 Financial analysis II: annuities, sinking funds and growth models   396

	Learning Objectives	396
E3.1	Annuities	396
E3.2	The value of an annuity	397
E3.3	NPV of an annuity	399
E3.4	Repayment annuity	400
E3.5	Sinking funds	400
E3.6	The mathematical constant e and rates of growth	401
E3.7	Calculus and e	406
E3.8	Rates of growth	408
E3.9	Summary	410
	Learning Check	410
	Worked Example	410
	Exercises	411

E4 An introduction to dynamics   413

	Learning Objectives	413
E4.1	Difference equations	413
E4.2	The equilibrium position	415
E4.3	The solution to a difference equation	416
E4.4	Stability of the model	418
E4.5	A macro model with a government sector	423
E4.6	Harrod−Domar growth model	424
E4.7	Market equilibrium	424
E4.8	Summary	427
	Learning Check	427
	Worked Example	427
	Exercises	428

E5 Probability in economic analysis   430

       Learning Objectives   431

E5.1 **Uncertainty and probability**   431

E5.2 **Understanding probability**   432

E5.3 **Basic rules of probability**   433

E5.4 **Bayes' theorem**   437

E5.5 **Probability distributions**   439

E5.6 **Decision-making under uncertainty**   444

E5.7 **Summary**   448

       Learning Check   448

       Worked Example   449

       Exercises   451

Appendix 1: The Greek alphabet in mathematics   454

Appendix 2: Solutions to Knowledge Check activities   455

Appendix 3: Solutions to Progress Check activities   457

Appendix 4: Outline solutions to end-of-module exercises   478

Index   510

Preface

There are a number of reasons why I decided to write this textbook and also why I wrote it in the way that it appears. The main motivation stems from my own experience as a student when I first encountered mathematics and economics together for the first time.

I'd taken a number of introductory economics classes as an undergraduate student and found the subject intellectually stimulating and challenging while at the same time it gave me real insight into how, and why, economic decisions were taken at the individual level, by the firm and by governments. The classes I took – micro- and macroeconomics – were taught using the principles of descriptive, verbal logic supported by simple graphs and diagrams. They helped me understand the general principles involved in economic models and economic analysis: for example, that marginal cost and marginal revenue would be equal at profit maximization; or how introducing a tax on a product will affect equilibrium supply and demand.

However, these classes also left me a little empty. They had introduced simple economic models and, through verbal logic, reached an economic conclusion that could be applied in that specific situation. But I was more interested in generalizations. Would profit be maximized when marginal cost equals marginal revenue in every economic situation, not just the one we explored in class? Would the effect of a tax on equilibrium supply and demand always be the same? Although I didn't realize at the time, I was looking for ways to reach general economic conclusions, not just specific, individual ones. One of my tutors suggested I should study mathematical economics to enable me to do this – hence my first class in the subject.

And that was a real shock. I'd last studied maths at secondary school. It wasn't my favourite subject since I hadn't fully understood it as it was taught and I couldn't see its relevance in the real world. However, I needed to pass school maths to apply for university, so I managed to pass the exam (at the second attempt). But the first classes in mathematical economics at university were even more difficult; it was like being taught in a foreign language that you didn't understand. The lecturers used symbols I'd never seen before (never mind knowing how to pronounce them), they all had a really strong maths background (as did most of my fellow students) and all had a keen interest in maths itself (which I did not). So I looked round for a textbook that would help me understand what mathematical economics was about. Even they were not much help, however. They were written by academics who were good at maths for students who were good at maths. The assumption seemed to be that if you didn't have a strong maths background at the beginning you shouldn't be studying mathematical economics. After a lot of hard work – and a bit of luck – I got through the mathematical economics class and eventually the maths started to make sense and I could appreciate how it helped me as an economist. But I told myself that if I ever got the chance to write a textbook on maths and economics for students like myself I would. This is it.

The book has been written for those whose main interest is in economics and economic analysis but who wish to use mathematics as a tool to help that analysis. The aim throughout the text is to show how mathematics allows us to undertake more robust analysis in economics, not in mathematics per se. This is why we introduce and explain mathematical principles not for their own sake but in order to develop our skills and knowledge of economics. This is achieved in a gradual and incremental way. The text begins by introducing the basic mathematics needed and shows its value in economic analysis. Gradually, more advanced mathematical topics are introduced, but, as ever, looking at how they add value to our understanding of economic theory and practice. By the time you get to the end of the text, I hope that, as happened to me, you will have been converted into an economist who sees the necessity for mathematical analysis and who has the ability and confidence to use mathematics as an integral part of such analysis. Let's start the journey.

A quick tour of the book

The textbook is split into five sections. Within each section the content is broken down into a series of individual modules. Each module covers a specific topic or technique and can be studied over a relatively short period.

In **Section A,** *The building blocks of economic analysis*, we begin by introducing some of the essential mathematical concepts and skills that immediately allow us to consider specific applications of mathematics in economics. Students with existing mathematical skills will be able to move through this material quickly and concentrate on the economic application of these techniques. Those whose grasp of such concepts is more limited to begin with are able to move at a slower pace to ensure that they develop an adequate understanding of this material before proceeding further. In **Section B,** *Linear models in economic analysis*, we examine in detail the principles of linear models since these are particularly common in economic analysis. Through the use of such linear models we examine the mathematical principles underpinning the economic concept of equilibrium and look at equilibrium at both the market analysis level and the national income level. We then move on to the area of matrix algebra. Given that economic models are frequently concerned with large sets of equations, a method of dealing with, and manipulating, such equation systems is needed: matrix algebra provides this framework. We introduce the principles of matrix algebra and see how these can be applied to the equilibrium analysis completed so far. We also see how matrix algebra can be applied to a particularly powerful type of economic analysis, that of input–output modelling. **Section C,** *Optimization in economic analysis*, explores how mathematics can be used in a particularly important area of economic analysis, that of optimization. This may apply to a firm wishing to maximize (optimize) its profits or market share; or a firm wishing to minimize its production costs; or a government wishing to maximize tax revenue. Optimization is a key part of economic theory and modelling, and we will look in detail at how mathematics can help particularly through the application of calculus. **Section D,** *Optimization with multiple variables*, looks at how we can undertake analysis into economic optimization with more complex, realistic models that involve multiple variables. Again, we'll be applying the mathematical principles to a number of common areas of economic analysis such as market equilibrium, production theory, utility theory and national income economics. The final **Section, E,** *Further topics in economic analysis*, introduces a variety of more

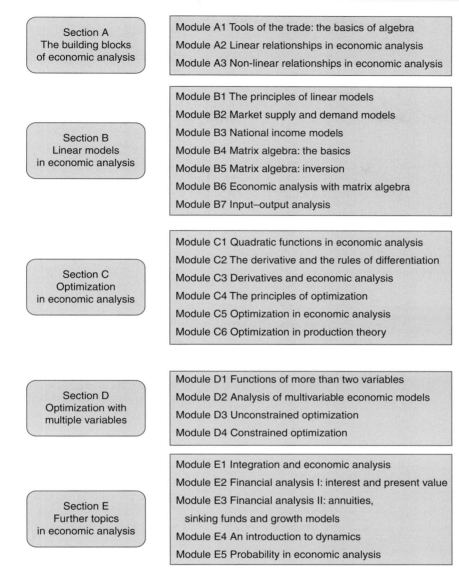

Figure P.1 Overview of the book

specialized areas of application. We shall be looking at the principles of integration and how these can be applied to analysis such as consumers' and producers' surplus and to capital stock formation. Then we'll explore how mathematics and economics can be used in the area of financial analysis. We'll look at how economic analysis can be further extended through the use of dynamic models that study how economic change occurs over time. Finally, we'll see how the principles of probability and uncertainty relate to economic analysis.

The approach taken in the book

Each section begins by outlining why we need to develop a particular mathematical concept or technique. The need for such skills is illustrated with reference to specific examples from the study of economics. This approach will help you to appreciate from the very beginning of your studies why we are examining a specific technique as *economists* and *not* as mathematicians. We shall then consider in detail the key principles underpinning each mathematical topic – again using a number of illustrative examples from economics – and at a pace that can be adapted to your own level of understanding. Naturally, this pace may be relatively leisurely at the beginning, but will quickly gather speed as you progress and develop a cumulative set of skills and knowledge. Finally, we shall return to consider the application of the mathematical techniques we have developed in the context of economics. A number of examples will be drawn from different areas of economics to illustrate the extensive potential application.

Throughout the text, detailed examples are used and, wherever relevant, graphical development of key concepts. The following features are also of note.

Learning Objectives

By the end of this module you should be able to:

- Confirm that $MR = MC$ at profit maximization
- Use differential calculus to determine the profit-maximizing position for a firm in perfect competition and for a firm in a monopoly
- Assess the effect of different taxes on profit maximization
- Determine the level of tax that will maximize tax revenue.

Learning Objectives

Each module sets out a list of *Learning Objectives* that outline what you should have learned on completion of that module. They serve as an indicator of what the module covers and also help you review and check your knowledge at the end of each module.

Knowledge Check A2

If you think you're already familiar with the mathematics of linear equations, try answering the following. If:

$$Q_d = f(P) = 1250 - 6P$$

where Q_d is quantity demanded of a product and P is the price charged for the product, then:

(i)   What will this function look like when plotted on a graph?

(ii)   What does this intercept represent in terms of economic behaviour?

(iii)   What does this slope/gradient represent in terms of economic behaviour?

Check your answers in Appendix 2. If you got these right, try some of the exercises at the end of this module and then move on to module A3.

Knowledge Check

In the first few modules there's a *Knowledge Check* activity. This allows you to see whether you're already familiar with the maths in that module. This enables students to advance at their own pace, according to their existing maths knowledge.

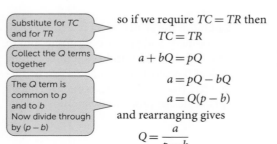

Substitute for *TC* and for *TR*

Collect the *Q* terms together

The *Q* term is common to *p* and to *b*
Now divide through by *(p − b)*

so if we require $TC = TR$ then

$$TC = TR$$

$$a + bQ = pQ$$

$$a = pQ - bQ$$

$$a = Q(p - b)$$

and rearranging gives

$$Q = \frac{a}{p - b}$$

Hints

Hints are given, particularly in the earlier modules, to help you follow the maths calculations and related economic analysis.

Progress Check B6.2

Return to the equation systems shown in Progress Check B1.3. Assuming that each system represents a market model, confirm the solutions using matrix algebra.

(i) $Y = 100 - 18X$
$Y = -75 + 17X$

(ii) $Y = 100 - 10X$
$Y = -50 + 5X$

(iii) $Y = -20 + 3X$
$Y = 200 - 5X$

(iv) $Y = -60 + 3X$
$Y = 50 - 2X$

Progress Checks

Progress Check activities are given throughout each module. As you will soon begin to appreciate, the development of mathematical skills for economics students is a cumulative process: that is, the skills developed in the early modules will be taken as given in later modules as more complex topics are introduced. It is essential that before you leave a specific module you fully understand what has been covered and are able to apply the mathematical skills and appreciate the mathematical concepts that have been introduced there. It is often tempting to skip over a topic that is proving particularly difficult. You may rationalize this by saying '*I can't understand this at the moment but I'll come back to it later on when I have the time (and patience) – and when the exam is closer!*'

All too often, however, this return does not take place and students find themselves at a later date in the position of being unable to understand a topic that builds upon the one that was omitted. To try to encourage you to make sure you do understand the material as it progresses, *Progress Check* activities appear throughout each module. The intention is that each such activity tests your understanding/skills of the material presented thus far. You're strongly encouraged to stop at that point and to complete the activity before proceeding. Solutions to these activities appear either immediately after the activity or in Appendix 3.

Worked Example

You have won first prize in a national competition run by a famous publishing company. You can take the prize of £100,000 now. Alternatively you can choose to receive £15,000 a year for the next ten years. Current interest rates are 3% per annum. Which would you choose and why?

You have a view that long-term interest rates over the next ten years are likely to average around 5%. How would this affect your decision?

Solution

The second option is effectively an annuity. To compare the two options you need to work out the present value of the annuity option and compare it with the £100,000 you could have now. If we assume a due annuity then Eq. E3.3 is appropriate:

$$PV = P\left(\frac{1(r^t - 1)}{r - 1}\right)$$

The relevant values are:

$P = £15000$
$r = 1/1.03 = 0.9709$
$t = 10$

Substituting and solving gives:

$$PV = 15000\frac{[1(0.9709^{10} - 1)]}{0.9709 - 1} = £131792$$

Clearly, the PV of the annuity outweighs the option of £100,000 now.

A rise in interest rates will generally lead to a fall in the PV. If we assume an interest rate of 5% over the whole of the next ten years then the PV of the annuity falls to £121,617.

Worked Example

Towards the end of each module you will find a *Worked Example*. Typically, this is a detailed problem highlighting, and pulling together, the key principles of what has been covered in that module but firmly in the context of economic analysis. We recommend that you work through such examples yourself. You can then check your own answer (and your understanding of what that module was about) with our detailed and fully worked solution.

Exercises

B3.1 Assume a simple national income model with:

$C = f(Y) = 750 + 0.75Y$ and $I = 500$

(i) Calculate the equilibrium levels of income, consumption and saving.

(ii) Calculate k and interpret the result.

(iii) If I changed to 510, what would be the effect on (i)?

(iv) Why has equilibrium changed in the way it has?

B3.2 In the model in Exercise B3.1 assume that the mpc changes to 0.8. Explain in detail the effect you would expect this to have on the equilibrium position. Calculate the new equilibrium to confirm your logic.

B3.3 The simple national income model now includes a government sector with $G = 150$ and $t = 0.25$. Calculate the new equilibrium and the new value for k. Why has the value for k decreased? What are the implications of this for the economy?

B3.4 For the model in Ex. B3.3 we now add a foreign trade sector with exports at 200 and with imports at 15% of disposable income. Calculate the new equilibrium and explain the changes in national income that have occurred.

B3.5 For the model in Ex. B3.3 find the level for G that will give a balanced budget (i.e. $G = T$).

B3.6 For the model in Ex. B3.3 find the level for G that will balance foreign trade (i.e. $X = M$).

Exercises

There are exercises at the end of each module. These are more detailed and thorough tests of your skills, knowledge and abilities and as such serve a number of purposes. They introduce larger-scale problems than those examined in the module itself. Such exercises will also help to reinforce the key points covered in the module and encourage you to develop your skills in both mathematical analysis and calculation and in terms of mathematical logic. One final purpose of the exercises is that they will frequently raise questions and issues addressed in subsequent modules, hence encouraging you to consider and evaluate critically what has been covered thus far. For these reasons you are strongly encouraged to undertake as many of these exercises as possible before proceeding to the next module. Brief solutions to the exercises are given in Appendix 4.

For lecturers using the book, there is a separate Solutions Manual available online. At over 250 pages, this contains full solutions to the exercises as well as detailed discussion and suggestions for further class discussion around that topic.

Appendix B5.1 Matrix inverse with Excel

Inverse of a matrix

The inverse of a matrix is obtained by using the MINVERSE function. This is illustrated in Figs B5.1 and B5.2 using the **S** matrix from the Worked Example. The matrix to be inverted is entered into the appropriate cells. The cells where the inverse will be calculated are selected. The MINVERSE function is entered together with the cells identifying the matrix to be inverted. The Ctrl Shift Enter keys are pressed at the same time to activate the MINVERSE function.

Determinants

Excel can also calculate the determinant of a matrix using the MDETERM function. This is shown in Figs B5.3 and B5.4.

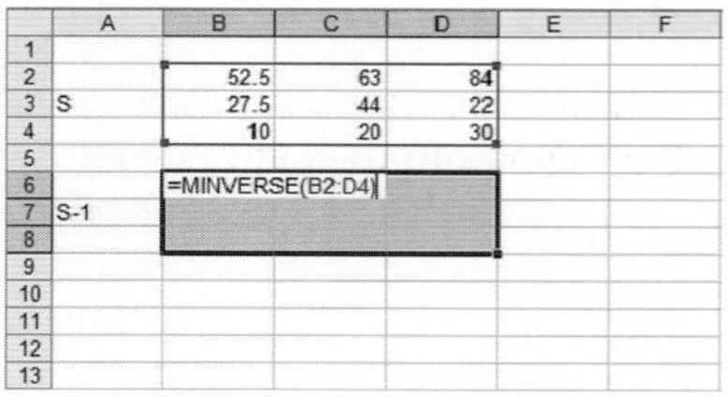

Excel

Finally, some modules contain detailed guidance on how MS Excel can be used to help with some of the maths calculations discussed in that module.

Figure B5.1 MINVERSE function

1
Introduction

You may be wondering what mathematics has to do with economic analysis. Like many students you have a serious interest in studying economics and understanding how economics and economic analysis contribute to both microeconomic and macro-economic activities. As we shall see throughout this text, serious students of modern economic analysis need a number of essential mathematical skills and techniques. Such skills and techniques are necessary to allow you to properly understand economic theory, economic behaviour and modern economic analysis. Let's consider the following scenarios.

Scenario 1

Following the banking crisis that began in 2008, particularly in the US and the UK, a number of governments had to put considerable emergency funding into their banking system to support banks and other financial institutions that were close to collapse. As a result, government expenditure and therefore borrowing increased dramatically. The Finance Minister has now decided that the government deficit (the difference between what the government collects in taxes and what it spends) needs to be cut back significantly to bring the government budget more into balance. However, the Minister is concerned about the impact that reducing government spending will have on particular sectors of the economy. Reducing government expenditure has consequences for the firms who supply the government with goods and services, for their employees, for their shareholders and often for the wider community as well. One sector in particular is under serious scrutiny: the government is thinking of cancelling a couple of major naval shipbuilding contracts. These defence cuts would initially save the government a good deal of money. However, the shipbuilding companies would be badly affected and would have to reduce their workforce considerably. In turn this would lead to a loss in tax revenue for the government and increased welfare payments for those who lost their jobs. The Minister has asked for your economic analysis of the overall impact of such a decision.

Scenario 2

You have been approached by both easyJet and Ryanair, two highly successful budget airlines operating in Europe. They're concerned that the European Union is considering imposing additional taxes on passengers who book short-haul flights by adding the tax to the ticket price charged by the airline. The declared purpose behind such taxes is to encourage passengers to switch to more environmentally friendly transport (such as electric trains) by making short-haul air travel more expensive, and thereby to reduce the carbon footprint of travel and contribute to a reduction in global warming. Once again, you've been asked to undertake an economic analysis to assess the impact that such a tax would have on their businesses. How will such a tax affect demand for airline travel? How will it affect airline revenue? How will it affect their profitability?

Scenario 3

The government is looking for ways of increasing both its tax revenue and its popularity with the public – not a combination that's easy to achieve. One option is to capitalize on the current unpopularity of senior executives in the banking sector among the public. There was considerable criticism that senior executives were awarded very large performance bonuses at the time when banks were struggling financially and had to be financially supported by the government. The government is now thinking of introducing a special tax on bankers' bonuses. It's looking for your economic advice as to what level of tax it should introduce in order to maximize the amount of tax revenue it collects in this way.

Scenario 4

As part of its economic growth strategy, the South African government is looking for ways to help small businesses start up and expand. It's thinking of encouraging the central bank (the South African Reserve Bank) to increase the money supply in the hope that this will reduce the interest rate that businesses borrowing money have to pay. Generally, an increase in the money supply in an economy makes it cheaper and easier to borrow money. The proposed measure is expected to increase the demand from firms for investment funding and so stimulate economic growth as firms borrow more money to help them expand their economic activities. What economic advice can you give on the impact such a policy would have on the economy?

These scenarios are all realistic – and real. They illustrate the situations that economists and economic analysis are frequently involved in. Some of the scenarios involve analysing and assessing what will happen at a *microeconomic* level – at the level of individual markets, organizations or people. Some of the scenarios involve analysing and assessing at the *macroeconomic* level – at the level of the whole economy or some part of it. At both the micro- and macro-levels it's likely that you will need to do a number of things. First, you will need to analyse each scenario in order to establish the general economic impact that we would expect to happen – that is, using economic theory to predict in general what economic changes are likely to occur. For example, in the easyJet/Ryanair scenario you want to be able to explain in general the effects that introducing a tax would have regardless of the precise value of the tax. Second, you want to quantify the exact effect at the micro- or macroeconomic level – in other words, be able to accurately predict for easyJet/Ryanair the impact of a specific tax level on their business. This combination of understanding the *general* effects of an economic change as well as being able to quantify the *exact* effects of a specific change is important in economics.

Through our economic analysis we want to be able to understand the general principles at work in a given scenario as well as the specific details. For example, you wouldn't want to be in a situation where you analysed the impact of, say, a €10 tax on each flight and then have to repeat the analysis if the tax changed to €15 or then do it all again because the tax was now going to be €20. What you do need to be able to do is to assess the impact no matter what the exact tax might be. And this is where mathematics comes into economic analysis.

1.1 The need for mathematics in economics

We begin with a bold statement: in order to develop a comprehensive understanding of both economic theory and economic analysis you need a detailed understanding of key mathematical principles and of the role that mathematics can play in the study of economics. You may have opened this text on mathematics and economics with a degree of uncertainty, being unsure what to expect, and possibly even some concern. As part of your studies of economics you may well have been surprised to realize that it is necessary to undertake a formal course in mathematical economic analysis (often under the name of applied economics, quantitative economics or similar) and that the use of mathematics in economics is more widespread than you realized. It may also be the case that the prospect of having to recollect and use key mathematical principles and skills acquired at school is not one that fills you with much enthusiasm. Mathematics in general has a poor reputation with many students, who simply cannot see its relevance in the real world.

However, it is an inescapable feature of the serious study of economics that you need to be familiar and comfortable with key mathematical methods and you need to develop the skills necessary to apply such methods to the economic models that you will gradually build and explore. But it's important for us to stress from the very beginning that this text is *not* a text on mathematical economics as such but rather on the *use* of mathematics in economic analysis. You may be forgiven at this stage in your studies for wondering what the difference is and whether it really matters. In this textbook our main focus is on:

- Seeing how mathematics is used and the value it adds to economic analysis
- Helping you develop your own skills in using such mathematics to improve your own economic analysis
- Increasing the level of your own mathematical confidence
- Developing your awareness of the widespread and typical uses of mathematics in economics.

As you work through the material in this book you will gradually recognize that mathematics need not be viewed as a discipline separate from economics but, rather, one that can be used in an integrated way to help develop economic models and economic theory. We stress again, however, that the purpose of this text is not to turn you into a mathematician but to allow you to develop the mathematical skills and knowledge that you will require as an economist.

There are a number of reasons why the use of mathematics in economics has steadily increased over the years. One important reason is that mathematics is a useful tool in the study of economics. While it is possible to undertake some limited economic analysis by relying on verbal analysis and logic without much use of mathematics, an appropriate use of mathematical notation and solution methods can make life much, much easier for the economist.

Let's return to the easyJet scenario. As a first step in trying to assess the impact that an EU tax might have on passenger numbers, we might consider thinking about the factors that would affect the number of people flying on one of easyJet's routes, say from Edinburgh to London. At this stage we do not need to know the precise effects, only to grasp what might influence the number of passengers choosing to fly this route. In standard economic terms, we'd say we want to identify the key factors affecting the demand for seats on this route.

Progress Check 1.1

Before reading on, take a few minutes to list the main factors you think could affect the demand for seats on this route.

Applying basic common sense, and possibly some personal experience, you may have said that the demand for airline seats on this route will depend on a variety of factors: the price charged by easyJet for the seat, the price charged by its competitors, such as British Airways, who also fly this route, the cost of alternative travel such as the rail fare from Edinburgh to London, or people's income levels. You might have suggested other factors as well. In other words, we can build up a *verbal* picture of the economic situation. But, as we all know, words can sometimes get in the way of understanding, with different people reading different things into a particular phrase, and it can sometimes take a lot of words to describe a relatively straightforward situation. A much more concise and unambiguous way of summarizing such an economic situation is provided through simple mathematical notation, such as:

$$Q_d = b_1 P + b_2 P_C + b_3 P_A + b_4 Y \tag{1.1}$$

where we use letters to stand for some of the factors we've thought of. Here we use:

Q_d = the total number of easyJet seats people want to buy on this route (often referred to as the *quantity demanded* and pronounced 'queue dee')
P = the price of easyJet's airline seats on this route
P_C = the price of competitor airlines' seats on this route
P_A = the price of alternative travel such as railways
Y = level of consumer income.

In economics we refer to these factors as *variables* – since they vary or change according to the economic situation under consideration. We use other letters (b_1, b_2, b_3, b_4) to represent what are called the *parameters* of the relationship (frequently these are the specific numerical values that are appropriate to the particular economic relationship). Notice also that we show Eq. 1.1 using *italics*. There is no particular reason for this other than the fact that it makes them stand out in the text and so helps you to realize that they are referring to parts of a mathematical expression.

Such a mathematical presentation offers a number of advantages to the economic analyst, once you get used to them. First, to those who understand the mathematical symbols used, the use of mathematical notation to describe such economic relationships provides a definitive and unambiguous statement of the relationship. A purely verbal description of an economic relationship is more prone to misinterpretation and confusion than a mathematical one. It is for this reason that relationships such as the example above are shown in mathematical terms. However, not only can we use mathematics to describe such a relationship, but we can also apply mathematical reasoning and logic. Mathematics is a particularly powerful tool in enabling us to make logical *deductions* about economic behaviour patterns. In the above example an economist with the appropriate mathematical understanding can work out the effect of, say, a change in consumer income on the quantity demanded of the product under the critical assumption that the other factors in the equation remain unchanged. This is a very common assumption used in economic analysis and one that we'll use often. If we wanted to work out the general effect on Q_d (demand for easyJet seats on this route) if Y (consumer income) changed, then the only way we can do this is to make the assumption that all the other factors stay exactly as they are. If we did not make this assumption but allowed other factors to change at the same time, it would be impossible to work out what was causing Q_d to change. Economists refer to this assumption using the phrase 'other things being equal' or with the Latin expression '*ceteris paribus*' (pronounced 'ketter-iss parry-bus'), which literally means 'with other things the same' or 'other things being equal'.

Progress Check 1.2

Suppose British Airways lowers its prices on this route. Other things being equal, what effect would you expect this to have on demand for easyJet seats?

Given that the expression $b_2 P_C$ in (1.1) is used to show the effect of competition on Q_d, what numerical value would you expect b_2 to take: negative, positive or zero?

Other things being equal, it seems reasonable to assume that if BA increase their prices, easyJet's prices will appear cheaper and so more attractive to the customer. In other words, we would expect an increase in demand for easyJet seats as a result of an increase in BA prices. This suggests that the numerical value for b_2 would be positive – an increase in a competitor's price, P_C, would lead to an increase in Q_d. This is our first mathematical economic analysis. You may also have worked out that we'd expect b_1 to be negative – if easyJet themselves charge a higher price then we'd expect this to have a negative effect on demand; we'd expect b_3 to be positive since, again, an increase in the prices of alternative forms of travel is likely to boost demand for air travel; b_4 is slightly less clear but we'd probably conclude that, if people have more income to spend, they'd probably travel more so we might think that b_4 would be positive also.

These examples illustrate how mathematical economic analysis can help us in the scenario outlined at the beginning of the module where the EU was considering imposing a tax on the price charged for short-haul flights. Although we've only just started looking at mathematical economic analysis we can use expression (1.1) to work out that such a tax would affect P and P_C but not P_A and Y. In other words, the effect of the tax on passenger demand, Q_d, would come through the impact of a higher price that easyJet would have to charge, P, and through the impact of the higher price its competitors would also have to charge, P_C – assuming of course that all airlines were charged the same tax. But we also see that the two effects might counterbalance each other to some extent. The effect on Q of a higher value for P will be negative (through b_1), so easyJet will lose passengers thanks to the higher price they have to charge because of the tax imposed. On the other hand, airline competitors will also have to increase their prices and, as we already know through b_2, this would have a positive effect on easyJet demand – increasing passenger numbers, other things being equal. So, on the one hand easyJet would lose passengers and on the other would gain passengers. What would the net effect be? In part this would depend on the exact numerical values taken by b_1 and

b_2 (which of course we don't know). Although we don't have exact numerical values for the two parameters it's clear that there are three possibilities if we ignore the positive and negative signs:

- b_1 is bigger than b_2
- b_1 is the same as b_2
- b_1 is less than b_2.

Progress Check 1.3

Look at each of the three possibilities in turn. Overall, would easyJet lose passengers or gain passengers for each of these possibilities?

The three possibilities effectively show how competitive easyJet's prices are relative to those of its airline competitors. In the first possibility it would lose more customers than it gains. In the second possibility the gains and losses would leave it as it is. In the third possibility it would win more than it lost. You have now completed your second mathematical economic analysis.

An important point to note at this stage is that the relationship we've been looking in Eq. 1 is expressed mathematically but contains no actual numbers. This is a common misunderstanding of the role of mathematics in economics. Of course, there are frequent occasions when we wish to use specific numerical values in such an equation. A business organization – easyJet for example – would wish to obtain precise and accurate forecasts of quantity demanded given specific values for the other variables in the equation. From the viewpoint of studying economic principles and theory, however, such number values are frequently irrelevant. Economists are often concerned with establishing key principles of economic behaviour – independently of whatever specific numbers happen to be appropriate. They might wish to work out, for example, the general principles of individual consumer behaviour if income changes. They might want to understand how firms would react if their labour costs increased. They might want to work out how both consumers and firms would react if interest rates increased. Accordingly, in this book we shall frequently be using general mathematical notation to establish general conclusions about economic behaviour. Naturally, we shall also be illustrating such important deductions with specific numerical values, although these are generally used primarily as an aid to understanding. In the real world considerable effort and attention is paid to obtaining and using such numerical values. This is the area known as *econometrics* or *econometric analysis* – another important and related area of economics.

1.2 Economic theory, economic models and mathematics

This leads us to another important area: the link between economic theory, economic models and mathematics. In economics we typically begin by observing something that's happening in a certain section of the economy. How much are consumers paying for the latest Apple smartphone? How are firms responding to the changes in the currency exchange rate? How is the energy industry responding to the latest government incentives to invest in green energy production? Using the example we have been using so far, we might observe that a particular level of demand for easyJet flights occurs. The economist will ask why this product was purchased by consumers and why this particular quantity of the product at this price. Typically, we will then try to develop a theoretical explanation of this observed economic behaviour (which is what we provided in Eq. 1.1). Such a theoretical explanation will generally involve the construction of an economic *model* (again, as we have provided in Eq. (1.1)). Other professions use models in their work. An architect may create a scale model of a new building so that people can see what it will look like. An engineer may use a model to help with the design of a new aeroplane so that he can see how changes in design may affect the aeroplane's performance.

In economics, we use models to help us understand various aspects of economic behaviour. There is no particular reason why an economic model has to be mathematical or why the underpinning theory needs to be expressed in mathematical terms. Indeed, much early economic thinking did not make use of mathematics as such. However, as we have seen, there are factors that may strongly encourage us to make use of mathematics in the model-building process. In addition, if the model is mathematical it will involve an equation (or equations) linking certain economic variables together. Typically, we will then wish to examine the model in a mathematical manner. This will involve:

- Setting out the key assumptions on which the model is built
- Using these assumptions to examine the logical deductions to be obtained from the model
- Reaching conclusions about predicted economic behaviour
- Comparing our conclusions with actual economic behaviour.

Naturally, such a process is not usually as simple as it first appears. The whole process, in fact, will be iterative: we specify key assumptions, make logical deductions, reach conclusions and then we may find that the conclusions derived from the model are inconsistent with observed economic behaviour. We then have to return to the model for further development and refinement until we are satisfied that the model provides a reasonable explanation of the observed economic phenomenon (or until we abandon this theory because of its repeated failure to provide such an explanation). Mathematics in economics, therefore, is primarily concerned with the application of mathematical principles and logic to the theoretical aspects of economic analysis. Frequently, the next stage is a rigorous empirical investigation of the theory that has been developed thus far.

At this stage, econometrics comes into play. Econometrics is primarily concerned with the measurement of economic data and economic relationships. Using both mathematics and the principles of statistical inference, econometrics seeks to empirically evaluate a theoretical economic model. In this book we are not concerned with econometrics or indeed with empirical evaluation of economic models as such, although we do need to be aware of its critical role in the process of economic analysis. Figure I.1 illustrates the process.

We must remember, however, that any economic model – whether mathematical or not – is a simplified representation of a far more complex real-world situation. The purpose of models in this context is to reduce these real-world complexities to a level that can be understood and analysed. By definition, a model restricts its attention to

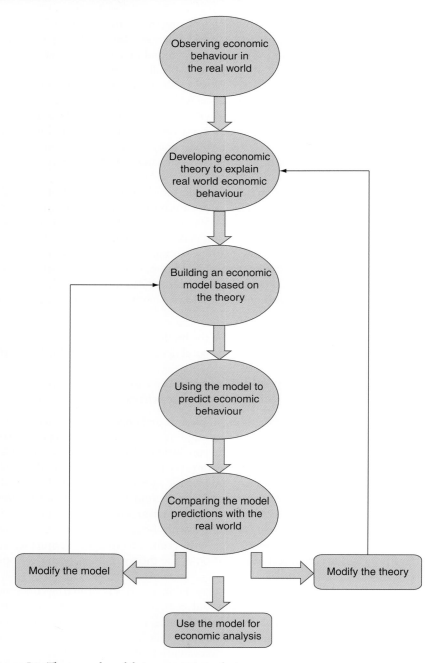

Figure I.1 Theory and models in economic analysis

what are seen to be the key features of the situation under investigation. So, in the context of our earlier example, there will be numerous factors influencing the quantity of a good that is purchased. An economic model will, however, focus on only a few of these factors – naturally, the ones thought to be most important in the context of the analysis. We did this earlier with Eq. 1.1 for easyJet.

1.3 Summary

We are now in a position to begin our investigation into the uses of mathematics in the study of economic analysis. Mathematics plays a critical role in providing economists with the logic and analytical tools needed to develop and investigate economic theories which are at the heart of economics and the study of economic behaviour. Without an adequate understanding of mathematics and its role in economics your career in this subject area will be severely curtailed. By the time you reach the end of this text we're convinced that your knowledge and appreciation of the usefulness of mathematics to the economist will have undergone a fundamental change.

Exercises

1.1 Earlier in this module we looked at the idea of a demand situation – considering the factors that will affect demand for a product. Consider the other side of the picture: the quantity of the good supplied by the individual firm. What variables do you think we would wish to link with the quantity supplied? What numerical values do you think each of these would take? Try using easyJet as an example again.

1.2 How do you think such numerical values could be obtained in practice?

1.3 Consider a variable, C, which represents the annual expenditure (consumption) of a particular individual. What variables do you think would influence consumption? Assess whether you would expect each variable to have a positive or a negative influence.

1.4 Consider an individual's consumption of a particular good – coffee. Identify a set of variables that you feel would influence such consumption and develop a simple model for determining such consumption. Consider the assumptions you are making – explicitly and implicitly – in your model. Practically, how could you test how good your model was?

1.5 In the context of Exercise 1.4 consider the annual national import of coffee. What variables do you think would influence imports of this good? How does your list of variables compare with that of Exercise 1.4 and how do you explain the differences?

Section A
The building blocks of economic analysis

In the introductory module we hope we convinced you that being able to use mathematics in economic analysis is essential if you want to study economics seriously. In this section we provide the necessary building blocks to enable you to understand and to start using mathematics and economic analysis effectively together. The section is divided into three modules.

Module A1 Tools of the trade: the basics of algebra

This module provides a refresher and reminder of the key principles of mathematics, in particular algebra and algebraic calculations, which are essential for the topics that follow.

Module A2 Linear relationships in economic analysis

This module looks at how we can express economic relationships using the simplest form of mathematics, which involves linear, or straight-line, equations. We'll look at the idea of functions and show how to use graphs to illustrate linear economic relationships.

Module A3 Non-linear relationships in economic analysis

Finally, in this section we look at non-linear relationships in economics. While linear equations are useful and easy to use, they're often restrictive in terms of building an accurate economic model. Frequently, economic relationships need to be modelled in a non-linear way. In this module we look at non-linear equations and equations involving several variables.

You may already be familiar and comfortable with the material in some of these modules. To help you check whether or not it's worth your while reading a particular module, we've included a Knowledge Check activity towards the start of each module. This is a short activity that will help you work out if you already know about the material of that module. If you answer the Knowledge Check correctly we suggest you don't need to read that module but move straight on to the exercises at the end of the module as they'll give you extra practice at seeing the connection between maths and economics. If you find any of the exercises especially challenging you can always go back and read the relevant part of that module.

Module A1
Tools of the trade: the basics of algebra

This module reviews a number of the basic principles in algebra. As we work through the text, you will see that economic analysis makes a lot of use of algebra to support and develop economic theory and to reach conclusions about economic behaviour: how firms will respond to a tax change; how consumers will respond to a change in interest rates; how government will respond to a change in exchange rates and so on. As mentioned in the Introduction, one of the main benefits of using mathematics in economic analysis is to help us to deduce general economic conclusions without having to resort to specific numerical values. Algebra allows us to do this, and although some algebra procedures may at first seem more like black magic than reasoned economic logic, you will find that, with practice, such manipulations begin to make sense. It may be some time since you last had to use algebra, so this module is intended to refresh your memory. The material that follows will allow you to gradually develop your own skills with algebra. However, if you find that you are unable to follow some of the algebraic manipulations that take place later in the text, you can return to the appropriate part of this module to help you.

Learning Objectives

By the end of this module you should be able to:

- Use algebraic notation to show economic relationships
- Work with brackets
- Work with inequalities
- Work with fractions
- Transpose an algebraic expression.

Knowledge Check A1

To check how comfortable you are with algebra already, try solving these:

(i) $y = \dfrac{3x + 3}{2x + 5}$

Find an expression for x

Knowledge Check A1 *(Continued)*

(ii) Simplify the expression $7x/4x^2 - 8x/2x^3$

Check your answers in Appendix 2. If you got the correct answers try out some of the exercises at the end of the module for extra practice and then move to module A2.

And, if you've no idea what to do, read on. You will be able to do these by the time you complete the end of this module.

A1.1 Algebraic notation

If you want to find out more about where algebra came from try http://en.wikipedia.org/wiki/Algebra

We start by looking at how algebra can be used to show a simple economic situation. For example, individual consumers would normally distinguish between their *gross* income and their *disposable* income. Gross income would mean all the income that they had: what they earned in wages or salaries; what they received in interest on their savings; or dividend payments from shares they had bought in companies. In most economies, though, your gross income is not what you actually have to spend. Typically, there are compulsory deductions from your gross income, such as government tax on your salary/interest/dividends, compulsory payments into a health insurance scheme in case you fall ill and compulsory payments into a pension scheme for when you retire. Disposable income is that income the consumer has left to spend after any deductions (such as tax) have been taken from their gross income. We've already seen in the Introduction how we can use mathematical notation to help illustrate simple economic models, and we will do the same here. We'll use Y_g to refer to gross income and D to refer to all deductions and we'll use Y_d for disposable income. Using algebraic notation we would then write:

$$Y_d = Y_g - D \tag{A1.1}$$

That is, disposable income, Y_d, is simply gross income, Y_g, less deductions, D.

As a slight digression, it is worth knowing that certain economic variables, like income, conventionally tend to be shown algebraically using specific letters. For example:

Y is used for income
P for price
C for consumption
G for government spending

and so on. We'll do the same throughout this book. And in case you're wondering why we use Y for income and not I, it is because I is used to refer to investment. It is also common practice to use subscripts with a variable when there may be different versions of that variable. That's why we have Y_g and Y_d.

A1.2 Arithmetic in algebra

Even with such a simple expression as Eq. A1.1 it is clear that we can obtain two related expressions:

$$D = Y_g - Y_d \tag{A1.2}$$

$$Y_g = Y_d + D \tag{A1.3}$$

Eq. A1.2 indicates that deductions, D, are simply the difference between gross income, Y_g, and disposable income, Y_d, and Eq. A1.3 indicates that gross income is equal to disposable income plus deductions. While Eqs A1.2 and A1.3 are easily obtained using some simple logic it will also be worth exploring the algebraic arithmetic. These principles will be useful when we look at more complex expressions.

To find an expression from Eq. A1.1 where D equals some combination of the other two variables, we can rearrange Eq. A1.1 (or any other algebraic expression) by understanding that if *one side* of an algebraic expression is altered we keep the algebraic relationship exactly the same *as long as* we alter the *other side* of the expression in exactly the same way. This is an important rule in algebra and one that we will use a lot. From Eq. A1.1 we have:

$$Y_d = Y_g - D$$

The rule says that the algebraic expression remains unchanged in terms of the underlying relationship if we alter both sides of the expression in the same way. If we add D to each side we have:

$$D + Y_d = Y_g - D + D$$

and by simple inspection we see that the two Ds on the right-hand side will cancel each other out to give:

$$D + Y_d = Y_g$$

If we now subtract Y_d from both sides (which again leaves the relationship unchanged as both sides of the equation are treated in the same way) this gives:

$$D + Y_d - Y_d = Y_g - Y_d$$

where, again, the two Y_d terms on the left-hand side cancel each other out to give

$$D = Y_g - Y_d$$

It is important to realize that this equation and Eq. A1.1 are identical.

We've deliberately taken a detailed, step-by-step approach, but you won't always need to be as methodical because it soon becomes obvious how to use this type of arithmetic with algebraic expressions.

Progress Check A1.1

Using the algebra we've just shown, try the following examples yourself and then carry on reading the text.

Rearrange each of the following expressions so that you have an expression in the form $Y =$

(i) $5Y + 3X - 10 = 25$
(ii) $A - C = Y + 10 - B$
(iii) $6A = 4Y - 5C$
(iv) $0.2X - 0.75Z = 0.3Y + 1512$

We'll work through each of these in the next section, but try them yourself first.

Taking each in turn, we have:

(i) $5Y + 3X - 10 = 25$

Using the rule from earlier, we can add 10 to both sides to give:

$$5Y + 3X - 10 + 10 = 25 + 10$$

with the two 10s on the left cancelling each other out to give

$$5Y + 3X = 35$$

Next we can subtract $3X$ from both sides to get:

$$5Y + 3X - 3X = 35 - 3X$$

Again, the two $3X$s on the left cancel each other out, giving:

$$5Y = 35 - 3X$$

Finally, we can divide both sides by 5:

$$\frac{5Y}{5} = \frac{35}{5} - \frac{3X}{5}$$

Which, if we do the maths, gives:

$$Y = 7 - \frac{3X}{5}$$

Once again, it is important to remember that, although this equation and the one we started with look very different, they are in fact identical.

(ii) $A - C = Y + 10 - B$

We want to rearrange this to get Y onto the left-hand side of the equation and everything else on the right-hand side. We can do this in several different ways, but let's first add B to both sides to get:

$$A - C + B = Y + 10 - B + B$$

And, with the two Bs on the right-hand side cancelling each other out, we get:

$$A - C + B = Y + 10$$

Now we can subtract 10 from both sides, giving:

$$A - C + B - 10 = Y + 10 - 10$$

or

$$A - C + B - 10 = Y$$

If we now simply swap over the left-hand and right-hand sides we get:

$$Y = A - C + B - 10$$

You might have done this in a different order, but should still have reached the same result.

(iii) $6A = 4Y - 5C$

Add $5C$ to both sides:

$$6A + 5C = 4Y - 5C + 5C$$
$$6A + 5C = 4Y$$

We now divide both sides by 4:

$$\frac{6A}{4} + \frac{5C}{4} = \frac{4Y}{4}$$

Simplifying and switching both sides gives:

$$Y = 1.5A + 1.25C$$

(iv)   Finally, we had $0.2X - 0.75Z = 0.3Y + 1512$

Subtracting 1512 we obtain:

$$0.2X - 0.75Z - 1512 = 0.3Y$$

Dividing through by 0.3 we obtain:

$$\frac{0.2X}{0.3} - \frac{0.75Z}{0.3} - \frac{1512}{0.3} = Y$$

Rearranging and simplifying gives:

$$Y = 0.67X - 2.5Z - 5040$$

The last example did not show all the detailed steps and calculations, but you should be able to follow what's happening.

A1.3 Brackets in algebra

The use of brackets in algebra is quite common, and we need to be familiar with how to use them. Let's go back to Eq. A1.1 where we had:

$$Y = S - D$$

Let's now define D, deductions, as:

$$D = f + tY_g \tag{A1.4}$$

where f is a fixed amount deducted from each person's gross income while t is a proportionate tax (expressed as a decimal) deducted from gross income Y_g. For example, suppose the government taxes everyone €100 and also sets income tax at 25% of gross income; f would be 100 and t would be 0.25, implying that deductions would be a fixed sum of €100 regardless of actual income plus 25% of gross income earned. We can now substitute Eq. A1.4 into Eq. A1.1:

$$Y_d = Y_g - D$$
$$Y_d = Y_g - (f + tY_g) \tag{A1.5}$$

Eq. A1.5 could be simplified by removing the brackets and rearranging the expression. However, we must remember that we cannot simply remove the brackets from the expression to give:

$$Y_d = Y_g - f + tY_g$$

You should be able to see what is wrong with this expression. We should subtract *both f and Y_g* and not just f. This gives a simple rule that, if we wish to remove brackets from an expression, then *all* the terms within the brackets must have the same arithmetical operation performed on them. In Eq. A1.5, for example, we must multiply each term within the brackets by a negative sign (since this is the mathematical operator immediately before the bracket expression). This then gives:

$$Y_d = Y_g - f - tY_g$$

We then collect all the Y_g terms together (collecting the common terms together in this way is something we will frequently want to do in economics):

$$Y_d = Y_g - tY_g - f$$

We now have two Y_g terms. We can now rewrite this equation as:

$$Y_d = 1Y_g - tY_g - f$$

or rearrange it as

$$Y_d = (1 - t)Y_g - f \qquad\qquad (A1.6)$$

If you look carefully at Eq. A1.6 you will note that it is the same as the previous equation. It may seem odd that we want to remove brackets first and then reintroduce them, but what we have been able to do with Eq. A1.5 is to derive an expression where similar terms appear together to help interpretation and evaluation of the expression. We can generalize the approach by saying that:

$$ab + ac = a(b + c)$$

where a is a term common to both parts. To see how this works let's go back to where we had:

$$Y_g - tY_g$$

or, as we wrote it

$$1Y_g - tY_g$$

The common term here is Y_g, so we have:

$$ab + ac = a(b + c)$$

In other words:

$$a = Y_g$$
$$b = 1$$
$$c = -t \text{ (remember the minus sign)}$$

so

> In Eq. A1.6 we showed this as $(1 - t)Y_g$, which is the same

$$a(b + c) = Y_g(1 - t)$$

We could just as well have had three, four or more terms inside the brackets and the same approach would be appropriate. Similarly, we could have had more than one term, a, before the bracket. For example:

$$(a + b)(c + d)$$

would give

$$ac + bc + ad + bd$$

and you can see that each term within the first set of brackets has, in turn, been multiplied by each term within the second set of brackets. Notice, though, that the order in which we multiply does not matter. This principle is readily extended to more than two sets of brackets or to brackets containing more than two expressions.

Progress Check A1.2

For each of the following expressions multiply out the brackets and, where relevant, simplify the expressions.

(i) $10x(3a - c)$

(ii) $(5x - 3y)(2x + 4y)$

(iii) $3(x + y - z) - (4y + 2)x$

Try these first before reading on.

Taking each in turn we have:

(i) $10x(3a - c)$

And we can multiply the two terms inside the brackets by $10x$ to give:

$30ax - 10cx$

Notice that it doesn't matter whether we write $30ax$ or $30xa$.

(ii) $(5x - 3y)(2x + 4y)$

We multiply each of the two terms in the second bracket first by $5x$ and then by $-3y$ (remember the minus sign):

Multiply by $5x$: $5x2x + 5x4y$
Multiply by $-3y$: $-3y2x - 3y4y$

When we multiply a variable like x by itself we get x^2 (x squared). (If you don't remember how to work with powers like x^2 you might want to read through the short appendix to this module on p. 31.) This would give us:

$5x2x + 5x4y = 10x^2 + 20xy$

and

$-3y2x - 3y4y = -6xy - 12y^2$

and combining these two expressions together we get

$10x^2 + 20xy - 6xy - 12y^2$

or

$10x^2 + 14xy - 12y^2$

(iii) $3(x + y - z) - (4y + 2)x$

If you think this appears complicated, remember to break it into parts and then add the parts together at the end. Let's take the first part of this and multiply the brackets through by 3:

$3(x + y - z) = 3x + 3y - 3z$

and now the second part (remembering the minus sign)

$-(4y + 2)x = -4xy - 2x$

and if we now collect both parts together we have

$3x + 3y - 3z - 4xy - 2x$

and collecting common terms together we have

$x + 3y - 3z - 4xy$

Multiple brackets

We have seen how we can multiply out brackets in an expression. There are times when we have multiple sets of brackets. For example:

$3x(4 - y(15 - x))$

Again, this looks complicated but if we do it part by part it's straightforward. We multiply this out in much the same way, but making sure that we start with the *inside* set of brackets first – those around $(15 - x)$ – and then gradually work outwards. So, multiplying out the inside set first we have:

$$-y(15 - x) = -15y + xy$$

and then

$$3x(4 - 15y + xy)$$

and then

$$12x - 45xy + 3x^2y$$

Expressions involving multiple sets of brackets can be simplified using this approach: find the innermost set of brackets, work out that expression, find the next innermost set of brackets, work that out – and so on.

Progress Check A1.3

Simplify each of the following expressions:

(i) $15x(3x - 2y(y - x))$

(ii) $(4x - 3y(4x + 3y)(5x))$

(iii) $(2x - 3y + 4z(2x + 3(15y)))$

For (i) we have:

$$15x(3x - 2y(y - x)) = 15x(3x - 2y^2 + 2xy)$$

(multiplying the $(y - x)$ term by $2y$ and remembering the change in sign when we have two negatives multiplied). This then becomes:

$$15x(3x - 2y^2 + 2xy) = 45x^2 - 30xy^2 + 30x^2y$$

Note that we cannot simplify further: the last two terms are not identical.

(ii) $(4x - 3y(4x + 3y)(5x))$

Multiplying together the two bracket terms inside the outside bracket, $(4x + 3y)$ and $(5x)$, we have:

$$(4x - 3y(20x^2 + 15xy))$$

Multiply through by $-3y$:

$$4x - 60x^2y + 45xy^2$$

(iii) $(2x - 3y + 4z(2x + 3(15y)))$

Multiply through the two terms on the right of the expression $3(15y)$:

$$(2x - 3y + 4z(2x + 45y))$$

Multiply through by $4z$:

$$2x - 3y + 8xz + 180yz$$

A1.4 Inequalities

So far we have explored algebraic expressions in the form of *equations*, where an expression on the left-hand side is set exactly equal to another expression on the right-hand side. Occasionally we will wish to explore relationships that are expressed in the form of an *inequality*. For example, we may have:

$$x > y$$

which is read as 'x is greater than y' and where the symbol $>$ indicates that x must take values greater than y at all times. Similarly, we may have:

$x < y$ x always takes a value less than y
$x \geq y$ x always takes a value which is greater than or equal to y (i.e. x values cannot be less than y but they could be the same as y or greater than y)
$x \leq y$ x always takes a value which is less than or equal to y (i.e. x values cannot be greater than y).

Let's go back to Eq. A1.4 where we had:

$$D = f + tY_g$$

where t is a tax imposed on gross income, Y_g. If we express the tax as a decimal (e.g. a tax that took 25% of income would be shown as 0.25) then we would have:

$t \geq 0$ i.e. the tax rate could not be negative
$t < 1$ the tax rate must be less than 1 (or less than 100%).

The first inequality could be rewritten instead as:

$$0 \leq t$$

so we could merge the two inequalities together to give

$$0 \leq t < 1$$

That is, t must lie within a range between 0 but less than 1.

It will also be worth exploring how inequalities are affected if we manipulate them using the algebraic principles developed earlier. We have already seen that we can manipulate equations in any way we wish as long as we alter both sides of the equation in the same way. Let us see if the same principle applies to inequalities. Consider:

$$x < y$$

where $x = 2$ and $y = 10$. Then:

$$2 < 10$$

which is clearly correct. Suppose we add 4 to both sides:

$$2 + 4 < 10 + 4$$
$$6 < 14$$

which is still correct. Suppose we now subtract 20 from both sides:

$$6 - 20 < 14 - 20$$
$$-14 < -6$$

which is still correct (although you may have to think about this one: -14 is lower (less) on the negative scale than -6 so the inequality holds true).

So addition and subtraction do not affect the inequality. What about multiplication and division? We had:

$$2 < 10$$

If we multiply both sides by 5:

$$2 \times 5 < 10 \times 5$$
$$10 < 50$$

which is correct. Suppose we now multiply by -2:

$$10 \times -2 < 50 \times -2$$
$$-20 < -100$$

which is clearly *incorrect* since -100 is a larger negative number and is less than -20. This leads us to a simple manipulation rule when dealing with inequalities: *if both sides of an inequality are multiplied/divided by a negative number, the direction of the inequality is reversed.*

So, if we had:

$$x < y$$

and multiplied through by $-n$, we would have

$$-nx > -ny$$

Progress Check A1.4

Simplify the following expressions by collecting all variable terms on one side and all numerical values on the other:

(i) $4x + 7 < 3x - 5$

(ii) $4x - 3 > 6x + 2$

(iii) $-4x + 5 \geq 6 - 3x$

For (i) we have:

$$4x + 7 < 3x - 5$$

Subtracting 7 gives:

$$4x + 7 - 7 < 3x - 5 - 7$$
$$4x < 3x - 12$$

Subtracting $3x$:

$$4x - 3x < 3x - 12 - 3x$$
$$x < -12$$

That is, x must always take values that are less than -12.

(ii) $4x - 3 > 6x + 2$

Add 3 to give:

$$4x > 6x + 5$$

Subtract $6x$:
$$4x - 6x > 5$$
$$-2x > 5$$
Divide through by -2:
$$x < -2.5$$
remembering that as we divide through by a negative value we must reverse the inequality sign. That is, x is less than or equal to -2.5.

(iii) $\quad -4x + 5 \geq 6 - 3x$

Add $3x$:
$$-4x + 3x + 5 \geq 6$$
$$-x + 5 \geq 6$$
Subtract 5:
$$-x \geq 6 - 5$$
$$-x \geq 1$$
Divide through by -1:
$$x \leq -1$$
again remembering to reverse the direction of the inequality.

A1.5 Fractions

We now look at the use of fractions in algebra. You will already be familiar with numerical fractions such as:
$$\frac{2}{3} \text{ or } \frac{1}{10} \text{ or } \frac{72}{100}$$
You may also remember that the number on the top of the fraction expression is referred to as the *numerator* and the one on the bottom as the *denominator*. In algebra we may have fractions such as:
$$\frac{a}{b} \text{ or } \frac{a^2 - 3b}{2a - b^2} \text{ or } \frac{15 - b}{3a^2 - 2ab}$$
The rules for manipulation of algebraic fractions are virtually the same as those for numerical fractions.

Multiplication

To multiply two or more fractions we multiply the numerator terms together and then multiply the denominator terms together. For example:
$$\frac{a}{b} \times \frac{c}{d} = \frac{a \times c}{b \times d} = \frac{ac}{bd}$$

Division

To divide one fraction by another, we invert (turn upside down) the fraction we are dividing by and then multiply the two fractions together:
$$\frac{a}{b} \Big/ \frac{c}{d} = \frac{a}{b} \times \frac{d}{c} = \frac{ad}{bc}$$

Addition/subtraction

To add or subtract two fractions, we put them over a *common denominator* and add/subtract the numerators. We will illustrate this with a numerical example first. Suppose we want:

$$\frac{3}{4} + \frac{1}{2}$$

A common denominator is a number of which 4 and 2 (the two original denominators) are exact multiples. In this case one common denominator would be 4 since the denominator 4 goes into this exactly once and the other denominator 2 goes into this exactly twice. We then use these multiples (1 and 2) to multiply the respective numerators. That is:

$$\frac{3}{4} + \frac{1}{2} = \frac{(1 \times 3) + (2 \times 1)}{4} = \frac{3+2}{4} = \frac{5}{4}$$

Note that we have multiplied the first numerator, 3, by 1 since its denominator (4) goes into the common denominator exactly once. We have multiplied the second numerator (1) by 2 since its denominator goes into the common denominator exactly twice.

Choosing a common denominator

When deciding which common denominator to use there's frequently an obvious number that will be exactly divisible by each of the two fraction denominators. There are times, however, when such a number is not immediately obvious. In such a case an easy approach is simply to use a common denominator that is the result of multiplying the two fraction denominators together. For example:

$$\frac{3}{7} + \frac{2}{3}$$

As there is no obvious common denominator that springs to mind, we choose 21 (7 × 3). The arithmetic would then be:

$$\frac{(3 \times 3) + (2 \times 7)}{21} = \frac{9 + 14}{21} = \frac{23}{21}$$

Progress Check A1.5

Simplify each of the following expressions:

(i) 3/5 + 8/4

(ii) 2/6 + 3/7

(iii) 4/5 + 2/3 + 6/8

For (i) we use a common denominator of 20 (5 × 4) to give:

$$\frac{(3 \times 4) + (8 \times 5)}{20} = \frac{12 + 40}{20} = \frac{52}{20}$$

Notice that while we can leave the result as 52/20 we can simplify further since both the numerator and denominator can be divided through by a common factor.

For example, divide both through by 2 (and since we are applying the same arithmetic to top and bottom it will leave the expression unchanged):

$$\frac{52}{20} = \frac{26}{10}$$

26/10 can be further simplified, again dividing by 2 to give:

$$\frac{26}{10} = \frac{13}{5}$$

Of course, we could have divided the top and bottom of 52/20 through by 4 straightaway. This type of simplification is quite common in economics, and so it is worthwhile familiarizing yourself with it, particularly with algebraic rather than arithmetic examples.

(ii) $2/6 + 3/7$

A common denominator of 42 (6×7) gives:

$$\frac{(2 \times 7) + (3 \times 6)}{42} = \frac{14 + 18}{42} = \frac{32}{42}$$

This can be simplified again by dividing through by 2:

$$\frac{32}{42} = \frac{16}{21}$$

(iii) $4/5 + 2/3 + 6/8$

Although we have not explicitly looked at three fractions being added together, we can simply add the first two and then add this product to the third (although with practice we might be able to perform the arithmetic in one step rather than two). We have:

$$\frac{(4 \times 3) + (2 \times 5)}{15} = \frac{22}{15}$$

> We use 5×3 as a common denominator for the first two fractions

and then

$$\frac{22}{15} + \frac{6}{8} = \frac{(22 \times 8) + (6 \times 15)}{120} = \frac{176 + 90}{120} = \frac{266}{120}$$

> We use 15×8 as a common denominator for the next two fractions

Simplifying gives:

$$\frac{266}{120} = \frac{133}{60} \quad \text{(dividing through by 2).}$$

We could have performed the arithmetic in one step as:

$$\frac{4}{5} + \frac{2}{3} + \frac{6}{8}$$

$$\frac{4(3 \times 8) + 2(5 \times 8) + 6(5 \times 3)}{(5 \times 3 \times 8)} = \frac{96 + 80 + 90}{120} = \frac{266}{120}$$

Subtraction

So far we have looked only at the addition of fractions; but exactly the same approach applies to subtraction. For example:

$$\frac{3}{5} - \frac{2}{3} = \frac{(3 \times 3) - (2 \times 5)}{15} = \frac{9 - 10}{15} = \frac{-1}{15}$$

For (i) we have:

$$\frac{3}{4} - \frac{2}{3} = \frac{(3 \times 3) - (2 \times 4)}{4 \times 3} = \frac{9 - 8}{12} = \frac{1}{12}$$

For (ii):

$$\frac{2}{5} - \frac{1}{9} = \frac{(2 \times 9) - (1 \times 5)}{45} = \frac{18 - 5}{45} = \frac{13}{45}$$

For (iii):

$$\frac{2}{5} - \frac{4}{7} + \frac{1}{8}$$

$$\frac{2(7 \times 8) - 4(5 \times 8) + 1(5 \times 7)}{(5 \times 7 \times 8)} = \frac{112 - 160 + 35}{280} = \frac{-13}{280}$$

Fractions with algebraic expressions

The same principles apply to algebraic expressions. For example:

$$\frac{x}{x+2} \times \frac{3x}{2x^2}$$

Multiplying the two denominators gives:

$$(x + 2)(2x^2) = 2x^3 + 4x^2$$

and then multiplying the two numerators gives

$$\frac{3x^2}{2x^3 + 4x^2}$$

However, if we divide both the numerator and denominator by x^2 we have:

$$\frac{3}{2x + 4}$$

Note that when we are cancelling out terms in an algebraic expression we must be careful to ensure that the term being used appears in all parts of the expression, as in this case.

Taking each in turn, for (i) we have:

$$\frac{(3x-6)}{x^2} \Big/ \frac{5x}{3x^2}$$

Recollecting that if we invert the second term and then multiply we have:

$$\frac{(3x-6)}{x^2} \times \frac{3x^2}{5x}$$

Notice that we can cancel the x^2 term on both top and bottom to give:

$$\frac{(3x-6)}{1} \times \frac{3}{5x} = \frac{9x-18}{5x}$$

We cannot cancel the x terms since they do not appear in each part of the final expression (the -18 term does not have an x attached to it).

For (ii):

$$\frac{5x}{4x^2} + \frac{3x^3}{5x}$$

we have a common denominator of $(4x^2)(5x)$ which is $20x^3$:

$$\frac{5x(5x) + 3x^3(4x^2)}{20x^3} = \frac{25x^2 + 12x^5}{20x^3}$$

If we wished we could simplify further as:

$$\frac{25 + 12x^3}{20x}$$

> We can divide through by the common term x^2

One useful way of checking whether we can simplify by cancelling a common term is to break the fraction into its component parts:

$$\frac{25x^2 + 12x^5}{20x^3} = \frac{25x^2}{20x^3} + \frac{12x^5}{20x^3}$$

It will then be apparent that both parts of the expression have a common term which can be cancelled (x^2 in this case).

For (iii):

$$\frac{7x}{4x^2} - \frac{8x}{2x^3}$$

we have a common denominator of $(4x^2)(2x^3)$ or $(8x^5)$ giving:

$$\frac{7x(2x^3) - 8x(4x^2)}{8x^5} = \frac{14x^4 - 32x^3}{8x^5}$$

Cancelling through by $2x^3$ we have:

$$\frac{7x - 16}{4x^2}$$

A1.6 Transposing an expression

The last aspect of algebra that we shall examine relates to the *transposition* of an expression (basically, rearranging it into another form). For example, consider the expression:

$$-ax = bx - cy + d \tag{A1.7}$$

We wish to rearrange this into an expression such that:

$x =$ an expression involving all other terms.

The first step is to collect x terms together. From Eq. A1.7 we can subtract bx from both sides to give:

$$-ax - bx = -cy + d$$

The two terms on the left-hand side have an x term in common, so we have:

$$x(-a - b) = cy + d$$

Dividing both sides through by $(-a - b)$ gives:

$$x = \frac{cy + d}{-a - b}$$

Progress Check A1.8

From Eq. A1.7 derive an expression for y.

We have:

$$-ax = bx - cy + d$$

Subtracting bx gives:

$$-ax - bx = -cy + d$$

Subtracting d:

$$-ax - bx - d = -cy$$

Multiplying through by -1:

$$ax + bx + d = cy$$

Dividing through by c:

$$y = \frac{ax + bx + d}{c}$$

We may also apply these principles to a more complex expression. Suppose we wish to derive an expression for x from:

$$y = \frac{x + 2}{x - 4}$$

Multiplying through by $(x - 4)$:

$$y(x - 4) = x + 2$$

Multiplying out the left-hand side:

$$yx - 4y = x + 2$$

Adding $4y$ to both sides:

$$yx = x + 2 + 4y$$

Subtracting x:

$$yx - x = 2 + 4y$$

The left-hand side terms have x in common, so:

$$x(y-1) = 2+4y$$

and dividing through by $(y-1)$:

$$x = \frac{2+4y}{y-1}$$

Although this type of manipulation looks complicated it is simply a matter of practice and applying a few basic rules. Use the algebraic principles we have developed to:

- Remove any fractions by cross-multiplication
- Multiply out any brackets
- Collect x terms on one side
- Find any factors/multiples of x
- Divide through by the x coefficient.

If you're in any doubt as to whether you've applied these principles correctly, choose a couple of numerical values for x and solve for y using the original expression. Then use these y values in your transposed result and see whether you get the same x values (which, of course, you will if you've not made a mistake anywhere).

Progress Check A1.9

Find an expression for x from:

(i) $y = \dfrac{x-5}{x+3}$

(ii) $y = \dfrac{3x+3}{2x-5}$

For (i), using the steps above:

$$y(x+3) = x-5$$
$$yx+3y = x-5$$
$$yx-x = -3y-5$$
$$x(y-1) = -3y-5$$
$$x = \frac{-3y-5}{y-1}$$

For (ii):

$$y = \frac{3x+3}{2x-5}$$
$$y(2x-5) = 3x+3$$
$$2yx-5y = 3x+3$$
$$2yx-3x = 5y+3$$
$$x(2y-3) = 5y+3$$
$$x = \frac{5y+3}{2y-3}$$

A1.7 Summary

This brings us to the end of this module on basic algebra and, although at times it might have looked complicated, algebra follows a set of basic rules. As long as you know what the rules are and have a steady, methodical approach to working with algebraic expressions, you will soon see how it works. If you've been able to follow what we've been doing in this module then you're ready to move on to where we can really start seeing how mathematics can be used in economic analysis. If, at any stage in the text, you have difficulty following the algebraic manipulations, return to the relevant part of this module and re-read that section.

Learning Check

Having read this module you should have learned that:

- A basic rule in algebra is that if both sides of an expression are changed in the same way the expression remains unchanged
- When you're working with multiple brackets, start with the ones on the inside and work outwards
- If both sides of an expression are multiplied or divided by a negative value, the direction of an inequality is reversed
- To divide by a fraction, turn it upside down and multiply
- To add/subtract fractions, put them over a common denominator and add/subtract the numerators.

Exercises

A1.1   For each of the following equations find the simplest form:

i) $y = \dfrac{3x + 3}{2x - 5}$

ii) $7x/4x^2 - 8x/2x^3$

(These were in the Knowledge Check at the start of this module.)

A1.2   For each of the following expressions find the simplest form:

i) $5(x - y) + 2(y - 3x)$

ii) $4x(3x - 2) + 0.5(x - 4y)$

iii) $(x - 2y)(3y - 5x)$

iv) $z(2x - y) - z(5x - 2)$

v) $3x(5 - 2x(y - x(3x - 6)))$

vi) $0.4y(3x(2 - 4y) + 2y(5 - 3x(x - 10)))$

A1.3   For each of the following expressions find the simplest form:

i) $x/(x - 1) \times 2/x(x - 4)$

ii) $7x/2x^3 + 5x/2x$

iii) $15x^3/3x^2 - 0.5x^2/3x$

iv) $6x/3x(5x - 10) + 2x^3/4(3 - 10x)$

Exercises *(Continued)*

A1.4   A company selling a particular product knows that the quantity of the product demanded by customers is given by the expression:

$$Q_d = 100 - 5P$$

where Q_d is the quantity of the product demanded and P is the price charged. Similarly, the quantity that the company is willing to supply is given by:

$$Q_s = -100 + 20P$$

where Q_s is the quantity supplied and P is the price charged. Equilibrium is defined as the price charged so that $Q_d = Q_s$. Find the price that will give equilibrium. What quantity will be demanded/supplied at this price?

A1.5   For the firm in A1.4, we now have:

$$Q_d = a - bP$$
$$Q_s = c + dP$$

Find an algebraic expression that will allow you to determine equilibrium price. Check this using the parameters in A1.4.

Appendix A1 Powers and exponents

When using mathematics in economic analysis we frequently come across terms such as x^2 or x^5 or $x^{-0.5}$. You will need to be able to use expressions like these. This is relatively straightforward once you understand that such notation is in fact a form of mathematical shorthand. Suppose we want to show some simple arithmetic:

$$10 \times 10 = 100$$
$$10 \times 10 \times 10 = 1000$$
$$10 \times 10 \times 10 \times 10 = 10,000$$

and so on. There's nothing wrong with showing such arithmetic in this way. However, it can be more convenient at times to use mathematical shorthand:

$$10 \times 10 = 10^2$$

where we say that the result of multiplying 10 by itself is 10^2 where the term ^{2} is known as the *power* or *exponent*. The power/exponent simply shows how many times we multiply a number/variable by itself. So, from above, we have:

$$10 \times 10 = 100 = 10^2$$
$$10 \times 10 \times 10 = 1000 = 10^3$$
$$10 \times 10 \times 10 \times 10 = 10,000 = 10^4$$

If we were using variables rather than numbers we'd have:

$$a^2 = a \times a$$
$$a^3 = a \times a \times a$$
$$a^4 = a \times a \times a \times a$$

Sometimes we'll come across exponents that appear a little odd, for example a^{-1}. This looks like a multiplied by itself -1 times. Earlier we saw that:

$$10^4 = 10,000$$

$$10^3 = 1000$$

$$10^2 = 100$$

Clearly there is a pattern here. As the exponent drops from 4 to 3 to 2 a zero is 'lost' from the actual number on the right. So, if we continue this pattern, we obtain:

$$10^4 = 10,000$$

$$10^3 = 1000$$

$$10^2 = 100$$

$$10^1 = 10$$

$$10^0 = 1$$

$$10^{-1} = 0.1$$

$$10^{-2} = 0.01 \text{ and so on.}$$

Now let's consider the items we have added. Normally we wouldn't bother writing 10 as 10^1 but write just 10 instead. $10^0 = 1$ might seem odd at first but it follows from the logic of the sequence. In fact, we'll state without proof that any number/variable to the power 0 equals 1: this is worth remembering. The negative exponents are just as logical. Negative exponents show decimals in exponent form. Sometimes these are written in a different way. Recollect that:

$$0.1 = \frac{1}{10}$$

and

$$10 = 10^1$$

so

$$0.1 = \frac{1}{10} = \frac{1}{10^1}$$

So:

$$10^{-1} = 0.1 = 1/10^1$$

Similarly:

$$10^{-2} = 1/10^2$$

and a^{-3} would be $1/a^3$.

Just as we can carry out algebraic arithmetic on ordinary numbers or variables, so we can do much the same when dealing with exponents. There are four simple rules for doing algebraic arithmetic with exponents.

Rule 1

$$a^n \times a^m = a^{n+m}$$

For example:

$$10^2 \times 10^4 = 10^6$$

$$a^5 \times a^3 = a^8$$

> Here $n = 2$ and $m = 4$
> Try it out using the actual numbers if you're not sure

Rule 2

$$a^n / a^m = a^{n-m}$$

For example:

$$10^6 / 10^3 = 10^3$$
$$a^5 / a^4 = a^1 = a$$

A

Rule 3

$$(a^n)^m = a^{nm}$$

For example:

$$(10^3)^2 = 10^6$$
$$(a^2)^4 = a^8$$

> We're squaring the number 10^3 so this is actually Rule 1: $10^3 \times 10^3$

Rule 4

$$(ab)^n = a^n b^n$$

For example:

$$(3 \times 10)^3 = 3^3 10^3$$

This may be seen more clearly if we write:

$$(3 \times 10)^3 = (3 \times 10) \times (3 \times 10) \times (3 \times 10)$$

The order in which we multiply is unimportant, so we can rearrange this as:

$$(3 \times 10)^3 = (3 \times 3 \times 3) \times (10 \times 10 \times 10) = 3^3 10^3$$

An example involving variables rather than numbers is:

$$(ab)^4 = a^4 b^4$$

Powers and exponents are easy to work with if you remember the rules.

Module A2

Linear relationships in economic analysis

This module develops our understanding of economic relationships that can be expressed and understood in mathematical terms. We will start with the simplest mathematical form of a relationship – linear relationships, which can be shown as a straight line on a graph. You will learn to recognize these relationships, see how they are used in economic analysis and learn how linear mathematical equations and graphs can be used interchangeably.

Learning Objectives

By the end of this module you should be able to:

- Construct and use graphs
- Explain what is meant by a function
- Use functional notation
- Use linear functions.

Knowledge Check A2

If you think you're already familiar with the mathematics of linear equations, try answering the following. If:

$$Q_d = f(P) = 1250 - 6P$$

where Q_d is quantity demanded of a product and P is the price charged for the product, then:

(i)   What will this function look like when plotted on a graph?

(ii)   What does this intercept represent in terms of economic behaviour?

(iii)   What does this slope/gradient represent in terms of economic behaviour?

Check your answers in Appendix 2. If you got these right, try some of the exercises at the end of this module and then move on to module A3.

A2.1 Economic relationships

As we began to see in the Introduction, economics – in terms of theory, models and analysis – is concerned with the relationships that exist between sets of economic variables. Examples of such relationships are common. For example, the price charged for a product and the quantity demanded by consumers; the price of a product and the quantity produced by firms; consumer disposable income and consumer spending; the level of imports and the exchange rate; production levels and labour costs; and so on – and we would expect all these to be related in some way. In economic analysis we'll often want to examine such relationships in three related ways:

- Through a graph
- Through a function
- Through an equation.

Although these are effectively alternative ways of looking at the same relationship, you need to be proficient at each of them. You should also note that you may not want to use all three approaches every time. You can examine a graphical representation, or introduce a mathematical function or investigate an equation.

Let's look at Table A2.1. This shows a firm that has monitored the demand for one of its products by consumers over the last four months. You can see both the price charged per unit (which we can see has altered or varied over this period) and the quantity demanded (which has also varied). Given our current knowledge of economics, our interest would be to examine the relationship between these two economic variables – that is, to see how the two variables have reacted to each other over this period. From the table itself it's difficult to draw detailed conclusions.

The first task is to simplify the relationship by using simplifying symbols for each of the variables. We will show price as P and quantity demanded as Q_d. The second step is to distinguish between the *dependent* variable and the *independent* variable. That is, we might expect one of the variables to *depend* on, or be influenced by, the other. Logically, from our understanding of economics, it seems reasonable to specify P as the independent variable and Q_d as the dependent variable. This indicates that Q_d depends on P: that is, the quantity demanded of a product will depend on the price charged per unit. We now wish to show this relationship visually in the form of a graph.

A2.2 Using graphs to show economic relationships

There are a number of reasons why you may want to illustrate an economic relationship in the form of a graph. Graphs provide a quick and easy way of illustrating a given economic situation that we're analysing – as the old saying goes, 'a picture is worth a thousand words'. We can easily see the key features of an economic relationship when

Table A2.1   Prices and quantities over a four-month period

	Month 1	Month 2	Month 3	Month 4
Price per unit (£)	10	7	9	5
Quantity demanded (daily average 000s)	50	65	55	75

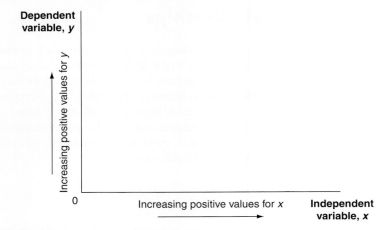

Figure A2.1 x and y axes

it is shown in the form of a graph and, more importantly, it is usually quite easy to assess what effect a specific change might have on the economic relationship. Fig. A2.1 shows two straight lines, known as the axes of the graph. The horizontal line is conventionally referred to as the x axis and is used to show the independent variable, while the vertical line is known as the y axis and shows the dependent variable. The point where the two axes meet is referred to as the *origin*, and at this point both variables take a zero value. On the x axis as we move from the origin to the right the independent variable will take increasingly higher, positive values. The same happens for the dependent variable as we move upwards from the origin along the y axis. The two axes – and the numerical scales that we will shortly draw on them – allow us to locate any specific point on the graph.

Now look at Fig. A2.2. This shows a point C which takes a value of a for the x variable and a value of b for the y variable. These numerical values for point C enable us to plot the point in terms of its *coordinates*, and we would refer to point C as C(a, b) where the first coordinate, a, shows the numerical value on the x axis and the second

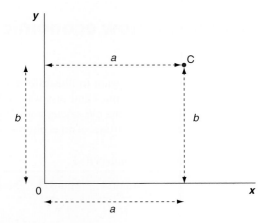

Figure A2.2 Plotting point C

coordinate, b, shows the numerical value on the y axis. To plot this point we need to find the exact numerical value for a on the x axis, the exact numerical value for b on the y axis and then find the exact point in the graph that lines up with both these values.

Progress Check A2.1

Return to Table A2.1, which shows prices and quantities.

(i)   Which variable – P or Q_d – would we show on the x axis and which on the y axis?

(ii)   For the four combinations of price and quantity shown in the table, write each point using the coordinate notation.

A

In the case of Table A2.1 we have already indicated that Q_d is the dependent variable, so this would be shown on the y axis while the independent variable, P, would be shown on the x axis. The four points would then be:

C_1 (5, 75)
C_2 (7, 65)
C_3 (9, 55)
C_4 (10, 50).

To locate these four points on the graph we clearly need appropriate numerical scales for both the x and y axes. In the case of the x axis (P), looking back at Table A2.1, a scale from zero (the origin) to 10 seems sensible because P takes a maximum value of 10. For y (Q_d) a scale from 0 to 75 is required, although we might round the 75 to 80 to make calculations slightly easier or we might even use a scale up to 100 for convenience. The numerical scales would then be drawn as shown in Fig. A2.3, where the four points are also plotted. It will be evident on inspection of Fig. A2.3 that these four points fall on a straight line: that is, we could join these points together with a straight line, as shown in Fig. A2.4. There are a number of things to observe about what we have just done here. The first is to emphasize the importance of graphs in economic analysis. We can see straightaway that Fig. A2.3 shows a straight-line or linear relationship between price and quantity demanded – something we could not see from the data in the original table. The second is that not all such relationships will give such a straight line. Many economic relationships are *non-linear* – they do not give a linear relationship, but some other sort. We will look at these in a later module. The third point is that in real life such a neat relationship rarely exists. In the real world you will often find a relationship that looks *almost* linear, like that in Fig. A2.5 where the data points almost make a straight line but not quite. In such a situation we would probably *approximate* the relationships with a straight line: that is, we'd assume the straight line was close enough to the actual points. So let's have a closer look at the relationship in Fig. A2.4.

Progress Check A2.2

From Fig. A2.4, what quantity will be demanded at the following prices?

- £6
- £3

If the quantity demanded is 40 what must the price be?

(Solution on p. 457)

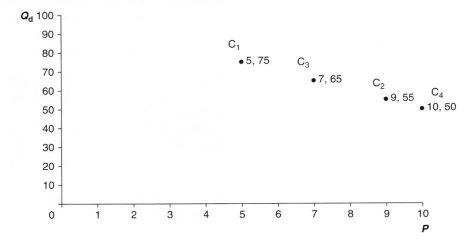

Figure A2.3 Plotting the four months' data

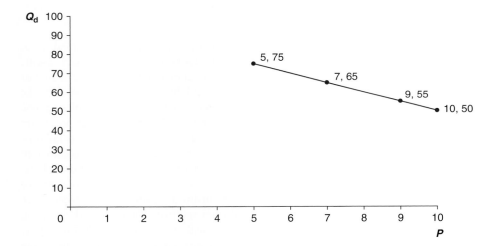

Figure A2.4 Price and quantity line

For a price of £6, we can use the graph to work out that 70 units will be demanded. For a price of £3, however, it's more difficult because the line drawn in Fig. A2.5 doesn't go that far. However, we can extend the line joining the four points, as in Fig. A2.6. The line has been extended both on the right (beyond $P = 10$) and to the left (below $P = 5$). We can now work out that with a price of £3 the quantity demanded will be about 85 units. (One of the problems with graphs is that it's often difficult to be exact and accurate when reading values.) Extending the line is an example of *extrapolation* – suggesting a pattern of economic behaviour that goes beyond that which we have observed directly. In this case we have observed consumer behaviour between a price of £5 per unit and of £10 per unit. We have not directly observed consumer behaviour at prices outside this range. We might hypothesize, however, that consumer behaviour would follow the same pattern as in the price range £5 to £10. Conversely, deducing a combination of P and Q_d, which occurs within the range of previously observed behaviour, is known as *interpolation* (a practice we used with a price of £6). Note that

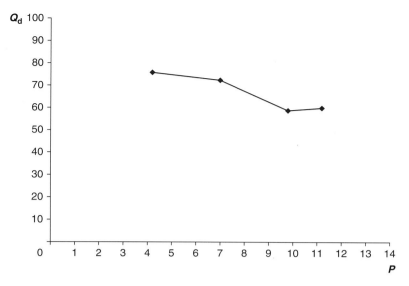

Figure A2.5 An almost linear relationship

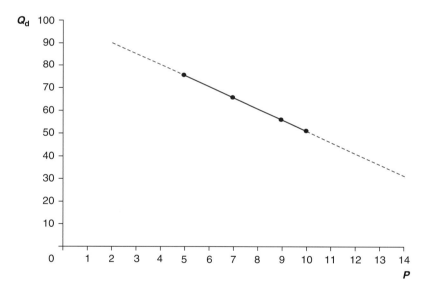

Figure A2.6 Price and quantity line extended

the line we have drawn now shows us all the P, Q combinations between $P = 2$ and $P = 14$. The graph can now be used to deduce P, Q_d combinations even if they have not been directly observed.

Quadrants

In this example, the coordinates of both variables that we needed to plot on the graph have all been positive. A graph can be drawn using some, or all, of the four *quadrants*, as shown in Fig. A2.7. Each quadrant shows different combinations of numerical values for the x and y variables. The x axis to the right of the origin shows positive values as

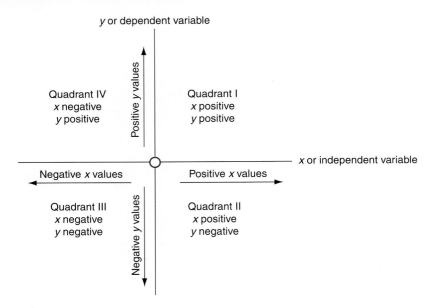

Figure A2.7 Quadrants

before. The x axis to the *left* of the origin shows negative x values (with these values becoming increasingly negative as we move further to the left). The y axis above the origin shows positive y values, but the y axis *below* the origin shows negative values (again with the negative values increasing in size as we move further away from the origin).

So the four possible combinations of positive and negative values for the x and y variables form the four quadrants. Inspection of Fig. A2.7 reveals that, in terms of much economic analysis, many of the graphs used will concentrate on quadrant I given that many economic variables can take only positive values. (It makes little sense, after all, to talk of negative Q_d and P values in the context of economics.) Occasionally we will use quadrant II and, still less frequently, quadrants III and IV.

Progress Check A2.3

On a single graph plot the following points:

A(6, 10)
B(6, −10)
C(−6, −10)
D(−6, 10)

(Solution on p. 457)

A2.3 Functions

In the situation we explored in Section A2.2 we can readily obtain a graph of the data that we have collected. But we may wish to examine an economic relationship without worrying about specific numbers. This may at first seem odd, but we may wish to consider the underlying relationship between two variables such as P and Q_d that will apply no matter what the actual price and quantity numerical values are. In other words, we may wish to study the general rather than the specific case. In such economic analysis we first need to specify which variables we are examining. Mathematically speaking, the first step is to establish a suitable *function*. If, for example, we show the price of a good as P and the quantity demanded as Q_d then we can write:

$$Q_d = f(P) \tag{A2.1}$$

Such an expression indicates that Q_d is a function of P: it should be understood as 'Q_d *is a function of P*', or 'Q_d *equals eff P*'. The implications of this expression are important. The term shown in Eq. A2.1 does not imply that Q_d equals f multiplied by P. Rather, the symbol $f(\ )$ is the standard notation for indicating that there is some (as yet undefined) relationship between the variables. The variable inside the brackets is referred to as the *argument* of the function. We are implying here that quantity demanded is in some way determined by price. Given a numerical value of P, therefore, we can derive the value for Q_d (as we did in Progress Check A2.2). A function provides us with a method, or rule, for obtaining the value of one variable given a value for the other. Formally we say that the function f provides a *mapping* rule from P to Q_d. Naturally, until we provide specific numerical values we cannot know precisely what this mapping rule is. Further than this, however, there is a hidden assumption behind a functional expression: that for any given value of P there is only *one* unique value for Q_d that can be determined. This is an important point and deserves clarification. Let's generalize a function such that:

$$Y = f(X) \tag{A2.2}$$

That is, some variable Y is a function of some other variable X. Let's assume that we can express such a function diagrammatically, as in Fig. A2.8.

We can see that for any given value of X we can determine a single, unique value for Y. x_1, for example, gives a single, unique value for Y of y_1 and a value x_2 gives a single, unique value of y_2. Now look at Fig. A2.9. This gives a different kind of relationship between X and Y, but still with a functional relationship. We see that for any

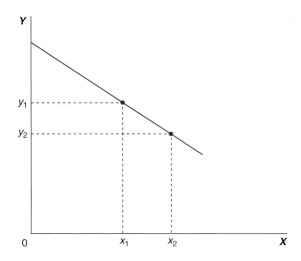

Figure A2.8 Mapping rule 1

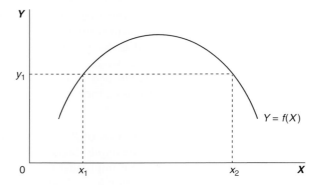

Figure A2.9 Mapping rule 2

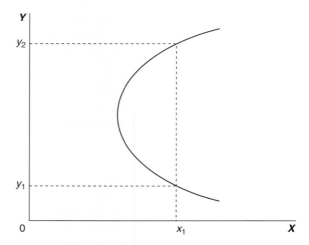

Figure A2.10 Non-functional relationship

given value of X there is only one unique value for Y. x_1, for example, continues to give only one Y value, y_1. The fact that y_1 can also result from a different X value, x_2, does not prevent the relationship being a functional one. Figure A2.10, however, shows a relationship where Y is *not* a function of X because for certain values of X more than one value of Y results. Two or more variables may be related, therefore, but not necessarily in a functional form. An example of this is given by the equation $y = \sqrt{x}$. If we set $x = 100$ then y will equal the square root. However, the square root of 100 could be either $+10$ or -10 (since both values when squared will give 100). Thus we obtain two y values from the same x value.

As we noted above, the function expressed in Eq. A2.1 involves two types of variable: a *dependent* and an *independent* variable. The independent variable is enclosed in the function brackets – here P is independent – while the dependent variable appears on the left-hand side of the function equation. The distinction between the two types of variable is itself important. As the name suggests, an independent variable is one that does not depend on other variables (or, to be more specific, on other variables detailed in the function). A dependent variable, by definition, does. However, we must distinguish between the economic and mathematical implications of dependency.

In mathematical terms a function simply establishes a rule or method for linking the two variables together: it does not examine *why* the variables move together in the stated way. In terms of economics, however, the choice of dependent/independent variable is usually of critical importance: it defines *causality*. We are implicitly assuming by our choice of variables that the value of the independent variable causes a change in the value of the dependent variable. Naturally, in terms of economic analysis we will wish to progress further and establish exactly what this causal link is and why it occurs. You will find it helpful to fully understand the distinction between mathematical and economic dependency.

Consider the situation between two economic variables that we define as:

W = annual percentage increase in average wage rates in the economy
Π = annual rate of inflation – that is, the increase in the price of goods and services.
  The symbol Π is pronounced 'pie'.

We could express the relationship in the form:

$$\Pi = f(W)$$

That is, the rate of inflation is dependent on the rate of wage increases. This implies, in an economic context, that W 'causes' I. This may seem logically reasonable given that for many goods the labour cost will be an important component of total costs. If these labour costs rise, businesses are likely to increase their prices to maintain profitability. However, we could equally write:

$$W = f(\Pi)$$

That is, inflation determines or causes the rate of wage increases. Once again this seem logical since the workforce may ask for higher wages if they notice that the prices of goods they wish to buy as consumers are increasing. It is important to realize that mathematics as such has no role to play in helping us decide which of these two functions is most appropriate. We must use our knowledge of economics, together with any empirical economic analysis that has been undertaken, to determine the appropriate direction of such causality. This aspect of functions leads us to ascertain exactly why we bother with functions in the first place. After all, you may think, a function in the form of Eq. A2.1 does little to help our economic understanding of a relationship. We are not, after all, specifying the exact form of the functional relationship between P and Q_d. Such notation, however, does offer a convenient, shorthand way of expressing an economic relationship or, perhaps more importantly, what we *believe* – or *hypothesize* – to be an economic relationship. To illustrate this point let us return to an example we looked at in the Introduction module. There we suggested that Q_d for a typical product would be affected not only by the price charged but also by a number of other factors. In functional form we could write:

$$Q_d = f(P, P_C, P_s, Y) \tag{A2.3}$$

That is, the quantity demanded is a function of several independent variables: the price of the product itself (P), the price of competitors' products (P_C), the price of substitute goods (P_s) and the level of consumer income (Y). Such an expression makes explicit at the start of any economic analysis the key assumptions underpinning the analysis. We assume, given the functional specification, that these four variables are the only factors affecting the dependent variable – or at least the only factors that we are explicitly considering in our economic model. Naturally, this is a convenient simplifying assumption that other economists may wish to challenge. However, by using the functional notation we are stating unequivocally what our initial assumptions are. We can then progress to deduce patterns of economic behaviour based on these assumptions. We may well be challenged on the validity of these assumptions – on the structure of the functional relationship specified – but we cannot be challenged on the deductive conclusions derived from these assumptions (providing, of course, that our logic and reasoning are correct).

A2.4 Functional notation

Although the usual method of denoting a functional relationship is in the form $Y = f(X)$, there are a number of other notational forms you should be aware of, since functions appear in a number of forms in the economics literature. Other common ways of representing functions are:

$$Y = g(X)$$
$$Y = y(X)$$

All state equally that Y is a function of X, but it is frequently a matter of personal preference as to which method of notation is used. It is important to remember that, even though the function has no numerical values, you can still undertake arithmetic operations on it. Consider, for example, a function such that:

$$Y = f(X)$$

Recollect that we have said that such a function represents a mapping rule to obtain Y, given a value for X, even though we do not know the precise form of the function; that is:

$$2Y = 2f(X)$$

still represents the same function (i.e. the same mapping rule) since a given X value will provide the same Y value. All that we have done is to multiply both parts of the functional expression by the same number, leaving the underlying relationship unchanged. We could, of course, have divided rather than multiplied, or subtracted or added or indeed undertaken most forms of arithmetic on the function (even though it currently involves no numbers). We shall frequently be making use of this concept as we progress through the book.

A2.5 Linear functions

While the expression of an economic relationship in functional form may be a useful first step in economic analysis, we will wish to go further in explicitly examining the form of the relationship. Typically, we will wish to examine the algebraic form of the function (the explicit equation) and we may also wish to represent this relationship diagrammatically in the form of a graph. First, let us examine those relationships that are *linear* in form. Consider a firm manufacturing a product for sale. We wish to examine the costs incurred in producing quantities of this item. It is logical to begin with:

$$TC = f(Q) \tag{A2.4}$$

where TC represent total costs incurred and Q represents units of output produced.

Progress Check A2.4

Why is Q set as the independent variable in this function? What other independent variables would you consider including to make the function more realistic?

Note that we imply that total costs depend upon output. We can logically assume that the firm will incur two separate types of costs. The first will be a set-up cost: a factory will have to be built, machinery acquired and resources obtained before any production can begin. We refer to these costs as *fixed* costs since they will be unaffected by the precise quantity of the product we actually decide to produce – that is, they will be independent of Q. The second type of cost will be directly related to what we actually produce: the more we produce, the more costs we incur for labour, materials, energy and so on. These costs are referred to as *variable* costs. Showing fixed costs as a and variable costs as b we can write:

$$TC = a + bQ \qquad (A2.5)$$

where a and b are referred to as the *parameters* of the equation. The values that these parameters take will give the equation its specific form and shape. While this equation does not yet involve specific numerical values, we can logically restrict the values that apply to a and b using not mathematics but our knowledge of economics. We can set:

$a > 0$

$b > 0$

That is, both costs can reasonably be assumed to be greater than zero. Naturally, we may wish to go one stage further and examine the precise effect of specific numerical values. Let us assume that, for the firm in question, fixed costs are £100,000 and variable costs are £5 per item produced. This gives the equation:

$$TC = 100 + 5Q \qquad (A2.6)$$

where both TC and Q are measured in thousands (£s and units respectively). As we shall soon discover, Eq. A2.6 is readily recognized as a linear equation and its graph can be obtained with a minimum of two pairs of coordinates. That is, if we derive two sets of coordinates for the equation and draw these on a graph we can join these two points together with a straight line which will then represent the linear Eq. A2.6. To obtain the two sets of coordinates we must define what is known as the *domain* of Q (the x, or independent, variable). The domain simply identifies the numerical limits for Q within which we wish to examine the economic relationship in Eq. A2.6. Assume that we limit Q to take a maximum value of 50 (measured in 000s units). A logical lower limit would be $Q = 0$. The domain of Q would then be $0 \le Q \le 50$ – that is, Q varies between (and including) 0 and 50. To determine the two sets of coordinates required for the graph it would then be logical to find the coordinates when $Q = 0$ and again when $Q = 50$. By substituting each value of Q in turn into Eq. A2.6 we can obtain the corresponding values for TC (and hence the two sets of coordinates):

$TC = 100 + 5Q$

$TC = 100 + 5(0) = 100$

$TC = 100 + 5Q$

$TC = 100 + 5(50) = 100 + 250 = 350$

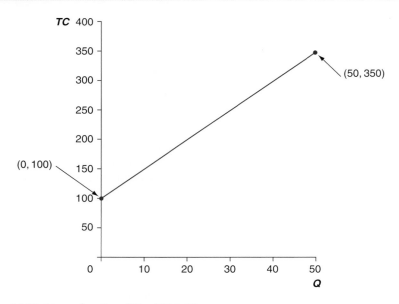

Figure A2.11 Linear function: $TC = 100 + 5Q$

That is, when $Q=0$, $TC=100$ and then when $Q=50$, TC takes the value 350. Therefore our two points have coordinates (0, 100) and (50, 350) and can be plotted onto the corresponding graph, shown in Fig. A2.11.

> Two sets of coordinates are all that are necessary to plot a linear equation
> However, until you get more practice it's worthwhile working out a third point and checking it falls on the line

The two points plotted have been joined together by a straight line (hence the term 'linear' equation). It is important to understand why this has been done. If we know that an equation results in a straight-line graph, we can derive any two points on that line from the equation. Joining the two points together gives the only straight line that can be drawn between the two points; hence giving the line of the equation. It is also important to realize that the graph and the original equation provide exactly the same information. Both allow us to quantify the value taken by the dependent variable (in this case total costs) for any given value for the independent variable (here quantity produced). From the graph we can see that the line starts from 100 on the vertical axis which, as we already know, shows the fixed cost part of total costs. Notice that at this point Q is zero, again confirming we are looking at fixed costs. You will also notice that the line slopes upwards as it goes from left to right. Again, this is consistent with what we know about the firm's cost function. We know that variable costs are £5; that is, each extra unit produced means an extra £5 cost for the company. This is confirmed on the graph since we see the TC line slopes upwards, implying that as Q increases so does TC (although we can't actually see from the graph that this is £5 per unit).

Progress Check A2.5

In the example we have just examined assume that:

(i) Fixed costs increase by £50,000. Draw the new TC function on a graph, together with the original function.

(ii) Variable costs now also increase by £2. Draw this third TC function on the same graph.

What observations can you make about the change on the graph as the a term and the b term change?

(Solution on p. 458)

A2.6 Summary

In this module we have begun to examine how mathematics can be applied in economics. We've looked at economic relationships which can be expressed and understood in mathematical terms. We've started with linear relationships which are the simplest mathematical form of a relationship. We've seen how to recognize a linear relationship and how to draw these on a graph. We've also introduced the idea of functions and functional relationships. A lot of basic economic analysis is undertaken using linear functions, and we'll see in Section B how linear economic models can be built and used. However, linear relationships can often be restrictive in modelling economic behaviour. So, in the next module, we'll develop our use of mathematics in economic analysis by looking at non-linear relationships.

Learning Check

Having read through this module you should have learned that:

- Economic variables are categorized into dependent or independent variables
- A dependent variable is plotted on the vertical, or y axis, on the graph, and the independent variable on the horizontal, or x axis
- Data points are plotted using a coordinate system
- A linear relationship is shown as a straight line on a graph
- Interpolation from a line on the graph means finding data values from within an already observed range
- Extrapolation means finding data values by extending the observed linear relationship
- Functional notation is away of linking variables together.

Worked Example

To reinforce the concepts introduced in this module, let us look at a Worked Example using the principles introduced so far. After we have introduced the problem (but before you examine the worked solution) you might wish to tackle the problem yourself and then compare your solution with the one presented here.

Let's return to the cost equation we used earlier:

$$TC = 100 + 5Q$$

The company concerned operate under very competitive conditions and the company is effectively a price-taker — it has to sell at the prevailing market price, which it cannot influence. The current market price is £7.50. The company wants to know what sales level will allow it to break even at that price (breakeven is where the company technically earns zero profit). The firm also thinks it may be able to cut its fixed costs to £90,000 and also wants to know the effect that this would have on breakeven. We want to use both algebra and graphs to examine the situation.

Worked Example *(Continued)*

Solution

Since breakeven is where profit is zero, we need to work out a profit function. Profit is defined as the difference between *TC*, total costs (which we already know) and *TR*, total revenue – which we have to work out. We're told that the company has to sell at whatever the prevailing market price is (you may realize from your studies of economics that this means the firm is operating under perfect competition market conditions) and that *TR* will simply be the market price multiplied by the quantity sold. That is:

$$TR = f(Q) = pQ$$

where *p* is the market prices and *Q* the quantity sold. The current market price, *p*, is £7.50, which gives:

$$TR = 7.5Q$$

Because both *TC* and *TR* are functions of *Q* we can now define profit as:

$$\text{Profit} = TR - TC = 7.5Q - (100 + 5Q)$$

or, by simplifying and rearranging

$$\text{Profit} = -100 + 2.5Q$$

We want to find the breakeven level of sales where Profit is zero. Setting our Profit equation to zero we get:

$$\text{Profit} = 0 = -100 + 2.5Q$$

Rearranging this using the algebra principles we developed in Module A1 we have:

$$Q = 40$$

as the breakeven level of sales. We can also show all three functions, *TC*, *TR* and Profit on a graph, as in Fig. A2.12. As usual, graphing the relationships makes a

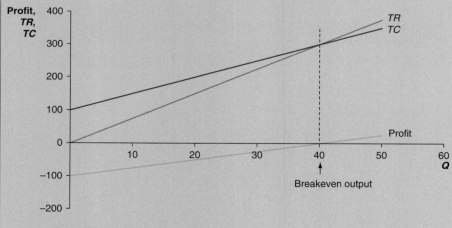

Figure A2.12 Breakeven analysis

Worked Example   *(Continued)*

number of things about the relationship clearer. Let's look at *TC* and *TR* first of all. The *TC* line is as before. The *TR* line on the other hand starts from the origin and slopes upwards as it moves from left to right. That is, when $Q = 0$, $TR = 0$. This makes sense both from the *TR* equation and from economics: sell nothing and you get nothing in revenue. The slope of the line also makes sense in that selling more (moving along the *Q* axis) means more revenue, *ceteris paribus*.

We can also see easily from the graph that the *TC* line and the *TR* line cross or intersect with each other. Inspection of the graph shows that this occurs when $Q = 40$. At this point both *TC* and *TR* take a value of 300. Obviously this is the breakeven point that we found earlier through algebra. By definition on the graph, the point where two lines cross must show they have the same value. It's also worth noting from the graph that for $Q < 40$ the *TC* line is above the *TR* line while for $Q > 40$ it's the opposite: the *TR* line is above the *TC* line. It is easy to understand what is happening here. For levels of *Q* less than 40 total costs are higher than revenue – in other words, the company would make a loss. For *Q* above 40 revenue is higher than costs, so the company would make a profit.

Let's now look at the third function on the graph, that for Profit. We see that the line starts at −100 on the vertical axis. In other words when $Q = 0$, profit is −100 – the company is losing £100,000. We can see the logic of this by using the other two lines for *TC* and for *TR*. *TC* takes a value of 100 at this value for *Q* and *TR* a value of 0. Given profit was defined earlier as the difference between total revenue and total costs, it's obvious that profit will have to be −100. We also see from the profit line that profit gradually increases as *Q* increases – increased production means increased profit. Looking carefully at the profit line we also see that it cross the horizontal, *Q*, axis at 40 – which is also the point where the cost and revenue lines cross – where $TC = TR$. Again, once we understand the graph this makes sense since this is the point where profit is zero – the breakeven point. The profit line also confirms what we've already seen. For $Q < 40$ profit will be negative (the firm is making a loss). We see this readily since the profit line is below zero all the way up to $Q = 40$. After this point we can also see that profit is positive and steadily increasing. You can probably understand now why economists like graphs so much.

Exercises

A2.1   For each of the following relationships obtain a graph for the range of *X* values indicated. Comment on the similarities and differences between the three.

  (i) $Y = 8 + 2X$, $X = 0$ to 20

 (ii) $Y = 8 + 4X$, $X = 0$ to 20

(iii) $Y = 8 + 0.5X$, $X = 0$ to 20

Exercises *(Continued)*

A2.2 Return to Eq. A2.6 where:

$$TC = f(Q) = 100 + 5Q$$

(i) If Q changes from 10 units to 11, what is the corresponding change in TC?

(ii) If Q changes from 40 to 41 units, what is the corresponding change in TC?

(iii) What is the economic interpretation of this change in TC?

(iv) How realistic is it that TC changes by the same amount regardless of the actual level of production?

A2.3 Return to the Worked Example in this module where:

$$TR = 7.5Q$$

$$TC = 100 + 5Q$$

For each of the following, find the new breakeven level of output using algebra and graphs and explain in economics terms why the breakeven point has changed in the way that it has:

(i) fixed costs increase by 10

(ii) variable costs fall by 1

(iii) price increases by 0.50

(iv) price falls by 0.50.

A2.4 We have collected some data on a cross-section of consumers in the economy to monitor their spending patterns and their income levels. Spending is generally referred to in economics as consumption (C). Typically these consumers had annual incomes (Y) of up to £40,000. Any income that is not spent they put into savings (S).

Income and spending for six individuals

	Income in £	Spending in £
Person A	10,000	10,500
Person B	32,000	25,900
Person C	22,000	18,900
Person D	18,750	16,625
Person E	34,000	27,300
Person F	15,500	14,350

Using graphs:

(i) Analyse the data to show income, consumption and savings

(ii) Comment on any relationships we can see

(iii) Predict what a consumer with an income of £30,000 would spend and how much they would save.

A2.5 For A2.4 extrapolate the consumption line back to the vertical axis. How do you explain what you can see?

Appendix A2 Graphs in Excel

Drawing graphs by hand can be dull, boring and time-consuming (but still good practice at getting to know how graphs work). These days you're more likely to use a spreadsheet to draw the graphs you will need to use. In this appendix we briefly outline how to draw straight-line graphs in Excel, using the inbuilt Chart Wizard. To do this, though, we have to set up the data we want Excel to graph in a table format. To show how to get a graph we'll use the same data we used in the module looking at Q_d and P.

The relevant data has been input into Excel as shown in Fig. A2.13. Notice that we've put the data into columns A and B, but you could put them anywhere in the spreadsheet. Similarly, we've put the data into columns, but it could just as easily go into rows. Note that we've put P – the independent variable – into the first column. The reason for this is that Excel automatically assumes the first column of data will go on the X axis of a graph. With the data now input we need to call up the Chart Wizard in Excel. The icon for this is a little graph symbol located somewhere in your toolbar as shown in Fig. A2.14. To start the Chart Wizard, first highlight the cells showing the data in the table that we want to graph and then click on the icon: you'll see the Chart Wizard starting up, as shown in Fig. A2.15.

Table A2.2 Prices and quantities over a four-month period

	Month 1	Month 2	Month 3	Month 4
Price per unit (£)	10	7	9	5
Quantity demanded	50	65	55	75

	A	B	C	D	E
1	*Price*	*Quantity*			
2	10	50			
3	7	65			
4	9	55			
5	5	75			
6					
7					
8					

Figure A2.13 Data input

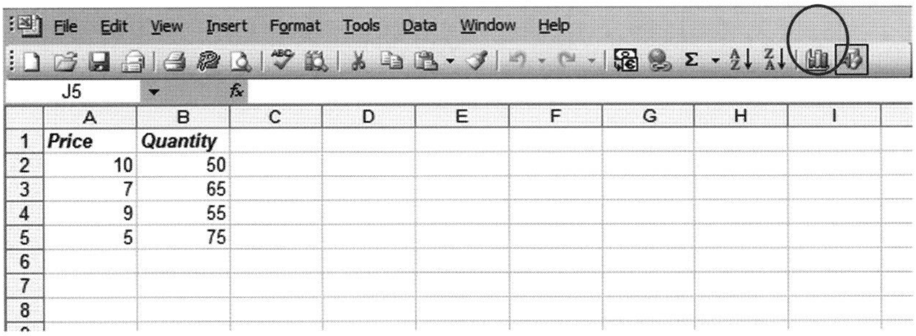

Figure A2.14 Chart Wizard

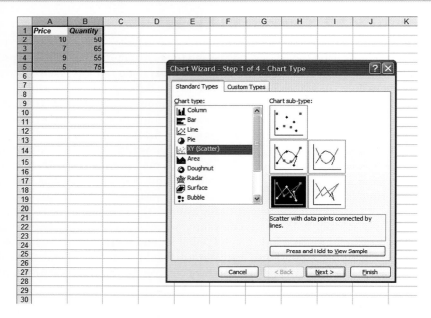

Figure A2.15 Chart Wizard dialogue box

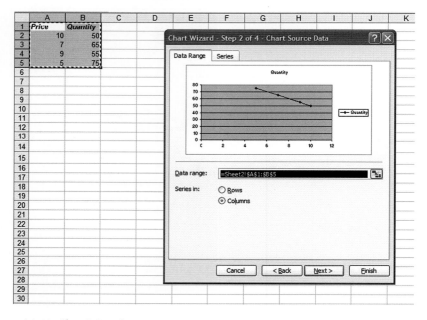

Figure A2.16 Chart Wizard preview

When the Chart Wizard starts up, it allows you to choose the type of chart you want and then the type of subchart. We need the XY (Scatter) chart and we want the points connected by lines. Click on Next to get a preview of how the chart will look – as in Fig. A2.16. If this looks OK, click on Next. If it doesn't look right it's probably because the wrong data cells have been selected, so you'd need to go back and correct

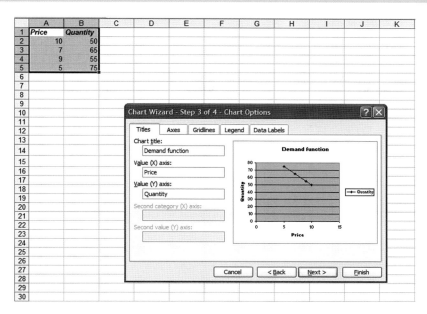

Figure A2.17 Chart Wizard options

this. Figure A2.17 shows the next stage of the wizard where you have various options to play around with as to how your graph will look. The labels we've chosen for the graph and the axes are just examples of the many available; you can explore these on your own.

Clicking Next again gives us Fig. A2.18, where we get the choice as to where the finished graph will be placed. You have the choice of having the graph put as an object into the worksheet you're working in or you can save it as a separate sheet in your worksheet file. I tend to do the second as it gives a better picture. The finished result is shown in Fig. A2.19. The Chart Wizard is very flexible, with lots of facilities, but can take a bit of getting used to.

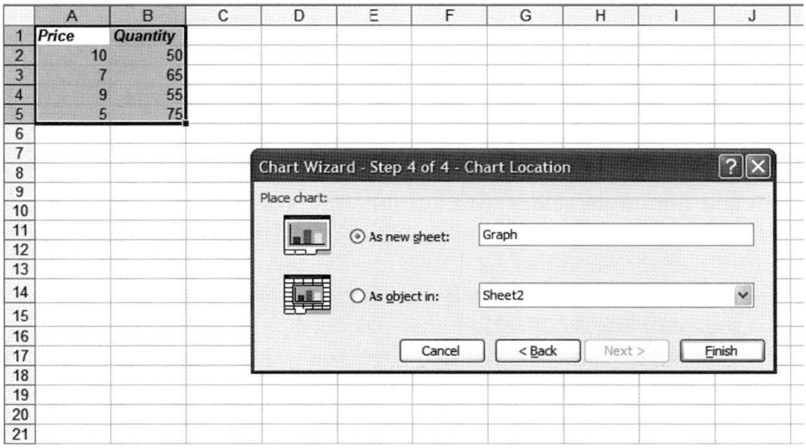

Figure A2.18 Chart Wizard location options

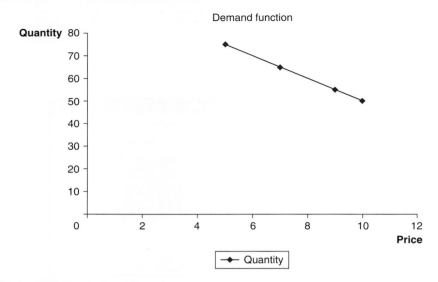

Figure A2.19 Finished graph

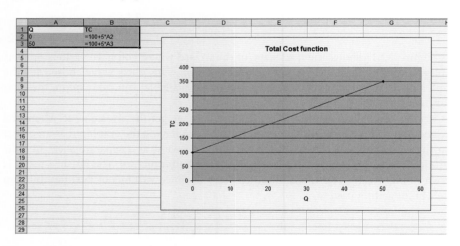

Figure A2.20 Formulae in Excel

Of course, if you want a graph of a linear equation, as opposed to data points, you have to set up your initial data table in a different way. We do this by inputting the maximum and minimum values we want for the x values in the equation and then entering the linear equation to get Excel to calculate the corresponding y values. Once we've done this, as shown in Fig. A2.20 where we've used the cost equation we used in the chapter, then the rest of the process for drawing the graph is as before (with the graph also shown in Fig. A2.20). Note that you need only two sets of coordinates for the linear equation but you could put more in if you want to be sure.

Module A3
Non-linear relationships in economic analysis

A

In the previous module we looked at linear relationships and saw how to use these in the form of graphs, functions and equations. While this type of function is common in economics, primarily because it has a number of useful properties as far as mathematical economic analysis is concerned, it will be apparent even from an elementary study of economics that it is far too simplistic to assume that all economic relationships can be represented as linear, straight-line functions. Many such relationships can be realistically represented only through the use of *non-linear* functions. In this module we look at some of the more common non-linear functions and learn how to use them.

Learning Objectives

By the end of this module you should be able to:

- Draw graphs of common non-linear equations
- Construct and use common non-linear functions
- Understand functions involving more than one independent variable.

Knowledge Check A3

If you think you're already familiar with the mathematics of non-linear equations, try answering the following:

(i) What type of non-linear function is:

$$y = 50 - x^3$$

(ii) Simplify the expression:

$$5^{-1/3}$$

(iii) Find the inverse of the function:

$$y = 100 - 5x$$

Check your answers in Appendix 2. If you have answered correctly, try some of the exercises at the end of this module and then move on to Section B.

A3.1 Polynomial functions

We have already seen that the general form of a linear function can be represented as:

$$Y = a + bX \tag{A3.1}$$

It will be useful to examine the structure of this equation in some detail in order to derive a general mathematical pattern. It is possible to represent each term in such an equation in terms of X. Equation A3.1 can be rewritten as:

$$Y = aX^0 + bX^1 \tag{A3.2}$$

> It you're not sure about this, go back and read the Appendix to Module A1.

given that $X^0 = 1$ and $X^1 = X$. There may appear to be little point in rewriting Eq. A3.1 in this way, but it does enable us to establish the pattern of polynomial equations (the word literally means 'many terms'). The pattern that becomes evident is:

$$Y = a \text{ (since } Y = aX^0 = a \text{ given that } X^0 = 1) \tag{A3.3}$$

$$Y = a + bX \tag{A3.4}$$

$$Y = a + bX + cX^2 \tag{A3.5}$$

$$Y = a + bX + cX^2 + dX^3 \tag{A3.6}$$

and so on, adding a new and higher power X term each time. In general, a polynomial function can be written as:

$$Y = a + b_1X + b_2X^2 + b_3X^3 + \ldots + b_nX^n \tag{A3.7}$$

We've already established that a polynomial of degree 1, where the 1 refers to the highest power of X in the function, as in Eq. A3.4, is a linear function. A polynomial of degree 2 (as in Eq. A3.5) is referred to as a *quadratic* function, while that of degree 3 (Eq. A3.6) is referred to as a *cubic* function. We shall examine the use of such polynomials in more detail as we progress through the text.

For now it is sufficient to know that a quadratic function will typically follow a pattern shown in Figs A3.1a and b. Which of the two patterns is followed will depend upon the exact parameters of the quadratic equation we're looking at. A cubic function will typically follow the sort of pattern shown in Fig. A3.2. We'll be seeing throughout the text how useful these functions can be in economic analysis.

Let us return to the four quadrants that are available for any graph. We may decide, for example, that in our illustration of a total cost function in the previous module it might be more realistic to use a quadratic function rather than a linear one. But if we look at Figs A3.1a and b we appear to have difficulties in using such a function to

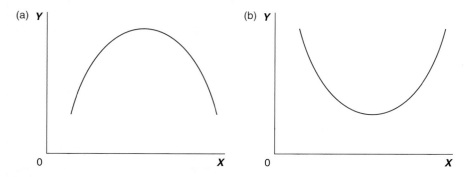

Figure A3.1 Graphs of quadratic functions

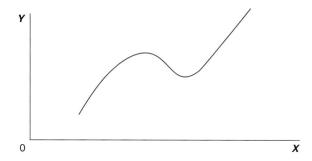

Figure A3.2 Cubic function

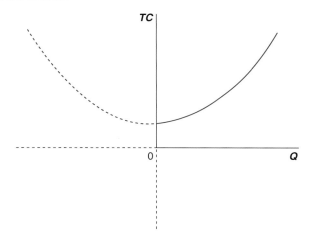

Figure A3.3 $TC = f(Q)$ as a quadratic function

model the economic relationship between TC and Q. If we look at Fig. A3.1a, the implications are that as output (on the X axis) increases, TC (on the Y axis) increases at first but then decreases. This doesn't seem a realistic pattern of economic behaviour for TC. Equally, with Fig. A3.1b, TC at first decreases as output increases and then increases again. Again, this doesn't seem unduly realistic either. However, through careful consideration of the existence of four quadrants and the economic implications of each we might use the quadratic relationship shown in Fig. A3.3. Although the function is quadratic, we're only using part of it for $Q \geq 0$. In terms of economic behaviour this now makes more sense. Using just this quadrant, the TC function starts on the vertical axis above the origin, implying fixed costs > 0, and increase as Q increase implying that variable costs > 0 also. Using those parts of non-linear functions that make economic sense is common in economic analysis.

A3.2 Graphs of non-linear functions

Drawing a graph of a non-linear function follows the same principles as those for a linear function we explored in the previous module, but with one major exception. For a linear function we required only two sets of x, y coordinates to be able to draw the straight line. For a non-linear function we require more. A rule of thumb is to determine about ten sets of coordinates. This is usually sufficient to determine the shape of the non-linear function reasonably accurately. A second difference is that while we join the coordinates for a linear function with a straight line, for a non-linear function we join the coordinates as best as we can with a curve. Let's illustrate with a function:

$$y = 50 - x^3$$

with $-10 \leq x \leq 10$. By substituting a range of x values into the equation and solving for y we can obtain a series of coordinates. The calculations are:

x	y
-10	1050
-8	562
-6	266
-4	114
-2	58
0	50
2	42
4	-14
6	-166
8	-462
10	-950

Note that we have taken 11 x values and spaced them equally over the x range. This provides a set of 11 x, y coordinates, which can be used to obtain the graph shown in Fig. A3.4. Notice also that we have drawn a smooth curve through the points rather than join them with a straight line.

Progress Check A3.1

Plot each of the functions shown below on one graph, with X from 0 to 50. What observations can you make about the three functions?

(i) $Y = 100 + 12X - 0.3X^2$

(ii) $Y = 500 + 12X - 0.3X^2$

(iii) $Y = 100 + 12X + 0.3X^2$

(Solution on p. 459)

A3.3 Other non-linear functions

The variety of other types of non-linear functions in addition to polynomials that we may encounter in economics is considerable. We shall focus attention here on two common groups: logarithmic and exponential functions (which we examine in sections A3.4 and A3.5) and non-linear functions derived from linear functions. Let's

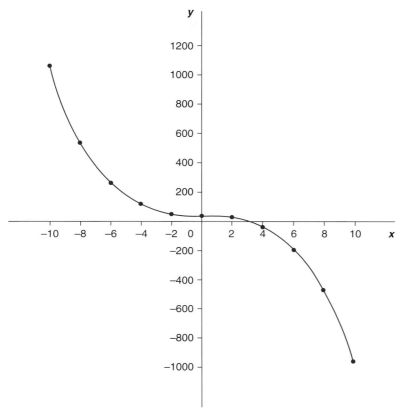

A

Figure A3.4 $y = 50 - x^3$

go back to the linear function we've been using showing the relationship between TC and Q:

$$TC = f(Q) = 100 + 5Q$$

It's common in economics to want to derive a related function from an equation such as this, and such derived functions may well be non-linear even though the original function is linear. For example, we may wish to derive a function showing average costs of production rather than the total. Given that the definition of an average cost (ATC) is the total cost divided by the quantity produced, we have:

$$ATC = \frac{TC}{Q} = \frac{100 + 5Q}{Q} = \frac{100}{Q} + 5$$

which is clearly non-linear even though the function from which it was derived is linear.

Progress Check A3.2

Plot this function on a graph, with Q from 0 to 50. (Take care with the graph coordinates when Q approaches 0.) What happens to ATC as Q gets larger over the range shown? How do you explain this in terms of economics?

(Solution on p. 459)

A3.4 Logarithms and logarithmic functions

We next turn to the use of *logarithms* and *logarithmic functions*. You may recollect encountering logarithms in your school studies. Logarithms are an invaluable aid to the economist both in terms of making complex arithmetical calculations easier and in developing mathematical economic models. We shall review their basic principles here before proceeding. You will find it useful to have a pocket calculator with logarithmic facilities available for this section. A logarithm is simply the power to which a given base number must be raised in order to obtain a specified numerical value. So, we say that the logarithm of 100 is 2 when using base 10. This probably makes more sense if we show that:

> *Look for keys on your calculator like 'log'*

$$100 = 10^2$$

since we see that, using the base number of 10, we must raise this to the power 2 in order to obtain the number of 100. Conventionally we would say that '2 is the log of 100'. Similarly, we would say that the log of 1000 was 3 ($1000 = 10^3$), the log of 10,000 was 4 ($10,000 = 10^4$) and so on. Logs of other numbers have the same logic but may be less obvious. For example, we can work out that the log of 56 is 1.7482 (you should check this on your own calculator). That is, $10^{1.7482} = 56$.

> *On your calculator, press log then 56 then =. You should get 1.7482*

Sometimes we already know the log value and wish to determine the actual number of which this is the logarithm. For example, suppose we knew that the log of a number is 1.2095. What is the number for which this is the logarithm? Effectively we have:

$$x = 10^{1.2095}$$

> *Look for keys on your calculator like 10^x. Press the 10^x key, then enter 1.2095 and press =*

so calculating the value of 10 to this power will provide the result. Such a process is known as finding the *antilog* of 1.2095 (and an appropriate key should be available on your pocket calculator to confirm the result of 16.199). So far, we have assumed that our logarithms have used a base of 10 (referred to as *common logarithms*). While computationally this is frequently very convenient we can in fact use any number as the base for the logarithm calculations. For theoretical model building there is an alternative to base 10 that is useful. This is the mathematical constant e (with a value of 2.71828). Using e as the base results in what is known as a *natural logarithm*, usually denoted either as ln or $\log_e$ to distinguish it from base 10 logarithms. As with exponents, there are a number of common and useful rules when dealing with logarithms (and the rules apply to both common and natural logarithms). Here we state what these are rather than show where they come from:

> *Look for keys on your calculator like 1n and e^x*

Rule 1

$$\log(ab) = \log a + \log b$$

Rule 2

$$\log(a/b) = \log a - \log b$$

Rule 3

$$\log a^n = n \log a$$

Rule 4

$$\log(\sqrt[n]{a}) = (\log a)/n$$

An illustration of the usefulness of logarithms in economic models may be of benefit at this stage. Consider the level of production of goods and services at a macroeconomic level. The output produced, Q, will depend on the inputs made available – knows as the factors of production, typically referred to as land, labour and capital (capital means things like buildings, machinery and equipment that is used in production). If we were to focus only on labour and capital as the two key inputs we could write:

$$Q = f(K, L)$$

where Q was production, L was labour and K was capital. In other words we have a *production function*. These are used a lot in economics. One particular type of production function takes the mathematical form:

$$Q = f(K, L) = AK^\alpha L^\beta \qquad \qquad \text{(A3.8)}$$

> *C* is generally used for consumption so we need another letter for capital

This particular production function is known as the *Cobb–Douglas production function* after the two economists who first tested it using econometrics. A, α and β are the parameters of the function (the sum of α and β indicates what is known as *the returns to scale effect*). Let's assume we have specific numerical values for the parameters so that:

> α (alpha) and β (beta) are letters from the Greek alphabet which are commonly used in mathematics. You'll find a list of common Greek letters in Appendix 1

$$Q = AK^\alpha L^\beta = 200K^{0.25}L^{0.5}$$

If we had 50 units of capital available and 100 units of labour then production, Q, would be:

$$Q = 200K^{0.25}L^{0.5} = 200(50^{0.25}100^{0.5})$$

Using logs this becomes:

$$Q = 200(2.66 \times 10) = 5320$$

That is, production would be 5320 units with the given level of inputs. However, the function in its current general form is not particularly easy to manipulate or develop further. As we have already seen, linear functions have certain properties that make them attractive to use in models, not least because they are easier to use and understand. So let's apply some of the logarithm rules we have just introduced to the production function (and we shall use logarithms to base e). Taking logarithms we have:

$$Q = AK^\alpha L^\beta$$
$$\ln Q = \ln A + \alpha \ln K + \beta \ln L$$

(A3.9)

or

$$Q' = A' + \alpha K' + \beta L'$$

(A3.10)

where we use the prime symbol (′) to denote a logarithmic variable. On inspection, it can be seen to have been transformed into a linear format. Not only is Eq. A3.10 easier to examine and understand but any numerical calculations required are more readily derived from the transformed function than the original. This use of logarithms to transform non-linear functions into a linear format is common in economics.

Progress Check A3.4

Assume that a variable Y changes over time. It has an initial value in period 1 of 100 and grows at 10% each subsequent period.

(i) Calculate the Y value up to period 10 and plot Y against time.

(ii) Take the logarithm of Y and plot this against time.

(iii) What observations do you make about the logarithmic relationship and how do you explain this?

(Solution on p. 460)

A3.5 Exponential functions

One further group of non-linear functions of special interest in economic analysis involves the use of *exponential* relationships. Such functions are particularly useful in examining economic growth problems and problems involving economic dynamics – looking at economic behaviour over time. We shall return to these functions in more detail later. Here we shall simply examine their basic features. We have already seen that polynomial functions involve a variable raised to some power. Mathematically, the value of the power is referred to as the *exponent*. So X^2 is said to be of exponent 2 and it is also evident that in such a case the exponent is a constant: no matter what the value of X, we always raise this value to the power 2. There is no reason, however, why the exponent itself could not be variable. When this occurs we have an *exponential* function. The simplest form of this type of function can be expressed as:

$$Y = f(X) = b^x$$

(A3.11)

where the b parameter is referred to as the fixed base of the exponent. Typically in economics, we might use x to denote a time variable and in such a case might replace the symbol x with t instead. The properties of such an exponential function are of considerable use in economic modelling. Let us consider the following:

$$Y = f(t) = 1.5^t$$

(A3.12)

We want to examine the relationship for $t = 0$ to 5. In order to do so we must ensure an adequate understanding of how we can mathematically manipulate exponents: a short digression will be profitable at this stage. We looked at powers and exponents in the Appendix to module A1 and introduced four rules for dealing with exponents and algebra. We repeat the rules here and add a couple more.

Rule 1

$$a^n \times a^m = a^{n+m}$$

Rule 2

$$a^n / a^m = a^{n-m}$$

Rule 3

$$(a^n)^m = a^{nm}$$

Rule 4

$$(ab)^n = a^n b^n$$

We will also need the following rules:

Rule 5

$$a^{-n} = 1/a^n$$

Suppose, for Rule 2, we require a^2/a^4. Applying Rule 2 we know this gives a^{-2} since:

$$\frac{a^2}{a^4} = \frac{a \times a}{a \times a \times a \times a} = \frac{1}{a \times a} = \frac{1}{a^2} = a^2$$

It is worth noting that this type of notation is frequently used. For example, we will usually write a^{-1} rather than $1/a$, although both are the same.

Rule 6

$$a^{1/n} = \sqrt[n]{a}$$

Assume we had an expression such as $a^{1/2}$. Using Rule 1 we know that:

$$a^{1/2} \times a^{1/2} = a^{(1/2+1/2)} = a^1$$

However, the interpretation of a square root of a (shown by $\sqrt{a}$, and pronounced as 'root a') is that we have a second number, say b, which when multiplied by itself gives the original number a. Thus we would say that 2 is $\sqrt{4}$ since $2^2 = 4$. We can, therefore, rewrite $a^{1/2}$ as $\sqrt{s}$ since this is also the definition of a square root. In fact, this rule can be generalized such that

$$a^{m/n} = \sqrt[n]{a^m}$$

Rule 7

$$a^{-1/n} = 1/\sqrt[n]{a}$$

Assume we had $a^{-1/4}$. Setting $n = 4$ and using Rule 5 we then have:

$$a^{-1/4} = \frac{1}{a^{1/4}}$$

but using Rule 6, $a^{1/4} = \sqrt[4]{a}$. So:

$$a^{-1/4} = \frac{1}{\sqrt[4]{a}}$$

Again, this can be generalized to:

$$a^{-m/n} = \frac{1}{\sqrt[n]{a^m}}$$

Progress Check A3.5

Using the rules we have just examined, simplify the following expressions:

(i) $8^6 \times 8^3$

(ii) $(7^2)^3$

(iii) $8^6/8^3$

(iv) $8^3/8^6$

(v) $5^{-1/3}$

(vi) $8^6 + 8^3$

(vii) $(10^3 \times 10^5)^2/10^4$

(Solution on p. 460)

Let's now go back to the exponential function where we had $Y = 1.5^t$, where t took values between 0 and 5. To graph this function we can now work out appropriate sets of coordinates using the rules we have just introduced:

t	Y	
0	1.5^0	$= 1$
1	1.5^1	$= 1.5$
2	1.5^2	$= 2.25$
3	1.5^3	$= 3.375$
4	1.5^4	$= 5.0625$
5	1.5^5	$= 7.59375$

and these produce a graph as in Fig. A3.5.

In fact, we can generalize such an exponential function into the form:

$$Y = f(t) = ab^{ct} \tag{A3.13}$$

where a, b and c are the parameters of the function, in this example taking the values $a = 1$, $b = 1.5$, $c = 1$. One specific example of this is frequently used in economics, where the b parameter is replaced by the mathematical constant e, which is known as an *irrational number* and always takes the same value: 2.71828. We cannot, at the moment, justify why such a number should be used – we must wait until certain other topics have been discussed before explaining this. However, the use of functions such as:

$$Y = f(t) = e^{0.25t} \tag{A3.14}$$

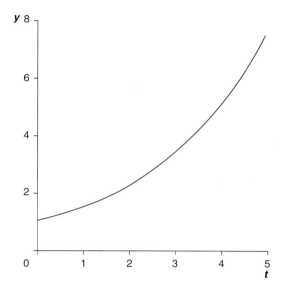

Figure A3.5 $Y = 1.5^t$

A

are common in mathematical economic models and this type of equation is evaluated and graphed in exactly the same way as before. Let's look at an example to see what they can tell us.

> Look for a key e^x on your calculator

Apple have just launched their latest i-gadget which is aimed globally at a target market of young professionals with a high disposable income. From previous product launches they estimate that cumulative sales over time are given by the function:

$$Q_d = 50 - 40e^{-0.75t} \tag{A3.15}$$

where Q_d is quantity demanded in hundreds of thousands of units and t is time in months. So Q_d in month 3 would show the cumulative sales from the time of the product launch up to month 3. The company also estimates that after four months one of its competitors is likely to bring out a competing product which is either technologically more advanced or at a substantially lower price. The company have asked us for advice as to what's likely to happen to demand over the next few months. We can readily calculate Q_d over the next 12 months using the demand function given (you may want to check our calculations to gain extra practice at this). The results are shown in Table A3.1 and the data has also been plotted in Fig. A3.6. Note that the time series actually starts at 0 which is effectively the time now at the product launch. There are a number of points that are now apparent from the graph. We see that initial sales are 10 million at the product launch time. Sales then rise sharply for the first couple of months, start to fall away from month 3 onwards and by month 5 have effectively reached a plateau. Such a curve is typical of many new products where there is initial high demand after the product launch but with sales then reaching a plateau at some stage in the future. Here we see that by month 6 global cumulative sales have reached their peak of 50 million units. In one sense we could advise the company not to worry too much about competition after month 4 since most of the potential cumulative sales will already have been achieved, around 96% according to Table A3.1.

Table A3.1 Cumulative sales of the i-gadget over the next 12 months

Months, t	Cumulative Sales, Q_d 000,000s
0	10
1	31.10534
2	41.07479
3	45.78403
4	48.00852
5	49.05929
6	49.55564
7	49.7901
8	49.90085
9	49.95316
10	49.97788
11	49.98955
12	49.99506

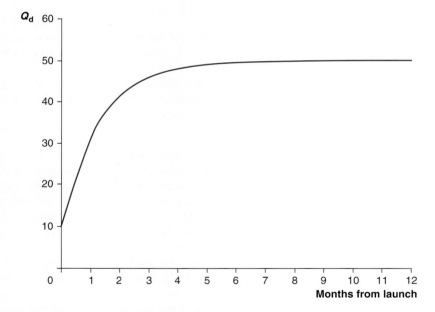

Figure A3.6 Sales, Q_d, over the next 12 months

A3.6 Functions with more than one independent variable

The Cobb–Douglas production function, which we looked at in Section A3.5, leads to the next topic we examine in this module: functions involving more than one independent variable. It's logical that we should wish to use such functions in economic analysis. After all, the purpose of modelling is to try to construct a theoretical model representing a real-world economic system. Given that such systems are typically complex, the models we develop will need to be able to cope with multiple independent variables. Let's consider in detail the function:

$$Q_d = f(P_x, P_s) \tag{A3.16}$$

which is a demand function indicating that the quantity demanded of a particular good X, Q_d, is a function of the price of that good, P_x, and the price of a substitute good, P_s. It is clear from the function that in order to determine the value of the dependent variable we now require a value for both the independent variables. For example, if we had specific numerical values for P_x and P_s, say P_{x1} and P_{s1}, we could work out the value for Q_d, Q_{d1}. Similarly, if we had a second set of numerical values, say P_{x2} and P_{s2}, we could again work out the value for Q_d, now Q_{d2}. But suppose we wanted to graph these coordinates and the Q_d function. Given we have three variables we would need three axes on the graph. In practice, we wouldn't normally do this given that we would need a 3D graph; but the principles involved are important and will help us to understand some of the things we'll be doing later. We effectively have two points represented by two sets of coordinates:

$$C_1(P_{x1}, P_{s1}, Q_{d1})$$
$$C_2(P_{x2}, P_{s2}, Q_{d2})$$

Figure A3.7 illustrates the principles involved.

The diagram shows Q_d on the vertical axis and the two price variables on the *two* horizontal axes that we now require. The first set of coordinates for C_1 requires us to plot P_{x1} on the P_X axis, P_{s1} on the P_s axis and Q_{d1} on the Q_d axis. The corresponding point for C_1 is shown in Fig. A3.7. The same approach would be needed for coordinate C_2, also shown in Fig. A3.7. If we were to construct a sufficient number of such points then we could obtain a graph of the function which would take the form of some three-dimensional *surface* rather than a two-dimensional *line* as it has been up to now. While we would not usually wish to do this for a specific numerical function, it will actually be informative to do so just this once, in order to reinforce the principles involved in dealing with these multivariable functions. Figure A3.8 illustrates the kind of surface we might obtain for such a demand function.

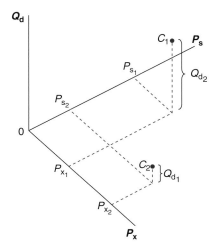

Figure A3.7 $Q_d = f(P_x, P_s)$

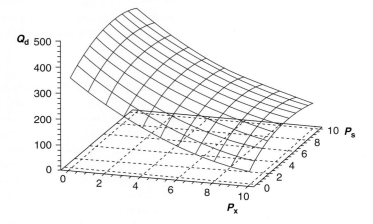

Figure A3.8 $Q_d = f(P_x, P_s)$

The diagram may at first appear somewhat complex, but will repay close attention. The three-dimensional surface that is shown represents the coordinates for the three variables in the function. As we progress through the text we shall be examining ways in which we can analyse a surface such as this. For the moment we explore a simple approach. Assume that we wish to examine the behaviour of Q_d with respect to P_x. Clearly we cannot just forget about P_s since it forms part of the demand function. What we can do, however, is to transform the *three*-dimensional diagram into a *two*-dimensional one. Assume that, as in Fig. A3.9, we take a series of 'slices' through the diagram and that these slices are parallel to the P_x axis. We could then 'transfer' the slices to a two-dimensional graph, as in Fig. A3.10. In such a way we can then build up a series of two-dimensional pictures showing the relationship between Q_d and P_x for different values of P. You will be able to appreciate how we can do this from Fig. A3.9. Each slice corresponds to a given value for P_s – in our example, at 2 and then at 4. Of course, what we are effectively doing is holding this variable constant in order to examine the economic relationship between the other two. In principle, this extends readily beyond three variable functions to functions involving any number of

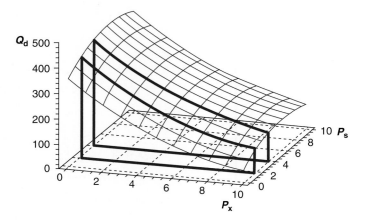

Figure A3.9 $Q_d = f(P_x, P_s)$

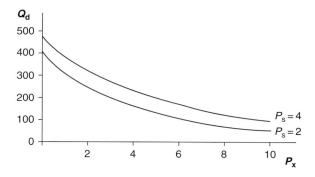

Figure A3.10 $Q_d = f(P_x, P_s)$

variables. While we would not be able to produce a corresponding graph for more than a three-variable function, the principles of examining slices of the function's surface (the slices are more formally known as *planes*) remain the same. You will probably have already encountered such principles in your study of economics even if they have not been explained in mathematical terms.

A3.7 Inverse functions

Finally in this module we consider the *inverse function*. Let's consider a function relating price and quantity demanded. Assume a function such that:

$$Q_d = f(P) = 100 - 5P \qquad (A3.17)$$

Now consider a situation where the firm wishes to derive a related function from this. It requires a function for total revenue, *TR*. Clearly, total revenue will simply be the product of price per unit times quantity demanded:

$$TR = P \times Q_d$$

but since we already have an expression for Q_d in Eq. A3.17 this becomes

$$TR = P(100 - 5P) = 100P - 5P^2 \qquad (A3.18)$$

where

$$TR = f(P)$$

and we have a mapping rule to determine *TR* given some value for *P*. However, assume that instead of determining *TR* from *P* we wished to determine *TR* from Q_d instead. From the perspective of a *TR* function this makes sense, as revenue will depend on quantity demanded as well as price. To proceed, we can find the *inverse* of Eq. A3.17. Since:

$$Q_d = 100 - 5P$$

we can rearrange this to get

$$5P = 100 - Q_d$$

$$P = 20 - 0.02Q_d \qquad (A3.19)$$

where Eq. A3.19 is the inverse of Eq. A3.17. Note that we are not implying that $P = f(Q)$ but have rearranged the original function into an equivalent form. We now have again:

$$TR = P \times Q_d$$

but substituting Eq. A3.19 for P now gives:

$$TR = f(Q) = (20 - 0.02Q_d) \, Q_d = 20Q_d - 0.02Q_d^2 \qquad\qquad\text{(A3.20)}$$

It is important to realize that both Eqs A3.20 and A3.18 will generate the same TR values for a specific P, Q_d combination.

A3.8 Summary

In this module we have begun to examine how mathematics can be applied in economics. We have examined and developed the fundamental principles of terminology and concepts that we shall require from now on. In the next section we shall immediately begin to put some of these principles to work as we examine a number of common mathematical models in economics. We shall be using the mathematics we have introduced so far to reveal aspects of these models – and the implicit economic behaviour patterns – that are not evident from any other perspective.

Learning Check

Having read this module you should have learned that:

- Polynomial functions are functions with a number of x terms where each x term is raised to a successively higher integer power
- Quadratic and cubic functions are commonly used in economics and take recognizable forms and shapes
- Graphing a non-linear function will take up to around ten sets of coordinates
- Exponential and logarithmic functions are used to analyse economic growth and economic behaviour over time
- Functions involving more than one independent variable cannot be graphed, but key aspects of their shape can be indentified by keeping some variables constant
- An inverse function rewrites the original function by rearranging the expression in terms of the dependent and independent variables.

Worked Example

A firm has been analysing its revenue and cost situations. A demand function for its product has been derived as:

$$Q = f(P) = 125 - P$$

and its total costs, TC, as

$$TC = f(Q) = 500 + 0.5Q^2$$

Worked Example *(Continued)*

The firm wishes to use graphs to:

(i) Derive a profit function $\Pi = f(Q)$ where Π is profit defined as the difference between TR and TC (note that the symbol Π, pronounced 'pie', is from the Greek alphabet and is typically used in economics for profit)

(ii) Use this profit function to determine the level of output which maximizes profit

(iii) Use this profit function to determine the breakeven level of output (where total costs are just equal to total revenue)

(iv) Determine the price to be set which will generate profit-maximizing output.

Output is not expected to exceed 100 units.

Solution

(i) Since we require a profit function where $\Pi = f(Q)$ we must have:

$$\Pi = TR - TC$$

and we require a function for TR and TC expressed in terms of Q. This implies that we require the inverse function of the demand function (since this is expressed in terms of P). The inverse function will be derived from:

$$Q = 125 - P$$

and this can be rearranged to give

$$P = 125 - Q$$

$$TR = f(Q) = P \times Q = (125 - Q) \times Q = 125Q - Q^2$$

and since $TC = 500 + 0.5Q^2$ this gives

$$\Pi = TR - TC$$
$$= (125Q - Q^2) - (500 + 0.5Q^2)$$
$$= -500 + 125Q - 1.5Q^2$$

The corresponding graph for the profit function for $0 \leq Q \leq 100$ is shown in Fig. A3.11.

(ii) We see from the graph that the profit function is quadratic and rises to reach a maximum value when Q is about 42 (although our solution from the graph might not be exactly correct given the limitations of the axis scales).

(iii) We can also note that the function takes a negative value when $Q = 0$ (implying the firm is making a financial loss). From our knowledge of economics this is logical since we know the firm faces fixed costs of 500 and, by definition, that these costs are incurred even when $Q = 0$. Since, also by definition, TR must equal 0 when $Q = 0$, this implies that $\Pi = -500$ at zero output. We also see that the firm will continue to make a loss until the profit curve crosses the x axis (technically this is the breakeven position where $\Pi = 0$). This occurs when Q is about 5 (again approximately given the graph). We also note, however, that a second

Worked Example *(Continued)*

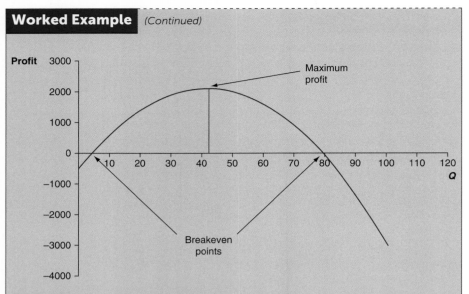

Figure A3.11 $\Pi = -500 + 125Q - 1.5Q^2$

breakeven level of output occurs when Q is about 80. You may wish to consider the economic explanation for this situation (and indeed the shape of the profit function itself). It is also instructive to show the relationship between the three functions: Π, TR and TC. All three functions are shown in Fig. A3.12. All three are quadratic (although with TC taking the opposite quadratic shape to Π and TR). The TR function starts from 0 while the TC function starts at 500 (linked to Π starting at -500). Notice that where TR and TC intersect is also where Π crosses the x axis – the two breakeven points, in other words. Notice also that Π reaches its maximum at the point where the gap between TR and TC reaches its widest. So, profit is maximized when output is around 42; the firm breaks even at levels of output of both 5 and 80; the firm is making a loss at output levels less than 5 and greater than 80; the firm makes a positive profit between 5 and 80 units of output.

(iv) Finally, we require the price that will equate to the profit-maximizing level of output. Since $Q = 42$ at the point of profit maximization we can use:

$$P = 125 - Q \qquad \text{and set} \qquad Q = 42$$

to give $P = 83$ as the price that will lead to the profit-maximizing level of output.

The problem illustrates two further points. The first is to highlight the limitations of graphical analysis in economics. Accurate numerical solutions are difficult, often impossible from graphs. We need to develop further mathematical ways of identifying the precise solutions to such problems. The second point is that it can be surprising how much economic analysis we can extract from of a couple of equations – if we know how.

Worked Example *(Continued)*

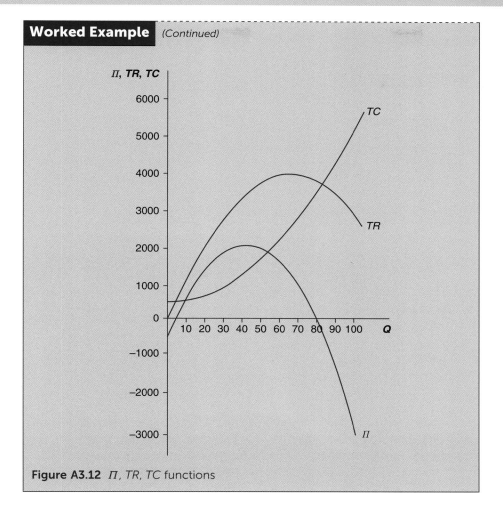

Figure A3.12 *Π*, *TR*, *TC* functions

A

Exercises

A3.1   Assume a function such that:

$$TC = f(Q) = 500 + 20Q - 6Q^2 + 0.6Q^3$$

where Q ranges from 0 to 15.

(i)   Plot this function and comment upon its shape.

(ii)   Derive functions for:

average total costs (ATC)
average variable costs (AVC)
average fixed costs (AFC)

and plot these functions on one graph.

(iii)   Comment on the economic explanation for the shape of the ATC function.

Exercises   *(Continued)*

A3.2   The market for a particular product is characterized by the following demand and supply functions:

$$Q_d = f(P) = 25 - 4P + 0.2P^2$$
$$Q_s = f(P) = -5 + 2P - 0.01P^2$$

(i)   Plot both functions on one graph for $P = 0$ to 50.

(ii)   In economic terms, over what range for P do these functions represent logical patterns of behaviour?

(iii)   Given that total revenue (TR) is defined as the quantity demanded multiplied by the price per unit, derive a function such that:

$$TR = f(P)$$

and plot this over the range for P that represents logical patterns of behaviour. Comment on the shape of this function.

A3.3   A firm expects that over the next decade its annual output will increase by 3% per year because of achievements in productivity. Its current annual output is 100,000 units.

(i)   For each of the next ten years calculate the annual output if this rate of growth is sustained.

(ii)   Show that this rate of growth can be represented by:

$$\text{Output} = 100{,}000(1.03)^t$$

where t is the number of years from the present.

A3.4   A Cobb–Douglas production function is given as:

$$Y = 0.6L^{0.3}K^{0.7}$$

where

   Y represents production
   L the input of labour
   K the input of capital.

(i)   Assume that K is fixed at 5 units. Plot the function for $L = 0$ to 10.

(ii)   On the same graph plot the function if K changes to 7.5 and then to 10 units.

(iii)   Repeat (i) and (ii) but now with L fixed at 5, 7.5 and 10 and K variable from 0 to 10.

(iv)   Comment on the shape of the functions you have produced.

A3.5   Plot the functions shown in (i) and (ii) below on one graph and those in (iii) and (iv) on a second graph. Use t from 0 to 10. What effect does the negative exponent term have?

(i) $Y = e^{0.25t}$

(ii) $Y = e^{0.3t}$

(iii) $Y = e^{-0.25t}$

(iv) $Y = e^{-0.3t}$

Exercises *(Continued)*

A3.6

(i) For the two functions used in Section A3.7, plot each over the range $P = 0$ to 15 and comment upon their relationship:

$$Q_d = 100 - 5P$$

$$TR = 100P - 5P^2$$

Assume the demand function now changes to:

$$Q_d = 150 - 5P$$

(ii) Plot this on the same graph as the original demand function and comment on the change in economic behaviour that this represents. What factors might have caused such a change?

(iii) The function now changes to:

$$Q_d = 150 - 10P$$

Plot this on the same graph and comment upon the observed change in economic behaviour and the factors that might have led to this change.

Appendix A3 Non-linear graphs in Excel

In Module A2 we saw how Excel could be used to create graphs of linear equations. Excel can also cope with non-linear equations, and we use Excel for this purpose in much the same way as for linear graphs. However, there's one important difference. For a linear graph we need a minimum of two sets of coordinates. For non-linear graphs we need more than that – typically around ten or so – although for more complex functions we may need more. Let's illustrate using the example used in Section A3.2:

$$y = 50 - x^3$$

and with $-10 \leq x \leq 10$. In the figure below, Fig. A3.13, you'll see we've started to create the data table in Excel for this function. We've set up the x variable column with x from -10 to $+10$ in steps of 2. We've also input a formula into cell C3 (which is the first of the y values) reading $= 50 - B3\^3$.

Given that B3 refers to the x variable and that the $\^$ symbol is Excel's way of showing powers or exponents this equates to $50 - x^3$. We can now Copy the formula in cell C3 to the other cells in the C column and call up the Chart Wizard as before (see Fig. A3.14).

Notice that, as before, we're choosing the XY scatter Chart type. This time, however, we've chosen a different chart subtype – that for the data points to be connected by smoothed rather than straight lines and without showing the markers (the actual data points). You could instead have chosen the subtype immediately to the left which would give you smoothed lines but also show the actual data points plotted. Clicking the Next option gives a preview of the graph, as shown in Fig. A3.15. If it looks OK then save it to the location of your choice. If it doesn't look OK – particularly if it doesn't look smooth enough – then all you have to do is to go back to your data table and

C3	▼		*fx* =-50-33^3		
	A	**B**	**C**	**D**	**E**	**F**
1						
2		x	y			
3		-10	950			
4		-8				
5		-6				
6		-4				
7		-2				
8		0				
9		2				
10		4				
11		6				
12		8				
13		10				
14						
15						
16						
17						
18						
19						

Figure A3.13 Setting up the data table for the function

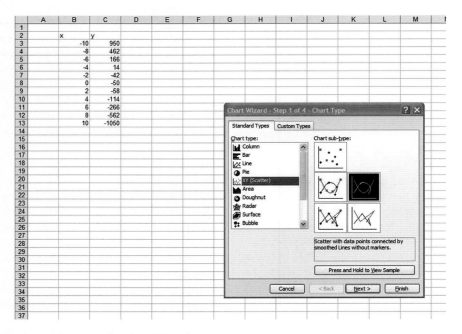

Figure A3.14 Using the Chart Wizard

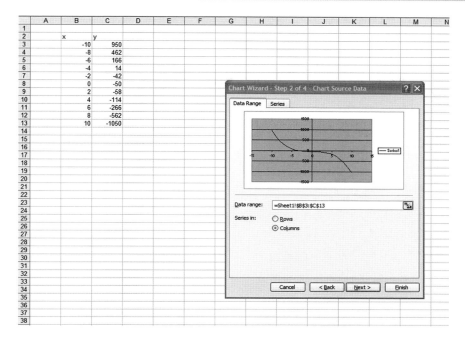

Figure A3.15 Graph preview

insert more data points for x and then calculate for y and bring up the Chart Wizard again.

There is a second method of drawing non-linear graphs in Excel. This can be used when you know the exact form of the polynomial function you are dealing with. Suppose you wanted a graph of the quadratic profit function we were looking at in this module: $Y = -500 + 125X - 1.5X^2$. Normally we'd need to set up a series of values for X and Y in Excel to be able to accurately draw the function. However, look at Fig. A3.16. In Excel we've calculated only three sets of coordinates and plotting an XY chart produces Fig. A3.17. It's difficult to see how we can get a quadratic curve from this. However, we can use one of Excel's chart options to help. In Excel you need to

	A	B	C	D	E
1					
2		x	y		
3		0	-500		
4		40	2100		
5		100	-3000		
6					
7					
8					
9					
10					
11					
12					

Figure A3.16 Data entry for the quadratic function

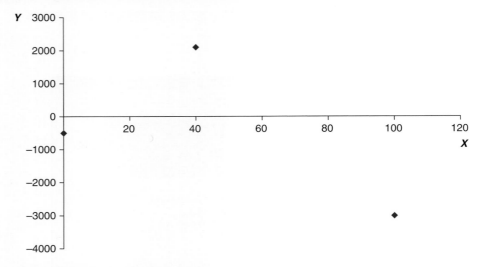

Figure A3.17 The three points plotted

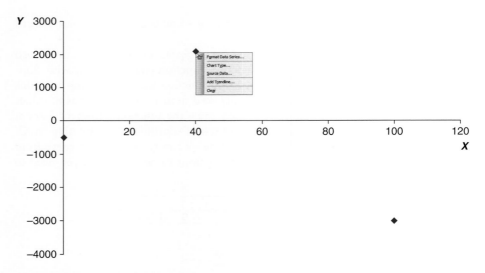

Figure A3.18 Trendline option

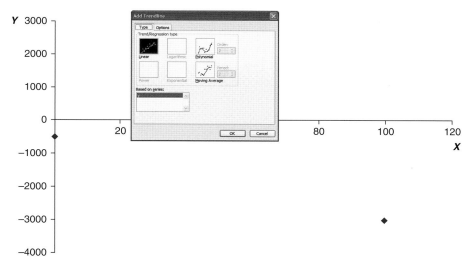

Figure A3.19 Choosing the trendline

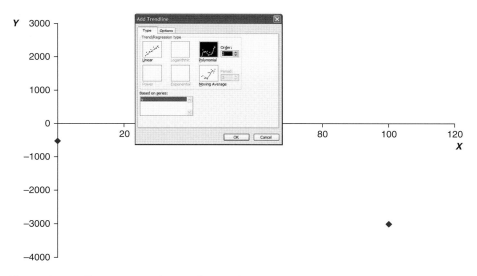

Figure A3.20 Choosing a quadratic polynomial

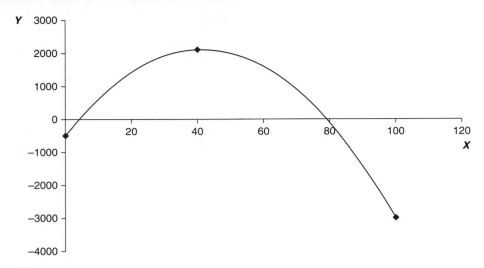

Figure A3.21 The quadratic trendline

move the cursor until it hovers over one of the plotted points and then right-click the mouse. This brings up a pop-up menu, as shown in Fig. A3.18; you should choose the Trendline option. Fig. A3.19 shows that you will have the option of choosing from several different trendlines – including polynomials. Here we choose a polynomial of the order 2 (a quadratic in other words) and press Enter. On doing so Excel fits a quadratic trendline to our three coordinates, with the result shown in Fig. A3.21.

Section B
Linear models in economic analysis

In Section A we provided the mathematical building blocks we shall need from now on. We also saw that linear equations and models are popular in economics because they are easy to work with and can be used to develop a number of important aspects of economic analysis. In this section we will look in detail at how linear mathematical models are used in economic analysis.

Module B1 The principles of linear models

This module looks at the key principles of linear models in economic analysis and makes sure you can use graphs and linear equations interchangeably.

Module B2 Market supply and demand models

In microeconomics, examining the conditions that generate an equilibrium between the quantity demanded of a product and the quantity supplied is an important aspect of economic analysis. In this module we look at how linear models help us to do this.

Module B3 National income models

In this module we turn our attention to macroeconomic analysis and look at a number of common national income models, seeing how equilibrium at the macroeconomic level can be analysed.

Module B4 Matrix algebra: the basics

If we wish to extend our analysis to large-scale linear economic models then ordinary algebra is not sufficient: we need to understand how to work with matrix algebra, a specialist form of algebra ideally suited to large linear models. In this module we introduce the basics of matrix algebra.

Module B5 Matrix algebra: inversion

In this module we complete our coverage of matrix algebra by looking at the topic of matrix inversion. This allows us to find solutions to large linear models.

Module B6 Economic analysis with matrix algebra

Having developed an understanding of matrix algebra we now see how it can be used in economic analysis. In this module we look again at market equilibrium and national income equilibrium analysis.

Module B7 Input–output analysis

In this module we extend our analysis to look at a very powerful type of economic modelling known as input–output analysis, which examines the interrelationships between different sectors of the economy.

Module B1
The principles of linear models

We have already seen that linear functions are particularly attractive in economic analysis because they are easy both to use and to understand – at least once you get used to them. So it's hardly surprising that a considerable number of economic models are built on linear functions. In this module we'll develop the necessary mathematical skills to be able to use and interpret these linear economic models.

Learning Objectives

By the end of this module you should be able to:

- Work out and explain the intercept/constant
- Work out and explain the slope/gradient
- Find the equilibrium solution using both algebra and graphs.

Knowledge Check B1

If you're already familiar and comfortable with linear maths, you may want to jump straight to the Worked Example at the end of this module. To check, try solving this:
   Sketch the two equations: $Y = 75 - 3X$; $Y = 25 + 5X$
Find the solution using simultaneous equations.
   Check your answer in Appendix 2.

B1.1 Linear functions

Let's go back to one of the linear functions we looked at previously. This and its corresponding graph (Fig. B1.1) are shown below:

$$TC = f(Q) = a + bQ = 100 + 5Q \tag{B1.1}$$

The function relates to a total cost equation for a firm where fixed costs were 100 and variable costs 5 per unit produced. It is clear that there are two parameters to this,

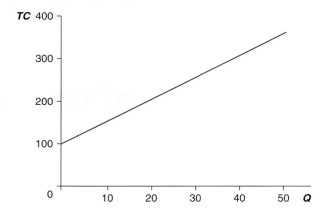

Figure B1.1 $TC = 100 + 5Q$

and any other, linear equation a and b. The exact numerical values taken by these parameters will vary, but in general each will fall into one of three categories:

Possible values for a		Possible values for b	
(i)	$a < 0$	(i)	$b < 0$
(ii)	$a = 0$	(ii)	$b = 0$
(iii)	$a > 0$	(iii)	$b > 0$

That is, a could be negative, zero or positive and similarly b could be negative, zero or positive.

In our example both parameters fall into category (iii). However, let's examine the general principles involved in such a function. The a parameter is generally referred to as the *intercept* or *constant* of the function. Referring to Fig. B1.1, it's clearly no coincidence that the line representing this function starts from a point on the vertical axis equal to 100, the value of a. Inspection of the linear function reveals that this will always be the case: the line will intercept the y axis at a value equal to a. Generalizing to $Y = a + bX$, if we set X to zero, then clearly $Y = a$. The line on the graph will always intercept the vertical axis at this value. Given that a could be negative, zero or positive, we have three possibilities, as shown in Fig. B1.2. The value taken by a will move the line up or down the vertical, Y, axis. So, simply by inspecting the a term in a linear equation, we know where the line will intercept the Y, or vertical, axis.

The second parameter of the function, b, refers to the *slope* or *gradient* of the line. Literally, it indicates the steepness of the line. As we shall see, the gradient is particularly important in economic analysis and will repay further detailed attention here. Let's look at Fig. B1.3. If we examine the linear function $Y = a + bX$ we see two points on the line with coordinates respectively of (x_1, y_1) and (x_2, y_2).

We have:

$$y_1 = f(x_1) = a + bx_1 \qquad\qquad\qquad (B1.2)$$
$$y_2 = f(x_2) = a + bx_2 \qquad\qquad\qquad (B1.3)$$

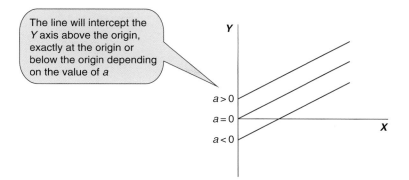

Figure B1.2 Changes in *a*

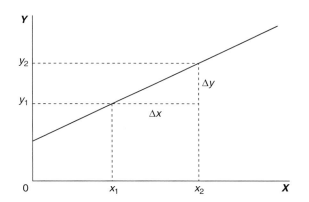

Figure B1.3 $Y = a + bX$

If we now wish to work out the change in Y that has occurred due to the change in X from x_1 to x_2 we have:

Change in X: $x_1 - x_2$

Change in Y: $y_1 - y_2 = (a + bx_1) - (a + bx_2)$

$$= a + bx_1 - a - bx_2$$

$$= bx_1 - bx_2$$

giving $y_1 - y_2 = b(x_1 - x_2)$

This shows that the change in Y is equal to b times the change in X. Now we need to introduce a new symbol, Δ (pronounced 'delta'), which is used in economics to indicate a *change* in the variable we are analysing. Here we have:

$$\Delta y = y_1 - y_2 \quad \text{and} \quad \Delta x = x_1 - x_2$$

so we now have

$$\Delta y = b\Delta x$$

giving

$$b = \frac{\Delta y}{\Delta x} \tag{B1.4}$$

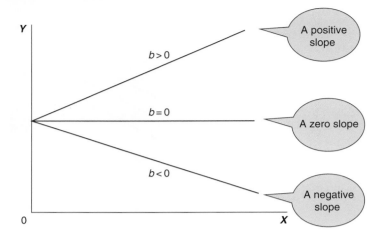

Figure B1.4 Change in b

That is, the slope b is given by the ratio of the change in Y to the change in X. The expression $\Delta y / \Delta x$ is often referred to as the *difference quotient*. We can also confirm from this that, for a linear function, the slope is constant – the slope is always equal to b. The implication of this is important for economics: the rate of change of Y to a change in X remains the same anywhere on the line representing the function. We shall see the economic implications of this shortly. In general, the exact numerical value of b could be negative, zero or positive. The three alternatives are shown in Fig. B1.4.

A linear function with a positive slope moves upwards, as we view it, from left to right. A function with a negative slope moves downwards (the change in Y brought about by a change in X represents a *decrease* in the Y value). A zero value for b indicates a line parallel to the X axis. Here a change in X brings about no change in Y; Y is actually independent of X in such a case.

To summarize, now we know about the a and b values in a linear function we can work out generally what the graph of a linear equation will look like just by looking at the a and b values and without any calculations.

Progress Check B1.1

Look at the following pairs of linear functions. Without drawing a detailed graph, sketch each pair of equations in terms of their relative intercepts and slopes.

(i) $Y = -75 + 12X$
$Y = -100 - 6X$

(ii) $Y = 75 - 15X$
$Y = 75 + 10X$

(iii) $Y = 100 - 5X$
$Y = 100 - 10X$

(iv) $Y = -100 + 12X$
$Y = -100 + 6X$

(Solutions on p. 461)

B1.2 A simple breakeven model

Now we understand the basics of linear equations let's develop the first of our linear economic models: that relating to breakeven analysis. We looked briefly at this in Module A2, but we are now able to apply more analysis to it. We already have a linear function, Eq. B1.1, representing total costs. We can also introduce a linear function showing the revenue that a firm obtains from selling the goods it produces. If we assume that the firm in question operates under conditions of perfect competition, then we know it has to sell at whatever price is fixed by the market, where P is used to show price. It is fairly obvious that at zero output the firm's revenue will also be zero. Think about this in the context of the two parameters of a linear function a and b, and the corresponding graph of total revenue. With zero production and zero revenue the line representing total revenue would go through the origin. In other words, the a parameter equals zero. This gives a function:

$$TR = f(Q) = a + bQ = pQ \tag{B1.5}$$

where TR refers to total revenue with parameters $a = 0$, $b = p$. If we now define the breakeven point as the level of output where total costs are equal to total revenue, then clearly we are seeking to work out a point where:

$$TC = TR$$

and visually this would be illustrated in Fig. B1.5 where we are looking for the value for q_1 – the level of output at which the firm breaks even and where, by definition, $TC = TR$.

It is worth noting that the expression $TC = TR$ does not represent a functional relationship in the way we have previously discussed, but is, rather, a requirement we are imposing on the model and is often referred to as a *conditional equality*. Clearly, we are not implying that $TC = f(TR)$ with this expression, but simply indicating that we seek a position where the two functions take identical values.

While we could examine this in numerical terms (as we shall shortly do to reinforce the key principles), as usual we are more interested in establishing general conclusions from this simple model. After all, numerical values will vary from one firm to another, from one country to another, or will vary over time. We seek to establish the general principles that apply to a breakeven analysis model so that they can be applied to any

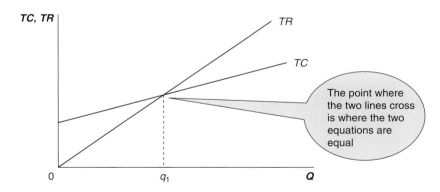

Figure B1.5 Breakeven point

such situation regardless of the precise numerical parameters used. Let us indulge in some simple algebra. We require:

$$TC = TR$$

However:

$$TC = f(Q) - = a + bQ$$

and

$$TR = f(Q) = pQ$$

so if we require $TC = TR$ then

Substitute for TC and for TR

$$TC = TR$$

Collect the Q terms together

$$a + bQ = pQ$$

The Q term is common to p and to b

$$a = pQ - bQ$$

$$a = Q(p - b)$$

Now divide through by $(p - b)$

and rearranging gives

$$Q = \frac{a}{p - b} \tag{B1.6}$$

where Q is the quantity such that total costs and total revenue will be equal.

This leads us to the conclusion that, in general, the breakeven level of output can be found by:

$$\frac{a}{p - b} = \frac{\text{fixed costs}}{\text{price} - \text{variable costs}}$$

since, in this model, a represents fixed costs and b represents variable costs. We have an immediate illustration of the usefulness of mathematics in evaluating economic models and this should not be underestimated. We have used some simple mathematics to reach a conclusion that would have been difficult to establish in any other way. Regardless of the exact numerical values in this type of model, Eq. B1.6 gives us a general solution method.

We can readily confirm our conclusion using a simple numerical example. If the firm we have examined sells its product for a price of €10 per unit then we have:

$$\text{Breakeven point} = \frac{a}{p - b} = \frac{100}{10 - 5} = 20 \, \text{units}$$

Equally, confirmation that this is, in fact, the correct solution can be obtained by substitution of $Q = 20$ into both the TC and TR equations. We have:

$$TC = 100 + 5(20) = 200$$

$$TR = 10(20) = 200$$

confirming that our solution method is correct.

Progress Check B1.2

Assume the firm now faces the following situation:

$$TR = 12Q$$

That is, the price charged per unit increases to €12. Plot this new function on the same graph as $TR = 10Q$, and $TC = 100 + 5Q$. Determine the new breakeven point using the general solution obtained in Eq. B1.6. Explain, in economic terms, why the breakeven level of output has fallen.

(Solution on p. 461)

B1.3 Simultaneous equations

The situation where we require a solution to two linear equations is one that occurs frequently in economic analysis. It will be worthwhile deriving a general solution method for the other models we shall be examining. If we have two linear equations such that

$$Y_1 = a_1 + b_1 X \tag{B1.7}$$

$$Y_2 = a_2 + b_2 X \tag{B1.8}$$

and we require a solution such that $Y_1 = Y_2$, then we can derive the following:

$$Y_1 = Y_2$$

$$a_1 + b_1 X = a_2 + b_2 X$$

$$a_1 - a_2 = b_2 X - b_1 X$$

$$a_1 - a_2 = X(b_2 - b_1)$$

$$\frac{a_1 - a_2}{b_2 - b_1} = X \tag{B1.9}$$

This expression, Eq. B1.9, allows us to find the solution to X that satisfies both equations simultaneously. This is referred to as the *method of simultaneous equations*. To find the corresponding Y value we have

$$Y_1 = a_1 + b_1 X$$

and using Eq. B1.9 we then have

$$Y_1 = a_1 + b_1 X$$

$$Y_1 = a_1 + b_1 \frac{a_1 - a_2}{b_2 - b_1}$$

$$= a_1 \frac{b_2 - b_1}{b_2 - b_1} + \frac{b_1 a_1 - b_1 a_2}{b_2 - b_1}$$

Multiply a_1 by $(b_2 - b_1) / (b_2 - b_1)$ (which = 1)
Multiply the second part through by b_1
Both parts now have the same denominator

$$= \frac{a_1 b_2 - a_1 b_1 + a_1 b_1 - a_2 b_1}{b_2 - b_1}$$

Multiply out the top terms
The two $a_1 b_1$ terms cancel

$$= \frac{a_1 b_2 - a_2 b_1}{b_2 - b_1} \tag{B1.10}$$

which, by definition, must give the same value for Y_2. Summarizing this gives a solution such that:

$$X = \frac{a_1 - a_2}{b_2 - b_1} \tag{B1.11}$$

and

$$Y_1 = Y_2 = \frac{a_1 b_2 - a_2 b_1}{b_2 - b_1} \tag{B1.12}$$

We now have a general method for deriving the solution for the problem we have already examined. We had:

$$TC = 100 + 5Q$$

$$TR = 10Q$$

so here we have

$$a_1 = 100 \qquad b_1 = 5$$

$$a_2 = 0 \qquad b_2 = 10$$

Using the two solution equations, Eqs B1.9 and B1.10, we have:

$$X = \frac{a_1 - a_2}{b_2 - b_1} = \frac{100 - 0}{10 - 5} = 20 \ (= Q \text{ in the context of our problem})$$

$$Y = \frac{a_1 b_2 - a_2 b_1}{b_2 - b_1} = \frac{100(10) - 0(5)}{10 - 5} = \frac{1000}{5} = 200 \ (= TC = TR)$$

Progress Check B1.3

For each set of functions derive the simultaneous equations' solution and sketch each pair of equations.

(i) $Y = 100 - 18X$
     $Y = -75 + 17X$

(ii) $Y = 100 - 10X$
      $Y = -50 + 5X$

(iii) $Y = -20 + 3X$
       $Y = 200 - 5X$

(iv) $Y = -60 + 3X$
      $Y = 50 - 2X$

(Solution on p. 461)

Two points are worth noting at this stage. First, there is no guarantee that an equation system actually has a simultaneous solution. Consider two equations such that:

$$Y = 100 + 5X$$

$$Y = 200 + 5X$$

Clearly, the two functions have the same slope and, in graphical terms, would be parallel to each other. Consider further that, since a simultaneous solution is effectively determining the point at which the two lines intersect, no such solution actually exists. Second, the equations in a model for which we require a simultaneous solution must be *functionally independent* of each other; that is, one equation must not be a function of another. Consider the two equations:

$$Y = 100 + 5X \tag{B1.13}$$

$$-2.75Y = -275 - 13.75X \tag{B1.14}$$

At first it may appear that we have two different equations and so we can find a unique solution. In fact, however, the second equation is a function of the first (it equals -2.75 times the first function). So in fact there is only one functional equation. Given that there are two unknowns, X and Y, no unique solution is possible. Naturally, in more complex equation systems it will not always be readily apparent that we face such problems. Fortunately, in Module B2 we shall be developing methods for determining whether a unique solution to a set of linear equations is possible.

Progress Check B1.4

Plot Eqs B1.13 and B1.14 on a graph for $X = 0$ to 100. Comment on the relationship between the two. Using the method of simultaneous equations attempt to find the values for X and Y for these two equations.

Exercises *(Continued)*

B1.3   Assume the following market model where Q_s shows the quantity of a product that will be supplied at a particular price and Q_d the quantity of the product that will be demanded at a particular price:

$$Q_d = 500 - 9P$$

$$Q_s = -100 + 6P$$

(i)   Sketch the model.

(ii)   Determine the equilibrium price and quantity.

B1.4   Assume that the demand function used in B1.3 changes to:

$$Q_d = 500 - 10P$$

(i)   Sketch both demand functions and the supply function.

(ii)   What would you expect to happen to the equilibrium price?

B1.5   Return to Exercise A2.4. We've collected some data on a cross-section of consumers in the economy to monitor their spending patterns and their income levels. As we have seen, spending is typically referred to in economics as consumption (C). Typically, these consumers had annual incomes (Y) of up to £40,000. Any income that's not spent they put into savings (S).

Income and spending for six individuals

	Income in £	Spending in £
Person A	10,000	10,500
Person B	32,000	25,900
Person C	22,000	18,900
Person D	18,750	16,625
Person E	34,000	27,300
Person F	15,500	14,350

Derive an equation for both the consumption function and the savings function. What would be the economic interpretation of the slope for each?

B1.6   For a particular product it's been noted that when the price was £4 per unit, 210 million units were demanded. When the price was £20 per unit, only 50 million units were demanded. Similarly, at a price of £22 per unit, firms were willing to supply 20 million units but at a price of £30 per unit were willing to supply 100 million units. Determine equilibrium price and quantity.

B

Module B2
Market supply and demand models

We have already seen that linear functions are particularly attractive because they are easy to both use and understand. Equally, there are a considerable number of areas of economic analysis where we can approximate some relationship using a linear function. It is not surprising, therefore, that a considerable number of economic models are built on linear functions, and in this module we shall examine some of the more common of these relating to market supply and demand, developing our mathematical skills as we do so. In particular we shall be examining the concept of *equilibrium* from both a mathematical and an economic viewpoint.

Learning Objectives

By the end of this module you should be able to:

- Solve and interpret a partial market equilibrium model
- Assess the effect of an excise tax on market equilibrium
- Explain the concept of elasticity.

B2.1 Market demand and supply

The first linear model we shall examine is the familiar one of market supply and demand. We have already discussed the type of demand function that is likely to exist for a particular product:

$$Q_d = f(P_x, P_c, P_s, Y, T) \tag{B2.1}$$

The quantity demanded, Q_d, of a product, X, will be a function of the price charged, P_x, the price of complementary goods, P_c, the price of substitute goods, P_s, consumer income, Y, and consumer tastes, T. For example, suppose we wanted to analyse the quantity demanded (sales) of a new DVD from a popular music group. Equation B2.1 indicates that the quantity demanded will be a function of several variables. The first is the price charged for the DVD itself. The price of complementary products – such as DVD players – will also, other things being equal, affect Q_d. So will the price of substitute products. These might be the price of competing DVDs from other artists or the price of downloading the group's album tracks from the internet. How much income consumers have available will affect how much they're willing to spend on this, and other, DVDs. Finally, consumer taste will have an impact – is this band still in fashion and in the public spotlight?

Note that our attention is focused upon market demand and supply and that, further, we assume that the market operates under competitive conditions. Naturally, the more complex we wish the model to be (and the more realistic), the more independent variables we can introduce into the function. By doing this, however, we make the function more difficult to use in terms of deducing patterns of economic behaviour. At this stage we shall assume that our prime interest lies in examining the relationship between the quantity demanded of the good and its price. This means that we are effectively assuming all other variables in the function remain constant (recollect the discussion on functions of more than one independent variable in Module A3). If we further assume that the demand function takes a linear form, then we have:

$$Q_d = f(P) = a + bP \tag{B2.2}$$

For a normal good we would expect the parameters of the function to be $a > 0$ and $b < 0$, that is, the intercept will be positive, implying that at zero price there will be some positive level of demand. Similarly, the slope/gradient is negative, implying that as the price increases quantity demanded will decrease and vice versa. This will give the familiar demand line shown in Fig. B2.1. The line slopes downwards with the negative slope equal to b and intercepts the vertical axis at a. Equally, we can develop a function for market supply – that is the amount that firms are willing to supply at particular prices. In linear form the function will be:

$$Q_s = f(P) = c + dP \tag{B2.3}$$

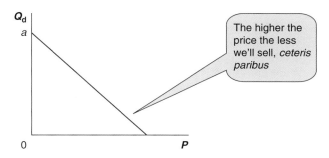

Figure B2.1 Demand function $Q_d = a + bP$

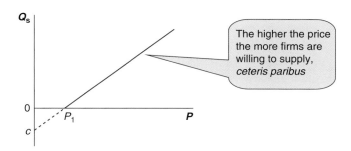

Figure B2.2 Supply function $Q_s = c + dP$

Here we can expect the slope to be positive (an increase in price leads to an increase in supply and hence $d > 0$) while the intercept will take a negative value ($c < 0$) as shown in Fig. B2.3.

Progress Check B2.1

Why, in economic terms, does the intercept of the supply function take a negative value?

The immediate logic of this may be less apparent until we examine Fig. B2.2. This shows a typical, linear supply function. We see that the function starts at a point on the horizontal axis below the origin. This implies, quite logically, that supply of the good will not commence until the price has reached some minimum level. Firms will simply be unwilling to supply this good at a price below P_1. Mathematically, this requires a negative constant in the supply function. It is evident that we shall wish to examine both functions together to build a simple economic model of supply and demand. To ensure that we recognize which parameters relate to which function we shall adopt the subscript notation:

$$Q_d = a_1 + b_1 P \tag{B2.4}$$

$$Q_s = a_2 + b_2 P \tag{B2.5}$$

with subscript 1 referring to the parameters of the first equation and so on.

B2.2 A partial equilibrium model

We are now in a position to analyse this model, to derive a number of principles of economic behaviour from it and to introduce the concept of equilibrium. You will already be aware that in such a market model equilibrium is defined as:

$$Q_d = Q_s \tag{B2.6}$$

That is, where the quantity of the good demanded by consumers is exactly matched by the quantity of the good supplied. In terms of our analysis such an equilibrium position is formally known as a *partial* equilibrium since we are examining only one good available in the market and not the totality of all goods available (where we would be trying to establish a *general* equilibrium). Therefore we have a model comprising:

$$Q_d = Q_s$$

$$Q_d = a_1 + b_1 P$$

$$Q_s = a_2 + b_2 P$$

Mathematically, we require values for the three variables, Q_d, Q_s, P, that satisfy all three equations simultaneously. Effectively, however, since we insist by definition that the two quantity variables must be equal, we shall require the values for P and Q that satisfy the model. Such values, naturally, are known as the *equilibrium* values: the equilibrium price, P_e, and the equilibrium quantity, Q_e. An examination of the appropriate graph (Fig. B2.3) for such a system reveals that the solution we seek will occur at the intersection of the two functions and that only one such solution exists (there is, after

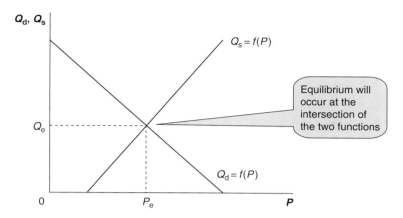

Figure B2.3 Market equilibrium

all, only one point where two straight lines can cross). You should also ensure that you understand why such a position will be an equilibrium.

Progress Check B2.2

Explain in detail why, under the conditions shown, the price can deviate only temporarily from the equilibrium level P_e.

Figure B2.4 illustrates these principles at work. At a price below P_e, quantity demanded will exceed quantity supplied and there will be a shortage of the product in the marketplace. Under shortage conditions the price will rise and as it does so the quantity demanded will decrease while that supplied will increase. Equally, if the price exceeds P_e there will be excess supply and pressure will arise for the price to fall, thereby stimulating quantity demanded but reducing quantity supplied. The only

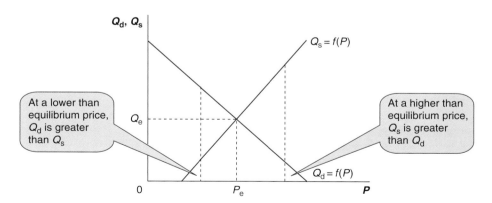

Figure B2.4 Equilibrium pressure

stable position, therefore, will be at the equilibrium point where both quantity supplied and demanded are equal. Algebraically, of course, we already have the ability to determine the general solution to such a model. We derived in Module B1 the general solution to two simultaneous equations as:

$$X = \frac{a_1 - a_2}{b_2 - b_1}$$

$$Y = \frac{a_1 b_2 - a_2 b_1}{b_2 - b_1}$$

for two linear equations of the form $Y = f(X)$. In the context of our market model, Q is the dependent variable and P the independent. So, the equilibrium can be found from:

$$P_e = \frac{a_1 - a_2}{b_2 - b_1} \qquad \text{(B2.7)}$$

$$Q_e = \frac{a_1 b_2 - a_2 b_1}{b_2 - b_1} \qquad \text{(B2.8)}$$

where P_e and Q_e denote the equilibrium values of the two variables. The equilibrium solution expression is worth further inspection. The parameters of the model have already been specified in terms of general value:

$a_1 > 0 \quad b_1 < 0 \qquad$ (relating to demand)

$a_2 < 0 \quad b_2 > 0 \qquad$ (relating to supply)

Looking at Eqs B2.7 and B2.8 we see that the denominator in the equations, $b_2 - b_1$, must be positive, given the restrictions on the values taken by b_1 and b_2. As b_2 is positive and b_1 negative, then subtracting a negative number from a positive must leave a positive result. Equally, in Eq. B2.7 the numerator must also be positive given the restrictions on a_1 and a_2. Hence P_e must also be positive. Examination of Eq. B2.8 also leads to the general conclusion that in order for Q_e to be positive (which makes sense economically) we must have the additional restriction:

$$a_1 b_2 - a_2 b_1 > 0$$

or

$$a_1 b_2 > a_2 b_1$$

With the restrictions on the parameters we have specified we have derived a simple mathematical method for determining the solution for any linear partial equilibrium market model. You should not underestimate the importance of this. It has not been necessary to use numerical examples to develop the general principles that we have obtained. In fact, the use of specific numerical examples would rarely allow us to make such generalized deductions about economic behaviour. But we have been able to show, for the simple model considered, what general conditions are required in order to establish an economically meaningful equilibrium solution.

Progress Check B2.3

Return to Progress Check B1.1. Assume that each pair of equations relates to supply and demand. Apply the principles we have just developed to determine which sets of equations will lead to an economically meaningful market equilibrium.

(i) $\quad Y = -75 + 12X$
$\quad\quad Y = -100 - 6X$

Progress Check B2.3 *(Continued)*

(ii) $Y = 75 - 15X$
     $Y = 75 + 10X$

(iii) $Y = 100 - 5X$
     $Y = 100 - 10X$

(iv) $Y = -100 + 12X$
     $Y = -100 + 6X$

(Solution on p. 461)

B2.3 An excise tax in a competitive market

We can develop our market model further in order to analyse a particular aspect of economic behaviour. Consider the situation where a government decides to impose a sales tax on a product. Assume that such a tax is imposed as a constant amount (known as an *excise tax*) regardless of the price. The government might impose a tax of £2 on each bottle of whisky, £1 on each pack of cigarettes or 10 pence on a litre of petrol. You may recollect that in the Introduction module we used a scenario looking at the government imposing such a tax on short-haul flights in Europe. As usual, we wish to analyse the general effects of such a policy. This brings us to a form of analysis that is particularly important in economics: *comparative static analysis*. Effectively, we wish to determine two equilibrium positions: one in the market where no tax is imposed and one in the market after the imposition of the tax. We shall then have two static, equilibrium positions and we shall be able to compare these to deduce the effect on the equilibrium brought about by the change that has been introduced into the model – in this case the tax imposed. Such comparative static analysis is frequently adopted in economic analysis to allow us to work out the effect that a specific change in a model will have on the solution to that model.

   This is a particularly important point in mathematical economic analysis and one worth reinforcing yet again. What we're able to do in terms of economic analysis and the use of mathematics is to assess the changes that will occur in an economic model regardless of the specific numerical values for the parameters of the model. Consider the importance and value of this. You have been asked by the government Finance Minister for advice. She's thinking of putting a 5-cent tax on a litre of petrol as part of the government's initiative to discourage car use because of its impact on global warming. She wants to know what the effect will be on equilibrium in this market. A few days later, she comes back asking about the effect of a 10-cent tax. And then about a 15-cent tax. Clearly, we could simply carry out analysis to assess the effect of the different policies using the exact values of the model parameters. But, as we shall now see, a much more appropriate method is to use mathematics to obtain the general implications for equilibrium regardless of the exact numerical parameters.

   In this scenario, the tax is imposed on sales, or supply. Clearly then, the demand equation will be unchanged. However, on the supply side we must now incorporate the effect of the tax imposed. The firm supplying the good will receive the market price, P, per item sold. However, from this it must pay the government the tax that has been imposed. Let's show this as t. From the supply side, therefore, we have:

$$P_t = P - t \tag{B2.9}$$

where P_t (the difference between the market price P and the excise tax t) is the price that is actually relevant to the firm's supply decisions. This is the price they get to keep after paying the government tax. We now have a supply function such that:

$$Q_s = a_2 + b_2 P_t \qquad \text{(B2.10)}$$

which can be rewritten using Eq. B2.9 as

$$Q_s = a_2 + b_2(P - t) \qquad \text{(B2.11)}$$

and the complete model becomes

$$Q_d = Q_s$$
$$Q_d = a_1 + b_1 P$$
$$Q_s = a_2 + b_2(P - t)$$

> We require the demand function to have a positive intercept and a negative slope

with restrictions on the values of the parameters such that

$$a_1 > 0 \quad b_1 < 0$$
$$a_2 < 0 \quad b_2 > 0$$

> We require the supply function to have a negative intercept and a positive slope

and

$$t > 0$$

Graphically, we might expect a situation as illustrated in Fig. B2.5. The imposition of the tax affects the price from the suppliers' perspective. Suppliers will now require a higher market price to supply the same quantity of the good given that part of this price will go to the government and not the firm. Effectively, therefore, the whole supply function will shift to the right as indicated. Mathematically we can see why this has happened if we look in more detail at the new supply function Eq. B2.11:

$$Q_s = a_2 + b_2(P - t) \qquad \text{(B2.11)}$$

If we multiply out the second part we get:

$$Q_s = a_2 + b_2 P - b_2 t$$

and rearrange to give

$$Q_s = (a_2 - b_2 t) + b_2 P$$

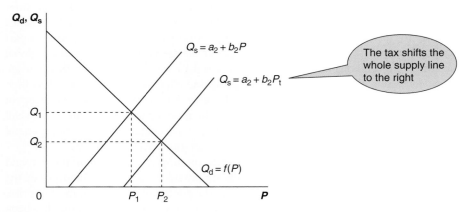

Figure B2.5 Excise tax

We see that the new supply function has the same slope as the pre-tax function but a different intercept. The original intercept, a_2, was required to be <0. We can deduce that the new intercept will have a larger negative value since both b_2 and t are required to be positive. So the new supply function will intercept further down the vertical axis and be parallel to the original supply function as shown in Fig. B2.5.

The effect on equilibrium will be an increase in the equilibrium price (from P_1 to P_2) and a decrease in the equilibrium quantity (Q_1 to Q_2). That is, the new equilibrium will be at a higher price and a lower quantity. We can confirm this logic through some simple algebra.

We require:

$$Q_d = Q_s$$

Algebraic manipulation shows that:

$$a_1 + b_1 P = a_2 + b_2(P - t)$$ ⟵ Use Eqs B2.10 and B2.11

$$a_1 + b_1 P = a_2 + b_2 P - b_2 t$$

$$a_1 - a_2 = b_2 P - b_1 P - b_2 t$$ ⟵ Collect all the a terms on one side and all the b terms on the other

$$a_1 - a_2 + b_2 t = b_2 P - b_1 P$$ ⟵ Move the tax term to the left-hand side

$$a_1 - a_2 + b_2 t = P(b_2 - b_1)$$ ⟵ Divide both sides by $b_2 - b_1$

or

$$P = \frac{a_1 - a_2 + b_2 t}{b_2 - b_1}$$

giving

$$P_e = \frac{a_1 - a_2}{b_2 - b_1} + \frac{b_2 t}{b_2 - b_1} \tag{B2.12}$$

and having found P we can determine the equilibrium quantity by substituting Eq. B2.12 into the demand (or supply) function

$$Q_e = a_1 + b_1 P$$

$$= a_1 + b_1 \left(\frac{a_1 - a_2}{b_2 - b_1} + \frac{b_2 t}{b_2 - b_1} \right)$$

$$= \frac{a_1(b_2 - b_1) + b_1(a_1 - a_2 + b_2 t)}{b_2 - b_1}$$ ⟵ Multiply a_1 by $(b_2 - b_1)/(b_2 - b_1)$ (which equals 1)

$$= \frac{a_1 b_2 - a_1 b_1 + b_1 a_1 - b_1 a_2 + b_1 b_2 t}{b_2 - b_1}$$

$$= \frac{a_1 b_2 - b_1 a_2 + b_1 b_2 t}{b_2 - b_1}$$

$$Q_e = \frac{a_1 b_2 - b_1 a_2}{b_2 - b_1} + \frac{b_1 b_2 t}{b_2 - b_1} \tag{B2.13}$$

Therefore Eqs B2.12 and B2.13 again provide us with a general solution for the market model involving an excise tax. This general solution may look complex but, again, careful examination proves particularly revealing. Let us compare these two equations with those derived earlier for the market model without the tax.

Market model without tax   *Market model with tax*

$$P_e = \frac{a_1 - a_2}{b_2 - b_1}$$ $$P_e = \frac{a_1 - a_2}{b_2 - b_1} + \frac{b_2 t}{b_2 - b_1}$$

$$Q_e = \frac{a_1 b_2 - a_2 b_1}{b_2 - b_1}$$ $$Q_e = \frac{a_1 b_2 - b_1 a_2}{b_2 - b_1} + \frac{b_1 b_2 t}{b_2 - b_1}$$

We see quite clearly that the two general solutions are similar. The difference is that for both P_e and Q_e we have an added element involving t, the tax levied. In fact if we set $t = 0$ we see that Eqs B2.12 and B2.13 become identical to Eqs B2.7 and B2.8. Let's examine these tax elements in more detail. With reference to the restrictions on the function parameters we see that b_2 is positive and the denominator, $b_2 - b_1$, must be positive also (since b_1 is negative and therefore $-b_1$ must be positive). So in Eq. B2.12 the expression:

$$\frac{b_2}{b_2 - b_1}$$

must be positive also.

So we now know that for $t > 0$ the effect of the tax on the equilibrium price must be positive. That is, the new equilibrium price must be higher than the non-tax P_e. Further inspection reveals that the expression must also be less than 1 since $b_2 - b_1$ will be larger than b_2. Hence the increase in P_e must be less than the tax imposed. Let's think about this carefully because it's an important conclusion. The sales tax was imposed on the companies selling the product. As a result equilibrium price will be higher than it was before the tax was imposed. But the increase in price is less than the amount of tax. This means that firms are not passing the full amount of tax on to the consumer but paying some of it themselves. Exactly how much of the tax will be paid by the consumer and how much by the firms will depend on the exact numerical parameters of the supply and demand equations.

Let us now examine the tax element in Eq. B2.13. We have:

$$\frac{b_1 b_2}{b_2 - b_1}$$

and since the denominator is positive and the numerator negative the whole expression must be negative. In other words, the effect on the equilibrium quantity will be negative. The equilibrium quantity after the imposition of a tax must be lower than it was. Hence we know that the imposition of such a tax will raise the equilibrium price but by less than the amount of tax imposed. Naturally, this higher price will lead to a fall in the equilibrium quantity. Once again, therefore, we have a clear demonstration of the usefulness of mathematics in evaluating a change in an economic model. We are able to deduce the effects of such a tax on any market model that fits the general structure identified (that is, has parameters that take numerical values consistent with the restrictions we introduced).

B2.4 Elasticity

We have seen how the slope of a linear function measures the change in Y to a change in X. Economists often wish to compare such slopes between two or more functions.

Consider two demand functions, say the demand for electricity by domestic consumers and the demand for petrol by domestic consumers. We may pose the question: by how much will demand change if the price increases by, say, £0.10 per unit? One problem with such an approach is that we immediately encounter difficulties in terms of units of measurement. Electricity demand is likely to be measured in kilowatt-hours; demand for petrol in litres. Equally, the price per unit is likely to differ, making the price change of £0.10 relatively larger for one product than the other. Clearly, the slope again will be of little direct use.

The way around this in economics is to examine not the slope of such functions directly but rather their *elasticity*. We need to develop a method of allowing such a comparison that is independent of units of measurement. This is what elasticity tries to provide. The simplest approach would be to express such changes in percentages rather than absolute terms, that is, comparing the percentage change in Q_d with the corresponding percentage change in P. Units of measurement then become irrelevant. In fact we can define elasticity in such a way:

$$E_d = \frac{\text{percentage change in } Q_d}{\text{percentage change in } P} \tag{B2.14}$$

where E_d denotes the price elasticity of demand. To calculate a percentage change is straightforward. Given that we have $Q_d = f(P)$, then if we have two values for P (P_1 and P_2) we can obtain two comparable values for Q_d (Q_1 and Q_2). The percentage change in Q_d is then:

$$\frac{Q_2 - Q_1}{Q_1} \times 100$$

or, to generalize

$$\frac{\Delta Q}{Q} \times 100$$

> Remember we use Δ(delta) to refer to the change in a variable

and we therefore have

$$E_d = \frac{\Delta Q/Q \times 100}{\Delta P/P \times 100}$$

which simplifies to

$$E_d = \frac{\Delta Q/Q}{\Delta P/P}$$

$$= \frac{\Delta Q}{Q} \times \frac{P}{\Delta P}$$

> Rearrange using the inversion rule used in Section A3.7

$$= \frac{\Delta Q}{\Delta P} \times \frac{P}{Q} \tag{B2.15}$$

Given that the demand function will be:

$$Q_d = a + bP$$

then $\Delta Q = b\Delta P$, giving $b = \Delta Q/\Delta P$. Hence:

$$E_d = \frac{bP}{Q} \tag{B2.16}$$

Consider a demand function: $Q_d = 100 - 10P$. We wish to determine the elasticity of demand when $P = 4$. Clearly, when $P = 4$ then $Q = 60$ and with $b = -10$ we have:

$$E_d = \frac{-10(4)}{60} = -0.67$$

This means that at this particular price a given percentage change in the price will bring about a percentage change in Q_d of -0.67 times the percentage change in price. To confirm this, let us assume that P changed by 1%, that is, from 4 to 4.04. The new Q_d will be:

$$Q_d = 100 - 10(4.04) = 59.6$$

and the percentage change in Q_d

$$\frac{59.6 - 60}{60} \times 100 = \frac{-0.4}{60} \times 100 = -0.67$$

Consider further the effect on total revenue, which is given by:

$$TR = P \times Q = P(100 - 10P) = 100P - 10P^2$$

Using $P_1 = 4$ and $P_2 = 4.04$ we have:

$$TR_1 = 240 \quad \text{and} \quad TR_2 = 240.784$$

In other words, even though the price has risen and the quantity demanded has fallen, the total revenue from the reduced volume of sales has actually increased. We also note that demand elasticity can normally be expected to be negative and the sign is usually ignored. Thus, we would report an elasticity of 0.67 in this example and the negative sign would be taken for granted.

Progress Check B2.4

Explain in terms of economics why TR has increased in the example above even though the price has risen.

(Solution on p. 461)

Clearly, such an outcome in terms of revenue will depend upon the exact price elasticity figure that applies to a particular situation. In general, however, we can denote three general values for the price elasticity of demand (ignoring the negative sign):

$$E_d < 1$$
$$E_d = 1$$
$$E_d > 1$$

These three categories indicate the responsiveness of quantity demanded to a proportionate change in price. As we have seen, with elasticity less than 1 (referred to as an *inelastic* position), a proportionate change in P leads to a smaller proportionate change in Q_d. That is, if the price changes, demand will also change but by less than the change in price. Basic foodstuffs such as bread tend to be inelastic. Changing the price does little to change demand – there's only so much bread you can eat, after all.

Equally, if the elasticity is greater than 1 (highly *elastic*), there will be a greater proportionate change in Q_d. So a change in the price will bring about a proportionately greater change in demand. Products classed a luxury items where spending is discretionary tend to be highly elastic. Products such as alcoholic spirits are often highly elastic in many economies, for example.

Wikipedia has some interesting research results on actual elasticities: http://en.wikipedia.org/wiki/Price_elasticity_of_demand

When elasticity equals 1 (*unitary* elasticity), a proportionate change in price brings about the same proportionate change in Q_d. Although we have introduced elasticity here in terms of a demand function, the concept is equally useful to many other functions in economics; we shall be returning to this important topic later in the text.

We should note that the evaluation of elasticity is strictly appropriate for considering infinitesimally small changes in the price.

Progress Check B2.5

Calculate, and interpret, the elasticity of demand for $Q_d = 100 - 10P$ when:

(i) $P = 8$

(ii) $P = 2$

Comment on the implications for the individual firm considering raising its price at each of these two levels.

(Solution on p. 461)

B2.5 Summary

We have seen in this module a number of examples illustrating the usefulness of mathematics in deriving general conclusions about economic behaviour from an economic model. None of the examples introduced has actually involved numerical values and yet we have been able to derive important policy conclusions from our applications of a combination of mathematical and economic logic. Naturally, there are limitations in the realism of the simple models we have examined. This does not negate, however, the importance of mathematics. As we progress through the text, expansions to all these models will be incorporated as you develop the necessary skills.

Learning Check

Having read this module you should have learned that:

- Market equilibrium shows where Q_d and Q_s are in balance
- Comparative static analysis compares two, or more, equilibrium positions to assess the impact of an economic change
- An excise tax is a fixed tax, regardless of price
- An excise tax will typically lead to an increase in equilibrium price and a decrease in equilibrium quantity
- Elasticity measures the change in quantity demanded relative to a change in price
- Elasticity of demand is typically classed into elastic products, inelastic products or unitary elastic products.

Worked Example

A government Finance Minister is keen to raise additional revenue through taxation. She has identified one industrial sector in the economy and is considering introducing an excise tax of £3 per unit sold. The relevant demand and supply functions are:

$$Q_d = 250 - 8P$$

$$Q_s = -50 + 4P$$

Worked Example *(Continued)*

where Q and P are measured in millions. Someone has suggested that if the tax were doubled to £6 per unit the government would raise twice as much tax revenue. Using the functions given, can we assess the accuracy of this suggestion? Additionally, can we suggest an excise tax amount which would maximize the tax revenue obtained by the government?

Solution

We can denote the tax revenue raised as T so we have:

$$T = tQ_e$$

where t is the unit tax and Q_e the equilibrium quantity. From Eq. B2.13 earlier in the module we know the equilibrium solution will be:

$$Q_e = \frac{a_1 b_2 - b_1 a_2}{b_2 - b_1} + \frac{b_1 b_2 t}{b_2 - b_1}$$

Here we have:

$$a_1 = 250$$
$$a_2 = -50$$
$$b_1 = -8$$
$$b_2 = 4$$
$$t = 3$$

and substituting into Eq. B2.13 we get

$$Q_e = \frac{250(4) - (-8)(-50)}{4 - (-8)} + \frac{(-8)(4)(3)}{4 - (-8)}$$

$$= \frac{1000 - 400}{12} - \frac{96}{12} = 42$$

and we then have

$$T = tQ_e = 3(42) = 126$$

as the tax revenue raised. So £126 million would be raised in tax in total.

If $t = £6$ we have:

$$Q_e = \frac{250(4) - (-8)(-50)}{4 - (-8)} + \frac{(-8)(4)(6)}{4 - (-8)}$$

$$= \frac{1000 - 400}{12} - \frac{192}{12} = 34$$

and we then have

$$T = tQ_e = 6(34) = 204$$

as the tax revenue raised. So total tax revenue has increased to £204 million.

While the tax revenue has increased it clearly has not doubled, whereas the tax imposed has. It is also clear that we have the same principles at work as with elasticity of demand.

With regard to the second part of the problem, we are required to offer advice on a tax that will maximize the total tax revenue. We know that in general:

Worked Example *(Continued)*

$$T = tQ_e$$

In this case Q_e simplifies to:

$$Q_e = \frac{a_1 b_2 - b_1 a_2}{b_2 - b_1} + \frac{b_1 b_2 t}{b_2 - b_1}$$

$$Q_e = \frac{250(4) - (-8)(-50)}{4 - (-8)} + \frac{(-8)(4)t}{4 - (-8)}$$

$$= \frac{1000 - 400}{12} - \frac{32t}{12}$$

$$Q_e = 50 - 2.67t$$

giving

$$T = tQ_e = t(50 - 2.67t) = 50t - 2.67t^2$$

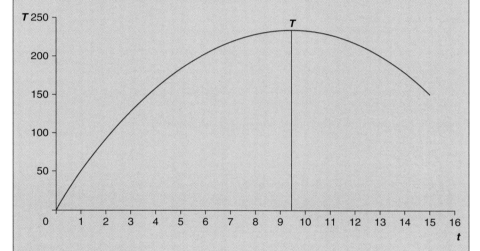

Figure B2.6 $T = 50t - 2.67t^2$

which we recognize as a quadratic taking the inverted U shape from Module A3. If we now plot this function we can use the graph to identify the maximum T position. The corresponding graph is shown in Figure B2.6 where we see the maximum value of T occurs when t is approximately £9.40 (in fact, the precise t value is £9.38 using solution techniques we shall develop later in the text).

Exercises

B2.1   Assume the following market model:

$$Q_d = 500 - 9P$$

$$Q_s = -100 + 6P$$

Exercises   *(Continued)*

(i)   Sketch the model.

(ii)   Determine the equilibrium price and quantity.

B2.2   For Ex. B2.1, if a tax of £5 per unit sold is now imposed, calculate the new equilibrium price and quantity.

 (i)   Sketch the new equilibrium.

 (ii)   What proportion of the tax is paid by the consumer?

 (iii)   What revenue does the government raise through imposition of the tax?

B2.3   Assume that the demand function changes to:

$$Q_d = 500 - 10P$$

(i)   Sketch both demand functions and the supply function.

(ii)   What would you expect to happen to the equilibrium price:
    (a)   before tax?
    (b)   after tax?

B2.4   For Ex. B2.3, calculate the new equilibrium price before and after tax.

 (i)   What proportion of the tax is paid by the consumer?

 (ii)   What has happened to the revenue raised from the tax?

 (iii)   How do you explain (i) and (ii)?

B2.5   For the previous exercises B2.1 and B2.3:

 (i)   Calculate elasticity of demand at the equilibrium

 (ii)   Explain what your answer means in terms of economic behaviour

 (iii)   Why has E_d changed in the way that it has?

B2.6   Return to Ex. B2.1, and determine the tax amount that will maximize tax revenue for the government.

Module B3
National income models

In the previous module we saw how market supply and demand models can be used to analyse equilibrium positions and change at the microeconomic level. In this module we do the same by looking at equilibrium at the macroeconomic level by building a national income model. We'll develop a series of such models, starting with the simplest and gradually adding more realism as we progress.

Learning Objectives

By the end of this module you should be able to:

- Solve and interpret a variety of national income models
- Calculate and explain the marginal propensity to consume
- Show national income models in diagram form
- Assess the impact on national income of changes in key parameters.

B3.1 A national income model

We start with a model that assumes what is known as a closed economy, where *firms* manufacture goods and services and *households* buy (or in economics, consume) the goods and services produced by firms. Households also supply firms with the factors of production – typically labour, land and capital – and in return are paid income for these by the firms. Of course, the households use this income to buy the goods and services produced by the firms and the firms use their income to buy the factors of production so that they can produce goods and services. This circular system is referred to as the *circular flow of income*. Figure B3.1 illustrates the flow of income, Y, from firms to households and the consumption expenditure, C, of households buying goods and services from firms.

We should also note that in the closed economy model we assume there is no foreign trade, no government sector, no inflation, and availability of unused resources. We can then define national income, Y, as comprising two elements, planned consumption and investment:

$$Y = C + I \qquad\qquad (B3.1)$$

where

Y = national income
C = consumption expenditure
I = investment expenditure.

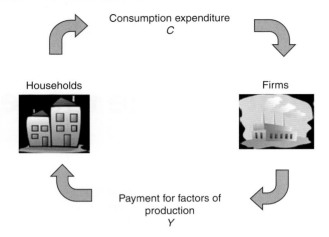

Figure B3.1 Circular flow of income in a closed economy

In other words, by definition, national income is the sum total of consumption and investment spending. Consumption refers to the expenditure planned by individuals and households. Investment refers to the amount firms invest in their own capacity – building factories, buying machinery and so on. In effect, Eq. B3.1 states that, in this simplest economic national income model, total national income is the combined total of what is spent on consumption and what is spent on investment. Let us make the further assumptions that:

$$C = f(Y) = a + bY \tag{B3.2}$$

$$I = i$$

where i is a constant value. It will be worth discussing the implications of these in more detail. We have already distinguished between dependent and independent variables. We now distinguish between *endogenous* and *exogenous* variables. Simply, an exogenous variable takes its value from outside the model we are investigating – in other words it is taken as given and known at the start. An endogenous variable, on the other hand, has its value determined from within the model – we need to work it out using the model. In this model I is exogenous – its value, i, is determined from outside the model – while Y and C are both endogenous. This is illustrated in Fig. B3.2, which shows the circular flow of income model but now with investment, I, coming from outside the model. (Don't worry about the savings element shown – we'll look at that later in this module.) Investment in such circumstances is often referred to as an *injection* into the model.

Let us now examine Eq. B3.2 in more detail. The function is an important one in macroeconomic theory, and is known as the *consumption function*. It is sensible to restrict the two parameters of this function so that:

$$a > 0 \quad \text{and} \quad 0 < b < 1$$

First, we require the intercept of the function to be positive. Think about what this means. When income is zero, some consumption still takes place – for example, you still need to eat, somewhere to live, and clothes to wear. Such consumption will be funded either from borrowing against future income or from savings derived from past income (a is often referred to as *autonomous* consumption). We also restrict the slope of the function to be positive and to lie between zero and 1. The positive restriction

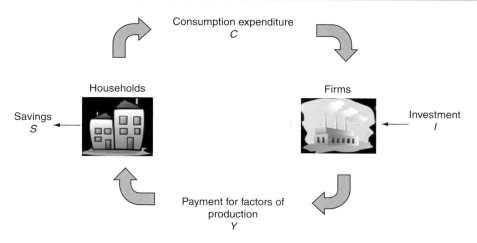

Figure B3.2 Circular flow of income in a closed economy with investment and savings

on b implies that as Y increases so does C (that is, $0 < b$). This appears logical, since generally if people's income rises then they tend to spend more. Equally we can restrict the maximum value for b to be less than 1. Consider the meaning of b in this context. It represents the change in C that occurs for a given change in Y. If Y increases by, say, €100, then we are restricting the increase in C to be a proportion less than this amount – that is, if people receive an increase in income they'll spend less than 100% of it (the rest goes into savings). In general, for a given change in Y, C will change by bY where bY shows the *change* in consumption arising from a *change* in income. Notice that, since we have a linear consumption function, its slope/gradient remains constant (at b) no matter the level of income. This has implications we need to consider. It indicates that regardless of their income, people will respond in exactly the same way to a change in that income. If b took a value, for example, of 0.75 it indicates that 75% of an increase in income would go on consumption expenditure no matter whether you had an income of €20,000 or €200,000. This may not always be realistic and is one of the reasons that, from Section C onwards, we'll be developing non-linear models.

In fact, the slope of the consumption function is more normally referred to as the *marginal propensity to consume* (mpc). Its value is an indication of the *extra* consumption arising from *extra* income. You may already be aware from your study of economics that the marginal concept is a particularly important one. It's a concept to which mathematical analysis is applied a lot, as we will discover. The mpc is given by:

$$\text{mpc} = \frac{\Delta C}{\Delta Y} = b \tag{B3.3}$$

Let us now consider equilibrium in the model. We have:

$$Y = C + I$$

$$C = a + bY$$

and substituting we obtain

$$Y = a + bY + I \quad \longleftarrow \boxed{\text{Substitute } a + bY \text{ for } C \text{ into the } Y \text{ function}}$$

$$Y - bY = a + I \quad \longleftarrow \boxed{\text{Collect the } Y \text{ terms together}}$$

$$Y(1 - b) = a + I \quad \longleftarrow \boxed{Y \text{ is common to both terms on the left}}$$

$$Y_e = \frac{a + I}{1 - b} \tag{B3.4}$$

Substituting Eq. B3.4 back into the consumption function, B3.2, we have:

$$C = a + bY$$

$$= a + b\frac{a+I}{1-b}$$

and multiplying a by $1 - b/1 - b$ (which is the same as 1) we then have

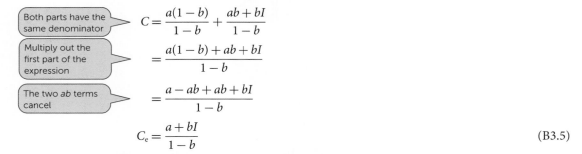

Both parts have the same denominator

Multiply out the first part of the expression

The two ab terms cancel

$$C = \frac{a(1-b)}{1-b} + \frac{ab+bI}{1-b}$$

$$= \frac{a(1-b) + ab + bI}{1-b}$$

$$= \frac{a - ab + ab + bI}{1-b}$$

$$C_e = \frac{a+bI}{1-b} \qquad\qquad (B3.5)$$

So from Eqs B3.4 and B3.5 we have:

$$Y_e = \frac{a+I}{1-b} \quad and \quad C_e = \frac{a+bI}{1-b}$$

as the equilibrium levels of national income and consumers' expenditure.

Progress Check B3.1

Given the restrictions on the equation parameters, what are the implications for the feasible values of Y_e and C_e?

Note that both endogenous variables (Y and C) can now be determined from given values (given that a and b are parameters and I is exogenous). Note also that given the restrictions on the parameter values the resulting equilibrium values for Y and C must be positive. The $a + I$ expression must be positive and so must the $1 - b$ part. We can also work out that as long as $I > 0$ then C must be less than Y (since $b < 1$).

Here we introduce a further interesting aspect by carrying out a comparative static analysis. Let us assume that in time period 1, investment takes some fixed value, I_1. Equilibrium national income will then be:

$$Y_1 = \frac{a+I_1}{1-b}$$

In period 2 investment changes to I_2. The new level of national income is then given by:

$$Y_2 = \frac{a+I_2}{1-b}$$

Accordingly, we have the change in income:

$$Y_1 - Y_2 = \frac{a + I_1}{1 - b} - \frac{a + I_2}{1 - b}$$

> Substitute for Y_1 and Y_2

$$= \frac{a + I_1 - a - I_2}{1 - b}$$

> Multiply out the second part on top and simplify the denominator

$$= \frac{I_1 - I_2}{1 - b}$$

$$\Delta Y = \frac{1}{1 - b} \Delta I$$

> Use ΔI for $I_1 - I_2$

$$\frac{\Delta Y}{\Delta I} = \frac{1}{1 - b} = \frac{1}{1 - \text{mpc}} \tag{B3.6}$$

which you may recognize as the familiar Keynesian investment *multiplier* (usually denoted in economics by k). Consideration of the parameter restrictions on b indicates that k must be positive. Think about the implications: an increase in exogenous investment will lead to an increase in equilibrium national income and a decrease in investment will lead to a decrease in equilibrium national income. The multiplier k also lies in the range greater than 1 but less than infinity, implying that a given change in I will lead to a greater, but finite, change in Y. This requires further explanation. In our model we restricted b to take a value above zero but less than 1. Any number for b which is greater than zero means the denominator in Eq. B3.6 will take a value less than 1. In turn this will mean that the value of the multiplier in Eq. B3.6 will be greater than 1 (since dividing the numerator of 1 by a number less than 1 gives a result greater than 1). So a given change in I will lead to a greater change in Y. But we said a short while ago that the change in Y would be greater – but finite. We already know that the multiplier will be greater than 1. But how much greater than 1 could it get? Let's try some numbers to see what's happening. If we set b at a particular value then we can easily work out k from Eq. B3.6. So, if we first set $b = 0.9$, then 0.99, then 0.999 ... we obtain the results shown below.

b	k
0.9	10
0.99	100
0.999	1000
0.9999	10,000
0.99999	100,000
0.999999	1,000,000

The larger the value that b takes as it approaches – but never reaches – the upper limit of 1, the larger k becomes. You may be able to work out that, as we add another decimal place to b, k adds another 0 at the end, becoming 10 times as big again. You may also be able to work out that, technically, there is no upper limit to the decimal places we can add to b and there is technically no upper limit to k – the number just keeps getting bigger and bigger. But however big k becomes it is still technically a *finite* number. This is why we said earlier that the multiplier k also lies in the range greater than 1 but less than infinity.

> Infinity is a tricky concept. Try http://en.wikipedia.org/wiki/Infinity

It is important to appreciate exactly how the multiplier effect works (we shall be returning to the multiplier concept a number of times through the text). It may at first appear odd that some change in investment can lead to a *larger* change in income – it seems as if we're getting something from nothing. The key to the puzzle lies in the model formulation. A given change in investment has, first, an immediate effect on Y, given Eq. B3.1, and then a subsequent effect on C through Eq. B3.2. However, the process does not stop there. Given that C has now changed, this again changes Y via Eq. B3.1, which again changes C, which changes Y – and so on. Eventually, of course, the process stops, given that each successive change in Y and C becomes smaller and smaller.

Let's look at the last Progress Check problem to show what's happening. Our model is:

$$Y = C + I$$
$$C = 1000 + 0.8Y$$
$$I = 250$$

From Eqs B3.4 and B3.5 we have:

$$Y_e = \frac{a + I}{1 - b} \quad \text{and} \quad C_e = \frac{a + bI}{1 - b}$$

and substituting for the parameters and the exogenous value for I we have

$$Y_e = \frac{1000 + 250}{1 - 0.8} = \frac{1250}{0.2} = 6250 \text{ as the equilibrium income}$$

and

$$C_e = \frac{1000 + 0.8(250)}{1 - 0.8} = \frac{1200}{0.2} = 6000 \text{ as the equilibrium consumption.}$$

That is, with a level of investment of 250, equilibrium national income will be 6250 and equilibrium level of consumption will be 6000 (with savings being 250). To calculate k, the multiplier, we use Eq. B3.5:

$$k = \frac{1}{1 - b} = 1/0.2 = 5$$

That is, a given change in I will lead to a fivefold change in Y.

Let's see what's happening on a step-by-step basis. Assume that I increases from 250 to 251. Y will initially increase from 6250 to 6251 through Eq. B3.1. However, the extra income, 1, has an effect on C, with 80% of extra income going into extra consumption (the other 20% will go into savings). So, C increases from 6000 to 6000.8. However, this in turn leads to another increase in Y through Eq. B3.1, with Y increasing again from 6251 to 6251.8. But this further increase in Y leads to another increase in C from 6000.8 to 6001.44. And so on. You can probably see that each successive change in Y and C is slightly smaller than the previous change, so eventually the changes will tend to zero. As they do so we will find the total cumulative change in Y will be 5 ($k \times 1$), the initial change in I. The calculations below show the first 25 iterations for the calculations for Y and C; by the final iteration, Y and C have already almost reached their final values.

Iteration	ΔY	Y	ΔC	C
		6250		6000
1	1.0000	6251.0000	0.8000	6000.8000
2	0.8000	6251.8000	0.6400	6001.4400
3	0.6400	6252.4400	0.5120	6001.9520
4	0.5120	6252.9520	0.4096	6002.3616
5	0.4096	6253.3616	0.3277	6002.6893
6	0.3277	6253.6893	0.2621	6002.9514
7	0.2621	6253.9514	0.2097	6003.1611
8	0.2097	6254.1611	0.1678	6003.3289
9	0.1678	6254.3289	0.1342	6003.4631
10	0.1342	6254.4631	0.1074	6003.5705
11	0.1074	6254.5705	0.0859	6003.6564
12	0.0859	6254.6564	0.0687	6003.7251
13	0.0687	6254.7251	0.0550	6003.7801
14	0.0550	6254.7801	0.0440	6003.8241
15	0.0440	6254.8241	0.0352	6003.8593
16	0.0352	6254.8593	0.0281	6003.8874
17	0.0281	6254.8874	0.0225	6003.9099
18	0.0225	6254.9099	0.0180	6003.9279
19	0.0180	6254.9279	0.0144	6003.9424
20	0.0144	6254.9424	0.0115	6003.9539
21	0.0115	6254.9539	0.0092	6003.9631
22	0.0092	6254.9631	0.0074	6003.9705
23	0.0074	6254.9705	0.0059	6003.9764
24	0.0059	6254.9764	0.0047	6003.9811
25	0.0047	6254.9811	0.0038	6003.9849

Progress Check B3.3

For the national income model in the last Progress Check, assume that, from equilibrium, I now changes from 250 to 240. Calculate the round-by-round changes in Y and C that occur. What do you observe happening to the successive changes? (Use a spreadsheet.)

(Solution on p. 462)

We can also derive the savings function for this model. Given that, by definition, income must either be spent or saved, we have:

$$Y = C + S$$

where S is savings, and it follows that $S = f(Y)$, giving

$$Y = C + S$$
$$Y = (a + bY) + S$$
$$S = Y - (a + bY) = -a + (1 - b)Y$$

as the savings function. Note that the function has a negative intercept and that for low levels of Y, S will be negative. Notice also that we have confirmation that at equilibrium income S must equal I. Since at equilibrium:

$$Y = C + I$$

and $Y = C + S$ it follows that $S = I$. From Fig. B3.2 we see that savings are effectively a *leakage* out of the model and that, at equilibrium, leakages, S, equals injections, I.

B3.2 The national income model in diagram form

It is now a straightforward task to represent the model in the form of a graph. If we examine Fig. B3.3 we can confirm the analysis we have just completed. First, we have a line showing investment, $I = i$. Notice that the line is parallel to the horizontal axis to indicate that I takes a constant value – it is fixed outside the model. We have the consumption function line, $C = f(Y)$, with an intercept of a and a slope equal to b (this is not shown). We then have a line representing $C + I$ to show the *actual* total of consumption and investment expenditure; that is, this line shows the actual level of $C + I$ determined by the model for differing values of Y. Notice that this line has an intercept of $(a + I)$ and also has the same slope as the consumption function (it is

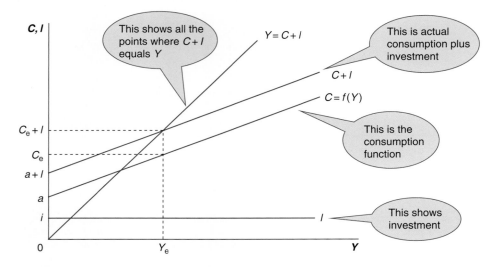

Figure B3.3 National income equilibrium

parallel). Finally, we have a line, $Y = C + I$, which shows all points where Y equals $(C + I)$ – that is, all possible equilibrium positions no matter what the exact national income model we are working with. This line is often referred to as *planned* consumption and investment (as opposed to actual). It relates to Eq. B3.3, starts from the origin and simply shows all points where Y and $(C + I)$ are equal. Naturally, our equilibrium position must occur *somewhere* on this line.

So we have to be on the $Y = C + I$ line to have an equilibrium but at the same time the $C + I$ line shows actual income. We require a solution that satisfies both of these at the same time. On the graph this will occur where the two lines intersect. This is shown by Y_e on Fig. B3.3. The corresponding level of equilibrium consumptions is shown as C_e.

Progress Check B3.4

For the model used in the last Progress Check ($C = 1000 + 0.8Y$ and $I = 250$) use a graph to confirm the equilibrium position.

B

The graph also allows us to confirm the general impact on the equilibrium of a change in any of the parameters. For example, suppose that there is an increase in the level of investment, I, from I_1 to I_2. An increase in I will increase the intercept of the $C + I$ line – that is, it will push the $C + I$ line higher up the vertical axis. This will have the effect of increasing equilibrium income, Y_e. Figure B3.4 shows the result. Exactly how much Y_e changes because of an increase in I will of course depend on the exact numerical parameters.

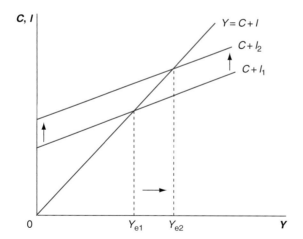

Figure B3.4 Change in I

Progress Check B3.5

For the model used in the last Progress Check ($C = 1000 + 0.8Y$ and $I = 250$) the marginal propensity to consume, mpc, falls to 0.75. Sketch the new model and assess the effect on equilibrium.
   Explain why equilibrium has changed in the way that it has.

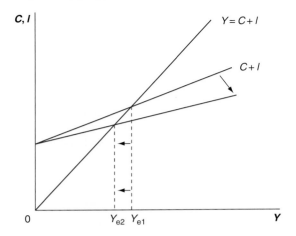

Figure B3.5 Change in mpc

If mpc falls, as in this case from 0.8 to 0.75, then the slope of the $C = f(Y)$ line falls and Y_e will also fall as we can see from Fig. B3.5, with the $C + I$ line swinging down (autonomous consumption doesn't change, only the mpc). The reason this has happened takes us back to the circular flow of income. The mpc falls to 0.75, indicating that consumers spend less of their income and consequently save more. As a result there is increased leakage in the form of savings. But if C is lower because of the fall in mpc then Y_e must also be lower.

B3.3 A national income model including a government sector

We are now in a position to make the national income model more realistic by including a government sector. Introducing a government sector has a twofold effect. First, the government itself will act as a consumer, introducing spending into the economic system by buying goods and services. Second, in order to spend, the government will need to raise revenue through the tax system. We shall make two assumptions: first that the level of government activity, G, is itself exogenous and, second, that tax is raised through a fixed rate imposed on income. Our model now becomes:

$$Y = C + I + G \tag{B3.7}$$

$$T = tY \tag{B3.8}$$

$$Y_d = Y - T \tag{B3.9}$$

$$C = a + bY_d \tag{B3.10}$$

Equation B3.7 is our equilibrium requirement, showing the equilibrium income is now made up of consumer spending, investment and government spending. Equation B3.8 shows that tax is a proportion, t, of income. Equation B3.9 indicates that disposable income, Y_d, is income Y less taxes, T, and the new consumption function shows C as a function of disposable income. If we show t in fractional terms then we would add a parameter restriction such that:

$$0 \leq t < 1$$

That is, the government must take less than 100% of income in tax. If we substitute Eq. B3.8 for T in Eq. B3.9 and then substitute this into the consumption function Eq. B3.10 we have:

$$C = a + b(Y - tY)$$

which then gives

$$Y = C + I + G$$

$$Y = a + b(Y - tY) + I + G \quad \longleftarrow \boxed{\text{Use } a + b(y - tY) \text{ for } C}$$

$$Y - b(Y - tY) = a + I + G \quad \longleftarrow \boxed{\text{Collect the } Y \text{ terms together on the left}}$$

$$Y - bY + btY = a + I + G$$

$$Y(1 - b + bt) = a + I + G \quad \longleftarrow \boxed{\text{Use } Y \text{ as a common term}}$$

$$Y[1 - b(1 - t)] = a + I + G$$

$$Y_e = \frac{a + I + G}{[1 - b(1 - t)]} \tag{B3.11}$$

We can also derive the equation for equilibrium consumption. Substituting Eq. B3.11 into Eq. B3.10 we have:

$$C = a + b(Y - tY) \quad \longleftarrow \boxed{\text{Substitute } (Y - tY) \text{ for } Y_d}$$

$$C = a + b\left[\frac{a + I + G}{1 - b(1 - t)} - t\left(\frac{a + I + G}{1 - b(1 - t)} \right) \right] \quad \longleftarrow \boxed{\begin{array}{l} \text{Substitute the right-hand side from} \\ \text{Eq. B3.11 for the two } Y\text{s} \end{array}}$$

Multiplying the first a by $1 - b(1 - t)/1 - b(1 - t)$ (which equals 1) and multiplying the term in square brackets through by b we have:

$$C = \frac{a[1 - b(1 - t)]}{1 - b(1 - t)} + \frac{ba + bI + bG}{1 - b(1 - t)} - \frac{bta + btI + btG}{1 - b(1 - t)}$$

$$C = \frac{a - ab + abt}{1 - b(1 - t)} + \frac{ba + bI + bG}{1 - b(1 - t)} - \frac{bta + btI + btG}{1 - b(1 - t)}$$

$$C = \frac{a + bI + bG - btI - btG}{1 - b(1 - t)} \quad \longleftarrow \boxed{\begin{array}{l} \text{Separate the } (I + G) \\ \text{term and the} \\ (b - bt) \text{ term} \end{array}}$$

$$C = \frac{a + b(I + G - t(I + G))}{1 - b(1 - t)} \quad \text{or} \quad \frac{a + (I + G)(b - bt)}{1 - b(1 - t)} \tag{B3.12}$$

Let's compare these equilibrium equations with those we derived earlier for an economy with no government activity – Eqs B3.4 and B3.5:

No government activity	Including a government sector
$Y_e = \dfrac{a + I}{1 - b}$	$Y_e = \dfrac{a + I + G}{1 - b(1 - t)}$
$C_e = \dfrac{a + bI}{1 - b}$	$C_e = \dfrac{a + (I + G)(b - bt)}{1 - b(1 - t)}$

We see that if $G = 0$ and $t = 0$ (i.e. there was no government sector) the two expressions for equilibrium income would be the same (we take G out of the Y_e equation and $(1 - t)$ becomes 1). Similarly, for C_e, we take out G, $(b - bt)$ becomes b, $(1 - t)$ becomes 1, and we see that without G and t the equations are again identical.

Equally, we could derive the equation for the final endogenous variable T, although this is left as an activity for you to check your own ability to manipulate a model in this way.

Progress Check B3.6

Derive a corresponding expression for T. Confirm that an increase in G will lead to an increase in T.

(Solution on p. 462)

Once again, if we wish to examine the parameter restrictions that we imposed on the model we see that Y, C and T must all be positive at equilibrium. Finally in this model, let us return to the multiplier. Following the same principles as before let us assume that G changes from G_1 to G_2, but with all other factors remaining constant. From Eq. B3.11 this gives:

$$Y_1 = \frac{a + I + G_1}{1 - b(1 - t)}$$

$$Y_2 = \frac{a + I + G_2}{1 - b(1 - t)}$$

$$Y_1 - Y_2 = \frac{a + I + G_1}{1 - b(1 - t)} - \frac{a + I + G_2}{1 - b(1 - t)}$$

$$Y_1 - Y_2 = \frac{G_1 - G_2}{1 - b(1 - t)}$$

$$\Delta Y = \frac{1}{1 - b(1 - t)} \Delta G \tag{B3.13}$$

where we see the new multiplier. Again, a quick confirmation reveals that if $t = 0$ then the new multiplier is the same as in the first model without government activity. Given that both b and t are required to be positive in the model we can also see that the denominator in the new multiplier is larger than in the old; hence the value of the multiplier will be less in this model than in the model without a government sector. We can rationalize this quite easily. An increase in one of the exogenous variables will now lead to a smaller increase than before in Y_e since some of the increase will 'leak out' of the system in terms of taxation revenue. That is, some of the income that people would have spent is now taken from them in tax so their disposable income is lower. However, on inspection of B3.13 it is evident that the multiplier, k, is still greater than 1: $(1 - t)$ will be less than 1; multiplying by b will still be less than 1 so the whole denominator will be less than 1, thus giving k greater than 1.

Progress Check B3.7

What effect will an increase in t have on k?

(Solution on p. 462)

B3.4 A national income model with a government sector and foreign trade

In terms of economic policy, governments are generally concerned about the effect of their own activities on the equilibrium level of national income. Equally, they have a keen interest in the balance of trade and its effect. The level of exports and the level of imports can have major effects on the national economy and hence on equilibrium. Let us expand the previous government model by introducing foreign trade in the form of exports, X, and imports, M. We shall assume that exports are exogenous (which is fairly realistic given that the demand for goods that we produce will frequently be determined by factors outside our own national economy). We also assume that imports are endogenous and take the form:

$$M = f(Y_d) = mY_d \qquad \text{(B3.14)}$$

where m represents the marginal propensity to import. Again, this is a realistic assumption indicating that the level of imports will depend on the level of national income. The equilibrium condition is now met when:

$$Y = C + I + G + X - M \qquad \text{(B3.15)}$$

Note that imports, M, reduce the level of national income, Y, since they represent payments that go out of the national economy. We then have:

$$Y_d = Y - T \qquad \text{(B3.16)}$$

$$T = tY \qquad \text{(B3.17)}$$

$$C = a + bY_d \qquad \text{(B3.18)}$$

$$M = mY_d \qquad \text{(B3.19)}$$

Substituting as appropriate we then derive:

$$Y = C + I + G + X - M$$

$$C = a + bY_d = a + b(Y - T) = a + b[Y(1 - t)]$$

$$M = mY_d = mY(1 - t)$$

giving at equilibrium

$$Y = a + b[Y(1 - t)] + (I + G + X) - mY(1 - t)$$

$$Y = a + bY - btY - mY + mtY + (I + G + X)$$

$$Y(1 - b + bt + m - mt) = a + I + G + X$$

$$Y = \frac{a + I + G + X}{(1 - b + bt + m - mt)} \qquad \text{(B3.20)}$$

and we see the new multiplier is given by

$$k = \frac{1}{(1 - b + bt + m - mt)} = \frac{1}{1 - (1 - t)(b - m)} \qquad \text{(B3.21)}$$

Progress Check B3.8

Confirm that the new multiplier would return to that shown in Eqs B3.13 and B3.6 if first m and then t took a zero value.

Clearly, our model is now more complex and enables us to examine a variety of potential policy issues. However, let us focus on the balance of trade, always a concern for governments. Let us define:

$$B = X - M$$

as the balance of trade, being simply the difference between exports and imports. Let us assume that the government is considering altering its own spending level, G, and wishes to evaluate the impact this will have on the balance of trade, that is, to assess ΔB. Given that exports are exogenous, clearly the impact in the model will occur through a change in income, consumption and then imports. Let's assume that $\Delta G > 0$: that is, the government increases its own spending. We know that:

$$\Delta M = m\Delta Y_d$$
$$= m\Delta Y(1-t)$$
$$= m(1-t)k\Delta G \quad \text{(since } \Delta Y = k\Delta G) \tag{B3.22}$$

and therefore $\Delta M > 0$ since m, t, k are > 0 in the model, $\Delta G > 0$ by definition and $t < 1$.

So we can see that an increase in G must lead to an increase in M and, in this model, a worsening of the balance of trade position. Exactly how much worse is, of course, dependent on the precise values taken by the model parameters. It is interesting to note that ΔM will be affected not only by the marginal propensity to import, m, but also by the income tax rate, t, and the marginal propensity to consume, b (which is hidden in the k term). In terms of policy instruments, therefore, the government would be able to affect the change in M through alterations in t as well as in G.

B3.5 A national income model with a monetary sector

In the final section of this module we look at a national income model that includes a financial or monetary sector. So far, we have assumed that investment, I, is exogenous to the national income model. It's more realistic to assume that the level of planned investment will depend primarily on the rate of interest, r. Given that firms may need to borrow money for investment, or raise it through issuing bonds or shares, the rate of interest determines the cost of doing this. Given we're examining the effects of the monetary sector on national income equilibrium, let's return to our simplest model where we have:

$$Y = C + I$$
$$C = a + bY$$

and we now have

$$I = c + dr$$

with $c > 0$ and $d < 0$; that is, as r increases I decreases and vice versa. Substituting the expressions for C and I into the Y expression we then have:

$$Y = C + I = (a + bY) + (c + dr)$$

or, collecting terms together

$$Y - bY = a + c + dr$$
$$Y(1 - b) = a + c + dr$$
$$Y = \frac{a + c}{(1 - b)} + \frac{dr}{(1 - b)} \qquad \text{(B3.23)}$$

Eq. B3.23 is referred to as the *IS schedule* (investment and savings schedule). Equilibrium in the monetary sector occurs when the supply of money, M_s, equals the demand for money, M_d:

$$M_s = M_d$$

In this basic model we assume that M_s is exogenous (determined by the central bank for example) while M_d will depend both on r and on Y:

$$M_d = m_1 + m_2 Y + m_3 r \qquad \text{(B3.24)}$$

with $m_1 > 0$, $m_2 > 0$ and $m_3 < 0$. Equation B3.24 is referred to as the *LM schedule* (liquidity-money schedule). Let us look at Eq. B3.24 in more detail. We require $m_1 \geq 0$, implying that there will be some amount of money that is required no matter what the level of national income or the interest rate. We then have $m_2 Y$, implying that demand for money is positively linked to the level of national income. This element of demand for money is often described as a combination of *transactions demand* and *precautionary demand.* Transactions demand for money is what individuals and firms need just to carry out their activities on a routine basis: money for shopping and consumption, money for paying workers and suppliers and so on. In fact, as national income increases more money will be required for these transactions. Precautionary demand arises from uncertainty: individuals and households put money aside in case of an emergency or an unexpected event – in case the TV breaks down and has to be replaced when you're watching the World Cup or Olympics; firms put money aside for the same reason – in case workers demand higher pay, or a customer doesn't pay their invoice on time. Again, it seems realistic to assume that as national income increases so will transactions demand. The third term, $m_3 r$, is referred to as *speculative demand* for money and is inversely linked to the interest rate. In this case individuals and firms are holding money/cash (on which they earn no return) in case they decide to invest in alternative assets such as government bonds (which pay interest). Again, it seems reasonable to assume that with higher interest rates speculative demand will fall as the opportunity cost of holding money increases. We could now, of course, find an expression to give equilibrium values for national income, Y, and for r. However, instead let's look at what would happen to Y if M_s, the money supply, changed. From B3.24 we have at equilibrium:

$$M_s = M_d = m_1 + m_2 Y + m_3 r$$

Let's rearrange this to show Y as a function of r:

$$M_s = m_1 + m_2 Y + m_3 r$$
$$m_2 Y = -m_1 + M_s - m_3 r$$
$$Y = \frac{-m_1 + M_s}{m_2} - \frac{m_3 r}{m_2}$$

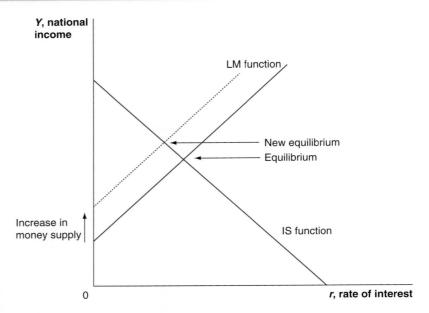

Figure B3.6 Impact of a change in M_s

We can identify this as a linear function with an intercept of $(-m_1 + M_s)/m_2$ and a slope of $-m_3/m_2$. A change in the money supply therefore will affect the intercept but not the slope. If we look at the values of the parameters in the intercept expression we know that m_1 and m_2 are both required to be positive. So as long as $M_s > m_1$ the intercept will be positive. It then follows that with a positive intercept an increase in M_s, *ceteris paribus*, will shift the LM function upwards and will cause an increase in Y, national income. A reduction in the money supply will have the opposite effect and will reduce Y. The overall effect is illustrated in Fig. B3.6. The IS function is shown as a downward-sloping function. From Eq. B3.23 we see that the intercept term will be positive, while the slope will be negative. The original LM function is shown as a solid line, giving an equilibrium level of income and an equilibrium rate of interest. With an increase in the money supply, the LM function shifts upwards but with the same slope or gradient. This has the effect of increasing the equilibrium level of national income and reducing the equilibrium rate of interest.

B3.6 Summary

We have seen in this module a number of examples of the usefulness of mathematics in deriving general conclusions about economic behaviour at a macroeconomic level. As in the previous module none of the examples we have introduced has actually involved numerical values, and yet we have been able to derive important policy conclusions from our applications of a combination of mathematical and economic logic. As we shall see as we progress through this book, expansions of all these models will be incorporated as you develop the necessary mathematical skills.

Learning Check

Having read this module you should have learned that:

- National income models show equilibrium levels of national income, consumption and savings. They can incorporate a government sector and foreign trade
- National income models can be used to show changes in national income as a result of changes in exogenous variables
- The multiplier shows the change in Y arising from a change in another variable.

Worked Example

A national income model is as follows:

- Autonomous consumption is £750 million
- Investment is exogenous and currently at £500 million
- Government expenditure is exogenous and currently £150 million
- mpc is 0.75
- Marginal propensity to import is 15% of disposable income
- Exports are exogenous and currently at £200 million
- The government taxes income at 25%.

The government has asked us to determine the current equilibrium level of national income. We have also been asked to provide advice on two policy options under consideration. The government is concerned about the size of its budget surplus. Option A would increase government spending by an extra £50 million in an attempt to reduce the size of the surplus. Option B would reduce the tax level to 20%. However, the government is also concerned about the effect of these two policy options on the balance of trade.

Solution

We have a national income model including government and foreign trade. The full model is then:

$$Y = C + I + G + X - M$$
$$Y_d = Y - T$$
$$T = 0.25Y$$
$$C = 750 + 0.75Y_d$$
$$M = 0.15Y_d$$
$$X = 200$$
$$G = 150$$
$$I = 500$$

From Eq. B3.20, equilibrium income is given as:

$$Y = \frac{a + I + G + X}{(1 - b + bt + m - mt)}$$

Worked Example *(Continued)*

Substituting gives:

$$Y_e = \frac{750 + 500 + 150 + 200}{(1 - 0.75 + 0.75(0.25) + 0.15 - (0.15)(0.25))} = \frac{1660}{0.55} = 2909.091$$

with an equilibrium income of £2909.091 million. We can just as easily determine the new level of Y_e under each of the two policy options again using Eq. B3.20. However, let us also show the results for the key variables in the model. (Check your maths against our answers to make sure you're able to use the model properly.)

Basic model		Option A: *G* increases by £50 million		Option B: *t* reduces to 20%	
Y_e	2909	Y_e	3000	Y_e	3076.92
Y_d	2181.75	Y_d	2250	Y_d	2461.54
T	727.25	T	750	T	615.38
C	2386.3125	C	2437.5	C	2596.15
I	500	I	500	I	500
G	150	G	200	G	150
X	200	X	200	X	200
M	327.2625	M	337.5	M	369.23
Budget surplus 577.25		Budget surplus 550		Budget surplus 465.3846	
Balance of trade −127.2625		Balance of trade −137.5		Balance of trade −169.23076	

We see that with the initial basic model and an equilibrium income of around £2909 million we will have a budget surplus of around £577 million and a balance of trade deficit of around £127 million. Option A, an increase in *G* of £50 million, will have the effect of boosting national income to £3000 million (*k*, the multiplier, is 1.82 so an increase in *G* of 50 leads to an increase in *Y* of 1.82 × 50 or £91 million). The budget surplus falls but only by £27.25 million and not by the £50 million of extra government expenditure. We know why this has happened, of course, as extra government spending has stimulated the economy through the multiplier leading to higher income and consequently to higher levels of tax income. *T*, we see, has also increased. As predicted by Eq. B3.22, the balance of trade worsens as higher national income leads to a higher level of imports. Again, using Eq. B3.22 we see that the increase in imports is around £10.24 million leading to a balance of trade deficit of £137.5 million.

$$\Delta M = m(1 - t)k\Delta G$$

$$= 0.15(0.75)1.82 \times 50 = 10.24$$

We can now consider Option B, reducing the tax rate to 20%. From Eq. B3.20 we determine the new equilibrium level of income to be around £3077 million

Worked Example *(Continued)*

with the other values as shown in the table. The budget surplus has now fallen by around £110 million. The tax reduction has had the effect of stimulating the economy and increasing national income. However, as the tax rate has fallen, tax income collected by the government has also fallen. Unfortunately for the government, the balance of trade has actually got much worse, with an increase in the deficit of over £40 million. The reason is that, as national income has increased due to the tax rate reduction, the economy has spent 15% of its extra disposable income on imports. So the bad news for the Finance Minister is that the two policy options will reduce the size of the government deficit but at the expense of a worsening in the balance of trade – at least according to this model.

Exercises

B3.1   Assume a simple national income model with:

$C = f(Y) = 750 + 0.75Y$ and $I = 500$

 (i)   Calculate the equilibrium levels of income, consumption and saving.
 (ii)   Calculate k and interpret the result.
(iii)   If I changed to 510, what would be the effect on (i)?
 (iv)   Why has equilibrium changed in the way it has?

B3.2   In the model in Exercise B3.1 assume that the mpc changes to 0.8. Explain in detail the effect you would expect this to have on the equilibrium position. Calculate the new equilibrium to confirm your logic.

B3.3   The simple national income model now includes a government sector with $G = 150$ and $t = 0.25$. Calculate the new equilibrium and the new value for k. Why has the value for k decreased? What are the implications of this for the economy?

B3.4   For the model in Ex. B3.3 we now add a foreign trade sector with exports at 200 and with imports at 15% of disposable income. Calculate the new equilibrium and explain the changes in national income that have occurred.

B3.5   For the model in Ex. B3.3 find the level for G that will give a balanced budget (i.e. $G = T$).

B3.6   For the model in Ex. B3.3 find the level for G that will balance foreign trade (i.e. $X = M$).

Module B4
Matrix algebra: the basics

In the previous modules we have looked at linear economic models and begun to see how we could obtain general economic conclusions based on the mathematics of these models, such as the impact of a tax on market equilibrium or the impact of a change in government expenditure on national income and the balance of trade. Economic analysis frequently tries, through comparative static analysis, to assess the impact of a change in the underlying conditions on an economic model. Typically, we wish to analyse the effect of a change to one of the parameter values in the model on the solution or equilibrium position. Obviously, with simultaneous equations it is necessary to recalculate the entire set of equations to determine the new solution. This makes the task of comparative static analysis both tedious and time-consuming. Additionally, it is apparent that the simple models we have developed so far in the book, involving only two or, at most, three equations, are far too restrictive in terms of economic analysis and model building. The task of analysing a national income model with several hundred equations (as is often the case in real life) using the mathematical tools we've developed so far is clearly a daunting one. For these reasons we require an alternative method of handling large systems of linear equations and of finding the unique solution to such sets of equations. Such a method is readily available through the use of *matrix algebra*. In this module we shall introduce the appropriate tools for dealing with matrix algebra and in the following modules we will learn how to use matrix algebra to develop a number of common economic models.

Health warning: there's no getting away from the fact that matrix algebra can be fairy dull, boring and heavy-going. We've tried to make the following modules as easy to read as possible. However, you may want to read the modules in stages rather than trying to get through them in one session.

Learning Objectives

By the end of this module you should be able to:

- Use matrix notation
- Use matrix arithmetic in addition, subtraction, multiplication
- Show economic models in matrix form.

Knowledge Check B4

If you're already familiar and comfortable with matrix algebra, you may want to jump straight to Module B6 to look at how more advanced matrix algebra is used in economic analysis and modelling. To test your ability, look at the two matrices shown below and calculate:

AB

BA

$$A = \begin{bmatrix} 6 & 2 & 1 \\ 3 & 4 & 5 \\ 1 & 7 & 2 \end{bmatrix} \qquad B = \begin{bmatrix} 2 & 3 & 4 \\ 1 & 2 & 1 \\ 0 & 3 & 1 \end{bmatrix}$$

Check your answer in Appendix 2.

B4.1 The vocabulary of matrix algebra

A *matrix* can be thought of simply as a rectangular array or table of numbers, numerical coefficients, parameters or variables. Let's look at a company that operates on a global basis and last year achieved the sales levels shown in Table B4.1. For example, in the Northern Europe region sales of product X were 1000 units, of product Y 500 units and of product Z 750 units. The matrix representing this data would be:

$$\text{Sales matrix } A = \begin{bmatrix} 1000 & 500 & 750 \\ 750 & 400 & 600 \\ 100 & 50 & 80 \end{bmatrix}$$

Conventionally, a matrix is denoted using a capital letter – **A** in this case – marked in bold type, and the values comprising the matrix denoted using square brackets [ ]. A matrix is, therefore, simply a format for showing the data used in the problem: regions and sales levels. It is our task to remember what the rows and columns of the matrix actually represent and also to remember, where appropriate, units of measurement being used. We can also use a matrix to denote a set of variables rather than numbers. We may have a matrix **P** denoting the selling price for each product in each region:

$$\text{Price matrix } P = \begin{bmatrix} P_{NX} & P_{NY} & P_{NZ} \\ P_{SX} & P_{SY} & P_{SZ} \\ P_{MX} & P_{MY} & P_{MZ} \end{bmatrix}$$

Matrix notation offers a convenient shorthand for describing large sets of data or variables. No matter how many regions or how many products, we can simply refer to matrix **A** and **P** rather than to a cumbersome multidimensional table of data. The potential usefulness of such notation in economic models is self-evident.

Note that the plural of matrix is matrices (pronounced 'may-tra-seas').

Table B4.1 Number of units of each product sold by region

Region	Product		
	X	Y	Z
Northern Europe	1000	500	750
Southern Europe	750	400	600
Middle East	100	50	80

The dimensions of a matrix

The *dimension*, or size, of a matrix is defined in terms of the number of rows (denoted by m) and the number of columns (n) that make up the matrix. In this example, matrix **A** is referred to as a 3 by 3 matrix since it has three rows and three columns. Conventionally, the first number in the dimension refers to the number of rows and the second to the number of columns. Note also that matrix **A** is symmetrical (that is, $m = n$). Such a matrix is known as a *square matrix* – but not all matrices are square. The items making up the matrix – in this example the set of numbers representing product sales in each region – are referred to as the *elements* of the matrix, or as the *cells* of the matrix. Each element can be uniquely identified by its row and column position using a suitable subscript notation:

$$\mathbf{A} = \begin{bmatrix} a_{11} & a_{12} & a_{13} \\ a_{21} & a_{22} & a_{23} \\ a_{31} & a_{32} & a_{33} \end{bmatrix}$$

So a_{23}, for example, refers to the matrix element in row 2, column 3 (here $a_{23} = 600$). It is also conventional to represent a matrix and its elements in a shorthand fashion:

$$\mathbf{A} = [a_{ij}] \qquad i = 1, 2, 3; \quad j = 1, 2, 3$$

or in general for a matrix of size m by n as

$$\mathbf{A} = [a_{ij}] \qquad i = 1, 2, \ldots, m; \quad j = 1, 2, \ldots, n$$

Vectors

One special type of matrix is that consisting of a single row or a single column. Such a matrix is more generally referred to as a *vector*. A column vector appears as:

$$\mathbf{c} = \begin{bmatrix} c_1 \\ c_2 \\ . \\ . \\ . \\ c_m \end{bmatrix}$$

and a row vector as

$$\mathbf{r}' = [r_1 r_2 \ldots r_n]$$

Notice that we show a vector by using a lower-case letter and that, conventionally, a row vector is distinguished from a column vector by using the prime (') symbol. You should note that a matrix is made up of a set of vectors. The sales matrix **A**, for example, can be broken into three column vectors (with each column representing sales of one product) or into three row vectors (with each vector representing sales in a particular region). This ability to manipulate a matrix as a series of vectors becomes useful at later stages of matrix algebra.

Scalars

One final term must be defined before we proceed to develop the use of matrices and matrix algebra. This is the term *scalar*, which represents not an array or matrix of numbers but only a single number, or a constant, which we shall occasionally wish to use in conjunction with a matrix.

B4.2 Special matrices

There are three special types of matrix that we introduce and we'll see why we need these later. The first of these is the *identity* matrix, denoted by **I**, which is a square matrix that consists solely of the values 1 and 0. The values of 1 occur in what is known as the main diagonal of the matrix, that is, the diagonal running from the top-left corner to the bottom-right corner. All other elements of the identity matrix take the value zero. So, for example, an identity matrix of size three would be:

$$\mathbf{I} = \begin{bmatrix} 1 & 0 & 0 \\ 0 & 1 & 0 \\ 0 & 0 & 1 \end{bmatrix}$$

Second, a *null* matrix, **N**, is one where all the elements take a zero value. Note that, unlike the identity matrix, the null matrix is not required to be square. Finally, there is the *transpose* matrix. Such a matrix is created by interchanging the rows and columns of a matrix. For example, let us return to the sales matrix, **A**:

$$\mathbf{A} = \begin{bmatrix} 1000 & 500 & 750 \\ 750 & 400 & 600 \\ 100 & 50 & 80 \end{bmatrix}$$

If we let row 1 of **A** become column 1 of a new matrix, row 2 become column 2 and row 3 become column 3, we have:

$$\mathbf{A}' = \begin{bmatrix} 1000 & 750 & 100 \\ 500 & 400 & 50 \\ 750 & 600 & 80 \end{bmatrix}$$

where **A**′ (pronounced 'A transpose' or 'A prime') is the transpose of **A**. In this example, the columns represent the regions and the rows represent the different products.

B4.3 Matrix algebra

The importance of matrices in economics is not simply a question of their usefulness in presenting data, variables or equations in a compact form, but, rather, in their ability to allow us to perform complex manipulations and algebra relatively easily. Just as we can carry out arithmetic with ordinary numbers, so we can undertake the equivalent arithmetic with matrices. In the rest of this module we shall focus upon a number of such types of matrix arithmetic:

- Matrix addition
- Matrix subtraction
- Multiplication by a scalar
- Matrix multiplication.

We shall look at each in turn. While much of the arithmetic performed with matrices is similar to that carried out with numbers, you should be cautious about thinking that exactly the same rules apply to matrix algebra as apply to ordinary algebra. There are some important differences.

B4.4 Matrix addition

We can add two matrices provided that they have the same dimensions – that is, provided they are *compatible* for addition. Assume that matrix **A** used earlier represents sales for last year and that we have a corresponding matrix, **B**, which represents sales achieved this month:

$$\mathbf{B} = \begin{bmatrix} 10 & 50 & 30 \\ 20 & 10 & 0 \\ 10 & 20 & 10 \end{bmatrix}$$

If we now require the total sales to date (that is, last year's sales plus this month's), we can add the two matrices simply by adding their corresponding elements. So:

$$\mathbf{C} = \mathbf{A} + \mathbf{B} = \begin{bmatrix} 1000 & 500 & 750 \\ 750 & 400 & 600 \\ 100 & 50 & 80 \end{bmatrix} + \begin{bmatrix} 10 & 50 & 30 \\ 20 & 10 & 0 \\ 10 & 20 & 10 \end{bmatrix}$$

$$\mathbf{C} = \begin{bmatrix} 1000+10 & 500+50 & 750+30 \\ 750+20 & 400+10 & 600+0 \\ 100+10 & 50+20 & 80+10 \end{bmatrix} = \begin{bmatrix} 1010 & 550 & 780 \\ 770 & 410 & 600 \\ 110 & 70 & 90 \end{bmatrix}$$

In general, therefore, we have:

$$\mathbf{C} = [c_{ij}] = [a_{ij}] + [b_{ij}] \tag{B4.1}$$

Given that a vector can be regarded as a particular type of matrix, this addition process can be applied equally to vectors, providing they are compatible. Note also that:

1 The **C** matrix resulting from the addition will be of the same size as the **A** and **B** matrices
2 $\mathbf{A} + \mathbf{B} = \mathbf{B} + \mathbf{A}$ $\qquad\qquad\qquad\qquad\qquad\qquad\qquad\qquad$ (B4.2)
3 $(\mathbf{A} + \mathbf{B}) + \mathbf{C} = \mathbf{A} + (\mathbf{B} + \mathbf{C})$, that is, when adding matrices, the order in which we add is irrelevant to the result.

Progress Check B4.1

For the three matrices shown below, determine which of the following can be undertaken and find the resulting matrix:

$\mathbf{D} + \mathbf{E}$

$\mathbf{E} + \mathbf{D}$

$\mathbf{D} + \mathbf{F}$

$\mathbf{F} + \mathbf{E}$

where

$$\mathbf{D} = \begin{bmatrix} 15 & 7 & 11 \\ 6 & 4 & 7 \\ 4 & 3 & 2 \end{bmatrix}$$

$$\mathbf{E} = \begin{bmatrix} 10 & 5 & 4 \\ -3 & 6 & 1 \\ 11 & 9 & 2 \end{bmatrix}$$

$$\mathbf{F} = \begin{bmatrix} -2 & 3 & 6 \\ 4 & 7 & 4 \end{bmatrix}$$

(Solution on p. 462)

B4.5 Matrix subtraction

Matrix subtraction is as straightforward as matrix addition. Again, as with addition, the two matrices to be subtracted must be compatible. In this case we have:

$$\mathbf{C} = [c_{ij}] = [a_{ij}] - [b_{ij}] \tag{B4.3}$$

That is, we simply subtract corresponding elements from each other.

Progress Check B4.2

Using **C** and **B**, derive the original **A** matrix (the sales matrix) we have been using.

B4.6 Multiplication by a scalar

As we have seen, a scalar is a single number or constant. When we multiply a matrix by a scalar the effect is to multiply each element in the matrix by that number. Assume that the firm has decided to establish regional sales targets for the future. Sales of each product in each region are to increase by 10% over and above last year's levels (as shown in **A**). We require the new sales target matrix. Given that the new sales levels will be 110% of the existing levels, the scalar takes a value of 1.1. Each element in turn in the matrix is then multiplied by the scalar:

$$\mathbf{B} = 1.1 \times \mathbf{A} = 1.1 \begin{bmatrix} 1000 & 500 & 750 \\ 750 & 400 & 600 \\ 100 & 50 & 80 \end{bmatrix} = \begin{bmatrix} 1100 & 550 & 825 \\ 825 & 440 & 660 \\ 110 & 55 & 88 \end{bmatrix}$$

Note that in general if we denote the scalar as k then:

1 $k\mathbf{A} = \mathbf{A}k$ (B4.4)

2 $k[a_{ij}] = [ka_{ij}] = [a_{ij}]k$ (B4.5)

In the terminology of matrix algebra, this implies that it is immaterial whether we *pre*multiply the matrix with the scalar or whether we *post*multiply the matrix with the scalar.

Progress Check B4.3

Using the appropriate scalar, transform **B** above back into the original **A** matrix, first by premultiplying and then by postmultiplying.

As an additional activity, derive a matrix showing the extra sales to be achieved per product per region in order to meet the sales target set.

B4.7 Matrix multiplication

The advantages of using matrix notation for large-scale economic models start to become apparent when we look at matrix multiplication. To illustrate, let's first look at the multiplication of a matrix and a vector.

Multiplying a vector and a matrix

Let's return to the sales matrix we have been using:

$$A = \begin{bmatrix} 1000 & 500 & 750 \\ 750 & 400 & 600 \\ 100 & 50 & 80 \end{bmatrix}$$

Let's also use the column vector, **b**:

$$b = \begin{bmatrix} 10 \\ 12 \\ 18 \end{bmatrix}$$

which represents the current market price of each of the three products: we see that product X sells for €10, product Y for €12 and product Z for €18. We want to calculate the current total sales revenue in each region. In terms of ordinary arithmetic we follow a simple process. For each region in turn we calculate the sum of the number of units of each product sold multiplied by the market price. So, for the Northern Europe region, we have:

$$(1000 \times 10) + (500 \times 12) + (750 \times 18) = £29\ 500$$

Let's show the vector and matrix by their cell references:

$$A = \begin{bmatrix} a_{11} & a_{12} & a_{13} \\ a_{21} & a_{22} & a_{23} \\ a_{31} & a_{32} & a_{33} \end{bmatrix} \qquad b = \begin{bmatrix} b_1 \\ b_2 \\ b_3 \end{bmatrix}$$

We now multiply each row in the **A** matrix by the column vector **b** and total the result. The product of this multiplication will be given by:

$$[a_{11}b_1 + a_{12}b_2 + a_{13}b_3 \qquad a_{21}b_1 + a_{22}b_2 + a_{23}b_3 \qquad a_{31}b_1 + a_{32}b_2 + a_{33}b_3]$$

where

$$a_{11}b_1 + a_{12}b_2 + a_{13}b_3 = 1000(10) + 500(12) + 750(18) = 29\ 500$$
$$a_{21}b_1 + a_{22}b_2 + a_{23}b_3 = 750(10) + 400(12) + 600(18) = 23\ 100$$
$$a_{31}b_1 + a_{32}b_2 + a_{33}b_3 = 100(10) + 50(12) + 80(18) = 3\ 040$$

giving

$$Ab = r = \begin{bmatrix} 29 & 500 \\ 23 & 100 \\ 3 & 040 \end{bmatrix}$$

where **r** represents a total revenue vector with the elements relating to sales revenue in a particular region.

Progress Check B4.4

Assume that the organization has data on the unit cost of each of the products sold:

Product X €8

Product Y €11

Product Z €15

(i)   Show these data in vector form.

(ii) Obtain a vector showing the total product cost for the sales achieved in each region.

(iii) Obtain a vector showing the total profit per region.

(iv) Construct a single matrix showing the price, cost and profit per product.

(Solution on p. 462)

Multiplying two matrices

Multiplying two matrices is as straightforward as the example shown of multiplying a vector and a matrix. Assume we have two matrices:

$$\mathbf{A} = \begin{bmatrix} a_{11} & a_{12} \\ a_{21} & a_{22} \end{bmatrix} \qquad \mathbf{B} = \begin{bmatrix} b_{11} & b_{12} & b_{13} \\ b_{21} & b_{22} & b_{23} \end{bmatrix}$$

and we wish to determine the product of $\mathbf{AB}$. If we regard matrix $\mathbf{A}$ as consisting of two row vectors, then we can perform exactly the same arithmetic as before. We take each *row* in turn in the $\mathbf{A}$ matrix and multiply by each *column* in turn in the $\mathbf{B}$ matrix, calculating the total of each row/column multiplication as we proceed. This results in matrix $\mathbf{C}$:

$$\mathbf{C} = \mathbf{AB} = \begin{bmatrix} a_{11}b_{11} + a_{12}b_{21} & a_{11}b_{12} + a_{12}b_{22} & a_{11}b_{13} + a_{12}b_{23} \\ a_{21}b_{11} + a_{22}b_{21} & a_{21}b_{12} + a_{22}b_{22} & a_{21}b_{13} + a_{22}b_{23} \end{bmatrix} \qquad \text{(B4.6)}$$

This process of multiplying rows and columns from the two matrices is readily applied to any two matrices of any size, although, naturally, the arithmetic for large matrices quickly becomes tedious.

Returning to the matrices in Progress Check B4.1, find the following:

(i)   **DE**

(ii) **ED**

(Solution on p. 462)

There are a number of important points about matrix multiplication that we need to be aware of. First, the two matrices to be multiplied must be *compatible*. It is clear that, given the nature of the multiplication process, the number of columns in the first matrix must be the same as the number of rows in the second matrix. In all the examples thus far the two matrices have been compatible. Not all matrices will be, however.

Second, the size of the matrix resulting from the multiplication will be determined by the sizes of the two matrices being multiplied. This matrix will have the same number of rows as the first matrix and the same number of columns as the second. If, for example, we multiply a 5×4 matrix by a 4×2 matrix the result will be a 5×2 matrix.

Third, the process of multiplying larger matrices together follows the same structure as in the simple examples used earlier – summing the products of multiplying successive rows by successive columns. To determine the position of the resulting elements we use the row/column combinations that have been used in the calculation – that is, if we want to multiply **A** and **B** and if we denote the resulting product matrix as **C**, the value of any cell, c_{ij}, will be the product of multiplying row i of the first matrix **A** and column j of the second matrix **B**. Thus each value produced from the multiplication takes its place according to the **A** row and **B** column used to produce it. Considerable care should be taken when multiplying large matrices manually.

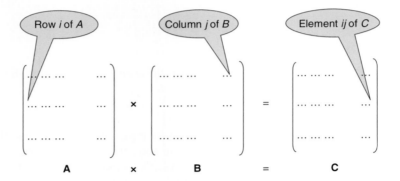

Fourth, it is important to note that, unlike ordinary algebra, the *order* of matrix multiplication is critical. In ordinary arithmetic the product of 2×5 is exactly the same as that of 5×2. In matrix algebra, however, this is generally not the case (as you will have realized in Progress Check B4.5); that is:

$$\mathbf{AB} \neq \mathbf{BA} \tag{B4.7}$$

However, the following property of multiplication does hold:

$$(\mathbf{AB})\mathbf{C} = \mathbf{A}(\mathbf{BC}) \tag{B4.8}$$

That is, the sequence of multiplication is immaterial.

B4.8 Using matrix algebra to represent economic models

Collecting the aspects of matrix algebra we have examined so far, we are now in a position to show how we can represent in matrix form the linear economic models we have previously developed. The next step, in Module B5, will be to show how we can use matrix algebra to find the solution to such models. But here let us return to the example we used earlier involving a sales matrix and a price vector. We show the sales matrix in numerical terms but the price vector simply in terms of the three variables:

$$\mathbf{A} = \begin{bmatrix} 1000 & 500 & 750 \\ 750 & 400 & 600 \\ 100 & 50 & 80 \end{bmatrix} \qquad \mathbf{p} = \begin{bmatrix} p_1 \\ p_2 \\ p_3 \end{bmatrix}$$

Similarly, we can represent the total sales revenue vector that we derived in Section 4.7 as:

$$\mathbf{r} = \begin{bmatrix} r_1 \\ r_2 \\ r_3 \end{bmatrix}$$

The relationship between sales, prices and revenue can then be conveniently represented as:

Ap = r

There are two aspects to the matrix representation of such an economic model to note. The first is that the matrix representation of the model remains the same no matter how large in terms of equations or variables the model becomes. Whether it's a three-equation system like this one or a 300-equation system, we can show the model in exactly the same compact way. We have a compact method of notation for the economic models we wish to examine. Second, the matrix notation actually represents a series of equations. In this example we would have:

$$\mathbf{Ap = r}$$

$$a_{11}p_1 + a_{12}p_2 + a_{13}p_3 = r_1$$
$$a_{21}p_1 + a_{22}p_2 + a_{23}p_3 = r_2$$
$$a_{31}p_1 + a_{32}p_2 + a_{33}p_3 = r_3$$

It will be useful to consider a second example, as it is central to much of what we shall be doing in the next module. Consider the market equilibrium model:

$$Q_d = Q_s$$
$$Q_d = a_1 + b_1 P$$
$$Q_s = a_2 + b_2 P$$

Let us rearrange these equations so that the variables (endogenous) are collected together on the left-hand side while the constants (exogenous) are on the right. We then have:

$$Q_d - Q_s = 0$$
$$Q_d - b_1 P = a_1$$
$$Q_s - b_2 P = a_2$$

and in matrix format this can be written as

$$\mathbf{Bx = a}$$

$$\begin{bmatrix} 1 & -1 & 0 \\ 1 & 0 & -b_1 \\ 0 & 1 & -b_2 \end{bmatrix} \begin{bmatrix} Q_d \\ Q_s \\ P \end{bmatrix} = \begin{bmatrix} 0 \\ a_1 \\ a_2 \end{bmatrix}$$

You should confirm for yourself that the matrix representation is identical to the equation system. The next stage is to determine the solution to such a model. In order to be able to do this we need to introduce the last aspect of matrix algebra: the matrix inverse. We'll look at this in the next module.

Progress Check B4.6

Represent the following two models in matrix format:

(i) $Y = C + I$
  $C = a + bY$
  where I is exogenous

Progress Check B4.6 *(Continued)*

(ii) $Y = C + I + G$
 $C = a + bY_d$
 $T = tY$
 $Y_d = Y - T$
 where I and G are exogenous.

(Solution on p. 463)

B4.9 Summary

In this module we've introduced the basic concepts and techniques associated with matrix algebra. We've seen that matrix algebra can be used to represent linear economic models in a very convenient and compact way – a type of shorthand – and that matrix algebra follows a number of simple rules.

Learning Check

Having read this module you should have learned that:

- A matrix is a rectangular array of numbers or coefficients
- A vector consists of a single row or column
- A scalar is a single number
- Matrix algebra consists of different ways of manipulating matrices and vectors
- Matrix algebra consists of a set of basic rules for each type of matrix algebra calculation that we want to do
- There are a number of special matrices including the identity matrix, the null matrix and the transpose matrix
- Matrix notation is a useful shorthand way of representing linear models in economics.

Worked Example

A firm produces three products, A, B and C, for sale both in the domestic market and in the export market and for sale to other firms to use in their own production process. Last year domestic sales were, respectively, 50, 60 and 80. Export sales were 25, 40 and 20. Sales to other firms were 10, 20 and 30. All figures are in units of thousands. This year domestic sales are expected to increase by 5% and export sales by 10%. Sales to other firms are expected to remain the same. The firm offers the products at the same price in all three markets. Prices are currently €3, €4 and €5. Production costs for the three products are €2, €3 and €4.

 We want to work out the following:

 (i) Profit for last year for the three products
 (ii) Projected profit for this year.

Worked Example *(Continued)*

Solution

First we must sort out the relevant matrices and vectors for the data given.

(i) We have:

$$S = \begin{bmatrix} 50 & 60 & 80 \\ 25 & 40 & 20 \\ 10 & 20 & 30 \end{bmatrix}$$

as the last year's sales matrix where the columns represent the three products and the rows the domestic market, the export market, and sales to other firms respectively. With a price vector, **p**, of:

$$p = \begin{bmatrix} 3 \\ 4 \\ 5 \end{bmatrix}$$

we have a revenue vector, **r**, of

$$r = Sp = \begin{bmatrix} 50 & 60 & 80 \\ 25 & 40 & 20 \\ 10 & 20 & 30 \end{bmatrix} \begin{bmatrix} 3 \\ 4 \\ 5 \end{bmatrix} = \begin{bmatrix} 790 \\ 335 \\ 260 \end{bmatrix}$$

Given a unit cost vector, **u**, of:

$$u = \begin{bmatrix} 2 \\ 3 \\ 4 \end{bmatrix}$$

we then have a total cost vector, **c**, of

$$c = Su = \begin{bmatrix} 50 & 60 & 80 \\ 25 & 40 & 20 \\ 10 & 20 & 30 \end{bmatrix} \begin{bmatrix} 2 \\ 3 \\ 4 \end{bmatrix} = \begin{bmatrix} 600 \\ 250 \\ 200 \end{bmatrix}$$

and a profit vector, **v**, of

$$v = r - c = \begin{bmatrix} 790 \\ 335 \\ 260 \end{bmatrix} - \begin{bmatrix} 600 \\ 250 \\ 200 \end{bmatrix} = \begin{bmatrix} 190 \\ 85 \\ 60 \end{bmatrix}$$

That is, the firm made profits of €190(000) for product A, €85(000) for product B and €60(000) for product C.

(ii) The projected profit matrix for this year can be obtained in the same way but now using an **S** matrix of:

$$S = \begin{bmatrix} 52.5 & 63 & 84 \\ 27.5 & 44 & 22 \\ 10 & 20 & 30 \end{bmatrix}$$

giving $v = \begin{bmatrix} 199.5 \\ 93.5 \\ 60 \end{bmatrix}$

That is, projected profit is €199,500 for A, €93,500 for B and €60,000 for C.

Exercises

B4.1 Using the sales matrix **A** which we have used in this module calculate:

AA′ and **A′A**

where

$$A = \begin{bmatrix} 1000 & 500 & 750 \\ 750 & 400 & 600 \\ 100 & 50 & 80 \end{bmatrix}$$

B4.2 Confirm that:

$$kA = Ak$$

using some numerical value of your choice for the scalar.

B4.3 For the following matrices complete the matrix arithmetic indicated (where possible):

$$A = \begin{bmatrix} 3 & 1 & 4 \\ 5 & -1 & 6 \\ 0 & 2 & 3 \end{bmatrix} \quad B = \begin{bmatrix} 7 & 2 & 3 \\ -1 & 2 & 2 \\ 5 & 9 & 1 \end{bmatrix} \quad C = \begin{bmatrix} 2 & 3 & 1 \\ 0 & 4 & 2 \\ 0 & 0 & 1 \end{bmatrix}$$

 (i) **AB**

 (ii) **BA**

(iii) **ABC**

(iv) **BAC**

B4.4 Supply and demand for a particular product, x, are given by:

$$Q_d = 1000 - 10P_x + 0.5P_y$$
$$Q_s = -500 + 4P_x - 0.2P_y$$

where P_x is the price of product x and P_y is the price of a substitute product.

Formulate the model in matrix form.

B4.5 For the model in Ex. B4.4, replace the numerical parameters with parameter symbols (a_1, b_1 etc.) and formulate the model in matrix form.

B4.6 A firm has four stores across the country and is doing a stock count of certain products. The table below shows the current number of items in stock across the stores. The products sell for £10, £15 and £23 respectively and cost the company £7, £12 and £20.

Items in stock

Product		Store		
	1	2	3	4
A	100	75	22	36
B	56	75	80	12
C	109	34	42	45

Exercises *(Continued)*

Using matrix algebra, work out the following:

(i)   The total cost of all items current held in stock

(ii) The potential revenue from all items held in stock

(iii) The potential profit from all items held in stock.

Appendix B4 Matrix algebra with Excel

Matrix algebra can be undertaken relatively easily in Excel (and other spreadsheet pro-
grammes). In this appendix we briefly outline how to use Excel for matrix calculations.
We did not explain this at the start of the module because, as has been emphasized a
number of times, the real benefit of matrix algebra in economic analysis lies in examining general economic problems rather than ones with specific numerical values; and
Excel cannot perform such general analysis.

How Excel handles matrix algebra

Matrix algebra is handled in two different ways in Excel, depending on exactly what
we want to do. Simple matrix algebra – addition, subtraction and multiplication by a
scalar – are handled by conventional cell arithmetic (that is, by copying cell formulae).
On the other hand, more complex matrix operations such as transposition and multiplication are handled by special matrix functions built into Excel. We'll show you how
to use both, taking the data from some of the matrix algebra we've looked at in this
chapter.

Simple matrix algebra

If we want to carry out fairly simple matrix algebra – such as addition, subtraction or
multiplication by a scalar – then we can use the normal formula calculations in Excel.
Let's look at the matrix addition we did at the beginning of Section B4.4, where we
wanted:

$$\mathbf{C} = \mathbf{A} + \mathbf{B}$$

where

$$\mathbf{A} = \begin{bmatrix} 1000 & 500 & 750 \\ 750 & 400 & 600 \\ 100 & 50 & 80 \end{bmatrix}$$

and

$$\mathbf{B} = \begin{bmatrix} 10 & 50 & 30 \\ 20 & 10 & 0 \\ 10 & 20 & 10 \end{bmatrix}$$

Figure B4.1 shows the Excel screenshot where we have input the data for the two
matrices. There are now two methods we can use in Excel.

	A	B	C	D	E	F
1						
2						
3	A		1000	500	750	
4			750	400	600	
5			100	50	80	
6						
7	B		10	50	30	
8			20	10	0	
9			10	20	10	
10						
11	C					
12						
13						
14						
15						
16						
17						

Figure B4.1 Excel screenshot of the matrices

Method 1

In cell C11 (the first cell of the new **C** matrix that we want to calculate) we can now enter the formula $= C3 + C7$ and press Enter, and the addition of the relevant two elements will be automatically completed. We now Copy the formula we input in cell C11 and Paste the formula into the other cells in the **C** matrix, cells C8–C9 and D11:E13, to give the resulting **C** matrix as shown in Fig. B4.2.

Method 2

The second method makes use of the *Named Ranges* feature in Excel. First, select the cells in the **A** matrix in the spreadsheet (cells C3:E5). Then go to the white cell in the top left immediately below the toolbar (just above the grey cell which is to the left of the A column and above row 1). Here, type 'A' to name the highlighted cells as range A, as shown in Fig. B4.3. Now do the same for the **B** matrix – highlighting cells C7:E9

	A	B	C	D	E	F
1						
2						
3	A		1000	500	750	
4			750	400	600	
5			100	50	80	
6						
7	B		10	50	30	
8			20	10	0	
9			10	20	10	
10						
11	C		1010	550	780	
12			770	410	600	
13			110	70	90	
14						
15						
16						

Figure B4.2 C matrix calculated

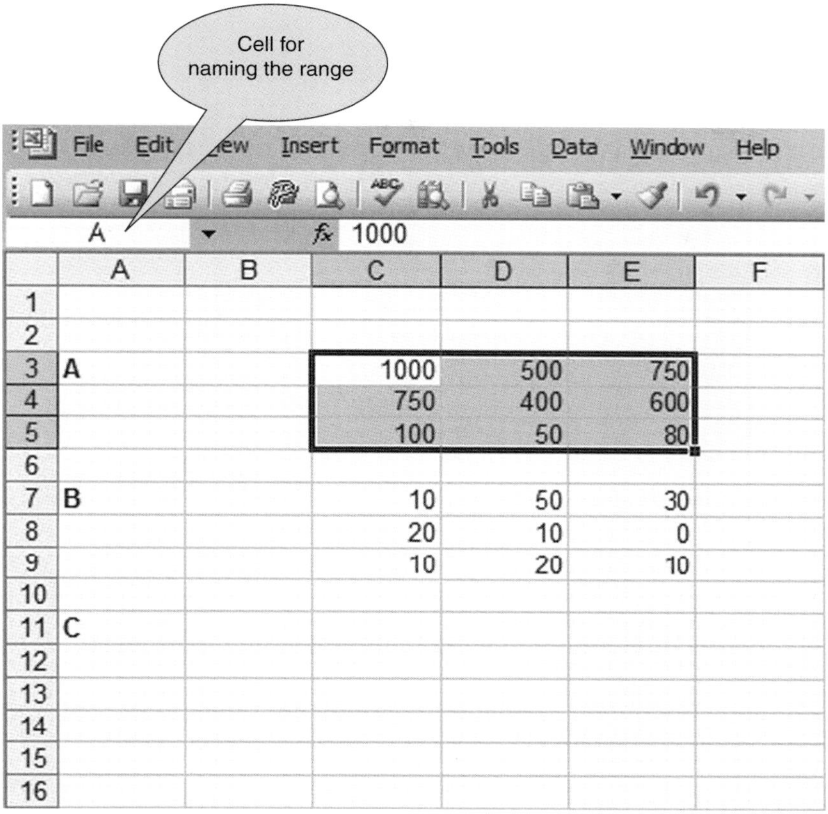

Figure B4.3 Named range A

and entering 'B' as the named range. Then highlight cells C11:E13 – the cells where the resulting **C** matrix will go – and type = **A** + **B** as shown in Fig. B4.4. At this stage don't press the Enter key as normal but instead press the three keys Ctrl Shift Enter at the same time. This results in all the cells in the **C** matrix being calculated by Excel, as shown in Fig. B4.5.

Using either Method 1 or Method 2 we can carry out addition, subtraction and scalar multiplication quite easily.

Matrix functions in Excel

For other types of matrix algebra we must use special matrix functions available in Excel. We'll look at each in turn.

Transposing a matrix

The mathematical operation of transposing a matrix is simply to switch the rows with the columns. To find the transpose of a matrix, use the TRANSPOSE function in Excel. Figure B4.6 shows a 2 × 3 **A** matrix that we want to transpose into **B** (which will be a 3 × 2 matrix). Cells B7:D8 have been highlighted as the destination cells for the transposed matrix and the formula = **TRANSPOSE(B3:C5)** has been typed in, showing the

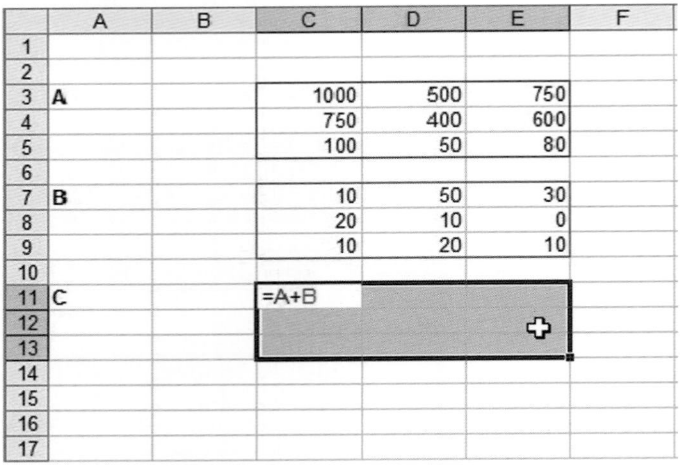

	A	B	C	D	E	F
1						
2						
3	A		1000	500	750	
4			750	400	600	
5			100	50	80	
6						
7	B		10	50	30	
8			20	10	0	
9			10	20	10	
10						
11	C		=A+B			
12					✛	
13						
14						
15						
16						
17						

Figure B4.4 Calculating the **C** matrix

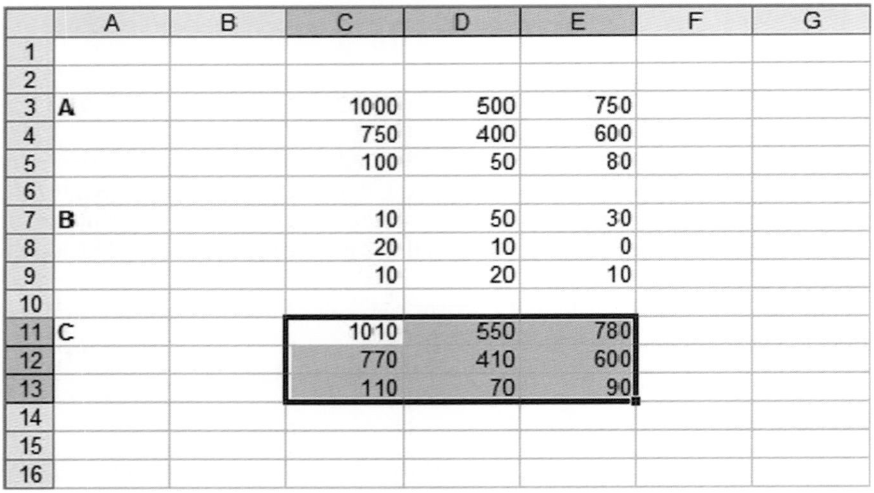

	A	B	C	D	E	F	G
1							
2							
3	A		1000	500	750		
4			750	400	600		
5			100	50	80		
6							
7	B		10	50	30		
8			20	10	0		
9			10	20	10		
10							
11	C		1010	550	780		
12			770	410	600		
13			110	70	90		
14							
15							
16							

Figure B4.5 **C** matrix calculated

	A	B	C	D	E	F
1						
2						
3	A	1000	500			
4		750	400			
5		100	50			
6						
7	B	=TRANSPOSE(B3:C5)				
8						
9						
10						
11						
12						
13						
14						

Figure B4.6 Transpose formula

	A	B	C	D	E	F
1						
2						
3	A	1000	500			
4		750	400			
5		100	50			
6						
7	B	1000	750	100		
8		500	400	50		
9						
10						
11						
12						
13						
14						
15						

Figure B4.7 Transposed matrix

	A	B	C	D	E	F
1						
2						
3	A	1000	500			
4		750	400			
5		100	50			
6						
7	B	1000	750	100		
8		500	400	50		
9						
10	C	=MMULT(B3:C5,B7:D8)				
11						
12						
13						
14						
15						

Figure B4.8 The MMULT function

	A	B	C	D	E	F
1						
2						
3	A	1000	500			
4		750	400			
5		100	50			
6						
7	B	1000	750	100		
8		500	400	50		
9						
10	C	1250000	950000	125000		
11		950000	722500	95000		
12						
13						
14						
15						

Figure B4.9 Result of matrix multiplication

cells from the original matrix. As before, use the Ctrl Shift Enter key combination to produce the transpose matrix shown in Fig. B4.7.

Matrix multiplication

Multiplying two matrices is done in much the same way but this time with the function MMULT as shown in Fig. B4.8, with the result shown in Fig. B4.9. Again, remember to use the Ctrl Shift Enter key combination.

Module B5
Matrix algebra: inversion

In the previous module we saw how matrix algebra can be used to build large economic models in an easy format and how some of the basic matrix algebra calculations can be done. Clearly, however, there is little point developing economic models in matrix format unless we can solve them. To do this we need to introduce some more matrix algebra, this time involving the *matrix inverse*.

Learning Objectives

By the end of this module you should be able to:

- Calculate the inverse of a matrix
- Use the inverse matrix to find the solution to a set of linear equations
- Use determinants.

Knowledge Check B5

If you're already familiar and comfortable with the matrix inverse, you may want to jump straight to Module B6 to look at how matrix algebra is used to develop and solve economic models.

To test your ability, find the inverse of:

$$\begin{bmatrix} 2 & 4 \\ 3 & 5 \end{bmatrix}$$

Check your answer in Appendix 2.

B5.1 The matrix inverse

The inverse matrix has much the same meaning as the inverse, or reciprocal, of a normal number. The inverse of the number 10, for example, is:

$$\frac{1}{10} \text{ or } 10^{-1}$$

One property of such an inverse is that:

$$10 \times 10^{-1} = 1$$

That is, a number multiplied by its inverse equals 1. In matrix terms the inverse of matrix **A** is shown as $\mathbf{A}^{-1}$ and has the equivalent property:

$$\mathbf{AA}^{-1} = \mathbf{I} \qquad \text{(B5.1)}$$

where **I** is the identity matrix. Alternatively, if we rearrange:

$$\mathbf{A}^{-1}\mathbf{A} = \mathbf{I} \qquad \text{(B5.2)}$$

That is, a matrix pre- or postmultiplied by its inverse will result in an identity matrix. However, do not be tempted at this stage to assume that the inverse of a matrix will simply be 1/**A**. The analogy with normal arithmetic is not appropriate, as we shall see. The following properties of inverse matrices should be noted:

- Only a square matrix can have an inverse
- Not all square matrices will have an inverse. A matrix that has an inverse is said to be *non-singular* and a matrix that has no inverse is said to be *singular*
- If an inverse exists it is unique
- Inverses have the following further properties:

$$(\mathbf{A}^{-1})^{-1} = \mathbf{A} \qquad \text{(B5.3)}$$

$$(\mathbf{AB})^{-1} = \mathbf{B}^{-1}\mathbf{A}^{-1} \qquad \text{(B5.4)}$$

$$(\mathbf{A}')^{-1} = (\mathbf{A}^{-1})' \qquad \text{(B5.5)}$$

Before we look at methods of determining the inverse of a matrix it is worth examining their use in order to understand their importance.

B5.2 Using a matrix inverse

Let us return to the sales matrix and price vector that we used in the previous module, where we had:

$$\mathbf{Ap} = \mathbf{r}$$

where

$$\mathbf{A} = \begin{bmatrix} 1000 & 500 & 750 \\ 750 & 400 & 600 \\ 100 & 50 & 80 \end{bmatrix}$$

and where **A** represents sales in the three regions last year, **p** represents the price vector and **r** represents the sales revenue vector. Let us assume that the firm has set a sales revenue target for next year of:

Region 1 €35,500

Region 2 €26,250

Region 3 €3450

and is investigating the implications of such a target for pricing policy. For simplicity, we shall assume that sales levels stay the same (that is, that the **A** matrix remains unchanged), although in practice we could readily simulate the effect of different growth rates in sales on the pricing policy. Management now wish to determine the market prices that must be charged for the three products, given the sales figures and the revenue targets. In matrix terms we require the appropriate values for the **p** vector given the values for **A** and **r**. Using what we know about the matrix inverse we can rearrange the model:

$$\mathbf{Ap} = \mathbf{r}$$

But if we multiply through by $\mathbf{A}^{-1}$ we have:

$$\mathbf{A}^{-1}\mathbf{Ap} = \mathbf{A}^{-1}\mathbf{r}$$

From Eq. B5.2 we have $\mathbf{A}^{-1}\mathbf{A} = \mathbf{I}$, so:

$$\mathbf{Ip} = \mathbf{A}^{-1}\mathbf{r}$$

Let us examine the term **Ip** in more detail. Given that the **A** matrix is of size 3×3, the **A** inverse matrix and the **I** matrix must also be of the same size. If we multiply out **Ip** we have:

$$\mathbf{Ip} = \begin{bmatrix} 1 & 0 & 0 \\ 0 & 1 & 0 \\ 0 & 0 & 1 \end{bmatrix} \begin{bmatrix} p_1 \\ p_2 \\ p_3 \end{bmatrix} = \begin{bmatrix} p_1 \\ p_2 \\ p_3 \end{bmatrix}$$

That is, multiplication of a vector by an identity matrix leaves the vector unchanged. Our model, therefore, can be written as:

$$\mathbf{p} = \mathbf{A}^{-1}\mathbf{r} \tag{B5.6}$$

That is, by multiplying the **A** inverse by the **r** vector we can obtain the numerical values for **p** that will satisfy the model. Given that such matrix notation is simply a shorthand way of representing a set of equations, what we have derived is a method of solving a simultaneous set of equations using matrix algebra and the matrix inverse. The potential of matrix algebra using the inverse in this way cannot be overemphasized, since the solution method is applicable to any size of matrix and the equation system it represents. To find the solution to the model we shall simply state (and later show the derivation) that the inverse of this particular **A** matrix is:

$$\mathbf{A}^{-1} = \begin{bmatrix} 0.016 & -0.02 & 0 \\ 0 & 0.04 & -0.30 \\ -0.02 & 0 & 0.20 \end{bmatrix}$$

Using this inverse we can now solve for the **p** vector values:

$$\mathbf{p} = \mathbf{A}^{-1}\mathbf{r} = \begin{bmatrix} 0.016 & -0.02 & 0 \\ 0 & 0.04 & -0.30 \\ -0.02 & 0 & 0.20 \end{bmatrix} \begin{bmatrix} 33,500 \\ 26,250 \\ 3450 \end{bmatrix}$$

giving

$$\mathbf{p} = \begin{bmatrix} 11 \\ 15 \\ 20 \end{bmatrix}$$

That is, the prices that must be charged to meet these sales targets are €11 for product X, €15 for product Y and €20 for product Z. The matrix inverse, therefore, can be used to determine the solution to a set of simultaneous equations. The advantages of the inverse method in terms of both economic theory and analysis are evident. Having seen the usefulness of the matrix inverse we now turn our attention to the method of derivation.

Progress Check B5.1

(i)   Using the **p** vector just obtained, confirm that **Ap** = **r**.

(ii) Assume that the firm has now set regional sales targets as:

   Region 1 €35,000

   Region 2 €27,400

   Region 3 €3595

Determine the new set of prices.

(Solution on p. 463)

B5.3 Calculating the matrix inverse

We have seen how the matrix inverse can be used to determine the solution to a matrix model. There are a number of alternative methods available for finding the matrix inverse. One method is the *Gauss–Jordan elimination method*, and we shall look at this first. However, it is also necessary to be familiar with a second method which is technically less efficient. This is the method of *determinants*. Determinants are widely used in mathematical economics and have an important role in theoretical analysis, as we shall shortly discover.

> It's named after Carl Friedrich Gauss and Wilhelm Jordan who first thought of this method

The Gauss–Jordan elimination method

This method is similar to the approach taken when we were solving a set of simultaneous equations in Module B1, and operates through a sequence of simple stages. First, we create what is known as an *augmented* matrix. This consists of the matrix for which we wish to find an inverse, matrix **A**, and the equivalent identity matrix. In this example we have:

> The **A** matrix

> The **I** matrix

$$\begin{bmatrix} 1000 & 500 & 750 & 1 & 0 & 0 \\ 750 & 400 & 600 & 0 & 1 & 0 \\ 100 & 50 & 80 & 0 & 0 & 1 \end{bmatrix}$$

where the left-hand part of the augmented matrix is **A** and the right-hand part the corresponding **I** matrix. We now undertake a series of arithmetic operations on the rows of this augmented matrix. At the end of all the calculations, the **A** part of this matrix will have been transformed into an identity matrix and what was the identity matrix will have been transformed into the inverse matrix. You should confirm the detailed arithmetic for yourself as we progress, using a pocket calculator. To begin the transformation of **A** into **I** we take the first row and force $a_{11} = 1$ (which is the value of the first diagonal element of the **I** matrix that we wish to create). This is achieved by dividing the entire row by the current a_{11} coefficient, 1000. This gives:

   Row 1 ÷ 1000   1   0.5   0.75   0.001   0   0

We now have to change the a_{21} coefficient into 0 (to correspond to the value required in the **I** matrix) and we use the new Row 1 to achieve this. We take the new Row 1, multiply by −750 (the a_{21} coefficient with reversed sign) and add this to the current Row 2:

−750 × Row 1	−750	−375	−562.5	−0.75	0	0
+ Row 2	750	400	600	0	1	0
New Row 2	0	25	37.5	−0.75	1	0

Perform the same process on Row 3, multiplying the new Row 1 by −100 (the a_{31} coefficient with reversed sign) and adding the result to the existing Row 3. This gives:

−100 × Row 1	−100	−50	−757	−0.1	0	0
+ Row 3	100	50	80	0	0	1
New Row 3	0	0	5	−0.1	0	1

to give a result at this stage of

B

Row 1	1	0.5	0.75	0.001	0	0
Row 2	0	25	37.5	−0.75	1	0
Row 3	0	0	5	−0.1	0	1

You will see that the effect of this arithmetic has been to transform the first column of the augmented matrix into a column appropriate for an identity matrix. We now repeat this process by transforming column 2 into an identity matrix format. This is achieved by dividing Row 2 by the a_{22} coefficient of 0.5 (changing it to the value 1) and then using this new Row 2 to alter Row 1 and Row 3 (changing the a coefficients to zero). Performing this arithmetic (and you are strongly urged to do this for yourself) produces the matrix:

Row 1	1	0	0	0.016	−0.02	0
Row 2	0	1	1.5	−0.03	0.04	0
Row 3	0	0	5	−0.1	0	1

You can see that the first *two* columns are now in identity matrix format. Finally, transform column 3 by using Row 3. Divide Row 3 by the a_{33} coefficient, 5, and use the new Row 3 to alter Row 1 and Row 2 (changing the a coefficients to zero). This gives a matrix:

Row 1	1	0	0	0.016	−0.02	0
Row 2	0	1	0	0	0.04	−0.3
Row 3	0	0	1	−0.02	0	0.2

which gives an inverse of

$$\mathbf{A}^{-1} = \begin{bmatrix} 0.016 & -0.02 & 0 \\ 0 & 0.04 & -0.3 \\ -0.02 & 0 & 0.2 \end{bmatrix}$$

The original **A** matrix has now been transformed into an **I** matrix, and the **I** matrix into the inverse of **A**. Because of its repetitive and sequential nature this process is readily extended to larger-sized matrices and is also ideally suited to solution via computer spreadsheet. Indeed, a number of commercial spreadsheets have an inbuilt matrix inverse function which performs such arithmetic automatically. The Appendix to this module shows how to use Excel to do this. To summarize the calculations:

1 Create an augmented matrix consisting of the **A** matrix (m by n, where $m = n$) and an identity matrix of the same size.
2 Divide the first row of the matrix through by the a_{11} coefficient.
3 Taking each subsequent row in turn, multiply the new row 1 by the a_{11} coefficient and subtract this from the existing ith row (to set a_{11} in the ith row to zero).
4 Repeat the calculation for each remaining row, 2 to m, in the **A** matrix:

  - Divide the row by its a_{11} coefficient
  - Taking all the other rows in turn, multiply the new row i by the relevant a_{ij} coefficient of the row being adjusted and subtract this from the existing ith row (to set the corresponding a in the row to zero).

Progress Check B5.2

Confirm the following using the original **A** matrix and the inverse that we have found:

(i) $AA^{-1} = I$

(ii) $A^{-1}A = I$

(iii) $(A^{-1})^{-1} = A$

B5.4 Determinants

The Gauss–Jordan method for finding an inverse is arithmetically straightforward. However, as we'll see later in this module, there are times when we want to look at matrix inverses in a different way. To be able to do this we need to be able to find an inverse using a different method – by using determinants. A *determinant* is a scalar associated with a square matrix. For a 2×2 matrix, **A**, the determinant would be defined as:

$$|A| = \begin{vmatrix} a_{11} & a_{12} \\ a_{21} & a_{22} \end{vmatrix} = a_{11}a_{22} - a_{21}a_{12} \tag{B5.7}$$

where $|A|$ (pronounced 'determinant A') is the standard notation for denoting a determinant. For example, suppose we had matrix **A** as:

$$A = \begin{bmatrix} 1 & 2 \\ 3 & 4 \end{bmatrix}$$

Then using Eq. B5.7, $|A| = (1 \times 4) - (3 \times 2) = -2$, that is, the determinant of matrix **A** equals -2. Such a determinant is known as a *second-order* determinant, given that it is associated with a 2×2 matrix, **A**. Determinants of an order higher than 2 can be evaluated using the *Laplace expansion*. Assume a matrix such that:

$$A = \begin{bmatrix} a_{11} & a_{12} & a_{13} \\ a_{21} & a_{22} & a_{23} \\ a_{31} & a_{32} & a_{33} \end{bmatrix}$$

then its determinant, $|\mathbf{A}|$, is found by expanding the first row in the manner

$$|\mathbf{A}| = +a_{11} \begin{vmatrix} a_{22} & a_{23} \\ a_{32} & a_{33} \end{vmatrix} - a_{12} \begin{vmatrix} a_{21} & a_{23} \\ a_{31} & a_{33} \end{vmatrix} + a_{13} \begin{vmatrix} a_{21} & a_{22} \\ a_{31} & a_{32} \end{vmatrix} \quad \text{(B5.8)}$$

At first sight, Eq. B5.8 might look somewhat daunting but such an expansion follows a simple set of rules. This third-order determinant comprises three parts, each of which consists of an element from the first row of the matrix (given that we are expanding the first row to obtain the determinant) and a 2×2 determinant. If we examine the first of these subdeterminants, we can see that it consists of the remaining cells of the $\mathbf{A}$ matrix after row 1 and column 1 have been deleted. Similarly, the second subdeterminant consists of those cells remaining after row 1 and column 2 have been deleted. Finally, the third subdeterminant is obtained from cells after row 1 and column 3 have been deleted. Such subdeterminants are more generally referred to as the *minors* of the elements of $\mathbf{A}$. To help see what's going on, let's show the following for the minor associated with element a_{12}:

$$\mathbf{A} = \begin{bmatrix} \cancel{a_{11}} & \cancel{a_{12}} & \cancel{a_{13}} \\ a_{21} & \cancel{a_{22}} & a_{23} \\ a_{31} & \cancel{a_{32}} & a_{33} \end{bmatrix}$$

Given we want the minor of a_{12}, we've crossed out the *first* row of the $\mathbf{A}$ matrix, given that a_{12} is in the first row, and then we've crossed out the *second* column, given that a_{12} is also in the second column. The elements that remain form the minor:

$$\begin{vmatrix} a_{21} & a_{23} \\ a_{31} & a_{33} \end{vmatrix}$$

Progress Check B5.3

Find the minor associated with element a_{31}.

(Solution on p. 463)

The calculation of a determinant using this approach is now a matter of simple arithmetic. Let us return to the sales matrix, $\mathbf{A}$, that we were using in the previous section:

$$\mathbf{A} = \begin{bmatrix} 1000 & 500 & 750 \\ 750 & 400 & 600 \\ 100 & 50 & 80 \end{bmatrix}$$

The determinant of $\mathbf{A}$ can now be calculated as:

$$|\mathbf{A}| = +a_{11} \begin{vmatrix} a_{22} & a_{23} \\ a_{32} & a_{33} \end{vmatrix} - a_{12} \begin{vmatrix} a_{21} & a_{23} \\ a_{31} & a_{33} \end{vmatrix} + a_{13} \begin{vmatrix} a_{21} & a_{22} \\ a_{31} & a_{32} \end{vmatrix}$$

giving

$$|\mathbf{A}| = 1000 \begin{vmatrix} 400 & 600 \\ 50 & 80 \end{vmatrix} - 500 \begin{vmatrix} 750 & 600 \\ 100 & 80 \end{vmatrix} + 750 \begin{vmatrix} 750 & 400 \\ 100 & 50 \end{vmatrix}$$

and calculating the values of the resulting 2×2 determinants we have

$$|\mathbf{A}| = 1000(2000) - 500(0) + 750(-2500) = 125{,}000$$

$$\text{So: } |\mathbf{A}| = 125{,}000$$

That is, the determinant of $\mathbf{A}$ equals 125,000.

This process of calculating the value of the determinant can be extended to higher-order determinants. To do so, however, it is worth introducing a new concept, that of a *cofactor*. Let's show the minor of a particular element of the determinant, a_{ij}, as M_{ij}. The expansion expression that we had earlier can then be written as:

$$|\mathbf{A}| = a_{11}M_{11} - a_{12}M_{12} + a_{13}M_{13} \tag{B5.9}$$

The cofactor, C_{ij}, of a_{ij} is defined as:

$$C_{ij} = (-1)^{i+j}M_{ij} \tag{B5.10}$$

and the determinant can be rewritten as

$$|\mathbf{A}| = a_{11}C_{11} + a_{12}C_{12} + a_{13}C_{13} \tag{B5.11}$$

If this seems to have appeared out of nowhere, look at the following using Eq. B5.10 for C_{11}:

$$C_{11} = (-1)^{1+1}M_{11} = (-1)^2 M_{11} = +M_{11}$$

Similarly, for C_{12} and C_{13}:

$$C_{12} = (-1)^{1+2}M_{12} = (-1)^3 M_{12} = +M_{12}$$
$$C_{13} = (-1)^{1+3}M_{13} = (-1)^4 M_{13} = +M_{13}$$

In other words, a cofactor is simply the corresponding minor with either a plus sign (if $i+j$ is even) or a minus sign (if $i+j$ is odd) attached. For higher-order determinants we can now provide a general expression for the expansion. For example, if we had a matrix **A** that was of size 4×4:

$$\mathbf{A} = \begin{bmatrix} a_{11} & a_{12} & a_{13} & a_{14} \\ a_{21} & a_{22} & a_{23} & a_{24} \\ a_{31} & a_{32} & a_{33} & a_{34} \\ a_{41} & a_{42} & a_{43} & a_{44} \end{bmatrix}$$

its determinant would be given by

$$|\mathbf{A}| = a_{11}C_{11} + a_{12}C_{12} + a_{13}C_{13} + a_{14}C_{14}$$

or

$$= a_{11}M_{11} - a_{12}M_{12} + a_{13}M_{13} - a_{14}M_{14}$$

In general, therefore, we can define the determinant as:

$$|\mathbf{A}| = \sum a_{1j}C_{1j}, \qquad j = 1, 2, \ldots, n \tag{B5.12}$$

A slight digression may be necessary to explain the symbol $\sum$. This is known as a summation operator (and called 'sigma') and indicates that you should add together whatever appears immediately after the symbol. So, in the example above, you add the $a_1 C_1$ terms for all the columns in the matrix.

The Laplace expansion has one particularly useful property: the determinant can be found by expanding *any* row or *any* column. No matter which row or column we use for the expansion we will arrive at the same determinant value. The expansion can, therefore, be undertaken across any row or down any column of the matrix. Expanding by a chosen row, *i* for example, would give:

$$|\mathbf{A}| = \sum a_{ij} C_{ij}, \qquad j = 1, 2, \dots, n$$

and by a chosen row, *j*, would give

$$|\mathbf{A}| = \sum a_{ij} C_{ij}, \qquad i = 1, 2, \dots, m$$

Progress Check B5.5

Referring back to the sales matrix, **A**, calculate the value of the determinant using:

(i)   Row 3

(ii)   Column 2.

B

Properties of a determinant

Determinants have a number of properties that will prove useful in mathematical economics. Among these are:

1   The determinant of a matrix **A** has the same value as that of its transpose, **A'**:

$$|\mathbf{A}| = |\mathbf{A}'| \tag{B5.13}$$

2   Multiplying a single row or column of a matrix by a scalar will cause the value of the determinant to be multiplied by the scalar:

$$k\mathbf{A} = k|\mathbf{A}| \tag{B5.14}$$

3   If one row (or one column) is a multiple of another row (or column) the value of the determinant is zero; that is, if two rows or columns are linearly dependent the value of the determinant is zero.

4   The expansion of a determinant by what are known as its *alien cofactors* will result in a value of zero for the determinant; that is, if we expand a determinant along a specific row (or column) but use the cofactors of a different row (or column) the value of the determinants will be zero. This may seem an illogical process to want to undertake but we shall see its relevance shortly when we examine the calculation of the matrix inverse using determinants.

To illustrate, assume a 3×3 matrix:

$$\mathbf{A} = \begin{bmatrix} a_{11} & a_{12} & a_{13} \\ a_{21} & a_{22} & a_{23} \\ a_{31} & a_{32} & a_{33} \end{bmatrix}$$

If we now decide to find the determinant by expanding with the second row elements but using the cofactors of the first row elements we have:

$$a_{21} C_{11} + a_{22} C_{12} + a_{23} C_{13} = 0$$

Alternatively:

$$\sum a_{2j}C_{1j} = 0. \qquad j = 1, 2, 3$$

B5.5 Calculating the matrix inverse using determinants

We are now in a position to use the determinant to calculate the matrix inverse. Let us return to the **A** matrix:

$$\mathbf{A} = \begin{bmatrix} a_{11} & a_{12} & a_{13} \\ a_{21} & a_{22} & a_{23} \\ a_{31} & a_{32} & a_{33} \end{bmatrix}$$

We can also define a matrix of the associated cofactors:

$$\mathbf{C} = \begin{bmatrix} C_{11} & C_{12} & C_{13} \\ C_{21} & C_{22} & C_{23} \\ C_{31} & C_{32} & C_{33} \end{bmatrix}$$

which, of course, would be determined from the relevant minors:

$$\mathbf{M} = \begin{bmatrix} M_{11} & -M_{12} & M_{13} \\ -M_{21} & M_{22} & -M_{23} \\ M_{31} & -M_{32} & M_{33} \end{bmatrix}$$

Transposing the **C** matrix we obtain:

$$\mathbf{C}' = \begin{bmatrix} C_{11} & C_{21} & C_{31} \\ C_{12} & C_{22} & C_{32} \\ C_{13} & C_{23} & C_{33} \end{bmatrix}$$

where **C'** is known as the *adjoint* of **A** and is denoted as adj **A**. Here we simply state that the inverse of **A** is given by:

> The Appendix to this module shows how B5.15 is obtained

$$\mathbf{A}^{-1} = \frac{1}{|\mathbf{A}|} \text{ adj } \mathbf{A} \tag{B5.15}$$

To illustrate the use of the inverse expression let's return to our original example where:

$$\mathbf{A} = \begin{bmatrix} 1000 & 500 & 750 \\ 750 & 400 & 600 \\ 100 & 50 & 80 \end{bmatrix}$$

The determinant of **A** was calculated earlier as 125,000. The **C** matrix for this **A** matrix will be:

$$\mathbf{C} = \begin{bmatrix} 2000 & 0 & -2500 \\ -2500 & 5000 & 0 \\ 0 & -37{,}500 & 25{,}000 \end{bmatrix}$$

$$\text{adj } \mathbf{A} = \begin{bmatrix} 2000 & -2500 & 0 \\ 0 & 5000 & -37{,}500 \\ -2500 & 0 & 25{,}000 \end{bmatrix}$$

So:

$$\mathbf{A}^{-1} = \frac{1}{|\mathbf{A}|} \text{adj } A$$

$$= \frac{1}{125{,}000} \begin{bmatrix} 2000 & -2500 & 0 \\ 0 & 5000 & -37{,}500 \\ -2500 & 0 & 25{,}000 \end{bmatrix}$$

giving

$$\mathbf{A}^{-1} = \begin{bmatrix} 0.016 & -0.02 & 0 \\ 0 & 0.04 & -0.3 \\ -0.02 & 0 & 0.2 \end{bmatrix}$$

again confirming that this is the inverse to the **A** matrix that we worked out in Section B5.3 using the Gauss–Jordan method.

The use of determinants allows us to calculate the inverse of a matrix and thereby determine the solution to a set of linear equations. It is apparent, however, that the use of determinants is more cumbersome than the Gauss–Jordan method. Why, then, do we bother with determinants when we have a computationally more efficient method of finding the inverse? The answer takes us back to one of the main elements of this text and of mathematical economics in general. As we shall see in the next module, the use of determinants is essential if we are to fully evaluate a theoretical, as opposed to a specific numerical, economic model. When we attempt to assess the implications and predictions of such a theoretical model we shall find that the determinant method is indispensable.

There is an additional reason why the determinant method may be useful. In some cases it may be easier to determine the numerical inverse using determinants. You will remember from the Laplace transformation that, to calculate the determinant of some matrix, we can expand along any row or any column. Consider the equation system detailed below:

$$\mathbf{Ax} = \mathbf{b}$$

where

$$\mathbf{A} = \begin{bmatrix} 2 & 3 & -1 \\ 5 & -4 & 2 \\ 0 & 0 & 2 \end{bmatrix} \quad \mathbf{x} = \begin{bmatrix} x_1 \\ x_2 \\ x_3 \end{bmatrix} \quad \mathbf{b} = \begin{bmatrix} 15 \\ 70 \\ 40 \end{bmatrix}$$

and we wish to solve for x. On inspection of the **A** matrix it is apparent that the calculation of the determinant using row 3 will involve very little arithmetic, given the two zero coefficients, whereas the Gauss–Jordan method requires arithmetic manipulation of the entire matrix.

B5.6 The determinant and non-singularity

When the concept of the inverse was first introduced we stated that inverses exist only for square matrices but that not every square matrix will have an inverse. A matrix without an inverse is said to be *singular*, and the determinant of such a matrix will have a zero value. We also stated, when summarizing the properties of determinants, that if a row (column) is a multiple of another row (column) in the matrix its determinant will take a zero value. Given our use of matrix algebra to represent, and solve, economic models, this feature of determinants is of particular importance. We've focused upon the use of the inverse matrix in finding the solution to a set of linear equations. If a matrix is singular – that is, if one row/equation is dependent upon another – then there can be no unique solution to the equation system represented by that matrix, and we can readily see this from the value of the determinant. Consider the following equation system:

$$x_1 + x_2 = 6$$
$$2x_1 + 2x_2 = 12$$

It is clear that the two equations are not independent, the second being a multiple of the first, and that we cannot find a unique solution. In matrix form we would have:

$$\begin{bmatrix} 1 & 1 \\ 2 & 2 \end{bmatrix} \begin{bmatrix} x_1 \\ x_2 \end{bmatrix} = \begin{bmatrix} 6 \\ 12 \end{bmatrix}$$

and the determinant of the **A** matrix is

$$(1 \times 2) - (2 \times 1) = 0$$

That is, the matrix is singular and hence has no inverse and the equation system has no unique solution. Consider now the following equation system:

$$X_1 + X_2 = 6$$
$$2X_1 + 2X_2 = 10$$

Careful inspection shows that these two equations are inconsistent in that there are no values for X_1 and X_2 that satisfy both equations simultaneously. Graphically, the two equations would appear as parallel lines and, given that a simultaneous solution occurs where two such lines cross, there can be no solution. Again, given that we have the same **A** matrix as before, this matrix is singular and again we know from the value of the determinant that no unique solution exists. In general, therefore, with a set of simultaneous equations, when the number of equations equals the number of unknowns a unique solution can be obtained only where no equation is either inconsistent or dependent on one of the others. This can be readily recognized from the value of the corresponding determinant being equal to 0. It is tempting to underestimate the usefulness of determinants in this context. In the illustrative examples used it is clear, even without calculating a numerical value for the determinant, that no solution exists. However, for larger-scale problems, and in particular for economic models that consist of theoretical parameters rather than numerical values, such a situation will be far less obvious and the use of the determinant in this way proves invaluable.

Progress Check B5.7

Consider the equation system:

$$4X_1 + 3X_2 + 5X_3 = 74$$
$$3X_1 + X_2 + 3X_3 = 42$$
$$-X_1 + 3X_2 + X_3 = 22$$

Show through the use of determinants that this system has no unique solution.

B5.7 Cramer's rule

As we have noted over the last few sections, matrix inversion provides a general method of finding the solution to a set of linear equations expressed in the form:

$$\mathbf{A}\mathbf{x} = \mathbf{b}$$

For certain applications there is a simpler method available, *Cramer's rule*, which is based on the determinant approach that we shall develop in this section. The general solution to the **x** vector in the equation system is given as:

> It's named after Gabriel Cramer, a Swiss mathematician active in the 1700s

$$\mathbf{x} = \mathbf{A}^{-1}\mathbf{b} = \frac{1}{|\mathbf{A}|}\text{adj } \mathbf{A}\mathbf{b} \qquad\qquad (B5.16)$$

For the 3×3 matrix problem we have been examining this can be rewritten as:

$$\begin{bmatrix} x_1 \\ x_2 \\ x_3 \end{bmatrix} = \frac{1}{|\mathbf{A}|}\begin{bmatrix} C_{11} & C_{21} & C_{31} \\ C_{12} & C_{22} & C_{32} \\ C_{13} & C_{23} & C_{33} \end{bmatrix}\begin{bmatrix} b_1 \\ b_2 \\ b_3 \end{bmatrix}$$

$$= \frac{1}{|\mathbf{A}|}\begin{bmatrix} C_{11}b_1 + C_{21}b_2 + C_{31}b_3 \\ C_{12}b_1 + C_{22}b_2 + C_{32}b_3 \\ C_{13}b_1 + C_{23}b_2 + C_{33}b_3 \end{bmatrix}$$

$$= \frac{1}{|\mathbf{A}|}\begin{bmatrix} \sum C_{i1}b_i \\ \sum C_{i2}b_i \\ \sum C_{i3}b_i \end{bmatrix} \qquad \text{for } i = 1, 2, 3$$

which gives

$$\begin{bmatrix} x_1 \\ x_2 \\ x_3 \end{bmatrix} = \frac{1}{|\mathbf{A}|}\begin{bmatrix} \sum C_{i1}b_i \\ \sum C_{i2}b_i \\ \sum C_{i3}b_i \end{bmatrix}$$

That is, any of the unknown x values can be determined by evaluating the appropriate cofactor expression. Cramer's rule takes us one stage further than this, however. Let us define a new determinant $|\mathbf{A}_1|$ such that:

$$|\mathbf{A}_1| = \begin{vmatrix} b_1 & a_{12} & a_{13} \\ b_2 & a_{22} & a_{23} \\ b_3 & a_{32} & a_{33} \end{vmatrix}$$

That is, $|\mathbf{A}_1|$ is simply the $|\mathbf{A}|$ determinant where the first column has been replaced by the **b** vector. Using the Laplace expansion on the b column we have:

$$|\mathbf{A}_1| = b_1 C_{11} + b_2 C_{21} + b_3 C_{31}$$

$$= \sum b_i C_{i1} \quad \text{for } i = 1, 2, 3$$

$$= \sum C_{i1}b_i \quad \text{for } i = 1, 2, 3$$

So we now have:

$$x_1 = \sum C_{i1}b_i = \frac{1}{|\mathbf{A}|}|\mathbf{A}_1|$$

In the same way we could define $|\mathbf{A}_2|$ with the **b** vector replacing column 2 of $|\mathbf{A}|$, and $|\mathbf{A}_3|$ where the **b** vector replaces the third column of the **A** determinant. This would give:

$$x_2 = \frac{1}{|\mathbf{A}|}|\mathbf{A}_2|$$

$$x_3 = \frac{1}{|\mathbf{A}|}|\mathbf{A}_3|$$

Generalizing this, we can state Cramer's rule as:

$$x_i = \frac{|\mathbf{A}_i|}{|\mathbf{A}|} \tag{B5.17}$$

That is, the value of the ith x value is given by the ratio of the two determinants. Let us illustrate by returning to the sales matrix we've been using:

$$\mathbf{A} = \begin{bmatrix} 1000 & 500 & 750 \\ 750 & 400 & 600 \\ 100 & 50 & 80 \end{bmatrix}$$

and

$$\mathbf{b} = \begin{bmatrix} 33,500 \\ 26,250 \\ 3450 \end{bmatrix}$$

which represents the sales revenue targets for each region. The determinant of **A** was calculated earlier as 125,000. The following further determinants are required:

$$|\mathbf{A}_1| = \begin{bmatrix} 33,500 & 500 & 750 \\ 26,250 & 400 & 600 \\ 3450 & 50 & 80 \end{bmatrix} = 1,375,000$$

$$|\mathbf{A}_2| = \begin{bmatrix} 1000 & 33,500 & 750 \\ 750 & 26,250 & 600 \\ 100 & 3450 & 80 \end{bmatrix} = 1,875,000$$

$$|\mathbf{A}_3| = \begin{bmatrix} 1000 & 500 & 33,500 \\ 750 & 400 & 26,250 \\ 100 & 50 & 3450 \end{bmatrix} = 2,500,000$$

Solving for x we have:

$$x_1 = \frac{1}{|\mathbf{A}|}|\mathbf{A}_1| = \frac{1,375,000}{125,000} = 11$$

$$x_2 = \frac{1}{|\mathbf{A}|}|\mathbf{A}_2| = \frac{1,875,000}{125,000} = 15$$

$$x_3 = \frac{1}{|\mathbf{A}|}|\mathbf{A}_3| = \frac{2,500,000}{125,000} = 20$$

confirming the solution to this equation system. The advantages of Cramer's rule are that it removes the need for the matrix inverse calculations and it allows us to solve for an individual x value if we do not require all the x solutions.

B5.8 Summary

This has been a challenging module. We have seen that, through the use of the matrix inverse, we can readily determine the solution (if it exists) to a set of linear equations. The inverse can be calculated using either the Gauss–Jordan elimination method or the determinants method. Although the Gauss–Jordan method is arithmetically easier when you start developing generic economic models through matrix algebra, you will also need to be able to use determinants.

Learning Check

Having read through this module you should have learned that:

- Matrix algebra can be used to find the solution to a linear model using the inverse matrix approach
- The inverse matrix can be found using the Gauss–Jordan elimination method or through the use of determinants
- A determinant is the scalar associated with a square matrix
- The Laplace expansion is used to find higher order determinants
- A minor of a matrix **A** is the determinant of a smaller square matrix after removal of one or more of its rows or columns
- Cramer's rule is a method of finding the solution to a set of simultaneous equations.

Worked Example

Here we look again at a Worked Example we used in the previous module.

A firm produces three products, A, B and C, for sale both in the domestic market and in the export market and for sale to other firms to use in their own production process. Last year domestic sales were, respectively, 50, 60 and 80. Export sales were 25, 40 and 20. Sales to other firms were 10, 20 and 30. All figures are in units of thousands. This year domestic sales are expected to increase by 5% and export sales by 10%. Sales to other firms are expected to remain the same. The firm offers the products at the same price in all three markets. Prices are currently €3, €4 and €5. Production costs for the three products are €2, €3 and €4.

In the previous module we wanted to work out the following:

(i) Profit for last year for the three products
(ii) Projected profit for this year.

Now we are also told that costs are expected to rise this year by 10%. If profit levels are to be maintained at the levels found in part (ii), what prices must the firm charge?

Solution

Let's use the following notation:

S is the sales matrix
p is the price vector

Worked Example *(Continued)*

u is the unit cost vector
v is the profit vector.

We then have:

$$\mathbf{v} = \mathbf{Sp} - \mathbf{Su}$$

or

$$\mathbf{Sp} = \mathbf{v} + \mathbf{Su}$$

giving

$$\mathbf{p} = \mathbf{S}^{-1}(\mathbf{v} + \mathbf{Su})$$

as the **p** vector that we need in order to keep profit levels at the projected values. However, we have a new **u** vector of:

$$\mathbf{u} = k\mathbf{u} = 1.1 \begin{bmatrix} 2 \\ 3 \\ 4 \end{bmatrix} = \begin{bmatrix} 2.2 \\ 3.3 \\ 4.4 \end{bmatrix}$$

and so **Su** as

$$\mathbf{c} = \mathbf{Su} = \begin{bmatrix} 52.5 & 63 & 84 \\ 27.5 & 44 & 22 \\ 10 & 20 & 30 \end{bmatrix} \begin{bmatrix} 2.2 \\ 3.3 \\ 4.4 \end{bmatrix} = \begin{bmatrix} 693 \\ 302.5 \\ 220 \end{bmatrix}$$

giving

$$\mathbf{v} + \mathbf{Su} = \begin{bmatrix} 199.5 \\ 93.5 \\ 60 \end{bmatrix} + \begin{bmatrix} 693 \\ 302.5 \\ 220 \end{bmatrix} = \begin{bmatrix} 892.5 \\ 396 \\ 280 \end{bmatrix}$$

$\mathbf{S}^{-1}$ is derived as follows:

$$\begin{bmatrix} 52.5 & 63 & 84 & 1 & 0 & 0 \\ 27.5 & 44 & 22 & 0 & 1 & 0 \\ 10 & 20 & 30 & 0 & 0 & 1 \end{bmatrix}$$

Transforming row 1 by 52.5 we next have:

$$\begin{bmatrix} 1 & 1.2 & 1.6 & 0.019048 & 0 & 0 \\ 0 & 11 & -22 & -0.523810 & 1 & 0 \\ 0 & 8 & 14 & -0.190476 & 0 & 1 \end{bmatrix}$$

then transforming row 2

$$\begin{bmatrix} 1 & 0 & 4 & 0.076190 & -0.109091 & 0 \\ 0 & 1 & -2 & -0.047619 & 0.090909 & 0 \\ 0 & 0 & 30 & 0.190476 & -0.727273 & 1 \end{bmatrix}$$

and finally row 3

$$\begin{bmatrix} 1 & 0 & 0 & 0.050794 & -0.012121 & -0.133333 \\ 0 & 1 & 0 & -0.034921 & 0.042424 & 0.066667 \\ 0 & 0 & 1 & 0.006349 & -0.024242 & 0.033333 \end{bmatrix}$$

Worked Example *(Continued)*

giving S^{-1}

$$
\begin{bmatrix}
0.050794 & -0.012120 & -0.133330 \\
-0.034920 & 0.042424 & 0.066667 \\
0.006349 & -0.024240 & 0.033333
\end{bmatrix}
$$

and then

$$
p = S^{-1}[v + Su] =
\begin{bmatrix}
0.050794 & -0.012120 & -0.133330 \\
-0.034920 & 0.042424 & 0.066667 \\
0.006349 & -0.024240 & 0.033333
\end{bmatrix}
\begin{bmatrix}
892.5 \\
396 \\
280
\end{bmatrix}
$$

$$
=
\begin{bmatrix}
3.20 \\
4.30 \\
5.40
\end{bmatrix}
$$

as the new price levels required to maintain profit levels given the cost increases and the sales increases. That is, prices should be set at €3.20, €4.30 and €5.40.

Exercises

B5.1 In the module the cofactor matrix **C** for the sales matrix **A** was given as:

$$
C =
\begin{bmatrix}
2000 & 0 & -2\,500 \\
-2500 & 5\,000 & 0 \\
0 & -37\,500 & 25\,000
\end{bmatrix}
$$

Confirm that it is correct.

B5.2 In the Worked Example we gave the inverse of the sales matrix S^{-1}. Confirm the inverse is correct by using the Gauss–Jordan method.

B5.3 For the S^{-1} confirm it is correct by finding the inverse of the **S** matrix using determinants.

B5.4 Return to the sets of equations that were given in Progress Check B2.3. Reformulate these into a matrix format and find the numerical solution using the Gauss–Jordan method. Compare these solutions with those obtained using the determinant approach.

(i) $Y = -75 + 12X$
   $Y = -100 - 6X$

(ii) $Y = 75 - 15X$
   $Y = 75 + 10X$

(iii) $Y = 100 - 5X$
   $Y = 100 - 10X$

(iv) $Y = -100 + 12X$
   $Y = -100 + 6X$

Exercises *(Continued)*

B5.5 Find the inverse of the following matrix:

$$\begin{bmatrix} 0.7 & -0.1 & 0 \\ -0.1 & 0.6 & -0.05 \\ -0.25 & -0.25 & 0.8 \end{bmatrix}$$

This solution will be required in the next module.

B5.6 For the following matrices complete the matrix arithmetic indicated (where possible):

$$A = \begin{bmatrix} 3 & 1 & 4 \\ 5 & -1 & 6 \\ 0 & 2 & 3 \end{bmatrix} \quad B = \begin{bmatrix} 7 & 2 & 3 \\ -1 & 2 & 2 \\ 5 & 9 & 1 \end{bmatrix} \quad C = \begin{bmatrix} 2 & 3 & 1 \\ 0 & 4 & 2 \\ 0 & 0 & 1 \end{bmatrix}$$

(i) $(AB)^{-1}$

(ii) $|AC|$

(iii) $|CA|$

(iv) $(CBA)^{-1}$

Appendix B5.1 Matrix inverse with Excel

Inverse of a matrix

The inverse of a matrix is obtained by using the MINVERSE function. This is illustrated in Figs B5.1 and B5.2 using the **S** matrix from the Worked Example. The matrix to be inverted is entered into the appropriate cells. The cells where the inverse will be calculated are selected. The MINVERSE function is entered together with the cells identifying the matrix to be inverted. The Ctrl Shift Enter keys are pressed at the same time to activate the MINVERSE function.

Determinants

Excel can also calculate the determinant of a matrix using the MDETERM function. This is shown in Figs B5.3 and B5.4.

	A	B	C	D	E	F
1						
2		52.5	63	84		
3	S	27.5	44	22		
4		10	20	30		
5						
6		=MINVERSE(B2:D4)				
7	S-1					
8						
9						
10						
11						
12						
13						

Figure B5.1 MINVERSE function

	A	B	C	D	E	F
1						
2		52.5	63	84		
3	S	27.5	44	22		
4		10	20	30		
5						
6		0.050794	-0.01212	-0.13333		
7	S-1	-0.03492	0.042424	0.066667		
8		0.006349	-0.02424	0.033333		
9						
10						
11						
12						
13						

Figure B5.2 The inverted matrix

B

	A	B	C	D	E	F
1						
2		52.5	63	84		
3	S	27.5	44	22		
4		10	20	30		
5						
6		=MDETERM(B2:D4)				
7						
8						
9						
10						
11						
12						
13						

Figure B5.3 The MDETERM function

	A	B	C	D	E	F
1						
2		52.5	63	84		
3	S	27.5	44	22		
4		10	20	30		
5						
6		17325				
7						
8						
9						
10						
11						
12						
13						

Figure B5.4 The determinant value

Appendix B5.2 Confirmation of the determinant method

Because of the importance of the determinant method of calculating the inverse in economic analysis that we looked at in B5.15, it's worth showing the derivation of this expression – that it is in fact true. Let's first examine a 2×2 matrix. Assume an **A** matrix such that:

$$\mathbf{A} = \begin{bmatrix} a_{11} & a_{12} \\ a_{21} & a_{22} \end{bmatrix}$$

Then **C**, the cofactors matrix, will be:

$$\mathbf{C} = \begin{bmatrix} a_{22} & -a_{21} \\ -a_{12} & a_{11} \end{bmatrix}$$

and adj **A** (which is simply **C**′) will be

$$\text{adj } \mathbf{A} = \begin{bmatrix} a_{22} & -a_{12} \\ -a_{21} & a_{11} \end{bmatrix}$$

We have already seen that:

$$|\mathbf{A}| = \begin{bmatrix} a_{11} & a_{12} \\ a_{21} & a_{22} \end{bmatrix} = a_{11}a_{22} - a_{21}a_{12}$$

and that $\mathbf{A}\mathbf{A}^{-1} = \mathbf{I}$. So, if we have:

$$\mathbf{A}^{-1} = \frac{1}{|\mathbf{A}|} \text{adj } \mathbf{A}$$

then premultiplying through by **A** gives

$$\mathbf{A}\mathbf{A}^{-1} = \frac{\mathbf{A} \text{ adj } \mathbf{A}}{|\mathbf{A}|}$$

$$= \frac{1}{|\mathbf{A}|} \begin{bmatrix} a_{11} & a_{12} \\ a_{21} & a_{22} \end{bmatrix} \begin{bmatrix} a_{22} & -a_{12} \\ -a_{21} & a_{11} \end{bmatrix}$$

which by matrix multiplication gives

$$\mathbf{A}\mathbf{A}^{-1} = \frac{1}{|\mathbf{A}|} \begin{bmatrix} a_{11}a_{22} - a_{12}a_{21} & -a_{12}a_{11} + a_{12}a_{11} \\ a_{22}a_{21} - a_{22}a_{21} & a_{21}a_{12} + a_{22}a_{11} \end{bmatrix}$$

$$= \frac{1}{|\mathbf{A}|} \begin{bmatrix} a_{11}a_{22} - a_{12}a_{21} & 0 \\ 0 & a_{11}a_{22} - a_{12}a_{21} \end{bmatrix}$$

and since earlier we saw that $|\mathbf{A}| = a_{11}a_{22} - a_{12}a_{21}$ this gives

$$\mathbf{A}\mathbf{A}^{-1} = \frac{1}{a_{11}a_{22} - a_{12}a_{21}} \begin{bmatrix} a_{11}a_{22} - a_{12}a_{21} & 0 \\ 0 & -a_{11}a_{22} - a_{12}a_{21} \end{bmatrix}$$

Remembering that the determinant of **A** is a scalar ($= a_{11}a_{22} - a_{12}a_{21}$) this gives:

$$\mathbf{A}\mathbf{A}^{-1} = \begin{bmatrix} 1 & 0 \\ 0 & 1 \end{bmatrix} = \mathbf{I}$$

which is the definition of an inverse matrix. So, for a 2×2 matrix, we've shown that Eq. B5.15 is correct. We can expand this to look at a 3×3 matrix. Now we have:

$$\mathbf{A} = \begin{bmatrix} a_{11} & a_{12} & a_{13} \\ a_{21} & a_{22} & a_{23} \\ a_{31} & a_{32} & a_{33} \end{bmatrix}$$

and

$$\mathbf{C}' = \begin{bmatrix} C_{11} & C_{21} & C_{31} \\ C_{12} & C_{22} & C_{32} \\ C_{13} & C_{23} & C_{33} \end{bmatrix}$$

Let's first work out the product of $\mathbf{AC}'$:

$$\mathbf{X} = \mathbf{AC}' = \begin{bmatrix} a_{11} & a_{12} & a_{13} \\ a_{21} & a_{22} & a_{23} \\ a_{31} & a_{32} & a_{33} \end{bmatrix} \begin{bmatrix} C_{11} & C_{21} & C_{31} \\ C_{12} & C_{22} & C_{32} \\ C_{13} & C_{23} & C_{33} \end{bmatrix}$$

Therefore x_{11}, for example, will be:

$$x_{11} = a_{11}C_{11} + a_{12}C_{12} + a_{13}C_{13}$$

or, alternatively, this can be written as

$$x_{11} = \sum a_{1j}C_{1j}, \qquad j = 1, 2, 3$$

Similarly, x_{21} will be:

$$x_{21} = a_{21}C_{11} + a_{22}C_{12} + a_{23}C_{13}$$
$$= \sum a_{2j}C_{1j}, \qquad j = 1, 2, 3$$

and the remaining elements of the resulting $\mathbf{X}$ matrix can also be expressed using summation notation as

$$\mathbf{X} = \mathbf{AC}' = \begin{bmatrix} \sum a_{1j}C_{1j} & \sum a_{1j}C_{2j} & \sum a_{1j}C_{3j} \\ \sum a_{2j}C_{1j} & \sum a_{2j}C_{2j} & \sum a_{2j}C_{3j} \\ \sum a_{3j}C_{1j} & \sum a_{3j}C_{2j} & \sum a_{3j}C_{3j} \end{bmatrix}$$

There are two aspects to note. First, the main diagonal elements represent the expansion of $|\mathbf{A}|$ that we have already used. Second, the remaining off-diagonal elements represent the expansion by alien cofactors. You will remember that one of the properties of determinants stated earlier was that such an expansion will result in a value of zero. We can therefore rewrite this product matrix as:

$$\mathbf{AC}' = \begin{bmatrix} |\mathbf{A}| & 0 & 0 \\ 0 & |\mathbf{A}| & 0 \\ 0 & 0 & |\mathbf{A}| \end{bmatrix}$$

In turn, remembering that $|\mathbf{A}|$ is a scalar, this gives:

$$\mathbf{AC}' = |\mathbf{A}| \begin{bmatrix} 1 & 0 & 0 \\ 0 & 1 & 0 \\ 0 & 0 & 1 \end{bmatrix} = |\mathbf{A}|\mathbf{I}$$

Rearranging gives:

$$\mathbf{AC}' = |\mathbf{A}|\mathbf{I}$$

$$\frac{1}{|\mathbf{A}|}\mathbf{AC}' = \mathbf{I}$$

Next, we premultiply both sides by $\mathbf{A}^{-1}$:

$$\frac{\mathbf{A}^{-1}\mathbf{AC}'}{|\mathbf{A}|} = \mathbf{A}^{-1}\mathbf{I}$$

but since $\mathbf{A}^{-1}\mathbf{A} = \mathbf{I}$ and $\mathbf{A}^{-1}\mathbf{I} = \mathbf{A}^{-1}$ we have

$$\frac{\mathbf{IC}'}{|\mathbf{A}|} = \mathbf{A}^{-1}$$

or

$$\mathbf{A}^{-1} = \frac{1}{|\mathbf{A}|}\mathbf{C}' = \frac{1}{|\mathbf{A}|} \text{ adj } \mathbf{A}$$

since $\mathbf{C}'$ is the adjoint of $\mathbf{A}$. So, again, we're able to show that Eq. B5.15 is true.

Module B6
Economic analysis with matrix algebra

In the previous two modules we have put a lot of hard work into understanding matrix algebra. In this module we examine a number of common and important economic models and show how, through the use of matrix methods, we can deduce a number of important economic conclusions from the relationships. The application of matrix algebra to theoretical economic models is a particularly important area in mathematical economics. While economists frequently wish to determine the solution to a numerical problem, they are often more interested in the underlying principles behind such a solution: what conditions must exist for a solution to be economically valid and what the implications of the solution are. We begin by returning to two simple microeconomic models that we introduced in Module B2.

Learning Objectives

By the end of this module you should be able to:

- Use matrix algebra to represent and solve market models
- Use matrix algebra to represent and solve national income models.

B6.1 A partial equilibrium market model

In Module B2 we developed a simple partial equilibrium market model which we present again as:

$$Q_d = Q_s \tag{B6.1}$$

$$Q_d = a_1 + b_1 P \tag{B6.2}$$

$$Q_s = a_2 + b_2 P \tag{B6.3}$$

where a_1, a_2, b_1 and b_2 are appropriate parameters for the linear demand and supply equations, and we restrict their values to those that are sensible in an economic context. As we have seen, it is useful to be able to derive the general implications from such a model, and we shall use the appropriate matrix algebra techniques to determine the appropriate equilibrium and examine its inherent implications. We can rearrange the model into a form more convenient for matrix representation. Collecting variables onto the left-hand side and single parameters (the exogenous elements of the model) onto the right, we can rewrite the model as:

$$1Q_d - 1Q_s + 0P = 0 \tag{B6.4}$$

$$1Q_d + 0Q_s - b_1 P = a_1 \tag{B6.5}$$

$$0Q_d + 1Q_s - b_2 P = a_2 \tag{B6.6}$$

This can be written in the standard matrix format of $\mathbf{Ax} = \mathbf{b}$ as:

$$\begin{bmatrix} 1 & -1 & 0 \\ 1 & 0 & -b_1 \\ 0 & 1 & -b_2 \end{bmatrix} \begin{bmatrix} Q_d \\ Q_s \\ P \end{bmatrix} = \begin{bmatrix} 0 \\ a_1 \\ a_2 \end{bmatrix} \tag{B6.7}$$

and we require a solution to the $\mathbf{x}$ vector (that is, we require the equilibrium values for Q_d, Q_s and P). The solution for the $\mathbf{x}$ vector is then given by:

$$\mathbf{x} = \mathbf{A}^{-1}\mathbf{b}$$

and, since we saw in Module B5 that $\mathbf{A}^{-1} = (1/|\mathbf{A}|)\text{adj}\,\mathbf{A}$, we can write

$$\mathbf{x} = \frac{1}{|\mathbf{A}|}\text{adj}\,\mathbf{Ab} \tag{B6.8}$$

So the solution to the model can be determined using the inverse to the $\mathbf{A}$ matrix. Before we find such an inverse, we must first test that a unique solution exists for this equation system. You will remember from the previous chapter that we stated that such a system will have a unique solution where $|\mathbf{A}| \neq 0$. The determinant of the $\mathbf{A}$ matrix in our system is readily found.

Progress Check B6.1

Find the determinant of $\mathbf{A}$ by expanding the third row.

We have a 3×3 matrix so we can expand, say, the first column:

$$|\mathbf{A}| = 1 \begin{vmatrix} 0 & -b_1 \\ 1 & -b_2 \end{vmatrix} - 1 \begin{vmatrix} -1 & 0 \\ 1 & -b_2 \end{vmatrix} + 0 \begin{vmatrix} -1 & 0 \\ 1 & -b_2 \end{vmatrix}$$

$$= 1[0 - (-b_1)] - 1(b_2 - 0) + 0$$

$$= b_1 - b_2$$

So, if this equation system has a unique solution then:

$$|\mathbf{A}| = b_1 - b_2 \neq 0$$

Given that b_1 and b_2 are the slopes of the demand and supply equations respectively, this implies that $b_1 \neq b_2$ and that the two equations cannot have the same slope if there is to be a unique solution. Since we would expect the slope of the demand equation to be positive and that of the supply equation to be negative, this requirement will normally be satisfied.

To find $\mathbf{A}^{-1}$ we now require adj $\mathbf{A}$. This can be obtained using the cofactor matrix that we introduced in Section B5.5. First we obtain the relevant minors of $\mathbf{A}$:

$$\mathbf{A} = \begin{bmatrix} 1 & -1 & 0 \\ 1 & 0 & -b_1 \\ 0 & 1 & -b_2 \end{bmatrix}$$

$$\mathbf{M} = \begin{bmatrix} \begin{vmatrix} 0 & -b_1 \\ 1 & -b_2 \end{vmatrix} & \begin{vmatrix} 1 & -b_1 \\ 0 & -b_2 \end{vmatrix} & \begin{vmatrix} 1 & 0 \\ 0 & 1 \end{vmatrix} \\[2ex] \begin{vmatrix} -1 & 0 \\ 1 & -b_2 \end{vmatrix} & \begin{vmatrix} 1 & 0 \\ 0 & -b_2 \end{vmatrix} & \begin{vmatrix} 1 & -1 \\ 0 & 1 \end{vmatrix} \\[2ex] \begin{vmatrix} -1 & 0 \\ 0 & -b_1 \end{vmatrix} & \begin{vmatrix} 1 & 0 \\ 1 & -b_1 \end{vmatrix} & \begin{vmatrix} 1 & -1 \\ 1 & 0 \end{vmatrix} \end{bmatrix}$$

> Each minor is obtained by crossing out the relevant row and column of **A** Check each one to help you follow what's going on

The cofactor matrix, **C**, is then obtained by using the +/− pattern from Eq. B5.18 in Module B5, which will give a pattern:

$$\begin{bmatrix} + & - & + \\ - & + & - \\ + & - & + \end{bmatrix}$$

Applying this to the matrix of minors, **M**, we get the cofactor matrix, **C**:

$$\mathbf{C} = \begin{bmatrix} +\begin{vmatrix} 0 & -b_1 \\ 1 & -b_2 \end{vmatrix} & -\begin{vmatrix} 1 & -b_1 \\ 0 & -b_2 \end{vmatrix} & +\begin{vmatrix} 1 & 0 \\ 0 & 1 \end{vmatrix} \\[2ex] -\begin{vmatrix} -1 & 0 \\ 1 & -b_2 \end{vmatrix} & +\begin{vmatrix} 1 & 0 \\ 0 & -b_2 \end{vmatrix} & -\begin{vmatrix} 1 & -1 \\ 0 & 1 \end{vmatrix} \\[2ex] +\begin{vmatrix} -1 & 0 \\ 0 & -b_1 \end{vmatrix} & -\begin{vmatrix} 1 & 0 \\ 1 & -b_1 \end{vmatrix} & +\begin{vmatrix} 1 & -1 \\ 1 & 0 \end{vmatrix} \end{bmatrix}$$

We can simplify **C** by working out each of the 2 × 2 determinants to give:

$$\mathbf{C} = \begin{bmatrix} b_1 & b_2 & 1 \\ -b_2 & -b_2 & -1 \\ b_1 & b_1 & 1 \end{bmatrix}$$

Remembering that the transpose of **C** is known as the adjoint of **A**, we have:

$$\mathbf{C}' = \text{adj } \mathbf{A} = \begin{bmatrix} b_1 & -b_2 & b_1 \\ b_2 & -b_2 & b_1 \\ 1 & -1 & 1 \end{bmatrix}$$

In Eq. B6.8 we said that the general equilibrium solution is given by:

$$\mathbf{x} = \frac{1}{|\mathbf{A}|}\text{adj } \mathbf{A}\mathbf{b}$$

So, substituting the expressions we have just worked out, this gives:

$$\begin{bmatrix} Q_d \\ Q_s \\ P \end{bmatrix} = \frac{1}{b_1 - b_2}\begin{bmatrix} b_1 & -b_2 & b_1 \\ b_2 & -b_2 & b_1 \\ 1 & -1 & 1 \end{bmatrix}\begin{bmatrix} 0 \\ a_1 \\ a_2 \end{bmatrix}$$

If we now multiply through by $1/b_1 - b_2$ we get:

$$\begin{bmatrix} Q_d \\ Q_s \\ P \end{bmatrix} = \begin{bmatrix} \dfrac{b_1}{b_1 - b_2} & \dfrac{-b_2}{b_1 - b_2} & \dfrac{b_1}{b_1 - b_2} \\[2ex] \dfrac{b_2}{b_1 - b_2} & \dfrac{-b_2}{b_1 - b_2} & \dfrac{b_1}{b_1 - b_2} \\[2ex] \dfrac{1}{b_1 - b_2} & \dfrac{-1}{b_1 - b_2} & \dfrac{1}{b_1 - b_2} \end{bmatrix}\begin{bmatrix} 0 \\ a_1 \\ a_2 \end{bmatrix}$$

which, when we multiply out, gives

$$Q_d = \frac{-a_1 b_2}{b_1 - b_2} + \frac{a_2 b_1}{b_1 - b_2} \tag{B6.9}$$

$$Q_s = \frac{-a_1 b_2}{b_1 - b_2} - \frac{a_2 b_1}{b_1 - b_2} \tag{B6.10}$$

$$P = \frac{-a_1}{b_1 - b_2} + \frac{a_2}{b_1 - b_2} \tag{B6.11}$$

These are the equilibrium values for our economic model.

While these solutions are perfectly adequate, it will be helpful to take them one stage further. Let's multiply each expression through by -1 and rearrange slightly (and you are strongly encouraged to do this yourself to confirm the results). We then get:

$$Q_d = \frac{a_2 b_1 - a_2 b_1}{b_2 - b_1} \tag{B6.12}$$

$$Q_s = \frac{a_2 b_1 - a_2 b_1}{b_2 - b_1} \tag{B6.13}$$

$$P = \frac{a_1 - a_2}{b_2 - b_1} \tag{B6.14}$$

It can now be seen that at the equilibrium solution Q_d and Q_s take exactly the same value. Using the determinant, we saw earlier that there will be a unique solution to this system, providing the two slopes are not the same. This does not guarantee, however, that the solution we obtain will be a meaningful one in an economic context. There is nothing in the model, for example, to prevent negative or zero values for P and Q. To make sense in an economic context both P and Q_d/Q_s must be greater than zero. Let's consider the values for the four parameters in the equations. For P this implies that both the numerator $(a_1 - a_2)$ and the denominator $(b_2 - b_1)$ take positive values and hence the ratio of these two must also result in a positive number, that is, at equilibrium $P > 0$. For Q a similar logic applies. The denominator is positive so in order for $Q > 0$ the numerator must be positive also; that is, $a_1 b_2 - a_2 b_1 > 0$ and therefore $a_1 b_2 > a_2 b_1$ in order for Q to take an economically meaningful value. You may also wish to compare the results we have obtained through the application of matrix algebra with those we obtained in Module B2 through the use of normal algebra. You will see that they are identical.

Progress Check B6.2

Return to the equation systems shown in Progress Check B1.3. Assuming that each system represents a market model, confirm the solutions using matrix algebra.

(i) $Y = 100 - 18X$
     $Y = -75 + 17X$

(ii) $Y = 100 - 10X$
      $Y = -50 + 5X$

(iii) $Y = -20 + 3X$
       $Y = 200 - 5X$

(iv) $Y = -60 + 3X$
      $Y = 50 - 2X$

B6.2 The effect of an excise tax on market equilibrium

In Module B2 we saw the effect that the imposition of an excise tax would have on the market equilibrium under competitive market conditions, and we compared that equilibrium with the one without the imposition of the tax. We saw that such a tax – where a fixed tax is imposed per unit of the product sold – would raise the equilibrium price and reduce the equilibrium quantity. We will now look at this model through the use of matrix algebra. Let's show the tax levied per unit sold as t and assume it is exogenous to the model. Then we have:

$$Q_d = Q_s$$
$$Q_d = a_1 + b_1 P$$
$$Q_s = a_2 + b_2 (P - t) \tag{B6.15}$$

again with all the parameters restricted to taking the usual values. The supply equation can be rewritten in a more convenient form by collecting terms together as:

$$Q_s = a_2 + b_2 (P - t)$$
$$= a_2 + b_2 P - b_2 t$$
$$= (a_2 - b_2 t) + b_2 P \tag{B6.16}$$

Comparison with the market model developed in the previous section (Eq. B6.3) reveals that the new supply equation has the same slope as before (b_2) but with a different intercept ($a_2 - b_2 t$). Given that $b_2 t > 0$ in terms of our model specification, then the second supply function will have a larger negative intercept than the first and will lie parallel and below the original on a graph. (Of course, this already allows us to predict that, with a given and fixed demand equation, the imposition of such an excise tax will change the equilibrium position to one where Q is lower and P higher than before.) What, however, are the general implications for equilibrium? Again developing the methods of the previous section, the answer to such a question is straightforward. We can rewrite the tax model as:

$$Q_d - Q_s = 0$$
$$Q_d - b_1 P = a_1$$
$$Q_s - b_2 P = a_2 - b_2 t \tag{B6.17}$$

and in matrix form

$$\mathbf{Ax = b}$$

where

$$\begin{bmatrix} 1 & -1 & 0 \\ 1 & 0 & -b_1 \\ 0 & 1 & -b_2 \end{bmatrix} \begin{bmatrix} Q_d \\ Q_s \\ P \end{bmatrix} = \begin{bmatrix} 0 \\ a_1 \\ a_2 - b_2 t \end{bmatrix} \tag{B6.18}$$

Comparison of this matrix formulation with that of the previous section (Eq. B6.7) shows that the only difference lies in the one cell of the **b** vector, reflecting the tax element, and this immediately illustrates one of the benefits of using matrix algebra. We do not have to rework the new model in full to determine the relevant basic principles and equilibrium conditions. We simply have to make relatively minor changes in the matrix structure. The general solution to the model, therefore, will be:

$$\mathbf{x} = \mathbf{A}^{-1}\mathbf{b}$$

where $\mathbf{A}^{-1}$ is exactly as before. So, to find the solution, we have:

$$
\begin{bmatrix} Q_d \\ Q_s \\ P \end{bmatrix} =
\begin{bmatrix}
\dfrac{b_1}{b_1 - b_2} & \dfrac{-b_2}{b_1 - b_2} & \dfrac{b_1}{b_1 - b_2} \\
\dfrac{b_2}{b_1 - b_2} & \dfrac{-b_2}{-b_2} & \dfrac{b_1}{b_1} \\
\dfrac{1}{b_1 - b_2} & \dfrac{1}{-1} & \dfrac{1}{b_1 - b_2}
\end{bmatrix}
\begin{bmatrix} 0 \\ a_1 \\ a_2 - b_2 t \end{bmatrix}
$$

giving

$$Q_d = Q_s = \frac{-a_1 b_2 + b_1 a_2 - b_1 b_2 t}{b_1 - b_2} \tag{B6.19}$$

$$P = \frac{-a_1 + a_2 - b_2 t}{b_1 - b_2} \tag{B6.20}$$

Once again we multiply through by -1 to get:

$$Q_d = Q_s = \frac{a_1 b_2 - b_1 a_2 + b_1 b_2 t}{b_2 - b_1} = \frac{a_1 b_2 - b_1 a_2}{b_2 - b_1} + \frac{b_1 b_2 t}{b_2 - b_1} \tag{B6.21}$$

$$P = \frac{a_1 - a_2 + b_2 t}{b_2 - b_1} = \frac{a_1 - a_2}{b_2 - b_1} + \frac{b_2 t}{b_2 - b_1} \tag{B6.22}$$

Let's look at the equilibrium position, and its implications, compared with the market model used above. It is apparent, examining P first, that the equilibrium price is as before but with an extra element involved:

$$\frac{b_2 t}{b_2 - b_1}$$

thanks to the imposition of the excise tax. Since all the elements of this expression are greater than zero (b_1 is the slope of the demand equation and will therefore be negative, but since it has a negative sign in the expression above it will then become positive), the value of this expression will be positive also. This implies that the equilibrium price after the imposition of an excise tax will always be higher than the equilibrium price without the tax. It is also apparent from this expression that since $t < 1$ then:

$$\frac{b_2 t}{b_2 - b_1} < t$$

so that the increase in the equilibrium price brought about by the excise tax will always be less than the full amount of the tax. In other words, part of the tax will be paid by the consumer of the product and part by the supplier, the exact proportions depending on the numerical b_1 and b_2 parameter values. Turning to the equilibrium quantity, it is evident that the difference between the new equilibrium and that prevailing before the imposition of the tax is given by:

$$\frac{b_1 b_2 t}{b_2 - b_1}$$

It is apparent that the denominator will be positive (thanks to the usual restrictions on the model parameters) while the numerator will be negative since b_1 is negative. This implies that the new equilibrium quantity must always be less than that prevailing before the excise tax. You may also realize that the results we have just obtained are the same as those in Section B2.3 for this model.

Progress Check B6.3

Return to Exercise B2.1. Work through the model we have developed in this section by substituting the appropriate numerical parameters, and thereby find the solution:

$$Q_d = 500 - 9P$$
$$Q_s = -100 + 6P$$

B6.3 A basic national income model

Let's now look at a macroeconomic model and return to the simplest national income model that we examined in Module B3. There we had a two-equation system such that:

$$Y = C + I \qquad\qquad\qquad\qquad \text{(B6.23)}$$
$$C = a + bY \qquad\qquad\qquad\qquad \text{(B6.24)}$$

where

Y = income
C = consumption
I = investment.

The second equation represents a linear consumption function and we would additionally specify that $0 < b < 1$ and $a > 0$. The Y and C variables are endogenous – that is, they are determined from within the model – while I is exogenous: it is determined independently of this model. If we rewrite the model in a form suitable for matrix representation by collecting endogenous and exogenous elements together, we have:

$$Y - C = I$$
$$-bY + C = a$$

which can be written as

$$\mathbf{Ax = b}$$

where

$$\begin{bmatrix} 1 & -1 \\ -b & 1 \end{bmatrix} \begin{bmatrix} Y \\ C \end{bmatrix} = \begin{bmatrix} I \\ a \end{bmatrix} \qquad\qquad \text{(B6.25)}$$

and the solution to the model – the equilibrium values for Y and C – will be given by

$$\mathbf{x = A^{-1}b}$$

We first require $|\mathbf{A}|$ to establish the conditions necessary for a unique solution. We have:

$$|\mathbf{A}| = 1 - b \neq 0$$

which confirms that b (the marginal propensity to consume) cannot equal 1 if there is to be a solution to the model. To determine $\mathbf{A^{-1}}$ we now require adj $\mathbf{A}$. Taking the minors of $\mathbf{A}$ we have:

$$\mathbf{M} = \begin{bmatrix} 1 & -b \\ -1 & 1 \end{bmatrix}$$

The cofactors are then found by using the $+/-$ pattern from Eq. B5.10 in Module B5, which will give a pattern:

$$\begin{bmatrix} + & - \\ - & + \end{bmatrix}$$

to give

$$C = \begin{bmatrix} 1 & b \\ 1 & 1 \end{bmatrix} \quad \text{and} \quad C' = \begin{bmatrix} 1 & 1 \\ b & 1 \end{bmatrix}$$

giving

$$A^{-1} = \frac{1}{1-b} \begin{bmatrix} 1 & 1 \\ b & 1 \end{bmatrix} = \begin{bmatrix} \dfrac{1}{1-b} & \dfrac{1}{1-b} \\ \dfrac{b}{1-b} & \dfrac{1}{1-b} \end{bmatrix}$$

and so giving a solution of

$$x = A^{-1}b = \begin{bmatrix} \dfrac{1}{1-b} & \dfrac{1}{1-b} \\ \dfrac{b}{1-b} & \dfrac{1}{1-b} \end{bmatrix} \begin{bmatrix} I \\ a \end{bmatrix}$$

$$= \begin{bmatrix} \dfrac{I}{1-b} + \dfrac{a}{1-b} \\ \dfrac{Ib}{1-b} + \dfrac{a}{1-b} \end{bmatrix} = \begin{bmatrix} \dfrac{I+a}{1-b} \\ \dfrac{a+bI}{1-b} \end{bmatrix} = \begin{bmatrix} Y \\ C \end{bmatrix} \qquad \text{(B6.26)}$$

The solution to the model, therefore, is readily determined from the matrix expression above giving the equilibrium values for Y and for C. What is more revealing, however, are the contents of A^{-1}. To show why, let's consider the impact of a change in I, investment. Assume that the level of investment changes from its current level, I, to $I + \Delta I$, where Δ is the usual symbol used in economics to indicate a change in the variable. From Eq. B6.26 we see that the new value of Y will be given by:

$$Y = \frac{(I + \Delta I) + a}{1-b}$$

So, as a result of a change in I from I to $I + \Delta I$, the change in Y will be:

$$\Delta Y = \frac{(I + \Delta I) + a}{1-b} - \frac{I + a}{1-b}$$

and cancelling terms we get

$$\Delta Y = \frac{\Delta I}{1-b}$$

or

$$\Delta Y = \frac{1}{1-b} \Delta I$$

which, on inspection, is the element of the A^{-1} matrix corresponding to the I and Y combination. So this expression is a multiplier showing the effect a change in investment will have on equilibrium national income.

Progress Check B6.4

Using the method immediately above, show the change in C from a change in I.

Following the same process, we have $I + \Delta I$ as the new level of investment. ΔC will be given by:

$$\Delta C = \frac{a + b(I + \Delta I)}{1-b} - \frac{a + bI}{1-b}$$

and cancelling gives

$$\Delta C = \frac{b\Delta I}{1-b}$$

or

$$\Delta C = \frac{b}{1-b}\Delta I$$

which again on inspection is the element of the $\mathbf{A}^{-1}$ matrix corresponding to the I and C combination. So this expression is a multiplier showing the effect a change in investment will have on equilibrium consumption. It is apparent that in $\mathbf{A}^{-1}$ we have the respective multipliers for the model that we originally derived using ordinary algebra in Module B3. The inverse neatly summarizes these impact multipliers in an obvious way. We have:

$$\begin{bmatrix} Y \\ C \end{bmatrix} = \begin{bmatrix} \dfrac{1}{1-b} & \dfrac{1}{1-b} \\ \dfrac{b}{1-b} & \dfrac{1}{1-b} \end{bmatrix} \begin{bmatrix} I \\ a \end{bmatrix} \tag{B6.27}$$

We can show this as:

	I	a
Y	Multiplier for Y given a change in I	Multiplier for Y given a change in a
C	Multiplier for C given a change in I	Multiplier for C given a change in a

(B6.28)

So, the multiplier impact of a change in I on the equilibrium level of income, Y, will be given by the corresponding cell of the $\mathbf{A}^{-1}$ matrix – here $1/(1-b)$ – and similarly for any other impact we wish to assess. The usefulness of this approach is further evidenced if we consider a slightly more developed national income model.

B6.4 A national income model with government activity

Let us consider an expanded model with government activity and government taxation:

$$Y = C + I + G \tag{B6.29}$$

$$C = a + bY_\mathrm{d} \tag{B6.30}$$

$$T = tY \tag{B6.31}$$

$$Y_\mathrm{d} = Y - T \tag{B6.32}$$

with

$$a > 0$$

$$0 < b < 1$$

$$0 < t < 1$$

and G representing government spending in the economy, t the rate of tax imposed on income and T the total tax collected by the government. Y_d is disposable income, as usual. I and G exogenously determined. Rewriting this, we have:

$$Y = C + I + G$$
$$Ca + b(Y - T) \qquad \text{(B6.33)}$$
$$T = tY$$

and in matrix form

$$\mathbf{Ax} = \mathbf{b}$$

$$\begin{bmatrix} 1 & -1 & 0 \\ -b & 1 & b \\ -t & 0 & 1 \end{bmatrix} \begin{bmatrix} Y \\ C \\ T \end{bmatrix} = \begin{bmatrix} I+G \\ a \\ 0 \end{bmatrix} \qquad \text{(B6.34)}$$

Before finding the solution to the model using the $\mathbf{A}$ inverse we need to test for the conditions necessary for a unique solution. Finding $|\mathbf{A}|$ by expanding the first row, we have:

$$|\mathbf{A}| = 1 \begin{vmatrix} 1 & b \\ 0 & 1 \end{vmatrix} + 1 \begin{vmatrix} -b & b \\ -t & 1 \end{vmatrix}$$

$$= 1 + (-b) + bt = 1 - b + bt$$

Therefore, for a unique solution to exist, $1 - b + bt \neq 0$. This is the same as:

$$1 \neq b - bt$$
$$1 \neq b(1 - t)$$

and, by definition of the model parameters, $b(1 - t)$ cannot equal 1 since both b and t are positive and less than 1. We now proceed to find the inverse of the $\mathbf{A}$ matrix. We have:

$$\mathbf{C} = \begin{bmatrix} \begin{vmatrix} 1 & b \\ 0 & 1 \end{vmatrix} & -\begin{vmatrix} -b & b \\ -t & 1 \end{vmatrix} & \begin{vmatrix} -b & 1 \\ -t & 0 \end{vmatrix} \\ -\begin{vmatrix} -1 & 0 \\ 0 & 1 \end{vmatrix} & \begin{vmatrix} 1 & 0 \\ -t & 1 \end{vmatrix} & -\begin{vmatrix} 1 & -1 \\ -t & 0 \end{vmatrix} \\ \begin{vmatrix} -1 & 0 \\ 1 & b \end{vmatrix} & -\begin{vmatrix} 1 & 0 \\ -b & b \end{vmatrix} & \begin{vmatrix} 1 & -1 \\ -b & 1 \end{vmatrix} \end{bmatrix}$$

giving

$$\mathbf{C} = \begin{bmatrix} 1 & b - bt & t \\ 1 & 1 & t \\ -b & -b & 1 - b \end{bmatrix}$$

$$\mathbf{C}' = \begin{bmatrix} 1 & 1 & -b \\ b - bt & 1 & -b \\ t & t & 1 - b \end{bmatrix}$$

which in turn gives $\mathbf{A}^{-1}$ as

$$\mathbf{A}^{-1} = \frac{1}{1 - b(1 - t)} \begin{bmatrix} 1 & 1 & -b \\ b - bt & 1 & -b \\ t & t & 1 - b \end{bmatrix}$$

$$
=
\begin{bmatrix}
\dfrac{1}{1-b(1-t)} & \dfrac{1}{1-b(1-t)} & \dfrac{-b}{1-b(1-t)} \\[2ex]
\dfrac{b-bt}{1-b(1-t)} & \dfrac{1}{1-b(1-t)} & \dfrac{-b}{1-b(1-t)} \\[2ex]
\dfrac{t}{1-b(1-t)1} & \dfrac{t}{-b(1-t)} & \dfrac{1-b}{1-b(1-t)}
\end{bmatrix}
\tag{B6.35}
$$

At this stage, of course, we could as usual derive the expressions for the equilibrium values for Y, C and T. Our interest, however, is rather in the inverse matrix and the multiplier expressions it contains. As a general statement it becomes clear, if we consider both this model and the previous national income model, that the inverse matrix coefficients are the multiplier coefficients linking the endogenous to the exogenous variables. If we show the inverse coefficients as α, then a particular coefficient, α_{ij}, links the ith endogenous variable with the jth exogenous variable in the model. So $(b-bt)/[1-b(1-t)]$, for example in Eq. B6.35, links Y with $(I+G)$. In general we would have for a three-equation model:

$$
\begin{bmatrix}
y_1 \\
y_2 \\
y_3
\end{bmatrix}
=
\begin{bmatrix}
\alpha_{11} & \alpha_{12} & \alpha_{13} \\
\alpha_{21} & \alpha_{22} & \alpha_{23} \\
\alpha_{31} & \alpha_{32} & \alpha_{33}
\end{bmatrix}
\begin{bmatrix}
x_1 \\
x_2 \\
x_3
\end{bmatrix}
\tag{B6.36}
$$

where x represents the exogenous variables in the model, y the endogenous, and the α matrix shows the multiplier coefficients linking each x to each y. It should be apparent that such an approach to multiplier analysis is readily extended to any sized model, given the two-dimensional nature of the inverse **A** matrix (which represents the multiplier coefficients).

Progress Check B6.5

Determine the appropriate expressions for the equilibrium values for Y, C and T. Compare these with those we derived in Module B3.

B6.5 Summary

In this module we've examined the area of matrix algebra and its potential application in the study of mathematical economics. In particular, in this module we have seen how matrix algebra can be used to examine the fundamental relationships inherent in a number of theoretical economic models, and we've been able to deduce the important implications of these models. The use of matrix methods allows the ready identification of economic multipliers and thereby the policy implications arising from the solution of a numerical model can be determined.

Learning Check

Having read this module you should have learned that:

- Matrix algebra allows us to analyses theoretical economic models as well as those with specific numerical parameters
- We can obtain the generic equilibrium conditions for a variety of market models.

Learning Check   *(Continued)*

- We can obtain the generic equilibrium conditions for a variety of national income models
- We can determine the generic multiplier effects of national income models.

Worked Example

We have been asked to examine a national income model that includes a financial and monetary sector and to assess the impact of changes in the money supply on national income equilibrium. We have a model where:

$$Y = C + I$$
$$C = a + bY$$

as usual, but also where

$$I = c + dr$$

showing that the level of investment in the economy is a function of r, the rate of interest. We place the usual restrictions on the individual parameters such that:

$$a > 0$$
$$0 < b < 1$$
$$c > 0$$
$$d < 0$$

For the investment function, this comprises a fixed level of investment, c, and a variable investment which is inversely linked to the rate of interest – the higher the rate of interest the lower the level of investment, other things being equal. There is also a monetary sector in the model:

$$M_s = m$$
$$M_d = m_1 + m_2 r + m_3 Y$$

M_s is the money supply which is assumed to be exogenous to the model. M_d is the demand for money in the economy linked to both the rate of interest and the level of national income. We place sensible restrictions on the parameters such that:

$$m_1 > 0$$
$$m_2 < 0$$
$$m_3 > 0$$
$$m > m_1$$

So the demand for money, M_d, is inversely linked to the rate of interest, but positively linked to the level of income. The autonomous demand for money, m_1, is less than the fixed supply.

We want to derive the equilibrium expressions for Y and r. The Finance Minister has also asked us to assess the effect of an increase in M_s on the equilibrium values of Y and r.

are used in the service sector to help it produce its own output. In short, some of the production industry's *output* is used as an *input* in other industries. On the other hand, some of the output of the production sector will be used directly by the final consumer. Cars produced by the *P* industry, for example, will be bought and used by the individual consumer. If we now turn to consider the other side of the production process – *inputs* as opposed to outputs – it is clear that the production industry, *P*, will require two broad categories of inputs. These will comprise:

1 Inputs from other industries

2 Inputs of primary factors of production (typically shown as land, labour and capital).

In this way the various sectors of an economy can be linked in terms of their inputs and outputs. Let's now consider the numerical example shown in Table B7.1.

Table B7.1 Input–output table (in £ billions)

Inputs	A	P	S	C	I	G	X	Total
				Outputs				
A	30	30	0	30	0	0	10	100
P	10	120	25	70	30	25	20	300
S	25	75	100	100	70	60	70	500
M	10	15	50	50	25	0	0	150
L	10	30	175	0	0	15	0	230
K	15	30	150	0	0	0	0	195
Total	100	300	500	250	125	100	100	1475

Key:

A = Agriculture
P = Production
S = Services
C = Private Consumption
I = Investment
G = Consumption by Government
X = Exports of goods and services
M = Imports of goods and services
L = Labour (measured in terms of wages and salaries)
K = Capital (measured in terms of profit)

You should make sure that you fully understand the structure and information content of the table before proceeding. The output destinations are shown at the top of the table. Let's take Agriculture, *A*, as an example. The total output of this sector is £100 billion.

Inputs	A	P	S	C	I	G	X	Total
				Outputs				
A	30	30	0	30	0	0	10	100

Of this £100 billion of output from Agriculture:

- £30 billion is used by the sector itself, e.g. farmers growing barley to feed to cattle $(A - A)$
- £30 billion is used by the Production sector, e.g. meat sold to food companies to turn into burgers $(A - P)$
- zero is used by the Services sector $(A - S)$
- £30 billion goes for private Consumption – people buying food $(A - C)$
- zero for Investment $(A - I)$
- zero for Government $(A - G)$
- £10 billion goes for Export $(A - X)$.

In terms of national income accounting, this *output* of £100 billion must be matched exactly by *inputs* of £100 billion. These are shown down the columns of the table. Using Agriculture as our example again, this sector uses £100 billion of inputs in the following way:

- £30 billion from Agriculture itself, as we have already seen $(A - A)$
- £10 billion from Production – tractors, for example $(P - A)$
- £25 billion from Services – banking services, for example $(S - A)$
- £10 billion of Imports $(M - A)$
- £10 billion of Labour – people working in the agriculture sector and being paid wages $(L - A)$
- £15 billion of Capital $(K - A)$.

We can examine the input–output pattern of the other sectors in exactly the same way. There are two important points to note about such an input–output table at this stage:

1 Although our example is a simplified representation, the input–output structure can easily be expanded into a more realistic, and larger, model. We can introduce additional industry sectors, we can subdivide the final demand categories, we can subdivide the primary factors of production. The basic structure of our simple model, however, will remain the same no matter how large the table becomes and is, therefore, eminently suitable for manipulation through matrix algebra.

2 The table shows that there is also a linkage between the primary factors of production and final demand. In our example, final demand consumers also require imports and labour.

B7.2 Input–output coefficients

The next stage in the development of a suitable model is to transform the data in Table B7.1 into a set of *input–output coefficients*. Our interest lies primarily in the links between the various sectors of the economy, and these can best be expressed in proportionate terms rather than in absolute terms as currently shown in Table B7.1. This can be achieved by showing, for a particular sector, the proportion of total inputs that came from each sector of economic activity. In the case of agriculture, for example, we can calculate the proportion of the total required from agriculture, production, services,

Table B7.2 Input–output table: input–output coefficients

			Outputs				
Inputs	**A**	**P**	**S**	**C**	**I**	**G**	**X**
A	0.30	0.10	0.00	0.12	0	0	0.10
P	0.10	0.40	0.05	0.28	0.24	0.25	0.20
S	0.25	0.25	0.20	0.40	0.56	0.60	0.70
M	0.10	0.05	0.10	0.20	0.20	0	0
L	0.10	0.10	0.35	0	0	0.15	0
K	0.15	0.10	0.30	0	0	0	0
Total	1.00	1.00	1.00	1.00	1.00	1.00	1.00

The coefficients are calculated from Table B7.1

imports, labour and capital. For the SA coefficient, this is the input from S, 25, divided by the total output for A at 100. These proportions – referred to as the *input–output coefficients* – are shown in Table B7.2.

For each of our three industry sectors (A, P, S), Table B7.2 effectively shows the input requirements for one unit of output of a particular sector. So, for example, for each unit of output from the production sector, P, a number of different inputs are required: 0.1 units of agriculture, 0.4 units of production, 0.25 units of services, 0.05 units of imports, 0.1 units of labour and 0.1 units of capital. Note that each column of input–output coefficients totals to 1 – we must show total inputs for each sector. We are now in a position to develop a matrix representation of the basic input–output model. First let us define vector $\mathbf{t}$ as the total outputs of the industry sectors. From Table B7.1 we have:

$$\mathbf{t} = \begin{bmatrix} t_1 \\ t_2 \\ t_3 \end{bmatrix} = \begin{bmatrix} 100 \\ 300 \\ 500 \end{bmatrix}$$

Let us show $\mathbf{f}$ as a vector of final demand for the outputs of the industry sectors. In our model this would comprise the total of $C + I + G + X$ to give:

$$\mathbf{f} = \begin{bmatrix} f_1 \\ f_2 \\ f_3 \end{bmatrix} = \begin{bmatrix} 40 \\ 145 \\ 300 \end{bmatrix}$$

Similarly, we define $\mathbf{y}$ as the total demand for primary factors of production, $\mathbf{h}$ as the vector of primary factors of production required by final users and $\mathbf{g}$ as the vector of final demand totals:

$$\mathbf{y} = \begin{bmatrix} y_1 \\ y_2 \\ y_3 \end{bmatrix} = \begin{bmatrix} 150 \\ 230 \\ 195 \end{bmatrix} \qquad \mathbf{h} = \begin{bmatrix} h_1 \\ h_2 \\ h_3 \end{bmatrix} = \begin{bmatrix} 75 \\ 15 \\ 0 \end{bmatrix}$$

and

$$\mathbf{g}' = \begin{bmatrix} 250 & 125 & 100 & 100 \end{bmatrix}$$

Turning now to Table B7.2, which shows the input–output coefficients, we define four matrices.

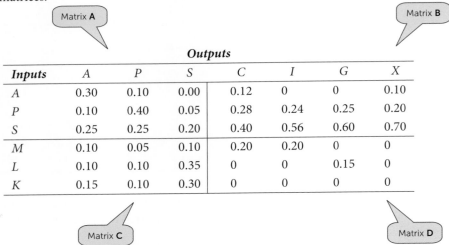

				Outputs			
Inputs	*A*	*P*	*S*	*C*	*I*	*G*	*X*
A	0.30	0.10	0.00	0.12	0	0	0.10
P	0.10	0.40	0.05	0.28	0.24	0.25	0.20
S	0.25	0.25	0.20	0.40	0.56	0.60	0.70
M	0.10	0.05	0.10	0.20	0.20	0	0
L	0.10	0.10	0.35	0	0	0.15	0
K	0.15	0.10	0.30	0	0	0	0

A is a matrix of the interindustry coefficients, **B** a matrix of the industry/final demand coefficients, **C** a matrix of the industry/factors of production coefficients and **D** a matrix of the factors of production/final demand coefficients. From Table B7.2 this gives:

$$\mathbf{A} = \begin{bmatrix} 0.30 & 0.10 & 0.00 \\ 0.10 & 0.40 & 0.05 \\ 0.25 & 0.25 & 0.10 \end{bmatrix} \quad \mathbf{B} = \begin{bmatrix} 0.12 & 0.00 & 0.00 & 0.10 \\ 0.28 & 0.24 & 0.25 & 0.20 \\ 0.40 & 0.56 & 0.60 & 0.70 \end{bmatrix}$$

$$\mathbf{C} = \begin{bmatrix} 0.10 & 0.05 & 0.10 \\ 0.10 & 0.10 & 0.35 \\ 0.15 & 0.10 & 0.30 \end{bmatrix} \quad \mathbf{D} = \begin{bmatrix} 0.20 & 0.20 & 0.00 & 0.00 \\ 0.00 & 0.00 & 0.15 & 0.00 \\ 0.00 & 0.00 & 0.00 & 0.00 \end{bmatrix}$$

Combining these coefficient matrices and the total vectors together would give the block structure shown in Table B7.3.

Table B7.3 Input–output block structure

				Outputs					*Total*
Inputs	*A*	*P*	*S*	*C*	*I*	*G*	*X*		*Total*
A									
P		A				B		f	t
S									
M									
L		C				D		h	y
K									
Total		t				g			

B7.3 Input–output analysis

To see how we can proceed from this stage we shall represent the relationships in the input–output structure as simple linear equations. Let's look at the outputs of the agriculture sector (which we denote as sector 1). From Table B7.2 we have:

$$t_1 = 0.30t_1 + 0.10t_2 + 0t_3 + f_1$$

This is readily confirmed from the vector definition:

$t_1 = 100, t_2 = 300, t_3 = 500$ and $f_1 = 40$. This gives:

$t_1 = 0.30(100) + 0.10(300) + 0(500) + 40 = 30 + 30 + 0 + 40 = 100$

Similarly, for the other two industry sectors we have:

$t_1 = 0.30t_1 + 0.10t_2 + 0t_3 + f_1$

$t_2 = 0.10t_1 + 0.40t_2 + 0.05t_3 + f_2$

$t_3 = 0.25t_1 + 0.25t_2 + 0.10t_3 + f_3$

So in matrix format this can be written as:

$$t = At + f$$

which in turn can be written as

$$t - At = f$$
$$t(I - A) = f$$
$$t(I - A)(I - A)^{-1} = (I - A)^{-1}f$$
$$t = (I - A)^{-1}f \tag{B7.1}$$

where $(I - A)^{-1}$ is known as the *input–output inverse*. Providing the $(I - A)$ matrix is non-singular, this implies that for a given f vector we can readily determine the corresponding t vector. This means that, given a level of final demand, we can work out the total output required to meet this final demand.

Before applying this to our problem it is worth reviewing the implications of this model so far. What we have obtained is a matrix expression that allows us to determine, for a given level of final demand, the corresponding total outputs of the various industry sectors. Further than this we can readily calculate the effect on total output for a given change in the f vector. For example, assume the government is concerned about the government deficit and is considering reducing the level of its own spending in the economy from £100 billion to, say, £90 billion. All other components of final demand are assumed to remain constant. The matrix expressions we have derived will allow us to determine the exact effect this will have on the various industry sectors – for example, the impact on the services sector.

Similarly, if exports are forecast to increase by 10%, the impact on each of the three industry sectors can be calculated. The model provides an extremely powerful economic planning and analysis tool. Let us return to our numerical example to illustrate this. $(I - A)$ will be given as:

$$(I - A) = \begin{bmatrix} 1 & 0 & 0 \\ 0 & 1 & 0 \\ 0 & 0 & 1 \end{bmatrix} - \begin{bmatrix} 0.30 & 0.10 & 0.00 \\ 0.10 & 0.40 & 0.05 \\ 0.25 & 0.25 & 0.20 \end{bmatrix} = \begin{bmatrix} 0.70 & -0.10 & 0.00 \\ -0.10 & 0.60 & -0.05 \\ -0.25 & -0.25 & 0.80 \end{bmatrix}$$

The inverse to this matrix can then be derived as:

$$(I - A)^{-1} = \begin{bmatrix} 1.4701260 & 0.2515723 & 0.0157233 \\ 0.2908805 & 1.7610060 & 0.1100629 \\ 0.5503145 & 0.6289308 & 1.2893080 \end{bmatrix}$$

We've not shown the calculation for the inverse but you should have this as the solution to Ex. B5.5

and we can confirm the logic of the model from the original input–output table

$$t = (I - A)^{-1}f = \begin{bmatrix} 1.4701260 & 0.2515723 & 0.0157233 \\ 0.2908805 & 1.7610060 & 0.1100629 \\ 0.5503145 & 0.6289308 & 1.2893080 \end{bmatrix} \begin{bmatrix} 40 \\ 145 \\ 300 \end{bmatrix} = \begin{bmatrix} 100 \\ 300 \\ 500 \end{bmatrix}$$

Let us return to one of the earlier illustrative examples. Assume that the government intends reducing its expenditure in terms of final demand in an attempt to reduce its deficit. The government final demand for production output, P, is expected to fall from its current level of £25 billion to £20 billion and for services output, S, is expected to fall from £60 billion to £55 billion. The new final demand vector ($\mathbf{f}_2$) therefore, *ceteris paribus*, will be:

$$\mathbf{f}_2 = \begin{bmatrix} 40 \\ 140 \\ 295 \end{bmatrix}$$

Final demand as a result of government reductions falls in total by £10 billion. Using the input–output inverse we can readily determine the new $\mathbf{t}$ vector, $\mathbf{t}_2$, which will be given by:

$$\begin{bmatrix} 1.4701260 & 0.2515723 & 0.0157233 \\ 0.2908805 & 1.7610060 & 0.1100629 \\ 0.5503145 & 0.6289308 & 1.2893080 \end{bmatrix} \begin{bmatrix} 40 \\ 140 \\ 295 \end{bmatrix} = \begin{bmatrix} 98.7 \\ 290.6 \\ 490.4 \end{bmatrix}$$

In this way, the precise changes such a decrease in government final demand would have on the three industry sectors can be quantified readily. We see that total output of Agriculture will fall to £98.7 billion, Production to £290.6 billion and Services to £490.4 billion as a result of a £10 billion reduction in government purchases of both production and services output. In total we see a reduction in overall final demand of £20.3 billion as a result of the reduction by government of £10 billion.

Progress Check B7.1

Explain why the reduction in the total output in each sector is larger than the initial reduction in G. Why has output of agriculture fallen even though the government purchases no output from this sector?

As we might expect from our understanding of macroeconomic multipliers, the overall reduction in G of £10 billion leads to a greater reduction in final demand of £20.3 billion. The largest impact of such a change in final demand is on the two sectors directly affected by the G reduction: P and S. Notice also that, because of the inter-relationships between the various sectors, total output of the agriculture sector also decreases, even though it is not directly affected by government spending changes.

Having found the new $\mathbf{t}$ vector we can determine the impact these changes in total outputs have on the rest of the input–output table. We know, for example, that agriculture's output requires a 10% input from labour (L). This is currently £10 billion. However, since the new agriculture output has fallen to £98.7 billion, the implication is that the new labour input will fall to £9.87 billion. Similar calculations are readily undertaken on the rest of the inputs for all three sectors. Should we require further detail of the precise impact of such a policy we could use the new $\mathbf{t}$ vector with the original input–output coefficients to construct the full, new, input–output table. It should be apparent that the use of the input–output inverse in this way provides an especially powerful tool for economic analysis and economic policy. The economic policymaker is able to assess in considerable detail alternative macroeconomic strategies and their impact on specific sectors of the economy. We could now, for example, compare the effects of this change in G with an alternative policy, for example a change in government tax policy which will impact on private consumption, C, by reducing disposable income. One further point to note at this stage is that we could have carried out the analysis on the various changes in the totals rather than on the actual totals – in other words, undertaking marginal analysis. Here, for example, we could have used an **f** vector such that:

$$\Delta \mathbf{f} = \begin{bmatrix} 0 \\ -5 \\ -5 \end{bmatrix}$$

and the **t** vector would now show changes in total outputs rather than the totals themselves. For comparative static analysis this may be more convenient than examining the totals as we did previously.

Progress Check B7.2

Confirm that such an **f** vector will produce the same results in the **t** vector as before.

B

We can easily expand the application of this analysis. So far, we have determined the change in total outputs that will be required as the result of some change in the final demand vector. From an economic planning viewpoint, what may be equally important is an assessment of the effect such a change in **f** will have on the demand for primary factors of production. The economic policymaker may, for example, be interested in the change in demand for labour (i.e. in employment levels) that such a change in final demand will bring about. Earlier we derived a matrix expression for the **t** vector:

$$\mathbf{t} = (\mathbf{I} - \mathbf{A})^{-1}\mathbf{f}$$

and in a similar way we can derive an equivalent expression for **y**, the vector of demand for primary factors of production. In terms of a linear equation system we have for the imports, labour and capital sectors respectively:

$$y_1 = 0.10t_1 + 0.05t_2 + 0.10t_3 + h_1$$
$$y_2 = 0.10t_1 + 0.10t_2 + 0.35t_3 + h_2$$
$$y_3 = 0.15t_1 + 0.10t_2 + 0.30t_3 + h_3$$

which in matrix form gives

$$\mathbf{y} = \mathbf{Ct} + \mathbf{h}$$

However, as we also have:

$$\mathbf{t} = (\mathbf{I} - \mathbf{A})^{-1}\mathbf{f}$$

this gives

$$\mathbf{y} = \mathbf{C}(\mathbf{I} - \mathbf{A})^{-1}\mathbf{f} + \mathbf{h} \tag{B7.2}$$

In other words, we can again use the input–output inverse to quantify the effects on the **y** vector of a given change in the **f** vector. To illustrate the calculations, let us return to the earlier example where the G element in the final demand vector was reduced. If we express the new **f** vector in terms of marginal changes we have:

$$\Delta \mathbf{f} = \begin{bmatrix} 0 \\ -5 \\ -5 \end{bmatrix} \quad \text{and} \quad \Delta \mathbf{h} = \begin{bmatrix} 0 \\ 0 \\ 0 \end{bmatrix}$$

since no change has occurred in terms of final demand for primary inputs. We now require the product of the **C** matrix multiplied by the input–output inverse. The product of this is:

$$\mathbf{C(I - A)}^{-1} = \begin{bmatrix} 0.10 & 0.05 & 0.10 \\ 0.10 & 0.10 & 0.35 \\ 0.15 & 0.10 & 0.30 \end{bmatrix} \begin{bmatrix} 1.4701260 & 0.2515723 & 0.0157233 \\ 0.2908805 & 1.7610060 & 0.1100629 \\ 0.5503145 & 0.6289308 & 1.2893080 \end{bmatrix}$$

$$= \begin{bmatrix} 0.2165881 & 0.1761006 & 0.1360063 \\ 0.3687107 & 0.4213836 & 0.4638365 \\ 0.4147013 & 0.4025157 & 0.4001572 \end{bmatrix}$$

and multiplying by the $\Delta\mathbf{f}$ vector gives

$$\Delta\mathbf{y} = \begin{bmatrix} -1.56 \\ -4.43 \\ -4.01 \end{bmatrix}$$

Interpretation of the $\Delta\mathbf{y}$ vector is straightforward. As a result of the reduction in G by £10 billion, the demand for imports will fall by £1.56 billion, for labour by £4.43 billion and for capital by £4.01 billion. In the context of the original problem, we could also determine the precise effect on each industry's labour requirements by returning to the original input–output coefficients. Finally, to complete the model we can develop the final matrix forms relating to the input–output table. We already have:

$$\mathbf{t} = \mathbf{(I - A)}^{-1}\mathbf{f}$$

and

$$\mathbf{y} = \mathbf{C(I - A)}^{-1}\mathbf{f} + \mathbf{h}$$

These can be written in an equivalent form as:

$$\mathbf{t} = \mathbf{(I - A)}^{-1}\mathbf{Bg}$$

since $\mathbf{f} = \mathbf{Bg}$, and as

$$\mathbf{y} = [\mathbf{C(I - A)}^{-1}\mathbf{B} + \mathbf{D}]\mathbf{g} \tag{B7.3}$$

since $\mathbf{h} = \mathbf{Dg}$. This means that we can determine the new $\mathbf{t}$ and $\mathbf{y}$ vectors not only from introducing a change in the $\mathbf{f}$ vector but also a change in the $\mathbf{g}$ vector (which relates to the final demand for primary factors). This would allow us to develop the following structure of coefficients:

$$\begin{array}{c|c} \mathbf{(I - A)}^{-1} & \mathbf{(I - A)}^{-1}\,\mathbf{b} \\ \hline \mathbf{C(I - A)}^{-1} & \mathbf{C(I - A)}^{-1}\mathbf{B} + \mathbf{D} \end{array} \tag{B7.4}$$

where the coefficients can be interpreted in the same general way as the multipliers that were discussed earlier. The two matrix expressions on the left will show the multiplier (or cumulative) impact of a change in the $\mathbf{f}$ vector (or any element of the $\mathbf{f}$ vector) on $\mathbf{t}$ and $\mathbf{y}$ respectively. The two matrix expressions on the right will show the multiplier impact of a change in the $\mathbf{g}$ vector on $\mathbf{t}$ and $\mathbf{y}$ respectively. Thus, these coefficients can be readily used to pinpoint a single multiplier impact on any of the elements in the $\mathbf{t}$ and $\mathbf{y}$ vectors arising from any element in the $\mathbf{f}$ and $\mathbf{g}$ vectors. For example, if we wished to determine the multiplier effect of a change in consumption, C, on total demand for imports, M, this is achieved through the appropriate multiplier coefficient. It can be seen, therefore, that input–output analysis provides the economic policymaker with a potentially extremely powerful comparative analysis tool. Through the use of matrix algebra, the input–output model can be easily constructed and, through the use of the input–output inverse, the solution to a numerical model found.

B7.4 Summary

In this module we have examined the area of matrix algebra and its potential application in the study of mathematical economics and, in particular, we have seen how matrix algebra can be used to examine the fundamental relationships inherent in a number of theoretical economic models. We have also been able to deduce the important implications of these models and to see that, in the area of input–output analysis and the development of macroeconomic models in general, the use of matrix algebra allows comparative static analysis to be undertaken on an economic structure. The use of matrix methods allows the identification of economic multipliers, and thereby the policy implications arising from the solution of a numerical model can be determined.

Learning Check

Having read this module you should have learned that:

- Through input–output analysis we can assess the impact of economic changes on the national economy
- An input–output table shows the outputs from individual sectors of the economy and the inputs required by those sectors
- Input–output coefficients show the proportion of inputs from each sector required by a particular sector
- The input–output inverse is given by $(I - A)^{-1}$ where A is the matrix of inter-industry coefficients.

Worked Example

The Planning Minister of a small African republic has asked for your help. He's come across input–output models and the World Bank has developed a basic input–output table for the economy. Understandably, the economy is currently highly dependent on agriculture, but has recently started to develop its tourist industry, targeting western economies. There is no manufacturing to speak of and only a small service sector. The input–output table is shown below. The Minister is considering two policy options to stimulate economic growth. The first is to increase government spending in the service sector by an extra $10 million. The second is to boost agricultural exports by $10 million. The Minister has asked for your advice on the overall impact of the two options and, in particular, the effect on the labour market (through wages and salaries) and on the balance of trade (through exports and imports).

Input–output table, $million

	Agriculture	Services	Tourism	C	I	G	X	Total
Agriculture	40	10	25	100	0	0	25	200
Services	5	10	20	5	10	10	0	60

Worked Example *(Continued)*

Input–output table, $million *(continued)*

	Agriculture	Services	Tourism	C	I	G	X	Total
Tourism	5	5	40	20	20	0	10	100
M	50	10	5	50	40	5	0	160
L	90	20	5	0	0	45	0	160
K	10	5	5	0	0	0	0	20
Total	200	60	100	175	70	60	35	700

Solution

The first thing we need to do is to work out the effects on the **t** and **y** vectors for each of the two options. To do that we need the $(\mathbf{I} - \mathbf{A})$ inverse and to get that we need the input–output coefficients. These are shown in the table below to four decimal places:

Input–output coefficients

	A	S	T	C	I	G	X
A	0.2000	0.1667	0.2500	0.5714	0.0000	0.0000	0.7143
S	0.0250	0.1667	0.2000	0.0286	0.1429	0.1667	0.0000
T	0.0250	0.0833	0.4000	0.1143	0.2857	0.0000	0.2857
M	0.2500	0.1677	0.0500	0.2857	0.5714	0.0833	0.0000
L	0.4500	0.3333	0.0500	0.0000	0.0000	0.7500	0.0000
K	0.0500	0.0833	0.0500	0.0000	0.0000	0.0000	0.0000

From the matrix of **A** coefficients, we can then obtain the $(\mathbf{I} - \mathbf{A})$ matrix as:

$$\begin{matrix} 0.8000 & -0.1667 & -0.2500 \\ -0.0250 & 0.8333 & -0.2000 \\ -0.0250 & -0.0833 & 0.6000 \end{matrix}$$

Using Excel, we then obtain the inverse. Note that this is calculated to several decimal places to ensure accuracy in subsequent calculations and is shown as $(\mathbf{I} - \mathbf{A})^{-1}$

$$\begin{matrix} 1.2864 & 0.3256 & 0.6445 \\ 0.0641 & 1.2610 & 0.4470 \\ 0.0729 & 0.1844 & 1.7585 \end{matrix}$$

From B7.1 we then have:

$$\Delta \mathbf{t} = (\mathbf{I} - \mathbf{A})^{-1} \Delta \mathbf{f}$$

$$\Delta \mathbf{f} = \begin{bmatrix} 0 \\ 10 \\ 0 \end{bmatrix}$$

Worked Example *(Continued)*

giving

$$\Delta t = \begin{bmatrix} 1.2864 & 0.3256 & 0.6445 \\ 0.0641 & 1.2610 & 0.4470 \\ 0.0729 & 0.1844 & 1.7585 \end{bmatrix} \begin{bmatrix} 0 \\ 10 \\ 0 \end{bmatrix} = \begin{bmatrix} 3.26 \\ 12.61 \\ 1.84 \end{bmatrix}$$

So, under option 1, increasing **G** by \$10 million in the service sector, total output will increase by \$3.2 million in Agriculture, \$12.61 million in Services and \$1.84 million in Tourism. However, there will also be an impact on the **y** vector. From Eq. B7.2 we have:

$$\Delta y = C(I - A)^{-1} \Delta f + \Delta h$$

However, $\Delta h = 0$, since there is no change in the final demand for primary inputs, so we have:

$$\Delta y \begin{bmatrix} 0.25 & 0.1667 & 0.05 \\ 0.45 & 0.33 & 0.05 \\ 0.05 & 0.083 & 0.05 \end{bmatrix} \begin{bmatrix} 1.2864 & 0.3256 & 0.6445 \\ 0.0641 & 1.2610 & 0.4470 \\ 0.0729 & 0.1844 & 1.7585 \end{bmatrix} \begin{bmatrix} 0 \\ 10 \\ 0 \end{bmatrix}$$
$$= \begin{bmatrix} 3.01 \\ 5.76 \\ 1.31 \end{bmatrix}$$

indicating that imports, M, will increase by \$3.01 million, wages and salaries, L, by \$5.75 million and capital, K, by \$1.31 million. The same arithmetic is readily done for option 2 but this time with an **f** vector:

$$\Delta f = \begin{bmatrix} 10 \\ 0 \\ 0 \end{bmatrix}$$

We can find the new Δt and Δy vectors in the same way (we're not showing the full calculations for this) to give:

\$ million

	Option 1	Option 2
Agriculture	203.26	212.86
Services	72.61	60.64
Tourism	101.84	100.73
M	163.01	163.36
L	165.76	166.04
K	21.31	20.73
Total	727.79	724.36

We see that, overall, the two options generate fairly similar economic changes. However, there are two areas in particular that are different. Option 1 stimulates a large increase in Services output while option 2 does the same in Agriculture (hardly surprising given what the two options are). The other main difference

Worked Example (Continued)

will be in the balance of trade. Both options lead to an increase in imports, M, of about $3 million. For option 1, exports were unchanged so this leads to a worsening of the balance of trade. Option 2, however, involved an initial increase in exports of $10 million so, even with an increase in imports of $6 million, the balance of trade has improved. As for the other area we were asked to look at, L, the two options again produce similar change.

Exercises

B7.1   Return to the input–output table shown in Table B7.1. The government is concerned about the level of economic growth in the economy and is trying to evaluate two policies that could be adopted to stimulate a higher growth rate.

   Policy 1 would lead to an increase in exports of the three sectors. Agricultural exports will rise by £2 billion, production exports by £3 billion and services exports by £5 billion.

   Policy 2 would lead to a 5% increase in private consumption, C, in each of the three sectors. For each policy, assess the effect on the total output of each sector.

B7.2   For Ex. B7.1, we have now also been asked to assess the impact of the two policy options on the demand for M, L, K.

B7.3   For Ex. B7.1, we have now also been asked to assess the impact of the two policy options on the balance of trade $(X − M)$.

B7.4   For Ex. B7.1, obtain a complete new table for each policy option, corresponding to that shown in Table B7.1.

B7.5   Return to the Worked Example in the module. A third option is to increase investment in tourism by $10 million. Evaluate the impact of this option on the economy.

B7.6   Return to Ex B7.5. What has been the impact on labour in each of the three industries?

Section C
Optimization in economic analysis

Up to now our attention has focused almost exclusively on the use of linear models in economic analysis. As you will appreciate from your study of economics, such models are useful because of their simple mathematical structure. However, they can also be limiting in the way they can be used to model economic behaviour. We clearly need to be able to develop *non-linear* models for use in economic analysis, and it is to these that we now turn. Examining them in detail, we shall look at the important economic principle of *optimization*. Optimization is important in economic analysis: firms want to optimize their profit or their production; consumers want to optimize their satisfaction, or utility, from consumption; governments wish to optimize tax revenue or national income. The analysis of economic optimization is made possible through the mathematical principles we shall develop in this section.

Module C1 Quadratic functions in economic analysis

The first module in this section brings us back to one of the functions we looked at in Module A3: the quadratic function. We'll look at this type of function in detail and explore how it is used in economic analysis to identify an optimum situation.

Module C2 The derivative and the rules of differentiation

This module introduces an important mathematical concept: the derivative. The derivative provides us with the analytical skills needed to be able to use non-linear models in economics. In this module we introduce some of the basic rules, focusing particularly on how the derivative is used to determine the slope of non-linear functions.

Module C3 Derivatives and economic analysis

Having seen how the derivative is calculated, in this module we use the derivative to analyse a number of economic models at both the micro- and macroeconomic level.

Module C4 The principles of optimization

As we've mentioned, the concept of optimization is a particularly important one in economic analysis. In this module we look at the mathematics behind the concept and show how differential calculus can be used to find an optimum position.

Module C5 Optimization in economic analysis

Following our exploration of the mathematical principles of optimization in the previous module, here we look at how these principles can be applied to a number of common economic models. We examine profit maximization under perfect competition and under monopoly; the effect of different taxes on profit maximization; and how the optimal level of tax can be determined.

Module C6 Optimization in production theory

In this final section we turn our attention to optimization in the context of the theory of production and costs.

Module C1
Quadratic functions in economic analysis

We shall focus our attention in this module on one particular type of non-linear function – the quadratic – because this has a number of useful properties for economic analysis, allowing us to illustrate many of the key features of non-linear models in general. We shall look at the general shape and characteristics of quadratics and at how we can find the *roots* of a quadratic equation. Such roots often have important economic meaning in the models we shall be developing and are a way of helping identify a maximum or minimum position for the quadratic function.

Learning Objectives

By the end of this module you should be able to:

- Sketch a quadratic function
- Work out the roots of a quadratic function
- Work out the turning point of a quadratic function
- Explain the roots and turning point in relation to economic analysis.

Knowledge Check C1

If you're already familiar and comfortable with quadratic algebra, you may want to jump straight to the exercises at the end of this module. For the following function, sketch the equation, and find the roots and turning point:

$$Y = -100 - 10X + 2.5X^2$$

Check your answer in Appendix 2.

C1.1 Quadratic functions

Quadratic functions were introduced briefly in Module A3 as a type of polynomial function. You will remember that such a function takes the general form:

$$Y = f(X) = a + bX + cX^2 \tag{C1.1}$$

where a, b and c are the numerical parameters of the function. It's the X^2 term that makes a function a quadratic. For example:

$$Y = a + bX + cX^2$$
$$Y = a + cX^2$$
$$Y = bX + cX^2$$

are all quadratic functions given that the highest polynomial term is a square, X^2. On the other hand:

$$Y = bX + cX^2 + dX^3$$

is not a quadratic since it involves a term higher than a square.

Note: some of you may be used to writing a quadratic in the form:

$$Y = c + bX + aX^2$$

Since we've used the notation $Y = a + bX$ for linear functions so far, we've shown the quadratic in the form:

$$Y = a + bX + cX^2$$

where the 'extra' X^2 term is added.

C1.2 Characteristics of quadratic functions

Quadratic functions have a number of characteristics that make them useful in economic analysis. We'll illustrate these using the function:

$$Y = 100 + 10X - 2X^2 \tag{C1.2}$$

The corresponding graph is shown in Fig. C1.1, plotted with X from -20 to $+20$.

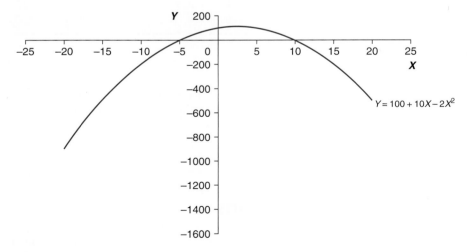

Figure C1.1 $Y = 100 + 10X - 2X^2$

We have already seen how to interpret the parameters a and b of a linear function. Can we interpret the quadratic parameters – a, b and c – in a similar way? Let's consider a first of all. On inspection, we see that the quadratic function intercepts the vertical axis at 100, the value for a in the quadratic equation. This is obviously no coincidence, since, as in a linear function, the a term indicates the intercept – where the quadratic function will cross the vertical axis. Figure C1.2 shows the function with different a values. We can see that the curve effectively stays the same except that it shifts up/down the Y axis according to the a value, which varies from 100 to -200 and then to -400.

We already know from Module A3 that a quadratic will take one of two general shapes, depending on the c value. In Fig. C1.3a the curve takes an inverted U shape ($\cap$) and will have a negative c term. In Fig. C1.3b the curve takes a U shape and c will have a positive value. But what happens to the quadratic curve if the c term changes? Figure C1.4 illustrates the general principles showing the c term increasing from -2 to -3 to -4. We see that as this happens the inverted U shape becomes more pronounced – the two ends of the curve are squeezed together. Equally, if the c term took smaller values the opposite would occur – the two ends will move further apart.

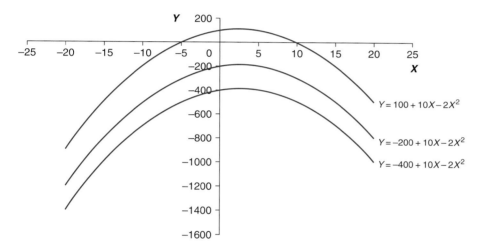

Figure C1.2 Varying the value of a in a quadratic function

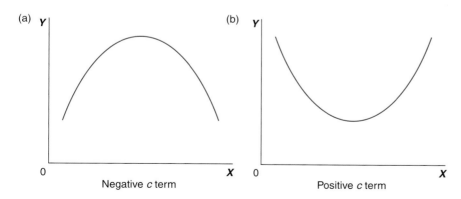

Figure C1.3 The two general forms of a quadratic function

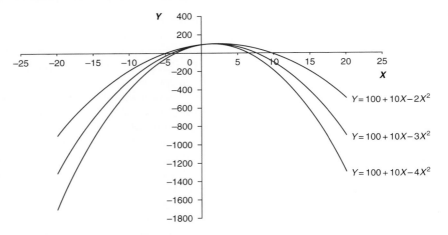

Figure C1.4 Varying the value of c in a quadratic function

This brings us finally to the bX term in a quadratic. Here we have:

$$Y = 100 + 10X - 2X^2 \tag{C1.2}$$

In this case, the b coefficient is positive. So when X takes positive values the effect on Y will be positive also. Let's change Eq. C1.2 to:

$$Y = 100 + 50X - 2X^2 \tag{C1.3}$$

As the b coefficient increases from 10 in Eq. C1.2 to 50 in Eq. C1.3, the effect is to increase the Y values where $X > 0$ and push this part of the quadratic curve higher up than it was. For $X < 0$ the opposite effect will occur, and the quadratic curve will be dragged downwards. This can be confirmed from Fig. C1.5 where we can see that the new quadratic curve is pushed up/down while pivoting on the a value of 100. If the b coefficient had been negative the new quadratic curve would be pushed in the reverse way: for $X > 0$ the curve would be pushed downwards compared with the original and with $X < 0$ the curve would be pushed up.

Progress Check C1.1

For each pair of functions, sketch both functions on the same graph. Don't worry about the precise numerical values on the graph; just sketch the two curves together:

(i) $Y = 100 + 10X - 4X^2$ and $Y = 500 + 10X - 4X^2$

(ii) $Y = 100 + 10X - 4X^2$ and $Y = 100 + 100X - 4X^2$

(iii) $Y = 100 + 10X - 4X^2$ and $Y = 100 + 10X - 10X^2$

(iv) $Y = 100 - 10X + 4X^2$ and $Y = 500 - 10X + 4X^2$

(v) $Y = 100 - 10X + 4X^2$ and $Y = 100 - 100X + 4X^2$

(vi) $Y = 100 - 10X + 4X^2$ and $Y = 100 - 10X + 8X^2$

Check your sketches in Excel.

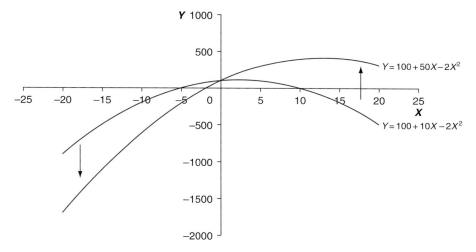

Figure C1.5 Varying the value of b in a quadratic function

C1.3 Breakeven analysis

Now that you understand the key characteristics of quadratic functions you are in a position to start using them for economic analysis. You will also see why they're popular in economics: they allow us to build more realistic models than linear functions do. Assume a firm faces a situation such that:

$$TR = f(Q) = 260Q \tag{C1.4}$$

$$TC = g(Q) = 1125 + 10Q + 5Q^2 \tag{C1.5}$$

where TR and TC represent total revenue and total costs respectively (both measured in £000s) and Q represents the units of output produced (measured in 000s). Figure C1.6 shows both these functions plotted for $Q = 0$ to 50.

> ### Progress Check C1.2
>
> Look at the *TR* function shown in Eq. C1.4. What does this imply about the demand function faced by this firm and the market conditions under which the firm operates?
>   Look at the *TC* function. How do you explain what's happening to *TC* as *Q* increases?
>
> (Solution on p. 463)

   A number of points become clear from the diagram. The *TR* function, as we know, is linear, while the *TC* function is quadratic (remember that we're only using one quadrant on the graph, so we see only part of the U shape). For the *TC* function we can make a number of observations. The first is that fixed costs are shown by the intercept at £1125(000). You will remember, however, that the other critical feature of a linear function was its slope or gradient – shown for a linear function by the b term. For a quadratic function, however, and indeed for non-linear functions in general, the slope is not as easily obtained. On inspection it is clear that the slope of the quadratic does not remain constant as it does in a linear function but changes according to where on the function we are – that is, it will vary depending on the value taken by the X variable.

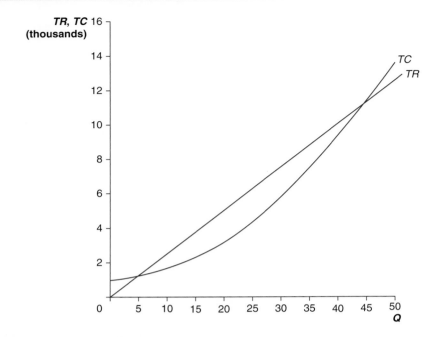

Figure C1.6 *TR* and *TC* functions

Fig C1.6 shows that for low values for *Q*, the slope of the *TC* function is positive but relatively shallow – that is, total costs are increasing as we increase output, but not by very much. We see, however, that gradually the slope of the *TC* function gets steeper and steeper, implying that as *Q* continues to increase then costs rise more and more quickly. Economic common sense suggests that for many companies this is reasonable. At low levels of output a company will have unused production capacity, so increasing output will add little to total costs. However, as output continues to rise and the firm gets close to production capacity, further output causes much larger increase in costs. Overtime may have to be paid to the workforce; additional machinery or equipment may have to be bought; repair costs start to escalate; and so on. One of the attractions of quadratic functions in economics is that they're often closer to economic reality than linear functions.

However, we also wish to find a solution to such an economic model (as we did with earlier, linear versions). In this example we require the breakeven level of output, defined as the level of output where $TR = TC$. It is evident from Fig. C1.6 that in this particular model there will be two such breakeven points and, from the graph, we see that these correspond to $Q = 5$ and $Q = 45$. However, such a graphical solution is not always possible or, indeed, desirable. We must turn to algebra as a general solution method. We have at breakeven:

$$TR = TC \tag{C1.6}$$

$$TR - TC = 0$$

$$260Q - (1125 + 10Q + 5Q^2) = 0$$

$$260Q - 1125 - 10Q - 5Q^2 = 0$$

$$-1125 + 250Q - 5Q^2 = 0 \tag{C1.7}$$

and we clearly require the values for Q that will cause the left-hand side of this equation to equal zero.

Progress Check C1.3

Plot the equation we have just derived, Eq. C1.7, for $X = 0$ to 50. What economic interpretation would you give this function? What interpretation would you give the two points where the function crosses the X axis? What interpretation would you give to the point where $X = 25$?

It may appear that finding such values algebraically as opposed to graphically will be no easy task. However, we can readily derive a suitable formula for finding such values for (almost) any quadratic function taking this general form. Let's show the general form of a quadratic as:

$$a + bX + cX^2 = 0 \qquad\qquad (C1.8)$$

The solution formula for a quadratic of the form of C1.8 is then given as:

$$X = \frac{-b \pm \sqrt{b^2 - 4ac}}{2c} \qquad\qquad (C1.9)$$

For those of you interested in seeing where this came from we show its derivation in Appendix C1. Note that in general the formula will provide *two* solution values for X: one when we evaluate the expression using the $+$ sign from the $\pm$ symbol and one when we use the $-$ sign. Effectively what Eq. C1.9 provides is a ready method of finding the X value for a quadratic function that will give $Y = 0$. Returning to our problem, we have:

$$-1125 + 250Q - 5Q^2 = 0$$

with

$$a = -1125$$
$$b = 250$$
$$c = -5$$

and substituting these into Eq. C1.9 (taking care with negative values) we have

$$
\begin{aligned}
Q &= \frac{-b \pm \sqrt{b^2 - 4ac}}{2c} \\
&= \frac{-250 \pm \sqrt{250^2 - 4(-1125)(-5)}}{2(-5)} \\
&= \frac{-250 \pm \sqrt{62{,}500 - 22{,}500}}{-10} \\
&= \frac{-250 \pm \sqrt{40{,}000}}{-10} = \frac{-250 \pm 200}{-10}
\end{aligned}
$$

and evaluating first for the $+$ sign and then for the $-$ sign we have

$$Q_1 = \frac{-250 + 200}{-10} = \frac{-50}{-10} = 5$$

$$Q_2 = \frac{-250 - 200}{-10} = \frac{-450}{-10} = 45$$

confirming that the two breakeven levels of output occur when $Q = 5$ and $Q = 45$.

In fact, the two values for Q that we have derived are more generally known as the *roots* of the quadratic expression from which they were derived. In general the roots represent the values for X that generate a value of zero for the quadratic function. There is another way to view the two roots, however. Assume that we were to graph the quadratic function for which we have just found the roots. The roots (the values for X that cause the function to take a zero value) will correspond to the two points on the X axis where the function crosses (much as the a term in a quadratic indicates where the function crosses the Y axis). Such an interpretation is not always useful for the economic model under analysis, although in this illustration it clearly will be. Consider the economic meaning of the quadratic function in Eq. C1.7. On reflection, it can be seen that this will represent a profit function for this firm given the definition of profit as the difference between total revenue and total costs. Let's now show this profit function on the same graph, Fig. C1.7, as the TR and TC functions.

Fig. C1.7 will repay close inspection, as it has a number of features that we shall develop over this and subsequent modules. The economic model we are examining here involves three functional relationships, with one of these, for profit, derived from the other two. The two roots of the profit function – at 5 and 45 – are the points where the profit function crosses the horizontal axis. Clearly, in this model the breakeven points are where profit equals zero. Note that, as must be the case, $TR = TC$ at these two output levels. The profit function also intercepts the vertical axis at -1125 (although this is difficult to see from the graph given the scale). It is evident that this represents the fixed cost the firm incurs even when it has a zero output. At such a point profit will be -1125; that is, the firm makes an operational loss. This loss-making situation continues up to an output level of 5, with the profit line staying below the horizontal axis representing negative profit levels. This is confirmed on examination of the TC and TR lines, with $TC > TR$ for output up to 5. After this point profit becomes positive

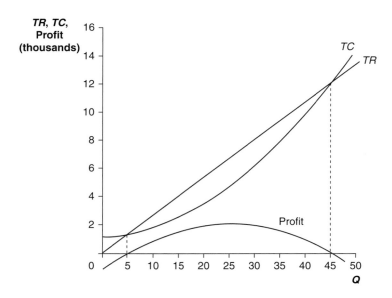

Figure C1.7 *TR, TC* and Profit functions

$(TC < TR)$ and it is also evident that profit continues to increase with extra output up to 25. At this level of output the situation reverses and while profits are still being made with increased output the total profit is gradually declining. At $Q = 45$ we again encounter breakeven, and after this level of output the firm is again in a loss-making situation. One point on the profit function will clearly be of considerable importance in economic analysis: the point where profit reaches its maximum. Here we can see from the graph that profit maximization occurs at $Q = 25$.

The concept of profit maximization in particular and optimization in general are of critical importance in economic analysis. It is evident that in our model the optimum level of profit occurs at the top of the quadratic profit curve. It is also evident on reflection that such a point occurs when the slope of the profit function is zero. Consider that for $Q < 25$ the slope of the profit function is positive while for $Q > 25$ the slope is negative. At $Q = 25$ we encounter what we can refer to as a *turning point*: where the slope is about to change from positive to negative (or vice versa depending on the exact nature of the quadratic function). For a quadratic function such a turning point is readily obtained: it occurs *midway* between the two roots. Here we see that 25 is equidistant from 5 and 45.

This is an important finding and worth summarizing. If we have a quadratic function then $Y = f(X)$:

- the two roots are the two X values that equate to Y taking a zero value ($Y = 0$)
- the turning point of the quadratic function occurs when the slope of the function equals zero
- the turning point is found midway between the two roots
- the turning point shows the maximum value of Y if the quadratic takes the inverted U shape ($\cap$) and shows a minimum value of Y if the quadratic takes a U shape.

For other types of non-linear functions, however, we need a more general approach to finding the maximum/minimum. We will explore this in later modules.

C1.4 Market equilibrium

Let's now look at a second example of quadratic functions, this time applied to market equilibrium. Assume a market model where:

$$Q_d = 100 - 2P$$
$$Q_s = -100 + 10P + 10P^2$$

As usual, we want to find the market equilibrium position. We require an equilibrium where $Q_d = Q_s$ or:

$$100 - 2P = -100 + 10P + 10P^2$$
$$0 = -200 + 12P + 10P^2$$

Because our equation is now in the form $= 0$, we can find the roots as before. Notice that unlike the previous example, where the quadratic we were analysing represented the profit function, in this case the quadratic function has no real economic meaning. Using the roots formula to solve we have:

$$a = -200$$
$$b = 12$$
$$c = 10$$

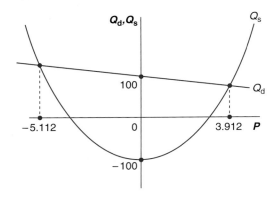

Figure C1.8 Q_d, Q_s

to give

$$Q = \frac{-12 \pm \sqrt{12^2 - 4(-200)(10)}}{2(10)}$$

$$= \frac{-12 \pm 90.244}{20}$$

which gives the two roots as $P_1 = 3.9122$ and $P_2 = -5.1122$. That is, mathematically there are two market equilibrium positions. That with a negative price, P_2, is clearly impossible in an economic context, so we would recognize the equilibrium price as 3.9122 and from either the demand or supply equation we can determine the equilibrium quantity to be 97.1756. It will be useful to show the situation graphically to ensure we understand what is going on. Figure C1.8 shows the analysis. The demand function is linear with an intercept of 100. The supply function is quadratic. It intercepts at -100 and takes the U shape given it has a positive c value. Mathematically we have used all four graph quadrants to show the two roots (where the supply and demand functions are equal). From an economic analysis perspective we would use only quadrant I, confirming equilibrium at P_1.

Progress Check C1.4

Assume the demand function changes to:

$Q_d = 200 - 2P$

Find the new market equilibrium.

(Solution on p. 463)

C1.5 Quadratic functions with no real roots

We should note that the algebraic method we have of finding the roots of a quadratic equation will not necessarily always find a solution. Recollect that one way of interpreting the roots is that they represent where the function crosses the X axis. Not all quadratic functions, however, will necessarily do this. Some may always lie above or below the X axis, and if a function does not cross it cannot have roots. We would normally recognize that this had occurred on inspection of part of Eq. C1.9:

$$\frac{-b \pm \sqrt{b^2 - 4ac}}{2c}$$

Let us examine the term involving the square root. It is possible that the term $4ac$ could take a larger value than b^2. If this were to happen the result would be a negative number. As far as we are concerned the square root of a negative number cannot be found; hence we cannot find the roots of such a function. This would indicate that the function did not intercept the X axis.

Progress Check C1.5

Return to the profit function we have been examining. Assume the firm's fixed costs increase to £4000. Reformulate the equation and attempt to find the roots. Graph this function to confirm that it always lies below the X axis.

C1.6 Summary

In this module we have begun to examine the principles involved in using non-linear functions in economic analysis, looking at quadratic functions specifically. Quadratic functions are useful in economics because of their specific characteristics, particularly that relating to the shape of a quadratic function that will show a maximum or a minimum turning point.

Learning Check

Having read this module you should have learned that:

- A quadratic function will take either a U shape or an inverted U shape depending on the value of the c parameter
- A negative value for c gives the inverted U and a positive value for c gives the U shape
- The two roots of a quadratic equation show where the function crosses the X axis and takes a zero value
- The turning point of a quadratic function occurs midway between the two roots.

Worked Example

The government is reviewing the tax rate it imposes on certain sources of personal income. It has estimated that the relationship between the tax rate, T, and the tax revenue collected, R, can be approximated by:

$$R = 100T - 1.5T^2$$

Worked Example *(Continued)*

where R is measured in \$ billion and T is measured as a percentage (e.g. a 10% tax rate would give $T=10$). The government has asked for advice as to the level of T to impose so as to maximize the tax revenue collected.

Solution

We have a quadratic function and with the c term negative we know the function will take the inverted U shape ($\cap$) and will have a maximum turning point. To find the turning point we need the two roots. In fact, we already have one of the roots. The a term is zero so the function will intercept the vertical axis at zero. The roots can be calculated from Eq. C1.7.

$$X = \frac{-b \pm \sqrt{-4ac + b^2}}{2c} \qquad (C1.10)$$

With $a=0$, $b=100$ and $c=-1.5$ we get:

$$X = \frac{-100 \pm \sqrt{0 + 100^2}}{-3}$$

Solving first for $+$ gives a value of 0. Solving next for $-$ gives a value of 66.7 for the second root. The turning point is midway between the two roots at 33.3. In other words a tax rate of 33.3% will optimize tax revenue in this model. The key features are shown also in Fig. C1.9.

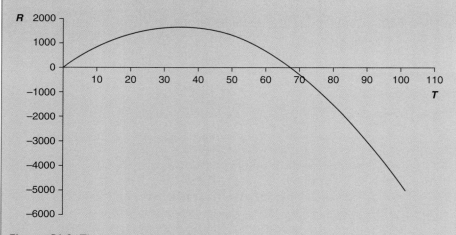

Figure C1.9 The tax revenue function

Exercises

C1.1 Find the roots and turning point of the following functions:

(i) $Y = -100 - 10X + 2.5X^2$

(ii) $Y = -100 + 50X - 5X^2$

Exercises *(Continued)*

(iii) $Y = -250 + 50X - 5X^2$

(iv) $Y = 250 + 50X - X^2$

C1.2   The market for a particular product is characterized by the following demand and supply functions:

$$Q_d = 50 - 3P$$

$$Q_s = -10 - 7P + 2P^2$$

 (i)   Sketch both these functions.

(ii)   Find the equilibrium position algebraically.

C1.3   Return to Ex. C1.2. Without performing any calculations, explain what would you expect to happen to equilibrium:

(i)   If Q_s changed to:

$$Q_s = -15 - 7P + 2P^2$$

(ii)   If Q_s changed to:

$$Q_s = -10 - 7P + 3P^2$$

(iii)   If Q_d changed to:

$$Q_d = 60 - 3P$$

C1.4   Return to Ex. C1.2. Find the price that would maximize total revenue.

C1.5   A firm faces the following total revenue and total cost functions. Find the breakeven levels of output.

$$TR = 15Q - 0.2Q^2$$

$$TC = 60 + 0.1Q + 0.05Q^2$$

C1.6   Return to Ex. C1.5. Derive the profit function. Determine the profit-maximizing level of output.

Appendix C1 Derivation of the roots formula

In Section C1.3 we showed the general form of a quadratic as:

$$a + bX + cX^2 = 0 \tag{C1.11}$$

and gave the roots formula as:

$$X = \frac{-b \pm \sqrt{-4ac + b^2}}{2c} \tag{C1.12}$$

If we divide Eq. C1.11 by c (given that it cannot equal zero by definition of being a quadratic), we have:

$$\frac{a}{c} + \frac{bX}{c} + X^2 = 0$$

and moving the a/c term to the right-hand side we get

$$\frac{bX}{c} + X^2 = \frac{-a}{c}$$

If we now add $b^2/4c^2$ to both sides we get:

$$\frac{bX}{c} + X^2 + \frac{b^2}{4c^2} = \frac{-a}{c} + \frac{b^2}{4c^2}$$

and rearrange the expression to get

$$X^2 + \frac{bX}{c} + \frac{b^2}{4c^2} = \frac{-a}{c} + \frac{b^2}{4c^2}$$

Now the left-hand side can be simplified to:

$$\left(X + \frac{b}{2c}\right)^2 = \frac{-a}{c} + \frac{b^2}{4c^2}$$

and the first part of the right-hand side can be multiplied by $4c$ to give

$$\left(X + \frac{b}{2c}\right)^2 = \frac{-4ca}{4c^2} + \frac{b^2}{4c^2}$$

$$\left(X + \frac{b}{2c}\right)^2 = \frac{-4ac + b^2}{4c^2}$$

Taking the square root of both sides we then have:

$$X + \frac{b}{2c} = \pm\sqrt{\frac{-4ac + b^2}{4c^2}}$$

Note that the $\pm$ term (meaning plus *and* minus) is necessary because the square of both a positive and negative number will produce the same result and there will effectively be two answers. The square root of $4c^2 = 2c$, so:

$$X + \frac{b}{2c} = \pm\frac{\sqrt{-4ac + b^2}}{2c}$$

$$X = \frac{-b}{2c} \pm \frac{\sqrt{-4ac + b^2}}{2c}$$

$$X = \frac{-b \pm \sqrt{-4ac + b^2}}{2c} \tag{C1.13}$$

Module C2
The derivative and the rules of differentiation

Non-linear models, like the quadratic, are clearly useful in economics since they allow us to develop more realistic economic models. As we saw in Module A3, you are likely to encounter a wide variety of different non-linear models, however, not just those that are quadratic. So you will need standard methods for analysing such non-linear models. In this module we turn to the important topic of *differential calculus* which provides us with the analytical skills required to cope with almost any type of non-linear model in economic analysis.

Learning Objectives

By the end of this module you should be able to:

- Explain what is meant by the derivative and its importance in economic analysis
- Calculate the derivative for a range of common non-linear functions
- Explain what is meant by a non-differentiable function.

Knowledge Check C2

If you're already familiar with the basics of differentiation and calculus, try solving the following. If you get the answers right then try the exercises at the end of the module.
For each of the following functions find the first and second derivatives:

(i) $Y = X^3 + 4X^2 - 9X + 10$

(ii) $Y = (5X - 10)(2X - 3)$

(iii) $Y = \dfrac{5X - 10}{2X - 3}$

(iv) $Y = (5X - 10)^4$

Check your answers in Appendix 2.

C2.1 The slope of linear and non-linear functions

As we have seen, the slope is an important concept in economic analysis. Let us return to the slope of a linear function. Figure C2.1 illustrates the principles involved. It shows

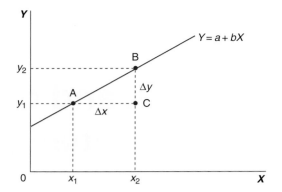

Figure C2.1 Slope of a linear function

a linear function whose slope can be determined graphically by locating two points, A and B, then finds the corresponding X and Y values and expresses the change in Y as a ratio to the change in X:

$$\frac{\Delta y}{\Delta x} = \frac{y_2 - y_1}{x_2 - x_1} = \frac{BC}{CA} \tag{C2.1}$$

and where we also know that $\Delta y / \Delta x$ (the *difference quotient*) is equal to the b parameter in the linear function. We also know that the slope of a linear function is constant. In other words, had point B in Fig. C2.1 been closer to, or further away from, point A, we would still obtain the same value for the slope of the function.

Let's now look at Fig. C2.2, which shows part of some non-linear function. Suppose we wanted the slope of this function at points A and B. To do this for point A we can draw an appropriate straight line that *just* touches the curve at this one point and nowhere else. Such a line is known as a *tangent*. A tangent line just touches, but does not cross, the curve, and there is only one possible tangent line for any single point on the curve. To work out the slope of the curve at point A we could now use the difference quotient to find the slope of the tangent line. Clearly, the slope of the tangent line and that of the curve at point A will be the same. In a similar way, if we required the slope of the curve at point B, we could determine its tangent line and then measure the slope

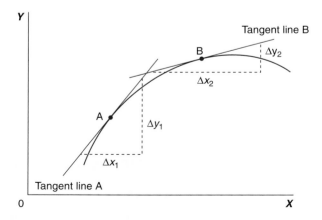

Figure C2.2 Slope of a non-linear function

of that line, which would be the same as that of the curve at point B. An inspection of Fig. C2.2 shows that the slope at points A and B will be different. That is, at point A the slope will have one particular value and at point B it will have another, different value.

Clearly, we do not wish to resort to a clumsy graphical method every time we wish to determine the slope at some point on a non-linear function. We need a method for working out the slope of a non-linear function for any given value of X. Let's introduce a further concept. In Fig. C2.3 we are still trying to determine the slope at point A, where X takes the value x_0, through the use of the tangent line, T. Let us return to the difference quotient. From point B_3 the slope of the line joining A to B_3 would be given by:

$$\frac{\Delta y}{\Delta x} \quad \text{where } \Delta x = x_3 - x_0$$

Similarly, the slope of the line B_2 would be given by:

$$\frac{\Delta y}{\Delta x} \quad \text{where } \Delta x = x_2 - x_0$$

and that of the line B_1 as

$$\frac{\Delta y}{\Delta x} \quad \text{where } \Delta x = x_1 - x_0$$

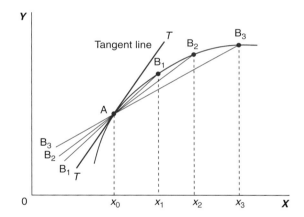

Figure C2.3 The tangent line

Consider what is happening as we move along our curve from point B_3 to B_2 to B_1. You will see that the slope of each corresponding line is getting closer and closer to the slope of the tangent line that we actually require. In other words, as Δx gets smaller and smaller (the difference between the appropriate x value and x_0) we get closer and closer to the slope of the tangent line at point A. Clearly, we could get to a position where the value for Δx was so infinitesimally small that the slope of the line from A to the corresponding B point is exactly the same as the slope of the tangent line. So, if we were to calculate the value of the difference quotient:

$$\frac{\Delta y}{\Delta x} \quad \text{where } \Delta x \text{ approaches zero}$$

we get the slope of the tangent line that we actually require. Formally we denote this as:

$$\lim_{\Delta x \to 0} \frac{\Delta y}{\Delta x} \tag{C2.2}$$

which means 'the limit of $\Delta y/\Delta x$ as Δx approaches zero'. The concept of a limit indicates the value that $\Delta y/\Delta x$ approaches as Δx itself approaches zero. If the concept of a limit, or a limiting value of a function, is new to you, you should make sure it's properly understood. Let's consider the function:

$$y = 1/x$$

Working out the value that y takes for different values for x isn't difficult. If $x=1$ then $y=1/1$, if $x=2$, $y=1/2$, if $x=3$ then $y=1/3$ and so on. We see that as x increases y decreases. In fact as x increases y not only decreases but gets closer and closer to zero (with $x=1000$, $y=0.001$, with $x=10,000$, $y=0.0001$, etc.). However, although y gets closer and closer to zero it will never actually *equal* zero. So as x increases y approaches (but never actually reaches) zero. This enables us to say that y approaches a limiting value of zero as x approaches infinity. In the language of calculus we show this as:

$$\lim_{x\to\infty} y = 0$$

That is, y approaches a limit of zero as x approaches infinity. Let's return to Eq. C2.2:

$$\lim_{\Delta x\to 0} \frac{\Delta y}{\Delta x} \tag{C2.2}$$

where this expression relates to the slope of the function at any point along its length and is formally referred to as the *derivative* of the function with respect to x. The notation appropriate for a derivative is:

$$\frac{dy}{dx} = \lim_{\Delta x\to 0} \frac{\Delta y}{\Delta x} \tag{C2.3}$$

where dy/dx (pronounced 'dee-y by dee-x') is the standard symbol used for the derivative. It is important to note that the derivative symbol does *not* represent d times y divided by d times x but is simply the standard notation used to denote a derivative. The process of obtaining the derivative of a function is known as *differentiation* and the formal study of derivatives is a branch of mathematics referred to as *differential calculus*. As we'll see shortly, the derivative allows us to calculate the slope of a non-linear function for a given value of X.

Progress Check C2.1

In Module C1 we used a profit function:

$$\text{Profit} = -1125 + 250Q - 5Q^2$$

where Q is output measured in 000's units.
We require the slope of the function when $Q=10$.

(i) Using a spreadsheet, calculate the profit for this level of output and also for the following levels:

$$Q = 11, 10.5, 10.25, 10.1, 10.01, 10.001, 10.0001$$

(ii) Taking Δy as the change in profit between $Q=10$ and each other value of Q in turn and Δx as the change in output from $Q=10$, calculate the difference quotient for each value of Q shown.

(iii) What comment can you make about the value of the difference quotient as Q approaches 10?

(iv) What would you infer the slope of the function to be when $Q=10$?

(Solution on p. 463)

Table C2.1   Difference quotients for profit $= -1125 + 250Q - 5Q^2$

Q	Profit	Quotient
10	875	
11	1020	145
10.5	948.75	147.5
10.25	912.1875	148.75
10.1	889.95	149.5
10.01	876.4995	149.95
10.001	875.15	149.995
10.0001	875.015	149.99995

Table C2.1 shows the relevant calculations. When $Q = 10$, Profit $= 875$. When $Q = 11$, Profit $= 1020$ and the difference quotient is 145; when $Q = 10.5$, the difference quotient is 147.5 and so on. It becomes apparent that as Q moves from 11 and closer and closer to 10 the difference quotient increases and gets ever closer to 150. Recollect that the difference quotient measures the slope of the line joining the point $Q = 10$ and each individual Q value. We conclude from these calculations that as Δx approaches zero we approach the slope of the profit function where $Q = 10$ and that the slope at this point will be 150.

C2.2 The derivative

We may not appear to be much further forward in terms of actually finding a value for the slope of a non-linear function, but in fact we now have all the concepts we need to put the finishing touches to our discussion. Let us return to the profit function we had earlier in Module C1 (Eq. C1.7):

$$\text{Profit} = -1125 + 250Q - 5Q^2$$

which we recollect is a quadratic following the inverted U shape. Clearly, in terms of our general discussion Q represents the X variable and Profit the Y variable. Looking at Fig. C2.2, we can assume this to represent some part of the profit function and that we wish to determine the slope of the profit function at point A. How can we proceed? First, let us rewrite the function in terms of X and Y:

$$Y = -1125 + 250X - 5X^2 \tag{C2.4}$$

At point A, $X = x_0$ and Y will be given by:

$$y_0 = -1125 + 250x_0 - 5x_0^2 \tag{C2.5}$$

If we now examine point B_3, we see that $X = x_3$. Let us show x_3 as $(x_0 + \Delta x)$, that is, as the original X value plus some change in X. Y will now be given as:

$$y_3 = -1125 + 250(x_0 + \Delta x) - 5(x_0 + \Delta x)^2 \tag{C2.6}$$

To work out the slope of the line AB_3 we require:

$$\frac{\Delta y}{\Delta x} = \frac{y_3 - y_0}{x_3 - x_0} = \frac{y_3 - y_0}{(x_0 + \Delta x) - x_0} = \frac{y_3 - y_0}{\Delta x}$$

$$= \frac{[-1125 + 250(x_0 + \Delta x) - 5(x_0 + \Delta x)^2] - [-1125 + 250x_0 - 5x_0^2]}{\Delta x}$$

$$= \frac{-1125 + 250x_0 + 250\Delta x - 5x_0^2 - 5\Delta x^2 - 10x_0\Delta x + 1125 - 250x_0 + 5x_0^2}{\Delta x}$$

$$= \frac{250\Delta x - 5\Delta x^2 - 10x_0\Delta x}{\Delta x} = 250 - 5\Delta x - 10x_0 = 250 - 10x_0 - 5\Delta x \quad (C2.7)$$

So we now have $\Delta y / \Delta x = 250 - 10x_0 - 5\Delta x$. Using the logic we introduced to derive the concept of a limit, as Δx gets smaller (that is, as $\Delta x \to 0$) then Eq. C2.7 will become:

$$\lim_{\Delta x \to 0} \frac{\Delta y}{\Delta x} = 250 - 10x_0 \quad (C2.8)$$

since $5\Delta x$ will tend to zero as Δx tends to zero. If we now generalize for any value of X and not simply for x_0, this gives:

$$\frac{dy}{dx} = \lim_{\Delta x \to 0} \frac{\Delta y}{\Delta x} = 250 - 10X \quad (C2.9)$$

That is, the derivative of this profit function is given by the expression $250 - 10X$. As we said above, the derivative, dy/dx, would allow us to calculate the slope of a non-linear function for a given value of X.

Progress Check C2.2

Using Eq. C2.9 calculate the slope of the profit function when $X = 10$. Compare this with your result from Progress Check C2.1.

We have the derivative:

$$\frac{dy}{dx} = 250 - 10X$$

which is the expression for calculating the slope of the original profit function for any given value of X. For $X = 10$, simple substitution gives $dy/dx = 150$. That is, the slope of the profit function when $X = 10$ is 150.

Let us review what we have accomplished. We began by seeking a general method of determining the slope of a non-linear function. We saw that difficulties arise as the slope of such a function will differ depending where on the curve we are (i.e. depending on which value for X we are considering). Through the use of logic and mathematical manipulation we have shown that the slope at a point on some non-linear function will be the same as that of the unique tangent line to that point. Similarly, as we take successively smaller changes in X we can approximate to this tangent line and hence to the slope of the point on the curve. This principle of a limit leads directly to the definition of a derivative of the original function: the derivative is the measure of the slope of a function.

Let us return to our example and examine in detail what we have achieved. We had the original function:

$$Y = -1125 + 250X - 5X^2$$

and obtained

$$\frac{dY}{dX} = 250 - 10X$$

where Y represents profit and X output. One important point to note at this stage is that the derivative of a function of X is itself a function of X, that is:

$$Y = f(X) = -1125 + 250X - 5X^2$$

and

$$\frac{dY}{dX} = f(X) = 250 - 10X$$

However, to denote that the derivative is actually derived from the profit function the standard notation used is:

$$\frac{dY}{dX} = f'(X) \tag{C2.10}$$

where f' (pronounced 'f prime') is used to show the derivative of a function of X. This point also helps explain what the derivative represents and how it can be used. For example, if $X = 10$ we have:

$$Y = f(X) = -1125 + 250X - 5X^2$$
$$= f(X = 10) = -1125 + 250(10) - 5(10)^2 = 875$$

Similarly, for the derivative when $X = 10$ we have:

$$\frac{dY}{dX} = f'(10) = 250 - 10(10) = 150$$

What does this value of 150 represent? Recollect how we obtained the derivative expression. It measures the slope of the original function at a given point. Here the given point is $X = 10$ so dY/dX measures the slope of the original function at this point. When $X = 10$ the profit function has a slope of 150. Consider further the meaning of the slope in the context of the profit function. At a level of output of 10 a marginal change in output will bring about a change in profit of 150 times the change in output. The derivative therefore allows us to determine the slope of the original function anywhere along its length (i.e. for any given value of X).

Progress Check C2.3

Using the difference quotient calculate the slope for the profit function between $Q = 9.99$ and $Q = 10$. Calculate the slope using the derivative for $Q = 9.99$. Why is there a difference between the two?

(Solution on p. 464)

There is one important point to note, however. The interpretation of the slope value is strictly correct only for *infinitesimally* small changes in X (recollect the limit concept). Technically the slope of 150 is strictly applicable only when X is *exactly* 10. If X were 10.01 or 9.99 then the slope of the profit function would not be 150 (although, of course, we could find its precise value from the derivative function as before). It will be helpful to show both the original function and its derivative on the same graph. We do this in Fig. C2.4, which shows both the profit function and its derivative. A number of points are worth noting. First, we note from the shape

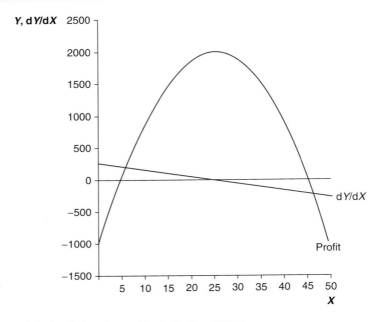

Figure C2.4 The Profit function and its derivative dY/dX

of the quadratic profit function that the function has a positive slope where $X < 25$ and a negative slope for $X > 25$. It can be seen from the line representing dY/dX that this is confirmed. The derivative, which measures the slope of the original function, takes positive values up to $X = 25$ and negative values thereafter. We can also see from Fig. C2.4 that the slope of the profit function as shown by the derivative takes a zero value when $X = 25$. At this level of output the derivative line crosses the X axis and must, therefore, take a zero value. In our example, this represents the level of output at which the firm will maximize profit. This point on the profit function where the slope is zero is referred to as a *stationary* point (since the slope is neither positive nor negative).

Second, note that the slope of the derivative is also negative. We see this also from Eq. C2.9 since the derivative, which is a linear function, has a slope of -10. How can this be interpreted? It is an indication of the rate of change of the slope of the original profit function. Given that, as we know, the original function is changing from a positive to a negative slope as X increases, it is clear that the direction of change of the slope is negative. This is confirmed by the slope of the derivative which is negative. This brings us to a further development. We have stated that the derivative is itself a function of X. As such we could find the derivative of this function – that is, an expression showing the slope of this function at any point. In other words, we have:

$$Y = f(X)$$
$$\frac{dY}{dX} = f'(X)$$

and we could determine the derivative of dY/dX. In this particular case algebra is not actually required. We know that dY/dX is itself a linear function and therefore has a constant slope represented by the b parameter (at -10). The derivative of dY/dX is known as the *second* derivative and is denoted by:

$$\frac{d^2Y}{dX^2} = f''(X) \tag{C2.11}$$

(pronounced as 'dee two Y by dee X squared' and as 'f double prime'). Note that, as before, the second derivative notation is not an indication of division or of squaring but simply the standard form of notation. If we collect these we have:

$$Y = f(X) = -1125 + 250X - 5X^2 \quad \boxed{\text{This is the original profit function}}$$

$$\frac{dY}{dX} = f'(X) = 250 - 10X \quad \boxed{\begin{array}{l}\text{This is the first derivative, showing the}\\ \text{slope of the profit function}\end{array}}$$

$$\frac{d^2Y}{dX^2} = f''(X) = -10 \quad \boxed{\begin{array}{l}\text{This is the second derivative, showing the slope}\\ \text{of the first derivative – the slope of the slope}\end{array}}$$

In Module C4 we shall examine the use of the second derivative in economic analysis.

Progress Check C2.4

A firm faces a marginal cost (*MC*) function:

$$MC = 50 - 10Q + Q^2$$

where Q represents units of output.

(i) Using the methods developed in this module find the derivative of this function.

(ii) Using the derivative calculate the point where the *MC* function takes a minimum value (where the slope is zero).

(iii) Attempt to find the roots of the *MC* function

(iv) Graph this function and comment on the suitability of the equation for representing typical economic behaviour in the context of marginal costs.

(Solution on p. 464)

C2.3 Rules of differentiation

Although we have developed a method for finding the derivative of a function, the approach so far is both clumsy and time-consuming. Clearly, we do not wish to have to go through the mathematical contortions of the previous section every time we wish to find the derivative of a function. Fortunately, we can develop simple rules for differentiating the kind of functions that we encounter in economic analysis. We shall not show the derivation of these rules but simply state them and illustrate their use. For the illustrative function we shall be using we shall assume that all functions are of the form $Y = f(X)$ and that we require $f'(X)$.

Rule 1: the power rule

Assume a function of the form:

$$f(X) = kX^n \tag{C2.12}$$

where k and n are any real numbers. Then $f'(X)$ is determined by:

$$f'(X) = nkX^{n-1} \tag{C2.13}$$

For example, for the function $f(X) = -5X^2$, we have $k = -5$ and $n = 2$, so:

$$f'(-5X^2) = 2(-5)X^{2-1} = -10X^1 = -10X$$

This rule can be applied to any function that can be expressed in the form of Eq. C2.12. For example:

$$f(X) = 15X^6 \qquad f'(X) = 90X^5$$
$$f(X) = 0.3X^{1/2} \qquad f'(X) = 0.15X^{-1/2}$$
$$f(X) = 250X \qquad f'(X) = 250$$
$$f(X) = -1125 \qquad f'(X) = 0$$

The last two examples require comment. $f(X) = 250X$ is clearly linear with a constant slope of 250. The derivative confirms this by producing a derivative function that takes a constant value equal to 250. Similarly, $f(X) = -1125$ is not actually a function of X at all (and would be represented by a line parallel to the X axis – i.e. with a zero slope). The derivative confirms the slope of such an expression to be zero: Y will not change as X changes. This will apply to any constant.

Progress Check C2.5

For the functions shown below obtain the first and second derivatives. Plot the original function and the first derivative together for $X = 0$ to 10.

(i) $Y = 0.6X^3$

(ii) $Y = 12X^6$

(iii) $Y = 100/X$

(iv) $Y = 7X^{1/3}$

(v) $Y = (1/3)X^{-1/3}$

(Solution on p. 464)

Rule 2: the generalized power rule

When we have a function so that:

$$f(x) = [g(x)]^n$$

then we have

$$f'(x) = n[g(x)]^{n-1}g^1(x)$$

For example, if we have:

$$f(X) = (x^3 + 2)^4$$

then

$$f'(X) = 4(x^3 + 2)^3 3x^2$$

which could also be written as $f'(X) = 12x^2(x^3 + 2)^3$.

This rule is known as the generalized power rule. You will find it useful when we apply calculus to algebraic rather than numeric expressions.

Rule 3: derivative of sums/differences of power functions

If we have a function that comprises the sums and/or differences of other functions, the derivative is simply the sum of the individual derivatives. In fact we have already used this rule. Let:

$$f(X) = -1125 + 250X - 5X^2$$

Then:

$$fd'(X) = \frac{d}{dX}(-1125) + \frac{d}{dX}(250X) + \frac{d}{dX}(-5X^2)$$
$$= 0 + 250 - 10X = 250 - 10X$$

Progress Check C2.6

Assume a total cost function such that:

$$TC = 500 + 50Q - 5Q^2 + 1/3Q^3$$

(i)   Obtain the derivative of this function.

(ii)   Interpret the derivative function in the context of economics.

(iii)   Find the value for Q that gives the minimum for the derivative function.

(iv)   Obtain a function for average cost.

(v)   Plot all three functions on one graph.

(Solution on p. 465)

Rule 4: derivative of a product of functions

If Y is the product of two functions so that:

$$Y = f(X) = g(X)h(X)$$

then the derivative is given as

$$f'(X) = g(X)h'(X) + h(X)g'(X) \tag{C2.14}$$

For example, let $g(X) = 6X^2 + 5X$ and let $h(X) = 2X^4 - 10$. We then have:

$$Y = f(X) = (6X^2 + 5X)(2X^4 - 10)$$

Then:

$$g(X) = 6X^2 + 5X \quad \text{and} \quad g'(X) = 12X + 5$$
$$h(X) = 2X^4 - 10 \quad \text{and} \quad h'(X) = 8X^3$$

and

$$f'(X) = (6X^2 + 5X)(8X^3) + (2X^4 - 10)(12X + 5)$$
$$= 48X^5 + 40X^4 + 24X^5 - 120X + 10X^4 - 50$$
$$= 72X^5 + 50X^4 - 120X - 50$$

Progress Check C2.7

Confirm the derivative obtained by first expanding in full the original function $(6X^2 + 5X)(2X^4 - 10)$ and then using the first rule of differentiation.

Rule 5: derivative of a quotient of functions

If Y is a function given by:

$$Y = f(X) = \frac{g(X)}{h(X)} \tag{C2.15}$$

then

$$f'(X) = \frac{g'(X)h(X) - h'(X)g(X)}{h(X)^2} \tag{C2.16}$$

For example, let $g(X)$ and $h(X)$ take the values as in the last rule. We then have:

$$Y = f(X) = \frac{6X^2 + 5X}{2X^4 - 10}$$

and

$$f(X) = \frac{(12X + 5)(2X^4 - 10) - 8X^3(6X^2 + 5X)}{(2X^4 - 10)^2}$$

$$= \frac{(24X^5 + 10X^4 - 120X - 50) - (48X^5 + 40X^4)}{(2X^4 - 10)^2}$$

$$= \frac{-24X^5 - 30X^4 - 120X - 50}{(2X^4 - 10)^2}$$

Progress Check C2.8

Assume a function such that

$$Y = \frac{2X^4 - 10}{6X^2 + 5X}$$

Obtain the first derivative.

(Solution on p. 465)

Rule 6: derivative of a function of a function (the chain rule)

If we have a function that is itself a function of X such that:

$$Y = f(g(x))$$

then the derivative is given by

$$\frac{dY}{dX} = \frac{dY}{dg} \frac{dg}{dX} \tag{C2.17}$$

Assume we have a function such that:

$$Y = (10X^2 - 3X + 25)^2$$

and we show

$$g(X) = 10X^2 - 3X + 25$$

Then we can write:

$$Y = g^2$$

Now:

$$\frac{dg}{dX} = g'(X) = 20X - 3$$

and:

$$\frac{dY}{dg} = f'(g^2) = 2g$$

We then have:

$$\frac{dY}{dX} = 2g(20X - 3) = 2(10X^2 - 3X + 25)(20X - 3)$$

$$= (20X^2 - 6X + 50)(20X - 3)$$

$$= 400X^3 - 120X^2 + 1000X - 60X^2 + 18X - 150$$

$$= 400X^3 - 180X^2 + 1018X - 150$$

Progress Check C2.9

Confirm this last derivative by first expanding the original function $Y = (10X^2 - 3X + 25)^2$ and then differentiating using the first rule of differentiation.

Rule 7: derivative of a logarithmic function

The derivative of a natural (base e) log function:

$$Y = f(X) = \ln X \tag{C2.18}$$

is given by

$$f'(X) = \frac{1}{X} \tag{C2.19}$$

Functions involving logarithms in economic analysis (usually to the base e because of their more useful theoretical properties) typically involve more complex functions than those shown. In such cases we can combine this rule with previous rules where appropriate. Consider the function:

$$Y = f(X) = \ln(3X^2 - 5X + 10)$$

Let:

$$g(X) = 3X^2 - 5X + 10$$

$$f(X) = \ln[g(X)]$$

Using the log rule and the product rule we have:

$$f'(X) = \frac{1}{g(X)}g'(X) = \frac{1}{3X^2 - 5X + 10}(6X - 5)$$

$$= \frac{6X - 5}{3X^2 - 5X + 10}$$

Rule 8: inverse function rule

Assume we have a function such that:

$$Y = f(X) = X^2$$

Then we have:

$$\frac{dY}{dX} = f'(X) = 2X$$

However, if we find the inverse of the original function we then have:

$$X = g(Y) = \sqrt{Y} = Y^{1/2}$$

and we have

$$g'(Y) = \frac{1}{2}Y^{-1/2} = \frac{1}{2\sqrt{Y}}$$

However:

$$2X = 2Y^{1/2}$$

Hence:

$$\frac{dY}{dX} = 2X = 2Y^{1/2} = 2\sqrt{Y}$$

and hence

$$\frac{dX}{dY} = \frac{1}{dY/dX} \tag{C2.20}$$

This result is known as the inverse function rule. Not all functions, however, will have an inverse that can be differentiated. In general, for a function to possess an inverse it must be *monotonic*. This simply means that if we have $Y = f(X)$ then if X increases then Y must increase/decrease successively. In other words, an increase in X will always lead to an increase/decrease in Y. A linear function, for example, is monotonic but a quadratic is not (Y will change in one direction with respect to X and then in the opposite direction). In the context of differential calculus, a monotonic function will always have the same type of slope, either always negative or always positive. These rules can be neatly summarized in tabular form: see Table C2.2.

Table C2.2   Derivative rules

Expression	Function	Derivative
	$y = f(x)$	$f'(x)$
Constant	$y = a$	0
Power term	$y = x^n$	$nx^{(n-1)}$
Constant times power term	$y = kx^n$	$knx^{(n-1)}$
Sum or difference	$y = g(x) \pm h(x)$	$g'(x) \pm h'(x)$
Product	$y = g(x)h(x)$	$g(x)h'(x) + h(x)g'(x)$
Quotient	$y = g(x)/h(x)$	$\dfrac{g'(x)h(x) - h'(x)g(x)}{h(x)^2}$
Chain rule	$y = f(g(x))$	$\dfrac{dY}{dg}\dfrac{dg}{dX}$
Natural logarithm	$y = \ln X$	$1/X$

C2.4 Non-differentiable functions

We must also appreciate that not all functions can be differentiated. Recollect that by differentiating we are finding an expression that allows us to quantify the slope of the original function for any value of X (and recollect this is the equivalent of finding the slope of the tangent line at that point). Consider the situations illustrated in Figs C2.5 and C2.6.

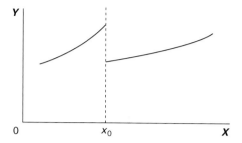

Figure C2.5 Discontinuity

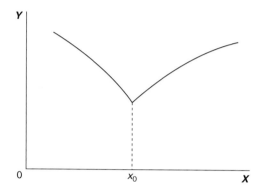

Figure C2.6 Non-differentiable function

Figure C2.5 shows a discontinuous function where the function takes a 'jump' at x_0, and clearly there will be no unique tangent at this point. Similarly, Fig. C2.6 shows that while the function is continuous there is a definite 'kink' at point x_0 where, again, there would be no unique tangent.

Fortunately we are usually able to develop suitable economic models with functions that are differentiable using the rules we have developed.

Progress Check C2.10

Plot the following function for $X = 0$ to 2 in steps of 0.2. Comment on whether you think it can be differentiated.

$$Y = 2 + \sqrt[3]{(x-1)^2}$$

(Solution on p. 465)

C2.5 Summary

In this module we have begun to examine the principles involved in using non-linear functions in economic analysis. We have seen that such functions involve two key principles: that of slope and that of optimization. Both these principles are of critical importance in economic theory, as we shall demonstrate in the following modules. In order to be able to deal with these we introduced the basics of differential calculus and saw that for any function we can obtain the derivative: a function showing the slope of the original function. In the next module we shall examine the opportunities that differential calculus offers economic analysis. Before proceeding, however, you should ensure that you have an adequate technical grasp of the topic.

Learning Check

Having read this module you should have learned that:

- A derivative is an expression showing the slope of a given function
- There are a variety of rules for finding the derivative depending on the type of original function
- Not all functions can be differentiated.

Worked Example

A small farming cooperative is examining its operations and has noted that its short-run production function, linking production and number of workers employed, is given by:

$$Q = -0.05L^3 + 3L^2$$

with $0 \leq L \leq 50$ where Q is production and L is the number of workers employed. Capital is assumed to be fixed in the short run. The cooperative is interested in assessing the impact on production of varying the number of workers employed and in trying to determine the number of workers to employ that will lead to maximum production. The cooperative is also interested in an explanation of its situation in this context.

Solution

The cooperative's interest is in assessing how production, Q, varies as the number of workers employed, L, varies. Effectively, this implies the cooperative is

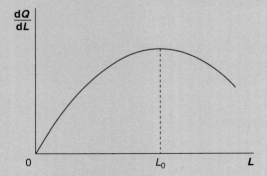

Figure C2.7 $dQ/dL = -0.15L^2 + 6L$

Worked Example   (Continued)

interested in assessing changes in Q brought about by changes in L, and it is clear that the derivative will be appropriate, since dQ/dL will provide a function showing the relationship between the changes in the two variables. We have:

$$\frac{dQ}{dL} = -0.15L^2 + 6L$$

(a)

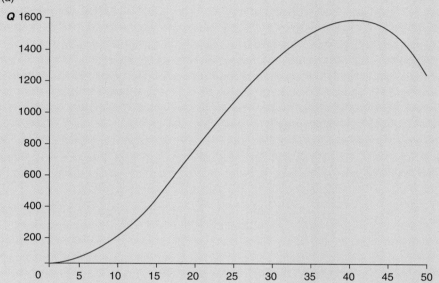

(b)

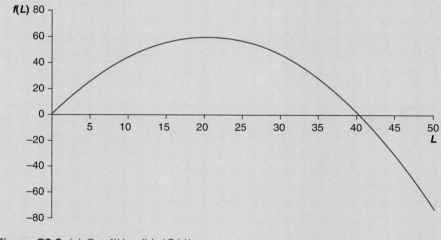

Figure C2.8 (a) $Q = f(L)$ (b) dQ/dL

Worked Example   (Continued)

We observe that the derivative is a quadratic with a zero intercept and will follow the inverted U shape giving a situation as in Fig. C2.7. Initially, as L increases so does dQ/dL: as the cooperative increases labour then total production increases (since dQ/dL represents additional production from additional labour). After some point, L_0, however, the derivative decreases in value: additional labour actually leads to a reduction in marginal production. This is predictable from economic theory. The law of diminishing returns (or diminishing marginal product) indicates that once the size of the labour input reaches a certain critical level (in part dependent on the available capital stock, which is fixed in the short run) then the additional output from additional labour will gradually decrease until the increase in labour actually has a negative impact on total production.

   We can confirm this through a graph of the original production function as in Fig. C2.8, which also shows the derivative. In fact it becomes more appropriate to refer to the derivative of the production function as the marginal product of labour (MP_L). We see that MP_L reaches its maximum at point L_m, which coincides with a point on the production function where diminishing returns begin to set in. We also see that at the point where Q reaches its maximum MP_L is zero and after this level of L, MP_L is negative and hence Q will actually decline after this point. We have, as yet, no tools other than the graph for obtaining a maximum value mathematically for the production function. However, we now know that $MP_L = 0$ at the maximum production point. We can then use the derivative:

$$MP_L = -0.15L^2 + 6L = 0$$

Using the roots approach from Module C1 we find:

$$L_1 = 0$$
$$L_2 = 40$$

and both from Fig. C2.8 and by substituting back into the production function we confirm that maximum production will occur when $L = 40$; that is, employing 40 workers will maximize production.

Exercises

C2.1   A firm has analysed demand for its product and obtained a demand function of the form:

$$Q_d = 100 + \frac{5}{P}$$

  (i)   Find the derivative of this function.
 (ii)   Calculate the slope when $P = 2$ and when $P = 5$. What observations can you make about the behaviour of the slope with respect to price?
(iii)   What use do you think could be made of the derivative in this context?

Exercises *(Continued)*

C2.2 Return to the TC and TR functions we were examining in Module C1:

$$TR = 260Q$$
$$TC = 1125 + 10Q + 5Q^2$$

(i) Find a derivative of the TR and TC functions.

(ii) What economic interpretation would you give to each of these?

(iii) Calculate the slope of the TR and TC functions at the profit-maximizing level of output ($Q = 25$).

(iv) How do you explain your result in (iii)?

(v) The selling price of the firm's product now increases to 300. What would you expect to happen to the profit-maximizing level of output?

(vi) Calculate the new profit-maximizing level of output.

(vii) The firm's fixed costs now increase to 1500. Calculate the new profit-maximizing level of output. How do you explain your result?

C2.3 For each of the following functions find the first and second derivatives:

(i) $Y = X^3 + 4X^2 - 9X + 10$

(ii) $Y = (5X - 10)(2X - 3)$

(iii) $Y = \dfrac{5X - 10}{2X - 3}$

(iv) $Y = (5X - 10)^4$

(v) $Y = (10X^3 - 12)(2X + 5)$

(vi) $Y = \dfrac{(10X^3 - 12)}{2X + 5}$

(vii) $(5X^3 - 7X^2)^2$

(viii) $Y = \sqrt{X - 1}$

(ix) $Y = 10\sqrt{X - 1}$

C2.4 A firm's cost function is given by:

$$TC = 500 + 20Q - 6Q^2 + 0.6Q^3$$

(i) Find an expression for marginal costs.

(ii) Find an expression for average costs.

(iii) Draw a graph of these two functions.

(iv) What do you notice about their intersection?

(v) Find this intersection algebraically.

C2.5 The market for a particular product is characterized by the following demand and supply functions:

$$Q_d = 25 - 3P + 0.2P^2$$
$$Q_s = -5 + 3P - 0.01P^2$$

(i) Sketch both these functions.

(ii) Find the equilibrium position algebraically.

(iii) Calculate total revenue at this point.

Exercises   *(Continued)*

C2.6   A Cobb–Douglas production function is given as:

$$Y = 0.6L^{0.3}K^{0.7}$$

(i)   If K is fixed at 10 units, derive a production function for labour.

(ii)   Find the derivative of this function.

(iii)   What is the economic meaning of this derivative?

(iv)   Plot this derivative together with the labour production function for $L=1$ to 10. Comment on the behaviour of the two functions.

(v)   Repeat the analysis but now with labour fixed at 10.

Module C3
Derivatives and economic analysis

In the previous module we introduced the important concept of the derivative. We saw how the derivative shows the slope of a function. In this module we start to explore how derivatives can be used in economic modelling and economic analysis; and this task will occupy us for much of the rest of the book. As we have seen, economic analysis is frequently concerned with relationships between variables and, in particular, the changes that occur in one variable when another variable changes. The derivative, as we have seen, is mathematically concerned with the same and it is apparent that we can use the derivative to examine such economic relationships. In this module we illustrate a number of common areas of economic application of the derivative and see how the ability to use the derivative allows us to reach important conclusions about those models.

C

Learning Objectives

By the end of this module you should be able to:

- Use the principles of calculus to help sketch typical functions
- Calculate elasticity using the derivative
- Explain the use of the derivative in the context of economic marginality
- Derive marginal expressions from a number of common economic models.

C3.1 Curve sketching

We can begin to use the principles of the first and second derivatives to help us sketch a particular mathematical function. As we have seen, it is often useful to sketch (as opposed to draw a detailed graph of) an economic function so that we have a picture of the corresponding relationship. Consider the function:

$$Q_d = \frac{100}{P} \tag{C3.1}$$

where

$P = $ price per unit
$Q_d = $ quantity demanded

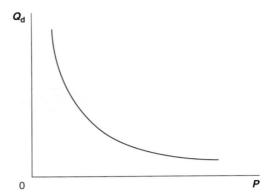

Figure C3.1 Sketch of $Q_d = 100/P$

Clearly, this is a demand function, but what shape will it take? Let us begin to put various pieces of information together. First, it is sensible in an economic context to restrict the values of P to be non-negative and greater than zero ($P \geq 0$). Then, as Eq. C3.1 shows, Q_d will take larger values as P decreases and Q_d will tend to infinity as P approaches zero. Equally, as P increases Q_d will approach, but never reach, zero. Similarly, using Rule 1 from Module C2, the first derivative of the function is:

$$f'(P) = -\frac{100}{P^2} \tag{C3.2}$$

and we see that with $P \geq 0$ then the first derivative must always take a negative value. The first derivative shows the slope of the function, so Eq. C3.2 indicates that the slope of Eq. C3.1 is always negative. That is, as P increases Q_d decreases and vice versa; this is hardly surprising for a demand function, but useful confirmation nevertheless. Moreover, we see from the derivative that the slope will take larger (negative) values when P decreases and smaller (negative) values as P increases. In other words, the function has a larger negative slope for lower prices than for higher. The second derivative confirms this. We have:

$$f''(P) = \frac{200}{P^3} \tag{C3.3}$$

which, again for $P \geq 0$, can give only positive values. Since the second derivative represents the rate of change in the first derivative (which in turn represents the gradient of the original function) we see that the function's slope is decreasing as P increases. Putting all these deductions together we can produce a sketch (Fig. C3.1) of Eq. C3.1. Note that we have not put any numerical values on the sketch but we do have a reasonably accurate picture of the general shape of the function. The function is downward sloping (first derivative), and has a large slope for small P values and a small slope for high P values (second derivative). Also, as P approaches zero, Q_d approaches infinity, and as P increases, Q_d approaches, but does not reach, zero.

What to think about when sketching a curve

When you sketch a curve you may find it helpful to consider the following:

- Does the curve fit any of the familiar functions that we've looked at? E.g. quadratic, cubic, exponential? If so, that will give you an idea of its general shape

- Does the curve intersect the Y and X axes and, if so, at what point(s)?
- Does the curve have any turning points and, if so, where?
- What happens to the Y value when X takes very large/small values?

Progress Check C3.1

(i) Plot both the demand function and its derivative for $P = 1.00$ to 2.00 in units of 0.1.

(ii) The function:

$$D = 400/W^2$$

shows the demand for labour, D, as a function of the wage rate, W. Obtain a sketch of this function. Confirm your sketch by drawing a detailed graph for $W = 5$ to 10 for both the function and its derivative.

C3.2 The derivative and the concept of marginality

Although using the derivative to sketch an economic function is useful, it cannot by itself justify the use of differential calculus in economics. However, we begin to appreciate the potential for using the derivative in economic analysis when we consider the link between the derivative and the economic concept of *marginality*. We have seen that the derivative allows us to determine the rate of change in some Y variable as the X variable changes. We have also seen that in this context the derivative is readily interpreted as the slope of the function. It will be apparent that there is a direct connection between the derivative and the economic concept of marginality. In economics, analysis is frequently concerned with decisions taken *at the margin*. This can be viewed as assessing the change that occurs in one economic variable as the result of a marginal change in another economic variable. So, for example, we interpret marginal cost as the *extra* cost incurred by a firm as an *extra* unit of output is produced. Marginal revenue is the *extra* revenue earned by the firm from producing and selling an *extra* unit of output. Economic analysis is littered with such marginal changes: marginal propensity to consume, marginal cost, marginal propensity to import, marginal rate of substitution, marginal product, marginal utility and so on. In terms of differential calculus, the derivative can be interpreted as a marginal change in the Y variable given some infinitesimally small change in X, and so is directly related to the marginal concepts that are so useful in economics. Throughout the rest of this module we shall be examining a number of such marginal relationships, and we shall use differential calculus to investigate them.

Some of the more common marginal functions in economics are summarized in Table C3.1.

Progress Check C3.2

(i) For the following function determine and interpret the function for marginal propensity to consume (mpc) and for marginal propensity to save (mps):

$$C = 100 + 5Y^{0.2}$$

Progress Check C3.2   *(Continued)*

(ii) A firm faces the following demand function. Determine a function for the firm's marginal revenue and interpret:

$$Q_d = 500 - 3P$$

(Solution on p. 465)

Table C3.1   Common marginal functions

Marginal Revenue (MR)	The change in total revenue as output changes	$MR = f'(TR)$
Marginal Cost (MC)	The change in total costs as output changes	$MC = f'(TC)$
Marginal Product of Labour (MP_L)	The change in production as labour input changes (*ceteris paribus*)	$MP_L = f'(Q) = dQ/dL$
Marginal Product of Capital (MP_K)	The change in production as capital input changes (*ceteris paribus*)	$MP_K = f'(Q) = dQ/dK$
Marginal Propensity to Consume (mpc)	The change in consumption as income changes	$mpc = f'(Y) = dC/dY$
Marginal Propensity to Save (mps)	The change in savings as income changes	$mps = f'(Y) = dS/dY$
Marginal Utility (MU)	The change in consumer utility as consumption changes	$MU = f'(U) = dU/dC$

C3.3 Analysing elasticity

We examined elasticity in Module B2, but only in the context of linear functions. We are now in a position to investigate the concept for any type of demand function. Let us examine the following demand function:

$$Q_d = f(P) = 250 - 10P \tag{C3.4}$$

We recognize this as a linear demand function and that its slope, given by the first derivative, will be:

$$\frac{dQ_d}{dP} = -10 \tag{C3.5}$$

From Section B2.4 we also have the general elasticity expression:

$$E_d = \frac{\Delta Q}{\Delta P}\frac{P}{Q} \tag{C3.6}$$

However, we saw in the previous module, when introducing the derivative concept, that for a function such as $Q_d = f(P)$ the limit of $\Delta Q/\Delta P$ as $\Delta P \to 0$ is the derivative of that function. In other words, when ΔP is infinitesimal we have:

$$E_d = \frac{dQ_d}{dP}\frac{P}{Q} \tag{C3.7}$$

where dQ_d/dP is the derivative of the demand function with respect to P. Since the change in P that we are evaluating is infinitesimally small, E_d is technically known as *point* elasticity. Such an elasticity is independent of any units of measurement and allows for a comparison of the responsiveness of quantity demanded to a change in price for any demand function. Let's look at Eq. C3.4 and use the elasticity formula to examine demand responsiveness. Assume that the current price, P, is 5. We see from Eq. C3.4 that the corresponding Q_d will be 200. Elasticity will then be calculated as:

$$E_d = \frac{dQ_d}{dP} \frac{P}{Q} = -10 \times \frac{5}{200} = -0.25 \qquad \text{(C3.8)}$$

We would conclude that the price elasticity of demand at this particular price level is -0.25, but what does this actually mean? It means that at the current price level, $P = 5$, a change in price (where the change is infinitesimally small) will bring about a corresponding proportionate change in Q_d of 0.25 *times* the change in price. Let's examine a simple illustration to confirm this. Assume that the price changes from 5 to 5.1. We calculate that the percentage change in P is 2% (0.1/5) and that the corresponding percentage change in Q_d is calculated as:

$$P = 5 \qquad Q_d = 200$$
$$P = 5.1 \qquad Q_d = 199$$

$$\text{Percentage change in } Q_d = \frac{200 - 199}{200} \times 100 = 0.5\%$$

which we can confirm is 0.25 of the change in the price, the elasticity value we calculated in Eq. C3.7.

It is important to realize that we are using elasticity to examine proportionate changes, not absolute changes. In terms of economics we would define the demand for this product at this particular price as *inelastic*: the quantity demanded is relatively unresponsive to a change in price. An increase in price of 2% brought about a reduction in demand of only 0.5%: in other words a proportionate change in price brought about a smaller proportionate change in Q_d. However, let us now consider elasticity at a different point on the same demand curve.

Progress Check C3.3

Calculate elasticity when $P = 15$. How do you interpret this?

Adopting the same approach we have:

$$P = 15 \text{ and } Q_d = 100$$

and then

$$E_d = -10 \times \frac{15}{100} = -1.5$$

which indicates that a change in price at this point on the demand curve will bring about a proportionate change in Q_d of 1.5 times the price change. In such a case we would denote that demand at this point was relatively *elastic* – that is, particularly responsive to a price change. A change in price at this price level will bring about a larger proportionate change in demand.

We can summarize the possibilities for elasticity of demand as:

$\|E_d\| < 1$	Inelastic	Demand is relatively unresponsive to a change in price	A marginal change in price will lead to a proportionately smaller change in demand
$\|E_d\| > 1$	Elastic	Demand is relatively responsive to a change in price	A marginal change in price will lead to a proportionately larger change in demand
$\|E_d\| = 1$	Unitary	Demand responds proportionately to a change in price	A marginal change in price will lead to a proportionately equal change in demand

The symbol around the E_d term, $|\quad|$, is known as a *modulus* (with the expression $|E_d|$ pronounced 'mod ee-dee') and indicates that we are interested only in the absolute value of E_d, not in whether it is positive or negative.

Progress Check C3.4

For the demand function we are examining, Eq. C3.4, determine what price must be charged for the elasticity to exactly equal (−)1.

(Solution on p. 465)

It is important to note that the elasticity value changes even though the slope of the linear function is constant. This occurs because elasticity is concerned with *relative* rather than absolute changes.

The same principles of price elasticity of demand can be applied to any type of demand function – linear or otherwise. One particular demand function worth noting at this stage returns us to Eq. C3.1, where we had:

$$Q_d = \frac{100}{P} \tag{C3.1}$$

Here we have:

$$E_d = \frac{dQ_d}{dP}\,\frac{P}{Q} = \frac{-100}{P^2}\,\frac{P}{Q}$$
$$= \frac{-100}{PQ}$$

which, if we substitute Eq. C3.1 for Q, gives

$$E_d = \frac{-100}{P(100/P)} = \frac{-100}{100} = -1$$

That is, for this demand function, point elasticity of demand is −1 at any price. This demand function has unitary elasticity anywhere along its length. As a further example consider the function:

$$Q_d = f(P) = \frac{a}{P^b} \tag{C3.9}$$

If a and b are > 0, then the demand function will have a constant elasticity of $-b$.

Progress Check C3.5

Show that the elasticity of this type of demand function will be $-b$. Sketch the demand function.

(Solution on p. 466)

C3.4 Analysing other types of elasticity

In previous sections we focused on price elasticity of demand; but the principles of elasticity are applicable to a number of different economic situations. For example, let us consider the following types of elasticity.

Elasticity of supply

$$E_s = \frac{dQ_s}{dP} \frac{P}{Q_s} \qquad (C3.10)$$

which would show the relative responsiveness of quantity *supplied* to a change in price. An inelastic situation, for example, would mean that suppliers would respond only slightly in terms of quantity supplied to a change in price; an elastic situation would mean that a small change in price would lead to a relatively large change in quantity supplied.

Cross-elasticity of demand

Assume we had a demand function such that:

$$Q_{dx} = f(P_y) \qquad (C3.11)$$

that is, where the quantity demanded of product X was a function of the price of product Y. Such a situation could arise, for example, if the two products were close substitutes or where X was regarded as a complementary good to Y. We can then define the cross-elasticity of demand for X as:

$$E_z = \frac{dQ_{dx}}{dP_y} \frac{P_y}{Q_{dx}} \qquad (C3.12)$$

and E_z would indicate the relative responsiveness of demand for good X in relation to a change in the price of good Y.

Income elasticity of demand

In a similar way we may have a demand function such that:

$$Q_d = f(Y) \qquad (C3.13)$$

where Y represents consumer income. Income elasticity of demand would then be given by:

$$E_y = \frac{dQ_d}{dY} \frac{Y}{Q_d} \qquad (C3.14)$$

and would indicate the relative responsiveness of quantity demanded to a change in consumer income.

Progress Check C3.6

For the functions shown below, obtain an expression for the appropriate elasticity and calculate the elasticity at the price required. Interpret your result.

(i) $Q_s = -10 + 5P$
   $P = 5$

(ii) $Q_{dx} = 200 - 3P_y$
   $P_y = 10$

(iii) $Q_{dx} = 200 + 3P_y$
   $P_y = 10$

What type of product is Y in (ii) and (iii)?

(Solution on p. 466)

C3.5 Analysing revenue

Understanding the relationship between different aspects of a firm's revenue is an important part of microeconomic analysis. Let's assume a demand function such that:

$$Q_d = 625 - 25P$$

While such a functional form is typical of consumer theory where consumer behaviour responds to price, when we wish to examine the theory of the firm it is generally more appropriate to rewrite the demand function in the form:

$$P = f(Q_d) \text{ which here gives } P = 25 - 0.04Q_d \tag{C3.15}$$

From now on we shall denote Q_d as Q to help keep the notation simpler. Given that a firm's total revenue, TR, will be determined by the quantity, Q, times the price per unit, P, we then have:

$$TR = f(Q) = PQ = (25 - 0.04Q)Q$$
$$= 25Q - 0.04Q^2 \tag{C3.16}$$

From the TR function we can obtain two related functions: average revenue, AR, and marginal revenue, MR. Average revenue, AR, is the total revenue received averaged over quantity sold and is given as:

$$AR = \frac{TR}{Q} = \frac{25Q - 0.04Q^2}{Q} = 25 - 0.04Q = P \tag{C3.17}$$

That is, average revenue is simply price per unit. Marginal revenue, on the other hand, is given by:

$$MR = \frac{d(TR)}{dQ} = 25 - 0.08Q \tag{C3.18}$$

That is, marginal revenue is the derivative of the TR function – the slope of the TR function. Note that the AR and MR functions are both linear, with the MR function having the steeper (negative) slope. This implies that, graphically, MR will always lie below the AR function.

However, these findings relate to a specific demand function. We can generalize these findings to any demand function. Assume a demand function:

$$Q = f(P) \tag{C3.19}$$

and its inverse

$$P = g(Q) \qquad \qquad \text{(C3.20)}$$

By definition $TR = PQ$ and using Eq. C3.20 we then have:

$$TR = g(Q)Q \qquad \qquad \text{(C3.21)}$$

Marginal revenue is the derivative of total revenue so we have, using the product rule:

$$MR = \frac{\mathrm{d}TR}{\mathrm{d}Q} = g(Q) + Qg'(Q) \qquad \qquad \text{(C3.22)}$$

But if we use Eq. C3.20, $P = g(Q)$, and its derivative, $g'(Q) = \mathrm{d}P/\mathrm{d}Q$, and substitute these into Eq. C3.22 we get:

$$MR = P + Q\frac{\mathrm{d}P}{\mathrm{d}Q} \qquad \qquad \text{(C3.23)}$$

Equation C3.23 shows the general relationship between marginal revenue, price and the slope of the inverse demand function for any demand function. We can then consider two typical economic situations.

Monopoly

In a monopoly the demand function is downward sloping, and in order to sell more the price must fall, implying that $\mathrm{d}Q/\mathrm{d}P < 0$. If, as is sensible, we restrict the analysis to positive values for Q, then from Eq. C3.23 we must have:

$$MR < P$$

That is, for a monopolist, marginal revenue is always less than price (which is also average revenue).

Perfect competition

For a firm operating under perfect competition, however, the individual firm is classed as a price-taker and can sell all they can produce at the prevailing market price. This implies that the demand function is horizontal and that $\mathrm{d}P/\mathrm{d}Q = 0$. From Eq. C3.23 this implies that:

$$MR = P$$

For a firm in perfect competition, marginal revenue exactly equals the market price.

Elasticity and revenue

We can now re-examine the price elasticity of demand that we introduced in Section C3.1. We can re-express the relationships as:

$$TR = PQ = f(Q)Q$$

$$MR = \frac{\mathrm{d}(TR)}{\mathrm{d}Q}$$

and using the differentiation product rule, Rule 3, from the previous module we then have

$$MR = \frac{\mathrm{d}[f(Q)Q]}{\mathrm{d}Q} = f(Q)(1) + Qf'(Q)$$

$$= f(Q) + Qf'(Q)$$

but since $P = f(Q)$ this gives

$$MR = P + Q\frac{dP}{dQ} \tag{C3.24}$$

From the earlier definition of elasticity, however, we had:

$$E_d = \frac{dQ}{dP}\frac{P}{Q}$$

which, when rearranged, gives

$$Q\frac{dQ}{dP} = \frac{P}{E_d} \tag{C3.25}$$

Therefore, using Eqs C3.24 and C3.25 we now have:

$$MR = P + \frac{P}{E_d} = P(1 + \frac{1}{E_d}) \tag{C3.26}$$

Let's look at the implied relationship between MR and E_d. It is evident from Eq. C3.26 that since E_d is always negative we reach the following general conclusions:

Elastic demand	MR will be positive	$E_d > -1$ and $1/E_d$ will be negative but less than 1 giving $(1 + 1/E_d) > 0$
Unitary elastic demand	MR will be zero	$E_d = -1$ and $1/E_d$ will be -1 giving $(1 + 1/E_d) = 0$
Inelastic demand	MR will be negative	$E_d < -1$ and $1/E_d$ will be negative but greater than 1 giving $(1 + 1/E_d) < 0$

If, at a particular price level, demand is elastic, we know that a change in price will lead to a proportionately greater change in quantity demanded. We now see that MR must be greater than zero. For example, a marginal decrease in P will lead to a proportionately larger increase in Q_d. MR will be positive – that is, extra units sold will lead to an increase in extra revenue. TR therefore will increase since, although the unit price is lower, extra sales more than compensate for this. Similar logic can be applied to inelastic and unitary elastic positions.

Progress Check C3.7

For Eq. C3.14, assume a current price of 5. Calculate E_d and MR. Now assume an initial price of 15. Repeat the calculations. Comment on the results.

(Solution on p. 466)

C3.6 Analysing production

While we would normally regard a production function as involving at least two main variable inputs, labour and capital, we can regard one of the inputs as fixed in the short term and then examine the implications of allowing the other to vary. Assume we have such a production function where we have:

$$Q = g(L) \tag{C3.27}$$

where Q represents output/production and L represents inputs of labour; that is, we are assuming that the supply of capital is currently fixed. We can obtain the derivative of such a production function:

$$\frac{dQ}{dL} = g'(L) \tag{C3.28}$$

and define this as the *marginal product of labour* (M_L) – the marginal product of the variable input. The marginal product of labour indicates the marginal change in production arising from a marginal change in the labour input. We would normally expect a positive marginal product – that is, $g'(L) > 0$. However, the *law of diminishing returns* (or diminishing marginal product) indicates that the increase in production following a marginal increase in labour will eventually decline. This implies that, while the marginal product may be positive, it will decrease as a function of labour input. In other words, the slope of the MP function will be negative. However, the slope of the MP function is the second derivative of the production function so that the assumption of diminishing marginal product implies that $g''(L) < 0$.

We are also in a position to link marginal product to marginal revenue. In the previous section we had a total revenue function such that:

$$TR = f(Q)$$

and we now have a production function such that

$$Q = g(L)$$

Clearly, it should be possible to determine the change in TR that will occur as we change L – that is, the change in total revenue brought about by a change in the variable input, labour, via a change in output, Q. Such a change will represent the *marginal revenue product* (MRP) of that input – the change in revenue arising from a change in labour input – and would be denoted as:

$$MRP = \frac{d(TR)}{dL} \tag{C3.29}$$

We have:

$$P = f(Q) = f(g(L)) \tag{C3.30}$$

However, $TR = PQ$ and $Q = g(L)$ so we have:

$$TR = f(Q)g(L) = f(g(L))g(L)$$

Using the chain rule for differentiation on $f(g(L))$ we have:

$$\frac{df(g(L))}{dL} = \frac{dP}{dL} = \frac{dP}{dQ}\frac{dQ}{dL} = f'(Q)g'(L)$$

and so, using the product rule

$$\frac{d(TR)}{dL} = g(L)\frac{d[f(g(L))]}{dL} + g'(L)f(g(L))$$

$$= g(L)f'(Q)g'(L) + g'(L)f(g(L))$$

However, from Eq. C3.28, $MP = g'(L)$ so that:

$$\frac{d(TR)}{dL} = g(L)f'(Q)MP + MPf(g(L))$$

$$= MP[g(L)f'(Q) + f(g(L))]$$

which, since

$$P = f(g(L)) \quad \text{and} \quad Q = g(L)$$

gives

$$\frac{d(TR)}{dL} = MP[Qf'(Q) + P]$$

but from Eq. C3.24 we have

$$MR = Qf'(Q) + P$$

which gives

$$\frac{d(TR)}{dL} = MP \times MR = MRP \tag{C3.31}$$

That is, the marginal revenue product, MRP, is given by the marginal product, MP, multiplied by marginal revenue, MR. Note that, importantly, we have derived such a relationship without any reference to numerical examples. The definition derived in Eq. C3.31, in other words, applies as a general result.

Progress Check C3.8

Assume that we now have a production function where labour is fixed and:

$$Q = h(K)$$

where K is capital input. Derive a comparable equation to Eq. C3.26 for capital.

C3.7 Analysing costs

Having seen how the derivative can be applied to revenue relationships and to production, let us now examine the cost side of the theory of the firm. If we have a total cost function such that:

$$TC = f(Q) \tag{C3.32}$$

it is evident that marginal cost (MC) will be given by

$$MC = \frac{d(TC)}{dQ} = f'(Q) \tag{C3.33}$$

That is, MC is the derivative of the TC function. It may also be apparent that if we break TC into fixed cost and variable cost elements then MC will be the same as marginal variable cost (MVC) since, by definition, fixed costs are independent of output, Q. We can also link marginal cost to marginal product. Assume, as we did earlier, that we have a production function:

$$Q = g(L)$$

If we define the cost per unit of labour as w (the wage rate paid), then variable cost (VC) will be:

$$VC = wL \tag{C3.34}$$

that is, the cost per unit of labour multiplied by the number of units of labour employed. The marginal cost of another unit of labour is also w, since:

$$\frac{d(VC)}{dL} = w \tag{C3.35}$$

However, let us investigate instead the marginal cost with respect to output, Q: that is, we require:

$$\frac{d(VC)}{dQ}$$

Through the use of the chain rule this gives:

$$\frac{d(VC)}{dQ} = \frac{d(VC)}{dL} \frac{dL}{dQ}$$

However, $Q = g(L)$ and, therefore:

$$\frac{dQ}{dL} = g'(L)$$

If we note that, using the inverse function rule:

$$\frac{dL}{dQ} = \frac{1}{dQ/dL} \frac{1}{g'(L)}$$

then we have

$$\frac{d(VC)}{dQ} = \frac{d(VC)}{dL} \frac{1}{g'(L)} = \frac{w}{g'(L)}$$

which, since $g'(L)$ is the marginal product, gives

$$MC = \frac{d(VC)}{dQ} = \frac{w}{MP} \qquad \text{(C3.36)}$$

That is, marginal cost (MC) is equal to the marginal cost (w) of the variable input L divided by its marginal product. MC is simply the ratio of extra labour cost to extra output produced by that extra labour.

Progress Check C3.9

Return to the production function for capital when labour is fixed. Derive a comparable expression to Eq. C3.36.

C3.8 The consumption function

So far, all the applications of the derivative have been on the microeconomic side. The derivative is equally applicable to macroeconomic relationships. Consider the consumption function:

$$C = f(Y) \qquad \text{(C3.37)}$$

where C is consumption and Y income. We can readily define:

$$\frac{dC}{dY} = f'(Y) \qquad \text{(C3.38)}$$

as the *marginal propensity to consume* (mpc) – the change in consumption that occurs with a change in income. If we also note that by definition any income that is not consumed is saved, we have an associated savings function:

$$S = g(Y) \qquad \text{(C3.39)}$$

since $Y = C + S$ and that

$$\frac{dS}{dY} = g'(Y) \tag{C3.40}$$

is the marginal propensity to save. Furthermore, it is logical to state that:

$$\frac{dC}{dY} + \frac{dS}{dY} = 1 \tag{C3.41}$$

That is, the change in consumption plus the change in savings must equal the change in income.

C3.9 National income

Finally in this module, let's consider how the derivative can help us assess one of the models we examined in Module B3. We will look at a macroeconomic national income model that involved a government sector but no foreign trade. We derived the value of the multiplier (Eq. B3.13) in this model as:

$$\Delta Y = \frac{1}{1 - b(1 - t)} \Delta G$$

where b represented the marginal propensity to consume and t the tax rate levied on income, Y. Clearly the equation allows us to determine the effect of a change in government expenditure on the equilibrium level of national income. However, let us examine the multiplier in a slightly different context. How will a change in the tax rate, t, affect the multiplier (and hence the impact effect of G)? Clearly, we can simply examine the multiplier expression and try to deduce what would happen if t increased or decreased. However, let us apply the principles we have been developing. If we denote the multiplier as k, then we have:

$$k = \frac{1}{1 - b(1 - t)} = \frac{1}{1 - b + bt} \tag{C3.42}$$

We require the effect on k of a change in t, that is:

$$\frac{dk}{dt}$$

If we denote $x = 1 - b + bt$, then we have:

$$\frac{dx}{dt} = b$$

but

$$k = \frac{1}{x} = x^{-1}$$

so

$$\frac{dk}{dx} = -1x^{-2} = \frac{-1}{x^2} = \frac{-1}{(1 - b + bt)^2}$$

and through the chain rule

$$\frac{dk}{dt} = \frac{dk}{dx}\frac{dx}{dt} = \frac{-1}{(1 - b + bt)^2} b = \frac{-b}{(1 - b + bt)^2} \tag{C3.43}$$

which can be rewritten as

$$\frac{dk}{dt} = -bk^2 \tag{C3.44}$$

From this, given that b, the marginal propensity to consume, and k, the multiplier, will be positive in the model, we see that the rate of change in the multiplier as the tax rate changes will always be negative. In other words, a change in the tax rate will have an inverse effect on the national income multiplier. Increasing the tax rate will decrease the multiplier and vice versa.

C3.10 Summary

In this module, we have seen how the derivative can be used in various areas of economic analysis at both the micro- and macroeconomic level. The derivative is useful in calculating various elasticities and is particularly important in economics for the concept of marginality. We have seen how the derivative can be used to obtain important general conclusions about economic behaviour that apply regardless of the specific numerical model we may be using.

Learning Check

Having read this module you should have learned that:

- The derivative is helpful in sketching the specific economic functions under analysis
- The derivative and the economic concept of marginality are directly related, making the derivative particularly useful in marginal economic analysis
- The derivative is used to calculate point elasticity of demand, supply and income
- Elasticity is classed as inelastic, elastic or unitary
- Average revenue is equal to market price
- Marginal revenue is the derivative of total revenue. For a monopolist marginal revenue is less than market price. For a firm in perfect competition marginal revenue is equal to market price
- Marginal revenue product is the change in revenue that occurs as we change a production function input and is equal to the marginal product multiplied by marginal revenue
- Marginal cost is the derivative of total cost and is also given by the wage rate divided by marginal product.

Worked Example

We shall return to the Worked Example we had in the previous module. There we had a farming cooperative facing a production function:

$$Q = -0.05L^3 + 3L^2$$

with $0 \leq L \leq 50$, where Q is production and L is the number of workers employed. We derived a MP_L function:

$$MP_L = f'(Q) = -0.15L^2 + 6L$$

Worked Example *(Continued)*

and concluded that when $L = 40$ total production is maximized. Let us investigate a different aspect of the problem. The cooperative has now expressed interest not in marginal product of labour but in average product (AP_L) and is interested in determining the level of output where AP_L is maximized. Try this yourself before reading further.

Solution

We can define:

$$AP_L = Q/L$$

That is, average product is production divided by the number of workers required to produce that output. So, in this case:

$$AP_L = \frac{-0.05L^3 + 3L^3}{L} = -0.05L^2 + 3L$$

Again by inspection we see that AP_L is quadratic and will reach a maximum point. This point will have a slope equal to zero so we require:

$$\frac{dAP_L}{dL} = -0.1L + 3 = 0$$

giving $L = 30$ as the number of workers where average product will be greatest. The second derivative helps us to confirm this:

$$\frac{d^2AP_L}{dL^2} = -0.1$$

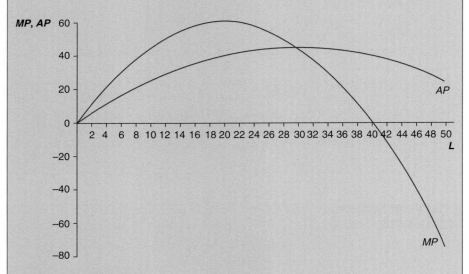

Figure C3.2 *MP* and *AP*

Worked Example *(Continued)*

The second derivative is a negative constant implying the slope of AP_L (the first derivative) is decreasing with respect to L. So $L = 30$ must equate to a maximum. AP_L will take its maximum value of 45 (units of production per worker) when we employ 30 workers. It will also be instructive to consider MP_L at this point:

$$MP_L = f'(Q) = -0.15L^2 + 6L$$

and when $L = 30$, $MP_L = 45$, that is, when average product is maximized, $MP = AP$. We shall see in Module C6 that this applies to production functions in general and not just to this specific numerical example. Fig. C3.2 shows the two functions.

Exercises

C3.1 Return to the national income model in Module B3, which involved both a government sector and foreign trade. From Eq. B3.21, which showed the multiplier for this model, determine the effect on the multiplier if the marginal propensity to import, m, changes.

$$k = \frac{1}{(1 - b + bt + m - mt)} = \frac{1}{1 - (1 - t)(b - m)} \tag{B3.21}$$

C3.2 We have the following market model:

$$Q_d = f(P) = 25 - 3P + 0.2P^2$$
$$Q_s = f(P) = -5 + 3P - 0.01P^2$$

(i) Derive an expression for elasticity of demand and of supply.
(ii) Calculate these two elasticities at the equilibrium price.
(iii) Derive an expression for marginal revenue.
(iv) Calculate marginal revenue at the equilibrium price.

C3.3 A firm's demand function is given by:

$$P = f(Q) = aQ^b$$

(i) Derive an expression for elasticity.
(ii) Derive an expression for marginal revenue.

C3.4 Assume a consumption function:

$$C = f(Y) = 100 + 2Y^{0.5}$$

(i) Sketch the shape of this function.
(ii) Comment on its general shape in the context of economic behaviour.
(iii) Derive an expression for marginal propensity to consume.
(iv) Comment on the behaviour of the mpc as Y increases. How do you explain this?

Exercises (Continued)

(v) Derive an expression for the marginal propensity to save.

(vi) Draw a graph for both the mpc and mps for Y up to 100. Comment on the relationship.

C3.5 A firm's production function is given as:

$$Q = 6L^{0.3}$$

and a demand function

$$P = 100 - 2Q$$

(i) Derive an equation for the marginal revenue product of labour.

(ii) Calculate the elasticity of demand when the marginal revenue is zero.

C3.6 Assume a production function:

$$Q = 100 + 0.1L^2 - 0.001L^3$$

with the wage rate set at 10. Find an expression for MC. Examine and comment upon its behaviour in relation to the production function. Plot both functions for L up to 65.

Module C4
The principles of optimization

In the previous modules we looked at the derivative and examined its applicability in economics. One of the main uses of differential calculus in economic analysis relates to the investigation of *optimization*. This concept is of particular importance and interest in economics at both the macro- and microeconomic level. In the theory of the firm a business organization is assumed to want to *maximize* profit. In cost theory the firm wishes to *minimize* costs. In consumer utility theory the individual consumer is assumed to want to *maximize* their utility derived from consumption. On the macro side, a government may wish to *maximize* the level of national income, to *minimize* the balance of trade deficit, to *minimize* inflation and/or unemployment, to *maximize* revenue from taxation. We saw in Module C1 how a quadratic function could be analysed to identify a maximum/minimum turning point. In this module we look at how we can determine such an optimum position for any function, whether it relates to a maximum or a minimum position. Fortunately, we already have all the tools we require to do this thanks to the principles of differential calculus that we have recently established. Now we simply have to put these together.

Learning Objectives

By the end of this module you should be able to:

- Find the stationary points of a function using the derivative
- Determine whether a stationary point represents a maximum or minimum using the second derivative
- Locate points of inflection.

C4.1 An example of optimization

Let us return to a profit function that we examined in Module C2. The function is shown in Fig. C4.1, together with the first and second derivatives and the corresponding profit function.

$$\text{Profit} = f(Q) = 1125 + 250Q - 5Q^2 \tag{C4.1}$$

$$f'(Q) = 250 - 10Q \tag{C4.2}$$

$$f''(Q) = -10 \tag{C4.3}$$

where Q represents the level of production.

In an economic context, we want to determine the level of output where the firm maximizes profit. We recognize the profit function as quadratic, and it can be seen from Fig. C4.1 that the point we require is the turning point of the profit function. We know from Module C1 that at this turning point the slope of the function will be zero. Given that the slope of the profit function is given by the first derivative we then require:

$$f'(Q) = 250 - 10Q = 0$$

which, on solving, gives $Q = 25$ as the level of output where $f'(Q)$ equals zero. This must also be the profit-maximizing level of output. However, let us consider a further aspect of the problem. The point we have found, $X = 25$, is technically a point where the slope of the original function is zero, often referred to as a *stationary* point – that is, a point where the function's value does not change but remains stationary or static. We were able to establish that this stationary point represented a *maximum* only because of our knowledge of economics and by visual inspection of the relevant graph. Generally, however, we may not be able to confirm this in the same way, since some functions could equally have a turning point that represents a minimum position. We clearly require a general method for determining which type of optimum the stationary position represents. This can be achieved by examining the behaviour of the derivative itself.

Let's look at Fig. C4.2, which shows some function, $Y = f(X)$, taking a maximum value (it happens to be a quadratic but the general principles apply to other functions

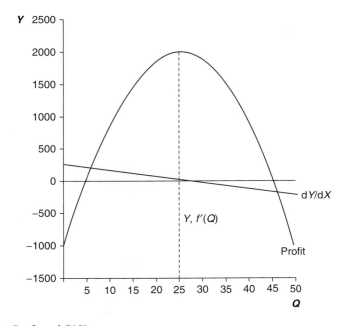

Figure C4.1 Profit and $f'(Q)$

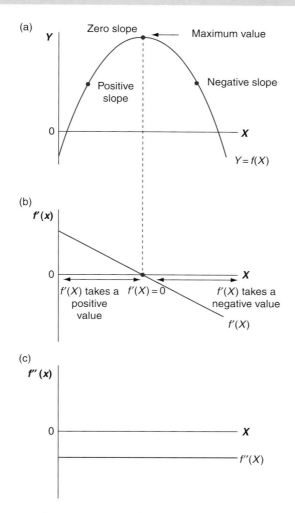

Figure C4.2 Function taking a maximum value

as well). Fig. C4.2a shows that the slope of the function behaves in a very specific way as X changes, moving from a positive slope through zero slope at the maximum point and then to a negative slope. Fig. C4.2b shows the first derivative of the function, $f'(X)$. Given that the first derivative measures the slope of the original function, we also see that the derivative is downward sloping – gradually changing from positive values to negative values as X increases and obviously taking a zero value at some point as it does so. Obviously, when the first derivative takes a zero value the corresponding X value also shows the optimum value for the original function. But how do we know without resorting to a graph whether this optimum point is a maximum or a minimum point? The answer lies with the *second* derivative. Consider that any derivative shows the slope of a function. The second derivative, therefore, must show the slope of the function represented by the first derivative (if you like, it shows the slope of the slope). Effectively, therefore, the second derivative can be interpreted as showing the rate of change of the first derivative, and the direction of the change of the first derivative can be obtained by inspection of the sign of the second derivative. In our example, the second derivative, shown in Fig. C4.2c, is negative, indicating that the slope of the first derivative is negative (sloping downwards from left to right). Such a second-derivative type can occur only if we have a stationary point representing a maximum, since it indicates a change from a large positive slope to a small positive or negative slope.

Let's now consider a function that has some minimum turning point (as illustrated in Fig. C4.3). We can see that the function itself (see Fig. C4.3a) moves from negative to positive slope as X increases. The first derivative, Fig. C4.3b, first takes negative values and then positive as X increases – exactly the opposite to when we had a maximum turning point. The positive slope of the first derivative is confirmed by the second derivative, Fig. C4.3c, which is positive.

Therefore, we can establish whether a stationary point represents a maximum or minimum by inspecting the behaviour of the first and second derivative. We can summarize what we have found so far:

1 A stationary point occurs at the value(s) for X that gives a zero value for the first derivative, $f'(X)$.

2 This stationary point represents:

a maximum if $f''(X) < 0$

a minimum if $f''(X) > 0$.

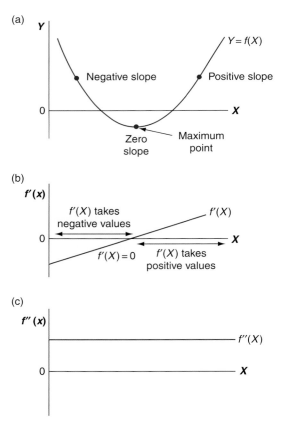

Figure C4.3 Function taking a minimum value

As we see later in this module, these rules will need a slight modification to make them generally applicable to any function, but they serve our purpose here. Point 1 is frequently referred to as the *first-order condition* to determine an optimum point, while point 2 is referred to as the *second-order condition*. Use of these principles allows us to find a turning point for a function and to determine whether this point represents a maximum or minimum position.

Progress Check C4.1

For the function:

$$Y = -20X^2 + 13X - 50$$

find the turning point of the function and determine whether it represents a maximum or minimum.

(Solution on p. 467)

C4.2 Optimization in general

Since economic functions will not always be quadratic, we need to develop a general approach to finding turning points for other functions. Let's progress by examining a slightly more complex function. Consider the function:

$$Y = -200 + 250X - 50X^2 + 3X^3 \tag{C4.4}$$

For $X = 0$ to 10, the function and its first and second derivatives are shown in Fig. C4.4. We have:

$$f'(X) = 250 - 100X + 9X^2 \tag{C4.5}$$

$$f''(X) = -100 + 18X \tag{C4.6}$$

In this example we see from the graph a function that has both a minimum and a maximum point. Using the first-order and second-order conditions, we first require:

$$f'(X) = 250 - 100X + 9X^2 = 0$$

to determine the stationary point(s). In this case the first derivative is itself a quadratic, so to find the values for X that give $f'(X) = 0$ we clearly require the two roots of the quadratic function. Applying the relevant solution formula that we derived in Module C1 we obtain:

$$X_1 = 3.80 \quad \text{and} \quad X_2 = 7.31$$

These are the two X values where the original function takes a stationary value. It is important to note that we *cannot* assume that $X_1 = 3.80$ is the minimum point simply because it takes a smaller value than X_2. We must examine the second-order conditions to determine whether the two stationary points represent a maximum or a minimum. We know that the stationary point represents:

a maximum if $f''(X) < 0$

a minimum if $f''(X) > 0$

With $X_1 = 3.80$ we then have:

$$f''(X_1) = -100 + 18X_1 = -100 + 18(3.80) = -31.6$$

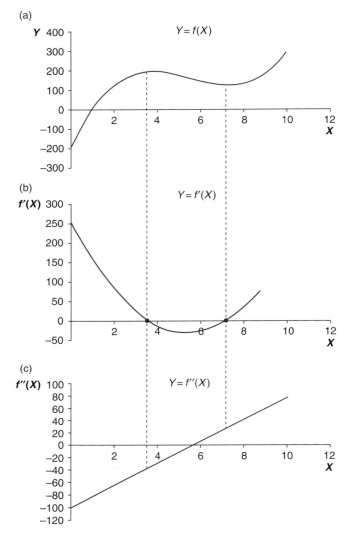

Figure C4.4 $Y, f'(X), f''(X)$

which, since the second derivative is negative, indicates that when $X = 3.80$, Y reaches a maximum position. Similarly, when $X_2 = 7.31$ we have:

$$f''(X_2) = -100 + 18(X_2) = -100 + (131.58) = 31.58$$

and, using the same logic, this value for X must indicate where Y takes a minimum value. The relationships between the original function, the two derivatives and the relevant X values are evident from Figs C4.4a to C4.4c.

Progress Check C4.2

For the function:
$$Y = X^3 - 20X^2 + 13X - 50$$
find the turning point(s) of the function and determine whether they represent a maximum or minimum.

(Solution on p. 467)

C4.3 Local and global maxima and minima

As we have seen, the principles of the first- and second-order conditions can be applied to virtually any type of function to establish maximum and/or minimum points. This establishes an important principle concerning optimization. In Eq. C4.4 we have two stationary points, one representing a maximum and the other a minimum. In general, however, we may well face functions that give several such stationary points. Consider the function illustrated in Fig. C4.5. It is evident that this function, in addition to having both maximum and minimum points, also has multiple maxima and minima. Point A clearly represents a maximum position *within that region of X values* but a second, and higher, maximum also occurs at point C. Points B and D are similar in terms of minimum positions. Points A and C are referred to as *local*, or relative, maxima, indicating that, although they are the maximum turning points relative to this range of X values, they may not be the *global* or absolute maximum. Points B and D are referred to as local minima for the same reason. If we examine the first and second derivatives in Fig. C4.5, we see that the first- and second-order conditions are clearly being met for all such optimum points regardless of whether they are local or global. On reflection, it is evident that these conditions are unable to distinguish between global optima and must be viewed as the condition for finding a local optimum (or a series of local optima if there is more than one). At present we have no method of determining whether an optimum point represents a local or a global position. The only method available is to compare all the local optima we have found for a function and determine which of

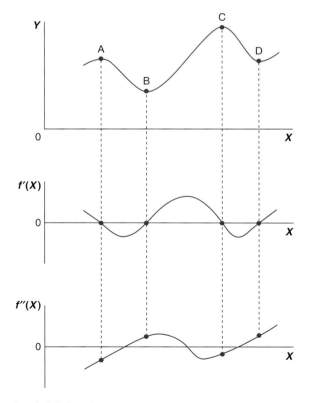

Figure C4.5 Local and global optima

these generates the highest (or lowest) value for the Y variable. This optimum point would then represent the global.

C4.4 Points of inflection

One further aspect of optimization must be considered. We have seen that, when we have located a stationary point where $f'(X) = 0$, we can use the second derivative rule to determine whether this point represents a local maximum or minimum. If the second derivative is positive, the stationary point represents a local minimum; while if it takes a positive value, the point represents a local maximum. But what if the second derivative is neither positive nor negative but zero? In such a situation we face a position where the stationary point may represent not a maximum or minimum but what is referred to as a *point of inflection*.

Consider the function shown in Fig. C4.6. A point of inflection on the original function is shown at point A (shown with the corresponding tangent line superimposed). This is clearly a stationary point as the first derivative, $f'(X)$, takes a zero value; that is,

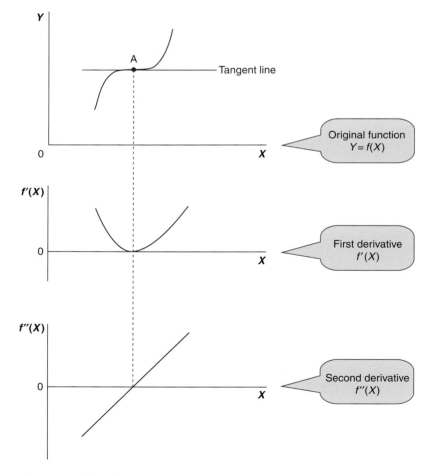

Figure C4.6 $Y = f(X)$: inflection point

the slope of the original function at this point is zero. The first derivative, however, is always non-negative so does not change its sign as we would normally expect (that is, the first derivative does not change from positive to negative values or from negative to positive values). Clearly at point A the second derivative will take neither a positive nor a negative value but will be zero. To illustrate the arithmetic involved let us consider the function:

$$Y = f(X) = 10 + (X - 4)^3 \tag{C4.7}$$

where

$$f'(X) = 3(X - 4)^2 \tag{C4.8}$$

$$f''(X) = 6(X - 4) \tag{C4.9}$$

The three functions are plotted in Fig. C4.7 over the range $X = 1$ to 7. To locate the point of inflection let us examine the second derivative, Eq. C4.8. At such a point $f''(X) = 0$. Setting Eq. C4.9 to zero and solving gives $X = 4$. When $X = 4$ we see that the first derivative takes a value of zero, indicating that we have a stationary point on the original function. However, there exists another type of inflection point that we need

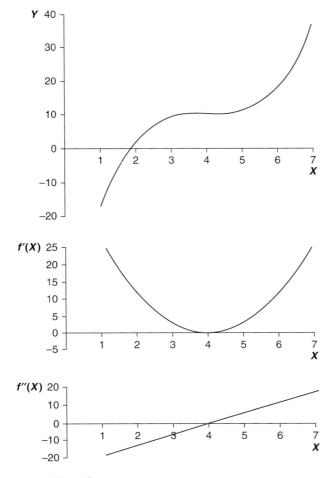

Figure C4.7 $Y = 10 + (X - 4)^3$

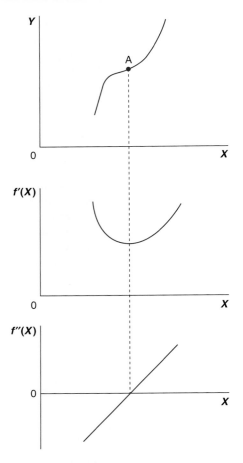

Figure C4.8 $Y = f(X)$: non-stationary inflection point

to consider. This can arise at a *non-stationary* point on the original function. Consider Fig. C4.8. At point A we again have a point of inflection, where $f''(X) = 0$. However, at this value of X the slope of the original function is not zero (as indicated by the first derivative) and hence cannot be a stationary point. To summarize our discussion to date, therefore, we can say that a local optimum point must also be a stationary point but that a stationary point could be either a local optimum or a point of inflection. If the stationary point is a local optimum then we can use the first- and second-order rules to determine both the X value at this point and whether we face a maximum or minimum local optimum.

C4.5 Summary

This has been a relatively short module, but the concepts relating to optimization are critical for what follows in the book and crucially important for many areas of economic analysis. You should ensure that you have thoroughly understood the concepts we have introduced here before proceeding.

Learning Check

Having read this module you should have learned that:

- We can use the first derivative of a function to find the optimum point in the original function
- Setting the first derivative to zero and solving identifies the optimum point(s)
- The second derivative allows us to determine whether an optimum point represents a maximum or minimum in the original function
- An optimal point represents a maximum value if the second derivative is negative
- An optimal point represents a minimum if the second derivative is positive
- An optimum point may represent a local or a global optimum.

Worked Example

A firm faces a total revenue function such that:

$$TR = 50Q - 2Q^2$$

and a total cost function

$$TC = 20 + 0.25Q^3 - 10Q^2 + 100Q$$

For each of the following, work out whether the corresponding function has a maximum or minimum and if so of what type:

(i) Marginal cost
(ii) Average fixed cost
(iii) Average variable cost
(iv) Marginal revenue
(v) Total revenue
(vi) Profit.

Try these first before reading on.

Solution

Taking each in turn:

(i) $MC = f'(TC) = 0.75Q^2 - 20Q + 100$
Marginal cost is the derivative of the TC function but is also a function in its own right. Setting $f'(TC)$ to zero and solving gives:

$$f'(TC) = 1.5Q - 20 \quad \text{giving } Q = 13.3$$

$f''(TC) = 1.5$, so when $Q = 13.3$, MC is at a minimum point.

(ii) $AFC = FC/Q = 20/Q$
$f'(AFC) = -20/Q^2$
On inspection we see that, as Q increases, the term $-20/Q^2$ approaches zero but will in fact technically never reach zero. $f'(AFC)$ cannot then be solved for $f'(AFC) = 0$ and no maximum or minimum exists.

Worked Example *(Continued)*

(iii) $AVC = VC/Q = 0.25Q^2 - 10Q + 100$

This has a stationary point where $f'(AVC) = 0$:

$$f'(AVC) = 0.5Q - 10 = 0$$

so $Q = 20$ at this point. To check whether this represents a maximum or minimum we require the second derivative:

$$f''(AVC) = 0.5$$

so we confirm that when $Q = 20$, AVC reaches its minimum value.

(iv) $MR = f'(TR)$, so we have:

$$MR = 50 - 4Q$$

This function reaches a stationary value when $f'(MR) = 0$:

$$f'(MR) = -4$$

which clearly cannot take a zero value. The MR function has no maximum or minimum value (a conclusion we can confirm on inspection of MR since this is a linear function).

(v) For total revenue we require $f'(TR) = 0 = 50 - 4Q$

giving $Q = 12.5$ (the optimum value for TR is found where $MR = 0$). Using the second derivative $f''(TR) = -4$ confirms that when $Q = 12.5$, TR will take a maximum value.

(vi) Profit $= TR - TC$

Profit $= -0.25Q^3 + 8Q^2 - 50Q - 20$

We require $f'(\text{Profit}) = 0$:

$$f'(\text{Profit}) = -0.75Q^2 + 16Q - 50 = 0$$

and solving gives $Q_1 = 3.8$ and $Q_2 = 17.53$ as the two turning points. Using the second derivative:

$$f''(\text{Profit}) = -1.5Q + 16$$

substituting Q_1 gives $f''(\text{Profit}) = 10.3$, indicating that this value of Q gives a minimum profit. When Q_2 is substituted we derive $f''(\text{Profit}) = -10.3$, implying that this is a maximum.

Exercises

C4.1   For the following functions, determine the stationary point(s) and determine whether they represent a minimum or maximum. You will also find it useful to graph most of these functions and their derivatives.

(i) $Y = 10 - X^3$

(ii) $Y = 100 + 5X + 0.05X^2$

(iii) $Y = 50 - 30X + 10X^2 - 0.5X^3$

(iv) $Y = X + 20/X$

(v) $Y = (3X - 6)^3$

Exercises   *(Continued)*

(vi) $Y = 3X/(X+2)^2$

(vii) $Y = X + 10X^{-1}$

(viii) $Y = 40X - 8X^2 + X^3$

(ix) $Y = 20X^2 - 3X^3$

(x) $Y = 10 + 0.1(X-5)^2$

(xi) $Y = \sqrt{X} - 5X$

C

Module C5
Optimization in economic analysis

Armed with the various principles and techniques introduced over the previous modules, we are now in a position to examine some of the key models used in economic analysis that depend upon the concept of optimization. Some of these may be familiar to you already, at least in terms of their general principles and verbal description. In what follows we shall establish key conclusions using differential calculus, and introduce specific economic models that can be analysed only through such mathematics. In this module, we look at the relationships between revenue, costs and profit and the effects of different types of tax on market equilibrium.

Learning Objectives

By the end of this module you should be able to:

- Confirm that $MR = MC$ at profit maximization
- Use differential calculus to determine the profit-maximizing position for a firm in perfect competition and for a firm in a monopoly
- Assess the effect of different taxes on profit maximization
- Determine the level of tax that will maximize tax revenue.

C5.1 Profit maximization

We begin with the most well-known economic model: that involving profit maximization for an individual firm. You will be aware from your studies of economics that a general principle applies: a firm will maximize profit where marginal cost (MC) equals marginal revenue (MR). We shall use some of the mathematics we've introduced to look at this in more detail. Profit can be defined as the difference between total revenue (TR) and total costs (TC). If, as is usually assumed, revenue and costs can be expressed as functions of Q (output) then we have:

$$\text{Profit} = TR - TC \tag{C5.1}$$

$$TR = r(Q) \tag{C5.2}$$

$$TC = c(Q) \tag{C5.3}$$

and so

$$\text{Profit} = TR - TC = r(Q) - c(Q) \tag{C5.4}$$

From now on we shall use the symbol π to represent profit.

Note that Eq. C5.2 for total revenue is independent of the market conditions we may be examining. In other words, Eq. C5.2 is equally applicable to a firm in conditions of perfect competition or of monopoly, since we do not specify the precise form of the function. Nor is the precise form of the TC function specified. To find the level of output that maximizes profit we require the first derivative:

$$\frac{d\pi}{dQ} = r'(Q) - c'(Q) = 0 \tag{C5.5}$$

which is the same as

$$r'(Q) = c'(Q) \tag{C5.6}$$

which, given the economic meaning of the first derivative of the TR and TC functions, equates to

$$MR = MC \tag{C5.7}$$

That is, marginal revenue must equal marginal cost at the optimum point regardless of the market conditions under which the firm operates. For this level of output to be a local maximum, however, we also require:

$$\frac{d^2\pi}{dQ^2} = r''(Q) - c''(Q) < 0 \tag{C5.8}$$

or

$$r''(Q) < c''(Q) \tag{C5.9}$$

This indicates that the rate of change in MR must be less than the rate of change in MC. Graphically this implies that, for levels of output below the optimum, MC is less than MR, while the reverse is true for levels of output that are greater than optimum. Clearly the exact optimum position depends upon the exact equation parameters. We now examine these under two different sets of market conditions.

Progress Check C5.1

Assume a firm has cost and revenue functions:

$$TC = 500 + 5Q + Q^2$$
$$TR = 500Q - 5Q^2$$

where Q is output.

Find the level of Q where $MC = MR$ and confirm that this gives maximum profit.

(Solution on p. 467)

C5.2 Profit maximization: perfect competition

Let us first examine a firm operating under conditions of perfect competition. One of the key assumptions about this model is that the individual firm is a price-taker: that is, the price per unit is determined by the market and no individual firm – because of its small size vis-à-vis the total market – can directly influence this. In the context of mathematics, this implies that the TR function is given as:

$$TR = PQ \tag{C5.10}$$

that is, the quantity the individual firm is able to sell (Q) at the prevailing price (P). Clearly, since P is a constant, Eq. C5.10 is linear. Equally, the derivative of Eq. C5.10 is:

$$\frac{d(TR)}{dQ} = P = MR \tag{C5.11}$$

which, since the derivative of TR is MR, indicates that $P = MR$; that is, the prevailing price is equal to the firm's marginal revenue. Given the basic principles established in Section C5.1, that $MR = MC$, this indicates that for a firm in perfect competition to maximize profit the level of output must be set where $P = MC$; that is, the prevailing price exactly matches the firm's marginal cost of production. Figure C5.1 illustrates graphically the general relationships involved. In Fig. C5.1a we see both the TR and TC functions. As we have just seen, the TR function for this type of firm will be linear. The TC function follows the usual assumptions relating to returns to scale effects at different levels of output (you may recognize this type of function as a cubic). Figure C5.1b shows the corresponding profit function (graphically the difference between TR and TC at different levels of output). At points Q_2 and Q_4 we see that we have the breakeven level of output where profit $= 0$ (that is, $TR = TC$). For levels of output, less than Q_2 or greater than Q_4 we see that profit is negative (that is, $TR < TC$), while between the two levels of output, profit is positive (that is, $TR > TC$). The relevant first-order conditions require the derivative of profit to be zero. We see from Fig. C5.1b that this occurs at two points – Q_1 and Q_3. From Fig. C5.1a we see that the slopes of TR and TC are identical at these two output levels (as is confirmed from Fig. C5.1c, which shows MR and MC – the relevant two first derivatives). However, we clearly need to distinguish between these two stationary points given that, as indicated by Fig. C5.1a, one level of output represents the minimum profit position while the other represents the maximum. The second-order condition (Eq. C5.9) requires the total revenue second derivative to be less than the total cost second derivative. This implies that the slope of MR must be less than the slope of MC at the profit-maximizing point. Under perfect competition, the slope of MR is zero no matter the level of output (MR is, after all, equal to P and parallel to the Q axis). At output level Q_1 the MC curve has a negative slope and hence the slope of MC is less than the slope of MR. Conversely, at Q_3, MC has a positive slope and hence the slope of MC is greater than the slope of MR. This satisfies the second-order condition for a maximum turning point for profit.

Let us illustrate the general principles involved with a set of appropriate functions. First, let us assume that the prevailing market price for the product is £30. This gives a TR function such that:

$$TR = 30Q \tag{C5.12}$$

Assume further that the TC function is given by:

$$TC = 100 + 20Q - 5Q^2 + 0.5Q^3 \tag{C5.13}$$

The profit function is then:

$$\pi = -100 + 10Q + 5Q^2 - 0.5Q^3 \tag{C5.14}$$

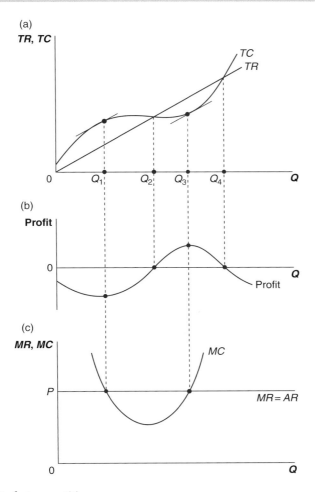

Figure C5.1 Perfect competition

while we have

$$MR = \frac{d(TR)}{dQ} = 30 \tag{C5.15}$$

$$MC = \frac{d(TC)}{dQ} = 20 - 10Q + 1.5Q^2 \tag{C5.16}$$

Progress Check C5.2

Plot all these functions on an appropriate graph (as Fig. C5.1).
Determine the profit-maximizing level of output.
Calculate MC and MR when $Q = 7.54$ and again when $Q = 7.56$. Comment on the results.
Confirm that the second-order conditions (Eq. C5.9) are satisfied.

The MC function gives a typical U-shaped curve, given that it is a quadratic function. We require the profit-maximizing level(s) of output. This requires the first derivative of the profit function, Eq. C5.14, to be set to zero and solved to give the stationary points of the function, giving $Q = -0.88$ and $Q = 7.55$. However, it is evident that one level of output represents a situation of minimum profit while the other represents a situation of maximum profit. To determine which is which mathematically, we require the second derivative:

$$\frac{d^2\pi}{dQ^2} = 10 - 3Q \tag{C5.17}$$

Using $Q = -0.88$, the second derivative is clearly positive and so this level of Q represents the minimum point. With $Q = 7.55$ the second derivative is negative, indicating a maximum stationary point.

C5.3 Profit maximization: monopoly

Let us now consider the opposite market condition of monopoly. Clearly, the situation will be similar in many respects. The cost functions facing the monopolist will be the same as those facing the perfectly competitive firm. However, the TR function will differ since the monopolist (and indeed any firm facing a less than perfect competition situation) will be faced with a downward-sloping demand function; that is, in order to sell more of the product the monopolist will be required, *ceteris paribus*, to lower the price per unit. This is in sharp contrast, of course, to the perfect competitive firm which can sell all it wishes at the prevailing price. If we show such a function in the form:

$$P = d(Q) = a - bQ \tag{C5.18}$$

then we also have

$$TR = r(Q) = PQ = (a - bQ)Q = aQ - bQ^2 \tag{C5.19}$$

which now gives a quadratic TR function. This function can be seen to have a zero intercept (zero production means zero revenue) and will take the standard inverted U shape since the parameter associated with the Q^2 term is negative. The appropriate relationships are shown in Fig. C5.2. Clearly the same logic applies as in the case of perfect competition. Figure C5.2a shows the TR and TC functions, with $TR < TC$ for levels of output below Q_2 and above Q_4. The relevant profit function (together with break-even points) is shown in Fig. C5.2b. The first-order condition requires the derivative of profit to be zero and clearly this will occur at Q_1 and Q_3 (where again from Fig. C5.2a we see that the slopes of TR and TC are equal at these points). These points are also confirmed from Fig. C5.2c, which shows MC, MR and AR. Note that both AR and MR must be downward-sloping, linear functions given by Eq. C5.1. At points Q_1 and Q_3, $MC = MR$. To determine which level of output represents the maximum profit position we apply the second-order condition requiring the slope of MR to be less than the slope of MC. Clearly, the slope of MR is negative for all Q. At point Q_1 the slope of MC is also negative but more so than that of MR. Conversely, at point Q_3 the slope of MC is positive while that of MR is still negative; hence this point must represent the profit-maximizing level of output. Note also from Fig. C5.2c that at this level of output the relevant price will be P_3 (since $P = AR$), and it can be seen that under such monopoly conditions $P > MR$ at the profit-maximizing level of output.

Again to reinforce these principles, let us examine a numerical example. Assume that the monopoly firm faces a demand function such that:

$$P = d(Q) = 50 - 0.5Q \tag{C5.20}$$

and

$$TC = 2 + 60Q - 8Q^2 + Q^3 \tag{C5.21}$$

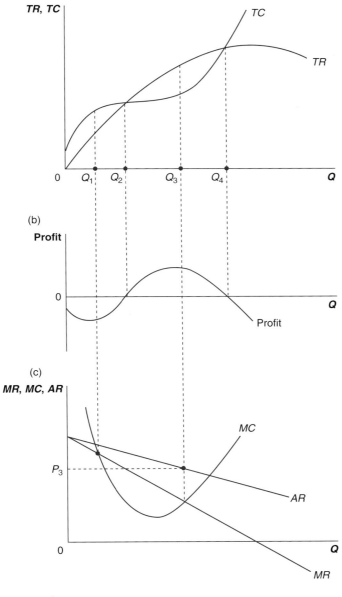

Figure C5.2 Monopoly

Progress Check C5.3

Derive the relevant equations for profit, *TR*, *MR* and *MC*.
Plot these on an appropriate graph as in Fig. C5.2.
Derive the profit-maximizing level of output.
Derive the price and marginal revenue at this level of output.
Explain why *P* > *MR* at the profit-maximizing point for a monopolist.

(Solution on p. 468)

Given Eq. C5.20 we have:

$$TR = PQ = 50Q - 0.5Q^2 \qquad (C5.22)$$

giving

$$\text{Profit} = -2 - 10Q + 7.5Q^2 - Q^3 \qquad (C5.23)$$

and

$$\frac{d(TR)}{dQ} = 50 - Q \qquad (C5.24)$$

$$\frac{d(TC)}{dQ} = 60 - 16Q + 3Q^2 \qquad (C5.25)$$

$$\frac{d\pi}{dQ} = -10 + 15Q - 3Q^2 \qquad (C5.26)$$

Setting Eq. C5.26 to zero and solving gives $Q = 0.792$ and $Q = 4.208$. Taking the second derivative of Eq. C5.23 gives:

$$\frac{d^2\pi}{dQ^2} = 15 - 6Q \qquad (C5.27)$$

and substituting the two Q values we see that $Q = 0.792$ represents minimum profit and $Q = 4.208$ maximum profit. Similarly from Eqs C5.20 and C5.24 we derive the price and marginal revenue as:

$$P = 50 - 0.5(4.208) = 47.896$$

and

$$MR = 50 - 4.208 = 45.792$$

confirming that $P > MR$. Figure C5.3 shows the relevant graphs.

C5.4 The effect of tax on profit maximization

In earlier modules we used comparative static analysis to examine the effect of the imposition of an excise tax on the market equilibrium. In Module B2, for example, we saw the effect such a tax would have in general on the market equilibrium under competitive conditions. Another aspect of this examination relates to the reasons why a government might impose such a tax on a product. Typically, the government will do so in order to raise revenue from the imposition of tax. But what effect will such a tax have on the profit-maximizing level of price and output? Let us begin by examining the effect of a lump-sum tax.

C5.5 The imposition of a lump-sum tax

A lump-sum tax is a fixed amount of tax imposed regardless of the quantity sold. Under monopoly conditions, for example, a government might view such a tax as an attractive method of penalizing supernormal profits arising from the existence of the monopoly. What effect will such a tax have? We now have:

$$TR = r(Q) \qquad (C5.28)$$

$$TC = c(Q) \qquad (C5.29)$$

$$T = t \qquad (C5.30)$$

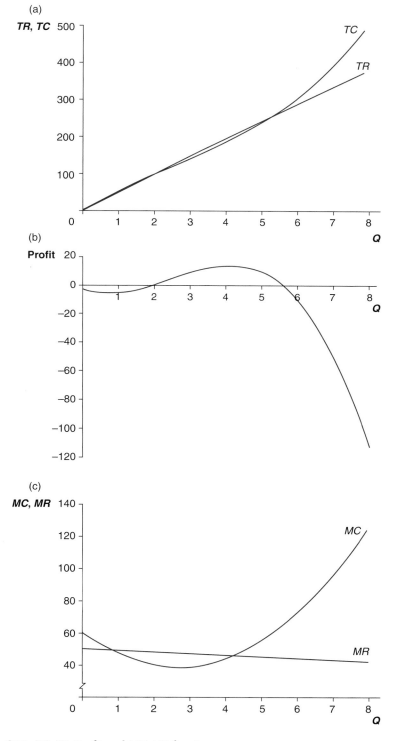

Figure C5.3 *TC*, *TR*, Profit, and *MC*, *MR* functions

where T (and t) is the lump sum imposed. We now need to distinguish between the profit earned by the firm and the profit retained after the tax has been paid. Retained profit will now be:

$$\text{Profit} = TR - TC - T$$

$$\pi = r(Q) - c(Q) - T \qquad (C5.31)$$

The firm will now want to maximize retained profit and, as usual, profit will be maximized where $d\pi/dQ = 0$ and $d^2\pi/dQ^2 < 0$. The first derivative will be:

$$\frac{d\pi}{dQ} = r'(Q) - c'(Q) - 0 = 0 \qquad (C5.32)$$

We see straightaway that this is effectively $MR = MC$ and is identical to Eq. C5.5, which related to market conditions before the imposition of the tax. Such a lump-sum tax will clearly not affect the profit-maximizing level of output (and hence price), although it will affect the profit retained at this level of output. Logically, we can view such a lump-sum tax as an addition to the firm's fixed costs. For this reason it is easy to see why some governments favour this type of tax for a monopoly firm since they can argue that they are not interfering in the market equilibrium process. Given that Eq. C5.5 involves *marginal* costs, the optimum point will remain unaffected.

Progress Check C5.4

Return to the activity C5.3. Confirm that a lump-sum tax of 2.5 will not affect the profit-maximizing level of output or the price for the monopolist.
Calculate the retained level of profit and compare this with that earned before the tax.

(Solution on p. 469)

C5.6 The imposition of a profit tax

Let us now examine the effect of a profit tax imposed on the firm. Such a tax typically takes a fixed percentage of the firm's profit. Again, such a tax system is frequently attractive to governments, since they can be seen to be actively taxing monopoly profits achieved, and is likely to have popular appeal with the electorate. Companies such as banks and utility companies are often the targets for such a tax. We now need to distinguish between pre-tax and post-tax profit for the firm. Our model is then:

$$TR = r(Q)$$

$$TC = c(Q) \text{ as before}$$

and

$$T = t\pi \qquad (C5.33)$$

where π now represents the pre-tax profits earned at the profit-maximizing level of output and t the proportion of tax levied on these profits (with $0 < t < 1$). We now have:

$$\pi = r(Q) - c(Q) \qquad (C5.34)$$

and hence post-tax profit is given by

$$\pi_t = r(Q) - c(Q) - t[r(Q) - c(Q)] \qquad (C5.35)$$

Clearly, the firm will seek to maximize post-tax profits. Rearranging Eq. C5.35 gives

$$\pi_t = (1 - t)[r(Q) - c(Q)] \tag{C5.36}$$

and hence we require

$$\frac{d\pi_t}{dQ} = (1 - t)[r'(Q) - c'(Q)] = 0 \tag{C5.37}$$

Since, by definition, $0 < t < 1$, then $(1 - t) > 0$, and hence we seek a value for Q such that:

$$r'(Q) - c'(Q) = 0 \tag{C5.38}$$

Again, we recognize that the imposition of a profit tax will leave the profit-maximizing level of output unchanged, since Eq. C5.38 is simply $MR = MC$.

Progress Check C5.5

Return to Progress Check C5.2. If the government imposes a profit tax of 60% on the monopolist, confirm that the profit-maximizing level of output is unchanged.

Compare the profit earned by the monopolist before the imposition of the tax with the post-tax profit.

(Solution on p. 469)

C5.7 The imposition of an excise tax

Let us now consider the imposition of an excise, or sales, tax which typically takes the form of a fixed amount (£) per unit sold. The government, for example, may levy a fixed tax of £1 per carton of cigarettes sold. Once again we have:

$$TR = r(Q)$$

$$TC = c(Q)$$

but now

$$T = tQ \tag{C5.39}$$

where T represents the total tax collected and t the per unit sales tax imposed. Retained profit π_t will now be:

$$\pi_t = TR - TC - tQ$$

$$= r(Q) - c(Q) - tQ \tag{C5.40}$$

Setting the first derivative to zero gives:

$$\frac{d\pi_t}{dQ} = r'(Q) - c'(Q) - t = 0 \tag{C5.41}$$

which, when rearranged, gives

$$r'(Q) = c'(Q) + t$$

$$MR = MC + t \tag{C5.42}$$

It can be seen that this type of tax, unlike the previous two types, will alter the profit-maximizing level of output. The tax imposed has the effect of shifting the MC function upwards by the amount of the per unit tax, t, imposed. Given the usual conditions associated with MR and MC, this must result in a profit-maximizing level of output that is lower than the non-tax model, and a price that is higher.

C5.8 Maximizing taxation revenue

Following on from this investigation we can clearly raise an associated question. We know that an excise tax will affect the profit-maximizing level of output. From the government's viewpoint (since it is the government that imposes the tax) can we determine the optimum value for t, that is, the per unit tax to be imposed that will maximize tax revenue? We shall illustrate with reference to a simple market structure. Assume a monopoly firm is facing the following TR and TC functions:

$$TR = b_1 Q + c_1 Q^2 \tag{C5.43}$$

$$TC = a_2 + b_2 Q + c_2 Q^2 \tag{C5.44}$$

with appropriate numerical restrictions on the parameters. The relevant TC function after the imposition of a tax will be:

$$
\begin{aligned}
TC_t &= TC + tQ \\
&= (a_2 + b_2 Q + c_2 Q^2) + tQ \\
&= a_2 + (b_2 + t)Q + c_2 Q^2
\end{aligned} \tag{C5.45}
$$

and retained profit will be given by

$$\pi_t = (b_1 Q + c_1 Q^2) - [a_2 + (b_2 + t)Q + c_2 Q^2] \tag{C5.46}$$

To find the profit-maximizing level of output we require the first derivative of the profit function:

$$
\begin{aligned}
\frac{d\pi_t}{dQ} &= b_1 + 2c_1 Q - [(b_2 + t) + 2c_2 Q] \\
&= b_1 - (b_2 + t) + 2(c_1 - c_2)Q
\end{aligned} \tag{C5.47}
$$

and rearranging gives

$$Q = \frac{-b_1 + (b_2 + t)}{2(c_1 - c_2)} \tag{C5.48}$$

as the profit-maximizing level of output. Using this we then have:

$$
\begin{aligned}
T = tQ &= t\left[\frac{-b_1 + (b_2 + t)}{2(c_1 - c_2)}\right] \\
T &= \frac{-t(b_1 - b_2) + t^2}{2(c_1 - c_2)}
\end{aligned} \tag{C5.49}
$$

To find the turning point of this function we require:

$$\frac{dT}{dt} = 0$$

and differentiating gives

$$\frac{dT}{dt} = \frac{-(b_1 - b_2) + 2t}{2(c_1 - c_2)}$$

Multiplying by $2(c_1 - c_2)$ gives:

$$\frac{dT}{dt} = -(b_1 - b_2) + 2t = 0 \tag{C5.50}$$

giving

$$2t = b_1 - b_2$$

$$t = \frac{b_1 - b_2}{2} \tag{C5.51}$$

where Eq. C5.51 indicates the optimal level of tax if the government wishes to optimize total taxation revenue. To determine whether this value of t gives a maximum or minimum turning point we require:

$$\frac{d^2 T}{dt^2} < 0$$

and from Eq. C5.50 this gives

$$\frac{d^2 T}{dt^2} = \frac{2}{2(c_1 - c_2)} = \frac{1}{(c_1 - c_2)} < 0 \qquad\qquad (C5.52)$$

which, given the usual restrictions on the numerical values for the parameters of this model ($c_1 < 0$, $c_2 > 0$), confirms that we have a maximum stationary point.

Progress Check C5.6

Assume a market model where:

$$TR = 125Q - Q^2$$

$$TC = 500 + 5Q + 0.5Q^2$$

Find the profit-maximizing level of output.
  Assume the government wishes to impose an excise tax. Find the optimal rate of tax. Calculate the new profit-maximizing level of output and price.

(Solution on p. 469)

Maximizing tax revenue in a competitive market

Finally, in the context of our examination of taxes, let us return to the model we derived in Module B2. There we had:

$$Q_d = Q_s \qquad\qquad (C5.53)$$

$$Q_d = a_1 + b_1 P \qquad\qquad (C5.54)$$

$$Q_s = a_2 + b_2(P - t) \qquad\qquad (C5.55)$$

with restrictions on the values of the parameters such that

$$a_1 > 0 \qquad b_1 < 0$$

$$a_2 < 0 \qquad b_2 > 0$$

and

$$t > 0$$

where t represented the excise tax levied per unit of the product sold. We derived the general equilibrium to be:

$$P_e = \frac{a_1 - a_2}{b_2 - b_1} + \frac{b_2 t}{b_2 - b_1} \qquad\qquad (C5.56)$$

and

$$Q_e = \frac{a_1 b_2 - b_1 a_2}{b_2 - b_1} + \frac{b_1 b_2 t}{b_2 - b_1} \qquad\qquad (C5.57)$$

From the government's perspective we can also introduce a new function:

$$T = t Q_e \qquad\qquad (C5.58)$$

which represents a tax revenue function with T being the total tax revenue (at £t per unit sold for each Q_e unit). However, substituting Eq. C5.57 this becomes:

$$T = t\left(\frac{a_1 b_2 - b_1 a_2}{b_2 - b_1}\right) + \left(\frac{b_1 b_2 t}{b_2 - b_1}\right)$$
$$= \frac{(a_1 b_2 - b_1 a_2)t + b_1 b_2 t^2}{b_2 - b_1} \tag{C5.59}$$

We then require the value for t that will generate the maximum value for T (total tax revenue). Clearly, in terms of the methodology we have developed, this requires:

$$\frac{dT}{dt} = 0 \quad \text{when} \quad \frac{d^2 T}{dt^2} < 0$$

Taking the first derivative of Eq. C5.59 with respect to t we have:

$$\frac{dT}{dt} = \frac{a_1 b_2 - b_1 a_2 + 2b_1 b_2 t}{b_2 - b_1} = 0 \tag{C5.60}$$

which gives

$$a_1 b_2 - b_1 a_2 + 2b_1 b_2 t = 0$$
$$a_1 b_2 - b_1 a_2 = -2b_1 b_2 t$$

and therefore

$$t = \frac{a_1 b_2 - b_1 a_2}{-2b_1 b_2} \tag{C5.61}$$

as the unit excise tax to be levied to maximize total tax revenue. For this to be a maximum we require $d^2 T/dt^2 < 0$, and from Eq. C5.60 we obtain:

$$\frac{d^2 T}{dt^2} = \frac{2b_1 b_2}{b_2 - b_1} < 0 \tag{C5.62}$$

To illustrate, let us return to one of the examples we used in Module B2 where we had:

$$Q_d = 500 - 9P \tag{C5.63}$$
$$Q_s = -100 + 6P \tag{C5.64}$$

Here we have the following values for the parameters:

$$a_1 = 500 \qquad b_1 = -9$$
$$a_2 = -100 \qquad b_2 = 6$$

and substituting into Eq. C5.61 gives

$$t = \frac{a_1 b_2 - b_1 a_2}{-2b_1 b_2}$$
$$= -\frac{500(6) - (-C9)(-100)}{-2(-C9)(6)} = \frac{2100}{108} = £19.44$$

as the unit tax required in order to maximize total tax revenue. To confirm that this gives a maximum tax revenue we also require:

$$\frac{d^2 T}{dt^2} = \frac{2b_1 b_2}{b_2 - b_1} < 0$$
$$= \frac{2(-9)(6)}{6 - (-9)} < 0$$
$$= -\frac{108}{15} < 0$$

which confirms that we have a maximum point on the tax revenue function.

Progress Check C5.7

Assuming this level of excise tax is imposed, find:

(i) The equilibrium price

(ii) The equilibrium quantity

(iii) The total tax revenue raised.

From Eq. C5.59 and using the numerical parameters for Eqs C5.63 and C5.64, derive a quadratic function for $T = f(t)$. Find the maximizing rate of excise tax directly from this function.

(Solution on p. 469)

C5.9 Summary

In this module we have examined a number of applications of the principles of optimization to economics and derived a number of well-known principles, as well as investigating a number of areas where we can reach definitive conclusions only through the use of calculus principles that we have developed. The topics we have examined are only a cross-section of those to which calculus could be applied.

Learning Check

Having read this module you should have learned that:

- At profit maximization $MC = MR$ regardless of the market conditions
- The imposition of a lump-sum tax leaves the profit-maximizing point unchanged although optimal profit is reduced by the amount of the lump-sum tax
- The imposition of a profit tax will also leave the profit-maximizing level of output unchanged
- The imposition of an excise tax alters the profit-maximizing level of output leading to a higher price and a lower level of output.

Worked Example

A firm produces a product at a single factory and sells the product in both the domestic and export markets. Its cost function is given by:

$$TC = 10,000 + 5Q$$

In the domestic market (d) it faces a demand function:

$$P_d = 250 - Q_d$$

and in the export market (x)

$$P_x = 200 - 2Q_x$$

(i) Determine the prices in the two markets that will maximize the firm's profit.

Worked Example *(Continued)*

(ii) The firm's exports are in fact to other countries forming part of a customs union, or common market, and the firm has been told that it cannot price-discriminate: that is, it must charge the same price in both its domestic market and its export market. Assess the new profit-maximizing level of output. Comment on the effect of the policy of non-price discrimination in this case.

Solution

(i) It is evident that the firm faces two demand functions in its two markets and that we seek a profit-maximizing level of output in each. It appears logical to seek a solution where:

$$MC_d = MR_d$$

and

$$MC_x = MR_x$$

In fact, with only one production source (the one factory), $MC_d = MC_x$
For the domestic market we then have:

$$TR_d = 250Q_d - Q_d^2$$
$$MR_d = f'(TR_d) = 250 - 2Q_d$$
$$MC = 5$$

and solving for Q_d when $MC = MR_d$ gives $Q_d = 122.5$ as the profit-maximizing level of output for the domestic market. For the export market we have:

$$TR_x = 200Q_x - 2Q_x^2$$

and

$$MR_x = f'(TR_x) = 200 - 4Q_x$$

Solving for $MC = MR_x$ gives $Q_x = 48.75$ as the profit-maximizing output for the export market. Total production for the firm will then be:

$$122.5 + 48.75 = 171.25$$

Note that the firm will actually discriminate in price terms between the two markets. For the domestic market we have:

$$P_d = 250 - Q_d$$

which for $Q_d = 122.5$ gives $P_d = 127.5$ as the domestic market price. For the export market we have:

$$P_x = 200 - 2Q_x$$

which gives $P_x = 102.5$ when $Q_x = 48.75$.

(ii) If the firm is now told that it must charge the same price in both markets, it will need to reassess its profit-maximizing position (particularly since in the domestic market it is able to earn considerably higher prices). We can arrange the two original demand functions to give:

$$P_d = 250 - Q_d$$

Worked Example (Continued)

which becomes

$$Q_d = 250 - P_d$$

and

$$P_x = 200 - 2Q_x$$

becomes

$$Q_x = 100 - 0.5P_x$$

Since $P_d = P_x$ because of the policy decision, then we have:

$$Q_d = 250 - P$$

and

$$Q_x = 100 - 0.5P$$

Total quantity will now be $Q_d + Q_x$ to give:

$$Q = Q_d + Q_x = 250 - P + (100 - 0.5P) = 350 - 1.5P$$

or

$$P = 233.33 - \frac{2Q}{3}$$

The new TR function will then be:

$$TR = 233.33Q - \frac{2Q^2}{3}$$

and

$$f'(TR) = 233.33 - \frac{4Q}{3}$$

We still require $MC = MR$, and as $MC = 5$ we derive $Q = 171.25$, and with $f''(Q) = -4/3$ this is the new profit-maximizing level of output. The destination of the total output has also changed. For this level of output the price required will be $P = 119.18$ as the price charged in both markets.

From the two market demand functions we can determine that $Q_d = 130.82$ and $Q_x = 40.41$. Note that the new price is in between the two original (and different), market prices and the overall effect has been to decrease export sales and increase domestic sales.

You may also find it instructive to calculate the firm's profit in parts (i) and (ii) and to consider through the use of the MR functions why the firm increases domestic sales at the expense of export.

Exercises

C5.1   Assume a function of the form:

$$TC = 2000 + 10Q - 3Q^2 + 0.5Q^3$$

relating total costs to output.

   (i)   Confirm that the function has 'sensible' numerical values for the parameters.
   (ii)   Find the level of output that minimizes MC.

Exercises *(Continued)*

(iii) Find the level of output that minimizes average costs, *AC*. Calculate *AC* and *MC* at this level of output.

(iv) Find the level of output that minimizes average fixed costs, *AFC*. Comment on the result.

(vi) Plot *MC,AC,AFC* on a single graph and comment upon their relationship.

C5.2 Assume the firm in Ex. C5.1 above can sell all its output at a price of 200. Find the profit-maximizing level of output. Calculate profit for this level of output. The government now imposes an excise tax, *t*, on sales of this product. Discuss how this will affect the firm.

C5.3 Assume a monopolist has the same *TC* function as in Ex. C5.1 above but faces a demand function:

$$P = 500 - 2.5Q$$

(i) Find the profit-maximizing level of output.

(ii) For the monopolist, find the revenue-maximizing level of output. Calculate the profit earned at this output level. Comment on why your solution to Ex. C5.3 is different.

C5.4 The government imposes a lump-sum tax of 1000 on the monopolist in Ex. C5.3. Confirm that this will not affect the optimum level of output. How would this affect the monopolist if he or she decided to maximize revenue instead?

C5.5 A firm faces the following:

$$TR = 300Q - 2Q^2$$
$$TC = 100 + 10Q + 5Q^2$$

The government now imposes an excise tax so as to maximize tax revenue. Assess the effect on the profit-maximizing level of output.

C5.6 A company manufactures a product with the relevant cost function:

$$TC = 75,000 + 20Q$$

It sells its product directly to domestic customers (d) and to non-domestic customers (n). The relevant demand functions are:

$$P_d = 1000 - Q_d$$
$$P_n = 4000 - 1.5Q$$

(i) Find the profit-maximizing level of output for the company.

(ii) The government now requires the company to charge the same price to all customers. Assess the effect of this policy on:
  (a) Profit
  (b) Equilibrium price
  (c) Equilibrium quantity.

Module C6
Optimization in production theory

In previous modules we saw how optimization can be applied to a number of areas of economic analysis. In this chapter we extend our examination of optimization to see how it can be applied to the theory of production and to the theory of costs, two important areas of economic analysis. As with the previous module, we'll use mathematics to confirm a number of significant economic conclusions that you may be familiar with from descriptive economic analysis.

Learning Objectives

By the end of this module you should be able to:

- Apply differential calculus to production theory
- Explain the relationship between average product (AP) and marginal product (MP)
- Explain the relationship between total cost (TC), average cost (AC) and marginal cost (MC)
- Explain the relationship between marginal cost (MC) and marginal product (MP).

C6.1 The theory of production

Assume that, in the short run at least, we can regard a firm's production function as being of the form:

$$Q = g(L) \tag{C6.1}$$

where Q refers to output and L to the labour input, with other possible inputs such as capital being regarded as fixed in the short term. The average product (AP) function will be given by:

$$AP = \frac{Q}{L} = \frac{g(L)}{L} \tag{C6.2}$$

that is, average product is total production divided by the units of labour employed. The marginal product (MP) function will be given by:

$$MP = \frac{dQ}{dL} = g'(L) \tag{C6.3}$$

that is, as the derivative of the production function. Let us investigate the maximum point on the AP function – where the firm maximizes average product. To find such a point we require:

$$\frac{d(AP)}{dL} = 0$$

but from Eq. C6.2 we have $AP = g(L)/L$. Applying the quotient rule from Module C2.3 we then have:

$$\frac{d(AP)}{dL} = \frac{Lg'(L) - g(L)}{L^2} = 0 \tag{C6.4}$$

which simplifies to

$$Lg'(L) - g(L) = 0$$
$$Lg'(L) = g(L)$$
$$g'(L) = \frac{g(L)}{L}$$

but from Eq. C6.2, since $AP = g(L)/L$, and from Eq. C6.3, since $MP = g'(L)$, this can be rewritten as

$$MP = g'(L) = \frac{g(L)}{L} = AP \tag{C6.5}$$

That is, $MP = AP$ when AP is at a maximum. In other words, the marginal product function passes through the point that is the maximum of the average product function. Again, this is a general deduction since we have not specified any particular mathematical form for the production function.

Progress Check C6.1

Assume a production function:

$$Q = -0.1L^3 + 5L^2$$

Confirm that $MP = AP$ when AP is at a maximum.

(Solution on p. 469)

However, it may have occurred to you that we have only found the turning point for AP, given that we have not yet examined the second derivative to confirm that we have actually found the maximum. From Eq. C6.4, and applying both the quotient and product rules, we obtain:

$$\frac{d^2(AP)}{dL^2} = \frac{L^2[Lg''(L) + g'(L) - g'(L)] - (2L)[Lg'(L) - g(L)]}{L^4}$$
$$= \frac{L^3 g''(L) - 2L^2 g'(L) + 2Lg(L)}{L^4}$$
$$= \frac{g''(L)}{L} - \frac{2g'(L)}{L^2} + \frac{2g(L)}{L^3} \tag{C6.6}$$

However, we already know that $Lg'(L) = g(L)$, so substituting gives:

$$\frac{d^2(AP)}{dL^2} = \frac{g''(L)}{L} - \frac{2g'(L)}{L^2} + \frac{2Lg'(L)}{L^3}$$
$$= \frac{g''(L)}{L} - \frac{2g'(L)}{L^2} + \frac{2g'(L)}{L^2}$$
$$= \frac{g''(L)}{L} \qquad\qquad\qquad\qquad\qquad\qquad (C6.7)$$

Hence we require:

$$\frac{d^2(AP)}{dL^2} = \frac{g''(L)}{L} < 0 \qquad\qquad\qquad\qquad\qquad (C6.8)$$

However, it is sensible to consider only the range of values for which $L > 0$; hence we require $g''(L) < 0$. We know that:

$$g''(L) = \frac{d(MP)}{dL} \qquad\qquad\qquad\qquad\qquad\qquad (C6.9)$$

Hence for the MP function to cross the AP function at the latter's maximum point we require the slope of the MP function to be negative at this point.

Progress Check C6.2

Return to Progress Check C6.1.
Confirm that MP takes a negative slope when AP is at a maximum.

Consider Figs C6.1 and C6.2, which show graphically a typical set of functions: a production function and the related MP and AP functions. Naturally, the shape of these functions is determined by the appropriate economic principles that we wish them to convey – the concept of diminishing marginal physical product, for example.

Let us assume that we wish to represent the production function as a cubic function mathematically. We then have:

$$Q = g(L) = a + bL + cL^2 + dL^3 \qquad\qquad\qquad (C6.10)$$
$$MP = g'(L) = b + 2cL + 3dL^2 \qquad\qquad\qquad\qquad (C6.11)$$
$$AP = \frac{g(L)}{L} = \frac{a + bL + cL^2 + dL^3}{L} = \frac{a}{L} + b + cL + dL^2 \qquad (C6.12)$$

Let us examine the relevant parameters in terms of any restrictions we would require to place on these equations. First, it is evident that the production function itself should start from the origin (zero input = zero output). This requires $a = 0$. We also see that we require the MP function to start from the origin. From Eq. C6.11 this clearly requires $b = 0$ also. (Clearly, we could now simplify Eqs C6.10 to C6.12 if we wished by omitting all terms involving a or b.) It is also evident that MP takes a quadratic form (the

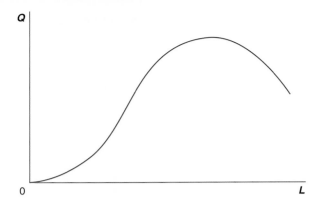

Figure C6.1 Production function

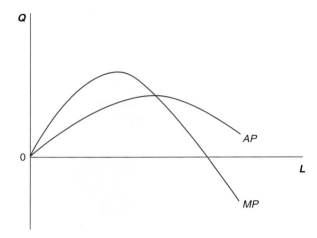

Figure C6.2 *AP* and *MP*

inverse U), giving a maximum for *MP* that is positive when $L > 0$. We know that such a maximum point will occur when:

$$\frac{d(MP)}{dL} = \frac{d[g'(L)]}{dL} = g''(L) = 2c + 6dL = 0 \qquad (C6.13)$$

$$\frac{d^2(MP)}{dL^2} = g'''(L) = 6d < 0 \qquad (C6.14)$$

The first-order conditions will then be satisfied when $L = -c/3d$. In order to meet the second-order conditions we require $d < 0$, and since we would expect L to be non-negative this implies that $c > 0$. Summarizing, we have:

$a = 0$

$b = 0$

$c > 0$

$d < 0$

which reduces the three equations to the form

$$Q = g(L) = cL^2 + dL^3 \qquad\qquad\qquad\text{(C6.15)}$$

$$MP = g'(L) = 2cL + 3dL^2 \qquad\qquad\qquad\text{(C6.16)}$$

$$AP = \frac{g(L)}{L} = cL + dL^2 \qquad\qquad\qquad\text{(C6.17)}$$

C6.2 The theory of costs

In the context of our examination of production, we now examine costs and, again, apply the mathematical principles we have developed so far. Consider the total cost function (TC) related to output (Q):

$$TC = c(Q) \qquad\qquad\qquad\text{(C6.18)}$$

$$MC = c'(Q) \qquad\qquad\qquad\text{(C6.19)}$$

$$AC = \frac{c(Q)}{Q} \qquad\qquad\qquad\text{(C6.20)}$$

and, again, diagrammatically we would often expect to see the relationships as they are shown in Figs C6.3 and C6.4. We see that the TC function is one that is monotonically increasing: cost always increases with output (although naturally at different rates). This further implies that MC must always be positive and, as we see, MC takes the typical U shape. Let us consider the logic behind this. Clearly, as we have seen previously, there are direct links between costs and production. If we assume a simplified short-run function of the form:

$$TC = F + wL \qquad\qquad\qquad\text{(C6.21)}$$

where F represents fixed costs, L the labour input into the production process and w the wage rate per unit of labour, then we can in turn express MC as

$$MC = c'(Q) = \frac{d(TC)}{dQ} = \frac{d(TC)}{dL}\frac{dL}{dQ}$$

However, from Eq. C6.21, $d(TC)/dL = w$ and $dL/dQ = 1/MP$. Hence:

$$MC = \frac{w}{MP} \qquad\qquad\qquad\text{(C6.22)}$$

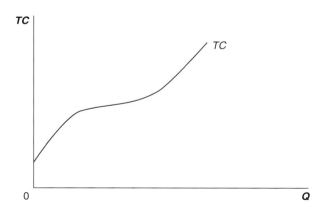

Figure C6.3 TC

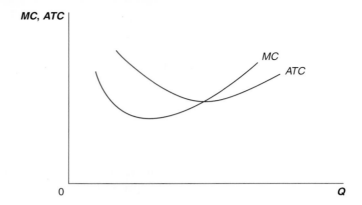

Figure C6.4 *ATC, MC*

That is, marginal cost is the wage rate divided by the marginal product of labour. Since, in the short term, w can be regarded as fixed, then MC will vary inversely with MP. In terms of the typical U shape for the MC function we can now see that as MP increases MC decreases and vice versa. Further, as MP approaches its maximum point, MC will approach its minimum; and logically when MP is at its maximum, MC is at its minimum. It is evident that there is a direct relationship between the theory of production and the theory of cost. As with the production function, we can consider numerical restrictions that we might wish to apply to a TC function. Consider the cubic function:

$$TC = a + bQ + cQ^2 + dQ^3 \qquad \text{(C6.23)}$$

which gives

$$MC = b + 2cQ + 3dQ^2 \qquad \text{(C6.24)}$$

which we recognize as a quadratic taking either the U or inverted U shape. The a term in Eq. C6.23 represents fixed costs and we would require $a > 0$. Since the TC function is monotonically increasing, MC must take positive values for non-negative values for Q. This implies that the required minimum value for MC must be positive. The minimum is given when:

$$\frac{d(MC)}{dQ} = 2c + 6dQ = 0 \qquad \text{(C6.25)}$$

and

$$\frac{d^2(MC)}{dQ^2} = 6d > 0 \qquad \text{(C6.26)}$$

Therefore MC will have a minimum when $Q = -c/3d$ and when $d > 0$. Additionally, since we require $Q > 0$, then from Eq. C6.25 we also require $c < 0$. Taking $Q = -c/3d$ and substituting into Eq. C6.24 we then have:

$$MC = b + 2c(-\frac{c}{3d}) + 3d(-\frac{c}{3d})^2$$

which we require to be positive. Simplifying this gives:

$$MC = b - \frac{2c^2}{3d} + \frac{3d(c^2)}{3d^2} = b - \frac{2c^2}{3d} + \frac{c^2}{3d} = b - \frac{c^2}{3d} = \frac{3db - c^2}{3d}$$

From this it is clear that the restrictions we have so far ($c < 0$ and $d > 0$) are insufficient to ensure a positive minimum value for MC. Additionally we require:

$$3db - c^2 > 0$$

which further implies that $b > 0$ and $3db > c^2$. Thus we require:

$$a > 0$$
$$b > 0$$
$$c < 0$$
$$d > 0$$
$$3db > c^2$$

to ensure the form of TC that we require to suit the economic model.

C6.3 Relationship between the cost functions

Finally, let us examine the relationship between the AC and MC functions. If we have:

$$TC = c(Q) \quad \text{then AC} = \frac{TC}{Q} = \frac{c(Q)}{Q} \tag{C6.27}$$

Assume we wish to find the point where AC is minimized. Following our usual approach we require the first derivative of ATC to be zero (and we can then solve for Q) and we require the second derivative to be positive to confirm that the turning point is a minimum. We then have, using the quotient rule:

$$\frac{d(AC)}{dQ} = \frac{Qc'(Q) - c(Q)}{Q^2} = 0$$
$$Qc'(Q) - c(Q) = 0$$
$$Qc'(Q) = c(Q)$$
$$c'(Q) = \frac{c(Q)}{Q} \tag{C6.28}$$

However, $MC = c'(Q)$ and $c(Q)/Q = AC$ so we have:

$$MC = AC \tag{C6.29}$$

at the turning point of the AC function; that is, the MC function intersects the AC function at the latter's turning point. To confirm that this turning point represents a minimum we examine the second derivative:

$$\frac{d^2(AC)}{dQ^2} = \frac{Q^2[Qc''(Q) + c'(Q) - c'(Q)] - [Qc'(Q) - c(Q)](2Q)}{Q^4}$$
$$= \frac{Q^3 c''(Q) - 2Q^2 c'(Q) + 2Qc(Q)}{Q^4}$$
$$= \frac{c''(Q)}{Q} - \frac{2c'(Q)}{Q^2} + \frac{2c(Q)}{Q^3}$$

Given that $MC = AC$, we have $c'(Q) = c(Q)/Q$, which can be written as $c(Q) = Qc'(Q)$. Substituting this gives:

$$
\begin{aligned}
\frac{d^2(AC)}{dQ^2} &= \frac{c''(Q)}{Q} - \frac{2c'(Q)}{Q^2} + \frac{2Qc'(Q)}{Q^3} \\
&= \frac{c''(Q)}{Q} - \frac{2c'(Q)}{Q^2} + \frac{2c'(Q)}{Q^2} \\
&= \frac{c''(Q)}{Q}
\end{aligned}
\tag{C6.30}
$$

which we require to be positive for a minimum. Logically $Q > 0$ and hence we require $c''(Q) > 0$. However, $c''(Q)$ is simply the second derivative of TC or the derivative of MC. Therefore, for this point on the AC function to represent a minimum we require MC to have a positive slope at this point. This confirms that MC will intersect AC at the latter's minimum point.

C6.4 Summary

Although this has been a relatively short module, we have confirmed a number of well-known economic principles and conclusions using differential calculus relating to production theory and costs.

Learning Check

Having read this module you should have learned that:

- $MP = AP$ when AP reaches a maximum value
- MC = the wage rate divided by MP
- $MC = AC$ when AC reaches a minimum value.

Worked Example

A firm faces a short-run production function of the form:

$$Q = 12L^2 - 0.4L^3$$

You have been asked to determine the optimal values for Q, MP and AP.

Solution

Note that:

$$MP = f'(Q) = 24L - 1.2L^2$$

and

$$AP = Q/L = 12L - 0.4L^2$$

From Section C6.1 we see that the equation parameters are as expected from the general solution (that is, $a = 0$, $b = 0$, $c > 0$ and $d < 0$).

Worked Example *(Continued)*

Q takes optimum values when $MP = 0$. Since MP is quadratic we will have two roots which can be found to be $L_1 = 0$ and $L_2 = 20$. The second-order condition, $f''(Q)$, indicates that when $L_2 = 20$, Q reaches a maximum value which can be calculated as 1600 units.

Similarly, MP reaches its turning point midway between the two roots that we've already calculated at $L = 10$. We can confirm this turning point is a maximum from inspection of the MP quadratic equation, which takes the inverted U shape. Equally, the second derivative of the MP function takes a negative value of -2.4 confirming this optimal point is a maximum. MP takes a maximum value when $L = 10$ of 120.

(a)

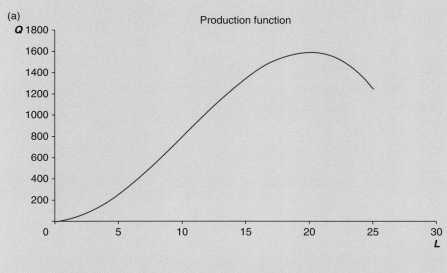

(b)

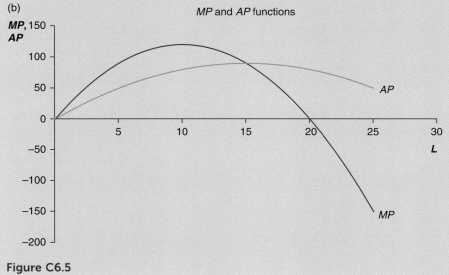

Figure C6.5

Worked Example *(Continued)*

Finally, AP is also quadratic. Its optimal value occurs when $L = 15$ and we can also confirm, either from the shape of the quadratic or the second derivative of the AP function, that this will be a maximum value giving $AP = 90$. We also show all the functions visually.

Exercises

C6.1 Assume a production function:

$$Q = g(L) = 12L^2 - 0.75L^3$$

 (i) Confirm that the numerical values for the parameters take 'sensible' values.

 (ii) Derive an expression for AP.

 (iii) Derive an expression for MP.

 (iv) Find the optimum values for AP and MP.

 (v) Plot all three functions on a single graph.

C6.2 Assume a production function of the form:

$$Q = h(K)$$

where K is capital input and L is fixed. Confirm that AP of capital equals MP of capital when AP is at a maximum.

C6.3 Assume a production function of the form:

$$Q = f(L) = 100 + 0.1L^2 - 0.001L^3$$

with a wage rate of £10 per unit of labour.

 (i) Derive the MC function.

 (ii) Plot the MP and the MC functions on a graph for L up to 50. Comment on the relationship between the two.

C6.4 We are told that a firm faces the function:

$$AP = 50 - 2L$$

Find the firm's MP function.

Section D
Optimization with multiple variables

Until now our analysis has largely been restricted to looking at optimization involving two variables – a dependent variable and a single independent or explanatory variable. This can be restrictive, given that economic models typically involve multiple explanatory variables. In this module we extend the principles of optimization in economic analysis to include models with multiple independent variables.

Module D1 Functions of more than two variables

The first module in this section expands the principles of calculus and differentiation to see how we can differentiate functions involving multiple independent variables. We do this by looking at the principles of partial differentiation, and also introduce the concept of the differential and the total derivative.

Module D2 Analysis of multivariable economic models

In this module we look at how the principles of partial differentiation can be applied to a variety of economic models in order to analyse economic behaviour with multiple variables.

Module D3 Unconstrained optimization

We now consider how we can determine optimality in economic models with multiple variables and see how partial differentiation can be used to determine such an optimal position.

Module D4 Constrained optimization

In this final section we examine a new type of economic model where we require an optimal position but subject to certain specified constraints. We see how the principles of constrained optimization can be developed through the introduction of Lagrange multipliers.

Module D1
Functions of more than two variables

In the previous modules we saw the importance and usefulness of differential calculus in economic analysis. However, the calculus methods introduced to date have focused only on the simplest of functions: those taking the form $Y = f(X)$. As we know, economic analysis is frequently concerned with functions involving more than two variables, and you need to be able to apply to such functions the useful principles you have developed. We begin in this module by looking at the principles involved in such functions and by examining the principle of a *partial* derivative, and then the concept of a *differential* and the *total* derivative.

Learning Objectives

By the end of this module you should be able to:

- Calculate first- and second-order partial derivatives
- Calculate the total differential
- Calculate the total derivative.

D1.1 Partial differentiation

In Module A3.6, we saw that economic models and economic analysis frequently require the use of more than one independent variable in order to capture the complexity of the real world in the economic model. We saw there the principles of three variable models, the corresponding 3D graphs and the concept of a surface that shows the relationship between the three variables. Consider the function:

$$Y = f(X_1, X_2) \tag{D1.1}$$
$$Y = -5 + 30X_1 - 3X_1^2 + 25X_2 - 5X_2^2 + X_1X_2 \tag{D1.2}$$

This may represent, for example, the profit function of a firm that makes two products where X_1 and X_2 represent the quantities of the two products sold. As we saw in Module A3, it is possible, but not easy, to plot such a function as a three-dimensional graph. Figure D1.1 shows the three-dimensional picture we would obtain for this function for

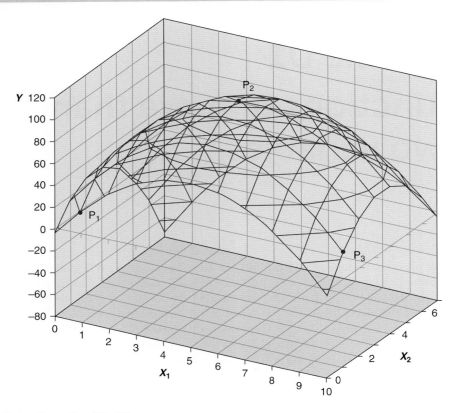

Figure D1.1 $Y = f(X_1, X_2)$

a range of values for X_1 and for X_2. We have highlighted three individual points on the surface of this function to help orientation:

> P_1 occurs when $X_1 = 1$, $X_2 = 0$, giving $Y = 22$
> P_2 occurs when $X_1 = 5$, $X_2 = 3$, giving $Y = 115$
> P_3 occurs when $X_1 = 10$, $X_2 = 1$, giving $Y = 25$.

If we look at the surface of this function we see that the slope follows a much more complex pattern than for the two-variable functions we have looked at so far. Clearly, the slope of this function changes not only as X_1 changes but also as X_2 changes. This makes our use of differential calculus more difficult when using such functions, given that we've been using derivatives to examine the slope of various functions.

One approach frequently adopted in economics with such complex functions is to choose a fixed value for one of the X variables – say, X_2 – and then to examine the relationship between Y and X_1. By keeping X_2 fixed, we can more easily see how Y and X_1 change in relation to each other. We can then repeat the analysis with the other X variable, X_1, taking fixed values to see how Y and X_2 change in relation to each other. Figure D1.2 shows the idea behind this. The figure shows the overall function again but now with certain parts highlighted. If we were to set $X_2 = 0$, the highlighted curve would show the relationship between Y and X_1 with X_2 fixed at zero. Similarly, we can set $X_2 = 1$ then $X_2 = 2$ then $X_2 = 3$. Figure D1.3 now shows the plot of Y and X_1 for

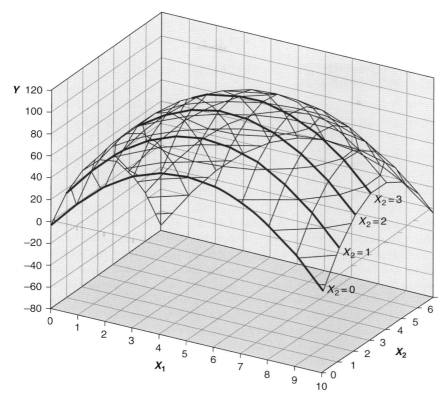

Figure D1.2 $Y = f(X_1, X_2)$ with $X_2 = 0, 1, 2, 3$

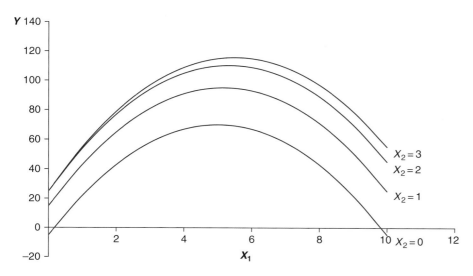

Figure D1.3 $Y = f(X_1, X_2)$ with X_2 constant

these fixed values of X_2, where we are effectively taking a series of slices through the 3D surface in Fig. D1.2.

Progress Check D1.1

Produce a diagram comparable to Fig. D1.3 but with X_1 fixed at 0, 2, 4.

(Solution on p 470)

However, the main difficulty for us in introducing functions of more than two variables is not with producing graphs but, rather, with the differential calculus we have started to use in our economic analysis. The techniques of differentiation that we have developed will not work here, since we have two X variables and the derivative applies only to one (recollect that the derivative is dY/dX). Recollect how we began the investigation of a simple derivative. We saw that the derivative indicated the change in Y given a change in X: in other words, the slope of the function at a specific X point. Consider the family of curves plotted in Fig. D1.3 for Y and X_1. Assume that we wished to find the slope of each of these functions when, for example, $X_1 = 6$. Clearly, we would not wish to have to resort to the approach of identifying the exact form of each associated function for each curve and then differentiating. It is apparent, however, that all these curves are related and that there should be some easier method of identifying the slopes. In fact, the approach we take is to obtain the *partial* derivative of the original multivariable function, as in Eq. D1.2. Consider how we obtained Fig. D1.3. We assumed that the other X variable, X_2, could be treated not as a variable but as a constant, and we assigned it a series of fixed values 0, 1, 2, 3. Remember, however, in our examination of calculus how we treated any constant in an expression that we wished to differentiate. Differentiating a constant gives a value of zero. It is clear, therefore, that we can obtain a derivative of Eq. D1.2 with respect to X_1, treating the other independent variable as a constant. Applying the basic rules that we have developed for differentiating we then get:

$$Y = -5 + 30X_1 - 3X_1^2 + 25X_2 - 5X_2^2 + X_1X_2$$

Differentiating the Y function in parts we see that we have:

Part	Derivative
-5	0
$30X_1$	30
$-3X_1^2$	$-6X_1$
$25X_2$	0 (since X_2 is assumed constant)
$-5X_2^2$	0 (since X_2 is assumed constant)
X_1X_2	X_2 (since X_2 is assumed constant)

Collecting these parts together we obtain:

$$\frac{\partial Y}{\partial X_1} = 30 - 6X_1 + X_2 \tag{D1.3}$$

Such an expression is referred to as a *partial derivative* of the original function and is denoted with the symbol $\partial Y/\partial X_1$ rather than the symbol dY/dX (this symbol is often referred to as 'the curly d'). It's pronounced 'partial dee Y by partial dee X one'.

Such a partial derivative indicates the change in Y as the X_1 variable changes, with the critical assumption that the other independent variable, X_2, remains unchanged. So, for example, if we set $X_2 = 2$ and $X_1 = 6$ we can calculate the partial derivative has a value of -4. That is, the slope of the original Y function, Eq. D1.2, at this point is -4. If you look back at Fig. D1.3 you will confirm the curve for Eq. D1.2 when $X_2 = 4$ has a negative slope when $X_1 = 6$.

Clearly, just as we have found the partial derivative with respect to X_1 we could find the partial derivative with respect to X_2 – that is, now keeping X_1 constant or fixed.

Progress Check D1.2

Take $X_1 = 0$, 1, 2, 3, 4. Substitute each value in turn into the original function (Eq. D1.2) to find $Y = f(X_2)$ for each X_1. Find the derivative of each of this series of functions and compare it with that for the partial derivative.
Find the partial derivative $\partial Y / \partial X_1$.

(Solution on p. 470)

So we can find the partial derivative of Y with respect to each X variable in the function. Just as we denoted the ordinary derivative of:

$$Y = f(X)$$

as dY/dX or $f'(X)$, so we have alternative notations for the partial derivatives. We have already seen that we can use the curly d. The alternative notation is:

f_{X1} to denote the partial derivative with respect to X_1
f_{X2} to denote the partial derivative with respect to X_2.

D1.2 Second-order partial derivatives

It will probably come as no surprise to realize that, as with our earlier functions, we can readily obtain the second derivative of a multivariable function such as that in Eq. D1.2, and that such second-order partial derivatives have much the same inter-pretation as any other second derivative, and they tell us how the first derivative is changing. Consider the partial derivative:

$$f_{X1} = 30 - 6X_1 + X_2$$

which indicates the change in Y from some change in X_1, assuming X_2 is fixed. Applying the same basic rules we can obtain the second-order partial derivatives with respect to X_1:

$$\frac{\partial^2 Y}{\partial X_1^2} = f_{X1X1} = -6 \tag{D1.4}$$

This second-order derivative tells us the rate at which the slopes of the family of curves in Fig. D1.3 changes as X_1 changes. In this example we note that the slope of Eq. D1.3 with respect to X_1 decreases as X_1 increases – graphically we see the slope generally changes from positive to negative.

Progress Check D1.3

Return to Progress Check D1.2. Find f_{X2X2} and interpret.

Similarly, we can obtain the first- and second-order partial derivatives with respect to X_2:

$$f_{X2} = 25 - 10X_2 + X_1 \qquad \text{(D1.5)}$$

$$f_{X2X2} = -10 \qquad \text{(D1.6)}$$

and these take a similar interpretation. Equation D1.5 shows how Y changes as X_2 changes, assuming X_1 is fixed. Equation D1.6 shows how Eq. D1.5 changes as X_2 changes. However, the matter of second-order derivatives for a multivariable function does not end there. Consider the first-order partial derivatives shown in Eqs D1.3 and D1.5. These in their own right are multivariable functions and it is clear that we could differentiate with respect *either* to X_1 or X_2 in both cases. In the case of Eq. D1.3 we then have:

$$f_{X1} = 30 - 6X_1 + X_2$$

and

$$f_{X1X2} = 1 \qquad \text{(D1.7)}$$

while for Eq. D1.5 we have

$$f_{X2} = 25 - 10X_2 + X_1$$

$$f_{X2X1} = 1 \qquad \text{(D1.8)}$$

It is particularly important to be aware of what we have done. Taking Eq. D1.2 – the original multivariable function – we differentiated first with respect to X_1 (to get Eq. D1.3). We then differentiated this function, Eq. D1.3, with respect to X_2 (to get Eq. D1.7). Such a derivative is known as a *cross-partial* derivative. Similarly, the other cross-partial derivative is obtained by differentiating first with respect to X_2 and then with respect to X_1. You may have noticed that both cross-partial derivatives produce the same result – Eqs D1.7 and D1.8. In fact, for any continuous function this will be the case, and this equality of the cross-partial derivatives is referred to as *Young's theorem*.

We examine below the use of such cross-partial derivatives in economic analysis. For the present, let's try to understand what they represent. We know that f_{X1} shows the slope of the Y function with respect to the X_1 variable, with the other X variable assumed constant. We know that the second-order partial derivative, f_{X1X1}, shows us the rate at which this slope, f_{X1}, is changing as X_1 changes. The cross-partial derivative, f_{X1X2}, tells us how the slope of f_{X1} is changing as X_2 changes. We'll show the general principle of what's happening with the cross-partial derivative using Fig. D1.4. This shows the surface of the Y function we've been looking at with four specific points marked: A, B, C and D. We can see that for these four points the X_1 value remains the same (the points are all on the same X_1 contour where $X_1 = 9$) while the X_2 value is varying from 0 to 1 to 2 to 3. At each point, we've drawn the appropriate tangent line that measures the slope at that point. So the tangent line for point A measures the slope of the Y function in relation to X_1 (with X_2 fixed at 0). The tangent line at point B measures the slope of the Y function in relation to X_1 (with X_2 fixed at 1). The same is true of the tangent lines at point C and D. So the four tangent lines all measure the slope of Y with respect to X_1 but for different values of X_2, which is exactly what f_{X1} measures. Let's now look at how the slope of these four tangent lines changes as X_2 changes. In Fig. D1.5 we've shown the value for the Y function for the same fixed values of X_2 with the four tangent lines for the four points superimposed. It's difficult to see precisely given the scale of the graph, but you should be able to observe from Fig. D1.5

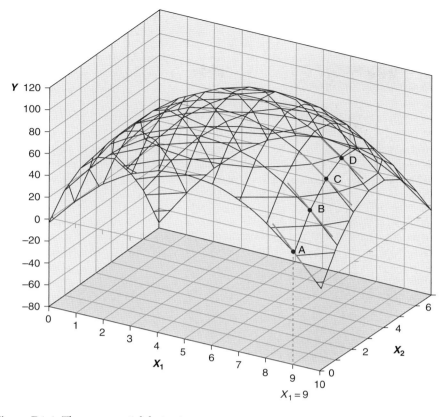

Figure D1.4 The cross-partial derivative

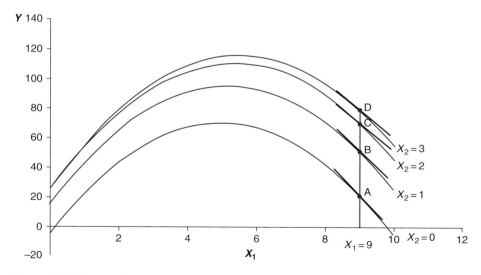

Figure D1.5 Tangent lines

that, as we move from A through to D, the slope of each tangent line changes slightly. This is what the cross-partial derivative f_{X1X2} measures – the change in f_{X1} as X_2 changes.

You may also be able to see how the tangent lines are changing in Fig. D1.5. The slope of all four lines is negative but is becoming less negative as X_2 increases. In other words, the slope of f_{X1} increases as X_2 increases. Let's look at the algebra to confirm this. We have:

$$f_{X1} = 30 - 6X_1 + X_2$$

At Point A we have $X_1 = 9$ and $X_2 = 0$ giving:

$$f_{X1} = 30 - 6X_1 + X_2 = -24$$

At Point B we have $X_1 = 9$ and $X_2 = 1$ giving:

$$f_{X1} = 30 - 6X_1 + X_2 = -23$$

At Point C we have $X_1 = 9$ and $X_2 = 2$ giving:

$$f_{X1} = 30 - 6X_1 + X_2 = -22$$

At Point D we have $X_1 = 9$ and $X_2 = 3$ giving:

$$f_{X1} = 30 - 6X_1 + X_2 = -21$$

It's obviously no coincidence that the slope is increasing by 1 as we move to subsequent points – this is what the cross-partial derivative of 1 in Eqs D1.7 and D1.8 also shows. However, we should remember that, as with any derivative, this is technically appropriate only for infinitesimally small changes in the X variables.

We can summarize what we've found out about partial derivatives in Table D1.1.

D1.3 Generalization to *n*-variable functions

The principles of partial differentiation are readily extended to functions involving more than three variables, although interpretation of these becomes more complex. Let's assume a function such that:

$$Y = f(X_1, X_2, X_3)$$

Table D1.1 Interpretation of partial derivatives

Which partial derivative?	What this tells us about point P on the surface of the function $Y = f(X_1, X_2)$
f_{X1}	Measures the slope at point P with respect to a change in X_1 with X_2 assumed constant The overall sign $(+/-)$ indicates whether the slope at this point is positive or negative
f_{X2}	Measures the slope at point P with respect to a change in X_2 with X_1 assumed constant The overall sign $(+/-)$ indicates whether the slope at this point is positive or negative
f_{X1X1}	Measures the change in the slope at point P as X_1 changes with X_2 assumed constant The overall sign $(+/-)$ indicates whether the change in the slope is positive or negative
f_{X2X2}	Measures the change in the slope at point P as X_2 changes with X_1 assumed constant The overall sign $(+/-)$ indicates whether the change in the slope is positive or negative
f_{X1X2}	Measures the change in the slope with respect to X_1 as X_2 changes The overall sign $(+/-)$ indicates whether the change in the slope is positive or negative
f_{X2X1}	Measures the change in the slope with respect to X_2 as X_1 changes The overall sign $(+/-)$ indicates whether the change in the slope is positive or negative

that is, there are three independent variables affecting Y. We now have three partial derivatives:

$$f_{X1}, f_{X2}, f_{X3}$$

and each of these is based on the assumption that the other two X variables are held constant. So, for example, f_{X1} shows the slope of the Y function as X_1 changes, assuming *both* X_2 and X_3 are constant. We also have three second-order partial derivatives:

$$f_{X1X1}, f_{X2X2}, f_{X3X3}$$

As before, each of these indicates how the slope of the Y function as shown by the appropriate partial derivative changes. So, for example, f_{X2} shows the slope of the Y function with respect to X_2 assuming X_1 and X_3 are constant. f_{X2X2} shows how this slope is changing as X_2 changes, with X_1 and X_3 again assumed to be constant.

Progress Check D1.6

How many cross-partial derivatives will there be?

Explain what any one of them shows.

You should be able to work out that there will be six cross-partial derivatives. Let's consider the partial derivative f_{X3}. This shows the slope of Y as X_3 changes assuming X_1 and X_2 are constant. We could now assess how this slope, f_{X3}, changes as each of the X variables change. This would give:

f_{X3X1} as the cross-partial derivative showing how this slope changes as X_1 changes, assuming X_2 and X_3 remain constant

f_{X3X2} as the cross-partial derivative showing how this slope changes as X_2 changes, assuming X_1 and X_3 remain constant.

So each partial derivative has two cross-partial derivatives giving six in total. These principles can be extended to functions involving n X variables.

Progress Check D1.7

For the function:

$$Y = 4X_1^2 - 5X_2^3 + 2X_3^4 - X_1X_2X_3$$

(i)   Find the partial derivatives
(ii)   Find the second-order partial derivatives
(iii)   Find the cross-partial derivatives.

(Solution on p. 471)

D1.4 Differentials

In our examination of differential calculus so far, we have treated the expression dY/dX as the symbol for a single item. We shall now explore the term as a ratio of the two terms dY and dX, where these individual terms are referred to as *differentials*. Consider the function:

$$Y = f(X)$$

Then, as we have seen on a number of occasions, we can investigate the effect of some small change in X, ΔX, on the Y value, ΔY. The ratio of the two changes we have referred to as the difference quotient is $\Delta Y / \Delta X$. Using this we then have:

$$\Delta Y = \frac{\Delta Y}{\Delta X} \Delta X \tag{D1.9}$$

In our examination of calculus we then assumed that ΔX became infinitesimally small and we saw that the difference quotient, $\Delta Y / \Delta X$, will then become the derivative dY/dX as ΔX approached zero, giving:

$$\Delta Y = \frac{dY}{dX} \Delta X \tag{D1.10}$$

If we then denote the (infinitesimally) small changes in X and Y as dX and dY respectively, we then have:

$$dY = \frac{dY}{dX} dX = f'(X) dX \tag{D1.11}$$

where dX and dY are known as the *differentials* of X and Y. Note that we can find the differential of Y simply by multiplying the derivative of the function by the differential of X. Equally, dividing the differential of Y by the differential of X will equal the derivative of the function. For example, assume a function:

$$Y = 4X^2$$

Then:

$$\frac{dY}{dX} = 8X$$

and

$$dY = (8X)dX$$

which we could use to determine dY if we were given a specific value for X and a value for dX (which would be measured from the given X value). For example, consider that we wished to examine what happened as X increases from 4 to 4.01. In this case dX is 0.01 and dY is given by:

$$dY = 8XdX = 8(4.01)(0.01) = 0.3208$$

Note this is an approximation, given that dY and dX relate to infinitesimally small changes.

D1.5 The total differential

Clearly, we also need to be able to apply the differential concept to partial derivatives. Assume a function such that:

$$Y = f(A, B) \tag{D1.12}$$

where Y, A and B are variables. If we keep B constant then, following the previous procedure, we have:

$$\Delta Y = \frac{\partial Y}{\partial A} \Delta A \tag{D1.13}$$

which for infinitesimally small changes becomes

$$dY = \frac{\partial Y}{\partial A} dA = f_A dA \tag{D1.14}$$

and through the same logic if we keep A constant we have

$$dY = \frac{\partial Y}{\partial B} dB = f_B dB \tag{D1.15}$$

However, as we have seen, partial derivatives (and differentials) require one independent variable to be kept constant. Assume that we allowed both independent variables to change simultaneously. We could then have:

$$\Delta Y = \frac{\partial Y}{\partial A} \Delta A + \frac{\partial Y}{\partial B} \Delta B \tag{D1.16}$$

$$dY = \frac{\partial Y}{\partial A} dA + \frac{\partial Y}{\partial B} dB \tag{D1.17}$$

$$dY = f_A dA + f_B dB \tag{D1.18}$$

Such an expression is referred to as the *total differential*. Let us illustrate with reference to the profit function we have been using:

$$Y = -5 + 30X_1 - 3X_1^2 + 25X_2 - 5X_2^2 + X_1X_2$$

We have:

$$f_{X1} = 30 - 6X_1 + X_2$$
$$f_{X2} = 25 - 10X_2 + X_1$$

giving

$$dY = (30 - 6X_1 + X_2)dX_1 + (25 - 10X_2 + X_1)dX_2 \qquad \text{(D1.19)}$$

Consider when $X_1 = 5$ and $X_2 = 2$. We wish to determine the effect on Y of:

- A change in X_1
- A change in X_2
- A change in *both* X_1 and X_2.

Let us examine each in turn.

Assume X_1 changes from 5 to 5.02. We then have:

$$dY = \frac{\partial Y}{\partial X_1}dX_1 = f_{X1}dX_1 = (30 - 6X_1 + X_2)dX_1$$

where $X_1 = 5$, $X_2 = 2$ and $dX_1 = 0.2$. We then have:

$$dY = [30 - 6(5) + 2](0.02) = 0.04$$

which would be the (approximate) change in Y as X_1 changes between the two stated values. Similarly, assume X_2 changes from 2 to 2.02. We then have:

$$dY = \frac{\partial Y}{\partial X_2}dX_2 = f_{X2}dX_2 = (25 - 10X_2 + X_1)dX_2$$

where $X_1 = 5$, $X_2 = 2$ and $dX_2 = 0.02$. We then have:

$$dY = [25 - 10(2) + 5]0.02 = 0.2$$

as the approximate change in Y as X_2 changes. Finally, if we wish to assess the effect of both changes in X simultaneously we have:

$$dY = (30 - 6X_1 + X_2)dX_1 + (25 - 10X_2 + X_1)dX_2$$

where

$$X_1 = 5$$
$$X_2 = 2$$
$$dX_1 = 0.02$$
$$dX_2 = 0.02$$

to give

$$dY = [30 - 6(5) + 2](0.02) + [25 - 10(2) + 5](0.02) = 0.24$$

Let's put this into an economic context. In the example we have been using, Y equates to profit, X_1 to the quantity of product 1 and X_2 to the quantity of product 2. So, when $X_1 = 5$, a marginal increase in output from 5 to 5.02 will lead to an increase in profit of 0.04, *ceteris paribus*. Similarly, when X_2 is 2 a marginal change in output to 2.02 will lead to an increase in profit of 0.2, *ceteris paribus*. Finally, if output of both products changes then profit will increase by 0.24. Partial derivatives and differentials then allow us to assess the impact on Y of changes in either of the X variables whether individually or together.

From the original function calculate Y when $X_1 = 5$, $X_2 = 2$. Recalculate the solution when $X_1 = 5.02$, $X_2 = 2.02$. Comment on the change in Y.

Obtain the total differential for the function:

$$Y = 50 - 3X_1 + 6X_1^2 - 5X_2 - 10X_2^2 - 3X_1X_2$$

(Solution on p. 471)

D1.6 The total derivative

So far we have considered a multivariable function where the X variables are independent of each other. In some economic models this may not be appropriate. We may have a situation, for example, where:

$$Z = f(X, Y) \tag{D1.20}$$

$$Y = g(X) \tag{D1.21}$$

where the X and Y variables are not independent but functionally related. In such a situation, a change in X will affect Z in two ways. It will affect Z directly (via function f) but also indirectly through Y via function g. This is illustrated in Fig. D1.6. A change in X affects Z in two ways: directly through the function f and indirectly through the function g and then f.

The direct effect is given by the partial derivative, f_X. The total effect is given by the *total derivative*. This can be calculated using the total differential. The total differential of such a function will be as before:

$$dZ = \frac{\partial Z}{\partial X}dX + \frac{\partial Z}{\partial Y}dY \tag{D1.22}$$

Dividing through by dX, the differential of X, we have:

$$\frac{dZ}{dX} = \frac{\partial Z}{\partial X} + \frac{\partial Z}{\partial Y}\frac{dY}{dX} = f_X + f_Y\frac{dY}{dX} \tag{D1.23}$$

where dZ/dX is known as the *total derivative* of Z with respect to X (where X is the independent variable in the function). Naturally we now need to be careful to distinguish between the partial derivative with respect to X and the total derivative. The

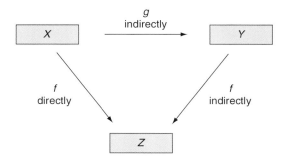

Figure D1.6 Direct and indirect effects on Z

partial derivative indicates the direct effect of a change in X on Z while the total derivative measures both the direct and indirect (via $Y = g(X)$) effects on Z of a change in X. Consider the example:

$$Z = f(X, Y) = 4X^3 - Y^2 \tag{D1.24}$$

$$Y = g(X) = X^2 - 5 \tag{D1.25}$$

$$\frac{dZ}{dX} = f_X + f_Y \frac{dY}{dX} \tag{D1.26}$$

where

$$f_X = 12X^2$$

$$f_Y = -2Y$$

$$\frac{dY}{dX} = 2X \qquad [\text{the derivative of } (X^2 - 5)]$$

giving

$$\frac{dZ}{dX} = 12X^2 - 2Y(2X) = 12X^2 - 2(X^2 - 5)(2X)$$

$$= 12X^2 - (4X^3 - 20X)$$

where the first term, $12X^2$, represents the direct effect of a change in X on Z, and the second term $(4X^3 - 20X)$ represents the indirect effects via $Y = g(X)$. Consider the situation when $X = 10$. Substituting into the total derivative expression we then have:

$$\frac{dZ}{dX} = 12X^2 - (4X^3 - 20X) = -2600$$

with $12X_2$ at 1200 and $-(4X^3 - 20X)$ at -3800. The total derivative, at -2600, shows the total change in Z as X changes. The direct effect on Z of a change in X will be $+1200$, and the indirect effects through Y will be -3800.

Progress Check D1.9

Using Eqs D1.24 and D1.25, calculate Z when $X = 10$ and again when $X = 10.0001$. Compare the change in Z with the total derivative at -2600.

(Solution on p. 471)

The principle can be readily extended to more complex situations. Consider the function:

$$Z = f(X, Y) \tag{D1.27}$$

where

$$X = g(W) \tag{D1.28}$$

$$Y = h(W) \tag{D1.29}$$

The total derivative is then denoted as dZ/dW (since W is the independent variable in the set), giving:

$$\frac{dZ}{dW} = f_X \frac{dX}{dW} + f_Y \frac{dY}{dW} \tag{D1.30}$$

For example, consider:

$$Z = 10X^4 - 3Y^2 \qquad \text{(D1.31)}$$
$$X = g(W) = 12W - 10 \qquad \text{(D1.32)}$$
$$Y = h(W) = 2W^3 \qquad \text{(D1.33)}$$

Then:

$$f_X = 40X^3$$
$$f_Y = -6Y$$
$$\frac{dX}{dW} = 12$$
$$\frac{dY}{dW} = 6W^2$$

giving

$$dW = 40X^3(12) - 6Y(6W^2) = 480(12W - 10)^3 - 6(2W^3)(6W^2)$$

as the total derivative, showing how Z will change with respect to W.

Progress Check D1.10

Find the total derivative for the function:

$$Z = 10X^{0.4}Y^{0.5}$$

where $Y = 0.8X^2$.

(Solution on p. 471)

D1.7 Implicit functions

Finally, before we examine the use of all these principles in economic analysis, let us consider an implicit function. Consider a function such that:

$$Z = f(X, Y) \qquad \text{(D1.34)}$$

where we arbitrarily set the value of the function to some constant value, k. We then have:

$$Z = f(X, Y) = k$$

which, although not immediately obvious, implicitly defines Y as a function of X. Consider, for example, the function:

$$Z = X^2Y - 5Y \qquad \text{(D1.35)}$$

where we set $Z = 100$. Then:

$$X^2Y - 5Y = 100$$
$$Y(X^2 - 5) = 100$$
$$Y = g(X) = \frac{100}{X^2 - 5}$$

confirming that $Y = f(X)$. Using the principles of total differentiation we can obtain dY/dX for such an implicit function. Given that $Z = k$ (a constant), then dZ (the change in Z) must be zero by definition. So we have:

$$dZ = f_X dX + f_Y dY = 0 \qquad \text{(D1.36)}$$

Dividing through by dX gives:

$$f_X + f_Y \frac{dY}{dX} = 0$$

and rearranging gives

$$\frac{dY}{dX} = \frac{-f_X}{f_Y} \qquad \text{(D1.37)}$$

Returning to the numerical example we have:

$$Z = X^2 Y - 5Y$$

with

$$f_X = 2XY$$
$$f_Y = X^2 - 5$$

and hence

$$\frac{dY}{dX} = \frac{-2XY}{X^2 - 5}$$

D1.8 Summary

In this module we have extended the application of calculus to functions involving more than two variables. The principles of this are generally extensions of the principles we had already developed using more cumbersome approaches. You should ensure, however, that you have an adequate understanding of the concepts of partial derivatives, differentials and the total derivative.

Learning Check

Having read this module you should have learned that:

- Partial differentiation is applied to multivariable functions
- A first-order partial derivative shows how the dependent variable changes as one of the independent variables changes, with the other independent variables assumed constant
- Second-order partial derivatives are obtained by differentiating the function first by one independent variable and then by the second independent variable
- Cross-partial derivatives will take the same value through Young's theorem
- The total differential shows the change in the dependent variable brought about by a change in each of the independent variables
- The total derivative shows the change in the dependent variables from both the direct and indirect effects of a change in a given independent variable.

Worked Example

A company manufactures two products, A and B, with a profit function given by:

$$Y = -100 + 80A - 0.1A^2 + 100B - 0.2B^2$$

where

Y = profit
A = output of product A
B = output of product B.

(i) Find the two first-order partial derivatives.
(ii) Find all the second-order partial derivatives. Find the total differential.
(iii) Explain what each of your answers means in an economic context.

Solution

For the first-order partial derivatives we have:

$$f_A = 80 - 0.2A$$
$$f_B = 100 - 4B$$

These show the change in profit, Y, as output of A or B changes. For example, consider f_A. We see this is a linear function so overall profit will increase as A increases but at a decreasing rate. We can also comment that if A increases beyond 400 units (80/0.2) then the change in profit will be negative.

For the second-order partial derivatives we have:

$$f_{AA} = -0.2$$
$$f_{BB} = -0.4$$
$$f_{AB} = 0$$

So f_{AA}, for example, shows the rate of change of profit as A changes, confirming the negative rate of change. f_{AB} shows the rate of change in profit with respect to one product as production of the other product changes. Here the rate of change is zero.

The total differential is given by:

$$dY = f_A dA + f_B dB$$

$$dY = -0.2dA - 0.4dB$$

This allows us to calculate the change in profit occurring from a change in both A and B.

D

Exercises

Before doing the following exercises you should read the Appendix to this module, which reviews the rules for partial differentiation.

D1.1 Find all the (first-, second-, cross-) partial derivatives for each of the following functions:

(i) $Z = w^3 X^4 Y^5 + 5Y^3$

(ii) $Z = 3X^2 + Y^4 - 4XY^2$

(iii) $Z = (X - 10Y)(4X + 2Y^2)$

Exercises (Continued)

D1.2 Find all the (first-, second-, cross-) partial derivatives for each of the following functions:

(i) $Z = W^3 X^4 Y^5$

(ii) $Z = Y/X^2 - 2X^3 + 4Y^2 X$

D1.3 Assume the following function:

$Z = 2X^4 + 10XY + 5Y^3$

(i) Find the total differential.

(ii) Let $X = 10$ and $Y = 5$. Find the effect on Z of a change in X, a change in Y and a change in both X and Y.

D1.4 Find the total derivative for the following functions:

(i) $Z = 5X^2 + 15XY + 5Y^2$ where $Y = 5X^2$

(ii) $Z = (10X - 5Y)^2$ where $Y = (X + 5)$

(iii) $Z = \dfrac{5X - 3Y}{2X + 4Y}$ where $Y = 2X - 10$

D1.5 Find the derivative, dY/dX, of the following functions:

(i) $Z = 10X^2 - Y$

(ii) $Z = 5X^4 - 7Y^3 - 100$

Appendix D1 Rules for partial differentiation

Without proof we state the following rules for partial differentiation of different types of function.

Rule 1: generalized power function rule

Given $Z = [f(X, Y)]^n$ then:

$$\partial Z/\partial X = n[f(X, Y)]^{n-1}\partial f/\partial X$$
$$\partial Z/\partial Y = n[f(X, Y)]^{n-1}\partial f/\partial Y$$

For example:

$$Z = (X^3 + 5Y^2)^5$$
$$\partial Z/\partial X = 5[X^3 + 5Y^2]^4 3X^2 = 15X^2[X^3 + 5Y^2]^4$$
$$\partial Z/\partial Y = 5[X^3 + 5Y^2]^4 10Y = 50Y[X^3 + 5Y^2]^4$$

Rule 2: product rule

Given $Z = f(X, Y)g(X, Y)$ then:

$$\partial Z/\partial X = f(X, Y)\partial g/\partial X + g(X, Y)\partial f/\partial X$$
$$\partial Z/\partial Y = f(X, Y)\partial g/\partial Y + g(X, Y)\partial f/\partial Y$$

For example:

$$Z = (5X + 10)(4X + 6Y)$$
$$\partial Z/\partial X = (5X + 10)4 + (4X + 6Y)5 = 40X + 30Y + 40$$
$$\partial Z/\partial Y = (5X + 10)6 + (4X + 6Y)0 = 30X + 60$$

Rule 3: quotient rule

Given $Z = f(X, Y)/g(X, Y)$ and $g(X, Y) \neq 0$ then:

$$\partial Z/\partial X = \frac{g(X, Y)\partial f/\partial X - f(X, Y)\partial g/\partial X}{g(X, Y)^2}$$

$$\partial Z/\partial Y = \frac{g(X, Y)\partial f/\partial Y - f(X, Y)\partial g/\partial Y}{g(X, Y)^2}$$

For example:

$$Z = (5X + 6Y)/(3X + 2Y)$$
$$\partial Z/\partial X = \frac{(3X + 2Y)5 - (5X + 6Y)3}{(3X + 2Y)^2} = \frac{-8Y}{(3X + 2Y)^2}$$
$$\partial Z/\partial Y = \frac{(3X + 2Y)6 - (5X + 6Y)2}{(3X + 2Y)^2} = \frac{8X}{(3X + 2Y)^2}$$

D

Module D2
Analysis of multivariable economic models

In the previous module we saw how the principles of calculus and differentiation can be applied to functions involving more than one independent variable. In this module we look at how partial differentiation can be applied to a number of economic models.

Learning Objectives

By the end of this module you should be able to:

- Use partial derivatives to assess the impact of parameter changes on market equilibrium
- Use partial derivatives to assess the impact of parameter changes on national income equilibrium
- Calculate direct price, cross-price and income elasticity
- Calculate elasticity of production
- Analyse consumer utility functions.

D2.1 Partial market equilibrium

To begin our exploration of how partial derivatives can be used in economic analysis we return to one of the earliest of our models, that relating to partial market equilibrium. The model is given as:

$$Q_d = Q_s \tag{D2.1}$$

$$Q_d = f(P) = a_1 + b_1 P \tag{D2.2}$$

$$Q_s = g(P) = a_2 + b_2 P \tag{D2.3}$$

with the usual restrictions that

$$a_1, b_2 > 0$$
$$a_2, b_1 < 0$$

and we previously derived market equilibrium solutions for P_e and Q_e such that

$$P_e = \frac{a_1 - a_2}{b_2 - b_1} \tag{D2.4}$$

$$Q_e = \frac{a_1 b_2 - a_2 b_1}{b_2 - b_1} \tag{D2.5}$$

We spent some time in Module B2 examining the effect on the solution of a change in each of the equation parameters (a_1, a_2, b_1, b_2). Let us now examine how this could be achieved through the application of the partial differentiation principles we introduced in the last module. Assume we wish to assess the effect of a change in a_1. This parameter is the intercept of the demand function, and any change will shift the whole function upwards or downwards. Such a change would be brought about by a structural change in the *ceteris paribus* conditions surrounding the model – that is, a change in one of the factors other than price affecting the demand function, which we have conveniently omitted from the function. If, for example, consumer income changed, then we would expect this to impact on the a_1 term, and we would wish to assess the impact such a change would then have on market equilibrium. If we wish to determine the effect of a change in a_1 on P_e then we require:

$$\frac{\partial P_e}{\partial a_1}$$

We can rewrite Eq. D2.4 as:

$$P_e = \frac{a_1 - a_2}{b_2 - b_1}$$

$$= a_1 \frac{1}{b_2 - b_1} - \frac{a_2}{b_2 - b_1} \tag{D2.6}$$

We then have:

$$\frac{\partial P_e}{\partial a_1} = \frac{1}{b_2 - b_1} \tag{D2.7}$$

If we examine this partial derivative we see that $(b_2 - b_1) > 0$, given the parameter restrictions, and hence the partial derivative itself must be positive. We conclude, therefore, that a change in the a_1 parameter will bring about a change in the same direction in P_e; that is, for example, an increase in a_1 will lead to an increase in P_e. Similarly, if we examine the effect on Q_e we require $\partial Q_e / \partial a_1$. We have:

$$Q_e = \frac{a_1 b_2 - a_2 b_1}{b_2 - b_1}$$

$$= \frac{a_1 b_2}{b_2 - b_1} - \frac{a_2 b_1}{b_2 - b_1}$$

giving

$$\frac{\partial Q_e}{\partial a_1} = \frac{b_2}{b_2 - b_1} \tag{D2.8}$$

Again, given the parameter restrictions, this implies that a change in the a_1 parameter will bring about a change in Q_e in the same direction – that is, an increase in a_1 will lead to an increase in Q_e. The use of the partial derivatives in this way allows us to assess the impact of change in a particular model parameter. In the same way we can examine the impact of a change in the slope parameters. Consider, for example, that we wish to evaluate the effect of a change in the slope of the supply function. We now want to look at:

$$\frac{\partial P_e}{\partial b_2} \quad \text{and} \quad \frac{\partial Q_e}{\partial b_2}$$

Using the quotient rule we have:

$$\frac{\partial P_e}{\partial b_2} = \frac{(b_2 - b_1)0 - (a_1 - a_2)1}{(b_2 - b_1)^2} = \frac{a_1 - a_2}{(b_2 - b_1)^2} \tag{D2.9}$$

which implies, given the parameter restrictions, that the partial derivative is less than zero. In other words, a change in b_2 will bring about a change in P_e of the opposite direction; an increase in the supply slope, for example, will lead to a decrease in P_e. Similarly, for Q_e we have:

$$\frac{\partial Q_e}{\partial b_2} = \frac{(b_2 - b_1)a_1 - (a_1 b_2 - a_2 b_1)}{(b_2 - b_1)^2}$$

$$= -\frac{a_1 b_1 + a_2 b_1}{(b_2 - b_1)^2} = \frac{b_1(a_2 - a_1)}{(b_2 - b_1)^2} \tag{D2.10}$$

and, once again given the parameter restrictions, we see that the partial derivative is negative, indicating an inverse relationship between a change in b_2 and Q_e.

Progress Check D2.1

Repeat this analysis for the parameter a_2.

(Solution on p. 472)

We can extend these principles to a more general model. Consider the model:

$$Q_d = f(a_1, P) \tag{D2.11}$$

$$Q_s = g(a_2, P) \tag{D2.12}$$

where we do not specify the exact form of either of the two functions – that is, whether they are linear, quadratic, cubic or any other form. We simply indicate that both Q_d and Q_s are functions of price and a shift factor (a_1 and a_2 respectively). The only requirements that we impose are that we face the usual downward-sloping demand function and upward-sloping supply function. Clearly, for equilibrium we require:

$$f(a_1, P) = g(a_2, P)$$

Assume that we wish to determine the effect of a change in either a_1 or a_2 on equilibrium. At equilibrium any change in Q_d must be matched by an identical change in Q_s. Expressing this in terms of differentials, therefore, we have:

$$dQ_d = dQ_s \tag{D2.13}$$

where

$$\partial Q_d = \frac{\partial Q_d da_1}{\partial a_1} + \frac{\partial Q_d dP}{\partial P} = f_{a1} \, da_1 + f_P dP \tag{D2.14}$$

and

$$\partial Q_s = \frac{\partial Q_s da_2}{\partial a_2} + \frac{\partial Q_s dP}{\partial P} = g_{a2} \, da_2 + g_P dP \tag{D2.15}$$

Substituting Eqs D2.14 and D2.15 into Eq. D2.13 gives:

$$f_{a1}\ da_1 + f_P dP = g_{a2}\ da_2 + g_P dP \tag{D2.16}$$

Since we are interested in the effect of a change in one of the shift parameters on equilibrium price we can rewrite this as:

$$dP(f_P - g_P) = g_{a2} da_2 - f_{a1}\ da_1 \tag{D2.17}$$

Hence:

$$dP = \frac{ga_2 da_2 - f_{a1}\ da_1}{f_P - g_P} \tag{D2.18}$$

Let us examine this in the context of some specific change. Assume, for example, that $da_1 > 0$ (that is, the demand function shifts upwards). Since we are introducing no change in the supply function we then have:

$$dP = -\frac{f_{a1} da_1}{f_P - g_P}$$

Since $da_1 > 0$ this implies that $f_{a1} > 0$ also – that is, an increase in a_1 leads to an increase in Q_d, *ceteris paribus*. Further, given a downward-sloping demand function we must have $f_P < 0$ (an increase in price, *ceteris paribus*, means a lower quantity is demanded). Equally, $g_P > 0$ since we assume an upward-sloping supply function. Examining the dP expression we then see that the denominator must take a negative value while the numerator is positive. The whole expression is preceded by a negative sign implying that $dP > 0$. Therefore, we conclude that, for any downward-sloping demand curve no matter what its precise numerical form, a shift upwards in the function must lead to an increase in equilibrium price. Once again we are able to deduce important economic conclusions through the application of mathematics.

Progress Check D2.2

Repeat this analysis for a_2.

D2.2 A national income model

Let us now look at the national income model we developed in Module B3 to see how partial differentiation can help in our analysis. We had a model involving a government sector such that:

$$Y = C + I + G \tag{D2.19}$$

$$Y_d = Y - T \tag{D2.20}$$

$$T = tY \tag{D2.21}$$

$$C = a + bY_d \tag{D2.22}$$

and with I and G exogenous. We further restrict the parameters so that:

$$0 < t < 1$$

$$a > 0$$

$$0 < b < 1$$

We previously derived an expression for equilibrium income such that:

$$Y_e = \frac{a + I + G}{1 - b(1 - t)} \qquad (D2.23)$$

We wish to evaluate the impact on Y_e (and thereby on C_e and T_e) of a change in any of the parameters in the model or in the exogenous variables. Through the use of partial derivatives this is now quite straightforward. Assume, for example, that we wish to assess the impact of a change in G. Taking the relevant partial derivative we have:

$$\frac{\partial Y_e}{\partial G} = \frac{1}{1 - b(1 - t)} \qquad (D2.24)$$

which, given the parameter restrictions, must be positive; that is, a change in G brings about a change in Y_e in the same direction. An increase in G leads to an increase in Y_e.

Progress Check D2.3

Investigate the impact of a change in I and a change in a.

(Solution on p. 472)

Clearly, the expression derived in Eq. D2.24 is a *multiplier* – the government expenditure multiplier in this case, showing the effect on equilibrium income of a change in G. It is evident that partial derivatives could be used to derive a whole series of such multipliers – showing the effect on Y_e of a change in any of the variables or coefficients. For example, the tax rate multiplier would be found from $\partial Y / \partial t$. From Eq. D2.23 we would have (using the quotient rule):

$$\frac{\partial Y}{\partial t} = \frac{-b(a + I + G)}{(1 - b(1 - t))^2} = \frac{-bY_e}{1 - b(1 - t)}$$

which from the model parameters must be less than zero. We can then readily assess the impact of a change in any of the model parameters in this way, not just on equilibrium income but also on C and on T – for example, assessing the change in T that would occur through a change in G. We can summarize the various multipliers as follows:

Multipliers

Change in a, autonomous consumption: positive

$$\frac{dY}{da} = \frac{1}{1 - b(1 - t)}$$

Change in b, marginal propensity to consume: positive

$$\frac{dY}{db} = \frac{(1-t)(a + I + G)}{(1 - b(1 - t))^2}$$

Change in I, autonomous investment: positive

$$\frac{dY}{dI} = \frac{1}{1 - b(1 - t)}$$

Change in G, autonomous government expenditure: positive

$$\frac{\partial Y}{\partial G} = \frac{1}{1 - b(1 - t)}$$

Change in t, tax rate: negative

$$\frac{\partial Y}{\partial t} = \frac{-b(a + I + G)}{(1 - b(1 - t))^2}$$

Clearly, we could follow the same principles for the more complex national income models – incorporating foreign trade and a monetary economy. These are left as exercises.

D2.3 Elasticity of demand

When we first introduced calculus we saw that we could examine elasticity of demand for a simple demand function of the form $Q = f(P)$ through the expression:

$$E_d = \frac{dQ}{dP} \frac{P}{Q} \qquad \text{(D2.25)}$$

where dQ/dP was the derivative of the demand function. In the more general case, however, we might wish to examine a more complex demand function:

$$Q_a = f(P_a, P_b, Y) \qquad \text{(D2.26)}$$

where

$Q_a =$ quantity demanded of good A
$P_a =$ price of good A
$P_b =$ price of some other good B
$Y =$ consumer income.

It is clear that we would now wish to examine the effect of each variable on Q_a and that we will be able to derive three elasticity expressions. Assume, for example, that we had a function such that:

$$Q_a = 100 - 10P_a + 15P_b + 0.3Y \qquad \text{(D2.27)}$$

and where $P_a = 5$, $P_b = 3$ and $Y = 200$.

Direct-price elasticity

This will show the proportionate effect of a change in the price of the good, A, itself:

$$E_{Pa} = \frac{\partial Q_a}{\partial P_a} \frac{P_a}{Q_a} \qquad \text{(D2.28)}$$

This assumes that both P_b and Y are constant. If we wish to find the direct-price elasticity for this numerical example we then have:

$$\frac{\partial Q_a}{\partial P_a} = -10 \qquad \text{(D2.29)}$$

$$E_{Pa} = -10 \frac{5}{155} = -0.32$$

At this particular price we have an inelastic demand.

Cross-price elasticity

Similarly, if we wish to find the cross-price elasticity with respect to a proportionate change in P_b we have:

$$E_{Pb} = \frac{\partial Q_a}{\partial P_b} \frac{P_b}{Q_a} \tag{D2.30}$$

assuming that now both P_a and Y are held constant. Here we can see that we are assessing the responsiveness of the demand for good A in the context of a change in the price of good B. With our numerical example we have:

$$E_{Pb} = 15\frac{3}{155} = +0.29$$

Note that since this cross-price elasticity is positive it implies that goods A and B are substitutes (at least at this level of prices). An increase in the price of good B will lead to an increase in the quantity demanded of good A, *ceteris paribus*. If this cross-price elasticity had been negative it would have indicated that the two goods were complementary. The size of the calculation again indicates a relatively inelastic situation.

Income elasticity

Finally, we can examine the income elasticity of demand – the responsiveness of demand to a change in consumer income, *ceteris paribus*. Following the same principles we have:

$$E_Y = \frac{\partial Q_a}{\partial Y} \frac{Y}{Q_a} \tag{D2.31}$$

which for our example gives

$$E_Y = 0.3\frac{200}{155} = 0.39$$

Since the income elasticity is positive we would class good A as a normal good (demand increases with income). Had this elasticity been negative the good would be seen as inferior (an increase in income leads to a [proportionate] decrease in quantity demanded). Note also that, in all three cases, the absolute size of the elasticity can be assessed in the usual way (inelastic, perfectly elastic, highly elastic).

Progress Check D2.4

Calculate and evaluate the elasticities for:

$$P_a = 10, P_b = 2, Y = 100$$

(Solution on p. 472)

D2.4 Production functions

We have previously examined production functions but have had to restrict our analysis to the short term so that we can assume that the supply of one of the two inputs is fixed. This was necessary to allow us to examine how output varied with the other input. Clearly, given the facility of partial derivatives this restrictive assumption is no longer necessary. Assume that we have a function:

$$Q = f(L, K)$$

where

Q = production
L = labour input
K = capital input.

Assume further that we generalize to examine a particular type of production function widely used in economic analysis, the Cobb–Douglas function. This takes the general form:

$$Q = AL^{\alpha}K^{\beta} \tag{D2.32}$$

where A is some positive constant and α and β are positive but less than 1. Let us first examine the two relevant marginal products: that of labour, MP_L, and of capital, MP_K. Clearly MP_L will relate to the extra production that can be obtained from an extra input of labour, but assuming the supply of capital is fixed. Similarly, MP_K will show how production changes with respect to a change in capital, assuming the labour input is fixed. We have, therefore:

$$MP_L = \frac{\partial Q}{\partial L} = \alpha AL^{\alpha-1}K^{\beta} \tag{D2.33}$$

and

$$MP_K = \frac{\partial Q}{\partial K} = \beta AL^{\alpha}K^{\beta-1} \tag{D2.34}$$

However, we also have, from Eq. D2.33:

$$AL^{\alpha-1}K^{\beta} = (AL^{\alpha}K^{\beta})L^{-1} = \frac{Q}{L}$$

giving

$$MP_L = \frac{\alpha Q}{L} \tag{D2.35}$$

Since we can logically restrict our attention to values of Q and L which are positive and since, by assumption, $\alpha > 0$, then this implies that $MP_L > 0$. In other words, for the Cobb–Douglas production function an increase (decrease) in labour input will always lead to an increase (decrease) in production, *ceteris paribus*. We can similarly derive:

$$MP_K = \frac{\beta Q}{K} \tag{D2.36}$$

and we reach the same conclusion regarding extra production arising from extra inputs of capital. However, it will be evident on reflection that we wish to examine these effects in more detail. Given that $MP_L > 0$, can we derive any conclusions about how MP_L changes as we change L (and obviously we wish to derive similar conclusions for MP_K)? Equally, however, we will wish to examine how MP_L changes as we now allow K to change. All of this is readily achieved through the partial derivatives. Let us examine MP_L:

$$MP_L = \frac{\partial Q}{\partial L} = f_L = \alpha AL^{\alpha-1}K^{\beta} \tag{D2.37}$$

We wish to examine the rate of change of this function first with respect to L and then again with respect to K. In the symbolism we have developed we require f_{LL} and f_{LK}. We then have:

$$f_{LL} = (\alpha - 1)\alpha AL^{\alpha-2}K^{\beta}$$

which from Eq. D2.35 gives

$$f_{LL} = (\alpha - 1)\frac{\alpha Q}{L^2} \tag{D2.38}$$

which, since Q and $L > 0$ and since $0 < \alpha < 1$ by definition, must give $f_{LL} < 0$. In other words, while MP_L is always positive it is also declining with increased labour input. Similarly we examine the change in MP_L as we now allow the capital input to change. We require f_{LK}. Since $f_L = \alpha AL^{\alpha-1}K^\beta$ then:

$$f_{LX} = \alpha\beta AL^{\alpha-1}K^{\beta-1}$$

$$= \alpha\beta\frac{Q}{LK} \tag{D2.39}$$

which again, given our assumptions, must be positive; that is, MP_L will increase if we increase the input of capital. Naturally we could readily derive similar conclusions for MP_K.

Progress Check D2.5

Obtain equivalent expressions for capital. Comment on f_{LK} and f_{KL}.

(Solution on p. 472)

Elasticity of production

Clearly, we may also wish to examine such changes not in absolute but in proportionate terms – this is comparable to elasticity of demand. In fact, this can be referred to as the *elasticity of production*. To determine this elasticity with respect to labour input we have:

$$E_L = \frac{\partial Q}{\partial L}\frac{L}{Q} = f_L\frac{L}{Q} = \left(\alpha\frac{Q}{L}\right)\frac{L}{Q} = \alpha \tag{D2.40}$$

That is, the elasticity of production with respect to labour is given by the α coefficient associated with that input in the production function.

Progress Check D2.6

Show that $E_K = \beta$.

Following on from this, we then face the question: if all inputs are changed in the same proportion, what will be the proportionate change in production? For example, what would happen if both L and K changed by 10%? Clearly, such a change will fall into one of three categories: the change in production could be proportionately larger than, smaller than or equal to the simultaneous change in inputs. Let us assume that we change both L and K by some proportion which we denote as λ (pronounced 'lamb-da'). We then have:

$$A(\lambda L)^\alpha(\lambda K)^\beta \tag{D2.41}$$

which can be rewritten as

$$\lambda^{\alpha+\beta}(AL^\alpha K^\beta) = \lambda^{\alpha+\beta}(Q) \tag{D2.42}$$

That is, a change in both inputs of λ gives rise to a change in production of $\lambda^{\alpha+\beta}$. Since, by definition, both α and β are between 0 and 1 then we face three possibilities.

Case 1 $\alpha + \beta < 1$

The proportionate change in output will be less than the proportionate change in both inputs. Clearly we would classify this as decreasing returns to scale.

Case 2 $\alpha + \beta = 1$

The proportionate change in output will be the same as the proportionate change in both inputs. This would represent constant returns to scale.

Case 3 $\alpha + \beta > 1$

The proportionate change in output will be greater than the proportionate change in both inputs. This would represent increasing returns to scale. In general such a function is said to be *homogeneous of degree n* if changing L and K by some proportion leads to a proportionate change in Q of λ^n.

D2.5 Utility functions

Our final area of application in this module brings us to *utility functions*. Economic theory relating to consumer behaviour is based on the assumption that a rational consumer will seek to maximize the satisfaction they obtain from the goods and services that they consume. Naturally, such satisfaction will be limited – or constrained – primarily by their available income, and we shall be exploring the principles of such *constrained maximization* later in this section. Here we can explore some of the principles behind such consumer behaviour using the principles of differential calculus. We can represent consumer behaviour with a utility function of the form:

$$U = u(X_1, X_2, \ldots, X_n)$$

where $X_1, X_2, \ldots, X_n$ represent the quantities of the various goods available consumed by the consumer and U shows the total utility obtained. You may appreciate, from your studies of economics, that this approach has a major practical problem. Unlike, say, a production function, we cannot actually *measure* utility directly. While we can measure what a firm's total production was given certain inputs of labour and capital, we cannot readily measure how much satisfaction a consumer obtained from, say, spending their income on a holiday. However, it is still worth assuming that such measurement could be carried out since we can then explore general principles of consumer behaviour. Let us assume a simplified case where the consumer faces a choice between two goods, X_a and X_b. The utility function will then be:

$$U = u(X_a, X_b)$$

If we apply the principles of partial differentiation to such a function we would derive:

$$\frac{\partial U}{\partial X_a} \quad \text{and} \quad \frac{\partial U}{\partial X_b}$$

as the two relevant partial derivatives. In an economics context it is evident that the two partial derivatives will actually represent *marginal utility*. That is, $\partial U / \partial X_a$ will represent the marginal utility obtained by the consumer derived from marginal consumption of good a when the consumption of good b remains unchanged. Similarly, $\partial U / \partial X_b$ represents the marginal utility obtained by the consumer derived from marginal consumption of good *b* when the consumption of good *a* remains unchanged. Without proof, although the logic is self-evident, we state two important principles relating to such utility functions:

- The law of diminishing marginal utility indicates that as consumption of one good increases then, *ceteris paribus*, the marginal utility of that good will eventually decrease
- A consumer will maximize satisfaction associated with a utility function when each good is consumed up to the point where the marginal utility derived from one good relative to the price of the good is the same for all goods.

Consider the function:

$$U = 5A^{0.3}B^{0.2}$$

where *A* and *B* are the quantities of good A and good B that are consumed. The two marginal utilities will then be:

$$MU_A = 1.5A^{-0.7}B^{0.2}$$

$$MU_B = A^{0.3}B^{-0.8}$$

On inspection of the two partial derivatives we see that, in the case of MU_A, as *A* increases then MU_A decreases; and similarly for MU_B, as *B* increases MU_B decreases. Clearly, there will come a time when extra consumption of a good, *ceteris paribus*, leads to a decrease in the extra satisfaction derived from it. Let us further assume that the consumer has an available income of £100 and that the price of good A, P_A, is £2 and the price of good B, P_B, is £10. Can we derive the combination of the two goods that will maximize consumer satisfaction? From the second principle that was stated we have:

$$\frac{MU_A}{P_A} = \frac{MU_B}{P_B} \qquad\qquad (D2.43)$$

at the point where the consumer maximizes satisfaction from available income. Effectively, this implies that the last pound spent on each good produces the same extra utility as the last pound spent on any other good. Substituting the appropriate values in Eq. D2.43 gives:

$$\frac{1.5A^{-0.7}B^{0.2}}{2} = \frac{A^{0.3}B^{-0.8}}{10}$$

Rearranging this gives:

$$15A^{-0.7}B^{0.2} = 2A^{0.3}B^{-0.8}$$

Dividing through by $B^{0.2}$ then gives:

$$15A^{-0.7} = 2A^{0.3}B^{-1}$$

while dividing through by $A^{0.3}$ gives

$$15A^{-1} = 2B^{-1}$$

which gives

$$15B = 2A$$

or

$$A = 7.5B$$

From the prices of the two goods and the consumer's available income we derive a budget constraint such that:

$$Y = P_A A + P_B B \qquad \text{(D2.44)}$$

where Y is available consumer income. Equation D2.44 then becomes:

$$100 = 2A + 10B$$

and substituting $A = 7.5B$ gives

$$100 = 15B + 10B$$

which solves as $B = 4$. Substituting back into the budget constraint we solve for A as 30. Thus, the combination of the two goods that will maximize consumer utility is $A = 30$ and $B = 4$. Note that we assume the consumer will spend all available income on the two available goods. If we wished to introduce the concept of saving part of income, we could actually denote savings as an additional 'good' generating additional satisfaction.

In the case of a utility function involving only two goods we can also represent a utility function through the *indifference map*. If we assume some fixed value for the utility function, U_1, then all the combinations of the two goods which generate this utility can be determined and the relationship between the two goods revealed. This is illustrated in Fig. D2.1. For the indifference curve U_1 this links all possible combinations of A and B that generate the same total utility, U_1. Thus, at point X the combination of A_1 and B_1 generates the same utility as the combination of A_2 and B_2 at point Y. Literally, given the assumption that the consumer wishes to maximize total utility, the consumer will be indifferent as to where on this particular line he or she will be.

A number of points emerge from the indifference map. The first is that we can derive a whole series of such curves, each representing a different total utility, U_n. While the consumer may be indifferent as to where on any particular indifference curve he or she actually is, the consumer will have a preference for moving between curves. U_2 would be preferable to U_1 since it represents a higher level of total utility (which can be achieved only through consumption of additional units of A and/or B). Similarly, U_3 would be preferred to U_2 and so on. What prevents the consumer moving from one curve to another higher curve will be his or her budget line. Effectively, the consumer's fixed income or the current prices of the two goods will act as a restraint.

D

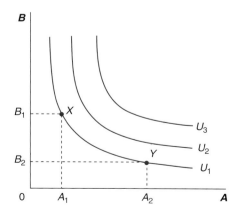

Figure D2.1 Indifference map

A second implication emerges from the shape of the curves, which are downward sloping. This implies that if consumption of B decreases then to maintain the same total utility the consumption of A must increase to compensate. However, the curve is clearly non-linear, further implying that this rate of substitution of one good for another in order to maintain total utility is not constant, as we would expect given the concept of diminishing marginal utility. At point X, for example, a relatively small decrease in A must be compensated for by a relatively large increase in B. We can explain this by the fact that at point X consumption of A is relatively low, so the opportunity cost of reducing consumption of A will be relatively high. In comparison, consumption of B at this point is relatively high, so the marginal utility associated with additional consumption will be relatively low. In comparison, at point Y a small decrease in A would require only a relatively small increase in B to maintain total utility. In fact, this relationship between A and B can be referred to as the *marginal rate of substitution*, MRS. The MRS will be the slope of the indifference curve, and where we have good B on the vertical axis the slope will be given by dB/dA. Hence:

$$MRS = \frac{dB}{dA}$$

Since the slope is negative it is common to represent MRS as:

$$MRS = \frac{-dB}{dA}$$

to give a substitution rate which is positive – for example, 3 units of A for 1 unit of B. However, in Module D1 we examined the use of implicit functions where the function was set to equal some constant value. Clearly, this is the case here with the indifference curves, and from Eq. D1.37 we had:

$$\frac{dY}{dX} = \frac{-f_X}{f_Y}$$

In our case this would be:

$$MRS = \frac{dB}{dA} = \frac{f_A}{f_B}$$

But $f_A = \partial U / \partial_A$ and $f_B = \partial U / \partial_B$, hence we have:

$$MRS = \frac{MU_A}{MU_B}$$

That is, the marginal rate of substitution is the ratio of the marginal utility of good A to the marginal utility of good B. In the context of our numerical example we have:

$$MU_A = 1.5A^{-0.7}B^{0.2}$$

$$MU_B = A^{0.3}B^{-0.8}$$

giving

$$MRS = \frac{1.5A^{-0.7}B^{0.2}}{A^{0.3}B^{-0.8}}$$

which simplifies to

$$MRS = 1.5\frac{B}{A}$$

If, for example, $B = 10$ and $A = 20$ then MRS = 0.75, implying that a one-unit decrease in A must be compensated for by a 0.75 unit increase in B in order to maintain total utility at its current value.

D2.6 Summary

In this module we have started to apply the principles of partial differentiation to a number of common economic models. We have seen that we are able to deduce important economic conclusions through the use of such mathematics and that we are also able to confirm a number of important economic principles through the application of such mathematics.

Learning Check

Having read this module you should have learned that:

- Partial derivatives allow us to determine the national income multipliers
- Direct-price elasticity shows the proportionate effect on quantity demanded of a change in the price of the good
- Cross-price elasticity shows the proportionate effect on quantity demanded of good A of a change in the price of the good B
- Income elasticity shows the proportionate effect on quantity demanded of a change in consumer income
- For a Cobb–Douglas production function, an increase/decrease in labour input will lead to an increase/decrease in total production. The same applies to capital input
- A utility function shows the utility/satisfaction obtained from consumption of goods and services
- The law of diminishing marginal utility indicates that as consumption of one good increases then, *ceteris paribus*, the marginal utility of that good will eventually decrease
- A consumer will maximize satisfaction associated with a utility function when each good is consumed up to the point where the marginal utility derived from one good relative to the price of the good is the same for all goods.

Worked Example

Assume we have a national income model with both a government sector and foreign trade such that:

$$Y = C + I + G + X - M$$
$$C = 100 + 0.7Y_d$$
$$M = 0.1Y_d$$
$$Y_d = (1 - t)Y$$

with $t = 0.25$; $G = 500$; $I = 250$; $X = 300$.

The Finance Minister has been told that the government in this situation currently has a budget surplus, and is subject to increasing public criticism for having such a surplus. Naively, the Minister suggests that the government should increase its own spending, G, by the exact amount of the surplus so as to avoid either a

Worked Example *(Continued)*

budget deficit or a budget surplus. We have been asked to provide confirmation that such a policy of spending the exact amount of the current surplus will not lead to a balanced government budget.

Solution

First, we should confirm the current equilibrium position. For this type of model we derived equilibrium income to be:

$$Y_e = \frac{a + I + G + X}{1 - (1 - t)(b - m)}$$

Substituting the relevant numerical values, we derive:

$$Y_e = \frac{1150}{0.55} = 2090.91$$

and

$$T = tY = 522.73$$

Given that G is 500, this implies a government budget surplus of 22.73.

We know from our examination of national income models and the multiplier effect that an increase in G of 22.73 will lead to an increase in Y_e (and we can calculate this through the appropriate multiplier). However, such an increase in Y_e will by default also lead to a further increase in T (since $T = tY_e$). Hence, although the increase in G will cause a temporary budget balance, once the economy reaches its new equilibrium income position then $T > G$ once again. Using the relevant partial derivative we would identify the G multiplier as:

$$\frac{\partial Y}{\partial G} = \frac{1}{1 - (1 - t)(b - m)} = \frac{1}{0.55} = 1.8182$$

So an increase in G of 22.73 would cause equilibrium income to rise by 41.33 and T to rise by 10.33 (0.25×41.33). Hence the government budget would soon move back to a surplus position. As an additional exercise you may wish to consider how you would put the economy into a balanced budget position.

Exercises

D2.1 Assume a production function of the form:

$$Q = 10L^{0.75}K^{0.25}$$

(i) Find the partial derivatives of labour and capital.

(ii) Find all the second-order partial derivatives.

(iii) Find the total differential.

(iv) For each of your answers, explain the meaning and provide an economic interpretation.

(v) Calculate from first principles the elasticity of production with respect to labour and then to capital.

Exercises *(Continued)*

D2.2   A production function is given as:

$$Q = f(L, K)$$

but where

$$L = g(t)$$
$$K = h(t)$$

where t represents time. Find the total derivative with respect to time and interpret.

D2.3   A consumer's utility function is given as:

$$U = f(A, B) = 10A + 30B - A^2 - B^2 + 5AB$$

where

   U represents total utility
   A represents units of product A consumed
   B represents units of product B consumed.

 (i)   Comment on the economic logic of this function.
 (ii)   Find the first-order partial derivatives.
 (iii)   Find the second-order partial derivatives.
 (iv)   Find the total differential.
 (v)   Explain and comment upon each of your answers in an economic context.

D2.4   Assume a demand function for product X where:

$$Q_x = 500 - 20P_x P_Y + 5P_Y Y$$

where

   P_x = price of product X
   P_Y = price of product Y
   Y = income.

 (i)   Find a general expression for the direct-price elasticity, the cross-price elasticity and the income elasticity.
 (ii)   If $Y = 500$, $P_x = 10$ and $P_Y = 20$, calculate each of these elasticities.
 (iii)   Interpret the results to (ii).

D2.5   Return to the numerical model used in Section D2.5. Assume the consumer's income rises to 150. Derive the new utility-maximizing combination of the two goods.

D2.6   Assume a national income model where:

$$Y = C + I + G + X - M$$
$$C = a + bY$$
$$M = m + cY$$

I, G, X are exogenous and the model parameters take the usual restricted values. Derive the relevant national income multipliers.

Module D3
Unconstrained optimization

It may be evident that in our examination of differential calculus that we have applied to multivariable functions to date, we have not yet considered the principles of optimization. When examining calculus principles for the simpler functions we saw that we could determine a maximum/minimum position for the function. Clearly, we require the same for the multivariable functions that we are now considering. In this module we shall introduce the relevant principles and, again, consider their use in economics.

Learning Objectives

By the end of this module you should be able to:

- Formulate optimization problems
- Find the solution to an unconstrained optimization problem
- Confirm whether the solution represents a maximum or minimum point
- Apply the principles of unconstrained optimization to a number of common economic models.

D3.1 General principles of unconstrained optimization

You will recollect that for a simple function of the form

$$Y = f(X)$$

we can find the stationary point(s) on such a function (if one exists) by taking the first derivative and setting it to zero:

$$f'(X) = 0$$

We referred to this as the *first-order condition* and then used the second derivative to determine whether this stationary point represents a (local) maximum or a minimum value:

If $f''(X) > 0$ we have a minimum

If $f''(X) < 0$ we have a maximum

which we referred to as a *second-order condition*. However, if we now have a function of the form:

$$Y = f(X_1, X_2) \qquad\qquad\qquad\qquad (D3.1)$$

we clearly seek the combination of X_1 and X_2 that will generate a maximum/minimum value for Y. Fortunately we can use the principles of partial derivatives in much the same way. Let us illustrate the principles by reference to the profit function we introduced in Module D1:

$$Y = -5 + 30X_1 - 3X_1^2 + 25X_2 - 5X_2^2 + X_1X_2 \qquad\qquad (D3.2)$$

which represents a firm's profit (Y) obtained from the manufacture of two products, X_1 and X_2. In this context the firm seeks the combination of the two production levels that will maximize profit. Figure D3.1 shows the generalized situation that we face for the function.

We see that this function takes the shape of a dome in three-dimensional space. Point A, at the top of the dome, is clearly the point we seek. At this point Y will be at its maximum and, somehow, we need to be able to determine the values of X_1 and X_2 that will generate this maximum point. But not all functions will give this type of three-dimensional picture. We may face the reverse situation – an inverted dome shape as in Fig. D3.2, where we would now be seeking a minimum Y value. There are two fundamental questions we need to resolve for multivariable functions:

1 How can we determine the relevant X_1 and X_2 values that correspond to such a point?

2 How can we establish whether such a point represents a maximum or a minimum position?

It will be helpful to consider the approach we adopted when introducing partial derivatives in the previous module. Assume, for example, that we fixed the value of X_2, say at 4. The relationship between Y and the other variable, X_1, could then be graphed as shown in Fig. D3.3. It is evident that, under such an assumption, we could find the first derivative with respect to X_1 in order to find the stationary point, and then use the second derivative to determine that we had obtained a maximum Y value. However, it is also evident that this optimum will relate only when $X_2 = 4$ and that, in fact, we face a whole series of such points for each possible value of X_2. Equally, of course, we would adopt the same approach with X_2. If we fixed X_1 at, say, 5, then we would

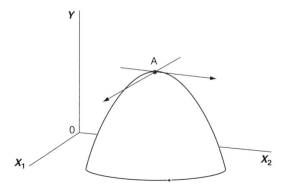

Figure D3.1 Maximum

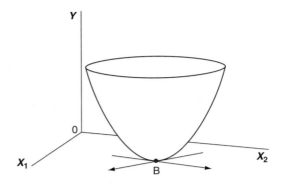

Figure D3.2 Minimum

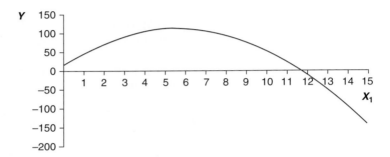

Figure D3.3 $Y = f(X_1, X_2)$ with $X_2 = 4$

face the situation shown in Fig. D3.4 and could follow the same approach as before. By combining these approaches, however, we can recognize intuitively how we can proceed. To hold X_2 constant to find the stationary point with respect to X_1 is the equivalent of finding the partial derivative with respect to X_1. With respect to X_1 we require:

$$fX_1 = 0$$

with $f_{X1X1} > 0$ for a minimum
   $f_{X1X1} < 0$ for a maximum

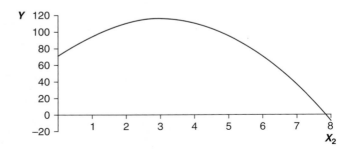

Figure D3.4 $Y = f(X_1, X_2)$ with $X_1 = 5$

and with respect to X_2

$$f_{X2} = 0$$

with $f_{X2X2} > 0$ for a minimum
$f_{X2X2} < 0$ for a maximum.

Let us return to our numerical example to illustrate this. Obtaining the relevant partial derivatives, we have:

$$f_{X1} = 30 - 6X_1 + X_2 \qquad\qquad (D3.3)$$
$$f_{X2} = 25 - 10X_2 + X_1 \qquad\qquad (D3.4)$$

Setting the two first partial derivatives to zero and solving simultaneously gives $X_1 = 5.5085$ and $X_2 = 3.05085$. It should be apparent why we require both partial derivatives to be zero at the same time. We cannot be at, say, a maximum if we can increase the value of Y by changing either of the variables, the other being held constant. However, how can we determine whether this point represents a maximum or a minimum position? Intuitively we might consider confirming that both second-order derivatives are negative, that is:

$$f_{X1X1} < 0 \quad \text{and} \quad f_{X2X2} < 0$$

However, this is in fact not sufficient by itself. We state without proof that for a maximum or minimum we also require:

$$f_{X1X1} f_{X2X2} > (f_{X1X2})^2 \qquad\qquad (D3.5)$$

For our example we have:

$$f_{X1X1} = -6$$
$$f_{X2X2} = -10$$

and

$$f_{X1X2} = 1$$

Note that from Young's theorem $f_{X1X2} = f_{X2X1}$, so that the order of differentiation is irrelevant. This gives:

$$f_{X1X1} f_{X2X2} > (f_{X1X2})^2$$
$$(-6)(-10) > 1$$

confirming that the point we have found does represent a maximum. Therefore profit is maximized when X_1 takes a value 5.5085 and X_2 a value of 3.050 85.

Progress Check D3.1

Calculate the value of Y for the given values of X_1 and X_2. Assume X_2 is fixed at 3.05085. Calculate the new profit if $X_1 = 5.6$ and again if it is 5.5. Comment on the results. Now assume X_1 is fixed at 5.5085. Repeat the analysis for $X_2 = 3.0$ and 3.1.

(Solution on p. 473)

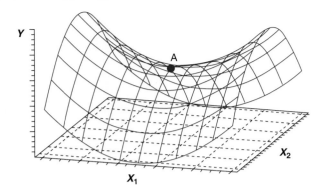

Figure D3.5 Saddle point

To summarize, therefore, we have the following conditions:

First-order conditions for a maximum or minimum:

$$f_{X1} = 0$$
$$f_{X2} = 0$$

Second-order conditions for a maximum:

$$f_{X1X1} < 0$$
$$f_{X2X2} < 0$$
$$f_{X1X1} f_{X2X2} > (f_{X1X2})^2$$

Second-order conditions for a minimum:

$$f_{X1X1} > 0$$
$$f_{X2X2} > 0$$
$$f_{X1X1} f_{X2X2} > (f_{X1X2})^2$$

Note that the condition that $f_{X1X1} f_{X2X2} > (f_{X1X2})^2$ is the same for both maximum and minimum points. This raises the interesting point of what happens if this last condition is not met. Suppose that we actually have:

$$f_{X1X1} f_{X2X2} < (f_{X1X2})^2$$

On reflection it can be seen that this could occur if f_{X1X1} and f_{X2X2} were of opposite signs (i.e. one positive and one negative). This would indicate that we had a position where the function takes a maximum with respect to one variable but a minimum with respect to the other. To help clarify this point, consider Fig. D3.5, which shows such a situation known as a *saddle point*. We see that when viewed against X_2, Y is at a maximum but when viewed against X_1, Y takes a minimum. At point A we see that if we move along the X_1 axis the value of Y will actually increase, while if we move along the X_2 axis the value of Y decreases.

Progress Check D3.2

Determine the optimum position of the following equations and determine whether this is a maximum or a minimum:

Progress Check D3.2 *(Continued)*

(i) $Z = 10 - 5X + 3X^2 - 8Y + 2Y^2 - XY$

(ii) $Z = 50 + 50X - 5X^2 + 30Y - 3Y^2 - 5XY$

(iii) $Z = 2Y^2 - 3X^2 + 100$

(Solution on p. 473)

D3.2 Profit maximization

Using these principles, we now examine some of the models we have developed thus far. Let us return to a firm that makes two products and its desire to maximize profit. Assume that we have:

$$TR = P_1 X_1 + P_2 X_2 \tag{D3.6}$$

$$TC = c(X_1, X_2) \tag{D3.7}$$

That is, while we do not specify the form of the cost function faced by the firm, it is evident from the TR function that the firm operates under conditions of perfect competition (since the prices are fixed). We then have:

$$\pi = TR - TC = (P_1 X_1 + P_2 X_2) - c(X_1, X_2) \tag{D3.8}$$

We want to determine the output levels that will maximize this function. Let us first consider the partial derivatives of the TC function. We can obtain

$$\frac{\partial(TC)}{\partial X_1} \quad \text{and} \quad \frac{\partial(TC)}{\partial X_2}$$

and it becomes apparent that these two derivatives actually refer to the two marginal costs: that is, $\partial(TC)/\partial X_1$ will be the marginal cost of product 1 assuming that the output of product 2 remains constant, while $\partial(TC)/\partial X_1$ will be the marginal cost of product 2 on the assumption that the output of product 1 is now fixed. Equally, by applying the same principles to the TR function, we have:

$$\frac{\partial(TR)}{\partial X_1} = P_1 \quad \text{and} \quad \frac{\partial(TR)}{\partial X_2} = P_2$$

which represent the marginal revenues of products 1 and 2 respectively. Note that we also have additional confirmation that the firm operates under perfect competition since, for both products, $P = MR$. We now have the necessary first-order conditions for the profit function as:

$$\frac{\partial \pi}{\partial X_1} = \frac{\partial(TR)}{\partial X_1} - \frac{\partial(TC)}{\partial X_1} = MR_1 - MC_1 = 0 \tag{D3.9}$$

$$\frac{\partial \pi}{\partial X_2} = \frac{\partial(TR)}{\partial X_2} - \frac{\partial(TC)}{\partial X_2} = MR_2 - MC_2 = 0 \tag{D3.10}$$

That is, we require the marginal revenue of each product to be equal to its marginal cost.

Progress Check D3.3

Assume the following *TC* function:

$$TC = 20 + 3X^2 + 2Y^2 - 0.5XY$$

where X and Y represent the output of two products. If the firm faces perfect competition with market prices of 10 for X and 5 for Y, determine the profit-maximizing combination of output.

(Solution on p. 473)

D3.3 Price discrimination

Through the use of partial derivatives we can also analyse the situation with regard to *price discrimination*. Consider a monopoly firm that makes a single product. The product can be sold in the domestic market or can be exported. Clearly, the firm will wish to determine the balance between the two markets in terms of the prices to be charged and the total profit to be maximized. Denoting output sold domestically as Q_1 and output sold abroad as Q_2, we then have:

$$Q = Q_1 + Q_2 \tag{D3.11}$$

$$TR = \mathrm{d}(Q_1) + x(Q_2) \tag{D3.12}$$

where $\mathrm{d}(Q_1)$ represents the revenue function for the domestic market and $x(Q_2)$ that for the export market. We also have:

$$TC = c(Q) \tag{D3.13}$$

The latter follows since we assume a single production plant. It also follows that the marginal cost of the product for each market must be the same. The profit function will then be:

$$\pi = TR - TC = \mathrm{d}(Q_1) + x(Q_2) - c(Q) \tag{D3.14}$$

We will then have:

$$MR_1 = \frac{\partial(TR)}{\partial Q_1} = \mathrm{d}'(Q_1) \tag{D3.15}$$

$$MR_2 = \frac{\partial(TR)}{\partial Q_2} = x'(Q_2) \tag{D3.16}$$

while for marginal cost we have (through the chain rule)

$$MC_1 = \frac{\partial C}{\partial Q_1} = c'(Q)\frac{\partial Q}{\partial Q_1} = c'(Q) \quad \text{(since } \partial Q/\partial Q_1 = 1 \text{ from Eq. D3.11)}$$

$$MC_2 = \frac{\partial C}{\partial Q_2} = c'(Q)\frac{\partial Q}{\partial Q_2} = c'(Q) \quad \text{(since } \partial Q/\partial Q_2 = 1\text{)}$$

which indicates that $MC_1 = MC_2$. The first-order conditions will then be that:

$$\frac{\partial(\pi)}{\partial Q_1} = \frac{\partial(\pi)}{\partial Q_2} = 0$$

$$MR_1 - MC_1 = 0$$

$$MR_2 - MC_2 = 0$$

or

$$MR_1 = MR_2 = MC$$

That is, the output levels in each market must be such that the marginal revenue in each market is the same as the marginal cost of total output.

We can now examine the implications for pricing policy. We know that $TR = PQ$ and so we have:

$$TR_1 = P_1 Q_1 \quad \text{and} \quad TR_2 = P_2 Q_2$$

Therefore:

$$MR_1 = \frac{\partial(TR_1)}{\partial Q_1} = P_1 \frac{dQ_1}{dQ_1} + Q_1 \frac{dP_1}{dQ_1}$$

$$= P_1 \left(1 + \frac{dP_1}{dQ_1} \frac{Q_1}{P_1} \right) \tag{D3.17}$$

and by the same logic we have

$$MR_2 = P_2 \left(1 + \frac{dP_2}{dQ_2} \frac{Q_2}{P_2} \right) \tag{D3.18}$$

However, bringing in elasticity we have:

$$E_{D1} = \frac{dQ_1}{dP_1} \frac{P_1}{Q_1} \tag{D3.19}$$

Hence:

$$1/E_{D1} = \frac{dP_1}{dQ_1} \frac{Q_1}{P_1}$$

and

$$MR_1 = P_1 \left(1 + \frac{1}{E_{D1}} \right) \tag{D3.20}$$

and

$$MR_2 = P_2 \left(1 + \frac{1}{E_{D2}} \right) \tag{D3.21}$$

However, we know that E_D will take a negative value. If, for example, E_{D1} is inelastic (taking values $< |1|$), MR_1 must take a negative value. Similarly, if $|E_{D1}| = 1$ then $MR_1 = 0$, while if $|E_{D1}| > 1$ then $MR_1 > 0$. However, we also know that MC must be positive; hence $MR_1 > 0$ also. It therefore follows that the optimum level of sales in each market must be such that the corresponding elasticity of demand is greater than 1. Given that we required $MR_1 = MR_2$, we now have:

$$P_1 \left(1 + \frac{1}{E_{D1}} \right) = P_2 \left(1 + \frac{1}{E_{D2}} \right) \tag{D3.22}$$

Clearly, $P_1 = P_2$ only when the elasticity of demand in each market is the same. If these elasticities differ then the firm must charge different prices in the two markets in order to maximize total profit. We can also infer that, *ceteris paribus*, the lower the elasticity in one market then the higher the price to be charged in that market, relative to the other available market. Let us examine the following example:

$$TC = f(Q) - = 500 + 10Q$$

$$Q = X + Y$$

$$P_X = 110 - 10X$$

$$P_Y = 80 - 5Y$$

We then have a profit function:

$$\pi = f(x, y) = 100X - 10X^2 + 70Y - 5Y^2 - 500$$

where

$$f_X = 100 - 20X$$

and

$$f_Y = 70 - 10Y$$

Setting both these to zero and solving gives $X = 5$ and $Y = 7$ as the profit-maximizing combination of output for the two products.

Progress Check D3.5

Calculate the elasticity of demand for each product at these levels of output. Confirm that the lower elasticity product has the higher price. Explain why this should be the case.

(Solution on p. 474)

D3.4 Profit maximization revisited

It will also be worthwhile examining the profit-maximizing situation from a slightly different perspective. We have seen on a number of occasions that costs are related to the firm's production function. Consider the production function:

$$Q = q(L, K)$$

relating output to inputs of labour and capital. Assume that we represent the price charged per unit sold as p, and w and i represent the prices of the labour and capital inputs respectively. We then have:

$$TR = pQ \tag{D3.23}$$

$$TC = wL + iK \tag{D3.24}$$

and

$$\pi = TR - TC = pQ - (wL + iK) \tag{D3.25}$$

which, on substituting the production function, gives

$$\pi = pq(L, K) - (wL + iK) \tag{D3.26}$$

which expresses profit purely in terms of the inputs of labour and capital. Let us assume further that w and i are fixed (perhaps because we are considering the short term or a firm under perfect competition). We can now examine the problem as one to determine the combination of L and K that will maximize the firm's profit. We then have:

$$\frac{\partial \pi}{\partial L} = p\frac{\partial Q}{\partial L} - w \qquad\qquad\qquad\qquad\text{(D3.27)}$$

$$\frac{\partial \pi}{\partial K} = p\frac{\partial Q}{\partial K} - i \qquad\qquad\qquad\qquad\text{(D3.28)}$$

Since both are required to be zero we have:

$$\frac{\partial Q}{\partial L} = \frac{w}{p} \quad \text{and} \quad \frac{\partial Q}{\partial K} = \frac{i}{p} \qquad\qquad\qquad\text{(D3.29)}$$

That is, the marginal product of labour must equal the factor input price divided by the product's selling price (what we can refer to as the real input price). We can view this ratio as the selling price expressed in terms of the production that it would buy, which must be equal to the marginal product. A similar interpretation can be given to capital.

A numerical example might be helpful at this stage. If we assume that $p = £2$ and $w = £10$, under the first-order conditions, $MP_L = 5$; that is, the extra unit of labour (for which we are paying £10) must produce 5 units of extra output to be worthwhile (given that we sell this output at £2 per unit). We now consider the second-order conditions for a maximum:

$$\frac{\partial^2 \pi}{\partial L^2} = p\frac{\partial^2 Q}{\partial L^2} < 0 \text{ (i.e. } \partial^2 Q/\partial L^2 < 0) \qquad\qquad\text{(D3.30)}$$

$$\frac{\partial^2 \pi}{\partial K^2} = p\frac{\partial^2 Q}{\partial K^2} < 0 \text{ (i.e. } \partial^2 Q/\partial K^2 < 0) \qquad\qquad\text{(D3.31)}$$

$$\frac{\partial^2 \pi}{\partial L^2}\frac{\partial^2 \pi}{\partial K^2} > \frac{(\partial^2 \pi)^2}{\partial K \partial L} \qquad\qquad\qquad\text{(D3.32)}$$

Let us consider these restrictions. Since the first partial derivative with respect to labour represents the marginal product, the second derivative shows the change in marginal product. We are being told that, at profit-maximization levels of output, an extra unit of labour input will lead to a change in output smaller than that of the previous level of labour input (with the same logic applying to capital). Since the marginal product of labour must, through the first-order condition, be equal to the real wage rate, then the marginal product of this extra labour unit will be less than the real wage rate. Hence extra labour at this point will reduce profit. Clearly the second-order conditions imply that diminishing marginal products for both inputs are necessary for profit maximization. Let us consider the following numerical example. We have a production function:

$$Q = f(L, K) = 5L^{0.25}K^{0.5}$$

and a total cost function

$$TC = 10L + 5K$$

That is, labour costs are £10 and capital costs are £5 per unit. If the product sells for £4 we then have a profit function:

$$\pi = 20L^{0.25}K^{0.5} - 10L - 5K$$

Taking the first-order derivatives, we require:

$$\pi_L = 5L^{-0.75}K^{0.5} - 10 = 0 \qquad\qquad\qquad\text{(D3.33)}$$

$$\pi_K = 10L^{0.25}K^{-0.5} - 5 = 0 \qquad\qquad\qquad\text{(D3.34)}$$

We then require values for K and L that satisfy Eqs D3.33 and D3.34. If we rewrite these, we have:

$$\frac{5K^{0.5}}{L^{0.75}} = 10$$

and

$$\frac{10L^{0.25}}{K^{0.5}} = 5$$

If we divide the first of these by the second and rearrange, we have:

$$\frac{5K^{0.5}K^{0.25}}{10L^{0.75}L^{0.25}} = \frac{10}{5}$$

giving

$$\frac{5K}{10L} = 2$$
$$5K = 20L$$
$$K = 4L$$

We can now substitute $K = 4L$ into either Eq. D3.33 or Eq. D3.34 and solve numerically for L and then for K. This turns out to be straightforward (if somewhat tedious) and gives $L = 1$ and $K = 4$ as the optimal combination of inputs. You may wish to check for yourself that the relevant first- and second-order conditions set out earlier are satisfied with this solution.

D3.5 Summary

We have examined how we can determine the optimal solution to some problem where there are no additional restrictions placed on the solution – an unconstrained optimization problem. We have seen that the principles involved are similar to those where we looked at two variable functions. Although we have examined only a limited number of economic applications, it will be evident that these principles are readily extended to a considerable variety of other multivariable economic models.

Learning Check

Having read this module you should have learned that:

- The first-order conditions for a maximum or minimum are:

$$f_{X1} = 0$$
$$f_{X2} = 0$$

- The second-order conditions for a maximum are:

$$f_{X1X1} < 0 \text{ and } f_{X2X2} < 0$$
$$f_{X1X1} f_{X2X2} > (f_{X1X2})^2$$

- The second-order conditions for a minimum are:

$$f_{X1X1} > 0 \text{ and } f_{X2X2} > 0$$
$$f_{X1X1} f_{X2X2} > (f_{X1X2})^2$$

Learning Check   *(Continued)*

- A saddle point is a stationary point but not a local extreme point
- The first-order condition for profit maximization is that $MR = MC$ for each product
- In production theory the marginal product of a factor of production is equal to the factor price divided by the product selling price.

Worked Example

An enterprising economics student was impressed by the concept of consumer utility detailed in the previous module. The student has derived a personal utility function such that:

$$U = 100W + 150L + 0.78WL - 2.5W^2 - 0.708L^2$$

where W refers to the hours per week the student spends in part-time paid work in order to raise income for course fees and L refers to the number of hours per week spent in 'leisure', where L is effectively non-paid work comprising time spent on all other activities during the week, including studying. The student is keen to determine the appropriate number of hours spent in paid work each week in order to maximize utility (U). Unfortunately, the student has been too busy earning money to understand the principles of optimization and has asked for help.

Solution

We have:

$$U = 100W + 150L + 0.78WL - 2.5W^2 - 0.708L^2$$
$$f_W = 100 + 0.78L - 5W$$
$$f_L = 150 + 0.78W - 1.416L$$

and solving gives $W = 40$ and $L = 128$ as the optimal combination of time spent in order to maximize utility (fortunately with the number of hours worked being considerably less than those classed as 'leisure').

We can confirm that this combination generates maximum utility since:

$$f_{WW} = -5$$
$$f_{LL} = -1.416$$

and

$$f_{WL} = 0.78$$

and hence

$$f_{WW} < 0$$
$$f_{LL} < 0$$
$$f_{WW} f_{LL} > (f_{WL})^2$$

confirming a maximum utility value.

Exercises

D3.1   Return to the function where we had:

$$Y = -100 + 80A - 0.1A^2 + 100B - 0.2B^2$$

where

Y = profit
A = output of product A
B = output of product B.

Determine the profit-maximizing combination of output.

D3.2   Assume a utility function:

$$U = f(A, B) = 50A + 200B - 0.05A^2 - 0.25B^2$$

where

U represents total utility
A represents units of product A consumed
B represents units of product B consumed.

Determine the combination of the two products that will maximize total utility. Examine the change in utility that will occur if we keep one of these optimal values constant but increase the other.

D3.3   Assume a production function:

$$Q = 10L^{0.5}K^{0.25}$$

With a selling price for the product of 10, and factor prices of 5 for L and 4 for K, determine the firm's profit-maximizing levels of inputs. Determine the level of output that this will produce. Determine the corresponding values for TC, TR and profit.

D3.4   Return to the problem in Progress Check D3.3. Assume the market prices now change to 12 and 7. Calculate the new solution.

D3.5   Return to the problem that formed the basis for Progress Check D3.5. Assume the cost function now changes to:

$$TC = f(Q) = 500 + 15Q$$

Calculate the new solution to the problem. Calculate the new elasticities. Explain why the solution has changed in the way that it has.

D3.6   Assume a situation where:

$$P_X = 20 - 2X$$
$$P_Y = 25 - 4Y$$
$$TC = 1000 + 10X + 5Y$$

Calculate the profit-maximizing combination of outputs for X and Y. Determine the relevant prices and elasticities at this combination.

Appendix D3 The Hessian matrix

In Section D3.1 we saw that the conditions for identifying an unconstrained optimum were:

First-order conditions for a maximum or minimum:

$$f_{X1} = 0$$
$$f_{X2} = 0$$

Second-order conditions for a maximum:

$$f_{X1X1} < 0$$
$$f_{X2X2} < 0$$
$$f_{X1X1} f_{X2X2} > (f_{X1X2})^2$$

Second-order conditions for a minimum:

$$f_{X1X1} > 0$$
$$f_{X2X2} > 0$$
$$f_{X1X1} f_{X2X2} > (f_{X1X2})^2$$

For the second-order conditions, we can adopt an approach using what is known as the *Hessian* matrix (named after the nineteenth-century German mathematician Ludwig Hesse). A Hessian is a matrix composed of all the second-order partial derivatives. The direct partial derivatives make up the main diagonal, and the cross-partial derivatives make up the rest. Assume a function:

$$Y = f(X_1, X_2)$$

Then the Hessian, **H**, will be:
$$\begin{bmatrix} f_{X1X1} & f_{X1X2} \\ f_{X2X1} & f_{X2X2} \end{bmatrix}$$

The determinant of **H** will then be given by:

$$|\mathbf{H}| = f_{X1X1}f_{X2X2} - f_{X1X2}f_{X2X1}$$

However, since:

$$f_{X1X2} = f_{X2X1}$$

this becomes

$$|\mathbf{H}| = f_{X1X1}f_{X2X2} - (f_{X1X2})^2$$

that is, the same as the second-order condition earlier. If f_{X1X1} is negative and $|\mathbf{H}|$ is positive then we have a maximum. If f_{X1X1} is positive and â $|\mathbf{H}|$ is positive we have a minimum. To illustrate the calculations, let us return to the profit function:

$$Y = -5 + 30X_1 - 3X_1^2 + 25X_2 - 5X_2^2 + X_1X_2$$
$$f_{X1X1} = -6$$
$$f_{X2X2} = -10$$

and

$$f_{X1X2} = 1$$

Then, **H** is:

$$\begin{pmatrix} -6 & 1 \\ 1 & -10 \end{pmatrix}$$

and with $f_{X_1X_1}$ negative and $|\mathbf{H}| = 59$, positive, indicating the optimum point is a maximum. The Hessian is readily applied to large sets of equations – one of the things we've seen previously that makes matrix algebra attractive to economic analysts and modellers. If we have n explanatory variables in a model then the Hessian would be made up of the following partial derivatives:

$$\mathbf{H} = \begin{pmatrix} f_{11} & f_{12} & \cdots & f_{1n} \\ f_{21} & f_{22} & \cdots & f_{2n} \\ \cdots & & & \\ f_{n1} & f_{n2} & \cdots & f_{nn} \end{pmatrix}$$

Module D4
Constrained optimization

So far our investigations into optimization have been in terms of simple unconstrained problems: we have a function and we wish to find its maximum/minimum value. In economic analysis, however, we do not always face such a straightforward problem. We may well have a function that we wish to optimize but, at the same time, we face certain constraints that limit the options available. A firm may wish to maximize profit, for example, but faces a constraint in terms of maximum production levels that can be attained with current levels of capital. A consumer may wish to maximize utility but faces a constraint imposed by a fixed budget or income. This type of problem lies at the heart of much economic analysis. It implies that there are restrictions imposed on the economic decision we can make and that we must choose between the alternatives that are available. Clearly, if we can approach such decision-making rationally through the use of relevant mathematics it will make our task of deciding what to do that much easier. It is to this type of *constrained optimization* problem that we now turn.

Learning Objectives

By the end of this module you should be able to:

- Formulate constrained optimization problems
- Use Lagrange multipliers to find the solution to a constrained optimization problem
- Interpret the meaning of a Lagrange multiplier in an economic context
- Apply Lagrange multipliers to a number of common economic models.

D4.1 The principles of constrained optimization

Consider the problem:

$$\pi = -100 + 80A - 0.1A^2 + 100B - 0.2B^2 \tag{D4.1}$$

which relates to the profit function (£s) for a firm and where A and B represent the levels of output of two products made by the firm. This is the type of problem we have examined thus far and, applying the principles we have developed, we can readily determine the profit-maximizing level of output. Taking the relevant partial derivatives, we have:

$$f_A = 80 - 0.2A \qquad \text{(D4.2)}$$

$$f_B = 100 - 0.4B \qquad \text{(D4.3)}$$

$$f_{AA} = -0.2$$

$$f_{BB} = -0.4$$

$$f_{AB} = 0$$

Setting Eqs D4.2 and D4.3 to zero and solving gives $A = 400$ and $B = 250$. We see that both second derivatives are negative and we can confirm that this output combination does represent a maximum through:

$$f_{AA}f_{BB} > (f_{AB})^2$$

$$(-0.2)(-0.4) > 0$$

and we calculate that the firm attains a profit of £28,400. However, let us further assume that the firm knows its maximum combined feasible production to be 325 – perhaps because of fixed labour or capital availability. That is, we face the constraint such that:

$$A + B = 325 \qquad \text{(D4.4)}$$

Clearly, our original solution is now unattainable. Somehow we must seek an optimum value for the profit function but still satisfy the constraint that we face. As a general rule, we might face a number of such constraints, and they must all be satisfied simultaneously while we seek an optimum value for what we refer to as the *objective function*. It will be useful to consider the graphical representation of the problem that we face. Figure D4.1 shows a series of objective function lines for different levels of profit. Each line indicates, for a given and fixed level of profit, the different combinations of output that will achieve this profit. For example, a profit of £20,000 can be achieved with a combination of (approximately) $A = 250$, $B = 75$; or $A = 150$, $B = 150$;

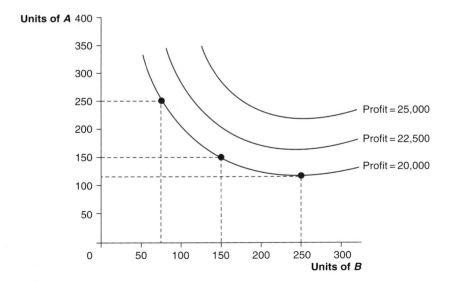

Figure D4.1 Iso-profit lines

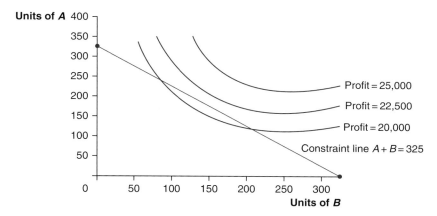

Figure D4.2 Iso-profit lines and constraint lines

or $A = 110$, $B = 250$ or indeed any of the specific combinations that occur on this line. Similarly, any of the output combinations falling on the second line will generate a profit of £22,500. Such a series of lines are generally referred to as *iso* lines (here we would refer to iso-profit lines) and each represents a constant and fixed value for the objective function. It is evident on inspection that the further the line moves outwards and away from the origin, the higher the profit it represents. Fig. D4.2 shows the same iso-profit lines together with the line representing the constraint Eq. D4.4. This line shows the various combinations of the two outputs that match the constraint specification. Any point on this line represents a combined output of 325. On examining Fig. D4.2, the general principles of what we are seeking to achieve become evident. In terms of the objective function we require the highest possible iso-profit line (since we seek to maximize profit, the objective function). However, it is also evident that, given the constraint, we must remain on the constraint line. Given the shape of the iso-profit lines it is also evident that we seek point X illustrated in Fig. D4.3. We seek to attain the highest possible iso line (and here we have $I_1 < I_2 < I_3$) but must also remain on the constraint line (line C). It is evident that all our solutions must occur on the

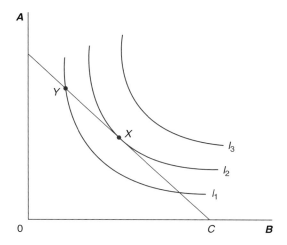

Figure D4.3 Optimum solution

constraint line. Point Y represents one possible solution since it falls on the line, as does point X. The highest iso line attainable will be that which is tangential to the constraint line, as at point X, which will, therefore, represent the optimum solution to the constrained problem. It is also worth recollecting that the objective function is actually three-dimensional (in our example; in general it would be n-dimensional). The issue remains unresolved, however, as to how we can find such a position (other than the usual cumbersome graphical approach).

D4.2 Lagrange multipliers

The method we introduce (there are others) utilizes *Lagrange multipliers* and offers considerable benefits to economic analysis. It is clear from Fig. D4.3 that, at the point we are seeking, the gradient of the relevant iso line will be equal to the gradient of the constraint line. Clearly, differential calculus is potentially a solution method that we can consider. We shall introduce the method of Lagrange multipliers through the numerical example we are currently examining and then we shall attempt to understand its justification. Let us show the objective function as:

$$Z = -100 + 80X - 0.1X^2 + 100Y - 0.2Y^2 \tag{D4.5}$$

with our constraint

$$X + Y = 325 \tag{D4.6}$$

The constraint is easily transformed into an implicit function:

$$X + Y - 325 = 0 \tag{D4.7}$$

and we can create a new function – known as a *Lagrange function* – such that

$$F = (-100 + 80X - 0.1X^2 + 100Y - 0.2Y^2) - \lambda(X + Y - 325) \tag{D4.8}$$

where λ is a new variable known as a *Lagrange multiplier*. The Lagrange multiplier method now proceeds as follows. We seek to establish the values of X, Y and λ that will solve the Lagrange function. If we do this then the X and Y values we obtain for this solution will be the values that maximize/minimize the original function, Z, subject to the constraint imposed. A formal mathematical proof of this is beyond our current capabilities but we can consider the logic of the method. In solving for F we seek values for X and Y that satisfy the imposed constraint, Eq. D4.7. However, from Eq. D4.7 such values for X and Y will cause the Lagrange function to become:

$$F = (-100 + 80X - 0.1X^2 + 100Y - 0.2Y^2) - \lambda(0) = Z \tag{D4.9}$$

That is, the value taken by the Lagrange function will be the same value as taken by the original objective function, Z. But if F and Z are identical then the values of X and Y that satisfy F must simultaneously satisfy Z. Therefore, solving F must be the same as solving Z subject to the imposed constraint, since it is only when this imposed constraint is satisfied that we find a value for F in the first place. We can now use the standard approach to finding the optimum value for Eq. D4.8. We require the relevant partial derivatives:

$$F_X = 80 - 0.2X - \lambda \qquad \text{(D4.10)}$$
$$F_Y = 100 - 0.4Y - \lambda \qquad \text{(D4.11)}$$
$$F_\lambda = -(X + Y - 325) \qquad \text{(D4.12)}$$

and we require all three partial derivatives to be zero simultaneously. Solving this as a straightforward set of simultaneous equations gives:

$$X = 183.3$$
$$Y = 141.7$$
$$\lambda = 43.3$$

and

$$F = 21{,}358.3$$

which, through our logic earlier, must also be the value for Z, that is, $Z = F = 21{,}358.3$. We also confirm that these values for X and Y satisfy the constraint equation. (Note that the solution with the constraint imposed generates a smaller profit than the unconstrained problem for which we found the solution originally.) The Lagrange multiplier method, therefore, can be used to determine the solution to a constrained optimization problem. However, it may have been noticed that we have not established a method for determining whether this solution represents a maximum or a minimum position. Once again, we have to state that the proof of how we can derive the relevant second-order conditions is beyond our present scope. All that we can do is to state that, for the typical economic problems we are considering, the method generates a maximum point for a maximization problem and a minimum point for a minimization problem.

Progress Check D4.1

Assume that the constraint equation changes to:

$$X + Y = 400$$

Find the new solution.

(Solution on p. 474)

D

D4.3 Interpretation of the Lagrange multiplier

It will be useful at this stage to examine the interpretation of the Lagrange multiplier itself, as this goes some way to illustrating why it is productive to get to grips with Lagrange functions in the first place. For the numerical example we have been considering we derived a value for λ of 43.3.

Progress Check D4.2

Assume the constraint equation alters to:

$$X + Y = 326$$

How would this affect the relevant graph? Find the new solution and the extra profit that has been attained.

Finding the new solution as before (in fact only F_λ alters), we have:

$$X = 184$$

$$Y = 142$$

$$\text{Profit} = 21{,}401.6$$

and we determine that the increase in profit brought about by increasing the constraint restriction by 1 unit has been 43.3 – exactly the same as the value for λ that we derived in the original formulation. Clearly, this is not simply coincidence. In fact if we denote the constraining equation in general as:

$$c(X, Y) = k$$

where k is some constant value (such as 325 or 326), then

$$\lambda = \frac{\partial Z}{\partial k} \tag{D4.13}$$

That is, λ, the Lagrange multiplier, shows the change that occurs in the optimal Z value given some marginal change in the constraint constant, k. Recollect, as is usual with derivatives, that the change in λ is technically infinitesimally small. The potential importance of this use of λ is self-evident. In the context of our example, λ indicates the opportunity cost of this constraint. We are being told that if we could reduce the constraint restriction (i.e. increase k) then production and hence profit will increase as a result. Clearly, to the economic decision-maker such information on opportunity costs is of considerable benefit. If we can increase production capacity to 326 at an extra cost of less than £43.33 then it will be beneficial to do so, given the resulting increase in profit. In the context of this problem, we might consider acquiring extra supplies of labour or capital to increase productive capacity. These extra resources have an opportunity cost of £43.33. Such opportunity cost information has an important role to play in economic analysis as we shall see later in this module. λ is also often referred to as a shadow price, the maximum price that the firm is willing to pay for an extra unit of a given limited resource.

To see how we arrive at Eq. D4.13, let us generalize the problem we have examined so that we require:

$$\text{Maximize } Z = f(X, Y)$$

$$\text{subject to } c(X, Y) = k$$

We then have a Lagrange function, F:

$$F = f(X, Y) - \lambda[c(X, Y) - k]$$

The two partial derivatives of F with respect to X and Y will then be:

$$\frac{\partial F}{\partial X} = \frac{\partial f}{\partial X} - \frac{\lambda \partial c}{\partial X}$$

and

$$\frac{\partial F}{\partial Y} = \frac{\partial f}{\partial Y} - \frac{\lambda \partial c}{\partial Y}$$

and the optimal values for X and Y will occur when the two partial derivatives are zero, hence

$$\frac{\partial F}{\partial X} = \frac{\partial F}{\partial Y}$$

But this can be rewritten as:

$$\frac{\partial f}{\partial X} - \frac{\lambda \partial c}{\partial X} = \frac{\partial f}{\partial Y} - \frac{\lambda \partial c}{\partial Y}$$

and rearranging then gives

$$\frac{\partial f/\partial X}{\partial c/\partial X} - \lambda = \frac{\partial f/\partial Y}{\partial c/\partial Y} - \lambda$$

and with the two λs cancelling, we then have

$$\frac{\partial f/\partial X}{\partial c/\partial X} = \frac{\partial f/\partial Y}{\partial c/\partial Y}$$

We shall use this result shortly. We require dZ/dk where dZ and dk are total differentials. Taking the total differential of $Z = f(X, Y)$ we then have:

$$dZ = \frac{\partial f}{\partial X} dX + \frac{\partial f}{\partial Y} dY$$

and taking the total differential of $c(X, Y) = k$ we have

$$dk = \frac{\partial c}{\partial X} dX + \frac{\partial c}{\partial Y} dY$$

However, let us multiply dk through by the expression derived earlier $(\partial f/\partial X)/(\partial c/\partial X)$:

$$\frac{\partial f/\partial X}{\partial c/\partial X} dk = \frac{\partial f/\partial X}{\partial c/\partial X} \frac{\partial c}{\partial X} dX + \frac{\partial f/\partial Y}{\partial c/\partial Y} \frac{\partial c}{\partial Y} dY$$

This simplifies to:

$$\frac{\partial f/\partial X}{\partial c/\partial X} dk = \frac{\partial f}{\partial X} dX + \frac{\partial f}{\partial Y} dY$$

But the right-hand side of this expression is identical to that which we had for dZ, hence:

$$\frac{\partial f/\partial X}{\partial c/\partial X} dk = dZ$$

But from the earlier partial derivatives we had:

$$\frac{\partial F}{\partial X} = \frac{\partial f}{\partial X} - \lambda \frac{\partial c}{\partial X} = 0$$

and hence

$$\lambda = \frac{\partial f/\partial X}{\partial c/\partial X}$$

Hence:

$$\frac{\partial f/\partial X}{\partial c/\partial X} dk = dZ$$

which can be written as

$$\lambda dk = dZ$$

and therefore

$$\frac{dZ}{dk} = \lambda$$

proving Eq. D4.13, that λ, the Lagrange multiplier, is the change in the optimal Z value given a marginal change in the constraint value, k.

It should be noted that our investigation of Lagrange multipliers only scratches the surface of their application. We have examined the application of only a single constraint, and might wish to extend the problem to involve several constraints. Equally, the constraints have taken the form of strict equations ($=$), while we may wish to impose minimum/maximum conditions on the constraints through the use of inequality signs ($<, >$). Such considerations are beyond our examination of the topic, although they do involve relatively little new material to allow their inclusion. Let us now turn to examine some of the economic applications of these principles. We shall consider two key applications: the first relating to the theory of the firm and the second to consumer behaviour. In practice, constrained optimization can be widely applied to economic analysis, and so reading around the topic is to be strongly encouraged.

D4.4 Output maximization subject to a cost constraint

Consider a firm facing a production function:

$$Q = q(L, K) \tag{D4.14}$$

and a cost function

$$TC = wL + rK \tag{D4.15}$$

We can establish a cost constraint of the form:

$$TC = c$$

where c is some specified value, perhaps through a limit on the firm's maximum cost expenditure. Our problem then becomes one of choosing the levels of factor inputs that will maximize output subject to the cost constraint imposed; that is:

Maximize $Q = q(K, L)$

subject to $wL + rK = c$ $\tag{D4.16}$

Diagrammatically we face a situation as in Fig. D4.4. Line C represents the cost constraint while we face a series of iso lines with each representing a given value for Q. The point we seek is Y, where the level of factor inputs occurs both on the cost constraint line and the production function. It is worth noting that the slope of the production function can be expressed by implicitly differentiating Eq. D4.14 as:

$$\frac{\partial L}{\partial K} = -\frac{\partial q/\partial K}{\partial q/\partial L} \tag{D4.17}$$

which represents the marginal rate of technical substitution between the two factor inputs; that is, it measures the rate at which we can substitute one input for another and leave output unchanged. The Lagrange function is:

$$F = q(L, K) - \lambda(wL + rK - c) \tag{D4.18}$$

and the relevant partial derivatives are

$$F_L = \frac{\partial q}{\partial L} - \lambda w = 0 \tag{D4.19}$$

$$F_K = \frac{\partial q}{\partial K} - \lambda r = 0 \tag{D4.20}$$

$$F_\lambda = -wL - rK + c = 0 \tag{D4.21}$$

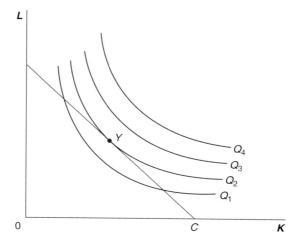

Figure D4.4 Optimizing output subject to cost constraint

Multiplying Eq. D4.19 by r and Eq. D4.20 by w and subtracting the two results gives:

$$\left(r\frac{\partial q}{\partial L} - \lambda wr \right) - \left(w\frac{\partial q}{\partial K} - \lambda wr \right) = 0$$

giving

$$r\frac{\partial q}{\partial L} - w\frac{\partial q}{\partial K} = 0$$

and rearranging gives

$$\frac{\partial q/\partial K}{\partial q/\partial L} = \frac{r}{w} \qquad\qquad (\text{D4.22})$$

Since this is an optimality condition it implies that we must choose values for L and K so that the ratio of their two marginal products is equal to the ratio of their prices. Let us now consider the optimal value for λ. Directly from Eqs D4.19 and D4.20 we see that we require:

$$\lambda = \frac{\partial q/\partial L}{w}$$

$$\lambda = \frac{\partial q/\partial K}{r}$$

and hence

$$\lambda = \frac{\partial q/\partial L}{w} = \frac{\partial q/\partial K}{r} \qquad\qquad (\text{D4.23})$$

Recollect that λ represents the change in output (the objective function) that will arise from a unit change in the factor inputs. We conclude that, from the optimal position, the change in output will be the same regardless of whether we change L or K (although of course we may require different quantities of L and K to generate this extra output). These conclusions are hardly those we could have obtained without the use of the calculus techniques we have developed.

D4.5 Cost minimization subject to an output constraint

Let us now examine the situation from a different perspective. Assume we now require:

$$\text{Minimize } C = wL + rK \tag{D4.24}$$

$$\text{subject to } q(L, K) = Q_0 \tag{D4.25}$$

where we now wish to minimize total costs while satisfying some imposed level of production, Q_0. Figure D4.5 shows diagrammatically the situation we now face. We now have the constraint represented by Q and are seeking the optimum C. The Lagrange function is now:

$$F = (wL + rK) - \lambda[q(L, K) - Q_0] \tag{D4.26}$$

and the relevant partial derivatives are

$$F_L = w - \lambda \frac{\partial q}{\partial L} = 0 \tag{D4.27}$$

$$F_K = r - \lambda \frac{\partial q}{\partial K} = 0 \tag{D4.28}$$

$$F_\lambda = q(L, K) + Q_0 = 0 \tag{D4.29}$$

Progress Check D4.3

Using the same principles as before, obtain an expression from Eqs D4.27 and D4.28 showing the optimal requirement. Obtain a comparable expression for λ.

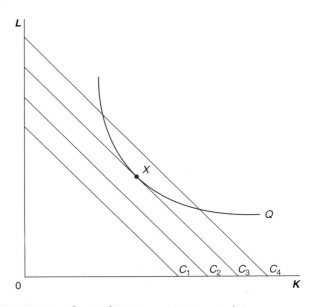

Figure D4.5 Optimization of cost subject to an output constraint

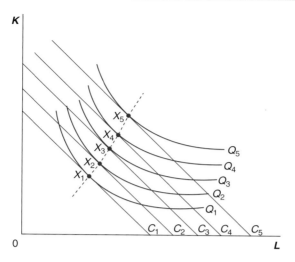

Figure D4.6 Iso-quants and iso-costs

We can derive an expression such that:

$$\frac{\partial q/\partial K}{\partial q/\partial L} = \frac{r}{w} \tag{D4.30}$$

which is identical to Eq. D4.22 that we derived from the output-maximization model. Equally, the value of the Lagrange multiplier in this cost-minimization model is seen to be:

$$\lambda = \frac{r}{\partial q/\partial K} = \frac{w}{\partial q/\partial L} \tag{D4.31}$$

which indicates that, at the optimal solution, the change in costs results from a unit change in Q_0; that is, λ represents marginal costs, and we see that, from the cost-minimizing position, the marginal cost will be the same no matter whether we obtain extra output from employing more labour or from more capital. It is evident that our two models are effectively mirror images of each other, and it is instructive to merge Figs D4.4 and D4.5 to examine the complete picture that we face.

Figure D4.6 shows both a series of iso-costs and iso-quants, and it is evident that if the firm is able to vary both its production *and* its total costs (as opposed to one of these being a fixed constraint) then we have a series of tangent points, marked as $X_1, \ldots, X_5$ in Fig. D4.6, which we can refer to as an *expansion path*, as it indicates a path through all the cost/production combinations. The firm seeking to maximize production/minimize costs will select a labour/capital combination that lies on this path.

D4.6 Maximizing consumer utility subject to a budget constraint

Finally, we turn to examine an aspect of consumer behaviour: utility. Consider a consumer who faces a function such that:

$$U = u(X, Y) \tag{D4.32}$$

where X and Y represent the quantities of products X and Y consumed, and U the total utility derived from such consumption. The graph of these iso curves would take the usual form, with the curves more generally referred to as *indifference curves* in this context. Given that on any one curve the consumer attains a constant level of utility, he or she will literally be indifferent as to where on this curve he or she will be. The slope of such an indifference curve will be given by:

$$\frac{\partial X}{\partial Y} = \frac{\partial U/\partial Y}{\partial U/\partial X} \tag{D4.33}$$

which we can refer to as the *marginal rate of substitution* of one good for the other. What will matter to the consumer will be the total utility obtained that we will seek to maximize. Clearly, the typical consumer does not face unlimited consumption of either good but rather will be constrained by the available income or budget. We have a problem where:

Maximize $U = u(X, Y)$

subject to $P_X X + P_Y Y = B$ (D4.34)

where P represents the price for each good and B the consumer's available budget. The Lagrange function is then:

$$F = u(X, Y) - \lambda(P_X X + P_Y Y - B) \tag{D4.35}$$

and

$$F_X = \frac{\partial u}{\partial X} - \lambda P_X = 0 \tag{D4.36}$$

$$F_Y = \frac{\partial u}{\partial Y} - \lambda P_Y = 0 \tag{D4.37}$$

$$F_\lambda = -P_X X - P_Y Y + B \tag{D4.38}$$

Eliminating λ from Eqs D4.36 and D4.37 and rearranging gives an optimality condition:

$$\frac{\partial u/\partial X}{\partial u/\partial Y} = \frac{P_X}{P_Y} \tag{D4.39}$$

which indicates that, to maximize utility, the consumer should ensure that the ratio of the marginal rate of substitution of one good for the other is the same as the ratio of their prices. Equation D4.39 can be rearranged into:

$$\frac{\partial u/\partial X}{P_X} = \frac{\partial u/\partial Y}{P_Y}$$

indicating that when utility is maximized given a budget constraint then the ratio of marginal utility to price is the same for all goods consumed. This further implies that if the price of a good altered then so would the optimal solution, *ceteris paribus*, since this equality requirement would no longer hold. Equally, we can derive an expression for λ such that:

$$\lambda = \frac{\partial u/\partial X}{P_X} = \frac{\partial u/\partial Y}{P_Y} \tag{D4.40}$$

The Lagrange multiplier indicates, at the optimum position, the change in utility that will occur with a unit change in the constraint limitation. Here λ will show the change in utility as income changes; hence we can refer to λ as the marginal utility of income.

D4.7 Summary

In this module we have been able to extend our analysis of optimization by considering constrained problems. We have seen how these can be solved through the use of the Lagrange multiplier and we have also seen that the multiplier has a particularly important meaning in the context of economics. The approach can readily be extended to include more than two variables and, indeed, more than one constraint (in which case we would have a separate Lagrange multiplier for each constraint). The calculation of such problems, however, quickly becomes tedious for manual solution. The exercises that follow will allow you to gain further practice in constrained optimization. You may wish to return to the unconstrained problems we examined in earlier modules and impose a sensible constraint on these to apply the Lagrange multiplier approach.

Learning Check

Having read this module you should have learned that:

- Constrained optimization is concerned with finding an optimum solution when there are one or more constraints imposed on the solution
- The Lagrange multiplier approach is used to find a constrained optimization solution
- The Lagrange multiplier shows the change in the optimal value of the function given a marginal change in the constraint
- In terms of economic analysis, the value of the Lagrange multiplier equates to an opportunity cost.

Worked Example

A firm produces two goods, 1 and 2, each of which faces a demand function:

$$P_1 = 100 - 2Q_1 + Q_2$$
$$P_2 = 75 + 2Q_1 - Q_2$$

where Q denotes the quantity of each good and P its price. The firm's total costs are given by:

$$TC = 1000 + 20Q_1 + 10Q_2 + 2Q_1Q_2$$

The firm wishes to determine profit-maximizing levels of production of the two goods but knows that its maximum combined production with its existing labour supply is 50.

Solution

We first need to derive a profit function:

$$\pi = TR_1 + TR_2 - TC$$
$$TR_1 = 100Q_1 - 2Q_1^2 + Q_1Q_2$$
$$TR_2 = 75Q_2 + 2Q_1Q_2 - Q_2^2$$

Worked Example *(Continued)*

giving

$$\pi = -1000 + 80Q_1 - 2Q_1^2 + Q_1Q_2 + 65Q_2 - Q_2^2$$

and we then have

Maximize $\pi = -1000 + 80Q_1 - 2Q_1^2 + Q_1Q_2 + 65Q_2 - Q_2^2$

subject to $Q_1 + Q_2 = 50$

The Lagrangian function is:

$$Z = -1000 + 80Q_1 - 2Q_1^2 + Q_1Q_2 + 65Q_2 - Q_2^2 - \lambda(Q_1 + Q_2 - 50)$$

We then have:

$$F_{Q1} = 80 - 4Q_1 + Q_2 - \lambda = 0$$
$$F_{Q2} = Q_1 + 65 - 2Q_2 - \lambda = 0$$
$$F_\lambda = -Q_1 - Q_2 + 50 = 0$$

Setting $Q_1 = 50 - Q_2$ and substituting into F_{Q1} and F_{Q2} we derive:

$$Q_1 = 20.625$$
$$Q_2 = 29.375$$
$$\lambda = 26.875$$

as the optimal values.

We can go one stage further, however. We are told that the production constraint arises because of a fixed supply of labour. The value of the Lagrange multiplier, 26.875, implies that profit will increase by this amount if we can improve the production constraint (i.e. to 51 or above). The value of the multiplier provides a maximum cost the firm should be willing to incur in order to allow the production to increase by an extra unit.

Exercises

In addition to the exercises detailed below you should return to any of the previous optimization problems we have examined. Impose a (sensible) constraint of your own and see what effect this has on the optimal solution.

D4.1 Explain in terms of economics the logic of Eq. D4.40.

D4.2 Assume a profit function:

$$\pi = -100 + 80A - 0.1A^2 + 100B - 0.2B^2$$

relating to the output of two products. If total production is limited to 500, find the solution that will maximize profit. Interpret the Lagrange multiplier obtained.

D4.3 Assume a utility function:

$$U = 50A + 200B - 0.05A^2 - 0.25B^2$$

Exercises *(Continued)*

If the price of good A is £10 per unit and that of B is £5 then determine the optimal combination of the two goods if the consumer has an income of:

(i) £5000

(ii) £6000

(iii) £7000.

How do you explain the change in the combination as income rises?

D4.4 Assume a utility function:

$$U = 4X^{0.5}Y^{0.25}$$

If the price of X is £2.50 and that of Y is £4, calculate the optimal combination for an income of £50. What interpretation can be given to the Lagrange multiplier?

D4.5 Return to the production function used in Exercise D3.3:

$$Q = 10L^{0.5}K^{0.25}$$

Assume that the firm has a fixed budget for its labour and capital costs. For each of the budgets shown below calculate the optimal level of inputs. Interpret the value of the Lagrange multiplier in each case.

(i) £38,000

(ii) £40,000

(iii) £45,000.

D4.6 Assume that the firm now wishes to minimize costs subject to an output constraint of 8000 units. Determine the optimal solution and interpret the Lagrange multiplier.

Appendix D4 The bordered Hessian matrix

In Section D3 we saw that the Hessian matrix can be used to evaluate the second-order conditions of an unconstrained optimization problem. The Hessian can also be applied to constrained optimization. If we wish to optimize a function $f(X, Y)$ subject to a constraint $c(X, Y)$ then the Lagrange function is:

$$F(X, Y, \lambda) = f(X, Y) - \lambda[c(X, Y) - k]$$

The second-order conditions can be expressed as a Hessian where:

$$H = \begin{pmatrix} F_{XX} & F_{XY} & F_{X\lambda} \\ F_{YX} & F_{YY} & F_{Y\lambda} \\ F_{\lambda X} & F_{\lambda Y} & F_{\lambda\lambda} \end{pmatrix}$$

However:

$$F_{X\lambda} = F_{\lambda X} = c_X$$
$$F_{Y\lambda} = F_{\lambda Y} = c_Y$$
$$F_{\lambda\lambda} = 0$$

giving

$$H = \begin{pmatrix} F_{XX} & F_{XY} & c_X \\ F_{YX} & F_{YY} & c_Y \\ c_X & c_Y & 0 \end{pmatrix}$$

which is referred to as the **bordered Hessian** since it comprises the ordinary Hessian

$$\begin{pmatrix} F_{XX} & F_{XY} \\ F_{YX} & F_{YY} \end{pmatrix}$$

bordered by the first derivatives of the constraint and a 0 on the main diagonal. Assuming all other conditions are met then a negative value for $|H|$ indicates a minimum for the optimum, and a positive value for $|H|$ indicates a maximum.

Section E
Further topics in economic analysis

In this final section of the book we cover a number of additional topics relevant to mathematical economic analysis.

Module E1 Integration and economic analysis

In this module we introduce the principles of integral calculus (as opposed to differential calculus, which we have used so far) and see how this can be used in different areas of economic analysis.

Module E2 Financial analysis I: interest and present value

Financial mathematical economics is an increasingly important topic in economic modelling. In this module we introduce some of the basic concepts behind this field, including the concepts of interest and present value.

Module E3 Financial analysis II: annuities, sinking funds and growth models

In this module we continue our examination of the use of mathematics in financial economic analysis. We look at the principles behind annuities and sinking funds and we also start to look at economic growth models.

Module E4 An introduction to dynamics

A focus on changes in equilibrium over time is an important part of economic analysis. In this module we outline the basic principles behind such dynamic models.

E

Module E5 Probability in economic analysis

In this final module we look at how probability can be used in economic analysis to deal with uncertainty and how we can incorporate such uncertainty into economic approaches to decision-making.

Module E1
Integration and economic analysis

Sections C and D have explored how differential calculus can be used in economic analysis. We now turn our attention away from differential calculus and towards *integral calculus*. Integration of a function can be seen as the reverse of the differentiation process. However, the use of integral calculus opens up areas of economic analysis that until now have been closed to us.

Learning Objectives

By the end of this module you should be able to:

- Use notation appropriate for integral calculus
- Use common rules of integrating
- Calculate definite integrals
- Calculate the area under a curve using integral calculus
- Apply integral calculus to common economic models.

E1.1 Notation and terminology

Let us assume we have a marginal cost function:

$$MC = 25 - 0.08Q \tag{E1.1}$$

where Q is quantity produced, and that we want to obtain the corresponding total cost function. Using our knowledge of differential calculus we know that:

$$TC = f(Q)$$

$$MC = f'(Q)$$

That is, that the derivative of the TC function is MC. It seems logical that, as we now know MC, we ought to be able to 'rediscover' the TC function from which it was obtained. Integration is concerned with this type of task and we say that we wish to *integrate the* MC *function*. From our knowledge of differential calculus we know that the derivative of $25Q$ is 25 and the derivative of $-0.04Q^2$ is $0.08Q$ and hence we can infer that if $MC = 25 - 0.08Q$ then

$$TC = 25Q - 0.04Q^2 \qquad \text{(E1.2)}$$

However, from both our knowledge of calculus and our understanding of the TC function in economics it is evident that Eq. E1.2 may well be incomplete. There is no value for the fixed cost element that we would expect in the TC function and we realize that the derivative of such a constant term would be zero, and hence there is no clue in the MC function itself as to what this constant value might have been. In other words, we have to specify the function as:

$$TC = 25Q - 0.04Q^2 + c \qquad \text{(E1.3)}$$

where c refers to an unknown constant, the value of which we can obtain only with additional information that may have been provided. The notation that we adopt to indicate the process of integration is:

$$TC = \int (25 - 0.08Q) dQ$$
$$= 25Q - 0.04Q^2 + c \qquad \text{(E1.4)}$$

or in general

$$Y = \int f'(X) dX = f(X) \qquad \text{(E1.5)}$$

The symbol $\int$ is known as an *integral sign*, $f(X)$ is known as the *integrand* and the dX symbol indicates that the integral operation is being undertaken with respect to the X variable, which may not be the only independent variable in more complex equations. While the process of integration involves some trial-and-error activity, there are a number of useful rules that we might be able to apply, depending on the type of problem faced.

E1.2 Rules of integration

Many of the rules for integration can be obtained simply by reversing the process of differentiation. These are stated briefly below, with a short explanation where necessary. It is recommended that you complete the Progress Check immediately following before proceeding with the rest of the material in this module. It is also useful to get into the habit of checking your solution by differentiating your answer (which should, of course, give you the original expression).

The power rule

If $Y = f(X)$ and $f'(X) = aX^b$, then:

$$\int aX^b \, dX = \frac{a}{b+1} X^{b+1} + c \qquad \text{(E1.6)}$$

For example, if $f'(X) = 2X^3$, then:

$$\int 2X^3 dX = \frac{2}{3+1} X^{3+1} + c = 0.5X^4 + c$$

The log rule

If $f(X) = 1/x$, then:

$$\int \frac{1}{X} dX = \ln X + c \qquad \text{for } X > 0 \tag{E1.7}$$

Integral of a constant times a function

If the function we wish to integrate is made up of some constant, k, and some function of X such as $kf(X)$, then:

$$\int kf(X) dX = k \int f(X) dX \tag{E1.8}$$

where k is some constant.

Integral of a sum or difference

If the function we wish to integrate is made up of two separable functions of X, $f(X) \pm g(X)$, then:

$$\int \left[f(X) \pm g(X) \right] dX = \int f(X) dX \pm g(X) dX$$

$$= \int f(X) dX \pm \int g(X) dX \tag{E1.9}$$

The substitution rule

Consider the function:

$$f(X) = 12X^2(X^3 - 10)^5 \tag{E1.10}$$

for which we seek the integral. The rules we have developed thus far are not readily applicable to such a complex function. However, under certain conditions, we can apply the substitution rule. Let:

$$u = X^3 - 10$$

Then $du/dX = 3X^2$ and therefore $dX = du/3X^2$. We require $\int 32X^2(X^3 - 10)^5 dX$ or, in general, $\int f(X) dX$. The rule is that:

$$\int f(X) dX = \int \left(u \frac{du}{dX} \right) dX \tag{E1.11}$$

We require $\int 12X^2(X^3 - 10)^5 dX$, but substituting for u and dX we have:

$$\int 12X^2 u^5 \frac{du}{3X^2}$$

which simplifies to

$$\int \frac{12X^2}{3X^2} u^5 du = \int 4u^5 du = \int 4u^5 du$$

However:

$$4 \int u^5 du = 4(1/6 \, u^6) + c$$

$$= 2/3(X^3 - 10)^6 + c$$

which is therefore the integral of the original function. It is important to realize that this rule can only be applied if we can express the required integral in the form of Eq. E1.11. For example, if we required:

$$\int 12X^2(X^4 - 10)dX$$

the rule cannot be applied as $du/dX = 4X^3$ is not a multiple of $12X^2$, which must be the case for the rule to be applicable.

Progress Check E1.1

Find the integrals for the following functions. Check your solution by differentiating it to confirm that the original function expression is obtained.

(i) X^6

(ii) $X^{-0.3}$

(iii) $X^3 - X^2$

(iv) $5X^4$

(v) $1/X$

(vi) $9X^2(X^3 + 10)^3$

(Solution on p. 474)

E1.3 Definite integrals

If this were the only aspect to integral calculus then you would probably be justified in the view that it was not really worth the effort. However, the type of integrals we have examined thus far are known as *indefinite integrals*. We now turn our attention to the *definite integral*. Consider the integral:

$$\int (10X + 5)dX = 5X^2 + 5X + c = f(X)$$

This is simply another example of the indefinite integral that we have examined. However, suppose we had instead:

$$\int_3^4 (10X + 5)dX \tag{E1.12}$$

What does this type of integral represent? In fact this is an example of a *definite integral* and is used to represent a situation where we require the value of the integral expression between the stated numerical limits – here between 4 and 3. That is, we require to evaluate the integral for $X = 4$ and again for $X = 3$. The definite integral is then the result of the difference between these two values. That is, we require:

$$f(X = 4) - f(X = 3)$$

Naturally, in this simple example this is easily obtained. We have:

$$f(X) = 5X^2 + 5X + c$$

$$f(X = 4) = 5(4)^2 + 5(4) + c = 80 + 20 + c = 100 + c$$

$$f(X = 3) = 5(3)^2 + 5(3) + c = 45 + 15 + c = 60 + c$$

$$\int_3^4 (10X + 5)dX = (100 + c) - (60 + c) = 40$$

That is, the value of the integral between the stated limits is 40. Note that the unknown *c* term in the integral is cancelled out in the process, which will always be the case. The standard notation for definite integrals takes the form:

$$\int_3^4 (10X + 5)dX = \left[\frac{10X^2}{2} + 5X \right]_3^4 \tag{E1.13}$$

or in general

$$\int_b^a f(X)dX = [F(X)]_b^a = F(a) - F(b) \tag{E1.14}$$

where *a* represents the upper limit and *b* the lower limit of the integral.

Progress Check E1.2

Calculate the value of the definite integral for (10X + 5) between the following values:

(i) $X = 0$ to 3

(ii) $X = 0$ to 4.

(Solution on p. 474)

E1.4 Definite integrals and areas under curves

Consider Figs E1.1 and E1.2, which show the integral function Eq. E1.12. Figure E1.1 relates to the upper limit of the integral we have just calculated, $X = 4$ (at which point $(10X + 5) = 45$). The total area under the curve to this point (i.e. for $X = 0$ to $X = 4$) has been divided into two to allow for easier calculation. Area *A* represents a triangle and its area is found by:

$$\frac{\text{Height} \times \text{width}}{2} = \frac{(45 - 5) \times (4)}{2} = \frac{160}{2} = 80$$

while *B* is a rectangle with area equal to height times width which here gives $5 \times 4 = 20$. Compare the values for the two areas with the values we had when evaluating the upper limit value for the integral expression. Clearly, they are the same and we would denote $A + B$ as the area under this line between $X = 0$ and $X = 4$ ($= 100$). Figure E1.2 repeats this process for $X = 3$. Area *A* is now:

$$\frac{(35 - 5) \times (3)}{2} = \frac{90}{2} = 45$$

and *B* is $(5 \times 3) = 15$, giving an area under the line from $X = 0$ to $X = 3$ of 60. If, as we did for the definite integral, we now find the difference between these two values, we have:

(Area from $X = 0$ to $X = 4$) − (area from $X = 0$ to $X = 3$) $= 100 - 60 = 40$

which must represent the area under the line between $X = 3$ and $X = 4$, as shown in Fig. E1.3. Clearly, therefore, when we are evaluating a definite integral we are actually finding the equivalent area under the curve between the upper and lower limits of the integral specified.

In fact this holds for non-linear functions also. For example, consider Fig. E1.4, showing some non-linear function. Finding the definite integral between points *a* and

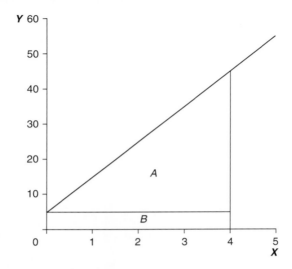

Figure E1.1 Area under $Y = 10X + 5$ for $X = 4$

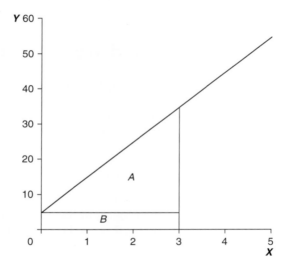

Figure E1.2 Area under $Y = 10X + 5$ for $X = 3$

b will be the equivalent of finding the area under the curve between these two values for X. One further point is worth noting. It is possible to obtain negative values when evaluating a definite integral. This would represent an area below the X axis, as shown between points c and d in Fig. E1.4. This can lead to possible difficulties. Consider that we required the integral between c and e. Clearly, evaluating the integral over this range will not produce the appropriate solution since the cd area will be negative and the de area positive, and there will be a cancelling effect. It is necessary, therefore, to evaluate the two parts of the area separately and then add them together – with an effective dividing point where the function crosses the X axis.

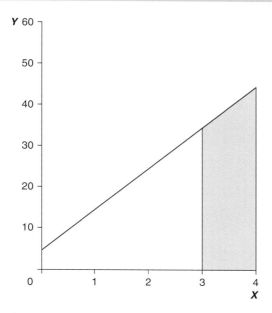

Figure E1.3 Area under $Y = 10X + 5$ for $X = 3$ to 4

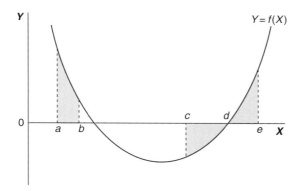

Figure E1.4 Non-linear function

Progress Check E1.3

For each of the integrals in activity E1.1, calculate the value of the definite integral between $X = 2$ and $X = 2.5$.

(Solution on p. 475)

E1.5 Consumer's surplus

Let us now see how integral calculus is used in economic analysis. First, we consider the application of these principles to the area of *consumer's surplus*. At market equilibrium all consumers pay the same price for the product. With a downward-sloping demand

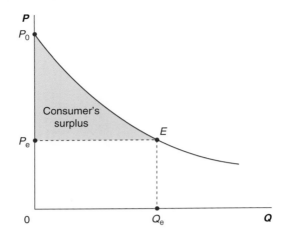

Figure E1.5 Consumer's surplus

curve some consumers would have been willing to pay a higher price for the product than the prevailing market price. The gap between the market price paid and the price that a consumer would have been willing to pay can be regarded as a measure of the consumer's surplus satisfaction and is accordingly known as *consumer's surplus*. For example, consumer's surplus of £1 occurs if I can buy an item for £5 at the current market price but would have been prepared to pay £6 for it. Consider the situation shown in Fig. E1.5.

P_e represents the prevailing market price, and consumers are able to purchase some quantity Q_e. Naturally, the consumer pays the same price for each of the units comprising this total quantity even though, as we see from the downward-sloping curve, he or she would have been willing to pay a higher per unit price to begin with. The area in Fig. E1.5 ($0 - P_0 - E - Q_e$) represents the amount the consumer would have been willing to pay in total for this quantity. The consumer's surplus is the difference between this total area and the area representing actual expenditure ($0 - P_e - E - Q_e$) and is clearly suitable for analysis through the definite integral approach we have just examined. Using integration we can find the total area under the curve from 0 to Q_e. This represents the total expenditure that consumers would have been willing to incur for this quantity of the good. If we then subtract the actual expenditure ($0 - P_e - E - Q_e$) from this we have the actual value of the consumer's surplus. Consider the function:

$$P = 100 - 5Q$$

with a current market price of £50 and hence a quantity demanded of 10. We then require:

$$\int_0^{10} (100 - 5Q)dQ - \text{actual expenditure}$$

$$\int_0^{10} (100 - 5Q)dQ - (50 \times 10)$$

$$[100Q - 2.5Q^2]_0^{10} - 500 = (750 - 0) - 500 = 250$$

as the size of the consumer's surplus. That is, there is a consumer's surplus of £250.

E1.6 Producer's surplus

The comparable situation applies to the firm and its supply function. At market equilibrium, the firm receives a uniform price per unit sold, whereas the firm would have been willing to sell some units for less than this. If we have a supply function such that:

$$P = 5Q$$

and a current market price as before of 50, then Q will again be 10. The producer's surplus will be:

$$\text{Actual revenue} - \int_0^{10} (5Q)dQ = 500 - [2.5Q^2]_0^{10}$$

$$= 500 - (250 - 0) = 250$$

The principle is illustrated in Fig. E1.6.

Total revenue will be given by the area $0 - P_e - E - Q_e$. However, the price the producer would have been willing to accept at lower levels for Q is given the supply function line. Hence the producer's surplus revenue is that shown shaded in the diagram: $P_0 - P_e - E$.

We can combine both consumer's surplus and producer's surplus, as shown in Fig. E1.7. This shows both demand and supply curves together with equilibrium price and quantity. Both consumer's surplus and producer's surplus are shaded.

E1.7 Capital stock formation

For our next use of integral calculus in economic analysis, we look at capital stock formation. Capital stock represents an economy's total quantity of capital goods (e.g. machinery, industrial and commercial buildings, roads, airports) that are available for use in the production process. Over a period of time we would expect the capital stock of an economy, K, to change, and looking at how an economy's capital stock changes

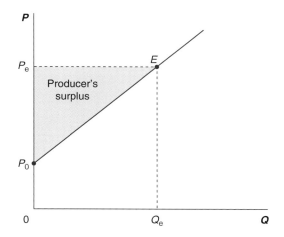

Figure E1.6 Producer's surplus

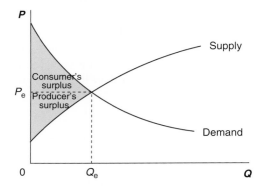

Figure E1.7 Consumer's surplus and producer's surplus

is an important part of economic analysis. In fact, we can define net investment, I, in the economy as:

$$I = \frac{dK}{dt}$$

where t is a time variable. That is, investment is the change in the capital stock over time. While K represents total capital stock at time t, I represents the net flow of investment at time t. If the net investment function is known then we can apply the principles of integration to derive capital stock formation in general or over a specified period of time. This would be given by:

$$\int_{t1}^{t2} I_t dt$$

For example, assume we have an investment function such that:

$$I_t = 1000t^{-0.5}$$

where I is measured in £ billions and we require the capital formation between years 4 and 5:

$$\int_{4}^{5} 1000t^{-0.5} dt$$

Integrating the function gives:

$$K = 2000t^{0.5}$$

and for $t = 5$ we derive $K = 4472$, while for $t = 4$, $K = 4000$. Hence between years 4 and 5 the capital stock increased by £472 billion.

Progress Check E1.4

Derive the change in the capital stock between years 7 and 8.

(Solution on p. 475)

E1.8 Summary

The principles of integration are straightforward, but the derivation of integrals can be difficult in practice. As with many of the topics we have covered, the only way forward is to practise the principles of integration on as many different functions as possible. Equally, we have examined three specific areas of definite integrals in economics. These principles can be applied where we wish to calculate the area under some function. For example, if we wished to calculate total cost, or total revenue, between specific levels of output, we can readily do so by obtaining the definite integral between those values. The exercises below illustrate a number of these applications.

Worked Example

A firm's marginal cost is given as:

$$MC = 150 - 10Q + 0.2Q^2$$

where Q is output. The firm wishes to estimate the increase in total costs as output increases from 30 to 32 units.

Solution

Clearly, the firm requires the change in total cost as output changes. Using the principles of integration we can derive TC as:

$$TC = \int MC \, dQ = \int (150 - 10Q + 0.2Q^2) dQ = 150Q - 5Q^2 + \frac{0.2Q^3}{3} + c$$

The TC function is incomplete since we have no information on fixed costs (the c term in this case). However, if we evaluate the definite integral of MC between

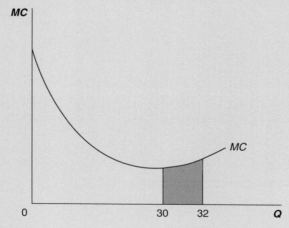

Figure E1.8 *MC*

Worked Example *(Continued)*

$Q = 30$ and $Q = 32$ then we will effectively evaluate the change in TC over this range. When $Q = 30$ the value of the definite integral is evaluated at 2300 and when $Q = 32$ at 2364.533. Therefore the increase in TC as Q increases from 30 to 32 will be 64.533. The principle is illustrated in Fig. E1.8 where the shaded area under the MC function equates to the value we have determined for the change in TC.

Exercises

In addition to the specific exercises below you should return to all the functions for which we obtained a derivative, in earlier modules. Taking the derivative, obtain the integral expression to check your ability to perform the relevant manipulations.

E1.1 Find the integrals for the following functions:

(i) $X^{2/3}$

(ii) $X^{-5/2}$

(iii) $6X^3 + 2X^2 + 5X$

E1.2 A firm faces the following marginal revenue function:

$$MR = 125 - 2Q$$

(i) Find the TR function.

(ii) Calculate the change in TR as Q changes from:

$$Q = 50 \text{ to } Q = 60$$
$$Q = 60 \text{ to } Q = 70$$
$$Q = 70 \text{ to } Q = 80$$
$$Q = 80 \text{ to } Q = 90.$$

You may find it useful to plot the TR function to check your solutions.

E1.3 A firm faces the following supply and demand functions:

$$Q_d = 500 - 9P$$
$$Q_s = -100 + 6P$$

Find the consumer's and producer's surpluses at equilibrium.

E1.4 We define the rate of investment (I) as the rate of capital formation dK/dt, where K is the total capital stock and t is time. If:

$$I = 3t^{0.8}$$

then find the total capital formation between periods $t = 10$ and $t = 15$.

E1.5 A monopolist faces the following:

$$P = 25 - 4Q$$
$$ATC = \frac{200}{Q} + 0.2Q + 10$$

Exercises *(Continued)*

Examine how both the consumer's and producer's surpluses are affected if the monopolist decides to maximize revenue rather than profit.

E1.6

(i) In an economy, the capital stock at time $t = 0$ is 100. The rate of investment, I, is given by:

$$I = 50t^{0.6}$$

Find the function for K, capital stock.

(ii) In a national income model we are told that autonomous consumption is 75 and that the marginal propensity to consume, mpc, is given by

$$mpc = 0.5 + 0.1^3\sqrt{Y}$$

where Y is income. Find an expression for the consumption function, C.

(iii) In a national income model we are told that the marginal propensity to save, mps, is given by:

$$mps = 0.5 - 0.2Y^{-0.5}$$

and that savings, S, is 12.17 when income, Y, is 50. Derive an expression for the savings function.

E

Module E2
Financial analysis I: interest and present value

This and the following module extend our examination of the usefulness of mathematics in economic analysis and economic models to look at financial economic analysis. In this module the concepts of interest, and arithmetic and geometric series are introduced, as well as those of discounting and present value. The module also examines the use of exponential functions in economics. You will need to use logarithms in this module, and access to a spreadsheet for the Progress Check activities will be helpful.

Learning Objectives

By the end of this module you should be able to:

- Perform a variety of interest calculations
- Evaluate an arithmetic and a geometric series
- Calculate the discounted values of a stream of financial data
- Calculate present value
- Explain the relationship between interest rates and bond prices.

E2.1 Financial mathematics

The necessity to be able to deal with, and understand, a variety of financial calculations in the world of business and economics is self-evident. Businesses – and the people who manage them – are primarily concerned with finance in one form or another. Businesses generate profits and business leaders have to determine where those profits should be invested for maximum return. Finance needs to be arranged to support investment plans and the cheapest sources of finance must be located. Equally, at a macroeconomic level, an understanding of financial mathematics – relating to capital stock formation, investment decisions, government taxation – is important. Underpinning most of the financial mathematics covered in this book is the concept of *interest*; and this is the focus of much of this module.

E2.2 Time preference

The principles of financial mathematics are based on a simple and obvious feature of behaviour. If you were offered the choice of receiving £1000 today or £1000 in 12 months' time you would almost certainly choose £1000 now. You would rationalize your decision on the grounds that, even ignoring inflation, £1000 now has more value to you than £1000 in 12 months' time. You could use the £1000 now to buy various goods and services which you could use over the next year and so derive utility and satisfaction. This preference for payment in the present rather than payment in the future is known as *time preference*. Other things being equal, we would prefer to have a sum of money now rather than the same sum of money at some time in the future. This has implications for the financial markets which bring together businesses and individuals who wish to borrow finance. Borrowers, by definition, wish to access money now with an intent to pay back what they have borrowed at some time in the future. Lenders, by definition, give up their money now in return for repayment at some time in the future. Lenders are effectively making a sacrifice since they could have used the money they are lending to buy goods and service now and derive satisfaction from them. Following on from the time preference concept, it is apparent that the person wishing to borrow money will have to offer the person lending the money some inducement or incentive for the sacrifice they are making. This incentive is the *rate of interest*. So, if you want to borrow £1000 from me now and repay me in a year's time you'll need to repay me more than the £1000 borrowed in order to encourage me to make the sacrifice of giving up the money for 12 months.

E2.3 Arithmetic and geometric series

To understand the principles and methods of calculation involved in financial mathematics it is necessary to examine two general mathematical principles: that of an *arithmetic series* and that of a *geometric series*.

Arithmetic series

Consider a sequence of numbers starting with the value a and progressing in the form:

a

$a + d$

$a + 2d$

$a + 3d$

$a + 4d$

and so on, where d is a fixed term added (or subtracted) to the previous value. Such a sequence is known as an arithmetic series. Without proof we state two general formulae for use with such a series:

1 To find the nth term in such a series:

$$a + (n - 1)d \qquad\qquad\qquad (E2.1)$$

2 To find the sum of the first n terms:

$$\frac{n}{2}(2a + (n - 1)d) \qquad\qquad\qquad (E2.2)$$

Let us illustrate with a simple problem. An individual is trying to plan for retirement. An investment broker has recommended a scheme whereby the individual pays a lump sum of money to the investment company and, in return, receives a guaranteed monthly income of £100. Moreover, the monthly income will increase by £10 per month. The individual wants to know what monthly income they will be receiving in five years' time. Here $a = 100$ and $d = 10$ with $n = 60$ (5 years × 12 months). Using Eq. E2.1 we have:

$$a + (n - 1)d$$
$$100 + (59)10 = £690$$

That is, in five years' time the individual will be receiving a monthly income of £690. The individual also wants to know what his total income from the scheme would be over the first five years. Here we use Eq. E2.2:

$$\frac{n}{2}(2a + (n - 1)d)$$
$$\frac{60}{2}(2(100) + (59)10) = 30(200 + 590) = £23{,}700$$

That is, the individual will receive total payments of £23,700 over the five-year period.

Progress Check E2.1

For the previous scenario:

(i) What would the individual be receiving as a monthly income after four years three months?

(ii) What would the total payments received be over this period?

(Solution on p. 475)

Geometric series

Not all series we may be interested in will be arithmetic, however. Some will be geometric. This occurs where we have:

a

ar

ar^2

ar^3

ar^4

and so on where a is the initial sum and r is a common ratio (rather than difference as before). Again without proof, we state three formulae:

1   To find the nth term in such a series:

$$ar^{(n-1)}$$ (E2.3)

2   To find the sum of the first n terms:

$$\frac{a(r^n - 1)}{r - 1}$$ (E2.4)

3 To find the sum of all terms (to infinity) *provided r < 1*:

$$\frac{a}{1-r} \qquad\qquad (E2.5)$$

Note that in the case of Eq. E2.5 it is necessary to specify that $r < 1$. In such a case as n increases the value of r^n approaches zero. To illustrate the use of such a series let us return to the individual contemplating their retirement. A second investment broker has found a scheme whereby, for the same lump-sum investment, a guaranteed monthly income of £100 is provided together with an increase in each month's income of 4%. Here $a = £100$ and $r = 1.04$ (expressed as a decimal). The individual again wishes to know his monthly income from the scheme in five years' time. Using Eq. E2.3 we have:

$$ar^{(n-1)}$$

$$100(1.04^{59}) = £1011.50$$

That is, in five years' time the monthly income from the scheme would be £1011.50. Similarly, the total income up to this time would be given using Eq. E2.4:

$$\frac{a(r^n - 1)}{r - 1}$$

$$\frac{100(1.04^{60} - 1)}{1.04 - 1} = \frac{100(10.51962741 - 1)}{0.04} = £23{,}799.07$$

That is, total income up to this moment would be £23,799.07. It is clear that, in this example, we cannot apply Eq. E2.5, as $r > 1$.

Progress Check E2.2

For the previous scenario assume that the monthly increase were now 5% not 4%.

(i) What would the individual be receiving as a monthly income after five years?

(ii) What would the total payments received be over this period?

(Solution on p. 475)

E2.4 Simple and compound interest

Assume that you have the sum of £100 in a bank account, attracting an interest rate of 5% per year (per annum). The initial sum deposited – your £100 – is known as the *principal* and it is this amount on which interest will be paid at a rate of 5% per annum. At the end of the first year your account would be credited with a further £5 representing the interest. Assume that you left the money (the principal plus first-year interest) in the account for a further year. What interest would you be entitled to at the end of the second year? You would not expect the interest to be £5 again. This amount would reflect interest paid on the principal. But you have had no reward for leaving your first year's interest untouched in the account. You would expect this sum to attract interest also. The appropriate interest credited at the end of year 2 should be:

£5 which is 5% of the principal

plus £0.25 which is 5% of the interest from year 1

Table E2.1   Interest calculations: principal of £100, interest rate of 5% per annum

	Principal at start of year (£)	Interest on principal at end of year (£)
Year 1	100	5.00
Year 2	105.00	5.25
Year 3	110.25	5.51
Year 4	115.76	5.79
Year 5	121.55	6.08
Year 6	127.63	*etc.*

The interest paid should be £5.25. The same process can be applied to years 3, 4, 5 and so on. Table E2.1 shows the relevant calculations.

The table shows the initial principal sum and the interest earned at the end of each year, which is then added to the account for the following year. You should ensure that you understand the timings implicit in the table as they are critical for such interest calculations. At the end of the five-year period (which is the same as the start of year 6) the original sum of £100 will have increased to £127.63. This method of interest calculation, where the interest from one period itself earns interest, is known as *compound interest*. If interest is based only on the original principal and not on subsequent interest payments as well, it is known as *simple interest*. From such principles of compound interest we can determine a number of useful formulae. We can express the calculations in Table E2.1 as a series:

$$\text{Value at end of period} = P(1 + i)^t \tag{E2.6}$$

where

$P =$ the original principal sum
$i =$ the rate of interest expressed as a decimal per period
$t =$ the appropriate number of periods.

You will see the similarity here to the geometric series. Hence, for the example in Table E2.1 we could have calculated the value of our original sum (£100) at the end of the five-year period as:

$$\text{Value} = 100(1 + 0.05)^5$$

$$= 100(1.05)^5 = 100(1.2763) = £127.63$$

This formula allows us to calculate the future value that a principal sum invested at a given rate of interest will have grown to by a specific period. At the end of, say, a ten-year period the equivalent calculation would show that the original investment would increase to £162.89. The basic formula can be presented in a different way to perform other related calculations. Let us suppose that we wish to invest a sum now, at a rate of interest of 5% per annum, such that it will be worth £127.63 in five years' time. What sum should we invest (i.e. what principal amount)? Of course, we already know the answer from the example, but the formula would also confirm this. Rewriting the original formula, we have:

$$P = \frac{V}{(1 + i)^t} \tag{E2.7}$$

Similarly, the formula could be expressed as:

$$i = \sqrt[t]{\frac{V}{P}} - 1 \tag{E2.8}$$

to determine the rate of interest that will turn a given principal into a known value after a specified number of periods. Thus the basic formula linking the variables (P, V, i) can be used to find any of the variables once we know the others.

Progress Check E2.3

(i) In four years' time you will require £10,000 as a deposit on a house purchase. The rate of interest is currently 8%. How much should you invest now?

(ii) You have decided that you cannot afford to invest the amount determined in (i) and have only £6000 to invest. What annual rate of return do you require on your investment?

(Solution on p. 475)

E2.5 Nominal and effective interest rates

The formula derived in E2.4 for compound interest can, as we have seen, be used for any combination of P, i and t. In the example used we assumed for simplicity that interest was added to the account at the end of each year. This will not necessarily be the case. Interest may be credited semi-annually, quarterly, monthly, even daily. The same formula can still be used but in such cases we need to distinguish between the *nominal rate* and the *effective rate*. Assume that, instead of paying interest annually, an account credits the accrued interest to your account on a monthly basis. You decide to invest the principal of £100 and leave the principal and accruing interest untouched for five years. What would the final value of your account be if the annual rate of interest is 10%? We have:

$$P = £100$$

$$i = 0.8333\% \text{ per period } (10\%/12) \text{ (or } 0.008333 \text{ as a decimal)}$$

$$t = 60 \text{ (12 months for 5 years)}$$

giving

$$V = 100(1.008333)^{60} = £164.53$$

If we had calculated the accrued amount in an account adding interest only once a year the amount would be £161.05 (you should confirm this yourself from the formula in the previous section). The difference, understandably, is that interest in the first case is being added to the account more frequently and this interest will in turn attract interest for the rest of the five-year period. The quoted rate of 10% per annum is known as the *nominal* rate. The rate actually earned is known as the *effective* rate or as the *annual percentage rate* (APR), or as the *annual equivalent rate* (AER). You may well see the APR/AER figure quoted in advertisements exhorting people to borrow money or take out credit to finance their consumer purchases. The APR can be calculated directly using the formula:

$$\text{APR} = \left(1 + \frac{i}{t}\right)^t - 1 \tag{E2.9}$$

where

$$t = 60$$

$$i = 0.10 \text{ (10\% as a decimal)}.$$

$$\text{APR} = \left(1 + \frac{0.1}{60}\right)^{60} - 1$$

$$\text{APR} = (1 + 0.001666667)^{60} - 1$$

$$= 1.1051 - 1 = 0.1051 \text{ or } 10.51\%$$

The effective or annual rate of interest is, therefore, 10.51%.

Progress Check E2.4

A credit card company publicizes that it charges only 2% per month interest on any out-standing debt. What is the company's APR?

(Solution on p. 475)

E2.6 Depreciation

Depreciation can be regarded as the gradual reduction in the value of capital assets of an organization or an economy. Typically, if a firm buys, say, a computer for use in the office, then over time the value of this item will reduce. Allowance has to be made in the value for wear and tear, usage and obsolescence. It is standard accounting practice to allow for such depreciation in financial analysis and we shall examine two of the common methods of determining depreciation.

Straight-line depreciation

This is the simplest method, where the value of the asset is averaged equally over the time period in which it is used. Let us suppose that a firm has purchased a new computer-based desktop publishing system for use within the accounts department. The system has cost £20,000 and is expected to have a useful life of four years, after which it will be obsolete and will need to be replaced by an up-to-date, state-of-the-art system. At that time the system will have a scrap value of £1000. Using this method the annual depreciation is simply calculated as:

$$\frac{(\text{Current value} - \text{value at end of period})}{\text{Number of periods}}$$

Here:

Current value is £20,000
Value at end of period = £1000
Number of periods is 4.

$$\text{Annual depreciation} = \frac{20,000 - 1000}{4} = £4750$$

Effectively, the asset is worth £4750 less each year. You will be aware that it is referred to as the 'straight-line' method because we are assuming a linear function for depreciation. A graph showing the current value and the final value would be joined by a straight line and the slope of the line would give the rate of depreciation.

The reducing-balance method

This second method assumes that the value of the asset is reducing not by a constant *amount* as in the straight-line method but rather by a constant *percentage* or proportion. The relevant formula is given by:

$$D = V(1-r)^t \tag{E2.10}$$

where D is the depreciated value at the end of a particular time period, V is the initial value of the asset, r is the rate of depreciation and t is the number of time periods. By rearranging the formula (as with the compound interest formula) we can determine any of the variables in the set:

$$V = \frac{D}{(1-r)^t} \tag{E2.11}$$

and

$$r = 1 - \sqrt[t]{D/V} \tag{E2.12}$$

To illustrate let us assume, in the earlier section on straight-line depreciation, that the firm has decided to depreciate the computer at the rate of 40% a year. At the end of the first year the depreciated value will be:

End year 1 $£20,000 - 0.40(20,000) = £12,000$

That is, although the asset started off with a value of £20,000 at the start of year 2, the asset is seen as having a value of £12,000. At the end of year 2 the depreciated value will then be:

End year 2 $£12,000 - 0.40(12,000) = £7200$

Subsequent calculations are shown below:

	Depreciated value
End of year 1	£12,000
End of year 2	£7200
End of year 3	£4320
End of year 4	£2592
End of year 5	£1555.20

and so on.

The depreciated values can easily be found using the formula in Eq. E2.10. Note that with such a geometric series the value of the asset will technically never reach zero. Assume that we wished to find the rate of depreciation to be used over a four-year period. Here we would use the formula:

$$\sqrt[n]{r} = 1 - \sqrt[t]{D/V}$$

$$r = 1 - \sqrt[4]{\frac{1000}{20\,000}}$$

$$r = 1 - \sqrt[4]{0.05} = 1 - 0.4729 = 0.5271$$

That is, $r = 52.71\%$.

E

Progress Check E2.5

A company has bought manufacturing equipment for a cost of £50,000. The equipment will have a useful life of six years, after which it has a zero value.

(i) Work out the depreciation each year using the straight-line method.

(ii) Assuming a depreciation rate of 15% per year, work out the annual depreciation each year.

(Solution on p. 476)

E2.7 Present value

In assessing financial alternatives we generally wish to compare different projects or investments with a view to deciding which is 'best'. The problem frequently arises that such projects generate cash flows at different periods of time, which means that direct comparison and evaluation is not possible. Accordingly, we determine the *present value* of the cash flows – literally their current worth – in order to facilitate such comparisons. We have already established the principle of time preference. That is, *ceteris paribus*, we would prefer a sum of money now (i.e. in the present) to the same sum of money at some stage in the future. Given the choice of £100 now or £100 in a year's time we would choose the £100 now. But suppose, instead, the choice were £100 now or £110 in a year's time. Would we still choose the £100 now? To answer such a question we need to assess the present value of the future sum of money. Literally, the present value is an indication of what some future sum is worth to us now, at present. Let us assume a rate of interest of 8%. The present value (PV) of £110 in one year's time is given by:

$$PV = \frac{V}{(1+i)^t} \qquad (E2.13)$$

where

   PV is the calculated present value
   V is the value at some time in the future (here £110)
   i is the rate of interest (here 0.08)
   t is the number of periods into the future we are examining (here 1).

So the PV is given as:

$$PV = \frac{110}{(1+0.08)^1} = \frac{110}{1.08} = £101.85$$

This means that the amount of £101.85 now and the amount of £110 in one year's time are identical and equal. Given a free choice between receiving £101.85 now and £110 in one year's time we would be indifferent, *ceteris paribus*. Effectively, both are worth the same to us. It is apparent that – from the compound interest formula introduced earlier – we could invest the principal of £101.85 at 8% per annum interest and in one year's time it will have increased to £110. Returning to the original alternatives, we were offered £100 now or £110 in one year's time. Which should we take? We should choose the £110 in one year's time because its present value (£101.85) is more than the alternative present value of £100 now. Such a decision, naturally, is based only on the financial information available. Under normal business circumstances a number of other factors would also be considered before reaching a decision: the risk involved in the alternatives, the rate of interest to be used, whether the rate of interest will remain the same over the entire period, and so on. The principles involved in present value remain the same, however.

Progress Check E2.6

For the previous example, assume the rate of interest changes to 7%. Work out the new PV. How do you explain the result?

(Solution on p. 476)

E2.8 Basic investment appraisal

Let us examine the use of such present value calculations with a simple illustration. A firm is considering investing in a new machine which will save on labour costs. The machine will cost £10,000 to purchase and install and will have a useful life of five years. It is estimated that the machine will reduce labour costs by £3000 each year. The current cost of capital to the company is 10%. What advice can we give on the viability of the investment? First, in Table E2.2 let us examine the relevant cash flows (we ignore aspects of the decision relating to depreciation and tax).

At first sight the project looks viable, generating a net cash flow of + £5000. However, this takes no account of the fact that the cash outflow takes place at the start of the project while the cash inflow (in the form of savings in labour costs) occurs throughout the life of the project. To determine whether the project is worthwhile we must determine its present value: the value of the future stream of cash flows now. We can determine in Table E2.3 the PV of each year's cash flow using the PV formula in Eq. E2.13.

The second column in the table shows the net cash flows as in Table E2.2. The third column shows the discount factor $(1/(1 + i)^t)$. This is taken from the PV formula and represents the rate at which we have to discount a future value to determine its present value. The final column shows the present value of each year's net cash flow determined by multiplying the net cash flow by the discount factor. So, for example, £3000 in one year's time has a present value of £2727.30.

There are two points to be noted about these present values. First, the present value for year 0 is the same as the net cash flow. This is not surprising as this cash flow is already taking place in the present. Second, the present value of £3000 decreases the further into the future we go. Again, this is not surprising. The longer we have to wait

Table E2.2 Project cash flows

Year	Cash inflow	Cash outflow	Net cash flow
0	0	10,000	−10,000
1	3000	0	3000
2	3000	0	3000
3	3000	0	3000
4	3000	0	3000
5	3000	0	3000
Total	15,000	10,000	5000

Table E2.3 Present value of cash flows

Year	Net cash flow (£)	Discount factor $1/(1+i)^t$	Present value Cash flow * DF
0	−10,000	1.0000	−10,000
1	3000	0.9091	2727.30
2	3000	0.8264	2479.20
3	3000	0.7513	2253.90
4	3000	0.6830	2049.00
5	3000	0.6209	1862.70
Total	5000		1372.10

to receive a given cash flow, the less it is worth to us compared with the present. The total present value (known as net present value, or NPV, as it deals with net cash flows) is £1372.10. What does this mean? It means that the present value of the net cash flows shown is equal to this amount. If you like, this is the present net worth of the cash flows generated by this project. If we were given the choice of a net cash flow now of £1372.10 or a net cash flow spread over the next five years of £5000 we would have no particular preference. The NPV is positive and this indicates that, *ceteris paribus*, the project is worthwhile in that the NPV of the cash inflows is greater than the NPV of the cash outflows. Had the NPV figure been negative it would indicate the reverse: the PV of the outflows was greater than that of the inflows. Similarly, an NPV $= 0$ would indicate that the PVs of the inflows and outflows were exactly the same. Such NPVs all take account of the timing of the various flows.

Progress Check E2.7

For the project in Table E2.2, assume the cost of capital rises to 12%. How does this affect the NPV? How do you explain this effect?

(Solution on p. 476)

E2.9 Internal rate of return

Partly because of the fact that the NPV will change if the rate of interest/cost of capital changes, it is often useful to calculate the *internal rate of return* (IRR). By definition, the IRR is simply the discount rate which yields an NPV of zero for a project, that is, a discount factor that gives an NPV which is neither negative nor positive. This IRR can then be compared to the actual cost of capital to determine at what rate of interest/cost of capital the project would cease to be profitable. By way of illustration, let us return to the example of a firm buying a labour-saving machine for £10,000. Earlier we used a discount rate of 10%. Let us use, instead, a rate of 15.24% (we shall see why shortly). The relevant calculations are shown in Table E2.4.

Allowing for arithmetic rounding (the discount factors are to only four decimal places) this rate gives an NPV effectively equal to zero. This means that, at a rate of discount of 15.24%, this stream of cash flows has a zero present value: the present value of the inflows is exactly the same as that of the outflows. More useful, however, is the

Table E2.4 Discount rate 15.24%

Year	Net cash flow	Discount factor	Present value
0	−10,000	1.0000	−10,000
1	3000	0.8678	2603.40
2	3000	0.7530	2259.00
3	3000	0.6534	1960.20
4	3000	0.5670	1701.00
5	3000	0.4920	1476.00
Total	5000		−£0.40

following evaluation. At 10% the project had a positive NPV; at 15.24% a zero NPV. It is apparent that at a rate above 15.24% the NPV will be negative (the present value of the outflows greater than that of the inflows). Accordingly, if the cost of capital to fund this project is more than 15.24% the project is not worthwhile. At rates of interest/cost of capital less than this, however, the project is viable. At exactly 15.24% the project is at breakeven (in present value terms that is, not in terms of costs and revenues). Similarly, the IRR of two or more projects can be compared to determine which is 'better'.

But how is the IRR determined? How did we know that the IRR of the project above was 15.24%? One could use a computer package, but it is possible to estimate the IRR by manual methods. There are two such methods available: one graphical, one mathematical. Both require the NPV of a project at two different discount rates to generate a positive NPV and a negative NPV, and we shall illustrate the mathematical method.

In Table E2.5 the NPV for the project has been evaluated with a discount rate of 10% and again with a rate of 16%. The IRR can now be estimated using a mathematical formula:

$$IRR = R_1 + (R_2 - R_1)\frac{|NPV_1|}{|NPV_1| + |NPV_2|} \tag{E2.14}$$

where
R_1 is the discount rate used for the first NPV
R_2 is the discount rate used for the second NPV
$|NPV_1|$ is the absolute value for the first NPV
$|NPV_2|$ is the absolute value for the second NPV.

Table E2.5 Present value of cash flows with two discount rates

Year	Net cash flow (£)	Present value DF 10%	Present value DF 16%
0	−10,000	−10,000	−10,000
1	3000	2727.30	2586.21
2	3000	2479.20	2229.49
3	3000	2253.90	1921.97
4	3000	2049.00	1656.87
5	3000	1862.70	1428.34
Total	5000	1372.10	−£177.12

E

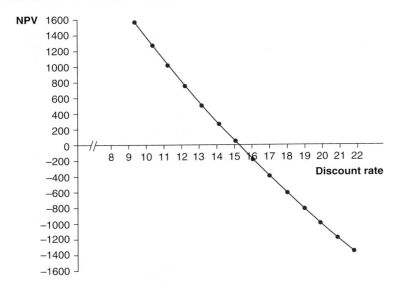

Figure E2.1 IRR

Here:

$$\text{IRR} = 10\% + (16\% - 10\%)\frac{1372.1}{(1372.1 + 177.12)}$$

$$= 10\% + 6(0.88567) = 15.3\%$$

This method should be seen as a linear approximation only to the true value of the IRR. In fact, the relationship between NPV and the discount rate is non-linear, so the approximation methods used here are valid only over small parts of the function. Figure E2.1 illustrates a range of NPV and discount rate values for this problem and the non-linear pattern is clearly evident. Accordingly, the IRR value should be treated as an approximation only and used with caution.

E2.10 Interest rates and the price of government bonds

Finally in this module we'll see how the financial analysis we have introduced helps us understand certain aspects of financial economics by looking at the relationship between interest rates in the economy and the price of government bonds. Understanding such a relationship is important in learning how global financial markets function and appreciating the principles of government monetary economic policy. A government bond is simply a financial product offered by a government, typically to financial institutions. If the government issued a new bond for, say, £1000 at 8% interest redeemable in five years' time, this simply means that you buy the bond for £1000, the government keeps your £1000 for the next five years but pays you 8% interest each year in return (obviously a fixed sum of £80), and at the end of the five years, the government repays you the £1000. It is important to appreciate that such bonds – and other financial products such as stocks and shares – are typically transferable and can be bought and sold on the open market. If you sold your government bond to someone else then the purchaser would receive all future payments from the government – the annual interest payments and the repayment of £1000. And that raises an interesting, and critical, question. How much would you be prepared to sell your bond for?

The answer for us is straightforward since we are looking at a future income stream and comparing it with a selling price now. Effectively, we would want to calculate the net present value of the future income stream from the bond. Assuming you've just bought the bond, the future income stream would be £80 per annum for the five years plus the repayment of £1000 in five years' time. Using the bond interest rate of 8% we can calculate that the bond would currently have an NPV of:

Year	Cash flow	NPV
1	£80	£74.07
2	£80	£68.59
3	£80	£63.51
4	£80	£58.80
5	£1080	£725.03
Total	£1400	£1000.00

That is, an NPV of £1000. So, you'd be prepared to sell the bond for £1000 – the NPV of the cash flow it will generate. However, assume that you think the actual interest rate in the economy over this period will average 9% per annum. Obviously your bond will still pay out £80 per annum (as agreed by the government when you bought the bond). With a change in the economy's interest rate, the NPV of the bond's cash flow will change.

Progress Check E2.8

Calculate the new NPV with an interest rate of 9%.
What price would you now be prepared to accept for selling the bond?

With a rate of now 9% the NPV changes to £961 and this would be the minimum price you would be prepared to sell at. Table E2.6 summarizes the NPV for a number of interest rates.

Table E2.6 confirms the inverse relationship between interest rates and bond prices. As interest rates rise, bond prices fall – and vice versa. However, let's return to the situation where you're expecting actual interest rates to average 9% over the life of the

Table E2.6   Present value of 8% £1000 bond redeemable in five years' time (£s)

Year	Cash flow	Interest rate % per annum					
		5	6	7	8	9	10
1	80	76.19	75.47	74.77	74.07	73.39	72.73
2	80	72.56	71.20	69.88	68.59	67.33	66.12
3	80	69.11	67.17	65.3	63.51	61.77	60.11
4	80	65.82	63.37	61.03	58.80	56.67	54.64
5	1080	846.21	807.04	770.03	735.03	701.93	670.06
PV		1129.89	1084.25	1041.10	1000.00	961.09	924.20

bond and so £961 is the minimum price at which you'd be prepared to sell. If you had sufficient confidence in your expectations you would try to sell the bond *now* (with its price of £1000) in anticipation of a rise in interest rates and a corresponding fall in the price of the bond. But would someone else be willing to pay this price? This depends on other people's expectations. If everyone else also expects interest rates to rise to 9% then no one will meet your asking price of £1000. On the other hand, if someone expected interest rates over this period to fall, they'd be happy to pay £1000 now since the future bond price will be higher. Whose expectations are correct will, of course only be known at a future date.

The relationship can also be examined from another angle by considering bonds issued not by government but also by companies wanting to raise capital. We can then consider the supply and demand relationship of bonds, as we can for any other economic good. The demand for bonds will depend, *ceteris paribus*, on the price. When bond prices are high (that is when interest rates are low), relatively few people will wish to buy. By contrast, when bond prices are low (interest rates are high), demand will be higher. The demand curve for bonds will therefore be downward sloping like that for any other product. The supply of bonds will also behave in the usual way. We can view the supply of bonds as the issuing of new bonds together with the stock of all previously issued bonds. At high rates of interest, few investment projects being considered by firms (opening a new factory for example) will be profitable, *ceteris paribus*, and so firms will issue relatively few bonds to raise capital. At low rates of interest, more projects become viable hence more new bonds are issued and the supply increases. So the supply of bonds will increase at lower rates of interest. Since lower interest rates imply higher bond prices, the implication is that the supply of bonds will increase with their price. The intersection of the bond supply and demand curves will naturally determine the equilibrium price of bonds and simultaneously the market rate of interest. This, in turn, has implications for government monetary policy. If the government monetary authorities want interest rates in the economy to rise they have to drive down the price of bonds. They can do this, of course, by increasing the supply of bonds. Conversely, if there is a desire to see interest rates fall then bond prices have to be pushed upwards. This can be achieved by increasing the demand for bonds – the government buying back bonds previously issued, for example.

E2.11 Summary

In this module we have extended the use of mathematics into the area of financial analysis and decision-making. The principles of interest calculations, depreciation and present value relate directly to many microeconomic decisions. Equally, at the macroeconomic level, policy decisions on interest rate changes, government borrowing and taxation and investment are directly influenced by the issues introduced in this module.

Learning Check

Having read this module you should have learned that:

- Time preference indicates that, *ceteris paribus*, a sum of money is preferred now rather than in the future

Learning Check (Continued)

- An arithmetic series is a sequence of numbers where the difference between any two successive numbers of the sequence is a constant
- A geometric series is a sequence of numbers with a constant ratio between successive numbers
- Simple interest is calculated only on the principal amount
- Compound interest is calculated when interest is added to the principal, so that from that moment, the interest that has been added also itself earns interest
- The effective interest rate shows the annual compound interest payable
- Present value is the value on a given date of a future payment or series of future payments
- Internal rate of return is the discount rate such that the net present value of a series of future payments equals zero.

Worked Example

You have inherited a government security as part of a relative's will. The security is a £1000 government stock at 7% per annum which is redeemable in six years' time. Effectively, what this means is that in six years' time the government will buy back the security for a price of £1000. Until then, at the end of the each year, it will pay the security owner £70 interest. If the current market rate of interest is 10%, for how much would you be prepared to sell the security now?

You have also heard a rumour that the central bank may be about to cut interest rates. How would this affect your decision on an acceptable price?

Solution

You have a security that will generate a stream of income over the next six years and you wish to ascertain its present value: the sum of money you would be prepared to accept now in exchange for the income stream in the future generated by the security. At a current interest rate of 10%, the relevant calculations are shown in the table below.

End of year	Income	Discounted income	Discount factor
1	70	63.64	0.909090
2	70	57.85	0.826446
3	70	52.59	0.751315
4	70	47.81	0.683013
5	70	43.46	0.620921
6	1070	603.99	0.564473

Worked Example *(Continued)*

At the end of each year you would receive £70 interest and additionally at the end of year 6 the government will buy back the security for £1000. In total, your income stream would be £1420. However, this is over a six-year period. By discounting (using the discount factors shown, at 10%) we can derive the discounted income stream as shown. This totals £869.34. This is the present value of the income stream from the security and would represent the minimum price you should be prepared to accept in exchange for the security (unless you are hugely in debt and require cash quickly, which will negate the usual 'rational' decision-making assumption used in economics).

If you believe the general interest rate is likely to fall, this will affect your view as to what is a 'fair' price for the security now. With a reduction in interest rates (bearing in mind that your income stream is fixed at £70 per year) then you would require a higher price, *ceteris paribus*, since you will need a larger amount in the present in order to generate the income stream shown.

Exercises

E2.1   The sum of £3100 is invested now. At a rate of interest of 12% per annum, calculate the value of the investment in ten years' time if interest is compounded:

(i)   Annually

(ii)   Quarterly

(iii)   Monthly

(iv)   Daily

(v)   Continuously.

E2.2   You know that an investment made now will mature in five years' time with a value of £750. If the current interest rate is 10%, what must you invest now to produce this maturity value? What assumptions have you made?

E2.3   You are offered one of the following:.

(i)   £100 now

(ii)   £120 in two years' time

(iii)   £150 in four years' time.

Which would you take and why? What assumptions have you made?

E2.4   A firm is considering replacing part of their computer network with the latest equipment. Two suppliers have been asked to tender for the project. The relevant costs of the project and the corresponding savings (e.g. in terms of reduced labour costs, increased efficiency) are shown in the table below

(i)   If the current rate of interest is 12%, which supplier would you recommend should be given the contract?

(ii)   What other factors would you wish to take into account before reaching a decision?

Exercises *(Continued)*

(iii) If the rate of interest were to fall, how do you think this would affect your recommendation?

(iv) For both suppliers, calculate the IRR.

(v) How could you use this information?

Year	Supplier A		Supplier B	
	Cost £	Savings £	Cost £	Savings £
Now	100,000	0	75,000	0
1	0	20,000	25,000	0
2	0	30,000	0	60,000
3	0	40,000	0	40,000
4	0	50,000	0	35,000
5	0	20,000	0	25,000

E2.5 A company is considering purchasing a labour-saving piece of equipment which will cost £40,000 and have a useful life of four years from now. Current cost of capital is 7.5%. Purchasing the machine will allow the company to cut its workforce by one person. At present average annual labour costs are £10,000 per person per year and are expected to increase by 5% per annum over the next few years.

(i) Advise the company as to whether it should purchase the machine.

(ii) At what cost of capital (%) would you change your mind about the recommendation made?

E2.6 Return to the government bond example in Section E2.10 where you had purchased an 8% £1000 government bond redeemable in five years' time. You have now held the bond for two years. You think interest rates in the economy are set to fall to 4%. What price would you sell the bond for?

Draft an explanation of your logic and thinking for your neighbour (who's not an economist).

Appendix E2 Financial calculations in Excel

E

Unsurprisingly, spreadsheets like Excel are essential for more complex financial calculations. It is quite easy to build spreadsheet models to automatically perform all the financial calculations we've done in this module (and that we'll be doing in the next). Alternatively, Excel has a large number of inbuilt financial formulae that require only the specification of appropriate parameters for the problem under examination. The more common of these are shown below.

Some of the content in this topic may not be applicable to some languages.

Function	Description
ACCRINT	Returns the accrued interest for a security that pays periodic interest
ACCRINTM	Returns the accrued interest for a security that pays interest at maturity
CUMIPMT	Returns the cumulative interest paid between two periods
CUMPRINC	Returns the cumulative principal paid on a loan between two periods
DB	Returns the depreciation of an asset for a specified period by using the fixed-declining balance method
DDB	Returns the depreciation of an asset for a specified period by using the double-declining balance method or some other method that you specify
DISC	Returns the discount rate for a security
EFFECT	Returns the effective annual interest rate
FV	Returns the future value of an investment
FVSCHEDULE	Returns the future value of an initial principal after applying a series of compound interest rates
IPMT	Returns the interest payment for an investment for a given period
IRR	Returns the internal rate of return for a series of cash flows
ISPMT	Calculates the interest paid during a specific period of an investment
NOMINAL	Returns the annual nominal interest rate
NPER	Returns the number of periods for an investment
NPV	Returns the net present value of an investment based on a series of periodic cash flows and a discount rate
PMT	Returns the periodic payment for an annuity
PPMT	Returns the payment on the principal for an investment for a given period
PV	Returns the present value of an investment
RATE	Returns the interest rate per period of an annuity
SLN	Returns the straight-line depreciation of an asset for one period
SYD	Returns the sum-of-years' digits depreciation of an asset for a specified period
VDB	Returns the depreciation of an asset for a specified or partial period by using a declining balance method
XIRR	Returns the internal rate of return for a schedule of cash flows that is not necessarily periodic
XNPV	Returns the net present value for a schedule of cash flows that is not necessarily periodic
YIELD	Returns the yield on a security that pays periodic interest
YIELDDISC	Returns the annual yield for a discounted security; for example, a Treasury bill
YIELDMAT	Returns the annual yield of a security that pays interest at maturity

The example below shows how Excel has been used to work out the internal rate of return (cell B13) for the cash flow in cells B6:B11 (we did this manually in Table E2.4).

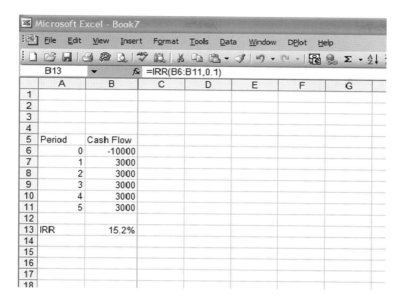

E

Module E3

Financial analysis II: annuities, sinking funds and growth models

In the previous module we looked at the ideas behind interest and present value. In this module we look at annuities and sinking funds – particular aspects of financial mathematics that help us understand how financial markets operate at both the micro- and macroeconomic level. We also look at the principles of growth models in economics.

Learning Objectives

By the end of this module you should be able to:

- Calculate values for an annuity
- Calculate values for a sinking fund
- Apply a number of economic growth models using the exponential function.

E3.1 Annuities

An *annuity* is a term for a series of fixed equal payments or receipts made at specified periods of time. Annuities (although they aren't always called this) can take many forms: payments of wages or salaries, repayments of loans, consumer credit repayments, repayments on mortgages, payments of insurance premiums and so on are all common examples. Calculations involving annuities use some of the formulae we explored in Module E2:

1 Eq. E2.6: Value of future amount $= P(1+i)^t$

2 Eq. E2.4: Sum of terms in a geometric progression $= \dfrac{a(r^n - 1)}{r - 1}$

3 Eq. E2.13: Present value $= \dfrac{V}{(1+i)^t}$

We shall examine a number of typical applications of annuities. Before doing so, however, it is necessary to be aware of a number of differing features of annuities:

1   The **term** of an annuity may be defined as:

   • Certain if it starts and ends on given fixed dates
   • Contingent if it depends on some event that cannot be fixed in time (e.g. insuring against a person's death).

2   The annuities may be paid/received:

   • On an **ordinary** basis if they are paid/received at the end of the payment intervals
   • On a **due** basis if they are paid/received at the beginning of payment periods.

3   An annuity may also carry on indefinitely: this is known as a *perpetual annuity*.

It is important to establish exactly which type of annuity is applicable to a given problem. To begin with, we shall concentrate on annuities that are due and certain.

E3.2 The value of an annuity

Let us suppose that a firm offers its employees the opportunity to invest part of their wages and salaries in an investment scheme. At the start of each year, for five years, an employee will pay the scheme £1000. This will be invested on his or her behalf and is expected to earn 8% per annum. The employee wishes to know what the investment is worth on an annual basis. Although this is similar to a compound interest problem, the difference is that the principal sum does not remain constant: £1000 is added to the scheme every year. However, the basic calculation is straightforward. We are dealing here with an annuity which is certain and due. The first payment, invested at the start of year 1, will attract interest for the first year at 8% per annum. This gives:

$$£1000(1.08) = £1080.00$$

Similarly, the second premium of £1000 will be added to this amount at the start of year 2. All this will now attract interest of 8% during year 2 to give:

$$£2080(1.08) = £2246.40$$

We could progress in the same way through the remainder of the period to produce the results shown in Table E3.1. At the end of five years, therefore, the fund contains

Table E3.1   Annuity value

Year	Premium (£)	Total in fund at start of year (£)	Interest (8%) (£)	Total in fund at end of year (t)
1	1000	1000.00	80.00	1080.00
2	1000	2080.00	166.40	2246.40
3	1000	3246.40	259.71	3506.11
4	1000	4506.11	360.49	4866.60
5	1000	5866.60	469.33	6335.93

£6335.93. In the same way we could use the geometric progression approach. The first payment will attract interest for the full five years:

$£1000(1.08)^5$
The second for 4 years: $£1000(1.08)^4$
The third for 3 years: $£1000(1.08)^3$
The fourth for 2 years: $£1000(1.08)^2$
The last for one year: $£1000(1.08)$.

Collecting these together we have:

$£1000[1.08 + 1.08^2 + 1.08^3 + 1.08^4 + 1.08^5]$

where the term in the square brackets is evidently a geometric progression with a at 1.08 and r at 1.08. Using the formula to find the sum of a geometric series we then have:

$$\text{Sum} = \frac{1.08(1.08)^5 - 1)}{1.08 - 1} = 6.33593$$

giving $£1000(6.33593) = £6335.93$. That is, the scheme would have a value of £6335.93 at the end of the 5 years. In general we have:

$$\text{Sum of an annuity} = \text{Payment} \frac{[a(r^n - 1)]}{r - 1} \tag{E3.1}$$

Progress Check E3.1

You have finished your college degree but you're £7500 in debt to your bank. You've been lucky enough to get your first job as an economist, and the bank manager has indicated that you can repay your debt with an annuity scheme. You propose to put £1500 a year into an investment scheme that should pay 4% interest per annum. Will you have enough to repay the debt after 4 years?

(Solution on p. 476)

Sum of an ordinary annuity

The appropriate formula for the sum of an ordinary annuity can be derived in the same way. Remember that ordinary annuities are paid/received at the end of the period, not at the beginning, like the due annuity. The relevant formula is then:

$$\text{Sum} = \text{Payment} \left[\frac{(1 + i)^t - 1}{i} \right] \tag{E3.2}$$

For example, assume that you are investing in an annuity for five years of £1000 at a rate of 10%, the sum to be invested at the end of each year. The corresponding final value will then be:

$$\text{Sum} = 1000 \left[\frac{(1.1)^5 - 1}{0.1} \right] = 1000(6.1051) = £6105.10$$

Progress Check E3.2

Assume the annuity in Progress Check E3.1 is now an ordinary annuity. Repeat your calculations.

(Solution on p. 476)

E3.3 NPV of an annuity

People often wish to determine the present value of an annuity – what is the present value of a future stream of annuity receipts? Assume that an employee who has retired from the firm has certain pension rights. These rights involve receipt of an annual income of £20,000 a year for the next ten years. Assume that the employee receives the payments at the start of the periods. We wish to determine the PV of this due, certain annuity. Let us assume a discount rate of 10%. It is apparent that the series of income receipts could be discounted individually:

	Receipt	PV
Start	£20,000	£20,000
Year 2	£20,000	$£\dfrac{20,000}{1.10}$
Year 3	£20,000	$£\dfrac{20,000}{1.10^2}$
Year 4	£20,000	$£\dfrac{20,000}{1.10^3}$

and so on through the series. This could be presented as:

$$\text{Sum of PV} = £20,000 \left(1 + \frac{1}{1.1} + \frac{1}{1.1^2} + \frac{1}{1.1^3} \ldots \right)$$

It is also apparent that we have a geometric series in the PV calculations with $a = 1$ and $r = 0.9091$.

To calculate the sum of such a series we have:

$$\text{Sum} = \frac{1(0.9091^{10} - 1)}{0.9091 - 1} = 6.759$$

$$\text{Sum of PV} = £20,000(6.759) = £135,180$$

The interpretation of this result is the same as for any present value calculation. This sum represents the value now of the stream of annuity income over the next ten years. In general we would have:

$$\text{PV} = \frac{P[1(r^t - 1)]}{r - 1} \tag{E3.3}$$

Present value of an ordinary annuity

Similarly, the formula for the PV of an ordinary annuity is given as:

$$\text{PV} = P\left[\frac{1 - 1/(1 + i)^t}{i}\right] \tag{E3.4}$$

and the present value is interpreted in the same way as any other PV result.

E

Progress Check E3.3

An elderly relative has died but has remembered you in their will. You will receive £500 at the start of each year for the next 20 years. Assuming an average rate of interest of 3%:

Progress Check E3.3 *(Continued)*

(i) What is the PV of this annuity?

(ii) Assume the annuity is now paid as an ordinary annuity. What is the new PV?

(Solution on p. 476)

E3.4 Repayment annuity

Annuity calculations are often applied to repayment of debt. For a sum of money borrowed for a fixed period of time, a certain and due annuity can be used to repay both capital and interest. Such a series of repayments is sometimes known as an *amortization annuity*. Typically, the problem faced relates to determining the periodic payment in order to repay the sum borrowed plus related interest in a stated number of periods. Assume that a firm offers its employees a mortgage facility whereby the employee can borrow money to purchase a house. One individual has borrowed £20,000. The rate of interest is 10% and the loan (and interest) is to be repaid over the next ten years. To calculate the annual payment needed to pay off the debt we can use the following approach.

If we denote the repayments as V, r as the rate of interest and the amount initially borrowed as P then we can relate P to the present value of the future stream of repayments:

$$P = \frac{V}{(1+i)} + \frac{V}{(1+i)^2} + \frac{V}{(1+i)^3} + \ldots + \frac{V}{(1+i)^t}$$

This can be rewritten as:

$$P = V\left[\frac{1}{(1+i)} + \frac{1}{(1+i)^2} + \frac{1}{(1+i)^3} + \ldots + \frac{1}{(1+i)^{10}}\right]$$

and the term in square brackets is seen to be a geometric series with a and r both equal to $1/(1+i)$. So here, with a rate of interest at 0.10, we have $1/(1+i) = 0.9091$ to give:

$$\frac{0.9091(0.9091^{10} - 1)}{0.9091 - 1} = 6.144567105$$

So with:

$$P = V\left[\frac{1}{(1+i)} + \frac{1}{(1+i)^2} + \frac{1}{(1+i)^3} + \ldots + \frac{1}{(1+i)^{10}}\right]$$

we have £20,000 = $V(6.144567105)$ to give $V = £3254.91$. That is, £3254.91 must be paid each year for 10 years to repay both the principal sum borrowed and the interest on the amount outstanding.

Frequently, it is necessary and useful to draw up a period repayment schedule to confirm the detailed payments, as in Table E3.2. Allowing for arithmetic rounding, it can be seen that the annual payment of £3254.91 repays the principal sum and the interest charged on the loan.

E3.5 Sinking funds

A *sinking fund* is another common method of debt repayment. If a sum of money is borrowed at a given rate of interest for a fixed period of time then the total amount

Table E3.2 Repayment annuity calculations

Year	Debt	Interest	Debt + interest	Payment made	Amount owing	Principal repaid
1	20,000.00	2000.00	22,000.00	3254.91	18,745.09	1254.91
2	18,745.09	1874.51	20,619.60	3254.91	17,364.69	1380.40
3	17,364.69	1736.47	19,101.16	3254.91	15,846.25	1518.44
4	15,846.25	1584.63	17,430.88	3254.91	14,175.97	1670.28
5	14,175.97	1417.60	15,593.57	3254.91	12,338.66	1837.31
6	12,339.66	1233.97	13,572.53	3254.91	10,317.62	2020.94
7	10,317.62	1031.76	11,349.38	3254.91	8094.47	2223.15
8	8094.47	809.45	8903.92	3254.91	5649.01	2445.46
9	5649.01	564.90	6213.91	3254.91	2959.00	2690.01
10	2959.00	295.90	3254.90	3254.91	−0.01	2959.01
Total		12,549.19		32,549.10		19,999.91

owing at the end of the period is easily calculated. An annuity can then be arranged with regular payments such that the value of the annuity at the end of the fixed time period is just sufficient to repay the debt. Such a scheme is known as a sinking fund. For example, let us consider an individual who takes out a mortgage of £200,000 over ten years at a rate of interest of 10%. She wishes to invest regularly in an investment scheme paying a rate of 12% per annum in order to use the proceeds from the scheme to repay the mortgage loan with a lump sum at the end of the period. How much per year should she invest in the scheme? At the end of ten years the person will owe the following amount in relation to the mortgage debt (principal plus interest):

$$200,000(1 + 0.10)^{10} = £518,748$$

The proceeds from the investment scheme must equal this sum in order to ensure repayment of both principal and accrued interest. It is clear that the investment scheme (the sinking fund) represents a geometric series. Using the appropriate formula to find the sum of such a series we have:

$$\text{Sum} = \frac{1.12(1.12^{10} - 1)}{1.12 - 1} = 19.65458328$$

Here $V = P(19.65458328)$ where V must equal £518,748 in ten years' time. This gives a value for P of £26,393.33. This is the annual amount to be invested in the sinking fund to generate the amount needed to repay the loan in ten years' time.

E3.6 The mathematical constant e and rates of growth

In section A2.3 we introduced the concept of a function. One of the types of function that we briefly examined was the general exponential function, together with a specific type of exponential function involving the mathematical constant e. We return to this type of function to examine its general principles and consider its use in economics in general and financial mathematics in particular. You will recollect that the general form of an exponential function is given by:

$$Y = a^X \tag{E3.5}$$

where $a > 1$. We also saw that one specific type of exponential function involved the mathematical constant e and took the form:

$$Y = ae^{bX} \tag{E3.6}$$

where a and b are the relevant numerical parameters. We shall now examine this function in more detail. We saw earlier that the mathematical constant e is given the value of approximately 2.71828. We did not at the time try to justify how this value had arisen. While we cannot provide a definitive mathematical proof we can illustrate the basic concepts. Consider a function:

$$Y = f(X) = \left(1 + \frac{1}{X}\right)^X \tag{E3.7}$$

Let us examine what happens as the value of X increases.

X	Function	Y
1	$\left(1 + \frac{1}{1}\right)^1$	2
2	$\left(1 + \frac{1}{2}\right)^2$	2.25
3	$\left(1 + \frac{1}{3}\right)^3$	2.37037
10	$\left(1 + \frac{1}{10}\right)^{10}$	2.59374
100	$\left(1 + \frac{1}{100}\right)^{100}$	2.70481
1000	$\left(1 + \frac{1}{1000}\right)^{1000}$	2.71692
10000	$\left(1 + \frac{1}{10,000}\right)^{10\,000}$	2.71815

It can be seen that as we take increasingly larger values of X then the Y values increase, but at a decreasing rate. In fact as X increases indefinitely Y will converge to the number $2.71828\ldots$ which, for convenience, we denote as e, the exponential constant. The principle behind this is visible in Fig. E3.1, which shows Y for successively larger values of X. In fact the value for $(1 + 1/X)^X$ will converge to e for any initial value for X.

Progress Check E3.4

(i) Take the initial value of X as 13.6. Calculate the value for Y using Eq. E3.7. Gradually increase X by a factor of 10 and find Y. Confirm that Y converges to e as X increases.

(ii) Choose your own initial value for X. Increase this in whatever size steps you wish and confirm that Y converges to e.

A spreadsheet is recommended for this activity.

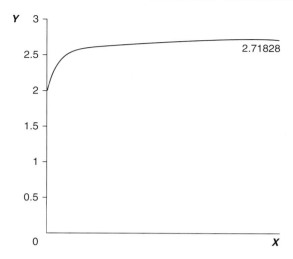

Figure E3.1 $(1 + 1/X)^X$

In general, therefore, we can define e as:

$$e = \lim_{X \to \infty} \left(1 + \frac{1}{X}\right)^X \approx 2.71828 \tag{E3.8}$$

indicating that as X approaches infinity the value of the function approximates to 2.71828 no matter what the value of X. It will be worth considering an application of the use of e in economics. Consider that we have invested a sum of money, say £100, in a bank account which pays interest of 10% annum. After one year the investment will be worth:

$$100 + 100(10\%) = 100(1 + 0.1) = £110$$

That is, the sum will have increased by 10%. If we left this amount invested then after a further year its value would be:

$$100 + 110(10\%) = 110(1 + 0.1) = £121$$

and we could clearly carry on calculating the value of the investment for further future time periods. However, let us begin to generalize. If we denote the initial investment as V_0 and the rate of interest as i (denoted as a decimal or fraction), then we have:

$$V_1 = V_0(1 + i) \tag{E3.9}$$
$$V_2 = V_1(1 + i) \tag{E3.10}$$

However, substituting Eq. E3.9 into Eq. E3.10 we have:

$$V_2 = [V_0(1 + i)](1 + i) = V_0(1 + i)^2$$

or in general

$$V_t = V_0(1 + i)^t \tag{E3.11}$$

where Eq. E3.11 allows us to work out the value in any period t of some initial investment V_0 at a given rate of interest.

You may be asking how this relates back to e, given that we may not be specifically interested in evaluating how an initial sum of money invested increases over time with a specified rate of interest. It will be evident that this general principle is readily applied

E

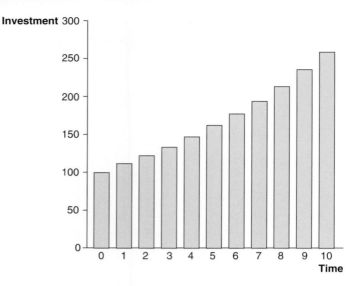

Figure E3.2 Yearly interest: $V_0 = 100$, $i = 0.1$

to any economic variable where we wish to be able to calculate the rate of growth. If, for example, we knew that investment in the economy was growing by 3% per year, then we can calculate the effect on total investment in, say, five years' time. We have made the assumption thus far, however, that in our monetary example the interest earned is added to the amount invested once each year; that is, the growth in the variable occurs at one specific moment in time. Figure E3.2 illustrates the general principles.

We see that once each year the value of the variable takes a step upwards (the size of the step, of course, determined by i). Consider the effect if interest on the investment were added not once each year but twice: say at six-monthly intervals. Equation E3.11 would now have to be amended to:

$$V_t = V_0 \left(1 + \frac{i}{2}\right)^{2t}$$

Note that we divide the interest rate, i, by two. In our example, the initial investment of £100 will earn interest of £5 for the first six months (i.e. half of 10%) and then 5% on £105 (=£110.25) at the end of the next six months and so on through time (hence the term $2t$). The general effect on the growth of the variable will be as shown in Fig. E3.3. The steps upwards in the value of the variable now occur at twice the frequency but, naturally, the size of each step is smaller than before. Continuing the logical process, if we consider that interest is now added quarterly the relevant equation becomes:

$$V_t = V_0 \left(1 + \frac{i}{4}\right)^{4t}$$

and the growth of the variables is as shown in Fig. E3.5. In general, therefore, we can calculate such changes with:

$$V_t = V_0 \left(1 + \frac{i}{n}\right)^{nt} \tag{E3.12}$$

where n refers to the number of times per year interest is added to the investment. It will be evident from the three figures we have examined that as n gets larger (i.e. as

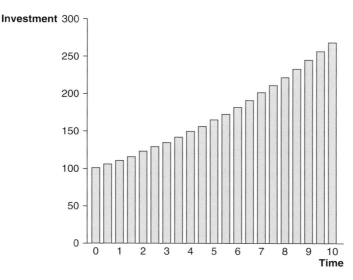

Figure E3.3 Semi-annual interest: $V_0 = 100$, $i = 0.1$

we add interest more frequently to the investment) the step changes in the variable get closer and closer together. If we allow n to tend to infinity, then the growth path of the variable will effectively become smooth and we can regard the value of the investment as changing *continuously* over time (rather than at discrete periods as we have up to now). We can also transform Eq. E3.12:

$$V_t = V_0 \left(1 + \frac{i}{n} \right)^{nt}$$

$$= V_0 \left[\left(1 + \frac{i}{n} \right)^{n/i} \right]^{it}$$

and letting $m = n/i$ gives

$$V_t = V_0 \left[\left(1 + \frac{1}{m} \right)^{m} \right]^{it}$$

However, if we allow $n \to \infty$ then $m \to \infty$ and we then have, through Eq. E3.8:

$$V_t = V_0 e^{it} \tag{E3.13}$$

or in general

$$Y = A e^{it} \tag{E3.14}$$

This indicates that if a variable has an initial value of A and grows continuously at a rate of i per year then its value after t years will be given by Y in Eq. E3.14.

While the compound interest formula (and its derivatives) is useful for financial mathematics applications, the continuous rate formula in Eq. E3.14 is useful in many economic models where the assumption that a variable changes continuously over time is an important one.

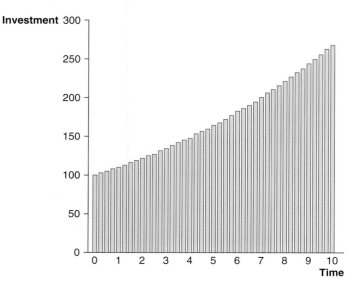

Figure E3.4 Quarterly interest: $V_0 = 100$, $i = 0.1$

Progress Check E3.5

Assume that investment in the economy is currently £250 billion and is estimated to grow at 3% per annum over the next five years on a continuous basis. Determine the total investment at the end of each of the next five years and hence derive the change in investment that has taken place each year.

(Solution on p. 476)

E3.7 Calculus and e

It will be useful to consider the application of both differential and integral calculus to the exponential function we have introduced. In general we have the function:

$$Y = Ae^{ix}$$

Let us begin with a simple example of:

$$Y = e^X$$

This implies that $X = \ln Y$ (since $\ln e = 1$) and recollects the derivative rule we introduced in Module C2.3 that:

If $Z = f(W) = \ln W$

then $f'(W) = 1/W$

In the case of our example we have $X = \ln Y$; hence $dX/dY = 1/Y$. Let us now consider the derivative of the exponential function $Y = e^X$:

$$\frac{dY}{dX} = \frac{1}{dX/dY} = \frac{1}{1/Y} = e^X$$

That is, the derivative of the exponential function is the exponential function! This turns out to be a useful property. If we now have:

$$Y = Ae^X$$

then

$$f'(X) = Ae^X \tag{E3.15}$$

and if we have

$$Y = Ae^{iX}$$

then if we let $u(X) = iX$ we have

$$Y = Ae^u$$

and via the chain rule and Eq. E3.15 we have

$$\frac{dY}{dX} = \frac{dY}{du}\frac{du}{dX} = Ae^u i = iAe^{iX} \tag{E3.16}$$

It is now a simple task to consider the integration of exponential functions. Since:

$$f'(e^X) = e^X \quad \text{then} \quad \int e^X dX = e^X + c \tag{E3.17}$$

where, as usual, we have to allow for a constant, c, in the integration process. These principles allow us to sketch exponential functions fairly readily. Consider the function which we can sketch as shown in Fig. E3.5:

$$Y = f(X) = 5e^{3X}$$

Then:

$$f'(X) = 15e^{3X}$$

and

$$f''(X) = 45e^{3X}$$

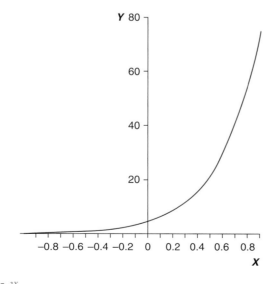

Figure E3.5 $Y = 5e^{3X}$

We know that the intercept of this function will be 5 ($= A$ when $X = 0$). Equally, we see that as X increases ($\to \infty$) then Y will also increase, but that when X takes larger negative values ($\to \infty$) then Y will tend to zero. Looking at the first derivative (showing the slope of the function) we see that this must be positive for all values of X while the second derivative indicates that the rate of change of the slope is positive for all values of X also. This implies that the slope (i.e. the first derivative) is increasing with X. Logically, therefore, this must give us the sketch that we have in Fig. E3.5.

E3.8 Rates of growth

One of the main areas of application of such functions to economic analysis is through models involving growth or change of some kind. We have already seen how the basic exponential formula can be used to calculate the future value of some variable, given its current level and a rate of growth. Let us consider the following. We have some economic variable, Y, such that:

$$Y_t = Y_0 e^{it}$$

The variable in question could relate, for example, to the labour supply, the capital stock or any variable that we would expect to change over time. It will be useful to consider r, the rate of change. We see that:

$$\frac{dY_t}{dt} = r\, Y_0 e^{rt} = r(Y_t) \tag{E3.18}$$

where dY_t/dt is the rate of change in the Y variable over time. However, we can define the proportional rate of change as:

$$\frac{dY_t/dt}{Y_t}$$

which can be expressed as

$$\frac{1}{Y_t}\frac{dY_t}{dt}$$

and, therefore, for any given period of time t the proportional rate of growth in Y is given as

$$\frac{1}{Y_t}\frac{dY_t}{dt} = \frac{rY_t}{Y_t} = r \tag{E3.19}$$

and we see that Y grows at a constant, proportional rate over time. We can go one stage further and use the exponential relationship to quantify the (continuous) rate of change that has occurred in some variable over time. Consider the following.

We observe that the capital stock now is £300 billion. Four years previously the capital stock was £250 billion. Assuming a continuous rate of change, what has been the rate of growth in the capital stock per year over this period? We have:

$$Y = Ae^{rt}$$

Hence:

$$300 = 250 e^{4r}$$

and rearranging to solve for r gives a general expression of

$$r = \frac{\ln(Y/A)}{t} = \frac{\ln(300/250)}{4} = 0.0456$$

This gives a rate of change of 4.56% per year over this period.

As a final example let us consider the following situation. We have:

$$Z = f(X, Y)$$

where

$$X = f(t)$$
$$Y = g(t)$$

and both X and Y grow exponentially at a rate of r for X and s for Y; that is:

$$X = X_0 e^{rt}$$

and

$$Y = Y_0 e^{st}$$

We then have:

$$dZ = \frac{\partial Z}{\partial X} dX + \frac{\partial Z}{\partial Y} dY$$

and hence we can express the rate of change in Z over time as

$$\frac{dZ}{dt} = \frac{\partial Z}{\partial X} \frac{dX}{dt} + \frac{\partial Z}{\partial Y} \frac{dY}{dt} \tag{E3.20}$$

However, we know from the exponential growth functions for X and Y that:

$$r = \frac{1}{X} \frac{dX}{dt} \quad \text{and hence} \quad \frac{dX}{dt} = rX$$

$$s = \frac{1}{Y} \frac{dY}{dt} \quad \text{and hence} \quad \frac{dY}{dt} = sY$$

From Eq. E3.20 we then have:

$$\frac{dZ}{dt} = \frac{\partial Z}{\partial X} rX + \frac{\partial Z}{\partial Y} sY$$

If we now require the proportionate rate of growth in Z we seek:

$$\frac{dZ/dt}{Z}$$

which gives

$$\frac{1}{Z} \frac{dZ}{dt} = \frac{1}{Z} \frac{\partial Z}{\partial X} rX + \frac{1}{Z} \frac{\partial Z}{\partial Y} sY \tag{E3.21}$$

Let us examine the term:

$$\frac{1}{Z} \frac{\partial Z}{\partial X} rX$$

and rearrange to

$$r \frac{\partial Z}{\partial X} \frac{X}{Z}$$

On reflection the term following r can be understood as the elasticity of Z with respect to X (given that we are considering proportionate changes in both Z and X)

and the equivalent expression for Y as the elasticity of Z with respect to Y. In general, therefore, we have:

$$\frac{1}{Z}\frac{dZ}{dt} = rE_x + sE_y \tag{E3.22}$$

From this we conclude that if X and Y are growing at their respective exponential rates and if the elasticities remain constant over time then Z will grow exponentially at the rate indicated in Eq. E3.22. Let us now consider an economic model. Assume a Cobb–Douglas production function:

$$Q = AL^{\alpha}K^{\beta}$$

and you will recollect that α and β represent the elasticities of output respectively of labour and capital. If we now assume that labour and capital are growing exponentially at rates r and s respectively, we now know that output will be growing at a rate of:

$$\alpha r + \beta s$$

Further, if we assumed that $r = s$ (that both labour and capital were changing at the same rate) and that the production function operated under constant returns to scale $(\alpha + \beta = 1)$ then output would be growing at the same exponential rate as labour and capital:

$$(\alpha + \beta)r = r$$

E3.9 Summary

Annuities and sinking funds lie at the heart of many activities in the financial markets, and understanding the principles of how they work and how they are calculated is important. Equally, much of economic analysis focuses on rates of growth and change. Understanding how exponential functions can be used in such economic models is essential.

Learning Check

Having read this module you should have learned that:

- An annuity is a series of fixed payments over a specified period of time
- An annuity may be certain, contingent, or perpetual. An annuity may also be due or ordinary
- A sinking fund is a fund or account into which money is deposited on a regular basis in order to repay a debt or other liability that will become due in the future
- A variety of economic growth models can be developed using exponential functions.

Worked Example

You have won first prize in a national competition run by a famous publishing company. You can take the prize of £100,000 now. Alternatively you can choose

Worked Example *(Continued)*

to receive £15,000 a year for the next ten years. Current interest rates are 3% per annum. Which would you choose and why?

You have a view that long-term interest rates over the next ten years are likely to average around 5%. How would this affect your decision?

Solution

The second option is effectively an annuity. To compare the two options you need to work out the present value of the annuity option and compare it with the £100,000 you could have now. If we assume a due annuity then Eq. E3.3 is appropriate:

$$PV = P\left(\frac{1(r^t - 1)}{r - 1}\right)$$

The relevant values are:

$P = £15000$

$r = 1/1.03 = 0.9709$

$t = 10$

Substituting and solving gives:

$$PV = 15000\frac{[1(0.9709^{10} - 1)]}{0.9709 - 1} = £131792$$

Clearly, the PV of the annuity outweighs the option of £100,000 now.

A rise in interest rates will generally lead to a fall in the PV. If we assume an interest rate of 5% over the whole of the next ten years then the PV of the annuity falls to £121,617.

Exercises

E3.1 You invest in an annuity paying a rate of 5% per annum. If you invest £500 per year, determine:

(i) The value after five years

(ii) The PV after five years.

E3.2 Assume for Ex. E3.1 that the annuity is now ordinary. Repeat the calculations and explain why the PV has changed.

E3.3 You have borrowed £10,000 from the bank at a rate of interest of 12%, the loan to be repaid over ten years.

(i) Determine the annual repayments.

(ii) Draw up a repayment schedule.

(iii) You wish to repay the loan via a sinking fund paying interest at 15%. Draw up a schedule of the sinking fund payments.

Exercises *(Continued)*

E3.4   A family are considering the cost of sending their child to university in ten years' time. They expect average interest rates to be 6%.

(i)   If they invest £2500 per year, how much will they have at the end of ten years?

(ii)   They estimate they will need £50,000 to send their child to university. How much will they need to invest annually?

(iii)   How much would they need to invest monthly?

Module E4
An introduction to dynamics

As we saw in the previous module, a number of interesting avenues of economic analysis begin to appear once we consider economic models over *time* rather than in a *static* position, as we have largely done up to now. Our analysis so far, in considering market equilibrium, for example, or macroeconomic equilibrium, has focused upon determining the change in equilibrium that occurs when the model we are examining changes. So, for example, if the intercept of the demand function alters, how will this affect equilibrium price and quantity? If marginal propensity to consume changes, how will this affect national income equilibrium? However, there is another related aspect to this: *how* do we move from one equilibrium position to another over time? Given that we may have an equilibrium now and a change in the model structure occurs, how do we reach the future new equilibrium position? It is this type of question that the area of economic dynamics tries to answer. In this module we shall introduce the basics of dealing with dynamic situations.

Learning Objectives

By the end of this module you should be able to:

- Find the solution to a difference equation
- Determine the stability of an economic model
- Solve common dynamic economic models.

E4.1 Difference equations

Let us examine the simplest macroeconomic model – with no government sector, no foreign trade and a simple equilibrium determined by:

$$Y = C + I \tag{E4.1}$$

It will be more appropriate, however, since we are concerned with changes over time, to ensure that we can identify the time period relevant to each variable. So we rewrite Eq. E4.1 as:

$$Y_t = C_t + I_t \tag{E4.2}$$

E

and we make the usual assumption that I_t is exogenous. All we are saying here is that income in period t is the sum of consumption in period t and investment in period t. Let us further define a consumption function such that:

$$C_t = a + bY_{t-1} \tag{E4.3}$$

This is different from the functions we have used before. We are saying here that consumption in the current period t is made up of an autonomous element, a, and an element that is determined from the income in the previous period $t - 1$. This is not unrealistic since we can logically argue that, from the perspective of the individual consumer, consumption spending will be influenced by past income since present income may not yet be known. My consumption expenditure this month is determined, *ceteris paribus*, by my income last month. Substituting Eq. E4.3 into Eq. E4.2 we then have:

$$Y_t = a + bY_{t-1} + I_t \tag{E4.4}$$

Equation E4.4 is referred to as a *difference equation* (since the equation relates to two [or more] periods of time). Equation E4.4 is technically known as a *first-order* difference equation since there is a difference of one period between the various elements of the equation. If, for example, we had specified a consumption function of the form:

$$C_t = a + bY_{t-1} + cY_{t-2}$$

we would have a *second-order* difference equation. We also have a linear difference equation (for the obvious reason) in Eq. E4.4. It will be useful to consider a numerical example of the model in Eq. 4.4 to examine its behaviour over time. Let us assume that I is fixed at 500, that a is 1000 and that b (the marginal propensity to consume) is 0.7. We then have:

$$Y_t = 1500 + 0.7Y_{t-1} \tag{E4.5}$$

If we wish to calculate Y_t, then clearly we require a value for Y_{t-1}. Let us assume an initial value, Y_0, of 3000. We then have:

$$Y_1 = 1500 + 0.7(3000) = 3600$$

Having obtained Y_1 we can proceed to calculate $Y_2, Y_3, \ldots, Y_{t-n}$. Shown below are the relevant results for the first few values of t:

Y_0	3000
Y_1	3600
Y_2	4020
Y_3	4314
Y_4	4520
Y_5	4664
.	
.	
.	
Y_{20}	4998.4
.	
.	
Y_{30}	4999.96

and it is apparent that over time the value for Y is approaching 5000 – that is, as $t \to \infty$ then $Y_t \to 5000$. Figures E4.1 and E4.2 show the movement of the variable over the first 30 periods. Figure E4.1 shows the value for Y in each period while Fig. E4.2 shows the change between successive periods. It is apparent that by period 20, successive values of Y are changing only in terms of their last few decimal places. (It will be apparent from the analysis we undertook earlier in the text into the multiplier process how and why

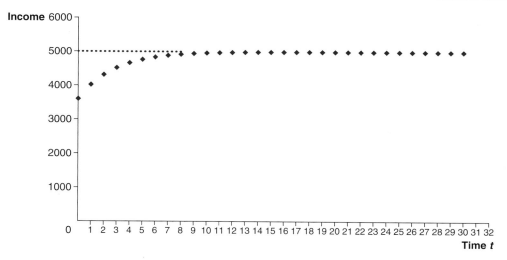

Figure E4.1 Income over time

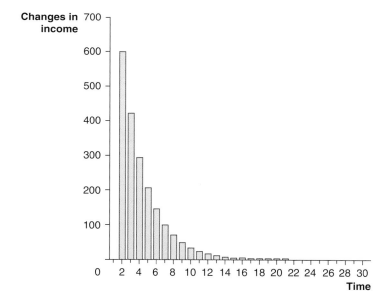

Figure E4.2 Changes in income

this is occurring.) It is clear, however, that we cannot rely on such a clumsy calculation approach to examine the behaviour of the model over time. We evidently require a suitable mathematical approach comparable to that which we examined in the previous module when re-examining exponential functions.

E4.2 The equilibrium position

If an equilibrium position for Y exists then we can assume that, once attained in a particular period, the equilibrium will be repeated in successive periods (assuming no further changes are introduced in any of the model parameters or exogenous values). In other words, once the model has reached an equilibrium we assume this to be a stable position, *ceteris paribus*. If we denote the equilibrium as Y^* then we have:

$$Y_t = Y^* = Y_{t-1}$$

and so

$$Y_t = Y_{t-1}$$

We then have:

$$Y^* = 1500 + 0.7Y^*$$

which can be solved in the usual way to give $Y^* = 5000$. In general, if we have a difference equation of the form:

$$Y_t = \alpha + \beta Y_{t-1} \tag{E4.6}$$

then such a solution (if it exists) can be found from

$$Y^* = \frac{\alpha}{1 - \beta} \tag{E4.7}$$

This confirms for our illustrative model that a solution exists, but still does not answer the question of determining how Y approaches this equilibrium over time. Clearly, what we require is a function of the form:

$$Y_t = f(t)$$

and not in the current form $Y_t = f(Y_{t-1})$; that is, we wish to be able to relate Y to t directly rather than indirectly through earlier values of Y. This will enable us more readily to examine the behaviour of Y over time.

E4.3 The solution to a difference equation

The derivation of such a solution equation is approached by identifying what is known as a *particular* solution and a *complementary* solution. We then state:

General solution = particular solution + complementary solution

The particular solution is in fact what we found in the previous section: the solution that provides the equilibrium position – here at 5000. The complementary solution is found by removing the constant from the difference equation, giving:

$$Y_t = 0.7Y_{t-1} \tag{E4.8}$$

Since we require a solution of the form $Y_t = f(t)$, let us consider the general exponential type of function:

$$Y_t = f(t) = km^t \tag{E4.9}$$

and we wish to determine suitable values for the parameters in Eq. E4.9.

Since $Y_t = f(Y_{t-1})$ then via Eq. E4.8:

$$km^t = km^{t-1}$$

and

$$km^t = 0.7km^{t-1}$$

and dividing through by km^{t-1} gives

$$\frac{km^t}{km^{t-1}} = 0.7\frac{km^{t-1}}{km^{t-1}}$$

which gives $m = 0.7$. We now have:

$Y_t = k(0.7)^t$

Therefore the general solution is given as:

$Y_t = 5000 + k(0.7)^t$

However, we know the initial value of Y, $Y_0 (= 3000)$, so we now have:

$Y_0 = 3000 = 5000 + k(0.7)^0$

Therefore:

$3000 = 5000 + k$

So $k = -2000$, giving the general solution as:

$Y_t = 5000 - 2000(0.7)^t$ \hfill (E4.10)

Equation E4.10 provides a general solution for finding Y_t for any particular time period. The solution provides us with a method for tracking the period-by-period changes in the model as it moves towards equilibrium.

Progress Check E4.1

Using Eq. E4.10, confirm the values we calculated earlier for Y_t when $t = 0, 1, 2, 3, 4, 5$.

It will be worth reviewing what we have accomplished. We started with a first-order difference equation expressed in general as:

$Y_t = \alpha + \beta Y_{t-1}$

and we have derived a related function where we relate Y_t only to t. In general such a solution can be derived as:

$$Y_t = \frac{\alpha}{1 - \beta} + \left(Y_0 - \frac{\alpha}{1 - \beta} \right) \beta^t$$ \hfill (E4.11)

providing that $\beta \neq 1$, which for convenience we can express as

$Y_t = a + k\beta^t$ \hfill (E4.12)

where

$$a = \frac{\alpha}{1 - \beta}$$

and

$$k = \left(Y_0 - \frac{\alpha}{1 - \beta} \right)$$

where Y_0 is taken as an initial value in the model.

Progress Check E4.2

For the equation:

$Y_t = 1500 + 0.8Y_{t-1}$

derive a function in the form of Eq. E4.12 with $Y_0 = 5000$.

(Solution on p. 476)

It is important to realize that the exact form of the difference equation we derive will, in part, depend on the Y_0 value that we use. Effectively, Y_0 indicates the initial starting point of the model, and since the new equilibrium will remain the same then we require an equation for tracing the movement of Y from a given value of Y_0 to the new equilibrium position. A different value for Y_0 in Progress Check E4.1 would generate a different difference equation.

E4.4 Stability of the model

In the example that we have examined we see that the simple model we have is stable over time; that is, it converges towards an equilibrium position and, once attained, will remain at that equilibrium, *ceteris paribus*. There is, however, no guarantee that a particular model will necessarily exhibit such stability over time. Let us consider the general model:

$$Y_t = a + kb^t$$

where a and b take the form shown earlier. We have already noted that the a term indicates the particular solution while the kb^t term represents the complementary solution. On reflection we can interpret the particular solution as representing an equilibrium level for Y over time. The complementary solution can then be interpreted as showing deviations from that equilibrium over time. We can test, therefore, whether a particular model will be dynamically stable (i.e. will tend to the equilibrium over time) by determining whether:

$$kb^t \to 0 \text{ as } t \to \infty$$

It is also clear that it is primarily the b^t term that will determine whether this convergence occurs, and we can naturally consider the effect on stability of different values for b.

Case 1 $0 < b < 1$
Assume a system such that:

$$Y_t = 1000 + 100(0.8)^t \tag{E4.13}$$

We note that b lies between 0 and 1 and we can calculate as before the period-by-period values for Y. Figures E4.3 and E4.4 show this system over a 30-period time scale.

Figure E4.3 shows the movement in the Y variable over time and it is evident that the Y value gradually converges towards the a term in the general expression (here $a = 1000$). We see the logic of this, since if b is positive but less than 1 then raising b to successively higher powers will cause it to tend to zero. This is also illustrated in Figure E4.4, which shows the period-by-period change in Y which clearly converges to zero. It may also be evident that the smaller the value of b between these limits then the faster the system will approach equilibrium.

Case 2 $b > 1$
Now consider the equation:

$$Y_t = 1000 + 100(1.1)^t \tag{E4.14}$$

(Note that we keep the a term and the k term constant in this and subsequent equations so we can more easily assess the effect of changing b.) In this case b is now greater than 1 and Figs E4.5 and E4.6 show the patterns for Y and changes in Y over time respectively. We now see that for this value of b the Y variable 'explodes' over time, with Y moving further and further away from equilibrium. Once again we recognize that the larger the value for b, then the faster the system explodes.

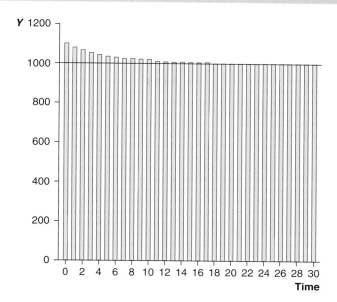

Figure E4.3 Convergence: $0 < b < 1$

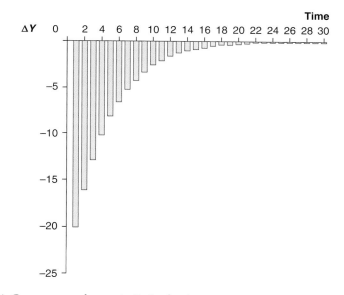

Figure E4.4 Convergence: changes in $Y: 0 < b < 1$

E

Case 3 $0 > b > -1$

Now consider the following equation:

$$Y_t = 1000 + 100(-0.8)^t \qquad\qquad (E4.15)$$

where b takes a negative value between 0 and -1. Clearly we have $b^t \rightarrow 0$, which implies that Y will tend to equilibrium. The system is clearly stable. However, since b is negative the b^t term will take negative values when t is an odd value, and positive values when t is even. The deviations for the equilibrium, therefore, will oscillate from period to

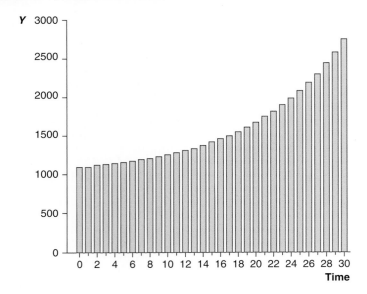

Figure E4.5 Explosion: $b > 1$

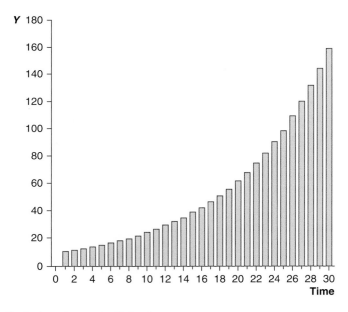

Figure E4.6 Explosion: changes in $Y : b > 1$

period. The situation is shown in Figs E4.7 and E4.8. Y can be seen to fluctuate around the equilibrium value over time although these fluctuations gradually diminish. Such a system is said to exhibit *damped oscillations*.

Case 4 $-1 > b$
We now have a model where the b term is negative but exceeds -1:

$$Y_t = 1000 + 100(-1.1)^t \tag{E4.16}$$

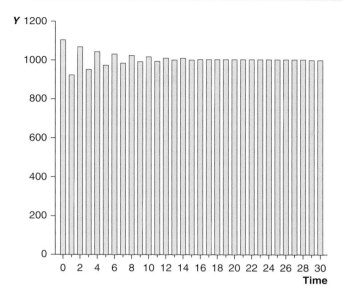

Figure E4.7 Damped oscillations: $0 > b > -1$

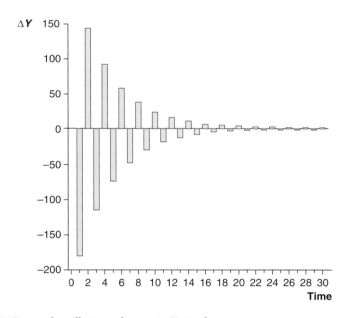

Figure E4.8 Damped oscillations: changes in $Y : 0 > b > -1$

Here as $t \to \infty$ then $\beta^t \to \infty$ also, that is, the model explodes. However, as with the previous model, the system will also exhibit oscillations as $b^t \pm \infty$. The situation is shown in Figs E4.9 and E4.10. Again, we see that the system is unstable and will move further away from equilibrium over time, alternating between positive and negative deviations, exhibiting an *explosive* oscillations pattern.

Finally, let us consider the other element of the complementary solution, the k term. In general this could be positive (as it has been in all our examples in this section) or

E

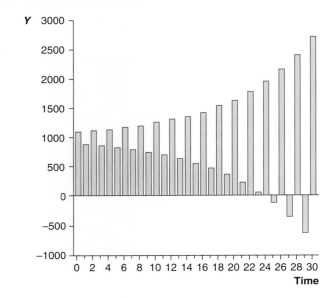

Figure E4.9 Explosive oscillations

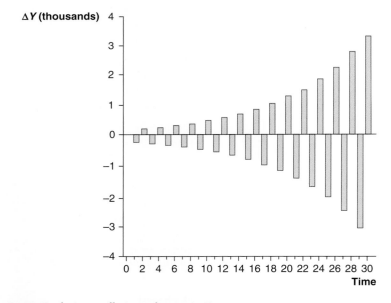

Figure E4.10 Explosive oscillations: changes in Y

negative (as it was in the original macroeconomic model). Since the term kb^t represents deviations from the equilibrium then effectively k indicates whether these deviations will be positive or negative. If we compare Figs E4.2 and E4.4, for example, we see that they are effectively mirror images of each other. Recollect that in the model for Fig. E4.2 the k term was negative while for Fig. E4.4 it was positive. Finally we should note that the a term in the system will determine the vertical intercept on the graph.

E4.5 A macro model with a government sector

Let us consider a slightly more complex macro model introducing a government sector. We now have:

$$Y_t = C_t + I_t + G_t \tag{E4.17}$$

$$YD_t = Y_t - xY_t \tag{E4.18}$$

$$C_t = c + d(YD_{t-1}) \tag{E4.19}$$

$$TX_t = xY_t \tag{E4.20}$$

where x represents the tax rate imposed, d the marginal propensity to consume, YD is disposable income, TX the total tax collected and I and G are exogenous. We then have:

$$Y_t = c + d[YD_{t-1}] + I + G$$
$$= c + d(Y_{t-1} - xY_{t-1}) + I + G$$
$$= c + d(1 - x)(Y_{t-1}) + I + G \tag{E4.21}$$

which collecting the exogenous terms together gives

$$Y_t = (c + I + G) + d(1 - x)Y_{t-1} \tag{E4.22}$$

which can be expressed in the standard difference equation form as

$$Y_t = \alpha + \beta Y_{t-1}$$

where $\alpha = c + I + G$ and $\beta = d(1 - x)$.

The general solution can be derived as:

$$Y_t = \frac{\alpha}{1 - \beta} + \left(\frac{Y_0 - \alpha}{1 - \beta}\right)\beta^t$$
$$= \frac{c + I + G}{1 - d(1 - x)} + \left[Y_0 - \frac{(c + I + G)}{1 - d(1 - x)}\right][d(1 - x)]^t \tag{E4.23}$$

Let us focus on the β^t term, $d(1 - x)^t$. Recollecting what we know about the stability of such a system we would require $d(1 - x)$ to be both positive and less than 1 for the system to be stable. This is entirely consistent with the usual economic assumptions of such a model, where we would expect both d and x (the marginal propensity to consume and the rate of tax) to be positive and < 1. Hence the β term will generate a stable system. Note also that this model – with a government sector – will converge at a faster rate than the model without the government sector. If x were zero, the β term would collapse to d, which must be larger than $c(1 - d)$. Recollect that the smaller the β term (when $0 < \beta < 1$) the faster the convergence process.

Progress Check E4.3

Assume a marginal propensity to consume of 0.7 and a tax rate of 0.25. Let $c = 100$, $I = 500$ and $G = 250$, $Y_0 = 800$. Analyse the model in terms of its movement over time.

(Solution on p. 477)

E4.6 Harrod–Domar growth model

Let us consider a macroeconomic growth model known as the *Harrod–Domar model*. The model is typically used to examine an economy's growth rate in terms of the level of savings and productivity of capital. It suggests that there is no reason for an economy to have balanced growth. We assume that:

$$S_t = sY_t \tag{E4.24}$$

$$I_t = p(Y_t - Y_{t-1}) \tag{E4.25}$$

Savings in period t, S_t, are some proportion, s, of income. Investment in period t, I_t, is some proportion, p, of the change in income since the last period. If we require $S_t = I_t$ for equilibrium, then we have:

$$sY_t = p(Y_t - Y_{t-1})$$

which on rearranging gives

$$Y_t = \frac{p}{p-s} Y_{t-1} \tag{E4.26}$$

and a general solution of

$$Y_t = k \left(\frac{p}{p-s} \right)^t \tag{E4.27}$$

but k will then be

$$Y_0 = k \left(\frac{p}{p-s} \right)^0 = k$$

giving a solution of

$$Y_t = Y_0 \left(\frac{p}{p-s} \right)^t \tag{E4.28}$$

We recognize that both p and s will be positive but less than 1; hence the term $[p/(p-s)]$ will be greater than 1, indicating that the system is explosive. Income will expand indefinitely unless there is some change in the parameters of the model over time (if, for example, the propensity to save altered). In order to assess whether the system oscillated we would need to assess which of p and s was the larger. If $s > p$ then the term $[p/(p-s)]$ becomes negative and the system oscillates.

Progress Check E4.4

Assume that $s = 0.1$, $p = 0.25$ and $Y_0 = 1000$. Draw a graph of the value of Y, over the first 10 periods.

(Solution on p. 477)

E4.7 Market equilibrium

Finally, let us examine a microeconomic application of difference equations. Consider the market model:

$$D_t = a + bP_t \tag{E4.29}$$

$$S_t = c + dP_{t-1} \tag{E4.30}$$

where we see that quantity demanded in the time period t, D_t is a function of the price in that period, while the quantity supplied in the period t, S_t is a function of the price in the previous period. This is not an unreasonable assumption, since firms may well take time to react to price changes and their output decisions may well lag behind the market price. Naturally, we could also apply the usual numerical restrictions to the equation parameters. If we assume there is an equilibrium price, P^*, then:

$$P_t = P^* = P_{t-1} \tag{E4.31}$$

and we have

$$a + bP^* = c + dP^*$$

which gives

$$P^* = \frac{a - c}{d - b} \tag{E4.32}$$

The difference equation can also be obtained. We require:

$$a + bP_t = c + dP_{t-1}$$

which on rearranging gives

$$P_t = \frac{c - a}{b} + \frac{dP_{t-1}}{b} \tag{E4.33}$$

fitting into our general form

$$Y_t = \alpha + \beta Y_{t-1}$$

This will then give a general solution (which you may want to confirm through your own calculations):

$$P_t = \frac{(c - a)/b}{1 - d/b} + \left[P_0 - \frac{(c - a)/b}{1 - d/b} \right] \left(\frac{d}{b} \right)^t \tag{E4.34}$$

and it is evident that the expression $(d/b)^t$ will control the stability of the system. It is evident first of all that the d/b term will be negative (since we usually require b, the slope of the demand function, to be negative). The system therefore will oscillate over time. Will the system converge to equilibrium or will it explode? Clearly, we require:

$$0 < d/b < -1$$

for a convergent system. If this condition were not met then the system would not converge to an equilibrium price/quantity combination. This value is simply the ratio of the slopes of the two functions. To illustrate, consider the model:

$$D_t = 90 - 0.8P_t$$

$$S_t = -10 + 0.2P_{t-1}$$

We have:

$$P_t = \frac{(-10 - 90)/-0.8}{1 - (0.2/-0.8)} + \left[P_0 - \frac{(-10 - 90)/-0.8}{1 - (0.2/0.8)} \right] \left(\frac{0.2}{-0.8} \right)^t$$

$$= 100 + (P_0 - 100)(-0.25)^t$$

We see that the d/b term is negative but does not exceed -1; hence the system will converge to an equilibrium which we confirm to be:

$$P^* = \frac{90 - (-10)}{0.2 - (-0.8)} = 100$$

Progress Check E4.5

If $P_0 = 80$ calculate the period-by-period change in P.

(Solution on p. 477)

However, consider the model:

$$D_t = 90 - 0.4P_t$$
$$S_t = -10 + 0.5P_{t-1}$$

Here we see that the ratio d/b is now $0.5/-0.4 = -1.25$, which would lead to an explosive oscillation. The price would never reach an equilibrium position, with quantity demanded and supplied getting further and further away from balance over time. These models are often referred to as *cobweb* models because of the web-like pattern that emerges if we were to plot the period-by-period movement in P on a graph (Fig. E4.11).

The movement in P over the first five periods for this model, with an initial price of 100, would be:

t	Pr
0	100
1	125.00
2	93.75
3	132.81
4	83.98
5	145.02

and it can be seen from Fig. E4.11 that D and S continue to move further and further apart over time.

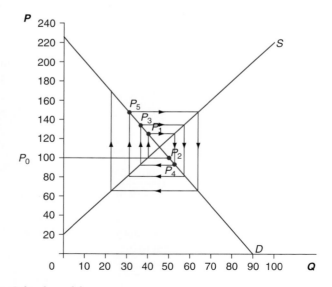

Figure E4.11 Cobweb model

E4.8 Summary

In this module, we have introduced some of the basic concepts that relate to the application of mathematics to dynamic economic models. It must be stressed that we have examined only some of the more fundamental and simpler economic models in this context. We have looked at the principles of simple linear first-order difference equations. While many of the more complex models will involve difference equations of higher order and will need to include non-linear relationships, the mathematical principles required to deal with these are only an extension of those we have developed.

Learning Check

Having read this module you should have learned that:

- A difference equation is a function linking the value of Y in a given period t to previous periods of t
- The general solution to a difference equation comprises the particular solution and the complementary solution
- The stability of a difference equation model over time depends on the specific values of the equation parameters
- Some models will converge to equilibrium; others show an explosive nature diverging from equilibrium over time
- Some models show a damped oscillation pattern; others show an explosive oscillations pattern.

Worked Example

Assume a simple national income model:

$$Y_t = C_t + I_t$$
$$C_t = 500 + 0.8Y_{t-1}$$

The economy is currently in equilibrium with I, exogenous, at 200:

I now increases to 250. Derive the level of national income five periods after this increase. How many periods will it take for the model to reach its new equilibrium position?

Solution

We can derive a suitable equation:

$$Y_t = C_t + I_t$$
$$C_t = 500 + 0.8Y_{t-1}$$

Hence with $I = 200$:

$$Y_t = 500 + 0.8Y_{t-1} + I_t$$
$$Y_t = 700 + 0.8Y_{t-1}$$

E

Worked Example (Continued)

and giving an equilibrium income of 3500. However, with the increase in I this becomes:

$$Y_t = 750 + 0.8Y_{t-1}$$

and we can quickly confirm that the new equilibrium would be 3750 (with a multiplier in this simple model of 5). This then allows us, using Eq. E4.11, to develop a difference equation such that:

$$Y_t = 3750 - 250(0.8^t)$$

With $t = 5$ we then have:

$$Y_t = 3668.08$$

as the income level in this period. However, we are also asked to determine how long it will be before the economy reaches its new equilibrium position. We have:

$$Y_t = 3750 - 250(0.8^t)$$

and we require to solve for t. In general, this would be:

$$Y_t - 3750 = -250(0.8^t)$$

$$\frac{Y_t - 3750}{-250} = 0.8^t$$

If we then took logarithms we would have:

$$\log\left(\frac{Y_t - 3750}{-250}\right) = t \log(0.8)$$

rearranging to give

$$t = \log\left(\frac{Y_t - 3750}{-250}\right) \times \frac{1}{\log(0.8)}$$

Initially we might set Y_t to 3750 since we know this will be the new equilibrium. However, this will require finding the log of 0. Instead we can set Y_t to a non-zero value as close to the equilibrium as we require, say $Y_t = 3749$. Substituting this then gives:

$$t = \log\left(\frac{3749 - 3750}{-250}\right) \times \frac{1}{\log(0.8)} = \frac{-2.39794}{-0.09691} = 24.7$$

Effectively, then, the economy will have reached its new equilibrium position when $t = 25$. You may wish to use a spreadsheet to show that the period-by-period changes using the difference equation are the same as those to be derived using the simple multiplier approach and calculating period-by-period changes for Y and C.

Exercises

E4.1   Return to the macro model with a government sector that we introduced in this module. Assume that G is no longer exogenous but takes the form:

$$G_t = gY_{t-1}$$

Exercises *(Continued)*

Assess the effect this will have on both the stability of the model and the time taken to converge to equilibrium.

E4.2 For the model in Section E4.7 we had a market system:

$$D_t = 90 - 0.4P_t$$
$$S_t = -10 + 0.5P_{t-1}$$

If $P_0 = 100$, examine the behaviour of this model over time. Plot the movement in P and Q on a graph showing both functions. Comment on the behaviour you observe and on how it could arise.

E4.3 Assume the following model:

$$D_t = 200 - 5P$$
$$S_t = -50 + 3P_{t-1}$$

Assume $P_0 = 25$. Assess the behaviour of the model over time. Plot the movement in P and Q on a supply and demand graph. How would this behaviour change if:

 (i) The slope of the demand function changed?

 (ii) The intercept of the supply function changed?

E4.4 Assume a national income model as in Section E4.5 involving a government sector where I and G are exogenous and the consumption function is a first-order difference equation with mpc $= 0.8$. Assume $I = 100$, $G = 50$ with a tax rate of 10%. If the autonomous level of consumption is 100 and $Y_0 = 750$, examine the behaviour of the model.

 (i) Plot the change in Y over time.

 (ii) If the tax rate changes to 20%, what effect will this have?

 (iii) If G increases to 75, what effect will this have?

 (iv) If I changes to 75, what effect will this have?

E4.5 From Exercise E4.4 derive a suitable savings function if we now assume that:

$$I_t = 0.05(Y_t - Y_{t-1})$$

Re-examine the models in Exercise E4.4.

E

Module E5
Probability in economic analysis*

So far in this book, we have looked at numerous examples of economic relationships and seen how these can be analysed and modelled. For example, let's consider a simple consumption function:

$$C = 1500 + 0.75Y$$

The numerical parameters in this equation are presented in a very precise way. The slope, for example, is 0.75 *exactly* – not 0.751 or 0.749, but exactly 0.75. We're implying that if consumer income increases by 1 then consumer expenditure will increase by 0.75 *exactly*. In reality, of course, the world is less exact and certain than this: we probably wouldn't expect consumption to increase precisely by 0.75, but by *about* 0.75. The parameter should therefore be seen as a probable value rather than as a certain, guaranteed value. This brings important implications for the mathematical analyses that we have undertaken throughout the text. Consider in practice how we might try to obtain a specific numerical value for a parameter like the mpc. In principle, your aim would be to collect data on every consumer's actual income and actual expenditure. You could then average these across the whole economy to obtain the mpc value. But this is unrealistic given the time, effort and cost involved. More practically, we would probably try to collect data from a representative sample of consumers instead. However, this brings its own difficulties given that we cannot be sure that such a sample result would be identical to that from the whole population. The sample mpc then would have to be viewed as an approximation to the 'true' mpc, which would remain unknown. There are other difficulties. Even if we focused on a sample set of data, this sample would relate to income and consumption for a given period of time – say last year. Who is to say that last year's mpc will be exactly the same as this year's? Or next year's? One reason to study probability theory is the fundamental role it plays in econometrics, allowing us to determine *probable* (but not certain) values for equation parameters.

However, there is a second reason to consider the use of probability theory in economics. Economic decisions often have to be made with incomplete information, especially about what might happen in the future. Should we launch a new product this year or wait until next year? Should we lend this company an extra £10 million to fund its expansion? Should we invest in new technology to improve productivity? Clearly,

*I could not have written this module without the considerable support of Ralph Bailey, assisted by Jacqueline Smith, University of Birmingham. Many thanks.

we don't know *for sure* what will happen in the future. If we wait until next year our competitors may bring out a competing product and we lose market share. If we lend the company money, it may be able to exploit new emerging markets profitably. If we invest in new technology today we might see even better technology emerging later. The problem is, we have to make decisions *now* without knowing what might happen *later*. In other words, we're making decisions in a situation where some things are uncertain.

However, as we'll see, although some aspects of the decision problem may be uncertain, we may be able to *quantify* that uncertainty; that is, we can attach a numerical value to indicate how likely an event is even if we don't know for certain what will happen. Economists use the subject of decision theory to analyse both how economic agents should react and how they do react to the problem of economic decision-making in a world full of uncertainty. Like econometrics, decision theory is based on probability theory. This module looks at probability largely in the context of economic uncertainty and decision-making.

Learning Objectives

By the end of this module you should be able to:

- Understand how probability theory relates to the more general problem of uncertainty
- Calculate the probability of an event, from information about related events and their probabilities, using the methods of conditional probability
- Understand the concept of a random variable
- Obtain descriptors of location and dispersion of random variables
- Understand, and be able to work with, probability theory and economic theories about decision-making.

E5.1 Uncertainty and probability

It will be worthwhile at this stage considering what we mean by *uncertainty* and by *probability*. Many things – in life generally as well as in economics – are uncertain. You do not know for sure, for example, whether you'll pass the Mathematical Economics exam. You don't know for sure when you'll get a job after graduation. We don't know for sure the economic growth rate next year, or the level of unemployment, or the balance of trade deficit. However, just because something's uncertain does not mean we can't *quantify* that uncertainty. Quantifying an uncertain event brings in the concept of probability.

Consider tossing a coin and seeing whether it comes down heads or tails. The outcome is uncertain – I can't be exactly sure which side of the coin will show. However, by applying simple logic you can quantify this uncertainty. If I ignore the possibility that the coin lands on its edge, then I'd rationalize by saying: there are two sides to the coin. Each has an equal chance of showing so there's a 50:50 chance the coin will show heads (and obviously a 50:50 chance that it shows tails). We'd normally refer to that chance as a *probability* – the probability that the coin shows a head. Once we understand certain probability concepts – which we'll outline in the rest of this module – we can start incorporating uncertainty into our economic analysis.

E

E5.2 Understanding probability

To develop our understanding of how probability can be used in economic analysis we need to introduce some new terminology. Mathematical analysis and modelling with probability typically involves random *experiments* – that is, activities with various possible outcomes that occur at random. Tossing a coin would be classed as an experiment – it has two outcomes (heads and tails) that occur by chance or at random. A *trial* is one occurrence of the experiment – tossing the coin once. We define the *sample space* for an experiment as the set of all possible outcomes from that experiment and each possible outcome is known as a *sample point*. For example, the experiment of rolling an ordinary six-sided dice would have sample points of 1,2,3,4,5,6, and a sample space:

$$S = \{1, 2, 3, 4, 5, 6\}$$

An *event* is a defined outcome which consists of a subset of the sample space. For example, the event of rolling a 6 would comprise the subset {6} while the event of rolling an odd number would comprise the subset {1,3,5}. The probability of an event is a numerical measure of the likelihood of that outcome occurring. Assume that a particular random experiment has outcomes $s_1, s_2, s_3, \ldots s_n$ and that to each outcome, s_k, we assign a real numerical value so that:

$$0 \leq P(s_k) \leq 1$$

and

$$P(s_1) + P(s_2) + P(s_3) + \ldots + P(s_n) = 1$$

then $P(s_k)$ is the probability of outcome s_k and will have a numerical value between 0 and 1. The first condition we imposed simply restricts a probability value to between 0 (impossible) and 1 (certain). The second condition indicates that whenever the random experiment is performed then one of the outcomes must occur.

Assigning probability

It is also important to be aware that probabilities can be determined or assigned in different ways. At one level we have *axiomatic* probabilities such as those relating to rolling a dice (sometimes referred to as an *a priori* probability). The probability can be obtained through logical deduction. A second category of probability is *empirical* or *observed* probability, sometimes referred to as *frequentist* probability. This is where observed data is used to determine a relative frequency. For example, I might record the actual number of sixes thrown from the total number of trials and use this as an empirical probability rather than the theoretical probability of 1/6. A third category of probability is *subjective* probability which is based on the subjective opinion of one or more people. If I'm a gambler, for example, and I've rolled the dice three times and each time it's shown a six, I may subjectively decide that the probability of the next throw being a six is not 1/6.

Progress Check E5.1

You want to figure out the probability that a student chosen at random in your class will pass the Mathematical Economics exam that you all have to take at the end of the class. How could you work out this probability and what category would it fall into?

Progress Check E5.1   *(Continued)*

You now want to work out the probability that you will pass this exam. What type of probability would this be?

(Solution on p. 477)

In fact, in economics there is some controversy as to how probability values should be assigned. A hard-line frequentist would argue that subjective probabilities are unscientific since they are not based on observations of repeated trials. Those preferring the subjective approach would argue that the frequentist approach uses historic information which may well be out of date or inappropriate, and that the frequentist approach cannot be used in new or one-off situations which have not occurred before. In such situations we still have to make a decision even if there are no historic data available.

E5.3 Basic rules of probability

As you might expect there are various rules for calculating common types of probability situations. To understand these we must introduce more terminology.

Mutually exclusive events

Two or more events are *mutually exclusive* if they cannot occur together – there is no sample point common to both events. Consider an experiment of rolling a six-sided dice. If we define event E_1 as the dice showing a six and Event E_2 as the dice showing an odd number then, by definition, E_1 and E_2 are mutually exclusive and this has the implications that:

$$P(E_1 \text{ and } E_2) = 0$$

that is, the probability of both events occurring together is zero. Clearly, not all events are mutually exclusive.

Independent and conditional events

Two events are said to be *independent* if their probabilities are not affected by each other. An event is said to be *conditional* if its probability is affected by whether or not another event occurs. Consider two events: E_1 is that you pass your exam in Mathematical Economics. E_2 is that you have red hair. There is no reason to assume that the two events are in any way connected and we would class them as independent: the probability of your passing the exam is in no way affected by the probability of your having red hair. However, some events may not be independent: one event may be conditional or dependent on another. Let E_1 stay the same. Let E_2 be the probability that you have carefully studied this learning material and completed all the exercises before the exam. It now seems reasonable to say that the probability of E_1 will depend on E_2.

The Multiplication Law

Consider a simple experiment. We throw a six-sided dice and note the number that is thrown. We then throw the dice a second time. What is the probability that on both occasions we threw a six? Let E_1 be that the first dice shows a six. Let E_2 be that the second dice shows a six. We then require:

$P(E_1 \text{ and } E_2)$

That is, the probability that both events occurred. It seems logical to say that:

$P(E_1) = 1/6$

$P(E_2) = 1/6$

so

$P(E_1 \text{ and } E_2) = P(E_1) \times P(E_2) = 1/6 \times 1/6 = 1/36$

That is, there is a probability of 1/36 that we will throw two sixes. For obvious reasons this is known as the *Multiplication Law*. When we are dealing with a situation where we require *both* events to occur – and the events are independent – then the Multiplication Law can be used. The Law is easily extended to cover more events:

$P(E_1 \text{ and } E_2 \text{ and } E_3) = P(E_1) \times P(E_2) \times P(E_3)$

and so on.

Progress Check E5.2

A firm manufactures a laptop. Three of the key parts are the screen, S, the keyboard, K, and the hard drive, H. The firm offers a money-back guarantee if any of these three components fails within 24 months. In the past it has found that 98% of component S lasts at least 24 months, 99% of component K and 95% of component H.

Calculate the probability for a product chosen at random that all three components will last at least 24 months.

What assumptions have you made?

(Solution on p. 477)

However, the Multiplication Law works only if the events we are dealing with are independent. But what if events are not independent – what if they are conditional? Then we must amend the law to take this into account. Let us illustrate with a different experiment. Take a pack of ordinary playing cards: there are 52 cards in the pack and 26 are black and 26 are red. What is the probability of choosing two cards at random and that both cards are red? At first sight we have another application of the Multiplication Law since we have a both/and situation. Let us define the two events as:

E_1: the first card is red
E_2: the second card is red.

We require:

$P(E_1 \text{ and } E_2)$

But a little thought reveals that the two events are not independent: the probability of E_2 will be affected by E_1.

$P(E_1) = 26/52 = 0.5$

$P(E_2)$, however, will not be 0.5 but will depend on E_1. If E_1 was red, then:

$P(E_2) = 25/51$

since there are now 25 red cards among the remaining 51. If E_2 was not red then:

$$P(E_2) = 26/52$$

since there are still 26 red cards among the 51 remaining. When dealing with conditional events we must amend the Multiplication Law such that:

$$P(E_1 \text{ and } E_2) = P(E_1) \times P(E_2|E_1) \tag{E5.1}$$

where $P(E_2|E_1)$ is known as the conditional probability of E_2 given that E_1 has occurred (the symbol | is read as 'given that'). Here we have:

$$P(E_2|E_1) = 25/51$$

so:

$$P(E_1 \text{ and } E_2) = P(E_1) \times P(E_2E_1)$$
$$= 26/52 \times 25/51 = 0.2451$$

Progress Check E5.3

Sony have been investigating consumer behaviour in relation to their latest plasma TV. At the time of the product launch they asked a representative sample of 1000 consumers whether they intended to buy the new product. 300 said 'Yes' and 700 said 'No'. Six months later Sony followed up the same 1000 consumers to find out whether they had actually purchased the new product. Of those that originally said 'Yes', 250 had actually bought the new model. Of those that originally said 'No', 660 had not bought the Sony TV but 40 had changed their minds and had bought the product.

Sony now want to interview those consumers who originally said they would buy the product but did not, in order to determine what factors changed their mind. What is the probability of choosing someone at random from the sample and finding they fall into this category?

Let us use the following notation:

S_1 – the probability that someone said originally they would buy the product
S_2 – the probability that someone said originally they would not buy the product
B_1 – the probability that someone did buy the new TV
B_2 – the probability that someone did not buy the new TV.

We then require $P(S_1 \text{ and } B_2)$.

It will be evident that the two events are conditional, so we require:

$$P(S_1 \text{ and } B_2) = P(S_1) \times P(B_2|S_1)$$
$$P(S_1) = 300/1000 = 0.3$$

We are told that of the 300 who originally said 'Yes', 250 went and bought the TV; therefore 50 did not. So:

$$P(B_2|S_1) = 50/300 = 0.1667$$

giving

$$P(S_1 \text{ and } B_2) = 0.3 \times 0.1667 = 0.05$$

That is, there is a 5% chance of choosing someone at random who falls into this particular category.

The Addition Law

The second law of probability is the *Addition Law*. Where the Multiplication Law is concerned with situations where two (or more) events both occur, the Addition Law is concerned with those situations where either of two events occurs. Consider the following example. We return to the pack of cards and we wish to calculate the probability that, on choosing one card at random, the card chosen is either an Ace or a King. If we use the following notation:

E_1: card is an Ace
E_2: card is a King

then we require

$P(E_1$ or $E_2)$ which is given by $P(E_1) + P(E_2)$

In this example:

$P(E_1) = 4/52$

$P(E_2) = 4/52$

so

$P(E_1$ or $E_2) = P(E_1) + P(E_2)$

$= 4/52 + 4/52 = 8/52 = 0.1538$

which we can confirm is correct since there are 8 cards out of 52 which are either Aces or Kings.

Progress Check E5.4

Using the Addition Law determine the probability that a card chosen at random is either an Ace or a Heart.
Is there any reason for thinking your answer using the law might be incorrect?

If we apply the law to find the probability that a card is either an Ace or a Heart we have:

E_1: card is an Ace
E_2: card is a Heart.

$P(E_1) = 4/52$

$P(E_2) = 13/52$

so

$P(E_1$ or $E_2) = P(E_1) + P(E_2)$

$= 4/52 + 13/52 = 17/52$

But on reflection this doesn't seem right. We are actually counting one card twice – the Ace of Hearts – which is both an Ace and a Heart, so the 17/52 result is incorrect. The reason for this is that the basic Addition Law works only where two events are mutually exclusive. If they are not – as in the Ace/Heart example – then the rule must be amended:

$$P(E_1 \text{ or } E_2) = P(E_1) + P(E_2) - P(E_1 \text{ and } E_2) \tag{E5.2}$$

where we subtract the probability that the card is both an Ace and a Heart. The probability given by $P(E_1 \text{ and } E_2)$ is determined using the Multiplication Law. In this case $P(E_1 \text{ and } E_2) = 1/52$ so we now have:

$$P(E_1 \text{ or } E_2) = P(E_1) + P(E_2) - P(E_1 \text{ and } E_2)$$
$$= 4/52 + 13/52 - 1/52 = 16/52$$

as the correct answer. The two laws we have developed in this section, Eqs E5.1 and E5.2, form the basis for complex problem-solving involving probability.

E5.4 Bayes' theorem

Bayes' theorem is a formula for determining conditional probability and provides a method for revising probabilities given new or additional evidence. Such situations are not uncommon in economics. Consider a scenario where the Finance Minister considers the probability of an economic downturn over the next few months to be 70% and is wondering what economic policy would be appropriate. The latest national income statistics show that key economic variables are all consistent with a downturn. However, these statistics are provisional and not guaranteed to be accurate. This new, additional information may lead the Finance Minister to revise their thinking about the 70% probability. But by how much? It is in situations such as these, where new information arrives and we need to incorporate this into our probability assessment, that Bayes' theorem applies.

We will show the formula for Bayes' theorem first and then illustrate how it is used to revise a probability given new or additional information. Let us define events $A_1, A_2 \ldots, A_n$ as comprising the sample space S where probabilities have been assigned to each A. The events $A_1, \ldots, A_n$ constitute what is known as a *partition* of the sample space – they are mutually exclusive but together cover all of the sample space, and one of the events must occur. Now an event B occurs. We wish to determine how the probabilities of $A_1, A_2 \ldots, A_n$ are affected by the information that B has occurred. By definition, the conditional probability of event A given B is:

$$P(A_i|B) = \frac{P(A_i \text{ and } B)}{P(B)} \tag{E5.3}$$

We also have:

$$P(A_i \text{ and } B) = P(B|A_i) \, P(A_i) \tag{E5.4}$$

Given that $A_1, A_2 \ldots, A_n$ form a partition of S then event $\{A_1, A_2 \ldots, A_n\}$ is equivalent to S. When B occurs only one of the events in the partition can occur, so:

$$P(B) = P(A_1 \text{ and } B) + P(A_2 \text{ and } B) + \ldots + P(A_n \text{ and } B) \tag{E5.5}$$

From Eq. E5.4 this can be re-written as:

$$P(B) = P(B|A_1) \, P(A_1) + P(B|A_2) \, P(A_2) + \ldots + P(B|A_n) \, P(A_n) \tag{E5.6}$$

Equation E5.6 is referred to as the Law of Total Probability. Substituting Eq. E5.5 into Eq. E5.3 then gives:

$$P(A_i|B) = \frac{P(B|A_i)P(A_i)}{P(B|A_1)P(A_1) + P(B|A_2)P(A_2) + \ldots + P(B|A_n)P(A_n)} \tag{E5.7}$$

E

which is the formula for Bayes' theorem where:

- $P(A_i)$ is the *prior* probability (or 'unconditional' or 'marginal' probability) of A_i. It is 'prior' in the sense that it does not take into account any information about $P(B)$
- $P(A_i|B)$ is the conditional probability of A_i, given B. It is also called the *posterior* probability because it is derived from or depends upon the specified value of B
- $P(B|A_i)$ is the conditional probability of B given A_i
- $P(B)$ is the prior or marginal probability of B.

We shall illustrate with an example. A company knows from previous experience that launching a new electronics product onto the market is uncertain in terms of its success. Historically, 30% of new product launches have been profitable with 70% being unprofitable. The company are developing a new HD/Blu-ray DVD player and are considering whether or not to launch the product. Initially, of course, the only information they have is that 30% of product launches turn out to be profitable. However, the company has an option to commission some in-depth – and expensive – market research. Such research is undertaken robustly across the company's key markets and each market research report is classed as either Favourable or Negative. A Favourable report concludes that a profitable launch is highly likely while a Negative report concludes that a profitable launch is highly unlikely. However, the reports themselves are not 100% reliable. 85% of profitable product launches have had Favourable reports while 20% of unprofitable product launches have also received Favourable reports. The company has just received the report on the proposed new DVD player and it is Favourable. How does this affect the probability that if we launch this new product it will be profitable?

Let us collect together what we have by using the following:

L_1 is the probability of a profitable product launch
L_2 is the probability of an unprofitable product launch
R_1 is the probability of a Favourable market research report
R_2 is the probability of a Negative market research report.

So we know that:

$$P(L_1) = 0.3$$
$$P(L_2) = 0.7$$

and

$$P(R_1|L_1) = 0.85$$
$$P(R_1|L_2) = 0.2$$

Substituting into Eq. E5.7 (where A is L and B is R) we get:

$$P(L_1|R_1) = \frac{0.85(0.3)}{0.85(0.3) + 0.2(0.7)} = \frac{0.255}{0.255 + 0.14} = 0.65$$

That is, given we have had a favourable market research report we revise the probability of a profitable product launch from 0.3 to 0.65.

Progress Check E5.5

You've analysed the share price performance of a particular company you're thinking of investing in. Historically, there's a 60% chance that the share price will rise over the next

Progress Check E5.5 *(Continued)*

three-month period. You've also been able to gather the expert opinion of an eminent economist. She has forecast that this particular company's share price will increase over the next three months. However, her forecasts aren't always right. In the past, 75% of companies have seen their share price increase when she's forecast that they would. However, 40% of companies that experienced a fall in share price had been forecast to see a rise.
    Calculate and explain the posterior probability.

(Solution on p. 477)

Controversy over Bayes' theorem

Bayes' theorem is a theorem that is accepted by everyone who studies and uses probability mathematics. Nonetheless, it has become the source of great controversy in economics. The controversy is not over the theorem itself, but over the uses to which it is put. The dispute is one we mentioned earlier: is it legitimate to use 'subjective' probabilities to represent degrees of belief? For instance, in the example we have been using, of the market research report, is it legitimate to write down probabilities if these are largely or solely subjective? Those who think that it is, 'subjectivists', are happy to use Bayes' theorem heavily, to convert their prior subjective probabilities into posterior subjective probabilities as new information arrives. It is because of this heavy use of the theorem that subjectivists are often called 'Bayesians'. As we have said, the opponents of subjectivism have no objection to the theorem itself. If the probabilities arose from a statistical study based on public data and a publicly agreed methodology, a frequentist would be as happy as a Bayesian to apply Bayes' theorem. In practice, however, such new information tends to have some degree of subjectivity in it.

E5.5 Probability distributions

Until now we have seen probability as an *event*. However, we can also view probability as a *variable*. Once we do this, opportunities arise for including such probability variables into our economic models alongside economic variables. Consider the experiment of rolling a six-sided dice. We can define a variable which shows the probability of a particular outcome. Given that the actual value of the variable cannot be predicted with certainty since probability is involved, we refer to such a variable as a *random variable*, and random variables have an important role in both economic analysis and econometrics. In such circumstances it makes sense to ask questions such as, on average, how large is the outcome likely to be? Or, on average, how scattered are the outcomes likely to be? The need to answer such questions is at the heart of the role played by probability in both decision-making and statistics.

Discrete random variables

We now introduce a simple example to explore the principles of random variables. A manufacturing company is bidding for two long-term supply contracts: one to a distributor in Germany, the other to a distributor in Japan. Clearly, the company could win 0, 1 or 2 of the contracts. It has calculated that if it wins one of the supply contracts this will have a net present value (NPV) of £2 million. If it wins both supply contracts then the combined NPV will be £6 million. Of course, if it wins neither contract the NPV will be zero. The company has calculated that it has a 10% chance of winning both contracts and a 50% chance of winning one (implying a 40% chance of winning neither). If we define V as a variable showing the NPV value of contracts then V is a random variable. For such a discrete random variable, V, we can state that:

$$p(v) = P(V = v)$$

for each value, v, taken by V. We also state that the function p is known as a *probability function* which satisfies the conditions that:

$$0 \le p(v) \le 1$$

and

$$p(v_1) + p(v_2) + \ldots + p(v_n) = 1$$

We can summarize the data as follows:

Contracts won	Probability	Value, £m
0	0.40	0
1	0.50	2
2	0.10	6

Expected value of the probability distribution

A probability distribution has certain statistical properties that describe the shape and form of the distribution. Two specific properties relate to the *arithmetic mean* of the distribution and to the *variance* of the distribution. The arithmetic mean is a measure of central tendency and can be used to give a sense of an average value in the distribution. The variance is a measure of variability around the mean and indicates the dispersion of the data set under examination. The mean of a random variable is referred to as the *expected value* and is written as E(X) where x is a random variable. The variance is shown as Var(X). For a discrete random variable, E(X) is a weighted average of the outcomes with the weights being the relevant probabilities with:

$$E(X) = \sum x\, p(x)$$

In our example, x represents the outcome value, V, in £ millions and we have:

$$E(V) = 0.40(0) + 0.50(2) + 0.10(6) = 1.6$$

Assuming it was possible to replicate the experiment multiple times, the average outcome would be £1.6 million. It is conventional to also show E(X) as μ_X where μ is the symbol used to represent the arithmetic mean. The variance shows variability around the mean and is given by:

$$\text{Var}(X) = \sum (x - \mu)^2\, p(x)$$

In our example we have:

$x =$ Value, £m	$(x - \mu)^2$
0	$(0 - 1.6)^2 = 2.56$
2	$(2 - 1.6)^2 = 0.16$
5	$(6 - 1.6)^2 = 19.36$

giving:

$$\mathrm{Var}(X) = \sum (x - \mu)^2 \, p(x) = 2.56(0.40) + 0.16(0.50) + 19.36(0.10) = 3.04$$

The variance, usually shown as σ^2, effectively shows how much the values of the random variable differ on average from the mean value. Other things being equal, the higher the variance the more variability from the mean. A related statistic is the standard deviation, σ, which is simply the square root of the variance. The standard deviation has the advantage that, by taking the square root, we are measuring variability in the same units as the random variable. Here, $\sigma = 1.74$ or £1.74 million.

Progress Check E5.6

In constructing a macroeconomic planning model for a developing economy we're looking at demographic analysis since this will affect labour supply and consumption patterns. Specifically, we're looking at the number of children in each economic household. From a sample of households we've obtained the following data:

No. of children per household	% of households
0	2
1	5
2	24
3	45
4	18
5	6
Total	100

Let x be the number of children in a household. Calculate and interpret the mean and the standard deviation.

(Solution on p. 478)

Continuous random variables

Of course, not all random variables are discrete: some are continuous. If a random variable is continuous then it can take any value in a given range or interval with a specified probability. The probability distribution can be viewed as a continuous function of the random variable. Consider the probability function shown in Fig. E5.1. Such a function must satisfy the conditions that $p(x) \geq 0$ and the total area under the curve must equal 1. If we wished to calculate a probability, for example, the probability of x taking a value between a and b, then we would need to determine the area under the curve in between these two parameters. How would we do this? The answer is by

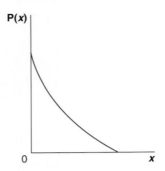

Figure E5.1 Continuous probability function

using the principles of integration we introduced in Module E1. In fact we can use integral calculus to define a continuous *probability density function*. A probability density function is a mathematical expression that defines the distribution of values for a continuous random variable and for the variable x is a function, f, that satisfies three conditions:

$$f(x) \geq 0 \text{ for all } x$$

$$\int_{-\infty}^{+\infty} f(x) \, dx = 1$$

and that the probability that x lies in the interval $a \leq x \leq b$ is given by

$$\int_a^b f(x) \, dx$$

To illustrate, let's look at the following example. A large fast-food restaurant has analysed the time taken to serve customers, from the customer placing their order to the order being served. It has been calculated that at peak times the probability density function showing how long you will have to wait for your order is given by:

$$f(t) = 0.5 - 0.125t$$

where t is the number of minutes waited. The restaurant knows that no customer waits more than 4 minutes. The restaurant wants to know how likely it is that a customer will wait no more than 1 minute. We then require:

$$P(t \leq 1) = \int_0^1 (0.5 - 0.125t) \, dt$$

$$= [0.5t - 0.0625t^2]_0^1$$

Evaluating for $t = 1$ and $t = 0$ gives

$$P(t \leq 1) = (0.5 - 0.0625) - 0 = 0.4375$$

That is, there is a 43.75% probability the customer will wait no more than a minute (with the implication that there is a 56.25% probability of waiting more than a minute).

Progress Check E5.7

For the restaurant scenario calculate the following probabilities:

(i) A wait between 2 and 3 minutes

(ii) A wait of at least 3 minutes.

(Solution on p. 477)

Expected value of a continuous probability distribution

Just as we can calculate the mean and variance/standard deviation for a discrete random variable, so we can calculate the same for a continuous random variable. Without proof we state that:

If X is a continuous random variable with probability density function, f, then:

$$E(X) = \int_{-\infty}^{+\infty} xf(x)\, dx$$

But $E(X) = \mu$, so

$$Var(X) = \int_{-\infty}^{+\infty} [x - \mu]^2\, f(x)\, dx$$

which can be re-written as

$$Var(X) = \int_{-\infty}^{+\infty} x^2\, f(x)\, dx - \mu^2$$

We can illustrate this by returning to the restaurant scenario. We had:

$$f(t) = 0.5 - 0.125t$$

and

$$E(t) = \int_{-\infty}^{+\infty} tf(t)\, dt = \int_0^4 t(0.5 - 0.125t)\, dt$$

since we know that t takes a maximum value of 4. This gives:

$$E(t) = \int_0^4 (0.5t - 0.125t^2)\, dt = [0.25t^2 - 0.0417t^3]_0^4$$

giving

$$E(t) = 1.33$$

as the mean waiting time, in minutes. Similarly the variance can be derived as:

$$Var(t) = \int_{-\infty}^{+\infty} t^2\, f(t)\, dt - E(t)^2 = \int_0^4 t^2(0.5 - 0.125t)\, dt - 1.33^2$$

$$= \int_0^4 (0.5t^2 - 0.125t^3)\, dt - 1.33^2 = [0.1667t^3 - 0.03125t^4]_0^4 - 1.33^2$$

$$= 0.90$$

If we take the square root, we have the standard deviation at 0.95. So, for this restaurant the average waiting time would be 1.33 minutes with a standard deviation of 0.95 minutes.

E

Progress Check E5.8

For the restaurant scenario, we now know that the maximum waiting time was 5 minutes not 4. Recalculate the mean and standard deviation and comment on why they have changed in the way that they have.

(Solution on p. 477)

E5.6 Decision-making under uncertainty

Finally in this module, we consider how probability can be used in economic decision-making. Consider a simple scenario. You're heading off to an important job interview nearby. A quick glance out of the window makes you realize that it might rain on your way to the interview. Should you take an umbrella or not? On the one hand, arriving wet at the interview because you didn't take an umbrella might not do your selection chances much good. On the other hand, you don't want to carry an umbrella unnecessarily. This is superficially a trivial problem but one that illustrates the basic dilemma in decision-making: how do we make a rational decision in the face of uncertainty? Such rational decision-making is at the heart of most economic analysis.

We realize that the problem involves two areas of difficulty: one is the uncertainty about whether it will rain or not. The second is to place a value on all the possible outcomes arising from the decision (and there are four possible outcomes here). In terms of whether it will rain or not, we can attach a probability to the two alternative events (rain, no rain). Such probabilities might be derived using a frequentist approach or they may be subjective. Such events are referred to as *states of nature* in decision-making – we have no control over them. As far as placing a valuation on the alternative outcomes, there are alternative approaches.

Expected monetary value (EMV)

Let's consider a scenario where as a budding entrepreneur you've set up your own company manufacturing a brand new electronics product. You're keen to get orders for your product from some of the big retail organizations as you don't have the capacity to sell direct to the public. To get your product noticed by these retailers you plan to attend one of the upcoming trade fairs: there's one in London and another in Dubai. Unfortunately, they're at the same time and in any event you don't have the resources to attend both. So you have to decide which event to attend in order to try to sell your new product. If you go to the London fair you reckon there's a 65% chance that it will be attended by the top retailers and as a result you expect to take orders for a net value of £40,000. This is the value of orders placed minus the costs you've incurred in attending the fair. If the London fair is not well attended you expect to take orders only for a net value of £10,000. Obviously, the probability of low attendance at the London fair is 35%. On the other hand, if you go to the Dubai fair, you figure there's only a 50% chance that it will be well attended. However, this would lead to net value of orders of £100,000. Low attendance in Dubai would, unfortunately, mean net orders of −£15,000 (because of the high cost of your attending and exhibiting). We can summarize the decision situation as follows:

Location	Possible states of nature	Probability	Outcome
London	High attendance	0.65	+£40,000
	Low attendance	0.35	+£10,000
Dubai	High attendance	0.5	+£100,000
	Low attendance	0.5	−£15,000

Note that for each location the relevant probabilities add up to 1. For each of the alternative decisions we can calculate the expected value arising from that decision. For London, there's a 65% probability of making £40,000 and a 35% chance of making £10,000. The expected value is then:

$$EV = 0.65(40,000) + 0.35(10,000) = £29,500$$

That is, the expected value of attending the London fair would be £29,500. As with other expected values we have calculated, this is not what you'd actually get in orders. And, like other expected values, it's an average of what you would get were you able to repeat the decision multiple times.

Progress Check E5.9

Calculate the EV of attending the Dubai fair.
  Based on this information, which fair would you attend?

The EV for Dubai is given as:

$$EV = 0.5(100,000) + 0.5(-15,000) = £42,500$$

Rationally, we would choose to attend the Dubai fair as this has the highest expected value. Note that the calculations above are often referred to as Expected Monetary Value (EMV) given we are calculating monetary outcomes.

Utility

The EMV approach is a standard method for looking at decision-making under uncertainty. However, there are two issues with this approach. The first is that we may have considerable difficulty in attaching sensible monetary values to outcomes in some circumstances. Consider the umbrella scenario we looked at earlier. How much is it worth to you to arrive dry at the job interview? Or wet? The second issue is that the EMV approach ignores risk, and the decision-maker's attitude to risk may be an important factor.

Progress Check E5.10

A very rich relative knows that you're a poverty-stricken student and has made you the following wager.

(i)   A neutral observer will toss a fair coin in the air. If the coin shows heads your relative will pay you £10. If it shows tails you will pay them £10.
      What's the EMV of the wager? Would you take it on?

(ii) The same rules apply to the wager, but the stakes have gone up. If the coin shows heads your relative will pay you £100,000. If it shows tails you pay them £100,000.
      What's the EMV of the wager? Would you take it on?

For (i) the EMV, assuming the coin is a fair one, is:

$$EMV = 0.5(1) + 0.5(-10) = £0$$

That is, on average you would break even but depending on your personal circumstances you might be willing to take a chance on winning £10. After all, in the worst case you'd only lose £10 anyway.

For (ii) the EMV is also £0. However, few of us would be willing to take the risk of losing £100,000 (that we probably don't have). In such a situation we'd say that the decision-maker was *risk-averse*. Let's return to the entrepreneur scenario from earlier. The EMV method suggested that Dubai was a better decision as it has the higher EMV. But looking at the decision situation carefully we see that London is a safer decision: both outcomes lead to a positive order value. For Dubai, however, although we stand to gain an order of £100,000 we also stand to lose £15,000 – and, as this may be a loss that the business cannot afford, you would be risk-averse. Some entrepreneurs, however, might be prepared to take such a risk in return for potentially higher rewards – they would be classed as risk-seeking.

The attitude of a decision-maker towards risk can be analysed by considering *utility* – more specifically their *utility function*. In economics, utility is generally a measure of satisfaction, referring to the total satisfaction received by a consumer from consuming a good or service. This allows us to analyse how someone's utility changes and so explain economic behaviour in terms of trying to increase one's utility. Utility is often analysed through consumption, wealth and time (spent on leisure as opposed to work for example). Utility theory in economics is an important topic and we can only introduce the basics here. There are a number of different ways of trying to determine a utility function in a specific scenario (over 20 methods at the last count). One important one is known as the *probability-equivalence* method. We start by showing the alternative outcomes ranked from best to worst and assign a utility of 1.0 to the best outcome and 0 to the worst:

Monetary outcome	Utility
£100,000	1.0
£40,000	
£10,000	
−£15,000	0

In fact, we could have assigned any two numbers as long as the highest goes to the best outcome. We now need to quantify the utilities for the intermediate monetary outcomes. We do this by saying to the decision-maker:

'Imagine you have won £40,000 in a lottery (one of the outcomes for which we currently have no utility value). You can now choose between keeping that £40,000, or receiving a lottery ticket with a chance to win a prize of £100,000 (the next highest outcome). How high would that chance to win £100,000 need to be so that you would prefer the lottery ticket to keeping the £40,000 that you had already won?'

Effectively we're offering the decision-maker a trade-off between a certain outcome, £40,000, and a higher outcome but which is not certain. We might say:

'Would a 10% chance be enough to persuade you to take the lottery ticket?'

If the answer were 'no, that's too risky', we might suggest 15% or 20% or 25% in turn. Eventually there would be a probability value – sometimes known as a *probability utility* – where the decision-maker was indifferent between the certain amount and the lottery ticket. Let's suppose this were 80%. This would then be the utility associated by the decision-maker to the outcome of £40,000, $u(40{,}000)$. We would repeat this for the other unknown utility outcome of £10,000. Let's suppose that we found $u(10{,}000) = 0.6$. We then have:

Monetary outcome	Utility
£100,000	1.0
£40,000	0.8
£10,000	0.6
−£15,000	0

We can now calculate the expect utility of the two alternative decisions (London or Dubai). For London we have:

$$EV(u) = 0.65(0.8) + 0.35(0.6) = 0.73$$

Progress Check E5.11

Calculate the EV(u) of attending the Dubai fair.
   Based on this information which fair would you attend?

For Dubai we have:

$$EV(u) = 0.5(1) + 0.5(0) = 0.5$$

Rationally we would choose the option that gave maximum utility, in this case London. In effect, we are saying that, based on our risk preference, Dubai is too risky an option. Figure E5.2 shows the utility function for this scenario. This particular function is concave which indicates risk aversion. Figure E5.3 shows the different types of attitude to risk that may be encountered.

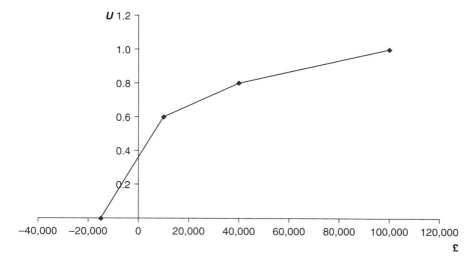

Figure E5.2 Utility function

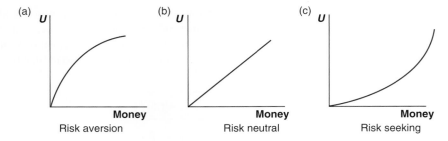

Figure E5.3 Attitudes to risk

Utility values in economics are often referred to as *von Neumann–Morgenstern* utilities after the two economists who first started to make use of expected utility maximization in their formulation of game theory. The calculations illustrate the central claim of normative expected utility theory, which is (to summarize) that every decision leads to a lottery yielding an expected utility, and that it is rational to take the decision leading to the largest expected utility. The word 'normative' means that the procedure is being advocated as an appropriate way to make decisions. A further claim, even more controversial, is that economic decision-makers do act, by and large, and usually unconsciously, in accordance with the theory. The claim, known as positive expected utility theory, is attractive to economists because it offers the possibility of understanding how decision-makers will behave when faced with uncertainty: whether and how they will gamble, how they might buy and sell stocks when prices are volatile; to what extent they will take out insurance; whether and at what rates of interest they might lend money to those undertaking risky enterprises. The word 'positive' here means that the method is being advanced as an accurate description of economic behaviour. 'Normative' and 'positive' are often contrasted in economics.

E5.7 Summary

In this module, we have introduced some of the basics of probability and begun to see how probability impacts on economic analysis and economic decision-making. Clearly, much of the real economic world is affected by uncertainty, and probability is a way of bringing such uncertainty into economics. We've shown in this module how probability can be incorporated into economic decision-making but we must stress we've only looked at the basics. Your studies of economics are likely to bring you into much more detailed contact with probability.

Learning Check

Having read this module you should have learned that:

- There is a debate about the interpretation of probability, over whether probabilities are subjective and personal, or whether they must be objective and scientific

Learning Check *(Continued)*

- Events can be thought of as sets of simple outcomes; set operations can be used to obtain new events from old; and the probability of an event can be obtained by adding up probabilities of outcomes
- The Law of Addition tells us the probability that an event occurs
- A conditional probability tells us the probability of one event, given that another occurs
- Useful applications of conditional probability are the Law of Multiplication, the Law of Total Probability, and Bayes' theorem
- Probability distributions and random variable are aspects of the same situation, which arises when the outcomes take numerical values
- Probability distributions can be summarized in several ways, by the use of important descriptors of location, dispersion and association
- Under the expected utility hypothesis, decision-makers are able to value (relative to each other) all possible outcomes in terms of 'utilities', and assign probabilities to all states of nature. These values and probabilities allow agents also to value as expected utilities the lotteries that arise from their choices. Then agents can be predicted, or recommended, to take decisions in accordance with the policy of maximizing their expected utility.

Worked Example

National income statistics are difficult, time-consuming and expensive to collect. In developing economies, policy- and decision-makers frequently have to take decisions at the macro- and micro-level with incomplete information as to what's happening in the economy. Frequently decision-makers have to use proxy measures instead. A proxy measure is a variable you can measure which you think indicates a variable that you can't easily measure. For example, it's difficult to measure consumer confidence directly. Perhaps by measuring the change in consumer spending we have a proxy measure for confidence, with the logic that if consumers are generally confident about their economic future, *ceteris paribus*, they will spend a sizeable portion of their disposable income. On the other hand, if consumer confidence is declining then expenditure might decline also.

You've been asked to advise the Minister of Finance in the developing economy of the Southern Bayesian Republic. She's had a report from the central bank that inflation in the economy appears to be higher than the target rate and could be threatening economic stability. She's considering what action, if any, to take to control the inflation rate. Some of her advisors have indicated that they think inflation is being caused by too high a rate of economic growth. This is stimulating demand and, given supply constraints, leading to higher prices. They're suggesting to her that the government should take action to reduce the rate of economic growth. However, one of the difficulties is that the next set of national statistics on production and growth is not due for several months and even

Worked Example *(Continued)*

then will be incomplete and inaccurate. There is the danger that taking action now to reduce economic growth might prove to have been the wrong policy when the national statistics do become available. However, research has shown that repayment of loans by small farmers is a proxy indicator of economic growth. Such loans are typically small and short-term. It has been found that the chance of such loans being repaid is higher with higher economic growth and lower when growth slackens off. Analysis has provided the following information:

Economic growth outcomes	Consensus probability for growth outcomes	Probability of loan repayments with this level of economic growth
1 Weak	0.20	0.62
2 Moderate	0.30	0.70
3 Average	0.20	0.85
4 Good	0.20	0.90
5 High	0.10	0.97

The table shows five possible levels of economic growth (E_i). A panel of government economists have produced a set of consensus probabilities as to how likely they consider each growth outcome. So, for example, the consensus view is that there is a 20% chance of Good economic growth. Note that these probabilities sum to 1. The final column shows the historic probability of agricultural loans being repaid for each growth outcome. So, for example, if economic growth turns out to be Good then typically there is a 90% probability that such loans will be repaid.

From the consensus probabilities it is clear that the probability that economic growth will be Good or High is 0.30 (0.20+0.10). The Minister has now been told that agricultural loans are in fact being repaid. Can this information be used to reassess the probability that the economy is experiencing Good/High growth?

Solution

The initial assessment is that the probability of Good/High economic growth is 0.30. We are also told that agricultural loan repayments tend to be correlated with economic growth. It seems logical to use the information that agricultural loan repayments are occurring to re-assess the probability that growth is Good/High. In fact this is an application of Bayes' theorem where we need to revise prior probabilities in the light of new information. If we denote E_i to represent the five growth outcomes in the table we then have five prior probabilities, $P(E_i)$. We also have five conditional probabilities linked to loan repayments, which we denote as R_i. These probabilities relate to $P(R_i|E_i)$. We require:

$$P(E_4|R) + P(E_5|R)$$

Worked Example   *(Continued)*

That is the probability that growth is Good given that loan repayments have occurred plus the probability that growth is High given that loan repayments have occurred. Using Eq. E5.7 we have:

$$P(E_4|R) = \frac{P(R|E_4)P(E_4)}{P(R|E_1)P(E_1) + P(R|E_2)P(E_2) + \ldots + P(R|E_5)P(E_5)}$$

and

$$P(E_5|R) = \frac{P(R|E_5)P(E_5)}{P(R|E_1)P(E_1) + P(R|E_2)P(E_2) + \ldots + P(R|E_5)P(E_5)}$$

From the data in the table we then have:

$$P(E_4|R) = \frac{0.90(0.20)}{0.62(0.2) + 0.70(0.30) + 0.85(0.20) + 0.90(0.20) + 0.97(0.10)} = 0.232$$

$$P(E_5|R) = \frac{0.97(0.1)}{0.62(0.2) + 0.70(0.30) + 0.85(0.20) + 0.90(0.20) + 0.97(0.10)} = 0.125$$

giving a revised probability that the economy is in a situation of Good or High growth of 0.354. As a result of this additional information we have revised our probability assessment of growth from 0.30 to 0.357.

Exercises

E5.1   An online company is trying to decide which credit cards to accept when customers are purchasing products. The company has collected data on a random sample of 2125 of its customers and found that the number of customers with the following credit cards is:

Card type	Number of customers
American Express	1360
MasterCard	1466
Visa	1679
Other	567
Store card	1211

(i)   What is the probability that a customer has a Visa card?

(ii)   Independent research shows that 58% of people have both a MasterCard and a Visa card. What is the probability that a customer has either of these?

(iii)   Looking at the data I conclude that at least 35% of customers hold both a Visa card and a store card. Am I right or wrong?

E5.2   A company operates 30-day terms for all its customers, meaning that customers are expected to pay their bills/invoices within thirty days of receipt. Experience has shown that 80% of all customer accounts are paid within one

Exercises *(Continued)*

month and 70% of the remainder are settled during the second month. Of those accounts still unpaid after two months, 50% are settled during the third month after a final demand has been sent. The company is trying to incorporate such uncertainty into its cash flow projection for the next three months.

(i) What is the probability for any particular account that payment is received during the second month?

(ii) What is the probability for any particular account that payment is received during the third month?

(iii) What proportion of payments for all accounts can the firm expect to have received by the end of the third month?

E5.3 Two local construction firms are in competition when bidding for work. In the recent past, of 20 contracts for which they have competed, ten were awarded to company A, six to company B and the remainder to other companies. Three new contracts have been offered for tender.

What is the probability that:

(i) A will win all three contracts?

(ii) B will obtain at least one contract?

E5.4 An insurance company specializes in providing insurance cover for students who own cycles. By paying an annual premium, students are covered in case the cycle is damaged in a traffic accident or is stolen. There is a maximum payout of £250. The company has analysed the amounts it has paid out over the last few years:

Amount paid out, £s	Number of claims
No claim	750
£50	75
£100	50
£150	50
£200	25
£250	50

(i) The company is reviewing how much it should charge as an annual premium for such cover. What should the premium be if the company wishes to break even on this policy?

(ii) The company has decided to charge a premium of £50. As a cyclist, what is the expected value of the policy to you? Would you take out such a policy? Why or why not?

E5.5 The government department in a developing country responsible for large infrastructure projects to support economic growth is considering funding a broadband and wireless expansion project. The project will extend broadband and wireless coverage in the country and make local industry more competitive.

Exercises *(Continued)*

The department has the option of funding a medium-sized project or a large-sized project. There is uncertainty about the uptake and demand from local businesses for additional coverage. Some market research has been done which shows that future demand could be Low, Medium or High with probabilities respectively of 0.2, 0.6 and 0.2. The net financial benefit to the economy has also been calculated.

	Net benefit, $ millions, from a medium expansion project	Net benefit, $ millions, from a large expansion project
Future demand		
Low	50	−50
Medium	150	150
High	200	500

What advice can you give the department as to which expansion project to choose?

E5.6   Returning to Exercise E5.5, we are now considering using a utility approach. Working with the department's Minister, we have derived her personal utility function as shown below:

Monetary outcome	Utility
$500 m	1.0
$200 m	0.3
$150 m	0.25
$50 m	0.1
−$50 m	0

(i)   What advice would you now give (and why)?

(ii) How would you describe the Minister's attitude to risk?

E

Appendix 1: The Greek alphabet in mathematics

There are 24 letters in the Greek alphabet.

Lower case	Upper case	Name	Pronunciation (where not obvious)
α	A	alpha	al-fa
β	B	beta	bay-ta
γ	Γ	gamma	
δ	Δ	delta	
ε	E	epsilon	
ζ	Z	zeta	zay-ta
η	H	eta	ay-ta
θ	Θ	theta	thay-ta
ι	I	iota	eye-ota
κ	K	kappa	
λ	Λ	lambda	
μ	M	mu	m-you
ν	N	nu	n-you
ξ	Ξ	xi	x-sigh
ο	O	omicron	
π	Π	pi	pie
ρ	P	rho	roe
σ	Σ	sigma	
τ	T	tau	tow
υ	Υ	upsilon	
φ	Φ	phi	fi
χ	X	chi	kye
ψ	Ψ	psi	p-sigh
ω	Ω	omega	

Appendix 2: Solutions to Knowledge Check activities

Knowledge Check A1

(i) $x = \dfrac{3 - 5y}{2y - 3}$

(ii) $\dfrac{7x - 16}{4x^2}$

Knowledge Check A2

(i) A straight line
(ii) The intercept represents the quantity demanded when price is zero
(iii) The slope at -6 indicates the change in quantity demanded as price changes.

Knowledge Check A3

(i) cubic
(ii) $1/^3\sqrt{5}$
(iii) $x = 20 - 0.02y$

Knowledge Check B1

$X = 6.25,\ Y = 56.25$

Knowledge Check B4

$$\mathbf{AB} = \begin{bmatrix} 14 & 25 & 27 \\ 10 & 32 & 21 \\ 9 & 23 & 13 \end{bmatrix}$$

$$\mathbf{BA} = \begin{bmatrix} 25 & 44 & 25 \\ 13 & 17 & 13 \\ 10 & 19 & 17 \end{bmatrix}$$

Knowledge Check B5

$$\begin{bmatrix} -2.5 & 2 \\ 1.5 & -1 \end{bmatrix}$$

Knowledge Check C1

$$X_1 = -4.633, \ X_2 = 8.633$$

Turning point $= 2$

Knowledge Check C2

(i) $f(X) = 3X^2 + 8X - 9$
      $f'(X) = 6X + 8$

(ii) $f(X)20X - 35$
      $f'(X) = 20$

(iii) $f(X) = 5(2X - 3)^{-2}$
      $f'(X) = -20(2X - 3)^{-3}$

(iv) $f(X) = 20(5X - 10)^3$
      $f'(X) = 300(5X - 10)^2$

Appendix 3: Solutions to Progress Check activities

Where no solution is shown, refer to the text in the section after the Progress Check.

Module A2 Linear relationships in economic analysis

A2.2

(i) Price = £6, quantity = 70
(ii) Price = £3, quantity = 85 (extrapolated)
(iii) Quantity = 40, price = £12 (extrapolated)

A2.3

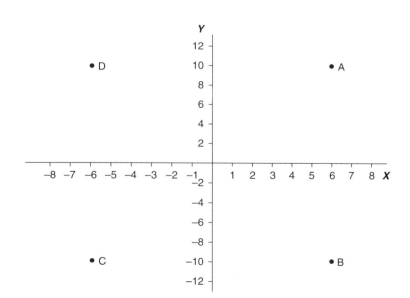

A2.5

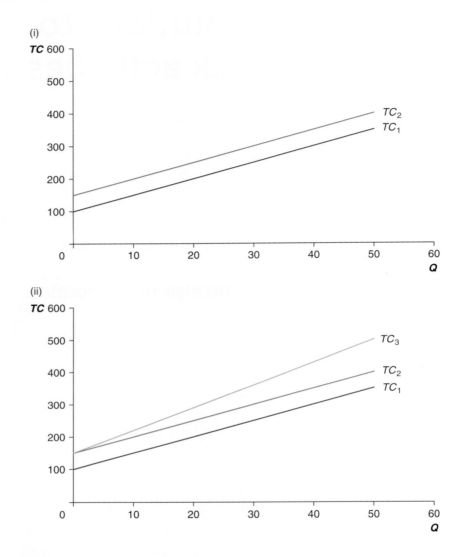

In (i) the whole line shifts upwards by £50 (000). In (ii) the line swivels or pivots upwards.

Module A3 Non-linear relationships in economic analysis

A3.1

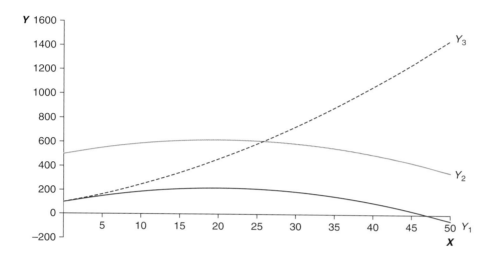

A3.2

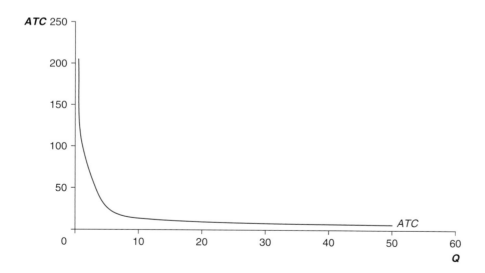

A3.4

(i)

Period	Y	Log Y
1	100.0	2.0000
2	110.0	2.0414
3	121.0	2.0828
4	133.1	2.1242
5	146.4	2.1656
6	161.1	2.2070
7	177.2	2.2484
8	194.9	2.2897
9	214.4	2.3311
10	235.8	2.3725

(ii)

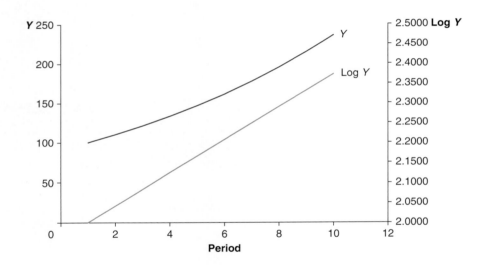

A3.5

(i) 8^9

(ii) 7^6

(iii) 8^3

(iv) $1/8^3$

(v) $1/^3\sqrt{5}$

(vi) None of the rules apply

(vii) 10^{12}

Module B1 The principles of linear models

B1.1

(i)
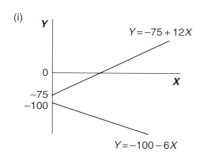
$Y = -75 + 12X$
$Y = -100 - 6X$

(ii)
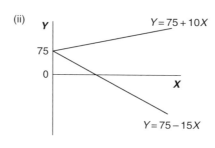
$Y = 75 + 10X$
$Y = 75 - 15X$

(iii)
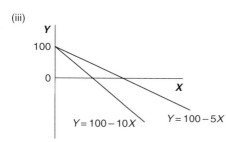
$Y = 100 - 10X$
$Y = 100 - 5X$

(iv)
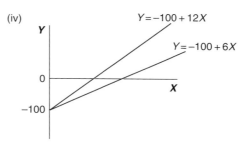
$Y = -100 + 12X$
$Y = -100 + 6X$

Module B2 Market supply and demand models

B1.2

Breakeven $= 14.3$

Breakeven output has fallen because a higher price means the firm needs to sell less to break even.

B1.3

(i) $Y = 10$
(ii) $Y = 0$
(iii) $Y = 62.5$
(iv) $Y = 6$

B2.3

None of them

B2.4

Because demand is relatively insensitive to price changes at this point.

B2.5

(i) $E_d = -4$
(ii) $E_d = -0.25$

Module B3 National income models

B3.2

(i) $Y = 6250$
(ii) $k = 5$
(iii) $Y = 5000$

B3.3

Y approaches 6200, the new equilibrium income.

B3.6

$$T = t\frac{(a + I + G)}{(1 - b)(1 - t)}$$

B3.7

If t increases then k will decrease.

Module B4 Matrix algebra: the basics

B4.1

$$\mathbf{D} + \mathbf{E} = \begin{bmatrix} 25 & 12 & 15 \\ 3 & 10 & 8 \\ 15 & 12 & 4 \end{bmatrix}$$

$$\mathbf{E} + \mathbf{D} = \mathbf{D} + \mathbf{E}$$

B4.4

(i)

$$p = \begin{bmatrix} 8 \\ 11 \\ 15 \end{bmatrix}$$

(ii)

$$c = \begin{bmatrix} 25750 \\ 19400 \\ 2550 \end{bmatrix}$$

(iii)

$$\text{Profit} = \begin{bmatrix} 4750 \\ 3700 \\ 490 \end{bmatrix}$$

(iv)

$$\begin{bmatrix} 10 & 12 & 18 \\ 8 & 11 & 15 \\ 2 & 1 & 3 \end{bmatrix}$$

B4.5

$$\mathbf{DE} = \begin{bmatrix} 250 & 216 & 89 \\ 125 & 117 & 42 \\ 53 & 56 & 23 \end{bmatrix}$$

$$\mathbf{ED} = \begin{bmatrix} 196 & 102 & 153 \\ -5 & 6 & 11 \\ 227 & 119 & 188 \end{bmatrix}$$

B4.6

(i) $\begin{bmatrix} 1 & -1 \\ -b & 1 \end{bmatrix} \begin{bmatrix} Y \\ C \end{bmatrix} = \begin{bmatrix} I \\ a \end{bmatrix}$

(ii) $\begin{bmatrix} 1 & -1 & 0 \\ -b & 1 & b \\ -t & 0 & 1 \end{bmatrix} \begin{bmatrix} Y \\ C \\ T \end{bmatrix} = \begin{bmatrix} I+G \\ a \\ 0 \end{bmatrix}$

Module B5 Matrix algebra: inversion

B5.1

$$\begin{bmatrix} 23 \\ 17.5 \\ 19 \end{bmatrix}$$

B5.3

$$\begin{vmatrix} a_{12} & a_{13} \\ a_{22} & a_{23} \end{vmatrix}$$

B5.4

$\mathbf{D} = -91$

$\mathbf{E} = -257$

Module C1 Quadratic functions in economic analysis

C1.2

With a linear *TR* function, the firm is a price-taker operating under perfect competition.

C1.4

$P_e = 4.91, Q_e = 190.18$

Module C2 The derivative and the rules of differentiation

C2.3

The difference quotient is 150.05. The derivative is 150.01.

The reason is that the quotient calculation relates to the line joining the two Q points together while the derivative calculation is technically accurate only at the specific point on the function when $Q = 9.99$. The derivative is therefore more accurate than the quotient.

C2.4

(i) $\dfrac{\mathrm{d}Y}{\mathrm{d}X} = -10 + 2X$

(ii) $X = 5$

(iii) We cannot derive the roots of this MC function. This implies that the function does not intercept the X axis but remains above it at all values for X. The sketch confirms that we have the familiar MC curve from economics: MC initially falls as Q increases (arising from economies of scale taking place), reaches a minimum value and then begins to increase (due to the diseconomies of scale effect).

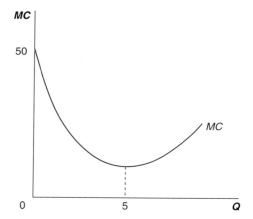

C2.5

We have:

(i) $f'(X) = 1.8X^2$ $f''(X) = 3.6X$

(ii) $f'(X) = 72X^5$ $f''(X) = 360X^4$

(iii) $f'(X) = \dfrac{-100}{X^2}$ $f''(X) = \dfrac{200}{X^3}$

(iv) $f'(X) = \dfrac{7X^{-2/3}}{3}$ $f''(X) = \dfrac{-14X^{-5/3}}{9}$

(v) $f'(X) = -1/9X^{-4/3}$ $f''(X) = 4/27X^{-7/3}$

C2.6

(i) We have:

$$f'(Q) = 50 - 10Q + Q^2$$

(ii) This derivative function is a marginal cost function in economics.

(iii) The minimum point (where the slope is zero) will be found when $Q = 5$.

(iv) $ATC = 500/Q + 50 - 5Q + 1/3Q^2$

(v)

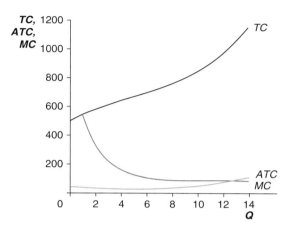

C2.8

$$f'(X) = \frac{24X^5 + 30X^4 + 120X + 50}{(6X^2 + 5X)^2}$$

C2.10

The function is non-differentiable.

Module C3 Derivatives and economic analysis

C3.2

(i) $\text{mpc} = Y^{-0.8}$

$\text{mps} = 1 - Y^{-0.8}$

(ii) $MR = 500 - 6P$

C3.4

$P = 12.5$

C3.5

We have:

$$Q_d = f(P) = aP^{-b}$$

$$f'(P) = -baP^{-b-1}$$

and

$$E_d = -baP^{-b-1}\frac{P}{Q} = \frac{-baP^{-b}}{Q}$$

But $Q = aP^{-b}$, hence:

$$E_d = \frac{-baP^{-b}}{aP^{-b}} = -b$$

C3.6

(i)   We have:

$$E_s = \frac{5(5)}{15} = 1.67$$

That is, at this price level a change in price will lead to a 1.67 times change in quantity supplied: supply is relatively responsive to a change in price at this point on the supply function.

(ii)   We have:

$$E_y = \frac{-3(10)}{170} = -0.18$$

Note that as the price of Y increases, quantity demanded of X decreases. This implies that X is complementary to good Y.

(iii)   Here we have:

$$E_y = \frac{3(10)}{230} = 0.13$$

In this case the two goods are direct substitutes since an increase in the price of Y leads to an increase in the quantity demanded of X.

C3.7

For $P = 5$, $Q_d = 500$:

$$E_d = \frac{-25(5)}{500} = -0.25$$

$$MR = 25 - 0.08Q = -15$$

but also $MR = P(1 + 1/E_d) = 5(1 - 4) = -15$, indicating that at this price level an increase in price is associated with a negative MR, implying that TR will fall if the price is increased.

When $P = 15$ we have:

$$Q_d = 250$$

$$E_d = \frac{-25(15)}{250} = -1.5$$

$$MR = 25 - 0.08Q = 5$$

but also $MR = P(1 + 1/E_d) = 15(1 - 0.67) = 5$, indicating that at this price level an increase in price is associated with a positive MR, implying that TR will increase if the price is increased.

Module C4 The principles of optimization

C4.1

$$f'(X) = -40X + 13$$

giving $X = -0.325$ when $f'(X) = 0$ so the turning point of the original function occurs at this X value.

$$f''(X) = -40$$

indicating that the turning point is a maximum.

C4.2

We have:

$$Y = X^3 - 20X^2 + 13X - 50$$

and

$$f'(X) = 3X^2 - 40X + 13$$
$$f''(X) = 6X - 40$$

Setting $f'(X)$ to zero and solving gives $X_1 = 1/3$ and $X_2 = 13$ as the two turning points. Substituting each into $f''(X)$ we find that X_1 gives a maximum turning point and X_2 a minimum.

Module C5 Optimization in economic analysis

C5.1

$$MC = f'(TC) = 5 + 2Q$$
$$MR = f'(TR) = 500 - 10Q$$

For $MC = MR$, $Q = 41.25$

From Eq. C5.9, for this to be a maximum we require:

$$f''(TR) < f''(TC)$$

We have $f''(TR) = -10$ and $f''(TC) = 2$, confirming $Q = 41.25$ is profit maximizing.

C5.3

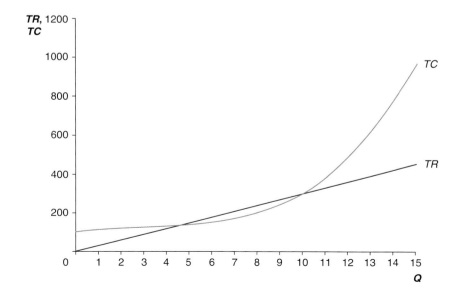

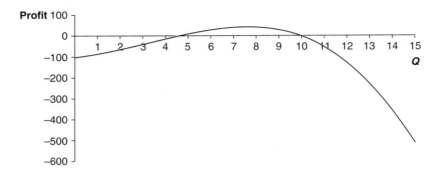

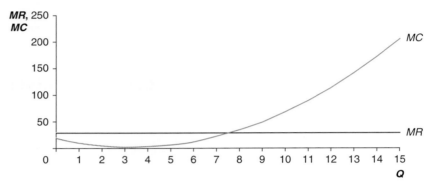

$Q = 7.55$

With $Q = 7.54$, $MC = 29.88$ and $MR = 30$ (i.e. $MC < MR$).

With $Q = 7.56$, $MC = 30.13$ and $MR = 30$ (i.e. $MC > MR$).

C5.4

The profit before tax is 14.21231 and that after tax is 2.5 less.

C5.5

The new profit will be 40% of the original: 5.685.

C5.6

We have:

$$TR = 125Q - Q^2$$

$$TC = 500 + 5Q + 0.5Q^2$$

$$\pi = -500 + 120Q - 1.5Q^2$$

$$f'(\pi) = 120 - 3Q, \text{ which gives } Q = 40$$

$f''(\pi) = -3$, confirming a maximum. From the TR function ($P = TR/Q$) we derive $P = 85$.

Tax maximization is when:

$$t = \frac{b_1 - b_2}{2} = \frac{125 - 5}{2} = 60$$

So the optimum tax amount is 60 per unit sold. This gives:

$$\pi = -500 + 120Q - 1.5Q^2 - 60Q = -500 + 60Q - 1.5Q^2$$

$$f'(\pi) = 60 - 3Q, \text{ which gives } Q = 20$$

$f''(\pi) = -3$, confirming a maximum. From the TR function $(P = TR/Q)$ we derive $P = 105$, confirming that the tax increases price and reduces quantity.

C5.7

The original equilibrium is given when $P = 40$ and $Q = 140$. The new equilibrium is found when

$$P = \frac{a_1 - a_2}{b_2 - b_1} + \frac{b_2 t}{b_2 - b_1} = 40 + \frac{6(19.44)}{15} = 47.78$$

(indicating that the consumer will effectively pay £7.78 of the tax and the firm the remainder):

$$Q = \frac{a_1 b_2 - b_1 a_2}{b_2 - b_1} + \frac{b_1 b_2 t}{b_2 - b_1} = 140 + \frac{(-9)(6)(19.44)}{15} = 70.02$$

With this new equilibrium quantity tax income will be $tQ = £1361.19$. From Eq. C5.59 we have:

$$T = 140t - 3.6t^2$$

$$f'(T) = 140 - 7.2t, \text{ which gives } t = 19.44$$

$f''(T) = -7.2$, confirming that this is a maximum.

Module C6 Optimization in production theory

C6.1

We have $Q = -0.1L^3 + 5L^2$

So $AP = -0.1L^2 + 5L$ and $MP = -0.3L^2 + 10L$

AP will have a turning point when $AP' = 0$ and solving gives $L = 25$. From AP'' we see that this turning point is a maximum. With $L = 25$ we have $AP = 62.5$ and $MP = 62.5$

Module D1 Functions of more than two variables

D1.1

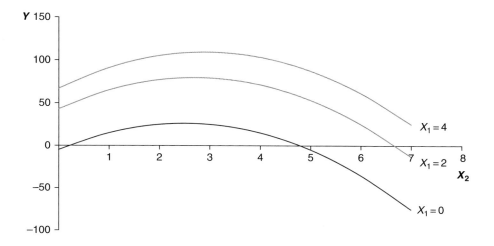

D1.2

We shall illustrate the solution only for $X_1 = 0$ since the method is then replicated for the remaining X_1 values. When $X_1 = 0$, Eq. D1.2 becomes:

$$Y = -5 + 25X_2 - 5X_2^2$$

and the derivative becomes

$$\frac{dY}{dX_2} = 25 - 10X_2$$

which is identical to the partial derivative. The partial derivative clearly defines a method of finding the derivative with respect to X_2 for any fixed value of X_1. The partial derivative of X_1 is:

$$\frac{\partial Y}{\partial X_2} = 25 - 10X_2 + X_1$$

D1.5

$$f_{X2} = 25 - 10X_2 + X_1$$

With $X_2 = 3$ we then have:

$$f_{X2} = 0 \text{ when } X_1 = 5$$

$$f_{X2} = 0.01 \text{ when } X_1 = 5.01$$

$$f_{X2} = 0.02 \text{ when } X_1 = 5.02$$

$$f_{X2} = 0.03 \text{ when } X_1 = 5.03$$

f_{X2} changes by 0.01 each time implying that the change in f_{X2} is directly proportional to the change in X_1, again confirming that $f_{X2X1} = 1$

D1.7

(i)

$$f_{X1} = 8X_1 - X_2X_3$$

$$f_{X2} = -15X_2^2 - X_1X_3$$

$$f_{X3} = 8X_3^3 - X_1X_2$$

(ii)

$$f_{X1X1} = 8$$

$$f_{X2X2} = -30X_2$$

$$f_{X3} = 24X_3^2$$

(iii)   All cross-partial derivatives are -1

D1.8

When $X_1 = 5$ and $X_2 = 2$ then by substitution back into the original function $Y = f(X_1, X_2)$ we derive $Y = 110$. When $X_1 = 5.02$ and $X_2 = 2.02$ we derive $Y = 110.2372$, an increase of 0.2372 compared with the differential of 0.24.

For the second function we have:

$$f_{X1} = -3 + 12X_1 - 3X_2$$

and

$$f_{X2} = -5 - 20X_2 - 3X_1$$

giving

$$dY = (-3 + 12X_1 - 3X_2)dX_1 + (-5 - 20X_2 - 3X_1)dX_2$$

D1.9

With $X = 10$, $Z = -5025$. With $X = 10.0001$, $Z = -5025.26$.

A change in X of 0.0001 leads to a change in Z of -0.26, 2600 times the change in X and the same value as the total derivative when $X = 10$.

D1.10

We have:

$$f_X = 4X^{-0.6} Y^{0.5}$$

$$f_Y = 5X^{0.4} Y^{-0.5}$$

$$\frac{dY}{dX} = 1.6X$$

and

$$\frac{dZ}{dX} = (4X^{-0.6} Y^{0.5}) + (5X^{0.4} Y^{-0.5})1.6X$$

$$= (4X^{-0.6} Y^{0.5}) + 8X^{1.4} Y^{-0.5}$$

Module D2 Analysis of multivariable economic models

D2.1

For a_2 we have:

$$\frac{dP}{da_2} = \frac{-1}{b_2 - b_1}$$

Since the denominator is positive then the effect on P must be the opposite to the direction of change in a_2. That is, if a_2 increases then P_e will decrease. We also have:

$$\frac{dQ}{da_2} = \frac{-b_1}{b_2 - b_1}$$

which again, given the model parameter restrictions, must be positive. An increase in a_2 leads to an increase in Q_e.

D2.3

For I we have:

$$\frac{dY}{dI} = \frac{1}{1 - b(1 - t)}$$

and for a

$$\frac{dY}{da} = \frac{1}{1 - b(1 - t)}$$

Clearly, these partial derivatives will all be the same since G, I, a are all exogenous to the model.

D2.4

For this combination of values we derive $Q_d = 60$, giving:

$$E_{Pa} = -10\frac{10}{60} = -1.67$$

$$E_{Pb} = 15\frac{2}{60} = 0.5$$

$$E_Y = 0.3\frac{100}{60} = 0.5$$

with the direct elasticity elastic and cross-price elasticity and income elasticity relatively inelastic.

D2.5

Following the same logic as for f_{LL} we derive f_{KK} as:

$$f_K = \beta AL^\alpha K^{\beta-1}$$

$$f_{KK} = (\beta - 1)\beta AL^\alpha K^{\beta-2}$$

$$= (\beta - 1)\beta\frac{Q}{K^2}$$

and f_{KL} as

$$f_{KL} = \alpha\beta\frac{Q}{LK}$$

and we note that $f_{KL} = f_{LK}$.

Module D3 Unconstrained optimization

D3.1

Substituting for X_1 and X_2 we derive $Y = 115.7627$. Keeping X_2 fixed when $X_1 = 5.6$, $Y = 115.7375$ and when $X_1 = 5.5$, $Y = 115.7624$. We see that for X_1 values less than 5.5085 and for values greater than 5.5085 the value of Y decreases, implying a maximum at this point. Similarly, when we fix X_1 and allow X_2 to vary we also confirm a maximum for Y when $X_2 = 3.05085$.

D3.2

(i) We have:

$$f_X = -5 + 6X - Y$$

$$f_Y = -8 + 4Y - X$$

and solving gives $Y = 2.304$ and $X = 1.216$. We also have:

$$f_{XX} = 6$$

$$f_{YY} = 4$$

and

$$f_{XY} = -1$$

confirming that the solution represents a minimum.

(ii) We have:

$$f_X = 50 - 10X - 5Y$$

$$f_Y = 30 - 9Y - 5X$$

and solving gives $Y = 0.7692$ and $X = 4.6154$. We also have:

$$f_{XX} = -10$$
$$f_{YY} = -9$$

and

$$f_{XY} = -5$$

confirming that the solution represents a maximum.

(iii) We have:

$$f_X = -6X$$
$$f_Y = 4Y$$

and solving gives $Y = 0$ and $X = 0$. We also have:

$$f_{XX} = -6$$
$$f_{YY} = 4$$

and

$$f_{XY} = 0$$

confirming that the solution represents a saddle point.

D3.3

We have $MR_X = 10$ and $MR_Y = 5$:

$$MC_X = 6X - 0.5Y$$
$$MC_Y = 4Y - 0.5X$$

Setting $MC_X = MR_X$ and $MC_Y = MR_Y$ and solving as a pair of simultaneous equations gives $X = 1.789474$ and $Y = 1.473684$ as the profit-maximizing level of output.

D3.5

For X we have an elasticity of:

$$E_X = -0.1\frac{60}{5} = -1.2$$

and for Y

$$E_Y = -0.2\frac{45}{7} = -0.1286$$

confirming that the lower elasticity is associated with the higher price. You may also wish to confirm the validity of Eq. D3.22 (with both expressions equal to 10).

Module D4 Constrained optimization

D4.1

In fact only F_λ changes:

$$F_\lambda = -(X + Y - 400)$$

Setting to zero and rearranging gives:

$$Y = 400 - X$$

Substituting back into F_Y gives:

$$F_Y = -60 + 0.4X - \lambda$$

and we can then solve for X using F_X and the derived F_Y expression to give $X = 233.33$. From F_λ, $Y = 166.67$ and from either F_X or F_Y, $\lambda = 33.33$.

Module E1 Integration and economic analysis

E1.1

(i) $f(X) = \dfrac{X^7}{7} + c$

(ii) $f(X) = \dfrac{X^{0.7}}{0.7} + c$

(iii) $f(X) = \dfrac{X^4}{4} - \dfrac{X^3}{3} + c$

(iv) $f(X) = X^5 + c$

(v) $f(X) = \ln X + c$

(vi) $f(X) = 0.75(X^3 + 10)^4 + c$

E1.2

$$f(X=3) = 60 + c$$
$$f(X=0) = c$$

Hence the value of the integral between these values equals 60. Similarly, between the values of 0 and 4 the integral takes a value of 100.

E1.3

Using the solutions from Progress Check E1.1 we have:

(i) $X = 2.5$ 87.1931
     $X = 2$ 18.2857
     Area $= 68.9074$

(ii) $X = 2.5$ 2.7131
      $X = 2$ 2.3207
      Area $= 0.3924$

(iii) $X = 2.5$ 4.5573
       $X = 2$ 1.3333
       Area $= 3.224$

(iv) $X = 2.5$ 97.6562
      $X = 2$ 32
      Area $= 65.6562$

(v) $X = 2.5$ 0.9163
     $X = 2$ 0.6931
     Area $= 0.2232$

(vi) $X = 2.5$ 323382
      $X = 2$ 78732
      Area $= 244650$

E1.4

365.4

Module E2 Financial analysis I: interest and present value

E2.1

(i) £600
(ii) £17,850

E2.2

(i) £1778.97
(ii) £35,358.37

E2.3

(i) With $V = 10,000$ and $i = 0.08$ we derive $P = 10,000/(1.08)^4 = £7350$ as the sum that must be invested now at 8% per annum to increase to £10,000 in four years' time.
(ii) With $P = 6000$ and $V = 1000$ we have:

$$i = \sqrt[4]{10,000/6000} - 1 = 0.136 \text{ or } 13.6\%$$

E2.4

With the nominal annual rate at 24% the APR is then derived as:

$$\text{APR} = (1 + 0.02)^{12} - 1 = 0.268 \text{ or } 26.8\%$$

E2.5

(i) £8333.33
(ii) £7500, £6375, £5419, £4606, £3915, £3328

E2.6

£102.8

E2.7

With a cost of capital of 12%, the NPV will be £814.33. The reason why the NPV has decreased as i increases is that a smaller value in the present is now needed to produce a fixed value at some stage in the future.

Module E3 Financial analysis II: annuities, sinking funds and growth models

E3.1

No: you'll have only £6624

E3.2

£6370

E3.3

(i)   £7662
(ii)   £7438

E3.4

(i)   £349,291
(ii)   £3579
(iii)   £305.1

Module E4 An introduction to dynamics

E4.2

$$Y_t = 7500 - 2500(0.8)^t$$

E4.3

$$Y_t = 1789.5 - 105.3(0.525)^t$$

We see that the model is stable since $0 < b < 1$.

E4.4

We derive an equation:

$$Y_t = 1000(1.67)^t$$

with the graph showing the results for the first 10 periods. We confirm that the model is explosive.

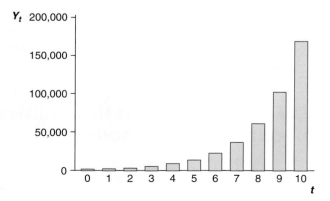

E4.5

The results from the model for the first 9 time periods are:

t	Pt
0	80
1	105
2	98.75
3	100.31
4	99.92187
5	100.02
6	99.99511
7	100.00
8	99.99969

Module E5 Probability in economic analysis

E5.1

If you took a frequentist approach you might work out the percentage of students in previous years who'd passed the exam. You might then assume that this percentage would apply to this year's exam. In terms of a probability relating to yourself, you'd probably be subjective perhaps using the frequentist calculation as a starting point.

E5.2

P(last 24 months) $= 0.98 \times 0.99 \times 0.95 = 0.92169$

Key assumption is that the three probabilities are independent.

E5.5

The posterior probability is 0.74. There's a 74% probability this share price will increase given it's had a positive forecast to do so.

E5.6

$E(x) = 2.9$, $\sigma = 1.03$

Average number of children per household is 2.9 with variability as measured by the standard deviation of 1.03 children.

E5.7

(i) 0.1875
(ii) 0.0625

E5.8

$\mu = 1.04$, $\sigma = 0.48$

Appendix 4: Outline solutions to end-of-module exercises

Note: only summary, outline solutions are given here. A full Tutor's Resource Manual available to academic staff contains fully worked solutions to all exercises.

Module 1 Introduction

1.1

A typical supply function for good X might be:

$$Q_x = \alpha + \beta_1 P_x + \beta_2 P_f + \beta_3 T + \beta_4 A$$

where

Q_x is the quantity supplied of good X
P_x is the price of the product
P_f is the price of factors of production used in the manufacture of the good
T is technology.

A relates to the profitability (possibly prices) of alternative products that the firm could produce.

α to be negative
β_1 to be positive
β_2 to be negative
β_3 to be positive
β_4 to be negative

1.2

Through data collection and econometric analysis

1.3

A typical function might be:

$$C = \alpha + \beta_1 Y_d + \beta_2 P + \beta_3 R + \beta_4 E$$

where

Y_d is disposable income
P is the general price level in the economy
R is interest rates
E is the individual's expectations about future income/prosperity.

1.4

The more obvious parameters would include:

P – the price of coffee
P_S – the price of substitute products
P_C – the price of complementary goods
Y – the individual's income
A – the level of advertising undertaken by companies trying to sell coffee
T – tastes or preferences of the individual for coffee and alternative products.

1.5

In addition to the variables above we could include:

- The exchange rate between the consuming country and the producing country
- Transport costs from the exporting country.

Module A1 Tools of the trade: the basics of algebra

A1.1

(i) $x = \dfrac{3 - 5y}{2y - 3}$

(ii) $\dfrac{7x - 16}{4x^2}$

A1.2

(i) $-x - 3y$
(ii) $12x^2 - 7.5x - 2y$
(iii) $13xy - 5x^2 - 6y^2$
(iv) $-3xz - yz + 2z$
(v) $15x - 6x^2y + 18x^4 - 36x^3$
(vi) $-2.4x^2 + 4y^2 - 2.4x^2y + 19.2xy$

A1.3

(i) $2/(x^2 - 3x + 4)$
(ii) $(7 + 5x^2)/2x^2$
(iii) $43.5x/9$
(iv) $(3 + x^2)/(-180 + 690x - 300x^2)$

A1.4

$P = 8;$

$Q_d = Q_s = 60$

A1.5

$(a - c)/(d + b)$

Module A2 Linear relationships in economic analysis

A2.1

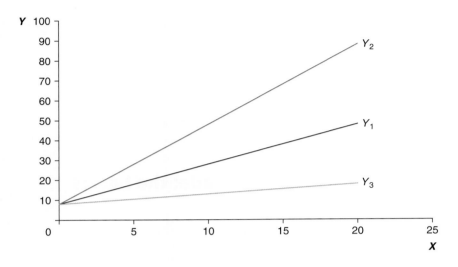

All have the same intercept but different (positive) slopes.

A2.2

   (i)   *TC* changes by 5.
  (ii)   *TC* changes by 5.
 (iii)   Total cost is changing by 5 as we change *Q* by 1.
        This is the marginal concept in economics, hence we have marginal cost – the extra cost of one extra unit.
  (iv)   It is unrealistic unless we are looking at only a small part of the *TC* function.

A2.3

Only the algebraic solutions are shown here.

   (i) $Q = 44$
  (ii) $Q = 28.6$
 (iii) $Q = 33.3$
  (iv) $Q = 50$

A2.4

(i)

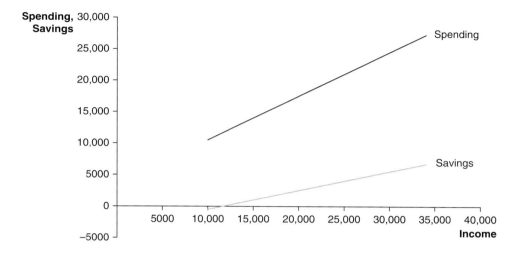

(ii) Both Spending and Savings increase as Income increases. By definition, Savings is Income minus Spending.

(iii) Spending = £24,000 (approx); Savings = £6000 (approx).

A2.5

This gives an intercept of (approx) £3500.

Module A3 Non-linear relationships in economic analysis

A3.1

(i)

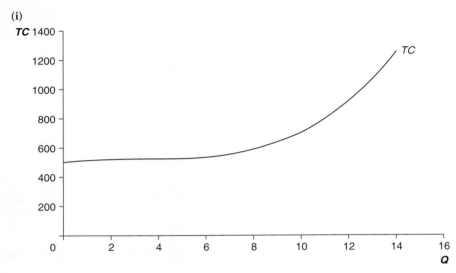

(ii)

$$ATC = \frac{TC}{Q} = 500/Q + 20 - 6Q + 0.6Q^2$$

$$AVC = VC/Q = 20 - 6Q + 0.6Q^2$$

$$AFC = FC/Q = 500/Q$$

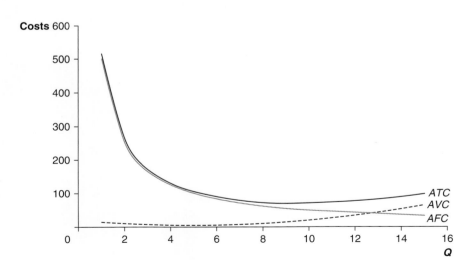

A3.2

(i)

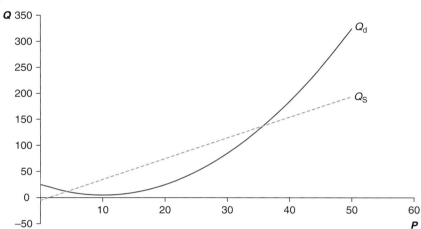

(ii) The supply function is 'sensible' over the entire price range. For a normal good, however, the demand function is realistic only over the price range 0 to 10.

(iii) $TR = 25P - 4P^2 + 0.2P^3$

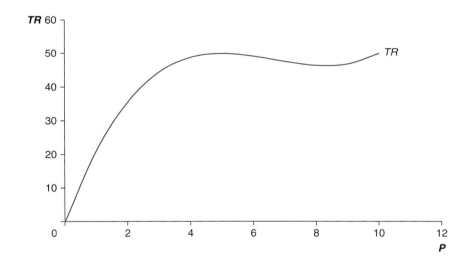

A3.3

(i)   For t from 0 to 10 we have, increasing output of 100,000 by 3% each year:

t	Output
0	100,000.00
1	103,000.00
2	106,090.00
3	109,272.70
4	112,550.88
5	115,927.41
6	119,405.23
7	122,987.39
8	126,677.01
9	130,477.32
10	134,391.64

(ii)   Using the equation:

$$\text{Output} = 100,000(1.03^t)$$

with $t = 0$ to 10 would give exactly the same values.

A3.4

(ii)   Effectively we have three functions such that:

$$K = 5: \qquad Y = 0.6L^{0.3}(5^{0.7}) = 1.8511L^{0.3}$$
$$K = 7.5: \qquad Y = 0.6L^{0.3}(7.5^{0.7}) = 2.4586L^{0.3}$$
$$K = 10: \qquad Y = 0.6L^{0.3}(10^{0.7}) = 3.0071L^{0.3}$$

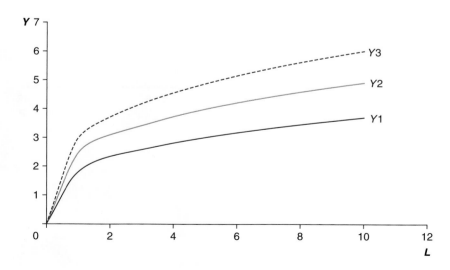

(iii)

$$L = 5: \qquad Y = 0.6(5^{0.3})K^{0.7} = 0.9724K^{0.7}$$
$$L = 7.5: \qquad Y = 0.6(7.5^{0.3})K^{0.7} = 1.0982K^{0.7}$$
$$L = 10: \qquad Y = 0.6(10^{0.3})K^{0.7} = 1.1972K^{0.7}$$

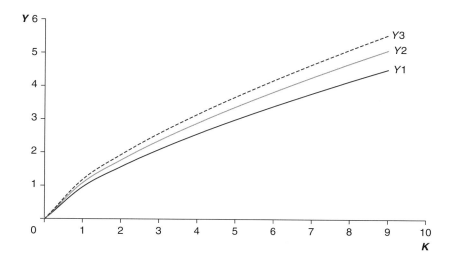

A3.5

We see that the larger the exponent term then the larger the slope of the curve. Similarly, a positive exponent generates an upward-sloping curve while a negative exponent produces a downward-sloping one.

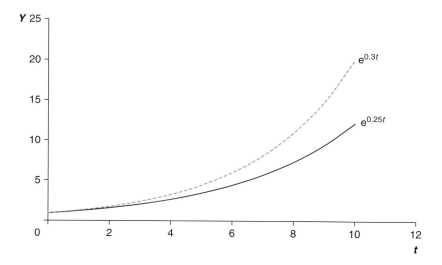

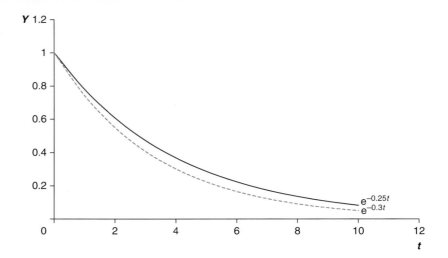

A3.6

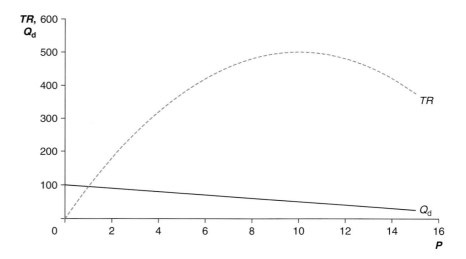

We note a downward-sloping demand curve (which is linear) with an intercept of 100 and a quadratic TR function reaching a maximum at $P = 10$.

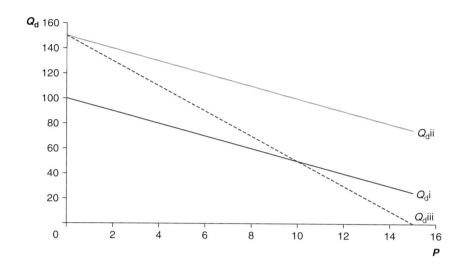

Module B1 The principles of linear models

B1.1

(i) $X = 7$; $Y = 29$
(ii) $X = 6$; $Y = 14$
(iii) $X = -5$; $Y = -75$

B1.2

Only (ii) gives an economically realistic model.

B1.3

$P_e = 40; Q_e = 140$

B1.4

Equilibrium price will fall.

B1.5

$C = 3500 + 0.7Y$

$S = -3500 + 0.3Y$

$0.7 = \text{mpc} : 0.3 = \text{mps}$

B1.6

$P = £22.5, Q = 25$ million units

Module B2 Market supply and demand models

B2.1

(i) $P_e = 40$, $Q_e = 140$

B2.2

(i) $P_e = 42$, $Q_e = 122$
(ii)   40%
(iii)   £610

B2.3

(i)   Lower price and lower quantity

    (a)   Before tax: price = £37.5
    (b)   After tax: price = £39.375

B2.4

(i)   37.5%
(ii)   £531.25

B2.5

(i)   B2.1: $E_d = 2.57$
    B2.3: $E_d = 2.85$

B2.6

£23.33

Module B3 National income models

B3.1

(i) $Y_e = 5000$, $C_e = 4500$ and $S_e = 500$
(ii) $k = 4$. A change in I will lead to a fourfold change in Y_e.
(iii) Y will change by 40.

B3.2

    $Y_e = 6250$

B3.3

    $Y_e = 3200$; $k = 2.286$

B3.4

    $Y_e = 2909$; $k = 1.82$

B3.5

G will need to be 1666.6 to balance the budget.

B3.6

G will need to be -716 to achieve a balanced trade.

Module B4 Matrix algebra: the basics

B4.3

$$\mathbf{AB} = \begin{bmatrix} 40 & 44 & 15 \\ 66 & 62 & 19 \\ 13 & 31 & 7 \end{bmatrix}$$

$$\mathbf{BA} = \begin{bmatrix} 31 & 11 & 49 \\ 7 & 1 & 14 \\ 60 & -2 & 77 \end{bmatrix}$$

$$\mathbf{ABC} = \begin{bmatrix} 80 & 296 & 143 \\ 132 & 446 & 209 \\ 26 & 163 & 82 \end{bmatrix}$$

$$\mathbf{BAC} = \begin{bmatrix} 62 & 137 & 102 \\ 14 & 25 & 23 \\ 120 & 172 & 133 \end{bmatrix}$$

B4.4

$$\begin{bmatrix} 1 & -1 & 0 & 0 \\ 1 & 0 & 10 & -0.5 \\ 1 & 1 & -4 & 0.2 \end{bmatrix} \begin{bmatrix} Q_d \\ Q_s \\ P_x \end{bmatrix} = \begin{bmatrix} 0 \\ 1000 \\ -500 \end{bmatrix}$$

B4.5

$$\begin{bmatrix} 1 & -1 & 0 & 0 \\ 1 & 0 & b_1 & b_2 \\ 1 & 1 & b_3 & b_4 \end{bmatrix} \begin{bmatrix} Q_d \\ Q_s \\ P_x \\ P_y \end{bmatrix} = \begin{bmatrix} 0 \\ a_1 \\ a_2 \end{bmatrix}$$

B4.6

$$\mathbf{cost} = \begin{bmatrix} 3552 \\ 2105 \\ 1954 \end{bmatrix}$$

$$\mathbf{revenue} = \begin{bmatrix} 4347 \\ 2657 \\ 2386 \end{bmatrix}$$

$$\mathbf{Profit} = \begin{bmatrix} 795 \\ 552 \\ 432 \end{bmatrix}$$

Module B5 Matrix algebra: inversion

B5.2

(i) $Y = -91.667, X = -1.389$
(ii) $Y = 75, X = 0$
(iii) $Y = 100, X = 0$
(iv) $Y = -100, X = 0$

B5.5

$$\begin{bmatrix} 1.470126 & 0.251572 & 0.015723 \\ -0.290881 & 1.761006 & 0.110063 \\ 0.550314 & 0.628931 & 1.289308 \end{bmatrix}$$

B5.6

(i) $(\mathbf{AB})^{-1}$

$$\begin{bmatrix} -0.53 & 0.05 & -0.03 \\ -0.07 & 0.03 & 0.08 \\ 0.42 & -0.23 & -0.14 \end{bmatrix}$$

(ii) $|\mathbf{AC}| = -160$
(iii) $|\mathbf{CA}| = -160$
(iv) $(\mathbf{CBA})^{-1}$

$$\begin{bmatrix} 0.01786 & -0.09375 & 0.20536 \\ 0.05119 & -0.08542 & 0.08869 \\ -0.01259 & 0.07083 & -0.14473 \end{bmatrix}$$

Module B6 Economic analysis with matrix algebra

B6.3

$$P_1 = 6, \ P_2 = 4, \ P_3 = 7$$

B6.4

$$Q_1 = 13, \ Q_2 = 16, \ Q_3 = 10$$

B6.5

$$Y_e = \frac{a + I + G + X - mk}{1 - (1 - t)(b - m)}$$

$$C_e = \frac{(I + G + X)(b - bt) + a(1 - mt + m) + k(-b + bt)}{1 - (1 - t)(b - m)}$$

$$T_e = \frac{t(a + I + G + x) - tk}{1 - (1 - t)(b - m)}$$

$$M_e = \frac{(a + I + G + X)(-tm + m) + k(1 - b - bt)}{1 - (1 - t)(b - m)}$$

B6.6

$$\begin{bmatrix} Y_1 \\ Y_2 \end{bmatrix} = \begin{bmatrix} \dfrac{1}{1-b_1+m_1} & \dfrac{m_2}{(1-b_1+m_1)(1-b_2+m_2)} \\ \dfrac{m_1}{(1-b_1+m_1)(1-b_2+m_2)} & \dfrac{1}{1-b_2+m_2} \end{bmatrix} \begin{bmatrix} I_1 \\ I_2 \end{bmatrix}$$

Module B7 Input–output analysis

B7.1

$$\mathbf{t1} = \begin{bmatrix} 103.8 \\ 306.4 \\ 509.4 \end{bmatrix}$$

$$\mathbf{t2} = \begin{bmatrix} 103.2 \\ 307.2 \\ 509.5 \end{bmatrix}$$

B7.2

$$\mathbf{y1} = \begin{bmatrix} 151.6 \\ 234.3 \\ 199.0 \end{bmatrix}$$

$$\mathbf{y2} = \begin{bmatrix} 151.6 \\ 234.3 \\ 199.0 \end{bmatrix}$$

B7.3

Policy 1: balance of trade $= -41.6$
Policy 2: balance of trade $= -51.6$

B7.4

Policy 1

31.13	30.64	0	30	0	0	12	103.8
10.38	122.57	25.47	70	30	25	23	306.4
25.94	76.6	101.89	100	70	60	75	509.4
10.38	15.32	50.94	50	25	0	0	151.6
10.38	30.64	178.3	0	0	15	0	234.3
15.57	30.64	152.83	0	0	0	0	199.0
103.8	306.4	509.4	250	125	100	110	1504.6

Policy 2

30.95	30.72	0	31.50	0	0	10	103.2
10.32	122.86	25.47	73.5	30	25	20	307.2
25.79	76.79	101.89	105	70	60	70	509.5
10.32	15.36	50.95	50	25	0	0	151.6
10.32	30.72	178.32	0	0	15	0	234.3
15.47	30.72	152.84	0	0	0	0	199.0
103.2	307.2	509.5	260	125	100	100	1504.8

B7.5

A	206.45
S	64.47
T	117.58
M	163.24
L	165.27
K	21.57
Total	730.61

B7.6

L in Agriculture is 92.90, in Services is 21.49 and in Tourism is 5.88.

Module C1 Quadratic functions in economic analysis

C1.1

(i)   Roots 8.63, −4.63
      Turning point 2
(ii) Roots 2.76, 7.24
      Turning point 5
(iii) No real roots
      Turning point 5
(iv) Roots −4.58, 54.58
      Turning point 25

C1.2

$P_e = 6.57$, $Q_e = 30.29$

C1.3

(i)   Higher price and lower quantity
(ii) Lower price and higher quantity
(iii) Higher price and lower quantity

C1.4

$P = 8.33$

C1.5

Breakeven at 4.34 and 55.26

C1.6

$Q = 29.8$

Module C2 The derivative and the rules of differentiation

C2.1

(i) $f'(Q) = -5P - 2$

(ii) When $P = 2$, $f'(Q) = -1.25$
      When $P = 5$, $f'(Q) = -0.2$

(iii) The slope is negative (increased price – decreased Q) but becomes less so as P increases (at least over the values calculated). Since the derivative shows the change in Y as X changes this implies Q becomes less responsive to changes in P as P increases (over the given range). If the firm is currently charging $P = 2$ then a prospective price increase would have a (relatively) large impact on Q. If the firm's price is currently 5, however, the same absolute price increase would have less effect on Q.

C2.2

(i) $f'(TQ) = 260$
       $f'(TQ) = 10 + 10Q$

(ii) MR and MC

(iii) When $Q = 25$, $f'(TQ) = 260$ and $f'(TQ) = 260$.

(iv)   By definition profit is maximized when $MR = MC$, which is what we are seeing here with the derivatives.

(v)   The TR function will shift upwards. The profit-maximizing level of Q will increase.

(vi) $Q = 29$

(vii) Q still equals 29. Given that profit maximization occurs when $MR = MC$, a change in fixed costs leaves MC unaltered.

C2.3

(i)
$$f'(X) = 3X^2 + 8X - 9$$
$$f''(X) = 6X + 8$$

(ii)
$$f'(X) = 20X - 35$$
$$f''(X) = 20$$

(iii)
$$f'(X) = 5(2X - 3)^{-2}$$
$$f''(X) = -20(2X - 3)^{-3}$$

(iv)

$$f'(X) = 20(5X - 10)^3$$
$$f''(X) = 300(5X - 10)^2$$

(v)

$$f'(X) = 80x^3 + 150x^2 - 24$$
$$f''(X) = 240x^2 + 300x$$

(vi)

$$f'(X) = \frac{40X^3 + 150X^2 + 24}{(2X + 5)^2}$$
$$f''(X) = \frac{160X^4 + 1600X^3 + 6000X^2 + 7300X - 500}{(2X + 5)^4}$$

(vii)

$$f'(X) = 150X^5 - 350X^4 + 196X^3$$
$$f''(X) = 750X^4 - 1400X^3 + 588X^2$$

(viii)

$$f'(X) = 0.5(X - 1)^{-1/2}$$
$$f''(X) = -0.25(X - 1)^{-3/2}$$

(ix)

$$f'(X) = 5(X - 1)^{-1/2}$$
$$f''(X) = -2.5(X - 1)^{-3/2}$$

C2.4

(i) $MC = 20 - 12Q + 1.8Q^2$

(ii) $ATC = 500/Q + 20 - 6Q + 0.6Q^2$

(iii)

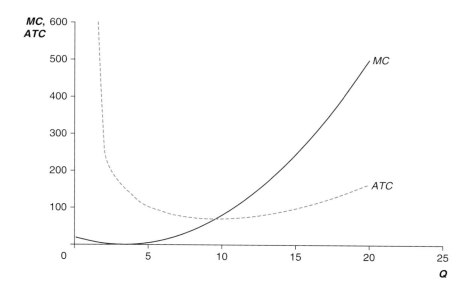

(iv)   The two intersect where ATC is at a minimum.

C2.5

(i) $P = 6.46$
(ii) $TR = 90.2$

C2.6

(i) $Y = 3L^{0.3}$
(ii) $f'(L) = 0.9L^{-0.7}$
(iii)   Marginal product of labour

(iv) It can be seen from the shape of the production function that the function is 'flattening out' as L increases. That is, the extra output from extra labour is increasing but at a decreasing rate. This is confirmed by the MP_L curve.

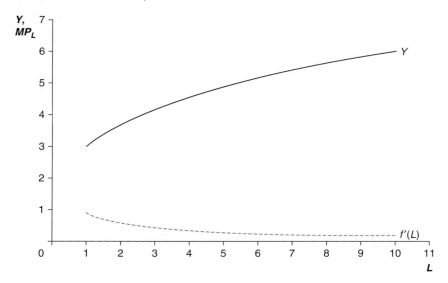

(v) $Y = 3K^{0.7}$

     $f'(K) = 2.1K^{-0.3}$

Module C3 Derivatives and economic analysis

C3.1

$$\frac{dk}{dm} = -k^2[1-t]$$

Since the multiplier, k, is positive the direction of the effect will depend on the sign of $[1-t]$. This is effectively 1 minus the tax rate. As long as t is less than 100% then a change in m will have an inverse effect on k.

C3.2

(i) $E_d = (-3 + 0.4P)(P/Q)$

      $E_s = (3 - 0.02P)(P/Q)$

(ii) $E_d = -0.19$

      $E_s = 1.33$

(iii) See Eq. C3.22

(iv) $MR = -27.54$

C3.3

(i) $\dfrac{1(P)^{1/b}}{bQa}$

(ii) $MR = (b+1)aQ^b$

C3.4

(ii) The consumption function takes a typical economic shape, flattening out at higher levels of income.

(iii) $\text{mpc} = Y^{-0.5}$

(iv) The value for mpc decreases as income increases. As consumers become wealthier their propensity to consume the extra income diminishes.

(v) $\text{mps} = 1 - \text{mpc} = 1 - Y^{-0.5}$

C3.5

(i) $180L^{-0.7} - 43.2L^{-0.4}$

(ii) $E_\text{d} = -1$

C3.6

$MC = w/MP$

The production function and *MC* function are obviously related. Closer examination of the *MC* function shows it takes the classic U shape and this can be linked to the concept of increasing/diminishing returns in the production function.

Module C4 The principles of optimization

C4.1

(i) Point of inflection when $X = 0$

(ii) Minimum when $X = -50$

(iii) Minimum when $X = 1.72$
Maximum when $X = 11.61$

(iv) Maximum when $X = -4.47$
Minimum when $X = 4.47$

(v) Point of inflection when $X = 2$

(vi) Maximum when $X = 2$

(vii) Maximum when $X = -3.16$
Minimum when $X = 3.16$

(viii) Inflection when $X = 2.67$

(ix) Minimum when $X = 0$
Maximum when $X = 4$

(x) Minimum when $X = 5$

(xi) No stationary point

Module C5 Optimization in economic analysis

C5.1

(ii) $Q = 2$
(iii) $Q = 13.7$
$AC = MC = 209$
(iv) AFC has no minimum position.

C5.2

$Q = 13.43$ at profit maximization.
Profit $= -118.346$
The excise tax will affect the profit function such that we must subtract tQ.
Given the shape of the function, however, over the sensible range of output the turning point will remain unaffected (the first derivative is quadratic and altered by $-t$, a constant). This implies that the optimum level of output will remain unaffected by the tax imposed although it will affect the firm's profit level.

C5.3

i) $Q = 18.41$
ii) $Q = 100$
Profit $= -448000$

C5.4

The lump-sum tax affects only fixed costs so the optimum Q will not be affected.

C5.5

Q before the tax is 20.71 and 10.36 after the tax.

C5.6

(i) $Q_d = 490; Q_n = 1326.67$

(ii)

(a) Profit falls by £1,223,534.
(b) In part (i) equilibrium prices were $P_d = 510$: $P_n = 2010$. In part (ii) the equilibrium price is 1542.92.
(c) In part (i) equilibrium quantities were $Q_d = 490$: $Q_n = 1326.67$. In part (ii) the equilibrium quantity is 1087.8.

Module C6 Optimization in production theory

C6.1

(ii) $AP = 12L - 0.75L^2$
(iii) $MP = 24L - 2.25L^2$

(iv)   for AP, $L = 8$
for MP, $L = 5.3$

(v)

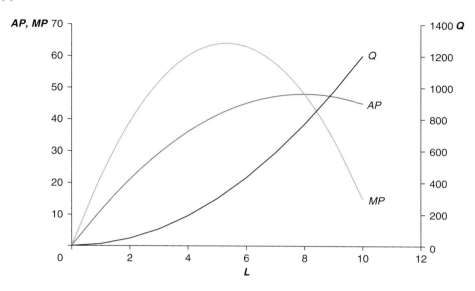

C6.2

See Section C6.1

C6.3

(i) $MC = \dfrac{10}{0.2L - 0.003L^2}$

(ii)

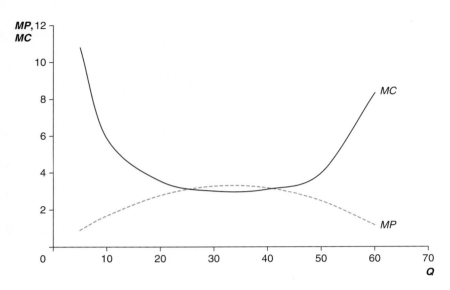

C6.4

$MP = 50 - 4L$

Module D1 Functions of more than two variables

D1.1

(i)

$$f_X = 8X$$
$$f_Y = 15Y^2$$
$$f_{XX} = 8$$
$$f_{YY} = 30Y$$
$$f_{XY} = 0$$

(ii)

$$f_X = 6X - 4Y^2$$
$$f_Y = 4Y - 8XY$$
$$f_{XX} = 6$$
$$f_{YY} = 4 - 8X$$
$$f_{XY} = -8Y$$

(iii)

$$f_X = 8X - 40Y + 2Y^2$$
$$f_Y = -40X + 4XY - 60Y^2$$
$$f_{XX} = 8$$
$$f_{YY} = 4X - 120Y$$
$$f_{XY} = -40 + 4Y$$

D1.2

(i)

$$f_W = 3W^2X^4Y^5 \quad f_X = 4W^3X^3Y^5 \quad f_Y = 5W^3X^4Y^4$$
$$f_{WW} = 6WX^4Y^5 \quad f_{XX} = 12W^3X^2Y^5 \quad f_{YY} = 20W^3X^4Y^3$$
$$f_{WX} = f_{XW} = 12W^2X^3Y^5$$
$$f_{WY} = f_{YW} = 15W^2X^4Y^4$$
$$f_{XY} = f_{YX} = 20W^3X^3Y^4$$

(ii)

$$f_X = -2YX^{-3} - 6X^2 + 4Y^2$$
$$f_Y = X^{-2} + 8XY$$
$$f_{XX} = 6YX^{-4} - 12X$$
$$f_{YY} = 8X$$
$$f_{XY} = -2X^{-3} + 8Y$$

D1.3

Assume the following function:

$$Z = 2X^4 + 10XY + 5Y^3$$

(i) $dZ = (8X^3 + 10Y)dX + (10X + 15Y^2)dY$

(ii) Let $X = 10$, $Y = 5$ and assume a change in X of 0.0001 and a change in Y of 0.0001.

$dZ = (8X^3 + 10Y)dX = 0.805$ as the change in Z as X changes
$dZ = (10X + 15Y^2)dY = 0.0475$ as the change in Z as Y changes
and 0.8525 as the (approximate) change in Z as both X and Y change.

D1.4

(i) $\dfrac{dZ}{dX} = 150X^2 + 10X + 100XY + 15Y$

(ii) $\dfrac{dZ}{dX} = 100X - 150Y$

(iii) $\dfrac{dZ}{dX} = \dfrac{-52X + 26Y}{(2X + 4Y)^2}$

D1.5

(i) $dY/dX = 20X$
(ii) $dY/dX = 20X^3/21Y^2$

Module D2 Analysis of multivariable economic models

D2.1

(i) $f_L = 7.5L^{-0.25}K^{0.25}$
$f_K = 2.5L^{0.75}K^{-0.75}$

(ii) $f_{LL} = -1.875L^{-1.25}K^{0.25}$
$f_{KK} = -1.875L^{0.75}K^{-1.75}$
$f_{LK} = f_{KL} = 1.875L^{-0.25}K^{-0.75}$

(iii) $dQ = f_L\,dL + f_K\,dK$

(v) 10.79

D2.2

$$\frac{dQ}{dt} = f_L\frac{dL}{dt} + f_K\frac{dK}{dt}$$

D2.3

(ii) $f_A = 10 - 2A + 5B$
$f_B = 30 - 2B + 5A$

(iii) $f_{BA} = 5$
$f_{AA} = -2 = f_{BB}$

(iv) $dU = f_A\,dA + f_B\,dB$

D2.4

Direct: $-20P_y\dfrac{P_x}{Q_x} = -0.089$

Cross: $(-20P_x + 5Y)\dfrac{P_y}{Q_x} = +0.99$

Income: $5P_y\dfrac{Y}{Q_d} = 1.075$

D2.5

$A = 45, B = 6$

D2.6

The partial derivatives for the exogenous variable and parameters are:

$1/(1 - b + m)$

$\partial Y/\partial b = -b(a + I + G + X)/(1 - b + m)^2$

$\partial Y/\partial m = -m(a + I + G + X)/(1 - b + m)^2$

Module D3 Unconstrained optimization

D3.1

$A = 400$

$B = 250$

D3.2

$A = 500$

$B = 400$

D3.3

$L = 6250$

$K = 3906$

D3.4

$X = 2.1684$

$Y = 2.021$

D3.5

$X = 4.75$

$Y = 6.5$

$E_x = -1.316$

$E_y = -1.462$

D3.6

$X = 2.5, \; P_x = 15, \; E_x = -3$

$Y = 2.5, \; P_y = 15, \; E_y = -1.5$

Module D4 Constrained optimization

D4.2

$A = 300$

$B = 200$

$\lambda = 20$

$F = 26{,}900$

λ is the opportunity cost of the output constraint.

D4.3

(i) $A = 318.2$
      $B = 363.6$
(ii) $A = 409.1$
      $B = 381.8$
(iii) $A = 500$
      $B = 400$

D4.4

$X = 13.33$
$Y = 3.33$

D4.5

(i) $K = 5066.7$, $L = 3166.7$
(ii) $K = 5333.3$, $L = 3333.3$
(iii) $K = 6000$, $L = 3750$

D4.6

$L = 1066.67$
$K = 666.7$

Module E1 Integration and economic analysis

E1.1

(i) $3/5X^{5/3} + c$
(ii) $\dfrac{-2}{3\sqrt{X^3}} + c$
(iii) $6/4X^4 + 2/3X^3 + 5/2X^2 + c$

E1.2

(i) $TR = 125Q - Q^2$
      since $c = 0$ by assumption.
(ii) Change in TR as Q changes: $-150, -50, -250, -450$

E1.3

Consumer surplus $= 1088.9$
Producer surplus $= 6300$

E1.4

113

E1.5

At profit max. consumer surplus $= 6.37$
At revenue max. consumer surplus $= 19.53$

E1.6

   (i) $K = 31.25t^{1.6} + 100$
  (ii) $C = 75 + 0.5Y + 0.15Y^{2/3}$
 (iii) $S = -10 + 0.5Y - 0.4Y^{0.5}$

Module E2 Financial analysis I: interest and present value

E2.1

    (i) £9628
   (ii) £10,112
  (iii) £10,231
  (iv) £10,290
   (v) £10,292

E2.2

£455, assuming continuous interest

E2.3

No definitive answer is given since the present values need to be calculated on an assumed rate of interest. Other critical assumptions are: constant rate of interest, no inflation effect, can afford to wait for future income.

E2.4

    (i) B
   (ii) Future interest rates; reliability of data; quality
  (iii) NPV of both projects will rise
  (iv) A = 16.9%, B = 18.1%
   (v) Confirms B is the preferred supplier

E2.5

  (i) Project has a positive NPV and is recommended
 (ii) IRR = 11.4%

E2.6

£1111

Module E3 Financial analysis II: annuities, sinking funds and growth models

E3.1

  (i) £2901
 (ii) £2273

E3.2

(i) £2763
(ii) £2165

E3.3

(i) £1769.84
(ii)

Year	Debt	Interest	Debt + Interest	Payment	Amount owed
1	10,000.00	1200.00	11,200.00	1769.84	9430.16
2	9430.16	1131.62	10,561.78	1769.84	8791.94
3	8791.94	1055.03	9846.97	1769.84	8077.13
4	8077.13	969.26	9046.38	1769.84	7276.54
5	7276.54	873.18	8149.72	1769.84	6379.88
6	6379.88	765.59	7145.47	1796.84	5375.63
7	5375.63	645.08	6020.70	1769.84	4250.86
8	4250.86	510.10	4760.96	1769.84	2991.12
9	2991.12	358.93	3350.06	1769.84	1580.22
10	1580.22	189.63	1769.81	1769.84	0.00
Total		7698.42		17,698.42	

(iii)

Year	Debt	Debt + Interest	Sinking fund			Fund value
			Payment	Total fund	Interest	
1	10,000.00	11,200.00	1330.17	1330.17	199.53	1529.70
2	11,200.00	12,544.00	1330.17	2859.87	428.98	3288.85
3	12,544.00	14,049.28	1330.17	4619.02	692.85	5311.87
4	14,049.28	15,735.19	1330.17	6642.04	996.31	7638.34
5	15,735.19	17,623.42	1330.17	8968.51	1345.28	10,313.79
6	17,623.42	19,738.23	1330.17	11,643.96	1746.59	13,390.55
7	19,738.23	22,106.81	1330.17	14,720.72	2208.11	16,928.83
8	22,106.81	24,759.63	1330.17	18,259.00	2738.85	20,997.85
9	24,759.63	27,730.79	1330.17	22,328.02	3349.20	25,677.23
10	27,730.79	31,058.48	1330.17	27,007.40	4051.11	31,058.51

E3.4

(i) £32,952
(ii) £3793
(iii) £305

cost minimization subject to an
output constraint   354–5
Lagrange multipliers   348–52,
353, 355, 356, 357, 358
output maximization subject to a
cost constraint   352–3
principles of   345–8
consumer income
gross and disposable   14–15
and quantity demanded   4, 5
consumer utility *see* utility
consumer's surplus   369–70, 371,
372
consumption   14, 111–14, 116–17,
121, 127, 178–9
multiplier   318
over time   413–14
consumption function   112–14, 430
analysis using derivatives   247–8
contingent annuities   397, 410
continuous interest rate   404–5
continuous random variables   441–3
convergence to equilibrium   418,
419, 423, 425–6, 427
coordinates   36–7, 45–6, 47, 57–8
cost
analysing using derivatives
246–7
average *see* average cost; average
fixed cost; average variable cost
constraint and output
maximization   352–3
fixed costs   45–6, 92, 93, 94
increases and pricing   163–5
marginal *see* marginal cost
minimization subject to an output
constraint   354–5
relationship between the cost
functions   289–90
theory of   287–9
total *see* total cost
variable costs   45–6, 92, 93–4
Cramer's rule   161–2, 163
cross-partial derivatives   300–2,
303, 303–4, 310
cross-price elasticity of demand
241, 320, 327
cubic functions   56, 57, 70
curve sketching   235–7

damped oscillations   419–20, 421,
427
debt repayment   400–1, 450–1

decision theory   431
decision-making under
uncertainty   444–8
decreasing returns to scale   323
deductions   14–15, 17
definite integrals   366–7, 373
and the area under a curve
367–9, 373
demand
for bonds   390
elasticity of   104–7, 107, 238–40,
243–4, 319–20, 327, 337–8
factors affecting   4–6, 43
final   186–8, 189, 191, 192–4,
196–7
market models   96–8
for money   125
multivariable functions   67–8
sketching a demand function
235–6
denominator   23
common   24–5, 30
dependent variable   35, 36, 37,
42–3, 47
depreciation   382–3
depreciation rate   383
derivatives   199–200, 218, 219–23,
230, 230–2
and the concept of marginality
237
cross-partial   300–2, 303, 303–4,
310
curve sketching   235–7
partial *see* partial derivatives
rules of differentiation   223–8,
229, 230
total derivative   307–9, 310
use in economic analysis   200,
235–52
analysing costs   246–7
analysing elasticity   238–41
analysing production   244–6
analysing revenue   242–4
consumption function   247–8
national income   248–9
destinations of output   186, 187
determinants   152, 154–60, 163
calculating the matrix inverse
158–9, 168–70
Cramer's rule   161–2, 163
in Excel   166, 167
and non-singularity   159–60
properties   157–8

difference equations   413–29
macroeconomic model   413–24,
427–8
equilibrium position   415–16,
418, 419, 427–8
Harrod–Domar growth model
424
model with government sector
423
solutions to a difference
equation   416–18, 427
stability of the model   418–22,
423, 427
market equilibrium   424–6
difference quotients   85–6, 216,
217–18, 219
differences/sums
derivatives of   225, 229
integrals of   365
differentials   304–6
exponential functions   406–7
total differential   305–6, 307, 310,
311, 351
differentiation   215–34
derivatives *see* derivatives
non-differentiable functions
228–9, 230
partial *see* partial differentiation
rules of   199, 223–8, 229, 230
slope of linear and non-linear
functions   215–20
dimensions of a matrix   132
diminishing marginal utility, law of
324, 327
diminishing returns, law of (or
diminishing marginal product)
232, 245
direct price elasticity of demand
319, 327
discontinuities   228
discount factor   385, 386, 387
discount rate   385, 386–8, 391
discrete random variables   439–41
disposable income   14–15
divergence from equilibrium   418,
420, 427
division
dealing with exponents   33
fractions   23, 30
inequalities   22
domain of an independent variable
45

due annuities   397, 397–8, 399, 410, 411
   repayment annuities   400, 401
dynamics   361, 413–29
   see also difference equations

e (mathematical constant)   60, 64–5
   calculus and   406–8
   and growth rates   401–6, 408–10
econometrics   6, 7
economic behaviour   7, 8
economic dependency   42–3
economic growth   449–51
economic models
   dynamics   361, 413–29
   economic theory, mathematics and   6–8
   market models *see* market models
   multivariable *see* multivariable economic models
   national income models *see* national income models
   representation with matrix algebra 138–9, 140
economic theory   2
   economic models, mathematics and   6–8
effective interest rate   381–2, 391
elastic demand   106, 107, 239, 240, 244, 249
elasticity   238–41, 249
   of demand   104–7, 107, 238–40, 243–4, 319–20, 327, 337–8
   elasticities and growth rates 409–10
   of production   322–3
elements of a matrix   132
empirical (frequentist) probability 432–3, 439, 448
EMV *see* expected monetary value
endogenous variables   112–14
equations   7, 34, 35
   linear   45–6, 54, 91–2
equilibrium
   market equilibrium *see* market equilibrium
   national income models   113–14, 118–20, 123, 125–6, 127, 127–9, 318
      difference equation model 415–16, 418, 419, 427–8

matrix algebra   178, 180–1, 182, 182–4
   with a government sector   121
events   432, 449
   conditional   433, 434–5
   independent   433, 434
   mutually exclusive   433
Excel
   determinants   166, 167
   financial calculations   393–5
   graphs in
      linear   51–4
      non-linear   75–80
   inbuilt financial formulae   393, 394
   matrix algebra   143–8
   matrix inverse   166–7
excise tax   107
   in a competitive market   101–4, 107, 175–6
   effect on market equilibrium 103, 175–6
   maximizing tax revenue   107–9, 276–8
   and profit maximization   275, 279
   on short-haul flights in Europe 1–2, 3–6
exogenous variables   112, 114–18, 127
expansion path   355
expected monetary value (EMV) 444–6
expected utility   447–8, 449
expected value   440–1, 443
experiments, random   432
explosive macroeconomic model 418, 420, 427
explosive oscillations   420–1, 422, 426, 427
exponential functions   62–6, 70
   differentiation   406–7
   growth models   401–10, 410
   integration   407–8
   rates of growth   408–10
exponents (powers)   31–3, 62–4
extrapolation   38, 47

final demand   186–8, 189, 191, 192–4, 196–7
financial analysis   361, 376–412
   annuities   396–400, 410, 410–11
   arithmetic series   377–8, 391

compound interest   379–81, 391, 403–5
depreciation   382–3
Excel and   393–5
geometric series   378–9, 380, 383, 391, 396, 398, 399, 400, 401
growth models   401–10, 410
interest rates and the price of government bonds   388–90, 391–2
investment appraisal   384, 385–8
nominal and effective interest rates 381–2, 391
present value *see* net present value; present value
simple interest   379–80, 391
sinking funds   400–1, 410
time preference   377, 384, 390
financial markets   377
financial (monetary) sector   124–6, 182–4
firms   111–13
first derivative   221–3, 236
   stationary points at zero value 254–5, 256, 263
first-order conditions   256–7, 259, 268, 286, 330
   profit maximization   335, 336–7, 341
   unconstrained optimization   334, 336–7, 339, 340, 343
first-order difference equations 414
first-order partial derivatives 298–9, 300, 303, 310, 311
fixed costs   45–6
   average fixed cost   263
   breakeven analysis   92, 93, 94
foreign trade   123–4, 127, 127–9, 195–8
fractions   23–7, 30
   with algebraic expressions   26–7
frequentist probability   432–3, 439, 448
function of a function, derivative of 226–7, 229
functional independence   90
functions   35, 40–6, 47
   implicit   309–10, 348
   linear *see* linear functions
   multivariable *see* multivariable functions

non-differentiable   228–9, 230
non-linear *see* non-linear
   functions
notation   44

Gauss–Jordan elimination method
   152–4, 159, 163
general equilibrium   98
generalized power rule for
   differentiation   224, 229
   partial differentiation   312
geometric series   378–9, 380, 383,
   391, 396, 398, 399, 400, 401
global maxima and minima
   259–60, 263
government bond prices   388–90,
   391–2
government expenditure   1, 14,
   120–2, 127–9
   input–output analysis   191,
      192–4, 195–8
   multiplier   122, 180–1, 318, 328
   spending the budget surplus
      327–8
government sector   120–4, 127
   budget surplus   127–9
      and balancing the budget
         327–8
   dynamic model   423
   effect of changes in the tax rate on
      the multiplier   248–9
   matrix algebra   179–81
   model including foreign trade
      123–4
   tax revenue maximization
      107–9, 211–12, 276–8
gradient (slope)
   linear functions   84–6, 92,
      112–13, 215–16
   non-linear functions   216–21
   quadratic functions   205–6
graphs   34, 35
   in Excel   51–4, 75–80
   functions with more than one
      independent variable   67–9
   linear *see* linear graphs
   non-linear functions   57–8, 59,
      70, 75–80
   obtaining linear equations from
      91–2
   national income model   118–20
   quadrants   39–40
   three-dimensional   67–9, 295–8

Greek alphabet   454
gross income   14–15
growth, proxy measures for
   449–51
growth models   401–10, 410
   growth rates   408–10
   Harrod–Domar macroeconomic
      model   424

Harrod–Domar growth model   424
Hessian matrix   342–4
   bordered   359–60
households   111–13

identity matrix   133, 140, 150, 151,
   152–4
implicit functions   309–10, 348
imports   123, 124
income
   circular flow of   111–13
   consumer income   4, 5, 14–15
   national income models *see*
      national income models
income elasticity of demand   241,
   320, 327
increasing returns to scale   323
indefinite integrals   364–6
independent events   433, 434
independent variable   35, 36, 37,
   42–3, 47, 51
   functions with more than one
      66–9, 70
indifference curves   325–6, 356
indifference map   325–6
inelastic demand   106, 107, 239,
   240, 244, 249, 319, 320
inequalities   21–3, 30, 352
inferior goods   320
inflection, points of   260–2
input–output analysis   82, 186–98
   input–output coefficients
      188–90, 195, 196
   input–output inverse   191–2,
      193–4, 195
   input–output tables   186–8, 195
integration   361, 363–75
   capital stock formation   371–2
   consumer's surplus   369–70, 371,
      372
   definite integrals   366–9, 373
   exponential functions   407–8
   notation and terminology   363–4
   probability density function   442

producer's surplus   371, 372
   rules of   364–6
intercept (constant)   84, 85, 92, 112,
   203, 205
interest   376–95
   compound   379–81, 391, 403–5
   depreciation   382–3
   exponential growth models and
      403–6
   investment appraisal   385–8
   simple   379–80, 391
   time preference   377
interest rate   124–5, 182–4, 377,
   380–1
   effective   381–2, 391
   nominal   381–2
   and the price of government
      bonds   388–90, 391–2
internal rate of return (IRR)   386–8,
   391, 394, 395
interpolation   38–9, 47
inverse function rule for
   differentiation   227–8
inverse functions   69–70, 70, 71
inverse matrix *see* matrix inverse
investment   111–12, 113, 118, 124–5
   appraisal   384, 385–8
   capital stock formation   372
   change in and national income
      114–17, 119, 178–9
   Harrod–Domar growth model
      424
   multiplier   115–17, 178–9, 318
IRR *see* internal rate of return
IS schedule (investment and savings
   schedule)   125–6
iso lines
   indifference curves   356
   iso-costs and iso-quants   353, 355
   profit   346–8

Keynesian multiplier   115–16

labour
   average product (*AP*) of labour
      250–51, 283–4,
   marginal product of labour (*MPL*)
      232, 237–8, 245–7, 250, 284,
      321, 339
   production maximization   230–2,
      249–51
   production theory   320–3
   profit maximization   338–40

labour market   195–8

Lagrange functions   348, 352, 354, 356, 358, 359

Lagrange multipliers   348–52, 353, 355, 356, 357, 358

  interpretation   349–52

Laplace expansion   154–5, 156–7, 161, 163

law of diminishing marginal utility   324, 327

law of diminishing returns (or diminishing marginal product)   232, 245

Law of Total Probability   437, 449

limit (limiting value of a function)   217–18, 220

linear equations   45–6, 54, 91–2

linear functions   44–6, 83–6, 92, 215

  gradient (slope)   84–6, 92, 112–13, 215–16

  integration and area under the line   367, 368, 369

  intercept   84, 85, 92, 112, 203, 205

  non-linear functions derived from   58–9

  transformation of non–linear functions to using logarithms   61–2

linear graphs   35–40, 47

  obtaining linear equations from   91–2

  plotting   45–6

  using Excel   51–4

linear models   81, 83–95

  simple breakeven model   87–8

  simultaneous equations   89–90

linear relationships   11, 34–54

  see also linear functions; linear graphs

LM schedule (liquidity–money schedule)   125–6

loan repayments   400–1, 450–1

local maxima and minima   259–60, 262, 263

logarithmic functions   60–2, 70

  derivatives of   227, 229

  log rule for integration   365

logarithms   60–2

logical deductions   4–5, 7

lump-sum tax   272–4, 279

macroeconomic growth model   424

marginal cost   237, 238, 246–7, 249, 263, 290

  cost minimization   355

  and marginal product   246–7

  price discrimination   336–7

  profit maximization   267, 268, 269, 270, 271, 273

    equality to marginal revenue   267, 279, 335

  relationship to average cost   289–90, 290

  and total cost   287–9, 373–4

marginal probability   437–8

marginal product

  and average product   283–7, 290, 290–2

  and marginal cost   246–7

  and marginal revenue   245–6

  unconstrained optimization   338–40, 341

marginal product of capital   238, 321–2, 339–40, 341

marginal product of labour   232, 238, 245, 250–1, 287–8, 321–2, 339–40, 341

marginal propensity to consume (mpc)   113, 120, 238, 247, 430

  multiplier   318

marginal propensity to save   238, 248

marginal rate of substitution   326, 356

marginal revenue   237, 238, 242–4, 249, 264

  and marginal product   245–6

  price discrimination   336–7

  profit maximization   267, 268, 269, 270, 271, 272, 273

    equality to marginal cost   267, 279, 335

marginal revenue product (MRP)   245–6, 249

marginal utility   238, 323–4, 327

marginal utility of income   356

marginality   237, 238, 249

market equilibrium   98–100, 107, 369

  difference equations   424–6

  effect of an excise tax   103–4, 175–6

  matrix algebra   173–4, 175–6

partial differentiation   315–17

quadratic functions   209–10

market models   81, 96–110

  dynamic model   424–6

  elasticity see elasticity

  excise tax in a competitive market   101–4, 107, 175–6

  market demand and supply   96–8

  matrix algebra   171–6, 181

  partial equilibrium model   98–100, 171–4, 314–17

mathematical dependency   42–3

mathematics

  economic theory, economic models and   6–8

  need for in economics   3–6

matrices   131–2, 140

  bordered Hessian matrix   359–60

  dimensions of a matrix   132

  Hessian matrix   342–4

  identity matrix   133, 140, 150, 151, 152–4

  null matrix   133, 140

  transpose matrix   133, 140, 145–8

matrix algebra   81, 130–48

  addition   134, 143–5, 146

  application to economic models   82, 171–85

    market model   171–6, 181

    national income model   177–81, 182, 182–4

  matrix multiplication   135–8, 147, 148

  multiplication by a scalar   135

  subtraction   135

  using Excel   143–8

  using to represent economic models   138–9

  vocabulary   131–2

matrix inverse   82, 149–70, 172

  calculating   152–4

    using determinants   158–9, 168–70

  Cramer's rule   161–2, 163

  using Excel   166–7

  using a matrix inverse   150–1

maxima   209, 254–6, 256–7, 257–8, 263

  global   259–60, 263

  local   259–60, 262, 263

  unconstrained optimization   330–5, 340, 343

  see also first-order conditions; second-order conditions

maximization 253
MDETERM function 166, 167
mean, arithmetic 440–1, 443
minima 209, 256–7, 257–8, 263
    global 259–60, 263
    local 259–60, 262, 263
    unconstrained optimization
        330–5, 340, 343
    see also first-order conditions;
        second-order conditions
minimization 253
minors of a matrix 155, 163, 172–3
MINVERSE function 166
MMULT function 147, 148
models 7
    economic see economic models
modulus 240
monetary sector (financial sector)
    124–6, 182–4
money
    demand for 125
    LM schedule (liquidity–money
        schedule) 125–6
money supply 2
    effect of changes in on national
        income equilibrium 125–6,
        182–4
monopoly 243, 249
    profit maximization 270–2, 273
monotonic functions 228
multiple brackets 19–20, 30
multiplication
    dealing with exponents 32, 33
    fractions 23
    inequalities 22
    matrices
        matrix multiplication 135–8
        multiplication by a scalar 135
        multiplying two matrices
            137–8, 147, 148
        multiplying a vector and a
            matrix 136
Multiplication Law 433–5, 449
multipliers 123, 127
    derivatives 248–9
    effect of changes in the tax rate
        248–9
    government expenditure 122,
        180–1, 318, 328
    input–output analysis 194
    investment 115–17, 178–9, 318
    matrix algebra 178–9, 180–1, 182

partial differentiation and
    318–19, 327
multivariable economic models
    293, 314–29
    elasticity of demand 319–20, 327
    national income model 317–19,
        327, 327–8
    partial market equilibrium
        314–17
    production functions 320–3, 327
    utility functions 323–6, 327
multivariable functions 293,
    295–313
    differentials 304–6
    implicit functions 309–10
    partial differentiation 295–304,
        310, 312–13
    total derivative 307–9, 310
mutually exclusive events 433

named ranges method 144–5, 146
national income models 81,
    111–29, 130
    analysis using derivatives 248–9
    closed economy 111–20
    diagram form 118–20
    difference equations model
        413–24, 427–8
    matrix algebra 177–81, 182,
        182–4
    multipliers see multipliers
    partial differentiation 317–19,
        327, 327–8
    proxy measures 449–51
    with foreign trade 123–4, 127,
        127–9, 195–8
    with a government sector see
        government sector
    with a monetary sector 124–6,
        182–4
natural logarithms 60, 227, 229
negative exponents 32
negative values 22
    in graphs 39–40
    inequalities 30
net present value (NPV) 386
    of an annuity 399, 411
    interest rates and the price of
        government bonds 388–90
    internal rate of return 386–8, 391
nominal interest rate 381–2
non-differentiable functions 228–9,
    230

non-linear functions 11, 55–80
    definite integrals and areas under
        curves 367–8, 369
    derived from linear functions
        58–9
    exponential functions see
        exponential functions
    functions with more than one
        independent variable 66–9, 70
    gradient (slope) 216–21
    graphs of 57–8, 59, 70, 75–80
    inverse functions 69–70, 70, 71
    logarithms and logarithmic
        functions 60–2, 70
    polynomial functions 56–8, 70,
        75–80, 201–2
non-singularity 150, 159–60
non-stationary inflection points
    262
normal goods 320
normative expected utility theory
    448
notation
    algebraic 14
    functional 44
    integration 363–4
    matrices 131–2
null matrix 133, 140
numerator 23
numerical values 6

objective function 346–8, 348
observed (frequentist) probability
    432–3, 439, 448
opportunity cost 350, 357
optimization 199–200
    constrained see constrained
        optimization
    example of 253–7
    in general 257–8
    maxima see maxima
    minima see minima
    points of inflection 260–2
    principles of 200, 253–65
    in production theory 200,
        283–92
    profit maximization see profit
        maximization
    tax revenue maximization
        107–9, 211–12, 276–8
    unconstrained see unconstrained
        optimization

ordinary annuities 397, 410
  present value 399
  sum 398
origin of a graph 36
oscillations 424
  damped 419–20, 421, 427
  explosive 420–1, 422, 426, 427
'other things being equal' (*ceteris
    paribus*) assumption 5
output 186–7
  breakeven analysis *see* breakeven
    analysis
  constraint and cost minimization
    354–5
  exponential growth model 410
  input–output analysis *see*
    input–output analysis
  maximization subject to a cost
    constraint 352–3
  profit-maximizing *see* profit
    maximization
  total cost as a function of 44–6

parameters 4, 5–6
  consumption function 112–14
  exponential functions 62, 64
  linear functions 45, 83–6
  quadratic functions 203–4, 205
partial derivatives 298–9, 307–8
  cross-partial derivatives 300–2,
    303, 303–4, 310
  first-order 298–9, 300, 303, 310,
    311
  general principles of
    unconstrained optimization
    330–4
  interpretation 303
  Lagrange multipliers 348–9,
    350–1
  second-order 299–302, 303, 310,
    311
partial differentiation 295–304, 310
  analysis of multivariable economic
    models 293, 314–29
  generalization to *n*-variable
    functions 302–4
  rules for 312–13
partial market equilibrium model
    98–100
  matrix algebra 171–4
  multivariable model 314–17
particular solution 416, 418, 427
partition of the sample space 437

perfect competition 243, 249
  profit maximization 267–70
perpetual annuities 397, 410
planes 68–9
planned consumption and
    investment 118–19
point elasticities 238–41, 249
points of inflection 260–2
polynomial functions 56–8, 70,
    201–2
  graphs of 57–8, 75–80
positive expected utility theory 448
posterior probability 438
power rule
  differentiation 223–4, 229
  integration 364
powers (exponents) 31–3, 62–4
precautionary demand for money
    125
present value 384–5, 391, 396
  annuities 399, 411
  investment appraisal 385–6
  net *see* net present value (NPV)
price 14
  breakeven analysis 92, 93, 94
  equilibrium price 98–100, 103–4,
    107, 174, 176, 210, 315–17
  consumer's and producer's
    surpluses 369–71, 372
  impact of a tax on short-haul
    flights 1–2, 3–6
  and profit maximization 279–81
  relationship with quantity 35,
    37–9, 235–6
  sales, profit and 140–1, 163–5
  sales, revenue and 138–9, 140–1,
    150–1
price discrimination 336–8
price elasticity of demand 105–7,
    238–40, 249, 319, 327
  cross-elasticity 241, 320, 327
  direct 319, 327
  and revenue 243–4
primary factors of production
    186–8, 193–4
  see also capital; input–output
    analysis; labour
principal sum 379–80
prior probability 437–8
probability 362, 430–53
  assigning 432–3
  basic rules 433–7

Bayes' theorem 437–9, 449,
    449–51
  decision-making under
    uncertainty 444–8
  uncertainty and 431
  understanding 432–3
probability density function 442
probability distributions 439–43,
    449
  continuous random variables
    441–3
  discrete random variables
    439–41
  expected value 440–1, 443
probability-equivalence method
    446–8
probability function 440, 441–2
probability utility 446–7
producer's surplus 371, 372
product launches 65–6, 438
product rule for differentiation
    225, 229
  partial differentiation 312–13
production
  analysing using derivatives
    244–6
  constrained optimization
    cost minimization subject to an
      output constraint 354–5
    output maximization subject to
      a cost constraint 352–3
    profit maximization 345–8,
      357–8
  elasticity of 322–3
  maximization and the number of
    workers 230–2, 249–51
  optimization in production theory
    200, 283–92
    relationship between the cost
      functions 289–90
    theory of costs 287–9
  unconstrained optimization
    338–40, 341
production functions 61–2, 283–7,
    290–2
  Cobb–Douglas 61–2, 320–3, 327,
    410
  partial differentiation 320–3, 327
productivity of capital 424
profit 264
  sales, price and 140–1, 163–5
profit function 48, 71–3, 208–9
  and its derivative 221–3

profit maximization   71–3, 208–9, 253–4, 266–75, 279, 279–81
  constrained   345–8, 357–8
  effect of tax on   272–5, 279
  monopoly   270–2, 273
  perfect competition   267–70
  and price discrimination   336–8
  unconstrained   335, 338–40, 341
profit tax   274–5, 279
project appraisal   384, 385–8
proxy measures   449–51

quadrants   39–40
quadratic functions   56–7, 70, 199, 201–14
  breakeven analysis   205–9
  characteristics   202–5, 211
  graphs in Excel   77–80
  market equilibrium   209–10
  roots of a quadratic equation 207–8, 209, 211
    derivation of the roots formula 213–14
  turning points   254–7
  with no real roots   210–11
quantity
  equilibrium quantity   98–100, 103–4, 107, 174, 176, 209–10, 315–16
  consumer's and producer's surpluses   369–71, 372
  relationship with price   35, 37–9, 235–6
quarterly interest   404, 406
quotient rule for differentiation 226, 229
  partial differentiation   313

random experiments   432
random variables   439–43, 449
  continuous   441–3
  discrete   439–41
real input price   339
reducing-balance method   383
repayment annuities   400, 401
retirement income planning   378, 379
returns to scale effect   61
revenue
  analysing using derivatives 242–4
  average   242, 249, 270, 271
  marginal see marginal revenue

sales, price and   138–9, 140–1, 150–1
  total see total revenue
risk, attitudes to   445–8
risk aversion   446, 447, 448
risk neutrality   448
risk seeking   446, 448
row vectors   132

saddle point   334, 341
sales
  price, profit and   140–1, 163–5
  price, revenue and   138–9, 140–1, 150–1
sales tax see excise tax
sample point   432
sample space   432
  partition of   437
savings   113, 118, 127, 247–8, 325
  Harrod–Domar growth model 424
  IS schedule (investment and savings schedule)   125–6
scalars   132, 140
  multiplication of a matrix by a scalar   135
scales, in graphs   37, 38
second derivative   222–3, 236
  and optimization   255–6, 263
second-order conditions   256–7, 257–8, 259, 268, 330–1
  bordered Hessian matrix   359–60
  Hessian matrix   342–4
  optimization of production 286–7
  unconstrained optimization   334, 339, 340, 342–4
second-order determinants   154
second-order difference equations 414
second-order partial derivatives 299–302, 303, 310, 311
semi-annual interest   404, 405
shadow price   350
simple interest   379–80, 391
simplification of fractions   24–5, 27
simultaneous equations   89–90, 130, 160
  Cramer's rule   161–2, 163
singular matrices   150, 159–60
sinking funds   400–1, 410
slope see gradient (slope)
special matrices   133, 140

speculative demand for money   125
square matrices   132, 150
stability over time   418–22, 423, 427
standard deviation   441, 443
states of nature   444
stationary points   222, 254
  points of inflection   260–1
  turning points see maxima; minima; turning points
  unconstrained optimization 330–4
straight-line depreciation   382
straight-line graphs see linear graphs
subjective probability   432–3, 439, 448
substitution rule for integration 365–6
subtraction
  fractions   25–6, 30
  inequalities   21, 22
  matrices   135
summation operator (sigma)   156–7
sums/differences
  derivatives of   225, 229
  integrals of   365
supply
  of bonds   390
  elasticity of   241
  market models   96–8
  money supply   2, 125–6, 182–4
surplus
  consumer's   369–70, 371, 372
  government budget surplus 127–9, 327–8
  producer's   371, 372

tangent lines   216–17, 300–2
tax
  bankers' bonuses   2
  effect of changes in the tax rate on the multiplier   248–9
  effect on profit maximization 272–5, 279
  excise tax see excise tax
  multiplier   318, 319
  national income models   120–2, 127–9, 179–81
  short-haul air travel tax   1–2, 3–6
  revenue maximization   107–9, 276–8
    tax rate and   211–12
term of an annuity   397

three-dimensional graphs 67–9, 295–8

time preference 377, 384, 390

total cost
  average 59
  breakeven analysis 48–9, 87–8, 205–6
  linear function 44–6, 47–9, 83–6
  and marginal cost 287–9, 373–4
  monopoly 270, 271
  non-linear function 56–7, 59
  perfect competition 268, 269
  total revenue, profit and 71–2, 73, 266–7

total demand for primary factors of production 189, 193–4, 197

total derivative 307–9, 310

total differentials 305–6, 307, 310, 311, 351

total output vector 189, 191, 192–4, 196–7

Total Probability, Law of 437, 449

total revenue 242, 264
  breakeven analysis 48–9, 87–8, 205–6
  monopoly 270, 271, 272, 273
  perfect competition 268, 269
  price elasticity of demand 106
  from quantity demanded function 69–70
  total cost, profit and 71–2, 73, 266–7

trade, foreign 123–4, 127, 127–9, 195–8

transactions demand for money 125

TRANSPOSE function 145–8

transpose matrix 133, 140, 145–8

transposition of an expression 27–9

trendlines 77–80

trials 432

turning points 254–8
  general approach to finding 257–8
  local and global 259–60, 262, 263
  maxima see maxima
  minima see minima
  quadratic functions 208, 209, 211, 212

uncertainty 430–1
  decision-making under 444–8
  and probability 431

unconditional probability 437–8

unconstrained optimization 293, 330–44
  general principles 330–4
  Hessian matrix 342–4
  price discrimination 336–8
  profit maximization 335, 338–40, 341

unitary elasticity 106, 107, 240, 244, 249

utility 446–7
  decision-making under uncertainty 445–8
  marginal 238, 323–4, 327
  marginal utility of income 356
  maximization subject to a budget constraint 355–6
  partial differentiation of a utility function 323–6, 327
  unconstrained optimization 341

value of a future amount 379–81, 396, 397–8

variable costs 45–6
  average variable cost 264
  breakeven analysis 92, 93–4

variables 4, 14
  dependent 35, 36, 37, 42–3, 47
  endogenous 112–14
  exogenous 112, 114–18, 127
  independent see independent variable
  random 439–43, 449

variance 440–1, 443

vectors 132, 140
  multiplying a vector and a matrix 136

x axis 36–7, 39–40, 47

y axis 36–7, 39–40, 47

Young's theorem 300, 333